OFFICIAL
BASEBALL CARD
PRICE GUIDE

PUBLICATIONS INTERNATIONAL, LTD.

Louis Weber, C.E.O.
Publications International, Ltd.
7373 North Cicero Avenue
Lincolnwood, Illinois 60646

Permission is never granted for commercial purposes.

Manufactured in USA.

8 7 6 5 4 3 2 1

ISBN: 0-56173-009-2

Library of Congress Catalog Card Number: 90-63962

Contributing writer: Tom Owens
Photography: Sam Griffith Studio, Inc.
Special thanks to: AU Sports Memorabilia, Skokie, Illinois; Sports
Collectors Store, LaGrange, Illinois; Steve Gold.

CONTENTS

INTRODUCTION

"What's it worth?"

Regardless of the baseball card, or the sophistication of the hobbyist asking the question, that simple phrase has become the motto of today's collector. Due to the dwindling supply of vintage collectibles and the increasing cost of new issues, the actual value of baseball cards is increasingly important to study. Thousands of collectors have hit the jackpot when certain cards in their possession soared in value. Speculators who used to dabble in stocks and bonds now look to Score, Topps, Upper Deck, and other companies for cardboard investment vehicles.

Skeptics may believe that the baseball card boom has been limited to 20- and 30-year-old products. Not so! Anyone wanting evidence of how cards can skyrocket in price need to look only at 1989. Upper Deck, a newly formed California company, defied the odds and produced an 800-card set to compete with the existing giants of the baseball card industry. Veteran hobbyists claimed that any set that would initially cost more than $30 couldn't be collectible. Those naysayers were silenced when the Upper Deck factory-collated set topped prices of $100 by Christmas.

Many similar surprises await card collectors in 1991 and beyond. That's why having a book like the *Official Baseball Card Price Guide* is so vital for survival in the hobby. This publication reviews all major card sets and offers values for selected cards that have been issued during the last 43 years, from 1948 Bowman through 1990 Upper Deck. Individual values are given for all major sets and for various series within a set.

In order to cover such a wealth of data, the first priority is to include the most notable cards of stars and rookies. Many cards of secondary players, of lesser interest to collectors and known as "commons," are also listed. This way readers will have the information they need the most. In all, more than 33,000 cards have been chosen for listing in this book.

Unlike other price guides, the *Official Baseball Card Price Guide* does more than simply list prices. Much more. Nearly 800 color photos throughout the book show important cards from every set. And each list is preceded by an introduction to provide valuable background information about that specific set.

To help serve collectors better, "best buys" are designated in nearly every set. Denoted by an asterisk, best buys are cards that are often available at bargain prices. More expensive best buys are key cards that could be enormous value gainers in the future. Overlooked rookies and Future Hall of Famers (including long-shot prospects like Bob Boone) are just two categories found in best buys. These evaluations, and prices of other sets listed in this publication, were established after thorough studies of previous card prices. Feedback from a number of card and hobby dealers helped to shape the price estimates that follow.

Do best buy suggestions help? Refer to the first edition of the Price Guide, and view the number of asterisks marking cards for Jim Palmer and Joe Morgan. Anyone who followed the tips before the pair were elected to the Hall of Fame could, in many cases, have tripled their money. Overlooked rookies, future Hall of Famers, and other forgotten stars are in this year's crop of best buys. Look them over and consider what future profits could be awaiting card investors.

The prices listed are estimated retail values. Hobbyists planning to sell their cards should expect dealers to pay anywhere from 50 to 60 percent of the prices given for star cards. Commons of poorer quality could be sold for about ten percent of the prescribed prices.

To make the most of the *Official Baseball Card Price Guide,* it's important to note that some names appear in italic type, and several abbreviations are frequently used.

Names in *italics:* Rookie cards. A rookie card is defined as the first appearance a player makes for any card company *during his rookie season.* When a player's name is printed in italic type, that card is considered to be a rookie card. However, a player who is shuttled between the majors and minors may not appear on a card for years. In that case he might not have a rookie card at all, though he would eventually have an "FC" (for "First Card"). A rookie card may be part of a specially designated rookie issue shared by other players, or it may be an ordinary card. In recent years, for example, Olympic cards (found in the 1985 Topps set) or First Round Draft Pick cards are considered rookie cards for stars like Mark McGwire.

In addition, fall extension sets like Topps Traded or Fleer Update have muddled the definition of rookie cards. Because they have not been sold individually through any sources outside of the hobby in the past, cards from fall-issued sets are not recognized by the *Official Baseball Card Price Guide* as genuine rookie cards. Topps and Donruss have sold complete sets of these late issues on a test basis through toy stores and by mail order. However, Upper Deck has been the only company through 1990 willing to include specially marked cards mixed in individual packages with other cards. When collectors have unlimited access to all the fall-issued cards, then rookie card definitions can be reworked.

(DK): Diamond Kings. This designation has been applied to a yearly 26-card set of painted portraits of one selected player from each team. They have been included as part of the Donruss sets since 1982.

(DP): Double-Printed cards. When Topps expanded its set size to more than 660 cards, uneven numbers neutralized the usual 132-card printing sheets. To compensate, the company printed certain cards twice on each sheet. As a result, the supply of some cards doubled. When star cards were involved, this lessened the demand and lowered their value. Common cards of marginal players take drastic price drops when double-printing occurs.

(FC): First cards. This means that a listed card marks a player's *first appearance* for a *certain card company.* Sometimes a player's first card is *not* his rookie card. For example, the first card for Padres pitcher Andy Benes appeared in the 1990 Donruss set and identified him as a "Rated Rookie." However, it was not a true rookie card at all since he had appeared in several sets in 1989. Those 1989 appearances constituted his genuine rookie cards.

FS: Future Stars. A number of cards for promising young players carry this designation, in 1982 Topps, for example.

IA: In-Action cards. On several occasions Topps has produced both standard cards and action-photo cards of selected popular players. In terms of value, however, IA cards don't climb as quickly as their regular card companions.

(RR): "Rated Rookies." These are specially-marked Donruss cards honoring young players.

In addition to these abbreviations, it is worth noting that many set profiles mention high-number and low-number cards. Before 1974, Topps issued cards throughout each summer in several series of approximately 110 cards each. Typically, the last 100-odd cards from a set are in shorter supply. This occurred because some retailers overstocked baseball cards early in the summer when demand was high. When the baseball season was winding down, the cards issued later in the season—those with higher numbers—were harder to find. Since fewer were sold in the past, there are fewer available today. As a result, such high-numbered cards tend to be more valuable.

A very different phenomenon took place when other retailers were slow to offer cards in larger numbers in the early part of the season. This means that the cards with low numbers became more valuable over time.

Condition, however, is even more important than supply and demand when determining card values. The prices listed in this guide are for cards in top condition— for all sets issued prior to 1980 that means Near Mint, and for all sets issued since 1980 that means Mint. These grades are the most sought-after by collectors. Obviously, cards in poorer condition will command lower prices. This makes proper grading of your cards of critical importance. The following guidelines on condition will be helpful in grading and thus estimating the value of your cards.

Mint cards are perfect, well-centered cards showing absolutely no wear, fading, scratches, printing flaws, loss of luster, or other imperfections. True Mint cards prior to 1980 may command values that are 40 to 50 percent higher than the Near Mint price listed. And don't assume that cards found in factory-collated sets or freshly removed from wax packs always will be graded as Mint. Cards with printing flaws, uneven borders, or gum stains (from Topps or Donruss wax packs) can be discounted by as much as 20 percent.

Near Mint cards are nearly perfect, with only a very minor flaw preventing a grade of full Mint. Such cards may be slightly off-center or have one corner that is less than perfect. Near Mint cards issued since 1980 may be worth 70 to 80 percent of the Mint value listed.

Excellent cards may have lost some original surface gloss but will display very little wear, have no serious defects, and still have sharp corners. Excellent cards may be off-center, but will have no creases or stains

corners, major creases, and other defects, but all parts of the cards will still be intact, without being defaced by holes, tears, tape, or writing. This is generally the poorest condition that most collectors would even consider. Cards in Good condition are worth approximately 10 to 15 percent of the Mint or Near Mint values listed.

Good cards show a great amount of handling and perhaps even some abuse. They may have softened from gum or wax. Cards in Excellent condition are generally worth approximately 40 to 60 percent of the Mint or Near Mint values listed.

Very Good cards will display some wear and have slightly rounded corners, minor creases, or stains. They will usually be valued at about 25 to 30 percent of the Mint or Near Mint values listed.

Fair and *Poor* cards show excessive wear, damage, and abuse. They are generally not considered collectible.

In addition to condition and scarcity, geographical demand influences card prices. While cards of players from universally popular teams like the Dodgers or Yankees may command higher prices nationwide, other stars bring different reactions from hobbyists. Most of the cards for the Seattle Mariners, for example, are considered commons because few fans across the nation pay much attention to this fledgling team. In the Pacific Northwest, however, collectors pay triple the national average value for Mariners cards.

Card pricing remains a new and inexact science. Prior to the 1980s, dealers knew little about rookie cards and often established blanket prices for nearly all players from popular teams. For a time, older sets identified stars with card numbers ending in 0 and 5. That system provided collectors with a temporary guideline for identifying valuable cards.

As you read the *Official Baseball Card Price Guide,* keep in mind that it should be used only as a general aide in determining the value of baseball cards. Altered distribution by card companies and successes (or failures) by teams and players themselves can cause quick fluctuations in card values. For instance, when Ken Griffey, Sr. joined his son on the Mariners in late 1990, collectors suddenly pursued his cards at a dime each, twice their previous value.

Finally, this publication does not represent an offer by the publishers or any other party to buy or sell cards. Reputable hobby dealers remain the best sources for collectors. They can be found at card shops, hobby conventions, or through advertisements in collector periodicals. And while every effort has been made to insure a high level of accuracy in the price estimates contained within this book, the publishers cannot assume any responsibility for errors that may occur.

Enjoy the *Official Baseball Card Price Guide,* but keep card price trends in perspective. While the cardboard stock used for these tiny creations has little intrinsic value, the loyalty and popularity you feel for individual teams and players create the ever-changing worth of each individual card.

1948 BOWMAN

The Philadelphia-based Bowman Company entered the baseball card market in 1948 with this 48-card set. Featuring black-and-white photos of players (with stadium backgrounds) on the front, with black printing on gray cardboard on the back, these 2¹/16- by 2¹/2-inch cards took Bowman to market dominance in one short year. The white-bordered cards were packaged with one card to a pack of gum. A total of 12 cards were short-printed (numbers 7, 8, 13, 16, 20, 22, 24, 26, 28, 29, 30, and 34). With the exception of Phil Rizzuto, number 8, all short-prints are lesser-known players today. Eight Hall of Famers are included: Kiner, Mize, Musial, Slaughter, Feller, Berra, Schoendienst, and Spahn.

5 Bob Feller

		NR MT
Complete set		**$2350.00**
Commons (1-36)		**12.00**
Commons (37-48)		**20.00**

1	Bob Elliott	$60.00
2	Ewell (The Whip) Blackwell	12.00
3	Ralph Kiner	75.00
4	Johnny Mize	60.00
5	Bob Feller	120.00
6	*Larry (Yogi) Berra*	360.00
7	Pete (Pistol Pete) Reiser	40.00
8	Phil (Scooter) Rizzuto	150.00
9	Walker Cooper	12.00
10	Buddy Rosar	12.00
12	Johnny Sain	30.00
13	Willard Marshall	30.00
14	Allie Reynolds	36.00
16	Jack Lohrke	30.00

6 Larry (Yogi) Berra

18 Warren Spahn

17	Enos (Country) Slaughter	75.00
18	Warren Spahn	135.00
19	Tommy Henrich	20.00
20	Buddy Kerr	30.00
22	Floyd (Bill) Bevins	40.00
24	Emil (Dutch) Leonard	30.00
25	Barney McCoskey	12.00
26	Frank Shea	40.00
28	Emil (The Antelope) Verban	30.00
29	Joe Page	40.00
30	"Whitey" Lockman	30.00
34	Sheldon (Available) Jones	30.00
35	George (Snuffy) Stirnweiss	17.00
36	Stan Musial	450.00
38	Al "Red" Schoendienst	75.00
40	Marty Marion	35.00
41	Rex Barney	22.00
42	Ray Poat	20.00
43	Bruce Edwards	20.00
44	Johnny Wyrostek	20.00
45	Hank Sauer	20.00
46	Herman Wehmeier	20.00
47	Bobby Thomson	40.00
48	George "Dave" Koslo	40.00

36 Stan Musial

8 Phil (Scooter) Rizzuto

1949 BOWMAN

Bowman's sophomore series of 240 cards for 1949 was one of the largest issues of that year. The 2 1/16- by 2 1/2-inch cards feature white-bordered, colorized photo portraits on solid color backgrounds. The backs are cream-colored with red-and-blue printing. Rookie cards for Hall of Famers Robin Roberts and Duke Snider are seen, as well as a rare set appearance by the great Satchel Paige. An unusual error occurs on number 240: It is supposed to be Babe Young, but in fact the photo is of Bobby Young.

226 Edwin "Duke" Snider

84 Roy Campanella

		NR MT
Complete set		$12,150.00
Commons (1-36)		10.00
Commons (37-73)		12.00
Commons (74-144)		10.00
Commons (145-240)		50.00

1	Vernon Bickford	$75.00
2	Carroll "Whitey" Lockman	17.00
3	Bob Porterfield	15.00
4	Jerry Priddy (no name on front)	13.00
4	Jerry Priddy (name on front)	35.00
5	Hank Sauer	12.00
6	Phil Cavarretta	14.00
7	Joe Dobson	10.00
8	Murry Dickson	10.00
9	Ferris Fain	13.00
10	Ted Gray	11.00
11	Lou Boudreau	50.00
12	Cas Michaels	10.00
13	Bob Chesnes	10.00
14	Curt Simmons	20.00
15	Ned Garver	12.00
16	Al Kozar	10.00
17	Earl Torgeson	10.00
18	Bobby Thomson	20.00
19	*Bobby Brown	35.00
20	Gene Hermanski	12.00
21	Frank Baumholtz	10.00
22	Harry "P-Nuts" Lowrey	10.00
23	Bobby Doerr	50.00
24	Stan Musial	425.00
25	Carl Scheib	10.00
26	George Kell	50.00
27	Bob Feller	100.00
28	Don Kolloway	10.00
29	Ralph Kiner	65.00
30	Andy Seminick	10.00
31	Dick Kokos	10.00
32	Eddie Yost	12.00
33	Warren Spahn	100.00
34	Dave Koslo	10.00
35	Vic Raschi	22.00
36	Harold "Peewee" Reese	150.00
37	John Wyrostek	12.00
38	Emil "The Antelope" Verban	12.00

39	Bill Goodman	12.00
40	George "Red" Munger	12.00
41	Lou Brissie	12.00
42	Walter "Hoot" Evers	12.00
43	Dale Mitchell	12.00
44	Dave Philley	12.00
45	Wally Westlake	12.00
46	Robin Roberts	135.00
47	Johnny Sain	20.00
48	Willard Marshall	12.00
49	Frank Shea	18.00
50	Jackie Robinson	535.00
51	Herman Wehmeier	12.00
52	Johnny Schmitz	12.00
53	Jack Kramer	12.00
54	*Marty "Slats" Marion	17.00
55	Eddie Joost	12.00
56	Pat Mullin	12.00
57	Gene Bearden	12.00
58	Bob Elliott	12.00
59	Jack "Lucky" Lohrke	12.00
60	Larry "Yogi" Berra	225.00
61	Rex Barney	14.00
62	Grady Hatton	12.00

224 Leroy "Satchell" Paige

63	Andy Pafko	14.00
64	Dom "The Little Professor" DiMaggio	20.00
65	Enos "Country" Slaughter	50.00

66	Elmer Valo	12.00
67	Alvin Dark	16.00
70	Carl Furillo	30.00
78	Sam Zoldak (no name on front)	12.00
78	Sam Zoldak (name on front)	30.00
82	Joe Page	16.00
83	Bob Scheffing (no name on front)	12.00
83	Bob Scheffing (name on front)	30.00
84	Roy Campanella	500.00
85	Johnny "Big John" Mize (no name on front)	50.00
85	Johnny "Big John" Mize (name on front)	110.00
86	Johnny Pesky	12.00
88	Bill Salkeld (no name on front)	12.00
88	Bill Salkeld (name on front)	30.00
98	Phil Rizzuto (no name on front)	80.00
98	Phil Rizzuto (name on front)	150.00

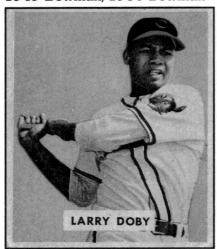

233 Larry Doby

100	Gil Hodges	150.00
110	Early Wynn	80.00
111	Al "Red" Schoendienst	60.00
114	Allie Reynolds	30.00
145	Sylvester "Blix" Donnelly	50.00
146	Myron "Mike" McCormick	50.00
147	Elmer "Bert" Singleton	50.00
148	Bob Swift	50.00
149	Roy Partee	55.00
150	Alfred "Allie" Clark	50.00
151	Maurice "Mickey" Harris	50.00
152	Clarence Maddern	50.00
153	Phil Masi	50.00
154	Clint Hartung	50.00
155	Fermin "Mickey" Guerra	50.00
156	Al "Zeke" Zarilla	50.00
157	Walt Masterson	50.00
158	Harry "The Cat" Brecheen	55.00
159	Glen Moulder	50.00
160	Jim Blackburn	50.00
161	John "Jocko" Thompson	50.00
162	Elwin "Preacher" Roe	125.00
163	Clyde McCullough	50.00
164	Vic Wertz	53.00

165	George "Snuffy" Stirnweiss	55.00
166	Mike Tresh	50.00
167	Boris "Babe" Martin	50.00
168	Doyle Lade	50.00
169	Jeff Heath	50.00
170	Bill Rigney	53.00
171	Dick Fowler	50.00
172	Eddie Pellagrini	50.00
173	Eddie Stewart	50.00
174	Terry Moore	55.00
175	Luke Appling	100.00
176	Ken Raffensberger	50.00
177	Stan Lopata	50.00
178	Tommy Brown	50.00
179	Hugh Casey	50.00
180	Connie Berry	50.00
181	Gus Niarhos	50.00
182	Hal Peck	50.00
183	Lou Stringer	50.00
184	Bob Chipman	50.00
185	Pete Reiser	55.00
186	John "Buddy" Kerr	50.00
187	Phil Marchildon	50.00
188	Karl Drews	50.00
189	Earl Wooten	50.00
190	Jim Hearn	50.00
191	Joe Haynes	50.00
192	Harry Gumbert	50.00
193	Ken Trinkle	50.00
194	Ralph Branca	100.00
195	Eddie Bockman	50.00
196	Fred Hutchinson	53.00
197	Johnny Lindell	53.00
198	Steve Gromek	50.00
199	Cecil "Tex" Hughson	50.00
200	Jess Dobernic	50.00
201	Sibby Sisti	50.00
202	Larry Jansen	50.00
203	Barney McCosky	50.00
204	Bob Savage	50.00
205	Dick Sisler	50.00
206	Bruce Edwards	50.00
207	Johnny "Hippity" Hopp	50.00
208	Paul "Dizzy" Trout	53.00
209	Charlie "King Kong" Keller	90.00
210	Joe "Flash" Gordon	53.00
211	Dave "Boo" Ferriss	50.00
212	Ralph Hamner	50.00

238 Bob Lemon

213	Charles "Red" Barrett	50.00
214	*Richie Ashburn*	400.00
215	Kirby Higbe	50.00
216	Lynwood "Schoolboy" Rowe	50.00
217	Marino Pieretti	50.00
218	Dick Kryhoski	53.00
219	Virgil "Fire" Trucks	53.00
220	Johnny McCarthy	50.00
221	Bob Muncrief	50.00
222	Alex Kellner	50.00
223	Bob Hoffman	50.00
224	Leroy "Satchell" Paige	1100.00
225	*Gerry Coleman*	90.00
226	*Edwin "Duke" Snider*	900.00
227	Fritz Ostermueller	50.00
228	Jackie Mayo	50.00
229	Ed Lopat	100.00
230	Augie Galan	50.00
231	Earl Johnson	50.00
233	*Larry Doby*	125.00
234	Truett "Rip" Sewell	53.00
236	Fred Sanford	50.00
238	Bob Lemon	200.00
239	Frank McCormick	50.00
240	Norman "Babe" Young (photo actually Bobby Young)	90.00

1950 BOWMAN

In its third year Bowman increased its set size to 252 cards. No double printing was necessary, since 36 cards of 2$^{1}/_{16}$- by 2$^{1}/_{2}$-inches fit on each printer's sheet, making an even series of seven sheets. For the first time Bowman featured its well-known paintings based on photographs, surrounded with a white border. The backs are cream-colored, with red-and-black print. Ted Williams made his Bowman debut, while Luke Appling made his farewell card appearance. No rookies of note are featured, but Bowman started something big by featuring non-playing managers Casey Stengel, Leo Durocher, and Frank Frisch.

	NR MT
Complete set	**$7550.00**
Commons (1-72)	**30.00**
Commons (73-252)	**10.00**

1	Mel Parnell	$200.00
2	Vern Stephens	35.00
3	Dom DiMaggio	30.00

4	Gus Zernial	25.00
5	Bob Kuzava	25.00
6	Bob Feller	135.00
7	Jim Hegan	25.00
8	George Kell	55.00
9	Vic Wertz	25.00
10	Tommy Henrich	45.00
11	Phil Rizzuto	95.00
12	Joe Page	32.00
13	Ferris Fain	27.00
14	Alex Kellner	25.00
15	Al Kozar	25.00
16	Roy Sievers	32.00
17	Sid Hudson	25.00
18	Eddie Robinson	25.00
19	Warren Spahn	115.00
20	Bob Elliott	25.00
21	Harold Reese	165.00
22	Jackie Robinson	525.00
23	*Don Newcombe*	75.00
24	Johnny Schmitz	25.00
25	Hank Sauer	25.00
26	Grady Hatton	25.00
27	Herman Wehmeier	25.00
28	Bobby Thomson	45.00
29	Ed Stanky	27.00
30	Eddie Waitkus	25.00
31	Del Ennis	25.00
32	Robin Roberts	80.00
33	Ralph Kiner	75.00
34	Murry Dickson	25.00
35	Enos Slaughter	55.00
36	Eddie Kazak	25.00
37	Luke Appling	60.00
38	Bill Wight	25.00
39	Larry Doby	45.00
40	Bob Lemon	55.00
41	Walter "Hoot" Evers	25.00
42	Art Houtteman	25.00
43	Bobby Doerr	55.00
44	Joe Dobson	25.00
45	Al "Zeke" Zarilla	25.00
46	Larry "Yogi" Berra	310.00
47	Jerry Coleman	37.00
48	Leland "Lou" Brissie	25.00
49	Elmer Valo	25.00
50	Dick Kokos	25.00

98 Ted Williams

21 Harold Reese

51	Ned Garver	25.00
52	Sam Mele	25.00
53	Clyde Vollmer	25.00
54	Gil Coan	25.00
55	John "Buddy" Kerr	25.00
56	*Del Crandell*	35.00
57	Vernon Bickford	25.00
58	Carl Furillo	45.00
59	Ralph Branca	45.00
60	Andy Pafko	27.00
61	Bob Rush	25.00
62	Ted Kluszewski	35.00
63	Ewell Blackwell	27.00
64	Alvin Dark	35.00
65	Dave Koslo	25.00
66	Larry Jansen	25.00
67	Willie Jones	25.00
68	Curt Simmons	27.00
69	Wally Westlake	25.00
70	Bob Chesnes	25.00
71	Al Schoendienst	65.00
72	Howie Pollet	25.00
73	Willard Marshall	10.00
74	Johnny Antonelli	15.00
75	Roy Campanella	250.00
76	Rex Barney	12.00
77	Edwin "Duke" Snider	200.00
78	Mickey Owen	10.00
79	Johnny Vander Meer	12.00
80	Howard Fox	10.00
81	Ron Northey	10.00
82	Carroll Lockman	10.00
83	Sheldon Jones	10.00
84	Richie Ashburn	45.00
85	Ken Heintzelman	10.00
86	Stan Rojek	10.00
87	Bill Werle	10.00
88	Marty Marion	12.00
89	George Munger	10.00
90	Harry Brecheen	15.00
91	Cass Michaels	10.00
92	Hank Majeski	10.00
93	Gene Bearden	10.00
94	Lou Boudreau	40.00
95	Aaron Robinson	10.00
96	Virgil "Fire" Trucks	12.00

97	Maurice McDermott	10.00
98	Ted Williams	500.00
99	Billy Goodman	10.00
100	Vic Raschi	20.00
101	Bobby Brown	20.00
102	Billy Johnson	15.00
103	Eddie Joost	10.00
104	Sam Chapman	10.00
105	Bob Dillinger	10.00
106	Cliff Fannin	10.00
107	Sam Dente	10.00
108	Rae Scarborough	10.00
109	Sid Gordon	10.00
110	Tommy Holmes	12.00
111	Walker Cooper	10.00
112	Gil Hodges	80.00
113	Gene Hermanski	12.00
114	Wayne Terwilliger	10.00
115	Roy Smalley	10.00
116	Virgil "Red" Stallcup	10.00
117	Bill Rigney	12.00
118	Clint Hartung	10.00
119	Dick Sisler	10.00
120	John Thompson	10.00
121	Andy Seminick	10.00
122	Johnny Hopp	10.00
123	Dino Restelli	10.00
124	Clyde McCullough	10.00
125	Del Rice	10.00
126	Al Brazle	10.00
127	Dave Philley	10.00
128	Phil Masi	10.00
129	Joe "Flash" Gordon	12.00
130	Dale Mitchell	10.00
131	Steve Gromek	10.00
132	James Vernon	12.00
133	Don Kolloway	10.00
134	Paul "Dizzy" Trout	12.00
135	Pat Mullin	10.00
136	Warren Rosar	10.00
137	Johnny Pesky	12.00
138	Allie Reynolds	25.00
139	Johnny Mize	60.00
140	Pete Suder	10.00
141	Joe Coleman	10.00
142	Sherman Lollar	12.00
143	Eddie Stewart	10.00

6 Bob Feller

144	Al Evans	10.00
145	Jack Graham	10.00
146	Floyd Baker	10.00
147	Mike Garcia	12.00
148	Early Wynn	60.00
149	Bob Swift	10.00
150	George Vico	10.00
151	Fred Hutchinson	12.00
152	Ellis Kinder	10.00
153	Walt Masterson	10.00
154	Gus Niarhos	10.00
155	Frank "Spec" Shea	15.00
156	Fred Sanford	15.00
157	Mike Guerra	10.00
158	Paul Lehner	10.00
159	Joe Tipton	10.00
160	Mickey Harris	10.00
161	Sherry Robertson	10.00
162	Eddie Yost	10.00
164	Sibby Sisti	10.00
165	Bruce Edwards	12.00
166	Joe Hatten	12.00
167	Elwin Roe	25.00
172	Peanuts Lowrey	12.00
180	Harry Walker	12.00
186	Ken Keltner	12.00
193	Harold "Pete" Reiser	12.00
194	Billy Cox	15.00
195	Phil Cavaretta	12.00

46 Larry "Yogi" Berra

203	Danny Murtaugh	12.00
212	Gerry Priddy	12.00
215	Ed Lopat	20.00
216	Bob Porterfield	15.00
217	Casey Stengel	100.00
218	Cliff Mapes	15.00
219	Hank Bauer	40.00
220	*Leo Durocher	40.00
222	Bobby Morgan	12.00
223	Jimmy Russell	12.00

224	Jack Banta	12.00
225	Eddie Sawyer	15.00
226	Jim Konstanty	12.00
229	Frank Frisch	40.00
232	Al "Flip" Rosen	40.00
234	Bobby Shantz	20.00
246	Walt Dropo	12.00
248	Sam Jethroe	12.00
251	John Lester Moss	15.00
252	Billy DeMars	70.00

1951 BOWMAN

At 324 cards, Bowman's 1951 baseball card set was the most complete issue up to that time. In addition to making the set larger for 1951, Bowman also made the individual cards larger. The 2¹/6- by 3¹/6-inch size would be maintained for two years. Each card provides the player name in a horizontal black box. Card backs use red-and-blue printing on gray cardboard, but use no statistics. Few changes were made from the 1950 Bowman edition. In fact, some of the same color paintings of the players from the 1950 issue were used in an enlarged version for the 1951 set. Incidentally, the attraction of the paintings is due in part to the fact that they are based on actual photographs. Bowman created a trend for the 1950s by issuing a card for each major league skipper. The rising expense of the 1951 Bowman set comes from a high-number series, which includes the ultra-popular rookie cards of Willie Mays and Mickey Mantle.

165 Ted Williams

		NR MT
Complete set		**$17,500.00**
Commons (1-36)		**13.00**
Commons (37-252)		**10.00**
Commons (253-324)		**40.00**

1	*Ed "Whitey" Ford*	$1500.00
2	Larry "Yogi" Berra	500.00
3	Robin Roberts	75.00
4	Del Ennis	13.00
5	Dale Mitchell	13.00
6	Don Newcombe	35.00
7	Gil Hodges	75.00

8	Paul Lehner	13.00
9	Sam Chapman	13.00
10	Al "Red" Schoendienst	65.00
11	George "Red" Munger	13.00
12	Hank Majeski	13.00
13	Ed Stanky	16.00
14	Alvin Dark	19.00
15	Johnny Pesky	16.00
16	Maurice McDermott	13.00
17	Pete Castiglione	13.00
18	Gil Coan	13.00
19	Sid Gordon	13.00
20	Del Crandall	16.00
21	George "Snuffy" Stirnweiss	13.00

22	Hank Sauer	13.00
23	Walter "Hoot" Evers	13.00
24	Ewell Blackwell	16.00
25	Vic Raschi	25.00

305 Willie Mays

253 Mickey Mantle

26	Phil Rizzuto	80.00
27	Jim Konstanty	14.00
28	Eddie Waitkus	13.00
29	Allie Clark	13.00
30	Bob Feller	125.00
31	Roy Campanella	300.00
32	Duke Snider	235.00
33	Bob Hooper	13.00
34	*Marty Marion	17.00
35	Al Zarilla	13.00
36	Joe Dobson	13.00
37	Whitey Lockman	10.00
40	Dave "Gus" Bell	13.00
41	Eddie Yost	13.00
46	George Kell	50.00
49	Jerry Coleman	16.00
50	Johnny Mize	50.00
51	Andy Seminick	10.00
52	Dick Sisler	10.00
53	Bob Lemon	42.00
54	Ray Boone	12.00
55	Gene Hermanski	12.00
56	Ralph Branca	30.00
58	Enos Slaughter	50.00
62	Lou Boudreau	50.00
65	Mickey Vernon	13.00
67	Roy Sievers	13.00
73	Tommy Byrne	15.00
74	Billy Johnson	12.00
76	Stan Lopata	10.00
78	Early Wynn	50.00
79	Jim Hegan	10.00
80	Harold "Peewee" Reese	135.00
81	Carl Furillo	25.00
86	Harry Brecheen	13.00
92	Vern "Junior" Stephens	12.00
100	Sherman Lollar	13.00
103	Andy Pafko	12.00
104	Virgil "Fire" Trucks	12.00
109	Allie Reynolds	25.00
110	*Bobby Brown	25.00
111	Curt Simmons	12.00
112	Willie Jones	10.00
113	Bill "Swish" Nicholson	10.00
114	Sam Zoldak	10.00
115	Steve Gromek	10.00
117	Eddie Miksis	12.00
118	Preacher Roe	25.00
119	Eddie Joost	10.00
120	Joe Coleman	10.00
121	Gerry Staley	10.00
122	Joe Garagiola	150.00
123	Howie Judson	10.00
125	Bill Rigney	12.00
126	Bobby Thomson	25.00
127	Sal Maglie	35.00
128	Ellis Kinder	10.00
129	Matt Batts	10.00
130	Tom Saffell	10.00
131	Cliff Chambers	10.00
132	Cass Michaels	10.00
133	Sam Dente	10.00
134	Warren Spahn	100.00
135	Walker Cooper	10.00
136	Ray Coleman	10.00
137	Dick Starr	10.00
138	Phil Cavarretta	12.00
139	Doyle Lade	10.00
140	Eddie Lake	10.00
141	Fred Hutchinson	12.00
142	Aaron Robinson	10.00
143	Ted Kluszewski	25.00
144	Herman Wehmeier	10.00
147	Ken Heintzelman	10.00
148	Granny Hamner	10.00
149	Emory "Bubba" Church	10.00
150	Mike Garcia	13.00
151	Larry Doby	25.00
152	Cal Abrams	12.00
153	Rex Barney	12.00
154	Pete Suder	10.00
155	Lou Brissie	10.00
156	Del Rice	10.00
157	Al Brazle	10.00
158	Chuck Diering	10.00
159	Eddie Stewart	10.00
160	Phil Masi	10.00
161	Wes Westrum	12.00
162	Larry Jansen	10.00
163	Monte Kennedy	10.00
164	Bill Wight	10.00
165	Ted Williams	525.00
166	Stan Rojek	10.00
167	Murry Dickson	10.00
170	Sibby Sisti	10.00
171	Buddy Kerr	10.00
172	Ned Garver	10.00
173	Hank Arft	10.00
174	Mickey Owen	10.00
175	Wayne Terwilliger	10.00
176	Vic Wertz	12.00
177	Charlie Keller	12.00
178	Ted Gray	10.00
179	Danny Litwhiler	10.00
180	Howie Fox	10.00
181	Casey Stengel	85.00
182	Tom Ferrick	15.00
183	Hank Bauer	25.00
184	Eddie Sawyer	10.00
185	Jimmy Bloodworth	10.00
186	Richie Ashburn	50.00
187	Al "Flip" Rosen	20.00
188	Roberto Avila	12.00
189	Erv Palica	11.00
190	Joe Hatten	11.00
195	Paul Richards	15.00
196	Bill Pierce	15.00
198	Monte Irvin	90.00
203	Vernon Law	17.00
207	Billy Southworth	10.00
217	Joe Page	16.00
218	Ed Lopat	25.00
219	Gene Woodling	27.00
223	Johnny Vander Meer	20.00
224	Billy Cox	16.00
225	Dan Bankhead	15.00
226	Jimmy Dykes	15.00
227	Bobby Schantz	15.00
228	Cloyd Boyer	10.00
230	Max Lanier	10.00
232	Nelson Fox	90.00
233	*Leo Durocher	50.00
234	Clint Hartung	10.00
238	Pete Reiser	15.00
242	Sam Jethroe	15.00
243	John Antonelli	15.00
245	John Beradino	15.00
248	Johnny Klippstein	15.00
253	Mickey Mantle	4500.00
254	Jackie Jensen	85.00
255	Milo Candini	40.00
256	Ken Silvestri	40.00
257	Birdie Tebbetts	40.00
258	Luke Easter	48.00
259	Charlie Dressen	45.00
260	Carl Erskine	90.00

2 Larry "Yogi" Berra

261	Wally Moses	40.00
262	Gus Zernial	40.00
263	Howie Pollett	40.00

264	Don Richmond	40.00
265	Steve Bilko	40.00
266	Harry Dorish	40.00
267	Ken Holcombe	40.00
268	Don Mueller	40.00
269	Ray Noble	40.00
270	Willard Nixon	40.00
271	Tommy Wright	40.00
272	Billy Meyer	40.00
273	Danny Murtaugh	45.00
274	George Metkovich	40.00
275	Bucky Harris	60.00
276	Frank Quinn	40.00
277	Roy Hartsfield	40.00
278	Norman Roy	40.00
279	Jim Delsing	40.00
280	Frank Overmire	40.00
281	Al Widmar	40.00
282	Frank Frisch	65.00
284	Gene Bearden	42.00
285	Johnny Lipon	40.00
286	Bob Usher	40.00
287	Jim Blackburn	40.00
288	Bobby Adams	40.00
289	Cliff Mapes	40.00
290	Bill Dickey	175.00
291	Tommy Henrich	60.00
292	Eddie Pellagrini	40.00
293	Ken Johnson	40.00
294	Jocko Thompson	40.00

295	Al Lopez	70.00
296	Bob Kennedy	40.00
297	Dave Philley	40.00
298	Joe Astroth	40.00
299	Clyde King	42.00
300	Hal Rice	40.00
301	Tommy Glaviano	40.00
302	Jim Busby	40.00
303	Marv Rotblatt	40.00
304	Allen Gettel	40.00
305	*Willie Mays*	1600.00
306	*Jim Piersall*	85.00
307	Walt Masterson	40.00
308	Ted Beard	40.00
309	Mel Queen	40.00
310	Erv Dusak	40.00
311	Mickey Harris	40.00
312	Gene Mauch	50.00
313	Ray Mueller	40.00
314	Johnny Sain	50.00
315	Zack Taylor	40.00
316	Duane Pillette	40.00
317	*Forrest Burgess*	50.00
318	Warren Hacker	40.00
319	Red Rolfe	40.00
320	Hal White	40.00
321	Earl Johnson	40.00
322	Luke Sewell	40.00
323	Joe Adcock	75.00
324	Johnny Pramesa	90.00

1951 TOPPS BLUE BACKS

In addition to the designations for series A and B on the card fronts, the only differences between the Topps Blue Back and Red Back sets are secondary border colors on the cards and scarcity in distribution. Both 52-card issues were sold at approximately the same time and packaged with two cards and a piece of candy for a penny. A large supply of Red Backs was discovered in a Philadelphia warehouse in the 1980s, but the Blue Backs are tougher to find. Fortunately, the cards were printed on heavy cardboard and are still found in top condition today. Each round-cornered card measures 2 by 2 5/8 inches.

50 Johnny Mize

		NR MT
Complete set		**$1800.00**
Commons		**26.00**
1	Eddie Yost	$30.00
3	Richie Ashburn	48.00
4	Del Ennis	28.00
5	Johnny Pesky	30.00
6	Albert (Red) Schoendienst	35.00
7	Gerald Staley	28.00
8	Dick Sisler	28.00
9	Johnny Sain	34.00
10	Joe Page	34.00
12	Sam Jethroe	28.00
13	James (Mickey) Vernon	25.00
15	Eddie Joost	28.00
16	Murry Dickson	28.00
17	Roy Smalley	28.00

18	Ned Garver	28.00
20	Ralph Branca	30.00
21	Billy Johnson	28.00
23	Paul (Dizzy) Trout	28.00
24	Sherman Lollar	28.00
25	Sam Mele	28.00
26	Chico Carresquel	28.00
27	Andy Pafko	25.00
28	Harry (The Cat) Brecheen	28.00
29	Granville Hamner	28.00
30	Enos (Country) Slaughter	60.00
32	Bob Elliott	28.00
34	Earl Torgeson	28.00
35	Tommy Byrne	28.00
36	Cliff Fannin	28.00
37	Bobby Doerr	53.00
39	Ed Lopat	28.00
40	Vic Wertz	25.00

41	Johnny Schmitz	28.00
43	Willie (Puddin' Head) Jones	30.00
45	Bill Pierce	30.00
48	Billy Cox	28.00
49	Henry (Hank) Sauer	28.00
50	Johnny Mize	60.00

1951 TOPPS RED BACKS

Although recognized as the first widespread baseball offering of the company, the 1951 Topps Red Backs set is one of the least appreciated of the early sets. The 52-card set was designed like a deck of playing cards, to be used in playing a basic baseball game because Bowman, at that time, held an exclusive contract to produce bubble gum cards. In addition to a black-and-white player photo set in a baseball diamond in the card center, each round-cornered card featured the player name, a short biography, and a number.

38 Ed (Duke) Snider

		NR MT
Complete set		**$700.00**
Commons		**8.00**
1	Larry (Yogi) Berra	$75.00
3	Ferris Fain	8.00
4	Verne Stephens	8.00
5	*Phil Rizzuto	23.00
6	Allie Reynolds	10.00
7	Howie Pollet	5.00
8	Early Wynn	25.00
9	Roy Sievers	6.00
10	Mel Parnell	6.00
12	Jim Hegan	5.00
13	Dale Mitchell	5.00
15	Ralph Kiner	25.00
16	Preacher Roe	8.00
17	Dave Bell	8.00
18	Gerry Coleman	8.00
20	Dominick DiMaggio	12.00
21	Larry Jansen	5.00
22	Bob Feller	25.00
23	Ray Boone	6.00
24	Hank Bauer	9.00
26	Luke Easter	8.00
29	Bob Kennedy	5.00
30	Warren Spahn	25.00
31	Gil Hodges	25.00
34	Grady Hatton	5.00
35	Al Rosen	10.00
36	Gus Zernial (Chicago in bio)	20.00
36	Gus Zernial (Philadelphia in bio)	11.00
37	Wes Westrum	6.00
38	Ed (Duke) Snider	55.00
39	Ted Kluszewski	10.00
40	Mike Garcia	8.00
41	Whitey Lockman	5.00
44	Sid Hudson	5.00
45	Andy Seminick	5.00
48	Eddie Stanky	6.00
50	Monte Irvin	22.00
51	Eddie Robinson	5.00
52	Tommy Holmes (Boston in bio)	20.00
52	Tommy Holmes (Hartford in bio)	20.00

1952 BOWMAN

The 1952 Bowman set follows a format similar to the 1951 issue. Players on the card fronts are depicted in paintings made from photographs. Unlike 1951, however, each player name appears as a facsimile autograph on card fronts. Backs show black printing on gray cardboard but maintain the 1951 format of the player name and vital data along with a brief biography. Some cards advertise a mail-in offer, which provided a baseball cap for five wrappers and 50 cents. Despite the reduced number of cards (just 252, compared to 324 in 1951), the 1952 Bowman set has enjoyed non-stop popularity because of its simple design and striking paintings.

101 Mickey Mantle

		NR MT
Complete set		**$7800.00**
Commons (1-36)		**12.00**
Commons (37-216)		**10.00**
Commons (217-252)		**20.00**
1	Larry "Yogi" Berra	$625.00
2	Bobby Thomson	30.00
3	Fred Hutchinson	14.00
4	Robin Roberts	45.00
5	*Orestes Minoso*	35.00
6	Virgil "Red" Stallcup	12.00
7	Mike Garcia	14.00
8	Harold "Pee Wee" Reese	150.00
9	Vern Stephens	12.00
10	Bob Hooper	12.00
11	Ralph Kiner	45.00
12	Max Surkont	12.00
13	Cliff Mapes	12.00
14	Cliff Chambers	12.00
15	Sam Mele	12.00

1952 Bowman

218 Willie Mays

196 Stan Musial

#	Player	Price
64	Roy Smalley	10.00
65	Hank Bauer	20.00
66	Sal Maglie	20.00
69	Joe Adcock	12.00
70	Carl Erskine	18.00
71	Vernon Law	12.00
73	Jerry Coleman	18.00
74	Wes Westrum	12.00
75	George Kell	40.00
76	Del Ennis	12.00
80	Gil Hodges	45.00
82	Gus Zernial	10.00
84	Sam Jethroe	10.00
85	*Marty Marion	12.00
86	Cal Abrams	12.00
87	Mickey Vernon	12.00
93	Paul Richards	12.00
94	Luke Sewell	10.00
95	Luke Easter	12.00
96	Ralph Branca	18.00
98	Jimmy Dykes	12.00
100	Sibby Sisti	10.00
101	Mickey Mantle	1500.00
102	Peanuts Lowrey	10.00
103	Joe Haynes	10.00
104	Hal Jeffcoat	10.00
105	*Bobby Brown	18.00
107	Del Rice	10.00
109	Tom Morgan	15.00
110	Max Lanier	10.00
111	Walter "Hoot" Evers	10.00
112	Forrest "Smokey" Burgess	12.00
113	Al Zarilla	10.00
114	Frank Hiller	10.00
115	Larry Doby	15.00
116	Duke Snider	150.00
120	Chet Nichols	10.00
126	Phil Cavarretta	12.00
127	Dick Sisler	10.00
128	Don Newcombe	20.00
131	Bob Swift	10.00
134	Al Brazle	10.00

1 Larry "Yogi" Berra

#	Player	Price
16	Omar Lown	12.00
17	Ed Lopat	25.00
18	Don Mueller	12.00
19	Bob Cain	12.00
20	Willie Jones	14.00
21	Nelson Fox	35.00
22	Willard Ramsell	12.00
23	Bob Lemon	45.00
24	Carl Furillo	20.00
25	Maurice McDermott	12.00
26	Eddie Joost	12.00
27	Joe Garagiola	70.00
28	Roy Hartsfield	12.00
29	Ned Garver	12.00
30	Al "Red" Schoendienst	55.00
31	Eddie Yost	12.00
32	Eddie Miksis	12.00
33	*Gil McDougald*	40.00
34	Al Dark	16.00
35	Gran Hamner	12.00
36	Cass Michaels	12.00
37	Vic Raschi	21.00
38	Whitey Lockman	10.00
39	Vic Wertz	12.00
40	Emory Church	10.00
41	Chico Carrasquel	10.00
43	Bob Feller	115.00
44	Roy Campanella	200.00
45	Johnny Pesky	12.00
48	Vern Bickford	10.00
49	Jim Hearn	10.00
50	Gerry Staley	10.00
51	Gil Coan	10.00
52	Phil Rizzuto	55.00
53	Richie Ashburn	40.00
54	*Billy Pierce	12.00
56	Clyde King	12.00
58	Hank Majeski	10.00
59	Murray Dickson	10.00
60	Sid Gordon	10.00
61	Tommy Byrne	10.00

#	Player	Price
139	Jerry Priddy	10.00
142	Early Wynn	45.00
145	Johnny Mize	50.00
146	*Leo Durocher	35.00
151	Al "Flip" Rosen	18.00
152	Billy Cox	12.00
154	Ferris Fain	12.00
156	Warren Spahn	70.00
158	Bucky Harris	30.00
159	Dutch Leonard	10.00
160	Eddie Stanky	12.00
161	Jackie Jensen	25.00
162	Monte Irvin	35.00
163	Johnny Lipon	10.00
164	Connie Ryan	10.00
165	Saul Rogovin	10.00
166	Bobby Adams	10.00
167	Bob Avila	10.00
168	Preacher Roe	18.00
169	Walt Dropo	10.00
170	Joe Astroth	10.00
173	Gene Bearden	10.00
174	Mickey Grasso	10.00
175	Ransom Jackson	10.00
176	Harry Brecheen	12.00
177	Gene Woodling	16.00
178	Dave Williams	10.00
179	Pete Suder	10.00
181	Joe Collins	15.00
184	Curt Simmons	12.00
188	Charlie Dressen	15.00
189	Jim Piersall	15.00
191	Bob Friend	15.00
196	Stan Musial	400.00
197	Charlie Silvera	13.00
198	Chuck Diering	10.00
199	Ted Gray	10.00
201	Ray Coleman	10.00
203	Steve Gromek	10.00
204	Andy Pafko	13.00
206	Elmer Valo	10.00

207	George Strickland	10.00
213	Monte Kennedy	10.00
214	Ray Boone	12.00
217	Casey Stengel	125.00
218	Willie Mays	725.00
219	Neil Berry	25.00
220	Russ Meyer	25.00
221	Lou Kretlow	25.00
222	Homer "Dixie" Howell	25.00
223	Harry Simpson	25.00
224	Johnny Schmitz	27.00
225	Del Wilber	25.00
226	Alex Kellner	25.00

227	Clyde Sukeforth	25.00
228	Bob Chipman	25.00
229	Hank Arft	25.00
230	Frank Shea	25.00
231	Dee Fondy	25.00
232	Enos Slaughter	60.00
233	Bob Kuzava	31.00
234	Fred Fitzsimmons	25.00
235	Steve Souchock	25.00
236	Tommy Brown	25.00
237	Sherman Lollar	27.00
238	Roy McMillan	26.00
239	Dale Mitchell	25.00

1952 Bowman/1952 Topps

240	*Billy Loes*	32.00
241	Mel Parnell	27.00
242	Everett Kell	25.00
243	George "Red" Munger	25.00
244	*Lew Burdette*	65.00
245	George Schmees	25.00
246	Jerry Snyder	25.00
247	John Pramesa	25.00
248	Bill Werle	25.00
249	Henry Thompson	25.00
250	Ivan Delock	25.00
251	Jack Lohrke	31.00
252	Frank Crosetti	125.00

1952 TOPPS

By far the most valuable *set* of baseball cards of the post-World War II period, the marvelous 1952 Topps set also contains the single most valuable *card* of that time: Number 311, showing the great Mickey Mantle, is currently valued at about $8500. Both in terms of size (2⅝ by 3¼ inches) and number of cards (407), the Topps set was the biggest baseball product of 1952. The cards offer colorized black-and-white photos along with the player name, facsimile autograph, and team logo on a movie marquee card front. The backs, for the first time, include both 1951 and lifetime statistics. The final series of cards (311-407) is extremely rare and commands premium prices. How popular is the 1952 Topps set? Even the reprinted set, issued by Topps in 1983, has grown in price from $40 to as much as $200 today.

311 Mickey Mantle

	NR MT
Complete set	$40,250.00
Commons (1-80)	50.00
Commons (81-250)	20.00
Commons (251-280)	40.00
Commons (281-300)	45.00
Commons (301-310)	40.00
Commons (311-407)	150.00

1	Andy Pafko	$1000.00
2	James E. Runnells	75.00
3	Hank Thompson	50.00
4	Don Lenhardt	50.00
5	Larry Jansen	55.00
6	Grady Hatton	50.00
7	Wayne Terwilliger	55.00
8	Fred Marsh	55.00
9	Bobby Hogue	60.00
10	Al Rosen	85.00
11	Phil Rizzuto	175.00
12	Monty Basgall	55.00
13	Johnny Wyrostek	55.00
14	Bob Elliott	50.00
15	Johnny Pesky	60.00
16	Gene Hermanski	55.00
17	Jim Hegan	55.00
18	Merrill Combs	50.00
19	Johnny Bucha	50.00
20	*Billy Loes*	150.00
21	Ferris Fain	60.00

22	Dom DiMaggio	90.00
23	Billy Goodman	55.00
24	Luke Easter	60.00
25	Johnny Groth	55.00
26	Monty Irvin	100.00
27	Sam Jethroe	55.00
28	Jerry Priddy	50.00
29	Ted Kluszewski	80.00
30	Mel Parnell	60.00
31	Gus Zernial	60.00
32	Eddie Robinson	50.00
33	Warren Spahn	190.00
34	Elmer Valo	50.00
35	Hank Sauer	55.00
36	Gil Hodges	150.00
37	Duke Snider	275.00
38	Wally Westlake	50.00
39	"Dizzy" Trout	55.00
40	Irv Noren	50.00
41	Bob Wellman	50.00
42	Lou Kretlow	50.00
43	Ray Scarborough	50.00
44	Con Dempsey	50.00
45	Eddie Joost	50.00
46	Gordon Goldsberry	50.00
47	Willie Jones	55.00
48	Joe Page (Johnny Sain bio)	225.00
48	Joe Page (correct bio)	90.00
49	Johnny Sain (Joe Page bio)	225.00
49	Johnny Sain (correct bio)	90.00

50	Marv Rickert	50.00
51	Jim Russell	50.00
52	Don Mueller	50.00
53	Chris Van Cuyk	50.00
54	Leo Kiely	50.00
55	Ray Boone	60.00
56	Tommy Glaviano	55.00
57	Ed Lopat	75.00
58	Bob Mahoney	50.00
59	Robin Roberts	135.00
60	Sid Hudson	55.00
61	"Tookie" Gilbert	55.00
62	Chuck Stobbs	55.00
63	Howie Pollet	55.00
64	Roy Sievers	70.00
65	Enos Slaughter	135.00
66	"Preacher" Roe	85.00
67	Allie Reynolds	90.00
68	Cliff Chambers	50.00
69	Virgil Stallcup	50.00
70	Al Zarilla	50.00

407 Ed Mathews

71	Tom Upton	50.00
72	Karl Olson	50.00
73	William Werle	50.00
74	Andy Hansen	50.00
75	Wes Westrum	55.00
76	Eddie Stanky	65.00
77	Bob Kennedy	50.00
78	Ellis Kinder	50.00
79	Gerald Staley	50.00
80	Herman Wehmeier	50.00
81	Vernon Law	25.00
88	Bob Feller	135.00
91	Al Schoendienst	55.00
98	*Bill Pierce	25.00
99	Gene Woodling	40.00
101	Max Lanier	20.00
106	Mickey Vernon	25.00
108	Jim Konstanty	25.00
117	Sherman Lollar	25.00
122	Jack Jensen	60.00
123	Eddie Yost	25.00
125	Bill Rigney	25.00
126	Fred Hutchinson	25.00
129	Johnny Mize	75.00
140	John Antonelli	25.00
162	Del Crandall	25.00
170	Gus Bell	25.00
175	Billy Martin	250.00
180	Charley Maxwell	25.00
189	Pete Reiser	25.00
191	Yogi Berra	335.00
195	Orestes Minoso	50.00
200	Ralph Houk	50.00
203	Curt Simmons	25.00
215	Hank Bauer	40.00
216	Richie Ashburn	60.00
219	Bobby Shantz	25.00
223	Del Ennis	25.00
224	Bruce Edwards	20.00
225	Frank Baumholtz	20.00
226	Dave Philley	25.00
227	Joe Garagiola	65.00
228	Al Brazle	20.00

229	Gene Bearden	25.00
230	Matt Batts	20.00
231	Sam Zoldak	20.00
232	Billy Cox	25.00
233	Bob Friend	25.00
234	Steve Souchock	20.00
235	Walt Dropo	25.00
236	Ed Fitz Gerald	20.00
237	Jerry Coleman	30.00
238	Art Houtteman	20.00
239	Rocky Bridges	25.00
240	Jack Phillips	20.00
241	Tommy Byrne	20.00
242	Tom Poholsky	20.00
243	Larry Doby	30.00
244	Vic Wertz	25.00
245	Sherry Robertson	20.00
246	George Kell	50.00
247	Randy Gumpert	20.00
248	Frank Shea	20.00
249	Bobby Adams	20.00
250	Carl Erskine	50.00
251	Chico Carrasquel	40.00
252	Vern Bickford	40.00
253	Johnny Berardino	50.00
254	Joe Dobson	40.00
255	Clyde Vollmer	40.00
256	Pete Suder	40.00
257	Bobby Avila	40.00
258	Steve Gromek	40.00
259	Bob Addis	40.00
260	Pete Castiglione	40.00
261	Willie Mays	1000.00
262	Virgil Trucks	45.00
263	Harry Brecheen	45.00
264	Roy Hartsfield	40.00
265	Chuck Diering	40.00
266	Murry Dickson	40.00
267	Sid Gordon	40.00
268	Bob Lemon	150.00
269	Willard Nixon	40.00
270	Lou Brissie	40.00
271	Jim Delsing	40.00
272	Mike Garcia	45.00

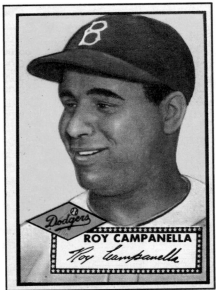

314 Roy Campanella

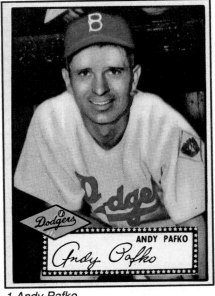

1 Andy Pafko

273	Erv Palica	40.00
274	Ralph Branca	60.00
275	Pat Mullin	40.00
276	Jim Wilson	40.00
277	Early Wynn	150.00
278	Al Clark	40.00
279	Ed Stewart	40.00
280	Cloyd Boyer	40.00
281	Tommy Brown	45.00
282	Birdie Tebbetts	50.00
283	Phil Masi	45.00
284	Hank Arft	45.00
285	Cliff Fannin	45.00
286	Joe DeMaestri	45.00
287	Steve Bilko	45.00
288	Chet Nichols	45.00
289	Tommy Holmes	50.00
290	Joe Astroth	45.00
291	Gil Coan	45.00
292	Floyd Baker	45.00
293	Sibby Sisti	45.00
294	Walker Cooper	45.00
295	Phil Cavarretta	50.00
296	"Red" Rolfe	45.00
297	Andy Seminick	50.00
298	Bob Ross	45.00
299	Ray Murray	45.00
300	Barney McCosky	45.00
301	Bob Porterfield	40.00
302	Max Surkont	40.00
303	Harry Dorish	40.00
304	Sam Dente	40.00
305	Paul Richards	45.00
306	Lou Sleator	40.00
307	Frank Campos	40.00
308	Luis Aloma	40.00
309	Jim Busby	40.00
310	George Metkovich	40.00
311	Mickey Mantle	8500.00
312	Jackie Robinson	800.00
313	Bobby Thomson	175.00
314	Roy Campanella	1250.00
315	Leo Durocher	225.00

316	Davey Williams	150.00	347	Joe Adcock	175.00	
317	Connie Marrero	150.00	348	Bob Kelly	150.00	
318	Hal Gregg	150.00	349	Bob Cain	150.00	
319	Al Walker	150.00	350	Cal Abrams	155.00	
320	John Rutherford	150.00	351	Al Dark	200.00	
321	*Joe Black*	200.00	352	Karl Drews	200.00	
322	Randy Jackson	150.00	353	Bob Del Greco	150.00	
323	Bubba Church	150.00	354	Fred Hatfield	150.00	
324	Warren Hacker	150.00	355	Bobby Morgan	150.00	
325	Bill Serena	150.00	356	Toby Atwell	150.00	
326	George Shuba	150.00	357	Smoky Burgess	175.00	
327	Archie Wilson	150.00	358	John Kucab	150.00	
328	Bob Borkowski	150.00	359	Dee Fondy	150.00	
329	Ivan Delock	150.00	360	George Crowe	150.00	
330	Turk Lown	150.00	361	Bill Posedel	150.00	
331	Tom Morgan	155.00	362	Ken Heintzelman	150.00	
332	Tony Bartirome	150.00	363	Dick Rozek	150.00	
333	Pee Wee Reese	500.00	364	Clyde Sukeforth	150.00	
334	Wilmer Mizell	150.00	365	"Cookie" Lavagetto	155.00	
335	Ted Lepcio	150.00	366	Dave Madison	150.00	
336	Dave Koslo	150.00	367	Bob Thorpe	150.00	
337	Jim Hearn	150.00	368	Ed Wright	150.00	
338	Sal Yvars	150.00	369	*Dick Groat*	250.00	
339	Russ Meyer	150.00	370	Billy Hoeft	150.00	
340	Bob Hooper	150.00	371	Bob Hofman	150.00	
341	Hal Jeffcoat	150.00	372	*Gil McDougald*	250.00	
342	*Clem Labine*	200.00	373	Jim Turner	150.00	
343	Dick Gernert	150.00	374	Al Benton	150.00	
344	Ewell Blackwell	155.00	375	Jack Merson	150.00	
345	Sam White	150.00	376	Faye Throneberry	150.00	
346	George Spencer	150.00	377	Chuck Dressen	175.00	

1952 Topps/1953 Bowman B&W

378	Les Fusselman	150.00
379	Joe Rossi	150.00
380	Clem Koshorek	150.00
381	Milton Stock	150.00
382	Sam Jones	150.00
383	Del Wilber	150.00
384	Frank Crosetti	250.00
385	Herman Franks	150.00
386	Eddie Yuhas	150.00
387	Billy Meyer	150.00
388	Bob Chipman	150.00
389	Ben Wade	150.00
390	Glen Nelson	150.00
391	Ben Chapman (photo is Sam Chapman)	150.00
392	*Hoyt Wilhelm*	400.00
393	Ebba St. Claire	150.00
394	Billy Herman	200.00
395	Jake Pitler	150.00
396	*Dick Williams*	175.00
397	Forrest Main	150.00
398	Hal Rice	150.00
399	Jim Fridley	150.00
400	Bill Dickey	500.00
401	Bob Schultz	150.00
402	Earl Harrist	150.00
403	Bill Miller	150.00
404	Dick Brodowski	150.00
405	Eddie Pellagrini	150.00
406	*Joe Nuxhall*	175.00
407	*Ed Mathews*	1800.00

1953 BOWMAN B&W

The 1953 Bowman black-and-white set was a separate issue from the Bowman color cards of the same year. The black-and-white cards came in a different wrapper and are numbered 1 through 64. In format, however, the sets are identical. Each one measures 2 1/2 by 3 3/4 inches, with a full photo surrounded by a black line and a white border. Card backs show a biography, stats for 1952, and lifetime stats. A blank line to write in statistics for the current year was included; thankfully, few youngsters took advantage of the opportunity. As a result, nearly all cards found today are free of any writing.

39 Casey Stengel

		NR MT
Complete set		**$2250.00**
Commons		**22.00**

1	Gus Bell	$80.00	12	Randy Jackson	22.00	
2	Willard Nixon	22.00	13	Joe Tipton	22.00	
3	Bill Rigney	26.00	14	Bill Nicholson	22.00	
4	Pat Mullin	22.00	15	Johnny Mize	125.00	
5	Dee Fondy	22.00	16	Stu Miller	22.00	
6	Ray Murray	22.00	17	Virgil Trucks	25.00	
7	Andy Seminick	22.00	18	Billy Hoeft	22.00	
8	Pete Suder	22.00	19	Paul LaPalme	22.00	
9	Walt Masterson	22.00	20	Eddie Robinson	22.00	
10	Dick Sisler	22.00	25	John Sain	50.00	
11	Dick Gernert	22.00	26	Preacher Roe	50.00	
			27	Bob Lemon	90.00	
			28	Hoyt Wilhelm	90.00	
			29	Sid Hudson	22.00	
			30	Walker Cooper	22.00	

31	Gene Woodling	40.00
32	Rocky Bridges	25.00

17

28 Hoyt Wilhelm

33	Bob Kuzava	25.00
36	Jim Piersall	35.00
37	Hal Jeffcoat	22.00
38	Dave Cole	22.00
39	Casey Stengel	300.00
40	Larry Jensen	22.00
41	Bob Ramazotti	22.00
42	Howie Judson	22.00
44	Jim Delsing	22.00
45	Irv Noren	22.00
46	Bucky Harris	50.00
51	Lou Burdette	40.00
52	Ralph Branca	40.00
53	Morris Martin	22.00
54	Bill Miller	22.00
56	Roy Smalley	22.00
57	Andy Pafko	28.00
58	Jim Konstanty	25.00
59	Duane Pillette	22.00
60	Billy Cox	30.00
61	Tom Gorman	22.00
62	Keith Thomas	22.00
63	Steve Gromek	25.00
64	Andy Hansen	35.00

27 Bob Lemon

1953 BOWMAN COLOR

Many collectors consider Bowman's 1953 set of 160 cards—the first ever to make use of color photography (as opposed to black-and-white colorized photos)—to be the most beautiful ever created. The jump in technology was due to competition from Topps, as was Bowman's increased card size (2 1/2 by 3 3/4 inches) and the inclusion of stats on the card backs, which are cream colored with red-and-black print. The splendid photographs are presented with a simple white border. Stan Musial made his farewell Bowman appearance in this set. Multiple player photos—a first in this century—include one card of Martin and Rizzuto; another of Mantle, Berra, and Bauer.

59 Mickey Mantle

		NR MT
Complete set		**$12,250.00**
Commons (1-112)		**25.00**
Commons (113-128)		**35.00**
Commons (129-160)		**30.00**

1	Davey Williams	$120.00
2	Vic Wertz	27.00
3	Sam Jethroe	25.00
8	Al Rosen	50.00
9	Phil Rizzuto	90.00
10	Richie Ashburn	75.00
11	Bobby Shantz	27.00
12	Carl Erskine	50.00
14	Billy Loes	27.00
16	Bob Friend	27.00
18	Nelson Fox	60.00
19	Al Dark	35.00
21	Joe Garagiola	75.00
24	Jackie Jensen	35.00
27	Vic Raschi	50.00

28	Forrest "Smoky" Burgess	27.00
30	Phil Cavarretta	27.00
31	Jimmy Dykes	27.00
32	Stan Musial	500.00
33	Harold "Peewee" Reese	300.00
36	Orestes Minoso	55.00
39	Paul Richards	27.00
40	Larry Doby	50.00
43	Mike Garcia	27.00
44	Hank Bauer, Yogi Berra, Mickey Mantle	425.00
46	Roy Campanella	300.00
48	Hank Sauer	25.00
49	Eddie Stanky	27.00
51	Monte Irvin	50.00
52	*Marty Marion	26.00
55	Leo Durocher	75.00
56	Bob Cain	25.00
57	Lou Boudreau	50.00

59	Mickey Mantle	1300.00
60	Granny Hamner	25.00
61	George Kell	50.00
62	Ted Kluszewski	50.00
63	Gil McDougald	50.00
65	Robin Roberts	60.00
68	Allie Reynolds	50.00
69	Charlie Grimm	27.00

117 Duke Snider

100	Bill Wight	25.00
101	Al "Red" Schoendienst	75.00
102	Jim Hegan	25.00
103	Del Ennis	25.00
104	Luke Easter	25.00
105	Eddie Joost	25.00
106	Ken Raffensberger	25.00
107	Alex Kellner	25.00
108	Bobby Adams	25.00
109	Ken Wood	25.00
110	Bob Rush	25.00
113	Karl Drews	35.00
114	Bob Feller	300.00
115	Cloyd Boyer	35.00
116	Eddie Yost	35.00
117	Duke Snider	500.00
118	Billy Martin	300.00
119	Dale Mitchell	35.00
120	Marlin Stuart	35.00
121	Yogi Berra	500.00
122	Bill Serena	35.00
123	Johnny Lipon	35.00
124	Charlie Dressen	45.00
125	Fred Hatfield	35.00

153 Ed "Whitey" Ford

70	Clint Courtney	25.00
73	Billy Pierce	27.00
78	Carl Furillo	50.00
79	Ray Boone	27.00
80	Ralph Kiner	65.00
81	Enos Slaughter	60.00
84	Hank Bauer	50.00
85	Solly Hemus	25.00
90	Joe Nuxhall	27.00
92	Gil Hodges	100.00
93	Billy Martin, Phil Rizzuto	225.00
94	Bob Addis	25.00
96	Sal Maglie	30.00
97	Eddie Mathews	100.00
98	Hector Rodriquez	25.00
99	Warren Spahn	135.00

44 Bauer, Berra, Mantle

126	Al Corwin	35.00
127	Dick Kryhoski	35.00
128	Whitey Lockman	35.00
129	Russ Meyer	35.00
130	Cass Michaels	30.00
131	Connie Ryan	30.00
132	Fred Hutchinson	35.00
133	Willie Jones	30.00
134	Johnny Pesky	35.00
135	Bobby Morgan	30.00
136	Jim Brideweser	30.00
137	Sam Dente	30.00
138	Bubba Church	30.00
139	Pete Runnels	35.00
140	Alpha Brazle	30.00
141	Frank "Spec" Shea	30.00
142	Larry Miggins	30.00
143	Al Lopez	75.00

144	Warren Hacker	30.00
145	George Shuba	35.00
146	Early Wynn	135.00
148	Billy Goodman	30.00
149	Al Corwin	30.00
150	Carl Scheib	30.00
151	Joe Adcock	35.00
152	Clyde Vollmer	30.00
153	Ed "Whitey" Ford	550.00
154	Omar "Turk" Lown	30.00
155	Allie Clark	30.00
156	Max Surkont	30.00
157	Sherman Lollar	35.00
158	Howard Fox	30.00
159	Mickey Vernon (photo is Floyd Baker)	40.00
160	Cal Abrams	100.00

32 Stan Musial

46 Roy Campanella

1953 TOPPS

Topps' second set was reduced to 274 cards due to player contract disputes with Bowman. Cards are numbered to 280, but due to last-minute legal considerations, six are missing (numbers 253, 261, 267, 268, 271, and 275). With no checklists to guide them, frustrated collectors pursued these non-existent cards in vain. Measuring 2⁵/₈ by 3³/₄ inches, the fronts feature a color painting, a team logo, and a panel for player identification. Backs are red and black printed on gray cardboard, with the first of Topps' popular Dugout Quiz series. Although the Mick's card is the most expensive, Willie Mays' is scarcer, as is a mint Jackie Robinson. Numbers 221-280 command premium value if the player's personal stats in the upper red panel are listed in black instead of white.

244 Willie Mays

82 Mickey Mantle

		NR MT
Complete set		**$12,500.00**
Commons (1-165) single-print		**25.00**
Commons (1-165) double-print		**20.00**
Commons (166-220)		**18.00**
Commons (221-280) single-print		**90.00**
Commons (221-280) double-print		**45.00**

#	Player	Price
1	Jackie Robinson	$700.00
2	Luke Easter	23.00
3	George Crowe	22.00
4	Ben Wade	22.00
5	Joe Dobson	23.00
6	Sam Jones	23.00
9	Joe Collins	30.00
10	Smoky Burgess	30.00
11	Sal Yvars	23.00
14	Clem Labine	24.00
15	Bobo Newsom	24.00
17	Billy Hitchcock	25.00
20	Hank Thompson	25.00
21	Billy Johnson	25.00
22	Howie Fox	25.00
24	Ferris Fain	25.00
25	Ray Boone	25.00
27	Roy Campanella	250.00
28	Eddie Pellagrini	25.00
29	Hal Jeffcoat	25.00
30	Willard Nixon	25.00
31	Ewell Blackwell	40.00
32	Clyde Vollmer	25.00
34	George Shuba	25.00
35	Irv Noren	25.00
37	Ed Mathews	100.00
39	Eddie Miksis	25.00
40	John Lipon	25.00
41	Enos Slaughter	75.00
42	Gus Zernial	21.00
43	Gil McDougald	35.00
44	Ellis Kinder	27.00
47	Bubba Church	20.00
50	Chuck Dressen	26.00
54	Bob Feller	100.00
57	Carl Scheib	25.00
58	George Metkovich	20.00
61	Early Wynn	85.00
62	Monte Irvin	35.00
64	Dave Philley	20.00
65	Earl Harrist	20.00
66	*Orestes Minoso	27.00
67	*Roy Sievers	21.00
68	Del Rice	20.00
69	Dick Brodowski	20.00
70	Ed Yuhas	20.00
71	Tony Bartirome	20.00
72	Fred Hutchinson	20.00
73	Eddie Robinson	20.00
74	Joe Rossi	20.00
75	Mike Garcia	20.00
76	Pee Wee Reese	100.00
77	John Mize	80.00
78	Al Schoendienst	50.00
79	Johnny Wyrostek	20.00
80	Jim Hegan	20.00
81	Joe Black	40.00
82	Mickey Mantle	2000.00
83	Howie Pollet	20.00
85	Bobby Morgan	20.00
86	Billy Martin	65.00
87	Ed Lopat	35.00
96	Virgil Trucks	20.00
99	Dave Madison	19.00
100	Bill Miller	19.00
101	Ted Wilks	19.00
102	Connie Ryan	19.00
103	Joe Astroth	19.00
104	Yogi Berra	175.00
105	Joe Nuxhall	19.00
106	Johnny Antonelli	19.00
107	Danny O'Connell	18.00
108	Bob Porterfield	18.00
109	Alvin Dark	25.00
110	Herman Wehmeier	18.00
111	Hank Sauer	18.00
112	Ned Garver	18.00
113	Jerry Priddy	18.00
114	Phil Rizzuto	75.00
115	George Spencer	18.00
116	Frank Smith	18.00
117	Sid Gordon	18.00
118	Gus Bell	19.00
119	*John Sain	35.00
120	Davey Williams	18.00
121	Walt Dropo	18.00
122	Elmer Valo	18.00
123	Tommy Byrne	18.00
124	Sibby Sisti	18.00
125	Dick Williams	23.00
126	Bill Connelly	19.00
127	Clint Courtney	19.00
128	Wilmer Mizell	21.00
129	Keith Thomas	19.00
130	Turk Lown	20.00
131	Harry Byrd	19.00
132	Tom Morgan	22.00
133	Gil Coan	19.00
134	Rube Walker	20.00
135	Al Rosen	30.00
136	Ken Heintzelman	20.00

137	John Rutherford	20.00
138	George Kell	60.00
139	Sammy White	19.00
140	Tommy Glaviano	19.00
141	Allie Reynolds	35.00
142	Vic Wertz	20.00
143	*Billy Pierce	20.00
144	Bob Schultz	19.00
145	Harry Dorish	19.00
146	Granville Hamner	20.00
147	Warren Spahn	100.00
148	Mickey Grasso	19.00
149	Dom DiMaggio	25.00
150	Harry Simpson	19.00
151	Hoyt Wilhelm	50.00
152	Bob Adams	19.00
153	Andy Seminick	20.00
154	Dick Groat	27.00
155	Dutch Leonard	20.00
156	Jim Rivera	19.00
157	Bob Addis	19.00
158	John Logan	20.00
159	Wayne Terwilliger	20.00
160	Bob Young	19.00
161	Vern Bickford	19.00
162	Ted Kluszewski	30.00
163	Fred Hatfield	19.00
164	Frank Shea	19.00
165	Billy Hoeft	20.00
167	Art Schult	19.00
169	Dizzy Trout	18.00
174	Billy Loes	19.00
176	Don Hoak	18.00
183	Stu Miller	19.00
184	Hal Brown	18.00
188	Andy Carey	20.00
190	Dixie Walker	18.00
191	Ralph Kiner	50.00
197	Del Crandall	21.00
206	Ed Bailey	18.00
207	Whitey Ford	100.00
210	Bob Cerv	20.00
213	Ray Scarborough	18.00

214	Bill Bruton	18.00
215	Gene Conley	18.00
216	Jim Hughes	18.00
219	Pete Runnels (photo is Don Johnson)	18.00
220	Satchell Paige	375.00
221	Bob Milliken	45.00
222	Vic Janowicz	45.00
223	John O'Brien	45.00
224	Lou Sleater	45.00
225	Bobby Shantz	60.00
226	Ed Erautt	45.00
227	Morris Martin	45.00
228	Hal Newhouser	100.00
229	Rocky Krsnich	45.00
230	Johnny Lindell	45.00
231	Solly Hemus	45.00

280 Milt Bolling

257	Bob Boyd	45.00
258	*Jim Gilliam*	250.00
259	Roy McMillan	45.00
260	Sam Calderone	45.00
262	Bob Oldis	45.00
263	*John Podres*	250.00
264	Gene Woodling	75.00
265	Jackie Jensen	125.00
266	Bob Cain	45.00
269	Duane Pillette	45.00
272	Bill Antonello	45.00
273	*Harvey Haddix*	100.00
274	John Riddle	45.00
276	Ken Raffensberger	45.00
277	Don Lund	45.00
278	Willie Miranda	45.00
279	Joe Coleman	45.00
280	Milt Bolling	300.00

220 Satchell Paige

232	Dick Kokos	45.00
233	Al Aber	45.00
234	Ray Murray	45.00
235	John Hetki	45.00
236	Harry Perkowski	45.00
237	Clarence Podbielan	45.00
238	Cal Hogue	45.00
239	Jim Delsing	45.00
240	Freddie Marsh	45.00
241	Al Sima	45.00
242	Charlie Silvera	45.00
243	Carlos Bernier	45.00
244	Willie Mays	1500.00
245	Bill Norman	45.00
246	*Roy Face*	90.00
247	Mike Sandlock	45.00
248	Gene Stephens	45.00
249	Ed O'Brien	45.00
250	Bob Wilson	45.00
251	Sid Hudson	45.00
252	Henry Foiles	45.00
254	Preacher Roe	80.00
255	Dixie Howell	45.00
256	Les Peden	45.00

1 Jackie Robinson

258 Jim Gilliam

21

1954 BOWMAN

Following the handsome 1953 set, Bowman's efforts in 1954 seem lackluster in comparison. The 224 cards (measuring 2 1/2 by 3 3/4 inches) again use colorized photographs. A pastel rectangle at the bottom contains a facsimile autograph of each depicted player. The 1954 Bowman set is best known for having two number 66 cards: The common number 66 is of Jimmy Piersall; the scarce version is of Ted Williams. Williams appeared in a Topps set for the first time in 1954, and it is believed that his contract with Topps prohibited Bowman from further picturing him on its baseball cards. His card was later pulled from circulation.

89 Willie May (Mays)

65 Mickey Mantle

		NR MT
Complete set		**$4000.00**
Commons		**7.00**

1	Phil Rizzuto	$150.00
2	Jack Jensen	10.00
3	Marion Fricano	7.00
4	Bob Hooper	7.00
5	William Hunter	7.00
6	*Nelson Fox	15.00
7	Walt Dropo	7.00
8	James F. Busby	7.00
9	Dave Williams	7.00
10	Carl Daniel Erskine	10.00
11	Sid Gordon	7.00
12	Roy McMillan	8.00
13	Paul Minner	7.00
14	Gerald Staley	7.00
15	Richie Ashburn	25.00
16	Jim Wilson	7.00
17	Tom Gorman	9.00
18	Walter "Hoot" Evers	7.00
19	Bobby Shantz	9.00
20	Artie Houtteman	7.00
21	Victor Wertz	8.00
22	Sam Mele	8.00
23	*Harvey Kuenn*	25.00
24	Bob Porterfield	7.00
25	Wes Westrum	7.00
26	Billy Cox	9.00
27	Richard Roy Cole	7.00
28	Jim Greengrass	8.00
29	Johnny Klippstein	7.00
30	Delbert Rice Jr.	7.00
31	"Smoky" Burgess	8.00
32	Del Crandall	8.00
33	Victor Raschi (with traded line)	25.00
34	Sammy White	7.00
35	Eddie Joost	8.00
36	George Strickland	7.00
37	Dick Kokos	7.00
38	*Orestes Minoso	10.00
39	Ned Garver	7.00
40	Gil Coan	7.00
45	Ralph Kiner	40.00
50	George Kell	25.00
57	Hoyt Wilhelm	25.00
58	"Pee Wee" Reese	50.00
62	Enos Slaughter	32.00

64	Ed Mathews	45.00
65	Mickey Mantle	700.00
66	Ted Williams	3000.00
66	Jimmy Piersall	85.00
67	Carl Scheib	7.00
68	Bob Avila	7.00
71	Ted Gray	7.00
72	Ed Yost	7.00
74	James Gilliam	10.00
75	Max Surkont	7.00
76	Joe Nuxhall	7.00
77	Bob Rush	7.00
78	Sal A. Yvars	7.00
79	Curt Simmons	7.00
80	John Logan	7.00
81	Jerry Coleman	8.00
82	Bill Goodman	8.00
83	Ray Murray	7.00
84	*Larry Doby	8.00
89	Willie May (Mays)	350.00
90	Roy Campanella	150.00
91	Cal Abrams	7.00
93	Bill Serena	7.00
94	Solly Hemus	7.00
95	Robin Roberts	25.00
96	*Joe Adcock	8.00

97	Gil McDougald	12.00
98	Ellis Kinder	7.00
99	Pete Suder	7.00
100	Mike Garcia	7.00
101	*Don James Larsen*	30.00
102	*Bill Pierce	7.00
103	Stephen Souchock	7.00
104	Frank Spec Shea	7.00
105	*Sal Maglie	9.00
106	"Clem" Labine	9.00
107	Paul E. LaPalme	7.00
108	Bobby Adams	7.00
109	Roy Smalley	7.00
110	Al Schoendienst	30.00
112	*Andy Pafko	7.00
113	Allie Reynolds	12.00
114	Willard Nixon	7.00
115	Don Bollweg	7.00
117	Dick Kryhoski	7.00
119	Fred Hatfield	7.00
121	Ray Katt	7.00
122	Carl Furillo	13.00
123	Toby Atwell	7.00
124	Gus Bell	8.00
127	Del Ennis	8.00
129	Hank Bauer	15.00
130	Milt Bolling	7.00
131	Joe Astroth	7.00
132	Bob Feller	75.00
134	Luis Aloma	7.00
135	Johnny Pesky	7.00
136	Clyde Vollmer	7.00
138	Gil Hodges	50.00
139	Preston Ward	7.00
140	Saul Rogovin	7.00
141	Joe Garagiola	40.00
142	Al Brazle	7.00
144	Ernie Johnson	7.00
145	Billy Martin	45.00
146	Dick Gernert	7.00
147	Joe DeMaestri	7.00
148	Dale Mitchell	7.00
149	Bob Young	7.00

151	Patrick J. Mullin	7.00
152	Mickey Vernon	8.00
153	Whitey Lockman	8.00
154	Don Newcombe	12.00
155	Frank Thomas	8.00
156	Everett Lamar Bridges	8.00
157	Omar Lown	7.00
158	Stu Miller	7.00
159	John Lindell	7.00
161	Yogi Berra	125.00
162	Ted Lepcio	7.00
163	Dave Philley (157 games with traded line)	7.00
163	Dave Philley (152 games w/o traded line)	25.00
164	Early "Gus" Wynn	35.00
165	Johnny Groth	7.00
170	Edwin D. Snider	125.00
174	Peter Paul Castiglione	7.00
177	Edward Ford	75.00
179	Morris Martin	7.00
180	Joe Tipton	7.00
182	Sherman Lollar	8.00
183	Matt Batts	7.00
184	Mickey Grasso	7.00
185	Daryl Spencer	7.00
186	Russell Meyer	8.00

187	Verne Law (Vern)	8.00
190	Joe Presko	7.00
191	Karl A. Drews	7.00
192	*Selva L. Burdette	8.00
193	Eddie Robinson	7.00
196	Bob Lemon	25.00
197	Lou Kretlow	7.00
198	Virgil Trucks	8.00
199	Steve Gromek	7.00
200	C. Marrero	7.00
201	Bob Thomson	9.00
202	George Shuba	8.00
203	Vic Janowicz	7.00
204	Jack Collum	7.00
207	Stan Lopata	7.00
208	Johnny Antonelli	8.00
209	Gene Woodling (photo reversed)	12.00
210	Jimmy Piersall	12.00
212	Owen L. Friend	8.00
214	Ferris Fain	8.00
215	Johnny Bucha	7.00
216	Jerry Snyder	7.00
217	Henry Thompson	7.00
218	Preacher Roe	12.00
219	Hal Rice	7.00
222	Memo Luna	7.00

90 Roy Campanella

223	Steve Ridzik	8.00
224	William Bruton	30.00

1954 TOPPS

Topps came up with a number of innovations for its 250-card set in 1954, including the introduction of coach cards. This year marked Topps' first use of more than one player to a card and the first-ever instance of two photographic images: These 2 5/8- by 3 3/4-inch cards feature both a colorized portrait and a black-and-white posed-action photo on the front. The backs have green, red, and black printing on white cardboard. Ted Williams appears twice to honor his exclusive new contract with Topps. Rookies include Al Kaline, Ernie Banks, Hank Aaron, and Tommy Lasorda. This is Lasorda's only card appearance as a player.

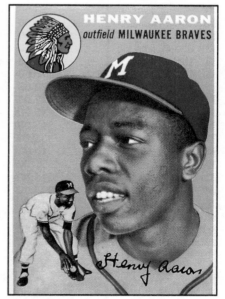

128 Henry Aaron

		NR MT
Complete set		**$7000.00**
Commons (1-50)		**15.00**
Commons (51-75)		**35.00**
Commons (76-250)		**15.00**

1	Ted Williams	$600.00
2	Gus Zernial	17.00
3	Monte Irvin	35.00
5	Ed Lopat	25.00
7	Ted Kluszewski	25.00
9	Harvey Haddix	17.00
10	Jackie Robinson	250.00
12	Del Crandall	17.00
13	Billy Martin	75.00
14	Preacher Roe	20.00
15	Al Rosen	20.00
17	Phil Rizzuto	75.00
20	Warren Spahn	90.00

21	Bobby Shantz	17.00
25	Harvey Kuenn	30.00
30	Ed Mathews	70.00
32	Duke Snider	125.00
35	Junior Gilliam	30.00
36	Hoyt Wilhelm	45.00
37	Whitey Ford	100.00
43	Dick Groat	18.00
45	Richie Ashburn	30.00
50	Yogi Berra	250.00
51	Johnny Lindell	35.00
52	Vic Power	35.00
53	Jack Dittmer	35.00
54	Vern Stephens	35.00
55	Phil Cavarretta	37.00
56	Willie Miranda	35.00
57	Luis Aloma	35.00
58	Bob Wilson	35.00
59	Gene Conley	35.00
60	Frank Baumholtz	35.00

61	Bob Cain	35.00
62	Eddie Robinson	35.00
63	Johnny Pesky	37.00
64	Hank Thompson	35.00
65	Bob Swift	35.00
66	Ted Lepcio	35.00
67	Jim Willis	35.00

1954 Topps

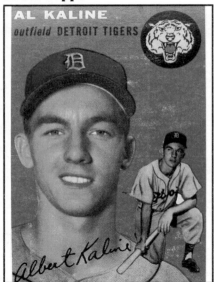

201 Al Kaline

117	Solly Hemus	15.00
119	Johnny Antonelli	15.00
120	Roy McMillan	15.00
121	Clem Labine	17.00
122	Johnny Logan	15.00
126	Ben Wade	15.00
127	Steve O'Neill	15.00
128	*Henry Aaron*	1100.00
129	Forrest Jacobs	15.00
130	Hank Bauer	30.00
131	Reno Bertoia	15.00
132	*Tom Lasorda*	150.00
133	Del Baker	15.00
134	Cal Hogue	15.00
135	Joe Presko	15.00
136	Connie Ryan	15.00
137	Wally Moon	16.00
138	Bob Borkowski	15.00
139	Ed & Johnny O'Brien	25.00
140	Tom Wright	15.00
141	Joe Jay	15.00
142	Tom Poholsky	15.00
143	Rollie Hemsley	15.00
144	Bill Werle	12.00
145	Elmer Valo	12.00
146	Don Johnson	12.00
147	John Riddle	12.00
148	Bob Trice	12.00
149	Jim Robertson	12.00
150	Dick Kryhoski	12.00
151	Alex Grammas	12.00
152	Mike Blyzka	12.00
153	"Rube" Walker	12.00
154	Mike Fornieles	12.00
155	Bob Kennedy	12.00
156	Joe Coleman	12.00
157	Don Lenhardt	12.00
158	"Peanuts" Lowrey	12.00
159	Dave Philley	12.00
160	"Red" Kress	12.00
161	John Hetki	12.00
162	Herman Wehmeier	12.00
163	Frank House	12.00

90 Willie Mays

68	Sammy Calderone	35.00
69	Bud Podbielan	35.00
70	Larry Doby	45.00
71	Frank Smith	35.00
72	Preston Ward	35.00
73	Wayne Terwilliger	35.00
74	Bill Taylor	35.00
75	Fred Haney	35.00
77	Ray Boone	15.00
79	Andy Pakfo	15.00
80	Jackie Jensen	18.00
81	Dave Hoskins	15.00
82	Milt Bolling	15.00
83	Joe Collins	15.00
84	Dick Cole	15.00
85	Bob Turley	17.00
86	Billy Herman	20.00
87	Roy Face	17.00
88	Matt Batts	15.00
89	Howie Pollet	15.00
90	Willie Mays	335.00
91	Bob Oldis	15.00
92	Wally Westlake	15.00
93	Sid Hudson	15.00
94	*Ernie Banks*	600.00
95	Hal Rice	15.00
96	Charlie Silvera	15.00
97	Jerry Lane	15.00
98	Joe Black	15.00
100	Bob Keegan	15.00
102	Gil Hodges	65.00
103	Jim Lemon	15.00
104	Mike Sandlock	15.00
105	Andy Carey	15.00
106	Dick Kokos	15.00
107	Duane Pillette	15.00
108	Thornton Kipper	15.00
109	Bill Bruton	15.00
110	Harry Dorish	15.00
112	Bill Renna	15.00
113	Bob Boyd	15.00
114	Dean Stone	15.00
115	"Rip" Repulski	15.00

94 Ernie Banks

164	Stu Miller	12.00
165	Jim Pendleton	12.00
166	Johnny Podres	25.00
167	Don Lund	12.00
168	Morrie Martin	12.00
169	Jim Hughes	12.00
170	Jim Rhodes	12.00
171	Leo Kiely	12.00
172	Hal Brown	12.00
173	Jack Harshman	12.00
174	Tom Qualters	12.00
175	Frank Leja	14.00
176	Bob Keely	12.00
177	Bob Milliken	13.00
180	Wes Westrum	13.00
181	Mel Roach	12.00
182	Chuck Harmon	12.00
183	Earle Combs	20.00
184	Ed Bailey	15.00
185	Chuck Stobbs	15.00
187	"Heinie" Manush	30.00
191	Dick Schofield	15.00
192	"Cot" Deal	15.00
193	Johnny Hopp	15.00
194	Bill Sarni	15.00
195	Bill Consolo	15.00
196	Stan Jok	15.00
197	"Schoolboy" Rowe	15.00
198	Carl Sawatski	15.00
200	Larry Jansen	15.00
201	*Al Kaline*	650.00
205	Johnny Sain	25.00
209	Charlie Thompson	15.00
210	Bob Buhl	15.00
211	Don Hoak	15.00
213	John Fitzpatrick	15.00
215	Ed McGhee	15.00
216	Al Sima	15.00
217	Paul Schreiber	15.00
218	Fred Marsh	15.00
219	Chuck Kress	15.00
220	Ruben Gomez	15.00
221	Dick Brodowski	15.00

10 Jackie Robinson

222	Bill Wilson	15.00
223	Joe Haynes	15.00
224	Dick Weik	15.00
225	Don Liddle	15.00
226	Jehosie Heard	15.00
227	Buster Mills	15.00
228	Gene Hermanski	15.00
229	Bob Talbot	15.00
230	Bob Kuzava	15.00
233	Augie Galan	15.00
234	Jerry Lynch	16.00
235	Vern Law	16.00
237	Mike Ryba	15.00
238	Al Aber	15.00
239	*Bill Skowron*	45.00
240	Sam Mele	15.00
241	Bob Miller	15.00
242	Curt Roberts	15.00
243	Ray Blades	15.00
245	Roy Sievers	15.00
246	Howie Fox	15.00
247	Eddie Mayo	15.00
248	Al Smith	15.00
250	Ted Williams	610.00

132 Tom Lasorda

1955 BOWMAN

Both color and baseball were relatively new to television in 1955 when Bowman came out with its "TV" set of cards, the last set issued by Bowman before being bought out by Topps. The front of each 2 1/2- by 3 3/4-inch card features a color photo framed to look as if the player were on television. The 320-card set has red-and-black printing on gray cardboard backs. In addition to the first umpire cards of the century, manager and coach cards were also released. Lots of superstars appear as well: The Mick, Pee Wee Reese, Whitey Ford, and Ralph Kiner.

		NR MT
Complete set		**$4500.00**
Commons (1-224)		**5.00**
Commons (225-320)		**14.00**

1	Hoyt Wilhelm	$90.00
2	Al Dark	14.00
3	Joe Coleman	5.00
4	Eddie Waitkus	5.00
5	Jim Robertson	5.00
6	Pete Suder	5.00
7	Gene Baker	5.00
8	Warren Hacker	5.00
9	Gil McDougald	10.00
10	Phil Rizzuto	40.00
11	Billy Bruton	5.00
12	Andy Pafko	6.00
13	Clyde Vollmer	5.00
14	Gus Keriazakos	5.00
15	Frank Sullivan	5.00
16	Jim Piersall	6.00
17	Del Ennis	5.00
18	Stan Lopata	5.00
19	Bobby Avila	5.00
20	Al Smith	5.00
21	Don Hoak	7.00
22	Roy Campanella	100.00
23	Al Kaline	100.00
24	Al Aber	5.00
25	Orestes "Minnie" Minoso	9.00
26	Virgil Trucks	6.00
27	Preston Ward	5.00
28	Dick Cole	5.00
29	Al "Red" Schoendienst	30.00
30	Bill Sarni	5.00
31	Johnny Temple	5.00
32	Wally Post	5.00
33	*Nelson Fox	17.00
34	Clint Courtney	5.00
35	Bill Tuttle	5.00
36	Wayne Belardi	5.00
37	Harold "Pee Wee" Reese	60.00
38	Early Wynn	20.00
39	Bob Darnell	5.00
40	Vic Wertz	5.00
41	Mel Clark	5.00
42	Bob Greenwood	5.00

202 Mickey Mantle

242 Ernie Banks

43	Bob Buhl	5.00
44	Danny O'Connell	5.00
45	Tom Umphlett	5.00
46	Mickey Vernon	6.00
47	Sammy White	5.00
48	Milt Bolling (Frank Bolling on back)	6.00
48	Milt Bolling (Milt Bolling on back)	15.00
49	Jim Greengrass	5.00
50	Hobie Landrith	5.00
51	Elvin Tappe	5.00
52	Hal Rice	5.00
53	Alex Kellner	5.00
54	Don Bollweg	5.00
55	Cal Abrams	5.00
56	Billy Cox	5.00
57	Bob Friend	6.00
58	Frank Thomas	5.00
59	Ed "Whitey" Ford	60.00
60	Enos Slaughter	25.00
61	Paul LaPalme	5.00
62	Royce Lint	5.00
63	Irv Noren	6.00
64	Curt Simmons	6.00
65	*Don Zimmer*	20.00
66	George Shuba	6.00
67	Don Larsen	15.00
68	*Elston Howard*	30.00
69	Bill Hunter	6.00
70	*Lou Burdette	7.00
71	Dave Jolly	5.00
72	Chet Nichols	5.00
73	Eddie Yost	5.00
74	Jerry Snyder	5.00
75	Brooks Lawrence	5.00
76	Tom Poholsky	5.00
77	Jim McDonald	5.00
78	Gil Coan	5.00
79	Willie Miranda	5.00
80	Lou Limmer	5.00
81	Bob Morgan	5.00
82	Lee Walls	5.00
83	Max Surkont	5.00
84	George Freese	5.00
85	Cass Michaels	5.00
86	Ted Gray	5.00
87	Randy Jackson	5.00
88	Steve Bilko	5.00

89	Lou Boudreau	20.00
90	Art Ditmar	5.00
91	Dick Marlowe	5.00
92	George Zuverink	5.00
93	Andy Seminick	5.00
94	Hank Thompson	5.00
95	Sal Maglie	10.00
96	Ray Narleski	5.00
97	John Podres	13.00
98	James "Junior" Gilliam	15.00
99	Jerry Coleman	7.00
100	Tom Morgan	8.00
101	Don Johnson (Braves' Ernie Johnson on front)	6.00
101	Don Johnson (Orioles' Don Johnson on front)	15.00
102	Bobby Thomson	8.00
103	Eddie Mathews	30.00
104	Bob Porterfield	5.00
105	Johnny Schmitz	5.00
106	Del Rice	5.00
107	Solly Hemus	5.00
108	Lou Kretlow	5.00
109	Vern Stephens	5.00
110	Bob Miller	5.00
111	Steve Ridzik	5.00
112	Gran Hamner	5.00
113	Bob Hall	5.00
114	Vic Janowicz	5.00
115	Roger Bowman	5.00

116	Sandalio Consuegra	5.00
117	Johnny Groth	5.00
118	Bobby Adams	5.00
130	Richie Ashburn	15.00
132	*Harvey Kueen (incorrect spelling on back)	7.00
132	Harvey Kuenn (correct spelling on back)	30.00
134	Bob Feller	75.00
143	Don Newcombe	8.00
157	Ernie Johnson (Braves' Ernie Johnson on front)	15.00
158	Gil Hodges	40.00
160	Bill Skowron	15.00
168	Larry "Yogi" Berra	85.00
169	Carl Furillo	15.00
170	Carl Erskine	9.00
171	Robin Roberts	20.00
179	Hank Aaron	200.00
184	Willie Mays	200.00
191	Bob Lemon	25.00
195	Erv Palica (traded line on back)	20.00
197	Ralph Kiner	30.00
201	Allie Reynolds	15.00
202	Mickey Mantle	400.00
204	*Frank Bolling* (Frank Bolling on back)	20.00
213	George Kell	25.00
225	Paul Richards	16.00
226	W.F. McKinley (umpire)	16.00
227	Frank Baumholtz	14.00
228	John M. Phillips	14.00
229	Jim Brosnan	16.00
230	Al Brazle	14.00
231	Jim Konstanty	18.00
232	Birdie Tebbetts	14.00
233	Bill Serena	14.00
234	Dick Bartell	14.00
235	J.A. Paparella (umpire)	16.00
236	Murray Dickson (Murry)	14.00
237	Johnny Wyrostek	14.00
238	Eddie Stanky	15.00
239	Edwin A. Rommel (umpire)	16.00
240	Billy Loes	15.00
241	John Pesky	15.00
242	Ernie Banks	350.00
243	Gus Bell	15.00
244	Duane Pillette	14.00

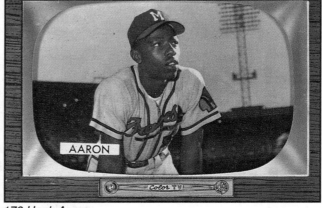

179 Hank Aaron

245	Bill Miller	14.00
246	Hank Bauer	25.00
247	Dutch Leonard	14.00
248	Harry Dorish	14.00
249	Billy Gardner	14.00
250	Larry Napp (umpire)	16.00
251	Stan Jok	14.00
252	Roy Smalley	14.00
253	Jim Wilson	14.00
254	Bennett Flowers	14.00
255	Pete Runnels	15.00
256	Owen Friend	14.00
257	Tom Alston	14.00
258	John W. Stevens (umpire)	16.00
259	Don Mossi	15.00
260	Edwin H. Hurley (umpire)	16.00
261	Walt Moryn	15.00
262	Jim Lemon	15.00
263	Eddie Joost	14.00
264	Bill Henry	14.00
265	Albert J. Barlick (umpire)	60.00
266	Mike Fornieles	14.00
267	George "Jim" Honochick (umpire)	50.00
268	Roy Lee Hawes	14.00
269	Joe Amalfitano	14.00
270	Chico Fernandez	15.00
271	Bob Hooper	14.00
272	John Flaherty (umpire)	16.00
273	Emory "Bubba" Church	14.00
274	Jim Delsing	14.00
275	William T. Grieve (umpire)	16.00
276	Ivan Delock	14.00
277	Ed Runge (umpire)	16.00
278	Charles Neal	17.00
279	Hank Soar (umpire)	16.00
280	Clyde McCullough	14.00
281	Charles Berry (umpire)	16.00
282	Phil Cavarretta	15.00
283	Nestor Chylak (umpire)	16.00
284	William A. Jackowski (umpire)	16.00
285	Walt Dropo	16.00
286	Frank E. Secory (umpire)	16.00
287	Ron Mrozinski	14.00
288	Dick Smith	14.00
289	Arthur J. Gore (umpire)	16.00
291	Frank Dascoli (umpire)	16.00
292	Marv Blaylock	16.00
293	Thomas D. Gorman (umpire)	17.00
294	Wally Moses	15.00
295	E. Lee Ballanfant (umpire)	16.00
296	*Bill Virdon*	25.00
297	L.R. "Dusty" Boggess (umpire)	16.00
298	Charlie Grimm	16.00
299	Lonnie Warneke (umpire)	16.00
300	Tommy Byrne	17.00
301	William R. Engeln (umpire)	16.00
302	*Frank Malzone*	17.00
303	J.B. "Jocko" Conlan (umpire)	75.00
304	Harry Chiti	14.00
305	Frank Umont (umpire)	16.00
306	Bob Cerv	17.00
307	R.A. "Babe" Pinelli (umpire)	16.00
308	Al Lopez	35.00
309	Hal H. Dixon (umpire)	16.00
310	Ken Lehman	15.00
311	Lawrence J. Goetz (umpire)	16.00
312	Bill Wight	16.00
313	A.J. Donatelli (umpire)	17.00
314	Dale Mitchell	14.00
315	Cal Hubbard (umpire)	60.00
317	Wm. R. Summers (umpire)	16.00
318	Sid Hudson	14.00
319	Albert B. Schroll	14.00
320	George D. Susce, Jr.	50.00

1955 TOPPS

Topps' first horizontally designed card again makes use of a combination of portraits and full-figure photos. Both photos on the 2⅝- by 3¾-inch fronts are colorized, with a horizontal bottom strip for player identification, a team logo in the upper right, and a facsimile autograph below. Unfortunately, many of the 206 portraits (Topps' smallest run ever) are reruns from the company's 1954 set. The backs feature red, black, and green printing on a white background. Rookies include Harmon Killebrew, Sandy Koufax, and Roberto Clemente.

		NR MT
Complete set		**$5000.00**
Commons (1-150)		**6.00**
Commons (151-160)		**7.00**
Commons (161-210)		**20.00**

1	"Dusty" Rhodes	$50.00
2	Ted Williams	400.00
3	Art Fowler	6.00
4	Al Kaline	150.00
5	Jim Gilliam	12.00
6	Stan Hack	7.00
7	Jim Hegan	6.00
8	Hal Smith	6.00
9	Bob Miller	6.00
10	Bob Keegan	6.00
11	Ferris Fain	7.00
12	"Jake" Thies	6.00
13	Fred Marsh	6.00
14	Jim Finigan	6.00
15	Jim Pendleton	6.00
16	*Roy Sievers	8.00
17	Bobby Hofman	6.00
18	Russ Kemmerer	6.00
19	Billy Herman	15.00
20	Andy Carey	8.00
21	Alex Grammas	6.00
22	Bill Skowron	12.00
23	Jack Parks	5.00

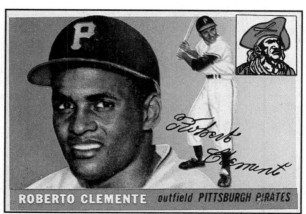

164 Roberto Clemente

1955 Topps

194 Willie Mays

24	*Hal Newhouser	7.00
25	Johnny Podres	15.00
26	Dick Groat	8.00
27	Billy Gardner	5.00
28	Ernie Banks	150.00
29	Herman Wehmeier	5.00
30	Vic Power	5.00
31	Warren Spahn	60.00
32	Ed McGhee	5.00
33	Tom Qualters	5.00
34	Wayne Terwilliger	5.00
35	Dave Jolly	5.00
36	Leo Kiely	5.00
37	Joe Cunningham	7.00
38	Bob Turley	12.00
39	Bill Glynn	5.00
40	Don Hoak	6.00
41	Chuck Stobbs	5.00
42	"Windy" McCall	5.00
43	Harvey Haddix	6.00
44	"Corky" Valentine	5.00
45	Hank Sauer	5.00
46	Ted Kazanski	5.00
47	Hank Aaron	350.00
48	Bob Kennedy	5.00
49	J.W. Porter	5.00
50	Jackie Robinson	225.00
51	Jim Hughes	6.00
52	Bill Tremel	5.00
53	Bill Taylor	5.00
54	Lou Limmer	5.00
55	"Rip" Repulski	5.00
56	Ray Jablonski	5.00
57	Billy O'Dell	6.00
58	Jim Rivera	5.00
59	Gair Allie	5.00
60	Dean Stone	5.00
61	"Spook" Jacobs	5.00
63	Joe Collins	8.00
64	Gus Triandos	7.00
65	Ray Boone	6.00
67	Wally Moon	6.00
70	Al Rosen	12.00
75	Sandy Amoros	6.00
80	Bob Grim	9.00
81	Gene Conley	6.00
84	Camilo Pascual	7.00
85	Don Mossi	7.00
88	Bob Skinner	7.00

90	Karl Spooner	9.00
92	Don Zimmer	20.00
99	Frank Leja	9.00
100	Monte Irvin	25.00
106	Frank Sullivan	6.00
108	"Rube" Walker	6.00
109	Ed Lopat	12.00
110	Gus Zernial	6.00
111	Bob Milliken	6.00
113	Harry Brecheen	6.00
120	Ted Kluszewski	15.00
123	"Sandy" Koufax	800.00
124	Harmon Killebrew	275.00
125	Ken Boyer	40.00
126	Dick Hall	6.00
127	Dale Long	6.00
139	Steve Kraly	9.00
140	Mel Parnell	6.00
146	Dick Donovan	6.00
151	"Red" Kress	7.00
152	Harry Agganis	75.00
153	"Bud" Podbielan	7.00
154	Willie Miranda	7.00
155	Ed Mathews	75.00
156	Joe Black	15.00
157	Bob Miller	6.00
158	Tom Carroll	12.00
159	Johnny Schmitz	6.00
160	Ray Narleski	7.00
161	Chuck Tanner	25.00

162	Joe Coleman	15.00
163	Faye Throneberry	15.00
164	Roberto Clemente	1000.00
165	Don Johnson	15.00
166	Hank Bauer	30.00
167	Tom Cassagrande	20.00
168	Duane Pillette	20.00
169	Bob Oldis	20.00
170	Jim Pearce	20.00
171	Dick Brodowski	20.00
172	Frank Baumholtz	20.00
173	Bob Kline	20.00
174	Rudy Minarcin	20.00
175	Not Issued	
176	Norm Zauchin	20.00
177	Jim Robertson	20.00
178	Bobby Adams	20.00
179	Jim Bolger	20.00
180	Clem Labine	23.00
181	Roy McMillan	20.00
182	Humberto Robinson	20.00
183	Tony Jacobs	20.00
184	Harry Perkowski	20.00
185	Don Ferrarese	20.00
186	Not Issued	
187	Gil Hodges	125.00
188	Charlie Silvera	20.00
189	Phil Rizzuto	125.00
190	Gene Woodling	22.00
191	Ed Stanky	22.00
192	Jim Delsing	20.00
193	Johnny Sain	35.00
194	Willie Mays	400.00
195	Ed Roebuck	20.00
196	Gale Wade	20.00
197	Al Smith	20.00
198	Yogi Berra	225.00
199	Bert Hamric	20.00
200	Jack Jensen	50.00
201	Sherm Lollar	21.00
202	Jim Owens	20.00
203	Not Issued	
204	Frank Smith	20.00
205	Gene Freese	20.00
206	Pete Daley	20.00
207	Bill Consolo	20.00
208	Ray Moore	20.00
209	Not Issued	
210	Duke Snider	400.00

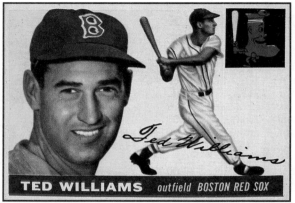

2 Ted Williams

1956 TOPPS

Topps continued to improve upon its double-photo format by superimposing a colorized portrait over an action shot. A facsimile autograph is displayed on these horizontal 2⅝- by 3¾-inch cards, which boast red, green, and black print on backs that are either white or gray. Three new types of cards were introduced in this 340-card set: teams, checklists, and league presidents. Of these, checklists are the most difficult to find today, although when issued they were thought of as disposable, of no value, and not tradable. Card backs in 1956 featured multiple humorous illustrations that depicted each player's career highlights.

		NR MT
Complete set (without checklists)		**$6000.00**
Commons (1-100)		**7.00**
Commons (101-180)		**10.00**
Commons (181-260)		**15.00**
Commons (261-340)		**10.00**

1	William Harridge	$150.00
5	Ted Williams	250.00
8	Walter Alston	30.00
10	Warren Spahn	35.00
14	Ken Boyer	10.00
15	Ernie Banks	75.00
20	Al Kaline	75.00
25	Ted Kluszewski	12.00
30	Jackie Robinson	150.00
31	Hank Aaron	200.00
33	Roberto Clemente	250.00
35	Al Rosen	10.00
61	Bill Skowron	9.00
63	*Roger Craig*	15.00
79	Sandy Koufax	250.00
101	Roy Campanella	100.00
102	Jim Davis	10.00
103	Willie Miranda	10.00
104	Bob Lennon	10.00
105	Al Smith	10.00
106	Joe Astroth	10.00
107	Ed Mathews	35.00
108	Laurin Pepper	10.00
109	Enos Slaughter	25.00
110	Yogi Berra	125.00
111	Red Sox Team	12.00
112	Dee Fondy	10.00
113	Phil Rizzuto	50.00
114	Jim Owens	10.00
115	Jackie Jensen	12.00
116	Eddie O'Brien	10.00
117	Virgil Trucks	11.00
118	"Nellie" Fox	20.00
119	*Larry Jackson*	11.00
120	Richie Ashburn	30.00
121	Pirates Team	12.00
122	Willard Nixon	10.00
123	Roy McMillan	10.00
124	Don Kaiser	10.00
125	"Minnie" Minoso	15.00
126	Jim Brady	10.00
127	Willie Jones	10.00
128	Eddie Yost	10.00
129	"Jake" Martin	10.00
130	Willie Mays	225.00
131	Bob Roselli	10.00
132	Bobby Avila	10.00
133	Ray Narleski	10.00
134	Cardinals Team	12.00
135	Mickey Mantle	700.00
136	Johnny Logan	10.00
137	Al Silvera	10.00
138	Johnny Antonelli	10.00
139	Tommy Carroll	10.00
140	*Herb Score*	20.00
141	Joe Frazier	10.00
142	Gene Baker	10.00
143	Jim Piersall	12.00
144	Leroy Powell	10.00
145	Gil Hodges	45.00
146	Senators Team	12.00
147	Earl Torgeson	10.00
148	Alvin Dark	12.00
149	"Dixie" Howell	10.00
150	"Duke" Snider	100.00
151	"Spook" Jacobs	10.00
152	Billy Hoeft	10.00
153	Frank Thomas	10.00
154	Dave Pope	10.00
155	Harvey Kuenn	12.00
156	Wes Westrum	10.00
157	Dick Brodowski	10.00
158	Wally Post	10.00
159	Clint Courtney	10.00
160	Billy Pierce	12.00
161	Joe DeMaestri	10.00
162	"Gus" Bell	11.00
163	Gene Woodling	11.00
164	Harmon Killebrew	75.00
165	"Red" Schoendienst	25.00
166	Dodgers Team	200.00
167	Harry Dorish	10.00
168	Sammy White	10.00
169	Bob Nelson	10.00
170	Bill Virdon	12.00
171	Jim Wilson	10.00
172	*Frank Torre*	11.00
173	Johnny Podres	15.00
174	Glen Gorbous	10.00
175	Del Crandall	11.00
176	Alex Kellner	10.00
177	Hank Bauer	15.00
178	Joe Black	11.00
179	Harry Chiti	10.00
180	Robin Roberts	25.00
181	Billy Martin	50.00
182	Paul Minner	15.00
183	Stan Lopata	15.00
184	Don Bessent	15.00
185	Bill Bruton	15.00
186	Ron Jackson	15.00
187	Early Wynn	30.00
188	White Sox Team	17.00
189	Ned Garver	15.00
190	Carl Furillo	19.00
191	Frank Lary	15.00
192	"Smoky" Burgess	15.00
193	Wilmer Mizell	15.00
194	Monte Irvin	30.00
195	George Kell	30.00
196	Tom Poholsky	15.00
197	Granny Hamner	15.00
198	Ed Fitzgerald (Fitz Gerald)	15.00
199	Hank Thompson	15.00
200	Bob Feller	90.00
201	"Rip" Repulski	15.00
202	Jim Hearn	15.00
203	Bill Tuttle	15.00
204	Art Swanson	15.00
205	"Whitey" Lockman	15.00
206	Erv Palica	15.00
207	Jim Small	15.00
208	Elston Howard	25.00

135 Mickey Mantle

31 Hank Aaron

209	Max Surkont	15.00
210	Mike Garcia	16.00
211	Murry Dickson	15.00
212	Johnny Temple	15.00
213	Tigers Team	18.00
214	Bob Rush	15.00
215	Tommy Byrne	15.00
216	Jerry Schoonmaker	15.00
217	Billy Klaus	15.00
218	Joe Nuxall (Nuxhall)	17.00
219	*Lew Burdette	18.00
220	Del Ennis	15.00
221	Bob Friend	15.00
222	Dave Philley	15.00
223	Randy Jackson	15.00
224	"Bud" Podbielan	15.00
225	Gil McDougald	20.00
226	Giants Team	45.00
227	Russ Meyer	15.00
228	"Mickey" Vernon	16.00
229	Harry Brecheen	16.00
230	"Chico" Carrasquel	16.00
231	Bob Hale	15.00
232	"Toby" Atwell	15.00
233	Carl Erskine	20.00
234	"Pete" Runnels	16.00
235	Don Newcombe	18.00
236	Athletics Team	16.00
237	Jose Valdivielso	15.00
238	Walt Dropo	16.00
239	Harry Simpson	15.00
240	"Whitey" Ford	90.00
241	Don Mueller	16.00
242	Hershell Freeman	15.00
243	Sherm Lollar	16.00
244	Bob Buhl	15.00
245	Billy Goodman	15.00
246	Tom Gorman	15.00
247	Bill Sarni	15.00
248	Bob Porterfield	15.00
249	Johnny Klippstein	15.00
250	Larry Doby	18.00
251	Yankees Team	225.00
252	Vernon Law	16.00
253	Irv Noren	15.00
254	George Crowe	15.00
255	Bob Lemon	25.00
256	Tom Hurd	15.00
257	Bobby Thomson	16.00

258	Art Ditmar	15.00
259	Sam Jones	15.00
260	"Pee Wee" Reese	90.00
261	Bobby Shantz	11.00
262	Howie Pollet	10.00
263	Bob Miller	10.00
264	Ray Monzant	10.00
265	Sandy Consuegra	10.00
266	Don Ferrarese	10.00
267	Bob Nieman	10.00
268	Dale Mitchell	10.00
269	Jack Meyer	10.00
270	Billy Loes	11.00
271	Foster Castleman	10.00
272	Danny O'Connell	10.00
273	Walker Cooper	10.00
274	Frank Baumholtz	10.00
275	Jim Greengrass	10.00
276	George Zuverink	10.00
277	Daryl Spencer	10.00
278	Chet Nichols	10.00
279	Johnny Groth	10.00
280	Jim Gilliam	11.00
281	Art Houtteman	10.00
282	Warren Hacker	10.00
283	Hal Smith	10.00
284	Ike Delock	10.00
285	Eddie Miksis	10.00
286	Bill Wight	10.00
287	Bobby Adams	10.00

288	Bob Cerv	12.00
289	Hal Jeffcoat	10.00
290	Curt Simmons	11.00
291	Frank Kellert	10.00
292	*Luis Aparicio*	100.00
293	Stu Miller	10.00
294	Ernie Johnson	10.00
295	Clem Labine	12.00
296	Andy Seminick	10.00
297	Bob Skinner	10.00
298	Johnny Schmitz	10.00
299	Charley Neal	11.00
300	Vic Wertz	10.00
301	Marv Grissom	10.00
302	Eddie Robinson	10.00
303	Jim Dyck	10.00
304	Frank Malzone	12.00
305	Brooks Lawrence	10.00
306	Curt Roberts	10.00
307	Hoyt Wilhelm	35.00
308	"Chuck" Harmon	10.00
309	*Don Blasingame*	12.00
310	Steve Gromek	10.00
311	Hal Naragon	10.00
312	Andy Pafko	11.00
313	Gene Stephens	10.00
314	Hobie Landrith	10.00
315	Milt Bolling	10.00
316	Jerry Coleman	11.00
317	Al Aber	10.00
318	Fred Hatfield	10.00
319	Jack Crimian	10.00
320	Joe Adcock	12.00
321	Jim Konstanty	12.00
322	Karl Olson	10.00
323	Willard Schmidt	10.00
324	"Rocky" Bridges	10.00
325	Don Liddle	10.00
326	Connie Johnson	10.00
327	Bob Wiesler	10.00
328	Preston Ward	10.00
329	Lou Berberet	10.00
330	Jim Busby	10.00
331	Dick Hall	10.00
332	Don Larsen	22.00
340	Mickey McDermott	25.00
—	Checklist 1/3 (unnumbered)	475.00
—	Checklist 2/4 (unnumbered)	475.00

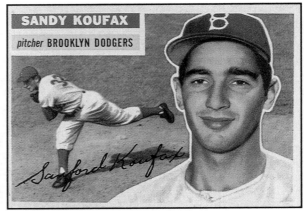

79 Sandy Koufax

1957 TOPPS

The 1957 Topps set was modernized in a number of ways. The cards were scaled down to a vertical 2 1/2 by 3 1/2 inches, the standard for today's sets. This edition also saw the first appearance of actual color photos in place of the colorized photos used earlier. While card fronts maintain simple designs, the backs are more sophisticated: Instead of giving statistics for only the previous season, complete year-by-year statistics for each player are now included. Hot rookies in this edition include Brooks Robinson, Don Drysdale, and Tony Kubek. Advanced collectors with an extra thousand dollars may want to pursue the four checklist series cards, scarce survivors from 1957.

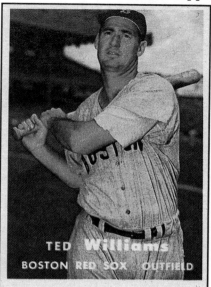

1 Ted Williams

	NR MT
Complete set (without checklists)	$7000.00
Commons (1-264)	5.00
Commons (265-352)	15.00
Commons (353-407)	6.00

#	Player	Price
1	Ted Williams	$450.00
2	Yogi Berra	150.00
3	Dale Long	5.00
4	Johnny Logan	5.00
5	Sal Maglie	8.00
6	Hector Lopez	5.00
7	Luis Aparicio	25.00
8	Don Mossi	5.00
9	Johnny Temple	5.00
10	Willie Mays	250.00
11	George Zuverink	5.00
12	*Dick Groat	6.00
13	Wally Burnette	5.00
14	Bob Nieman	5.00
15	Robin Roberts	20.00
16	Walt Moryn	5.00
17	Billy Gardner	5.00
18	*Don Drysdale*	200.00
19	Bob Wilson	5.00
20	Hank Aaron (photo reversed)	250.00
21	Frank Sullivan	5.00
22	Jerry Snyder (photo is Ed Fitz Gerald)	5.00
23	Sherm Lollar	5.00
24	*Bill Mazeroski*	25.00
25	Whitey Ford	45.00
26	Bob Boyd	5.00
27	Ted Kazanski	5.00
28	Gene Conley	5.00
29	*Whitey Herzog*	24.00
30	Pee Wee Reese	50.00
31	Ron Northey	5.00
32	Hersh Freeman	5.00
33	Jim Small	5.00
34	Tom Sturdivant	5.00
35	*Frank Robinson*	300.00
36	Bob Grim	5.00
37	Frank Torre	5.00
38	*Nellie Fox	12.00
39	Al Worthington	5.00
40	Early Wynn	18.00

95 Mickey Mantle

#	Player	Price
41	Hal Smith	5.00
42	Dee Fondy	5.00
43	Connie Johnson	5.00
44	Joe DeMaestri	5.00
45	Carl Furillo	9.00
46	Bob Miller	5.00
47	Don Blasingame	5.00
48	Bill Bruton	5.00
49	Daryl Spencer	5.00
50	Herb Score	6.00
51	Clint Courtney	5.00
52	Lee Walls	5.00
53	Clem Labine	6.00
54	Elmer Valo	5.00
55	Ernie Banks	70.00
56	Dave Sisler	5.00
57	Jim Lemon	5.00
58	Ruben Gomez	5.00
59	Dick Williams	6.00
60	Billy Hoeft	5.00
61	Dusty Rhodes	5.00
62	Billy Martin	40.00
63	Ike Delock	5.00
64	Pete Runnels	6.00
65	Wally Moon	5.00
66	Brooks Lawrence	5.00

#	Player	Price
67	Chico Carrasquel	5.00
68	Ray Crone	5.00
69	Roy McMillan	5.00
70	Richie Ashburn	15.00
71	Murry Dickson	5.00
72	Bill Tuttle	5.00
73	George Crowe	5.00
74	Vito Valentinetti	5.00
75	Jim Piersall	6.00
76	Bob Clemente	200.00
77	Paul Foytack	5.00
78	Vic Wertz	6.00
79	*Lindy McDaniel*	6.00
80	Gil Hodges	50.00
81	Herm Wehmeier	5.00
82	Elston Howard	10.00
83	Lou Skizas	5.00
84	Moe Drabowsky	5.00
85	Larry Doby	8.00
86	Bill Sarni	5.00
87	Tom Gorman	5.00
88	Harvey Kuenn	6.00
89	Roy Sievers	5.00
90	Warren Spahn	50.00
91	Mack Burk	5.00
92	Mickey Vernon	6.00
93	Hal Jeffcoat	5.00
94	Bobby Del Greco	5.00
95	Mickey Mantle	650.00
96	*Hank Aguirre*	6.00
97	Yankees Team	30.00
98	Al Dark	7.00
99	Bob Keegan	5.00
100	League Presidents (Warren Giles, William Harridge)	6.00
101	Chuck Stobbs	5.00
102	Ray Boone	5.00
103	Joe Nuxhall	6.00
104	Hank Foiles	5.00
105	Johnny Antonelli	5.00
106	Ray Moore	5.00
107	Jim Rivera	5.00

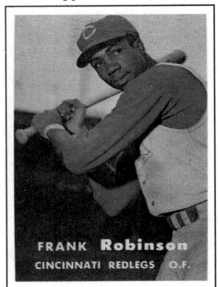

35 Frank Robinson

407 Yankees' Power Hitters

151	Willie Miranda	5.00
152	Jack Harshman	5.00
153	Karl Olson	5.00
154	Red Schoendienst	20.00
155	Jim Brosnan	5.00
156	Gus Triandos	5.00
157	Wally Post	5.00
158	Curt Simmons	6.00
159	Solly Drake	5.00
160	Billy Pierce	6.00
161	Pirates Team	8.00
162	Jack Meyer	5.00
163	Sammy White	5.00
164	Tommy Carroll	5.00
165	Ted Kluszewski	18.00
166	Roy Face	6.00
167	Vic Power	6.00
168	Frank Lary	6.00
169	Herb Plews	5.00
170	Duke Snider	85.00
171	Red Sox Team	9.00
172	Gene Woodling	6.00
173	Roger Craig	8.00
174	Willie Jones	5.00
175	Don Larsen	7.00
176	Gene Baker	5.00
177	Eddie Yost	5.00
178	Don Bessent	5.00
179	Ernie Oravetz	5.00
180	Gus Bell	5.00
181	Dick Donovan	5.00
182	Hobie Landrith	5.00
183	Cubs Team	8.00
184	*Tito Francona*	6.00
185	Johnny Kucks	6.00
186	Jim King	5.00
187	Virgil Trucks	5.00
188	Felix Mantilla	5.00
189	Willard Nixon	5.00
190	Randy Jackson	5.00
191	Joe Margoneri	5.00
192	Jerry Coleman	6.00
193	Del Rice	5.00
194	Hal Brown	5.00

108	Tommy Byrne	5.00
109	Hank Thompson	5.00
110	Bill Virdon	6.00
111	Hal Smith	5.00
112	Tom Brewer	5.00
113	Wilmer Mizell	5.00
114	Braves Team	10.00
115	Jim Gilliam	8.00
116	Mike Fornieles	5.00
117	Joe Adcock	6.00
118	Bob Porterfield	5.00
119	Stan Lopata	5.00
120	Bob Lemon	18.00
121	*Cletis Boyer*	10.00
122	Ken Boyer	8.00
123	Steve Ridzik	5.00
124	Dave Philley	5.00
125	Al Kaline	60.00
126	Bob Wiesler	5.00
127	Bob Buhl	5.00
128	Ed Bailey	5.00
129	Saul Rogovin	5.00
130	Don Newcombe	10.00
131	Milt Bolling	5.00
132	Art Ditmar	5.00
133	Del Crandall	6.00
134	Don Kaiser	5.00
135	Bill Skowron	12.00
136	Jim Hegan	5.00
137	Bob Rush	5.00
138	*Minnie Minoso	8.00
139	Lou Kretlow	5.00
140	Frank Thomas	5.00
141	Al Aber	5.00
142	Charley Thompson	5.00
143	Andy Pafko	6.00
144	Ray Narleski	5.00
145	Al Smith	5.00
146	Don Ferrarese	5.00
147	Al Walker	5.00
148	Don Mueller	5.00
149	Bob Kennedy	5.00
150	Bob Friend	6.00

328 Brooks Robinson

195	Bobby Avila	5.00
196	Larry Jackson	5.00
200	Gil McDougald	12.00
203	Hoyt Wilhelm	18.00
210	Roy Campanella	80.00
212	*Rocco Colavito*	40.00
215	Enos Slaughter	20.00
230	George Kell	18.00
240	Hank Bauer	10.00
250	Ed Mathews	25.00
252	Carl Erskine	10.00
265	Harvey Haddix	20.00
266	Ken Kuhn	15.00
267	Danny Kravitz	15.00
268	Jackie Collum	15.00
269	Bob Cerv	15.00
270	Senators Team	25.00
271	Danny O'Connell	15.00
272	Bobby Shantz	25.00
273	Jim Davis	15.00
274	Don Hoak	16.00
275	Indians Team	25.00
276	Jim Pyburn	15.00
277	Johnny Podres	60.00
278	Fred Hatfield	15.00
279	Bob Thurman	15.00
280	Alex Kellner	15.00
281	Gail Harris	15.00
282	Jack Dittmer	15.00
283	*Wes Covington*	18.00
284	Don Zimmer	20.00
285	Ned Garver	15.00
286	*Bobby Richardson*	90.00
287	Sam Jones	15.00
288	Ted Lepcio	15.00
289	Jim Bolger	15.00
290	Andy Carey	17.00
291	Windy McCall	15.00
292	Billy Klaus	15.00
293	Ted Abernathy	15.00
294	Rocky Bridges	15.00
295	Joe Collins	17.00
296	Johnny Klippstein	15.00

297	Jack Crimian	15.00	318	Mickey McDermott	15.00	
298	Irv Noren	15.00	319	Gino Cimoli	16.00	
299	Chuck Harmon	15.00	320	Neil Chrisley	15.00	
300	Mike Garcia	17.00	321	Red Murff	15.00	
301	Sam Esposito	15.00	322	Redlegs Team	40.00	
302	Sandy Koufax	400.00	323	Wes Westrum	16.00	
303	Billy Goodman	15.00	324	Dodgers Team	90.00	
304	Joe Cunningham	18.00	325	Frank Bolling	15.00	
305	Chico Fernandez	15.00	326	Pedro Ramos	15.00	
306	Darrell Johnson	17.00	327	Jim Pendleton	15.00	
307	Jack Phillips	15.00	328	*Brooks Robinson*	325.00	
308	Dick Hall	15.00	329	White Sox Team	25.00	
309	Jim Busby	15.00	330	Jim Wilson	15.00	
310	Max Surkont	15.00	331	Ray Katt	15.00	
311	Al Pilarcik	15.00	332	Bob Bowman	15.00	
312	*Tony Kubek*	125.00	333	Ernie Johnson	15.00	
313	Mel Parnell	17.00	334	Jerry Schoonmaker	15.00	
314	Ed Bouchee	15.00	335	Granny Hamner	15.00	
315	Lou Berberet	15.00	336	*Haywood Sullivan*	16.00	
316	Billy O'Dell	15.00	337	Rene Valdes	15.00	
317	Giants Team	40.00	338	*Jim Bunning*	90.00	

339	Bob Speake	15.00
340	Bill Wight	15.00
341	Don Gross	15.00
342	Gene Mauch	20.00
343	Taylor Phillips	15.00
344	Paul LaPalme	15.00
345	Paul Smith	15.00
346	Dick Littlefield	15.00
347	Hal Naragon	15.00
348	Jim Hearn	15.00
349	Nelson King	15.00
350	Eddie Miksis	15.00
400	Dodgers' Sluggers (Campanella, Furillo, Hodges, Snider)	150.00
407	Yankees' Power Hitters (Berra, Mantle)	300.00
—	Checklist Series 1/2	125.00
—	Checklist Series 2/3	175.00
—	Checklist Series 3/4	350.00
—	Checklist Series 4/5	425.00

1958 TOPPS

Topps stretched its 1958 set to 494 cards, which provide a vivid contrast to the mild-mannered 1957 issue. In 1958, the 21/2- by 31/2-inch vertical cards show portraits or posed-action photos set against plain but brightly colored backgrounds. Team cards include set checklists on the card backs. Interestingly, 33 cards (dispersed randomly between numbers 2 and 108) are famous as yellow-letter variations. Either the player name or the team name on the card front is printed in yellow. This is indicated in the following list with YP or YT, respectively, following the name. The more common style, with ordinary white printing, is marked WP or WT. One of the most popular subsets in the 1958 edition consists of the 20 cards of All-Star players selected by *Sport* magazine (shown with AS in list). An additional All-Star card shows the two 1957 World Series managers, Casey Stengel and Fred Haney.

150 Mickey Mantle

	NR MT
Complete set	**$4200.00**
Commons (1-110)	**6.00**
Commons (111-440)	**2.50**
Commons (441-494)	**2.00**

1	Ted Williams	$400.00
2	Bob Lemon (YT)	35.00
2	Bob Lemon (WT)	15.00
3	Alex Kellner	6.00
4	Hank Foiles	6.00
5	Willie Mays	125.00
6	George Zuverink	6.00
7	Dale Long	6.00
8	Eddie Kasko (YP)	15.00
8	Eddie Kasko (WP)	6.00
9	Hank Bauer	10.00
10	Lou Burdette	8.00
11	Jim Rivera (YT)	15.00
11	Jim Rivera (WT)	6.00
12	George Crowe	6.00
13	Billy Hoeft (YP)	15.00
13	Billy Hoeft (WP)	6.00

14	Rip Repulski	6.00
15	Jim Lemon	6.00
16	Charley Neal	6.00
17	Felix Mantilla	6.00
18	Frank Sullivan	6.00
19	Giants Team/ Checklist 1-88	11.00
20	Gil McDougald (YP)	25.00
20	Gil McDougald (WP)	10.00
21	Curt Barclay	6.00
22	Hal Naragon	6.00
23	Bill Tuttle (YP)	15.00
23	Bill Tuttle (WP)	6.00
24	Hobie Landrith (YP)	15.00
24	Hobie Landrith (WP)	6.00
25	Don Drysdale	30.00
27	Bud Freeman	6.00
28	Jim Busby	6.00
30	Hank Aaron (YP)	250.00
30	Hank Aaron (WP)	175.00
31	Tex Clevenger	6.00
32	J.W. Porter (YP)	15.00
32	J.W. Porter (WP)	6.00
33	Cal Neeman (YT)	15.00

33	Cal Neeman (WT)	6.00
34	Bob Thurman	6.00
35	Don Mossi (YT)	15.00
35	Don Mossi (WT)	6.00
36	Ted Kazanski	6.00
37	*Mike McCormick (photo is Ray Monzant)*	6.00
38	Dick Gernert	6.00
40	George Kell	12.00
41	Dave Hillman	6.00
42	*John Roseboro*	7.00
43	Sal Maglie	9.00
44	Senators Team/ Checklist 1-88	11.00

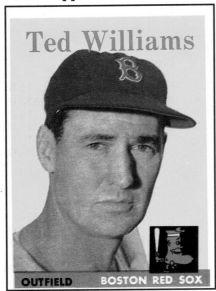

1 Ted Williams

45	Dick Groat	7.00
46	Lou Sleater (WP)	6.00
47	*Roger Maris*	350.00
48	Chuck Harmon	6.00
49	Smoky Burgess	7.00
50	Billy Pierce (YT)	20.00
50	Billy Pierce (WT)	7.00
51	Del Rice	6.00
52	Bob Clemente (YT)	250.00
52	Bob Clemente (WT)	125.00
53	Morrie Martin (YP)	11.00
53	Morrie Martin (WP)	6.00
54	*Norm Siebern*	7.00
55	Chico Carrasquel	6.00
57	Tim Thompson (YP)	15.00
57	Tim Thompson (WP)	6.00
58	Art Schult (YT)	15.00
58	Art Schult (WT)	6.00
59	Dave Sisler	6.00
60	Del Ennis (YP)	15.00
60	Del Ennis (WP)	6.00
61	Darrell Johnson (YP)	15.00
61	Darrell Johnson (WP)	6.00
62	Joe DeMaestri	6.00
63	Joe Nuxhall	7.00
64	Joe Lonnett	6.00
65	Von McDaniel (YP)	15.00
65	Von McDaniel (WP)	6.00
66	Lee Walls	6.00
67	Joe Ginsberg	6.00
69	Wally Burnette	6.00
70	Al Kaline (WP)	75.00
70	Al Kaline (YP)	200.00
71	Dodgers Team/ Checklist 1-88	15.00
72	Bud Byerly	6.00
73	Pete Daley	6.00
74	Roy Face	7.00
75	Gus Bell	6.00
76	Dick Farrell (YT)	15.00
76	Dick Farrell (WT)	6.00
77	Don Zimmer (YT)	15.00
77	Don Zimmer (WT)	6.00

78	Ernie Johnson (YP)	15.00
78	Ernie Johnson (WP)	6.00
79	Dick Williams (YT)	20.00
79	Dick Williams (WT)	7.00
80	Dick Drott	6.00
81	*Steve Boros* (YT)	15.00
81	*Steve Boros* (WT)	6.00
82	Ronnie Kline	6.00
83	Bob Hazle	6.00
84	Billy O'Dell	6.00
85	Luis Aparicio (YT)	45.00
85	Luis Aparicio (WT)	20.00
87	Johnny Kucks	7.00
88	Duke Snider	40.00
89	Billy Klaus	6.00
90	Robin Roberts	15.00
91	Chuck Tanner	7.00
92	Clint Courtney (YP)	15.00
92	Clint Courtney (WP)	6.00
93	Sandy Amoros	6.00
94	Bob Skinner	6.00
95	Frank Bolling	6.00
96	Joe Durham	6.00
97	Larry Jackson (YP)	15.00
97	Larry Jackson (WP)	6.00
98	Billy Hunter (YP)	15.00
98	Billy Hunter (WP)	6.00
99	Bobby Adams	6.00
100	Early Wynn (YT)	30.00
100	Early Wynn (WT)	15.00
101	Bobby Richardson (YP)	30.00
101	Bobby Richardson (WP)	10.00
102	George Strickland	6.00
103	Jerry Lynch	6.00
104	Jim Pendleton	6.00
105	Billy Gardner	6.00
106	Dick Schofield	6.00
107	Ossie Virgil	6.00
108	Jim Landis (YT)	15.00
108	Jim Landis (WT)	6.00
109	Herb Plews	6.00
110	Johnny Logan	6.00
111	Stu Miller	2.50
112	Gus Zernial	2.50

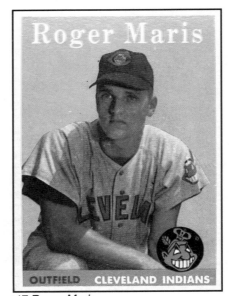

47 Roger Maris

30 Hank Aaron

113	Jerry Walker	2.50
114	Irv Noren	2.50
115	Jim Bunning	10.00
116	Dave Philley	2.50
117	Frank Torre	2.50
118	Harvey Haddix	2.50
119	Harry Chiti	2.50
120	Johnny Podres	4.00
121	Eddie Miksis	2.50
122	Walt Moryn	2.50
123	Dick Tomanek	2.50
124	Bobby Usher	2.50
125	Al Dark	4.00
126	Stan Palys	2.50
127	Tom Sturdivant	3.00
128	*Willie Kirkland*	3.00
129	Jim Derrington	2.50
130	Jackie Jensen	4.00
131	Bob Henrich	2.50
132	Vernon Law	4.00
133	Russ Nixon	2.50
134	Phillies Team/ Checklist 89-176	9.00
135	Mike Drabowsky	2.50
136	Jim Finigan	2.50
137	Russ Kemmerer	2.50
138	Earl Torgeson	2.50
139	George Brunet	2.50
140	Wes Covington	3.00
141	Ken Lehman	2.50
142	Enos Slaughter	18.00
143	Billy Muffett	2.50
144	Bobby Morgan	2.50
145	Not Issued	
146	Dick Gray	2.50
147	*Don McMahon*	3.00
148	Billy Consolo	2.50
149	Tom Acker	2.50
150	Mickey Mantle	500.00
151	Buddy Pritchard	2.50
152	Johnny Antonelli	3.00
153	Les Moss	2.50
154	Harry Byrd	2.50

155	Hector Lopez	2.50
157	Dee Fondy	2.50
158	Indians Team/	
	Checklist 177-264	8.00
159	Taylor Phillips	2.50
160	Don Hoak	3.00
161	Don Larsen	5.00
162	Gil Hodges	18.00
163	Jim Wilson	2.50
164	Bob Taylor	2.50
165	Bob Nieman	2.50
166	Danny O'Connell	2.50
167	Frank Baumann	2.50
168	Joe Cunningham	3.50
169	Ralph Terry	3.00
170	Vic Wertz	3.00
171	Harry Anderson	2.50
172	Don Gross	2.50
173	Eddie Yost	2.50
174	A's Team/	
	Checklist 89-176	8.00
175	*Marv Throneberry*	7.00
176	Bob Buhl	2.50
177	Al Smith	2.50
178	Ted Kluszewski	5.00
179	Willy Miranda	2.50
180	Lindy McDaniel	2.50
181	Willie Jones	2.50
182	Joe Caffie	2.50
183	Dave Jolly	2.50
184	Elvin Tappe	2.50
185	Ray Boone	2.50
186	Jack Meyer	2.50
187	Sandy Koufax	120.00
188	Milt Bolling (photo is	
	Lou Berberet)	2.50
189	George Susce	2.50
190	Red Schoendienst	15.00
191	Art Ceccarelli	2.50
192	Milt Graff	2.50
193	*Jerry Lumpe*	5.00
194	Roger Craig	3.00
195	Whitey Lockman	2.50
196	Mike Garcia	2.50

187 Sandy Koufax

197	Haywood Sullivan	2.50
198	Bill Virdon	3.50
199	Don Blasingame	2.50
200	Bob Keegan	2.50
201	Jim Bolger	2.50
202	*Woody Held*	3.00
203	Al Walker	2.50
204	Leo Kiely	2.50
205	Johnny Temple	2.50
206	Bob Shaw	3.00
207	Solly Hemus	2.50
208	Cal McLish	2.50
209	Bob Anderson	2.50
210	Wally Moon	2.50
211	Pete Burnside	2.50
212	Bubba Phillips	2.50
213	Red Wilson	2.50
214	Willard Schmidt	2.50
215	Jim Gilliam	5.00
216	Cardinals Team/	
	Checklist 177-264	7.00
217	Jack Harshman	2.50
218	Dick Rand	2.50
219	Camilo Pascual	2.75
220	Tom Brewer	2.50
221	Jerry Kindall	2.50
222	Bud Daley	2.50
223	Andy Pafko	3.50
224	Bob Grim	3.75
225	Billy Goodman	2.50
226	Bob Smith (photo is	
	Bobby Gene Smith)	2.50
227	Gene Stephens	2.50
228	Duke Maas	2.50
229	Frank Zupo	2.50
230	*Richie Ashburn	8.00
231	Lloyd Merritt	2.50
232	Reno Bertoia	2.50
233	Mickey Vernon	2.75
234	Carl Sawatski	2.50
235	Tom Gorman	2.50
236	Ed Fitz Gerald	2.50
237	Bill Wight	2.50

238	Bill Mazeroski	7.00
239	Chuck Stobbs	2.50
240	Moose Skowron	7.00
241	Dick Littlefield	2.50
242	Johnny Klippstein	2.50
243	Larry Raines	2.50
244	*Don Demeter*	2.75
245	*Frank Lary*	2.75
246	Yankees Team/	
	Checklist 177-264	30.00
247	Casey Wise	2.50
248	Herm Wehmeier	2.50
249	Ray Moore	2.50
250	Roy Sievers	3.50
251	Warren Hacker	2.50
252	Bob Trowbridge	2.50
253	Don Mueller	2.50
254	Alex Grammas	2.50
255	Bob Turley	5.00
256	White Sox Team/	
	Checklist 265-352	8.00
257	Hal Smith	2.50
258	Carl Erskine	5.00
259	Al Pilarcik	2.50
260	Frank Malzone	2.75
261	Turk Lown	2.50
262	Johnny Groth	2.50
263	Eddie Bressoud	2.50
264	Jack Sanford	2.50
265	Pete Runnels	2.75
266	Connie Johnson	2.50
267	Sherm Lollar	3.00
268	Granny Hamner	2.50
269	Paul Smith	2.50
270	Warren Spahn	35.00
271	Billy Martin	10.00
272	Ray Crone	2.50
273	Hal Smith	2.50
274	Rocky Bridges	2.50
275	*Elston Howard	8.00
276	Bobby Avila	2.50
277	Virgil Trucks	2.75
278	Mack Burk	2.50
279	Bob Boyd	2.50

70 Al Kaline

418 World Series Batting Foes

280	Jim Piersall	3.50
281	Sam Taylor	2.50
282	Paul Foytack	2.50
283	Ray Shearer	2.50
284	Ray Katt	2.50
285	Frank Robinson	60.00
286	Gino Cimoli	2.50
287	Sam Jones	2.50
288	Harmon Killebrew	50.00
296	*Ryne Duren*	6.00
304	*Tigers' Big Bats (Al Kaline, Harvey Kuenn)	8.00
307	Brooks Robinson	60.00
310	Ernie Banks	50.00
312	Red Sox Team/ Checklist 353-440	8.00
314	Dodgers' Boss and Power (Walt Alston, Duke Snider)	25.00
320	Whitey Ford	35.00
321	Sluggers' Supreme (Ted Kluszewski, Ted Williams)	15.00
324	Hoyt Wilhelm	15.00
340	Don Newcombe	6.00
343	*Orlando Cepeda*	50.00
351	Braves' Fence Busters (Hank Aaron, Joe Adcock, Del Crandall, Ed Mathews)	20.00
368	Rocky Colavito	10.00
370	Yogi Berra	70.00
375	Pee Wee Reese	50.00
377	Braves Team (numerical checklist)	60.00
386	Birdie's Young Sluggers (Ed Bailey, Frank Robinson, Birdie Tebbetts)	7.00
393	Tony Kubek	10.00
397	Tigers Team (numerical checklist)	60.00
400	*Nellie Fox	8.00
408	Orioles Team (numerical checklist)	60.00
417	Carl Furillo	6.00
418	World Series Batting Foes (Mickey Mantle, Hank Aaron)	100.00
420	*Vada Pinson*	15.00
424	Larry Doby	4.00
428	Redlegs Team (numerical checklist)	50.00
436	Rival Fence Busters (Willie Mays, Duke Snider)	35.00
438	Whitey Herzog	4.00
440	Ed Mathews	20.00
448	Charlie Lau	4.00
450	Preston Ward	4.00
457	Milt Pappas	4.00
462	Gary Geiger	7.00
464	*Curt Flood	12.00
475	AS Managers (Fred Haney, Casey Stengel)	20.00
476	Stan Musial AS	30.00
479	Nellie Fox AS	10.00
480	Eddie Mathews AS	15.00
482	Ernie Banks AS	20.00
483	Luis Aparicio AS	13.00
484	Frank Robinson AS	17.00
485	Ted Williams AS	45.00
486	Willie Mays AS	35.00
487	Mickey Mantle AS	55.00
488	Hank Aaron AS	30.00
494	Warren Spahn AS	20.00

1959 TOPPS

Topps closed out the 1950s with a 572-card set, the largest of the decade, and added many specialty subsets to the regular player cards. Normal cards feature a nearly round color photo on a solid-color background with a white outer border. A facsimile autograph appears across the photo. Card backs have year-by-year stats, a cartoon, and a short player biography. One specialty group is a ten-card subset highlighting events from the 1958 season. Other subsets include 31 Rookie Stars and 22 All-Star selections. Card number 550, called Symbol of Courage, portrays Roy Campanella in a wheelchair following his near-fatal car accident.

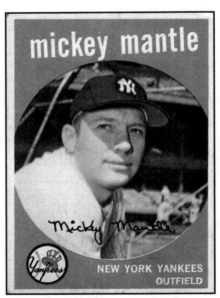

10 Mickey Mantle

		NR MT
Complete set		**$4150.00**
Commons (1-110)		**4.00**
Commons (111-506)		**2.50**
Commons (507-572)		**10.00**

1	Ford Frick	$60.00
2	Eddie Yost	4.00
3	Don McMahon	4.00
4	Albie Pearson	4.00
5	Dick Donovan	4.00
6	Alex Grammas	4.00
7	Al Pilarcik	4.00
8	Phillies Team/ Checklist 1-88	12.00
9	Paul Giel	4.00
10	Mickey Mantle	400.00
11	Billy Hunter	4.00
12	Vern Law	5.00
13	Dick Gernert	4.00
14	Pete Whisenant	4.00
15	Dick Drott	4.00
16	Joe Pignatano	4.00
17	Danny's All Stars (Ted Kluszewski, Danny Murtaugh, Frank Thomas)	5.00
18	Jack Urban	4.00
19	Ed Bressoud	4.00
20	Duke Snider	40.00
21	Connie Johnson	4.00
22	Al Smith	4.00
23	Murry Dickson	5.00
24	Red Wilson	4.00
25	Don Hoak	4.50
26	Chuck Stobbs	4.00
27	Andy Pafko	4.50
28	Red Worthington	4.00
29	Jim Bolger	4.00
30	Nellie Fox	10.00
31	Ken Lehman	4.00
32	Don Buddin	4.00
33	Ed Fitz Gerald	4.00
34	Pitchers Beware (Al Kaline, Charlie Maxwell)	9.00
35	Ted Kluszewski	7.00
36	Hank Aguirre	4.00
37	Gene Green	4.00
38	Morrie Martin	4.00
39	Ed Bouchee	4.00
40	Warren Spahn	40.00
41	Bob Martyn	4.00
42	Murray Wall	4.00
43	Steve Bilko	4.00
44	Vito Valentinetti	4.00
45	Andy Carey	5.00

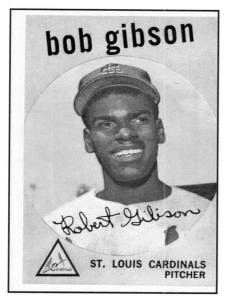

514 Bob Gibson

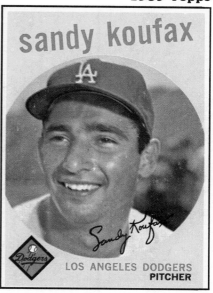

163 Sandy Koufax

85	Harry Anderson	4.00
86	Bob Keegan	4.00
87	Danny O'Connell	4.00
88	Herb Score	4.50
89	Billy Gardner	4.00
90	Bill Skowron	8.00
91	Herb Moford	4.00
92	Dave Philley	4.00
93	Julio Becquer	4.00
94	White Sox Team/ Checklist 89-176	15.00
95	Carl Willey	4.00
96	Lou Berberet	4.00
97	Jerry Lynch	4.00
98	Arnie Portocarrero	4.00
99	Ted Kazanski	4.00
100	Bob Cerv	4.00
101	Alex Kellner	4.00
102	Felipe Alou	6.00
103	Billy Goodman	4.00
104	Del Rice	4.00
105	Lee Walls	4.00
106	Hal Woodeshick	4.00
107	Norm Larker	4.00
108	Zack Monroe	4.00
109	Bob Schmidt	4.00
110	George Witt	4.00
111	Redlegs Team/ Checklist 89-176	8.00
112	Billy Consolo	2.50
113	Taylor Phillips	2.50
114	Earl Battey	2.50
115	Mickey Vernon	3.00
116	*Bob Allison	4.00
117	John Blanchard	3.00
118	John Buzhardt	2.50
119	John Callison	4.00
120	Chuck Coles	2.50
125	Ron Fairly	3.75
131	Deron Johnson	3.25
132	Don Lee	2.50
133	Bob Lillis	2.75
134	Jim McDaniel	2.50
135	Gene Oliver	2.50

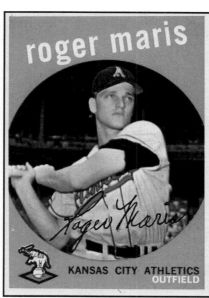

202 Roger Maris

46	Bill Henry	4.00
47	Jim Finigan	4.00
48	Orioles Team/ Checklist 1-88	10.00
49	Bill Hall	4.00
50	Willie Mays	125.00
51	Rip Coleman	4.00
52	Coot Veal	4.00
53	Stan Williams	4.00
54	Mel Roach	4.00
55	Tom Brewer	4.00
56	Carl Sawatski	4.00
57	Al Cicotte	4.00
58	Eddie Miksis	4.00
59	Irv Noren	4.00
60	Bob Turley	6.00
61	Dick Brown	4.00
62	Tony Taylor	4.00
63	Jim Hearn	4.00
64	Joe DeMaestri	4.00
65	Frank Torre	4.00
66	Joe Ginsberg	4.00
67	Brooks Lawrence	4.00
68	Dick Schofield	4.00
69	Giants Team/ Checklist 89-176	12.00
70	*Harvey Kuenn	5.00
71	Don Bessent	4.00
72	Bill Renna	4.00
73	Ron Jackson	4.00
74	Directing the Power (Cookie Lavagetto, Jim Lemon, Roy Sievers)	4.50
75	Sam Jones	4.00
76	Bobby Richardson	9.00
77	John Goryl	4.00
78	Pedro Ramos	4.00
79	Harry Chiti	4.00
80	Minnie Minoso	5.00
81	Hal Jeffcoat	4.00
82	Bob Boyd	4.00
83	Bob Smith	4.00
84	Reno Bertoia	4.00

136	Jim O'Toole	2.50
137	Dick Ricketts	2.50
138	John Romano	2.50
139	Ed Sadowski	2.50
140	Charlie Secrest	2.50
141	Joe Shipley	2.50
142	Dick Stigman	2.50
143	Willie Tasby	2.50
144	Jerry Walker	2.50
145	Dom Zanni	2.50
146	Jerry Zimmerman	2.50
147	Cubs' Clubbers (Ernie Banks, Dale Long, Walt Moryn)	9.00
148	Mike McCormick	2.50
149	*Jim Bunning	8.00
150	Stan Musial	120.00
151	Bob Malkmus	2.50
152	Johnny Klippstein	2.50
153	Jim Marshall	2.50
154	Ray Herbert	2.50
155	Enos Slaughter	15.00
156	*Ace Hurlers (Billy Pierce, Robin Roberts)	3.50
157	Felix Mantilla	2.50
158	Walt Dropo	2.50
159	Bob Shaw	2.50
160	Dick Groat	3.00
161	Frank Baumann	2.50
162	Bobby G. Smith	2.50
163	Sandy Koufax	120.00
164	Johnny Groth	2.50
165	Bill Bruton	2.50
166	*Destruction Crew (Rocky Colavito, Larry Doby, Minnie Minoso)	3.25
167	Duke Maas	3.00
168	Carroll Hardy	2.50
169	Ted Abernathy	2.50
170	Gene Woodling	3.00
171	Willard Schmidt	2.50
172	A's Team/ Checklist 177-242	7.00

150 Stan Musial

173	Bill Monbouquette	2.75
174	Jim Pendleton	2.50
175	Dick Farrell	2.50
176	Preston Ward	2.50
177	Johnny Briggs	2.50
178	Ruben Amaro	2.50
179	Don Rudolph	2.50
180	Yogi Berra	60.00
181	Bob Porterfield	2.50
182	Milt Graff	2.50
183	Stu Miller	2.50
184	Harvey Haddix	2.75
185	Jim Busby	2.50
186	Mudcat Grant	2.50
187	Bubba Phillips	2.50
188	Juan Pizarro	2.50
189	Neil Chrisley	2.50
190	Bill Virdon	3.00
191	Russ Kemmerer	2.50
192	Charley Beamon	2.50
193	Sammy Taylor	2.50
194	Jim Brosnan	2.75
195	Rip Repulski	2.50
196	Billy Moran	2.50
197	Ray Semproch	2.50
198	Jim Davenport	2.50
199	Leo Kiely	2.50
200	*Warren Giles	2.75
201	Tom Acker	2.50
202	Roger Maris	125.00
203	Ozzie Virgil	2.50
204	Casey Wise	2.50
205	Don Larsen	5.00
206	Carl Furillo	5.00
207	George Strickland	2.50
208	Willie Jones	2.50
209	Lenny Green	2.50
210	Ed Bailey	2.50
211	Bob Blaylock	2.50
212	Fence Busters (Hank Aaron, Eddie Mathews)	18.00
213	Jim Rivera	2.50
214	Marcelino Solis	2.50

215	Jim Lemon	2.50
216	Andre Rodgers	2.50
217	Carl Erskine	4.00
218	Roman Mejias	2.50
219	George Zuverink	2.50
220	Frank Malzone	2.50
221	Bob Bowman	2.50
222	Bobby Shantz	3.50
223	Cards Team/ Checklist 265-352	7.00
224	Claude Osteen	3.00
225	Johnny Logan	2.50
226	Art Ceccarelli	2.50
227	Hal Smith	2.50
228	Don Gross	2.50
229	Vic Power	2.50
230	Bill Fischer	2.50
231	Ellis Burton	2.50
232	Eddie Kasko	2.50
233	Paul Foytack	2.50
234	Chuck Tanner	3.00
235	Valmy Thomas	2.50
236	Ted Bowsfield	2.50
237	*Run Preventers (Gil McDougald, Bobby Richardson, Bob Turley)	4.00
238	Gene Baker	2.50
239	Bob Trowbridge	2.50
240	Hank Bauer	7.50
241	Billy Muffett	2.50
242	Ron Samford	2.50
243	Marv Grissom	2.50
244	Dick Gray	2.50
245	Ned Garver	2.50
246	J.W. Porter	2.50
247	Don Ferrarese	2.50
248	Red Sox Team/ Checklist 177-264	8.00
249	Bobby Adams	2.50
250	Billy O'Dell	2.50
251	Cletis Boyer	4.50
252	Ray Boone	2.50
253	Seth Morehead	2.50
254	Zeke Bella	2.50

550 Roy Campanella

561 Hank Aaron AS

255	Del Ennis	2.75
256	Jerry Davie	2.50
257	Leon Wagner	3.00
258	Fred Kipp	2.50
259	Jim Pisoni	2.50
260	Early Wynn	15.00
261	Gene Stephens	2.50
262	*Hitters' Foes (Don Drysdale, Clem Labine, Johnny Podres)	8.00
263	Buddy Daley	2.50
264	Chico Carrasquel	2.50
267	John Romonosky	2.50
268	Tito Francona	2.50
269	Jack Meyer	2.50
270	Gil Hodges	18.00
271	Orlando Pena	2.75
272	Jerry Lumpe	3.00
273	Joe Jay	2.50
274	Jerry Kindall	2.50
275	Jack Sanford	2.50
276	Pete Daley	2.50
277	Turk Lown	2.50
278	Chuck Essegian	2.50
279	Ernie Johnson	2.50
280	Frank Bolling	2.50
281	Walt Craddock	2.50
282	R.C. Stevens	2.50
283	Russ Heman	2.50
284	Steve Korcheck	2.50
285	Joe Cunningham	3.50
286	Dean Stone	2.50
287	Don Zimmer	2.75
288	Dutch Dotterer	2.50
289	Johnny Kucks	2.75
290	Wes Covington	2.75
291	Pitching Partners (Camilo Pascual, Pedro Ramos)	2.75
292	Dick Williams	2.75
293	Ray Moore	2.50
294	Hank Foiles	2.50
295	Billy Martin	9.00
296	Ernie Broglio	2.75

297	Jackie Brandt	2.50
298	Tex Clevenger	2.50
299	Billy Klaus	2.50
300	Richie Ashburn	9.00
301	Earl Averill	2.50
302	Don Mossi	2.50
303	Marty Keough	2.50
304	Cubs Team/ Checklist 265-352	7.00
305	Curt Raydon	2.50
306	Jim Gilliam	5.00
307	Curt Barclay	2.50
308	Norm Siebern	3.00
309	Sal Maglie	3.00
310	Luis Aparicio	15.00
311	Norm Zauchin	2.50
312	Don Newcombe	4.50
313	Frank House	2.50
314	Don Cardwell	2.50
315	Joe Adcock	3.00
316	Ralph Lumenti (with option statement)	2.50
316	Ralph Lumenti (w/o option statement)	80.00
317	NL Hitting Kings (Richie Ashburn, Willie Mays)	15.00
318	Rocky Bridges	2.50
319	Dave Hillman	2.50
320	Bob Skinner	2.75
321	Bob Giallombardo (with option statement)	2.50
321	Bob Giallombardo (w/o option statement)	80.00
322	Harry Hanebrink (with trade statement)	2.50
322	Harry Hanebrink (w/o trade statement)	65.00
325	Ken Boyer	5.00
326	Marv Throneberry	4.00
327	Gary Bell	2.75
329	Tigers Team/ Checklist 353-429	8.00
336	Billy Loes (with trade statment)	2.50

336	Billy Loes (w/o trade statement)	65.00
338	George Anderson	12.00
345	Gil McDougald	8.00
349	Hoyt Wilhelm	15.00
350	Ernie Banks	50.00
352	Robin Roberts	15.00
359	*Bill White	15.00
360	Al Kaline	50.00
362	Dolan Nichols (with option statement)	2.50
362	Dolan Nichols (w/o option statement)	80.00
380	Hank Aaron	100.00
383	Words of Wisdom (Don Larsen, Casey Stengel)	5.00
387	Don Drysdale	20.00
390	Orlando Cepeda	9.00
395	Elston Howard	7.00
397	Senators Team/ Checklist 430-495	7.00
408	*Keystone Combo (Luis Aparicio, Nellie Fox)	7.00

570 Bob Turley AS

419	Braves Team/ Checklist 353-429	8.00
428	Buc Hill Aces (Roy Face, Bob Friend, Ron Kline, Vern Law)	3.25
430	Whitey Ford	25.00
435	Frank Robinson	25.00
439	Brooks Robinson	30.00
440	Lou Burdette	8.00
444	Ronnie Hansen	2.75
450	Ed Mathews	20.00
457	Dodgers Team/ Checklist 430-495	12.00
461	Mantle Hits 42nd Homer for Crown	25.00
462	Colavito's Great Catch Saves Game	3.00
463	Kaline Becomes Youngest Bat Champ	8.00

464	Mays' Catch Makes Series History	12.00
465	Sievers Sets Homer Mark	2.75
466	Pierce All-Star Starter	2.75
467	Aaron Clubs World Series Homer	12.00
468	Snider's Play Brings L.A. Victory	9.00
469	Hustler Banks Wins MVP Award	8.00
470	Musial Raps Out 3,000th Hit	12.00
476	Indians Team/ Checklist 496-572	7.00
478	Bob Clemente	70.00
480	Red Schoendienst	12.00
505	Tony Kubek	8.00
507	Bob Hale	10.00
508	Art Fowler	10.00
509	Norm Cash	15.00
510	Yankees Team/ Checklist 496-572	45.00
511	George Susce	10.00
512	George Altman	10.00
513	Tom Carroll	10.00
514	Bob Gibson	300.00
515	Harmon Killebrew	110.00
516	Mike Garcia	11.00
517	Joe Koppe	10.00
518	Mike Cueller (Cuellar)	10.00
519	Infield Power (Dick Gernert, Frank Malzone, Pete Runnels)	12.00
520	Don Elston	10.00
521	Gary Geiger	10.00
522	Gene Snyder	10.00
523	Harry Bright	10.00
524	Larry Osborne	10.00
525	Jim Coates	10.00
526	Bob Speake	10.00
527	Solly Hemus	10.00
528	Pirates Team/ Checklist 496-572	25.00
529	George Bamberger	11.00
530	Wally Moon	11.00

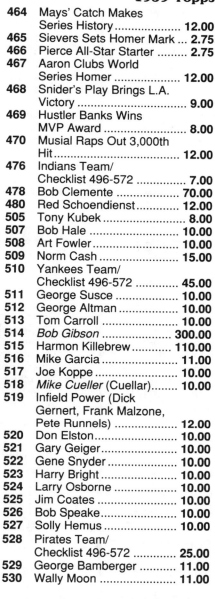

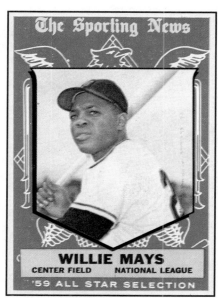
563 Willie Mays AS

478 Bob Clemente

531	Ray Webster	10.00
532	Mark Freeman	10.00
533	Darrell Johnson	10.00
534	Faye Throneberry	10.00
535	Ruben Gomez	10.00
536	Dan Kravitz	10.00
537	Rudolfo Arias	10.00
538	Chick King	10.00
539	Gary Blaylock	10.00
540	Willy Miranda	10.00
541	Bob Thurman	10.00
542	Jim Perry	15.00
543	Corsair Outfield Trio (Bob Clemente, Bob Skinner, Bill Virdon)	30.00
544	Lee Tate	10.00
545	Tom Morgan	10.00
546	Al Schroll	10.00
547	Jim Baxes	10.00
548	Elmer Singleton	10.00
549	Howie Nunn	10.00
550	Roy Campanella (Symbol of Courage)	100.00
551	Fred Haney AS	11.00
552	Casey Stengel AS	30.00
553	Orlando Cepeda AS	12.00
554	Bill Skowron AS	12.00
555	Bill Mazeroski AS	12.00
556	Nellie Fox AS	14.00
557	Ken Boyer AS	12.00
558	Frank Malzone AS	11.00
559	Ernie Banks AS	30.00
560	Luis Aparicio AS	20.00
561	Hank Aaron AS	90.00
562	Al Kaline AS	35.00
563	Willie Mays AS	90.00
564	Mickey Mantle AS	175.00
565	Wes Covington AS	11.00
566	Roy Sievers AS	11.00
567	Del Crandall AS	11.00
568	Gus Triandos AS	11.00
569	Bob Friend AS	11.00
570	Bob Turley AS	11.00
571	Warren Spahn AS	35.00
572	Billy Pierce AS	15.00

1960 TOPPS

In this 572-card set Topps revived the horizontal format used in 1955 and 1956. Color photos were used alongside smaller black-and-white photos on card fronts. The horizontal format and use of two photos, however, detract from the visual appeal of the cards. The backs are simpler than usual, with black-and-gold printing on gray or white cardboard. Card numbers 375-440 are slightly rarer in the white cardboard variety. For the first time, the 1960 set included World Series highlight cards from the previous year. Hot cards include rookies Carl Yastrzemski, Willie McCovey, and Jim Kaat, along with superstars Mickey Mantle, Roger Maris, and Bob Clemente.

	NR MT
Complete set	$3600.00
Commons (1-286)	1.50
Commons (287-440)	1.75
Commons (441-506)	3.50
Commons (507-572)	8.00

1	Early Wynn	$35.00
2	Roman Mejias	2.00
3	Joe Adcock	2.25
4	Bob Purkey	1.50
5	Wally Moon	1.75
6	Lou Berberet	1.50
7	Master & Mentor (Willie Mays, Bill Rigney)	8.00
8	Bud Daley	1.50
9	Faye Throneberry	1.50
10	Ernie Banks	30.00
11	Norm Siebern	1.75
12	Milt Pappas	1.75
13	Wally Post	1.50
14	Jim Grant	1.50
15	Pete Runnels	1.50
16	Ernie Broglio	1.50
17	Johnny Callison	1.75
18	Dodgers Team/ Checklist 1-88	10.00
19	Felix Mantilla	1.50
20	Roy Face	2.00
21	Dutch Dotterer	1.50
22	Rocky Bridges	1.50
23	Eddie Fisher	1.50
24	Dick Gray	1.50
25	Roy Sievers	3.50
26	Wayne Terwilliger	1.50
27	Dick Drott	1.50
28	Brooks Robinson	30.00
29	Clem Labine	1.75
30	Tito Francona	1.50
31	Sammy Esposito	1.50
32	Sophomore Stalwarts (Jim O'Toole, Vada Pinson)	3.50
33	Tom Morgan	2.25
34	George Anderson	2.50
35	Whitey Ford	25.00
36	Russ Nixon	1.50
37	Bill Bruton	1.75
38	Jerry Casale	1.50
39	Earl Averill	1.50
40	Joe Cunningham	2.00
41	Barry Latman	1.50
42	Hobie Landrith	1.50
43	Senators Team/ Checklist 1-88	6.00
44	Bobby Locke	1.50
45	Roy McMillan	1.50
46	Jack Fisher	1.50
47	Don Zimmer	2.25
48	Hal Smith	1.50
49	Curt Raydon	1.50
50	Al Kaline	25.00
51	Jim Coates	1.50
52	Dave Philley	1.50
53	Jackie Brandt	1.50
54	Mike Fornieles	1.50
55	*Bill Mazeroski	3.00
56	Steve Korcheck	1.50
57	Win Savers (Turk Lown, Gerry Staley)	1.75
58	Gino Cimoli	1.50
59	Juan Pizarro	1.50
60	Gus Triandos	1.50
61	Eddie Kasko	1.50

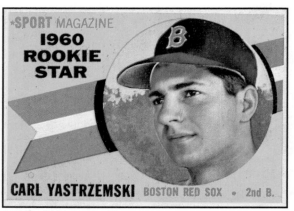

*SPORT MAGAZINE
1960 ROOKIE STAR
CARL YASTRZEMSKI   BOSTON RED SOX • 2nd B.

148 Carl Yastrzemski

62	Roger Craig	2.50
63	George Strickland	1.50
64	Jack Meyer	1.50
65	Elston Howard	6.00
66	Bob Trowbridge	1.50
67	*Jose Pagan*	1.75
68	Dave Hillman	1.50
69	Billy Goodman	1.50
70	Lou Burdette	3.25
71	Marty Keough	1.50
72	Tigers Team/ Checklist 89-176	8.00
73	Bob Gibson	25.00
74	Walt Moryn	1.50
75	Vic Power	1.50
76	Bill Fischer	1.50
77	Hank Foiles	1.50
78	Bob Grim	1.50
79	Walt Dropo	1.50
80	Johnny Antonelli	2.00
81	Russ Snyder	1.50
82	Ruben Gomez	1.50
83	Tony Kubek	4.50
84	Hal Smith	1.50
85	Frank Lary	1.75
86	Dick Gernert	1.50
87	John Romonosky	1.50
88	John Roseboro	1.75
89	Hal Brown	1.50
90	Bobby Avila	1.50
91	Bennie Daniels	1.50
92	*Whitey Herzog	3.25
93	Art Schult	1.50
94	Leo Kiely	1.50
95	Frank Thomas	1.50
96	Ralph Terry	2.50
97	Ted Lepcio	1.50
98	Gordon Jones	1.50
99	Lenny Green	1.50
100	Nellie Fox	7.00
101	Bob Miller	1.50
102	Kent Hadley	1.50
103	Dick Farrell	1.50
104	Dick Schofield	1.50
105	Larry Sherry	1.50
106	Billy Gardner	1.50
107	Carl Willey	1.50
108	Pete Daley	1.50
109	Cletis Boyer	3.00
111	Vic Wertz	1.75

250 Stan Musial

112	Jack Harshman	1.50
113	Bob Skinner	1.50
114	Ken Aspromonte	1.50
115	Fork & Knuckler (Roy Face, Hoyt Wilhelm)	4.00
119	*Chico Cardenas*	1.75
125	Dick Ellsworth	1.75
126	Chuck Estrada	1.75
132	*Frank Howard*	10.00
134	*Deron Johnson*	2.00
136	*Jim Kaat*	25.00
138	*Art Mahaffey*	1.75
148	*Carl Yastrzemski*	350.00
150	*Billy Pierce	2.25
151	Giants Team/ Checklist 177-264	6.00
153	Bobby Thomson	2.00
155	Charlie Neal	1.50
159	Jim Piersall	2.00
160	Rival All Stars (Ken Boyer, Mickey Mantle)	30.00
164	Reds Team/ Checklist 89-176	7.00
167	Valmy Thomas	1.50
168	Alex Grammas	1.50
169	Jake Striker	1.50
170	Del Crandall	2.00
171	Johnny Groth	1.50
172	Willie Kirkland	1.50
173	Billy Martin	7.00
174	Indians Team/ Checklist 89-176	6.00

176	Vada Pinson	3.25
177	Johnny Kucks	1.50
178	Woody Held	1.50
179	Rip Coleman	1.50
180	Harry Simpson	1.50
181	Billy Loes	1.75
182	Glen Hobbie	1.50
183	Eli Grba	1.75
188	Dick Williams	2.00
190	Gene Woodling	1.75
196	Andy Carey	2.00
200	Willie Mays	100.00
208	White Sox Team/ Checklist 177-264	6.00
210	Harmon Killebrew	20.00
212	Walt Alston	6.00
213	Chuck Dressen	1.75
216	Joe Gordon	1.75
217	Charley Grimm	1.75
219	Fred Hutchinson	1.75
221	Cookie Lavagetto	1.50
222	Al Lopez	5.00
223	Danny Murtaugh	1.75
224	Paul Richards	1.75
225	Bill Rigney	1.50
226	Eddie Sawyer	1.50
227	Casey Stengel	20.00
230	Mound Magicians (Bob Buhl, Lou Burdette, Warren Spahn)	6.00
235	Gus Bell	1.75
237	Elmer Valo	1.75
240	Luis Aparicio	10.00
241	Albie Pearson	1.50
242	Cards Team/ Checklist 265-352	6.00
245	Eddie Yost	1.75
247	Gil McDougald	4.50
249	*Earl Wilson*	1.75
250	Stan Musial	100.00
255	Jim Gilliam	3.25
258	Dick Groat	4.00
260	Power Plus (Rocky Colavito, Tito Francona)	3.00
262	Hank Bauer	2.00
263	Darrell Johnson	1.50
264	Robin Roberts	15.00
270	Bob Turley	3.00
275	Curt Flood	3.00
279	Chuck Tanner	2.25

350 Mickey Mantle

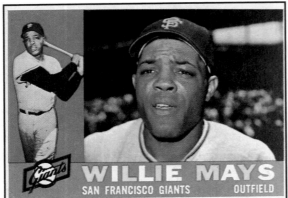

'200 Willie Mays

281	Ray Boone	1.75
282	Joe Nuxhall	1.75
283	John Blanchard	2.00
287	Felipe Alou	2.50
290	Jerry Lumpe	2.00
292	Dodger Backstops (Joe Pignatano, John Roseboro)	2.00
295	Gil Hodges	18.00
300	Hank Aaron	80.00
302	Phillies Team/ Checklist 353-429	7.00
305	Richie Ashburn	7.00
310	Frank Malzone	2.00
312	Charlie Lau	1.75
315	Bobby Shantz	3.00
316	*Willie McCovey*	150.00
320	Bob Allison	2.25
321	Ron Fairly	2.00
324	Jim Perry	2.50
326	Bob Clemente	75.00
330	Harvey Kuenn	2.75
332	Yankees Team/ Checklist 265-352	20.00
335	Red Schoendienst	10.00
340	Harvey Haddix	2.25
341	Carroll Hardy	1.75
343	Sandy Koufax	70.00
349	Moe Drabowsky	1.75
350	Mickey Mantle	325.00
351	Don Nottebart	1.75
352	Cincy Clouters (Gus Bell, Jerry Lynch, Frank Robinson)	5.00
353	Don Larsen	2.00
354	Bob Lillis	1.75
355	*Bill White	2.50
356	Joe Amalfitano	1.75
357	Al Schroll	1.75
358	Joe DeMaestri	2.25
359	Buddy Gilbert	1.75
360	Herb Score	2.25
361	Bob Oldis	1.75
362	Russ Kemmerer	1.75
363	Gene Stephens	1.75
364	Paul Foytack	1.75
365	Minnie Minoso	3.00
366	*Dallas Green*	3.00
367	Bill Tuttle	1.75

368	Daryl Spencer	1.75
369	Billy Hoeft	1.75
370	Bill Skowron	6.00
371	Bud Byerly	1.75
373	Don Hoak	2.00
374	Bob Buhl	2.00
375	Dale Long	1.75
376	Johnny Briggs	1.75
377	Roger Maris	90.00
378	Stu Miller	1.75
379	Red Wilson	1.75
380	Bob Shaw	1.75
381	Braves Team/ Checklist 353-429	7.00
382	Ted Bowsfield	1.75
383	Leon Wagner	1.75
384	Don Cardwell	1.75
385	World Series Game 1 (Neal Steals Second)	3.50
386	World Series Game 2 (Neal Belts 2nd Homer)	3.50
387	World Series Game 3 (Furillo Breaks Up Game)	3.50
388	World Series Game 4 (Hodges' Winning Homer)	3.75
389	World Series Game 5 (Luis Swipes Base)	3.75
390	World Series Game 6 (Scrambling After Ball)	3.50

391	World Series Summary (The Champs Celebrate)	3.50
392	Tex Clevenger	1.75
393	Smoky Burgess	2.25
394	Norm Larker	1.75
395	Hoyt Wilhelm	15.00
396	Steve Bilko	1.75
397	Don Blasingame	1.75
398	Mike Cuellar	2.00
399	Young Hill Stars (Jack Fisher, Milt Pappas, Jerry Walker)	2.25
400	Rocky Colavito	5.00
401	Bob Duliba	1.75
402	Dick Stuart	2.00
403	Ed Sadowski	1.75
404	Bob Rush	1.75
405	Bobby Richardson	6.00
406	Billy Klaus	1.75
407	*Gary Peters* (color photo is J.C. Martin)	2.50
408	Carl Furillo	4.00
409	Ron Samford	1.75
410	Sam Jones	1.75
411	Ed Bailey	1.75
412	Bob Anderson	1.75
413	A's Team/ Checklist 430-495	7.00
414	Don Williams	1.75
415	Bob Cerv	1.75
416	Humberto Robinson	1.75
417	Chuck Cottier	1.75
418	Don Mossi	1.75
419	George Crowe	1.75
420	Ed Mathews	25.00
421	Duke Maas	2.00
422	Johnny Powers	1.75
423	Ed Fitz Gerald	1.75
424	Pete Whisenant	1.75
425	Johnny Podres	1.75
426	Ron Jackson	1.75
427	Al Grunwald	1.75
428	Al Smith	1.75
429	*AL Kings (Nellie Fox, Harvey Kuenn)	2.25
430	Art Ditmar	1.75
431	Andre Rodgers	1.75
432	Chuck Stobbs	1.75
433	Irv Noren	1.75
434	Brooks Lawrence	1.75

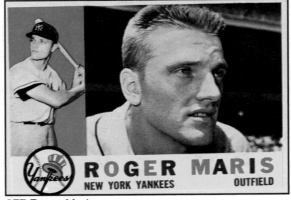

377 Roger Maris

435	Gene Freese	1.75
436	Marv Throneberry	2.00
437	Bob Friend	2.50
438	Jim Coker	1.75
439	Tom Brewer	1.75
440	Jim Lemon	1.75
441	Gary Bell	3.50
442	Joe Pignatano	3.50
443	Charlie Maxwell	3.50
444	Jerry Kindall	3.50
445	Warren Spahn	30.00
446	Ellis Burton	3.50
447	Ray Moore	3.50
448	*Jim Gentile*	4.00
449	Jim Brosnan	3.75
450	*Orlando Cepeda	8.00
451	Curt Simmons	3.75
452	Ray Webster	3.50
453	Vern Law	4.00
454	Hal Woodeshick	3.50
455	Orioles Coaches (Harry Brecheen, Lum Harris, Eddie Robinson)	3.75
456	Red Sox Coaches (Del Baker, Billy Herman, Sal Maglie, Rudy York)	4.00
457	Cubs Coaches (Lou Klein, Charlie Root, Elvin Tappe)	3.75
458	White Sox Coaches (Ray Berres, Johnny Cooney, Tony Cuccinello, Don Gutteridge)	3.75
459	Reds Coaches (Cot Deal, Wally Moses, Reggie Otero)	3.75
460	Indians Coaches (Mel Harder, Red Kress, Bob Lemon, Jo-Jo White)	4.00
461	Tigers Coaches (Luke Appling, Tom Ferrick, Billy Hitchcock)	4.00
462	A's Coaches (Walker Cooper, Fred Fitzsimmons, Don Heffner)	3.75
463	Dodgers Coaches (Joe Becker, Bobby Bragan, Greg Mulleavy, Pete Reiser)	4.00

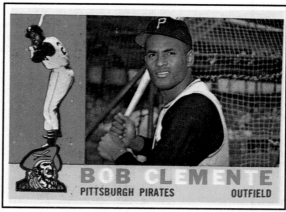

326 Bob Clemente

464	Braves Coaches (George Myatt, Andy Pafko, Bob Scheffing, Whitlow Wyatt)	3.75
465	Yankees Coaches (Frank Crosetti, Billy Dickey, Ralph Houk, Ed Lopat)	7.00
466	Phillies Coaches (Dick Carter, Andy Cohen, Ken Silverstri)	3.75
467	Pirates Coaches (Bill Burwell, Sam Narron, Frank Oceak, Mickey Vernon)	4.00
468	Cardinals Coaches (Ray Katt, Johnny Keane, Howie Pollet, Harry Walker)	3.75
469	Giants Coaches (Salty Parker, Bill Posedel, Wes Westrum)	3.75
470	Senators Coaches (Ellis Clary, Sam Mele, Bob Swift)	3.75
471	Ned Garver	3.50
472	Al Dark	4.50
473	Al Cicotte	3.50
474	Haywood Sullivan	3.50
475	Don Drysdale	25.00

476	Lou Johnson	3.50
477	Don Ferrarese	3.50
478	Frank Torre	3.50
479	Georges Maranda	3.50
480	Yogi Berra	40.00
481	Wes Stock	3.50
482	Frank Bolling	3.50
483	Camilo Pascual	3.75
484	Pirates Team/ Checklist 430-495	15.00
485	Ken Boyer	3.50
486	Bobby Del Greco	3.50
487	Tom Sturdivant	3.50
488	Norm Cash	4.50
489	Steve Ridzik	3.50
490	Frank Robinson	30.00
491	Mel Roach	3.50
492	Larry Jackson	3.50
493	Duke Snider	40.00
494	Orioles Team/ Checklist 496-572	7.00
495	Sherm Lollar	3.00
496	Bill Virdon	4.00
497	John Tsitouris	3.50
498	Al Pilarcik	3.50
499	Johnny James	3.50
500	Johnny Temple	3.50
501	Bob Schmidt	3.50
502	Jim Bunning	8.00
503	Don Lee	3.50
505	Ted Kluszewski	4.50
506	Lee Walls	3.50
507	Dick Stigman	8.00
508	Billy Consolo	8.00
509	*Tommy Davis*	17.00
510	Jerry Staley	8.00
511	Ken Walters	8.00
512	Joe Gibbon	8.00
513	Cubs Team/ Checklist 496-572	20.00
514	*Steve Barber*	9.00
515	*Stan Lopata*	8.00
516	Marty Kutyna	8.00
517	Charley James	8.00
518	*Tony Gonzalez*	8.50
519	Ed Roebuck	8.00
520	Don Buddin	8.00
521	Mike Lee	8.00

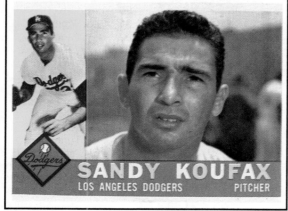

343 Sandy Koufax

522	Ken Hunt	8.00	538	Frank Barnes	8.00	556	Charlie Neal AS	14.00
523	*Clay Dalrymple*	8.50	539	Gene Baker	8.00	557	Frank Malzone AS	14.00
524	Bill Henry	8.00	540	Jerry Walker	8.00	558	Eddie Mathews AS	30.00
525	Marv Breeding	8.00	541	Tony Curry	8.00	559	Luis Aparicio AS	23.00
526	Paul Giel	8.00	542	Ken Hamlin	8.00	560	Ernie Banks AS	40.00
527	Jose Valdivielso	8.00	543	Elio Chacon	8.00	561	Al Kaline AS	40.00
528	Ben Johnson	8.00	544	Bill Monbouquette	8.50	562	Joe Cunningham AS	14.00
529	Norm Sherry	8.00	545	Carl Sawatski	8.00	563	Mickey Mantle AS	165.00
530	Mike McCormick	8.25	546	Hank Aguirre	8.00	564	Willie Mays AS	85.00
531	Sandy Amoros	8.00	547	*Bob Aspromonte*	8.50	565	Roger Maris AS	100.00
532	Mike Garcia	8.75	548	*Don Mincher*	9.00	566	Hank Aaron AS	100.00
533	Lu Clinton	8.00	549	John Buzhardt	8.00	567	Sherm Lollar AS	14.00
534	Ken MacKenzie	8.00	550	Jim Landis	8.00	568	Del Crandall AS	14.00
535	Whitey Lockman	8.00	551	Ed Rakow	8.00	569	Camilo Pascual AS	9.00
536	Wynn Hawkins	8.00	553	Bill Skowron AS	16.00	570	Don Drysdale AS	30.00
537	Red Sox Team/ Checklist 496-572	22.00	554	Willie McCovey AS	50.00	571	Billy Pierce AS	14.00
			555	Nellie Fox AS	20.00	572	Johnny Antonelli AS	20.00

1961 TOPPS

Topps returned to a vertical format again and issued a standard-sized edition of 589 cards. Although two planned All-Star cards (numbers 587 and 588) were never issued, the rest of the set is simple and attractive. A large color photo is accented only by small, multi-colored rectangles on each card bottom that list the player name, position, and team. Card backs again contain statistics by year and utilize black-and-green/gold printing on gray cardboard. The 1961 set features a unique 16-card subset honoring each MVP Award winner since 1951. Card numbers 523 through 589 are among the scarcest high numbers ever produced by Topps.

2 Roger Maris

		NR MT
Complete set		$4700.00
Commons (1-370)		1.00
Commons (371-522)		1.50
Commons (523-589)		20.00

1	Dick Groat	$12.00
2	Roger Maris	200.00
3	John Buzhardt	1.00
4	Lenny Green	1.00
5	Johnny Romano	1.00
6	Ed Roebuck	1.00
7	White Sox Team	2.50
8	Dick Williams	1.50
9	Bob Purkey	1.00
10	Brooks Robinson	30.00
11	Curt Simmons	1.25
12	Moe Thacker	1.00
13	Chuck Cottier	1.00
14	Don Mossi	1.25
15	Willie Kirkland	1.00
16	Billy Muffett	1.00
17	Checklist 1-88	5.00
18	Jim Grant	1.00
19	Cletis Boyer	2.25
20	Robin Roberts	10.00
21	*Zorro Versalles*	2.00
22	Clem Labine	1.25
23	Don Demeter	1.25
24	Ken Johnson	1.00

578 Mickey Mantle AS

25	Red's Heavy Artillery (Gus Bell, Vada Pinson, Frank Robinson)	9.00
26	Wes Stock	1.00
27	Jerry Kindall	1.00
28	Hector Lopez	1.25

29	Don Nottebart	1.00
30	Nellie Fox	6.00
31	Bob Schmidt	1.00
32	Ray Sadecki	1.00
33	Gary Geiger	1.00
34	Wynn Hawkins	1.00
35	*Ron Santo*	10.00
36	Jack Kralick	1.00
37	Charlie Maxwell	1.00
38	Bob Lillis	1.00
39	Leo Posada	1.00
40	Bob Turley	2.50
41	NL Batting Ldrs (Bob Clemente, Dick Groat, Norm Larker, Willie Mays)	4.00
42	AL Batting Ldrs (Minnie Minoso, Pete Runnels, Bill Skowron, Al Smith)	2.50

577 Hank Aaron AS

287 Carl Yastrzemski

65	Ted Kluszewski	4.00
68	Deron Johnson	1.50
69	Earl Wilson	1.00
70	Bill Virdon	2.00
71	Jerry Adair	1.00
72	Stu Miller	1.00
73	Al Spangler	1.00
74	Joe Pignatano	1.00
75	Lindy Shows Larry (Larry Jackson, Lindy McDaniel)	1.50
80	Harmon Killebrew	18.00
81	Tracy Stallard	1.00
82	Joe Christopher	1.00
83	Bob Bruce	1.00
84	Lee Maye	1.00
85	Jerry Walker	1.00
86	Dodgers Team	3.50
88	Richie Ashburn	6.00
89	Billy Martin	6.00
90	Jerry Staley	1.00
91	Walt Moryn	1.00
92	Hal Naragon	1.00
93	Tony Gonzalez	1.00
94	Johnny Kucks	1.00
95	Norm Cash	3.50
98	Checklist 89-176 ("Checklist" in red on front)	7.00
98	Checklist 89-176 ("Checklist" in yellow, "98" in black on back)	5.00
98	Checklist 89-176 ("Checklist" in yellow, "98" in white on back)	7.00
100	Harvey Haddix	1.50
101	Bubba Phillips	1.00
102	Gene Stephens	1.00
103	Ruben Amaro	1.00
104	John Blanchard	1.25
105	Carl Willey	1.00
106	Whitey Herzog	2.25
109	Johnny Podres	2.25
110	Vada Pinson	3.00
111	Jack Meyer	1.00

43	NL HR Ldrs (Hank Aaron, Ernie Banks, Ken Boyer, Eddie Mathews)	4.00
44	AL HR Ldrs (Rocky Colavito, Jim Lemon, Mickey Mantle, Roger Maris)	15.00
45	NL ERA Ldrs (Ernie Broglio, Don Drysdale, Bob Friend, Mike McCormick, Stan Williams)	3.25
46	AL ERA Ldrs (Frank Baumann, Hal Brown, Jim Bunning, Art Ditmar)	2.50
47	NL Pitching Ldrs (Ernie Broglio, Lou Burdette, Vern Law, Warren Spahn)	3.25
48	AL Pitching Ldrs (Bud Daley, Art Ditmar, Chuck Estrada, Frank Lary, Milt Pappas, Jim Perry)	2.50
49	NL SO Ldrs (Ernie Broglio, Don Drysdale, Sam Jones, Sandy Koufax)	4.00
50	AL SO Ldrs (Jim Bunning, Frank Lary, Pedro Ramos, Early Wynn)	3.00
51	Tigers Team	3.50
52	George Crowe	1.00
53	Russ Nixon	1.00
54	Earl Francis	1.00
55	Jim Davenport	1.00
56	Russ Kemmerer	1.00
57	Marv Throneberry	1.75
58	Joe Schaffernoth	1.00
59	Jim Woods	1.00
60	Woodie Held	1.00
61	Ron Piche	1.00
62	Al Pilarcik	1.00
63	Jim Kaat	8.00

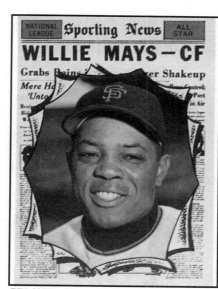

579 Willie Mays AS

112	Chico Fernandez	1.00
114	Hobie Landrith	1.00
115	Johnny Antonelli	1.25
116	Joe DeMaestri	1.25
117	Dale Long	1.25
119	A's Big Armor (Hank Bauer, Jerry Lumpe, Norm Siebern)	1.50
120	Ed Mathews	20.00
122	Cubs Team	2.50
123	Billy Gardner	1.00
124	J.C. Martin	1.00
125	Steve Barber	1.00
126	Dick Stuart	1.25
127	Ron Kline	1.00
128	Rip Repulski	1.00
129	Ed Hobaugh	1.00
130	Norm Larker	1.00
131	Paul Richards	1.25
132	Al Lopez	3.00
133	Ralph Houk	3.00
136	Walt Alston	4.00
141	*Billy Williams*	75.00
142	Luis Arroyo	1.50
143	Russ Snyder	1.00
144	Jim Coker	1.00
145	Bob Buhl	1.00
147	Ed Rakow	1.00
149	Julian Javier	1.25
150	Willie Mays	15.00
159	Orioles Team	2.50
160	Whitey Ford	25.00
167	Giants Team	2.50
168	Tommy Davis	3.00
173	Beantown Bombers (Jackie Jensen, Frank Malzone, Vic Wertz)	2.00
180	Bobby Richardson	5.00
184	Steve Bilko	1.00
185	Herb Score	1.50
186	Elmer Valo	1.00
189	Checklist 177-264	5.00
200	Warren Spahn	25.00

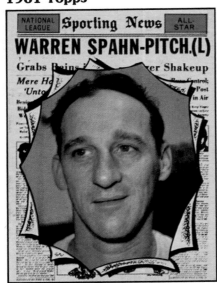

589 Warren Spahn AS

205	Bill Pierce	1.75
207	Dodger Southpaws (Sandy Koufax, Johnny Podres)	15.00
211	Bob Gibson	20.00
213	*Bill Stafford*	2.00
215	Gus Bell	1.25
219	Gene Mauch	2.50
220	Al Dark	1.25
221	Mike Higgins	1.00
222	Jimmie Dykes	1.00
223	Bob Scheffing	1.00
224	Joe Gordon	1.25
225	Bill Rigney	1.00
226	Harry Lavagetto	1.00
227	Juan Pizzaro	1.00
228	Yankees Team	10.00
230	Don Hoak	1.25
232	*Bill White	1.50
238	Jim Gilliam	2.50
245	Joe Adcock	2.00
249	Reds Team	4.00
250	*Buc Hill Aces (Roy Face, Vern Law)	2.00
251	Bill Bruton	1.00
260	Don Drysdale	15.00
261	Charlie Lau	1.25
265	Tony Kubek	5.00
273	Checklist 265-352	5.00
275	Gene Woodling	1.25
280	Frank Howard	2.50
281	Frank Sullivan	1.00
282	Faye Throneberry	1.00
285	Sherm Lollar	1.25
286	George Witt	1.00
287	Carl Yastrzemski	175.00
290	Stan Musial	65.00
295	Milt Pappas	1.25
297	Athletics Team	2.50
300	Mickey Mantle	300.00
306	World Series Game 1 (Virdon Saves Game)	3.50
307	World Series Game 2 (Mantle Slams 2 Homers)	20.00

308	World Series Game 3 (Richardson Is Hero)	4.00
309	World Series Game 4 (Cimoli Is Safe In Crucial Play)	3.00
310	World Series Game 5 (Face Saves the Day)	3.50
311	World Series Game 6 (Ford Pitches Second Shutout)	5.00
312	World Series Game 7 (Mazeroski's Homer Wins It!)	5.00
313	World Series Summary (The Winners Celebrate)	3.00
318	Danny O'Connell	1.00
319	Valmy Thomas	1.00
320	Lou Burdette	2.50
321	Marv Breeding	1.00
322	Bill Kunkel	1.00
323	Sammy Esposito	1.00
324	Hank Aguirre	1.00
325	Wally Moon	1.25
326	Dave Hillman	1.00
327	*Matty Alou*	4.00
328	Jim O'Toole	1.00
329	Julio Becquer	1.00
330	Rocky Colavito	3.00
337	*Al's Aces (Al Lopez, Herb Score, Early Wynn)	3.50
339	Gene Baker	1.00
340	Vic Wertz	1.25
344	Sandy Koufax	80.00
345	Jim Piersall	2.00
347	Cardinals Team	2.50
349	Danny McDevitt	1.25
350	Ernie Banks	30.00
355	Bob Allison	1.25
356	Ryne Duren	2.00
359	Dallas Green	1.25
360	Frank Robinson	20.00
361	Checklist 353-429 ("Topps Baseball" in black on front)	5.00

572 Brooks Robinson AS

580 Al Kaline AS

361	Checklist 353-429 ("Topps Baseball" in yellow on front)	6.00
365	Jerry Lumpe	1.25
369	Dave Philley	1.25
370	Roy Face	2.00
371	Bill Skowron	5.00
372	Bob Hendley	1.50
373	Red Sox Team	5.00
374	Paul Giel	1.50
375	Ken Boyer	4.00
376	Mike Roarke	1.50
377	Ruben Gomez	1.50
378	Wally Post	1.50
379	Bobby Shantz	2.50
380	*Minnie Minoso	3.00
381	Dave Wickersham	1.50
382	Frank Thomas	1.50
383	Frisco First Liners (Mike McCormick, Billy O'Dell, Jack Sanford)	2.00
384	Chuck Essegian	1.50
385	Jim Perry	2.50
386	Joe Hicks	1.50
387	Duke Maas	1.75
388	Bob Clemente	75.00
389	Ralph Terry	3.00
390	Del Crandall	2.25
391	Winston Brown	1.50
392	Reno Bertoia	1.50
393	Batter Bafflers (Don Cardwell, Glen Hobbie)	1.75
394	Ken Walters	1.50
395	Chuck Estrada	1.50
396	Bob Aspromonte	1.50
398	Hank Bauer	3.00
399	Cliff Cook	1.50
400	Vern Law	2.50
401	Babe Ruth Hits 60th Homer	15.00
402	Larsen Pitches Perfect Game	10.00
403	Brooklyn-Boston Play 26-Inning Tie	2.00

404	Hornsby Tops NL With .424 Average	3.50
405	Gehrig Benched After 2,130 Games	12.00
406	Mantle Blasts 565 Ft. HR	30.00
407	Jack Chesbro Wins 41st Game	2.50
408	Mathewson Strikes Out 267 Batters	2.50
409	Johnson Hurls 3rd Shutout in 4 Days	3.50
410	Haddix Pitches 12 Perfect Innings	2.50
411	Tony Taylor	1.50
412	Larry Sherry	1.50
413	Eddie Yost	1.50
414	Dick Donovan	1.50
415	Hank Aaron	90.00
416	*Dick Howser*	7.00
417	*Juan Marichal*	80.00
418	Ed Bailey	1.50
419	Tom Borland	1.50
420	Ernie Broglio	1.50
421	Ty Cline	1.50
422	Bud Daley	1.50
423	Charlie Neal	1.50
424	Turk Lown	1.50
425	Yogi Berra	60.00
426	Not Issued	
427	Dick Ellsworth	1.50
428	Ray Barker	1.50
429	Al Kaline	35.00
430	Bill Mazeroski	3.50
431	Chuck Stobbs	1.50
432	Coot Veal	1.50
433	Art Mahaffey	1.50
434	Tom Brewer	1.50
435	Orlando Cepeda	7.00
436	*Jim Maloney*	2.50
437	Checklist 430-506	6.00
438	Curt Flood	2.50
439	*Phil Regan*	1.75
440	Luis Aparicio	12.00

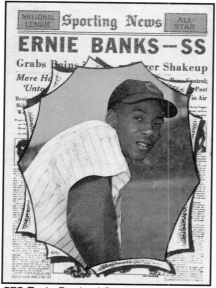

575 Ernie Banks AS

570 Nellie Fox AS

441	Dick Bertell	1.50
442	Gordon Jones	1.50
443	Duke Snider	35.00
444	Joe Nuxhall	1.75
445	Frank Malzone	1.75
446	Bob "Hawk" Taylor	1.50
447	Harry Bright	1.50
448	Del Rice	1.50
449	*Bobby Bolin*	1.75
450	Jim Lemon	1.50
451	Power for Ernie (Ernie Broglio, Daryl Spencer, Bill White)	1.75
452	Bob Allen	1.50
453	Dick Schofield	1.50
454	Pumpsie Green	1.50
455	Early Wynn	15.00
456	Hal Bevan	1.50
457	Johnny James	1.50
458	Willie Tasby	1.50
459	Terry Fox	1.50
460	Gil Hodges	18.00
461	Smoky Burgess	2.50
463	Braves Team (should be card 426)	4.00
463	Jack Fisher	1.75
464	*Leroy Thomas*	1.50
465	Roy McMillan	1.50
466	Ron Moeller	1.50
467	Indians Team	3.50
468	Johnny Callison	1.75
469	Ralph Lumenti	1.75
470	Roy Sievers	1.75
471	Phil Rizzuto MVP	8.00
472	Yogi Berra MVP	25.00
473	Bobby Shantz MVP	3.50
474	Al Rosen MVP	3.50
475	Mickey Mantle MVP	70.00
476	Jackie Jensen MVP	3.50
477	*Nellie Fox MVP	4.00
478	Roger Maris MVP	30.00
479	Jim Konstanty MVP	2.50
480	Roy Campanella MVP	20.00
481	Hank Sauer MVP	2.50

482	Willie Mays MVP	30.00
483	Don Newcombe MVP	3.50
484	Hank Aaron MVP	25.00
485	Ernie Banks MVP	15.00
486	Dick Groat MVP	3.50
487	Gene Oliver	1.50
488	Joe McClain	1.50
489	Walt Dropo	1.75
490	Jim Bunning	8.00
491	Phillies Team	3.50
492	Ron Fairly	3.50
493	Don Zimmer	2.00
494	Tom Cheney	1.50
495	Elston Howard	6.00
496	Ken MacKenzie	1.50
497	Willie Jones	1.50
498	Ray Herbert	1.50
499	Chuck Schilling	1.50
500	Harvey Kuenn	3.00
501	John DeMerit	1.50
502	Clarence Coleman	1.50
503	Tito Francona	1.50
504	Billy Consolo	1.75
505	Red Schoendienst	8.00
506	*Willie Davis*	7.00
507	Pete Burnside	1.50
508	Rocky Bridges	1.50
509	Camilo Carreon	1.50
510	Art Ditmar	2.50
511	Joe Morgan	1.50
512	Bob Will	1.50
513	Jim Brosnan	1.75
514	Jake Wood	1.50
515	Jackie Brandt	1.50
516	Checklist 507-587	6.00
517	Willie McCovey	45.00
518	Andy Carey	1.50
519	Jim Pagliaroni	1.50
520	Joe Cunningham	1.75
521	Brother Battery (Larry Sherry, Norm Sherry)	2.00
522	Dick Farrell	1.50
523	Joe Gibbon	20.00
524	Johnny Logan	20.00

417 Juan Marichal

525	Ron Perranoski	20.00	547	Leon Wagner	20.00	569	Frank Herrera AS	18.00
526	R.C. Stevens	20.00	548	Ted Wills	20.00	570	Nellie Fox AS	45.00
527	Gene Leek	20.00	549	Hal R. Smith	20.00	571	Bill Mazeroski AS	30.00
528	Pedro Ramos	20.00	550	Frank Baumann	20.00	572	Brooks Robinson AS	85.00
529	Bob Roselli	20.00	551	George Altman	20.00	573	Ken Boyer AS	30.00
530	Bobby Malkmus	20.00	552	Jim Archer	20.00	574	Luis Aparicio AS	50.00
531	Jim Coates	20.00	553	Bill Fischer	20.00	575	Ernie Banks AS	80.00
532	Bob Hale	20.00	554	Pirates Team	35.00	576	Roger Maris AS	95.00
533	Jack Curtis	20.00	555	Sam Jones	20.00	577	Hank Aaron AS	130.00
534	Eddie Kasko	20.00	556	Ken R. Hunt	20.00	578	Mickey Mantle AS	350.00
535	Larry Jackson	20.00	557	Jose Valdivielso	20.00	579	Willie Mays AS	130.00
536	Bill Tuttle	20.00	558	Don Ferrarese	20.00	580	Al Kaline AS	80.00
537	Bobby Locke	20.00	559	Jim Gentile	20.00	581	Frank Robinson AS	80.00
538	Chuck Hiller	20.00	560	Barry Latman	20.00	582	Earl Battey AS	20.00
539	Johnny Klippstein	20.00	561	Charley James	20.00	583	Del Crandall AS	20.00
540	Jackie Jensen	30.00	562	Bill Monbouquette	20.00	584	Jim Perry AS	25.00
541	Roland Sheldon	20.00	563	Bob Cerv	20.00	585	Bob Friend AS	24.00
542	Twins Team	40.00	564	Don Cardwell	20.00	586	Whitey Ford AS	80.00
543	Roger Craig	35.00	565	Felipe Alou	22.00	587	Not Issued	
544	George Thomas	20.00	566	Paul Richards AS	21.00	588	Not Issued	
545	Hoyt Wilhelm	60.00	567	Danny Murtaugh AS	20.00	589	Warren Spahn AS	125.00
546	Marty Kutyna	20.00	568	Bill Skowron AS	30.00			

1962 TOPPS

Topps used a woodgrain border design in 1962 that was repeated in 1987. At 598 cards, the 1962 set had a larger number of cards than any previous edition. A ten-card subset highlighting the career of Babe Ruth is included, although the cards are surprisingly undervalued. One of the most notable features of the set is the first use of multiplayer photos for rookie cards, grouping four or five players together by position. Many challenges are posed for collectors, with both a rare final series (cards 523-598) and several photo changes in later printings. All photo variations are found in cards 129-190.

		NR MT
Complete set		**$4400.00**
Commons (1-370)		**1.50**
Commons (371-522)		**2.50**
Commons (523-598)		**12.00**

200 Mickey Mantle

1	Roger Maris	$250.00
2	Jim Brosnan	1.75
3	Pete Runnels	1.50
4	John DeMerit	2.00
5	Sandy Koufax	85.00
6	Marv Breeding	1.50
7	Frank Thomas	2.00
8	Ray Herbert	1.50
9	Jim Davenport	1.50
10	Bob Clemente	75.00
11	Tom Morgan	1.50
12	Harry Craft	1.50
13	Dick Howser	1.75
14	*Bill White	1.50
15	Dick Donovan	1.50
16	Darrell Johnson	1.50
17	Johnny Callison	1.75
18	Managers' Dream (Mickey Mantle, Willie Mays)	85.00
19	*Ray Washburn*	1.50
20	Rocky Colavito	3.00

21	Jim Kaat	4.00
22	Checklist 1-88 (numbers 33-88 on back)	6.00
22	Checklist 1-88 (numbers 121-176 on back)	5.00
23	Norm Larker	1.50
24	Tigers Team	3.50
25	Ernie Banks	25.00
26	Chris Cannizzaro	2.00
27	Chuck Cottier	1.50
28	Minnie Minoso	2.50
29	Casey Stengel	15.00
30	Ed Mathews	12.00
31	*Tom Tresh*	7.00
32	John Roseboro	1.75
33	Don Larsen	1.75
34	Johnny Temple	1.75
35	*Don Schwall*	1.75
36	Don Leppert	1.50
37	Tribe Hill Trio (Barry Latman, Jim Perry, Dick Stigman)	1.75
38	Gene Stephens	1.50
39	Joe Koppe	1.50
40	Orlando Cepeda	5.00
41	Cliff Cook	1.50
42	Jim King	1.50
43	Dodgers Team	3.50

44	Don Taussig	1.50
45	Brooks Robinson	25.00
46	*Jack Baldschun*	1.50
47	Bob Will	1.50
48	Ralph Terry	2.50
49	Hal Jones	1.50
50	Stan Musial	65.00
51	AL Batting Ldrs (Norm Cash, Elston Howard, Al Kaline, Jim Piersall)	3.00
52	NL Batting Ldrs (Ken Boyer, Bob Clemente, Wally Moon, Vada Pinson)	3.50

1 Roger Maris

75	Milt Pappas	1.75
76	Howie Bedell	1.50
77	Tony Taylor	1.50
78	Gene Green	1.50
79	Ed Hobaugh	1.50
80	*Vada Pinson	2.50
81	Jim Pagliaroni	1.50
82	Deron Johnson	1.50
83	Larry Jackson	1.50
84	Lenny Green	1.50
85	Gil Hodges	12.00
86	*Donn Clendenon*	1.75
87	Mike Roarke	1.50
88	Ralph Houk	2.50
89	Barney Schultz	1.50
90	Jim Piersall	2.00
91	J.C. Martin	1.50
92	Sam Jones	1.50
93	John Blanchard	2.00
94	Jay Hook	2.00
95	Don Hoak	1.75
96	Eli Grba	1.50
97	Tito Francona	1.50
98	Checklist 89-176	4.00
99	*John Powell*	12.00
100	Warren Spahn	25.00
102	Al Schroll	1.50
103	Don Blasingame	1.50
104	Ted Savage	1.50
105	Don Mossi	1.50
106	Carl Sawatski	1.50
107	Mike McCormick	1.50
108	Willie Davis	2.50
109	Bob Shaw	1.50
110	Bill Skowron	5.00
111	Dallas Green	1.75
112	Hank Foiles	1.50
113	White Sox Team	2.50
114	Howie Koplitz	1.50
115	Bob Skinner	1.50
116	Herb Score	2.00
117	Gary Geiger	1.50
118	Julian Javier	1.75
119	Danny Murphy	1.50

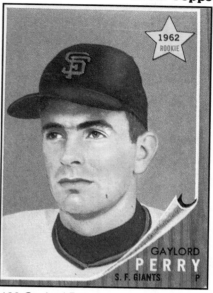

199 Gaylord Perry

53	AL HR Ldrs (Jim Gentile, Harmon Killebrew, Mickey Mantle, Roger Maris)	15.00
54	NL HR Ldrs (Orlando Cepeda, Willie Mays, Frank Robinson)	3.50
55	AL ERA Ldrs (Dick Donovan, Don Mossi, Milt Pappas, Bill Stafford)	2.50
56	NL ERA Ldrs (Mike McCormick, Jim O'Toole, Curt Simmons, Warren Spahn)	3.00
57	AL Win Ldrs (Steve Barber, Jim Bunning, Whitey Ford, Frank Lary)	3.00
58	NL Win Ldrs (Joe Jay, Jim O'Toole, Warren Spahn)	3.00
59	AL SO Ldrs (Jim Bunning, Whitey Ford, Camilo Pascual, Juan Pizarro)	3.00
60	NL SO Ldrs (Don Drysdale, Sandy Koufax, Jim O'Toole, Stan Williams)	3.50
61	Cardinals Team	2.50
62	Steve Boros	1.50
63	*Tony Cloninger*	2.00
64	Russ Snyder	1.50
65	Bobby Richardson	6.00
66	Cuno Barragon (Barragan)	1.50
67	Harvey Haddix	1.75
68	Ken L. Hunt	1.50
69	Phil Ortega	1.50
70	Harmon Killebrew	15.00
71	Dick LeMay	1.50
72	Bob's Pupils (Steve Boros, Bob Scheffing, Jake Wood)	1.75
73	Nellie Fox	7.00
74	Bob Lillis	1.50

425 Carl Yastrzemski

120	Bob Purkey	1.50
121	Billy Hitchcock	1.50
122	Norm Bass	1.50
123	Mike de la Hoz	1.50
124	Bill Pleis	1.50
125	Gene Woodling	1.75
126	Al Cicotte	1.50
127	Pride of the A's (Hank Bauer, Jerry Lumpe, Norm Siebern)	1.75
128	Art Fowler	1.50
129	Lee Walls (facing left)	8.00
129	Lee Walls (facing right)	1.50
130	Frank Bolling	1.50
131	*Pete Richert*	1.75
132	Angels Team (with inset photos)	10.00
132	Angels Team (w/o inset photos)	3.00
133	Felipe Alou	1.75
134	Billy Hoeft (green sky)	8.00
134	Billy Hoeft (blue sky)	1.50
135	Babe as a Boy	7.00
136	Babe Joins Yanks	7.00
137	Babe and Mgr. Huggins	7.00
138	The Famous Slugger	7.00
139	Hal Reniff (pitching)	35.00
139	Hal Reniff (portrait)	12.00
139	Babe Hits 60	7.00
140	Gehrig and Ruth	9.00
141	Twilight Years	7.00
142	Coaching for the Dodgers	7.00
143	Greatest Sports Hero	7.00
144	Farewell Speech	7.00
145	Barry Latman	1.50
146	Don Demeter	1.50
147	Bill Kunkel (pitching)	8.00
147	Bill Kunkel (portrait)	1.50
148	Wally Post	1.50
150	Al Kaline	25.00
151	Johnny Klippstein	1.50
152	Mickey Vernon	1.50
153	Pumpsie Green	1.50

10 Bob Clemente

154	Lee Thomas	1.50
156	Merritt Ranew	1.50
157	Wes Covington	1.50
158	Braves Team	3.00
159	Hal Reniff	2.00
160	Dick Stuart	1.50
161	Frank Baumann	1.50
162	Sammy Drake	2.00
163	Hot Corner Guardians (Cletis Boyer, Billy Gardner)	3.00
165	Jackie Brandt	1.50
166	Don Lee	1.50
167	Tim McCarver	10.00
168	Leo Posada	1.50
169	Bob Cerv	1.75
170	Ron Santo	3.50
171	Dave Sisler	1.50
172	Fred Hutchinson	1.50
173	Chico Fernandez	1.50
174	Carl Willey (with cap)	8.00
174	Carl Willey (w/o cap)	1.50
175	Frank Howard	3.00
176	Eddie Yost (batting)	8.00
176	Eddie Yost (portrait)	1.50
177	Bobby Shantz	1.75
178	Camilo Carreon	1.50
179	Tom Sturdivant	1.50
180	Bob Allison	1.75
181	Paul Brown	1.50
182	Bob Nieman	1.50
183	Roger Craig	3.00
184	Haywood Sullivan	1.50
185	Roland Sheldon	2.00
186	Mack Jones	1.50
187	Gene Conley	1.50
188	Chuck Hiller	1.50
189	Dick Hall	1.50
190	Wally Moon (with cap)	9.00
190	Wally Moon (w/o cap)	1.75
191	Jim Brewer	1.50
192	Checklist 177-264	4.00
193	Eddie Kasko	1.50

194	Dean Chance	3.00
195	Joe Cunningham	1.50
196	Terry Fox	1.50
198	Johnny Keane	1.50
199	Gaylord Perry	150.00
200	Mickey Mantle	500.00
208	Billy Martin	6.00
209	Jim Fregosi	5.00
213	Richie Ashburn	6.00
217	Walt Alston	4.00
218	Joe Torre	10.00
219	Al Downing	4.00
243	Robin Roberts	12.00
251	Yankees Team	8.00
288	Billy Williams	20.00
300	Willie Mays	150.00
310	Whitey Ford	25.00
312	Spahn Shows No-Hit Form	7.00
313	Maris Blasts 61st	15.00
315	Ford Tosses A Curve	6.00
316	Killebrew Sends One Into Orbit	5.00
317	Musial Plays 21st Season	12.00
318	The Switch-Hitter Connects (Mickey Mantle)	30.00
320	Hank Aaron	150.00
325	Luis Aparicio	15.00
340	Don Drysdale	25.00
350	Frank Robinson	25.00
360	Yogi Berra	60.00
371	Earl Battey	2.75
372	Jack Curtis	2.50
373	Al Heist	2.50
374	Gene Mauch	2.75
375	Ron Fairly	3.00
376	Bud Daley	2.75
377	Johnny Orsino	2.50
378	Bennie Daniels	2.50
379	Chuck Essegian	2.50
380	*Lou Burdette	4.00
381	Chico Cardenas	2.50

530 Bob Gibson

544 Willie McCovey

382	Dick Williams	3.50
383	Ray Sadecki	2.50
384	Athletics Team	3.50
385	Early Wynn	20.00
386	Don Mincher	2.50
387	Lou Brock	125.00
388	Ryne Duren	2.75
389	Smoky Burgess	2.75
390	Orlando Cepeda AS	5.00
391	Bill Mazeroski AS	3.50
392	Ken Boyer AS	3.50
393	Roy McMillan AS	3.50
394	Hank Aaron AS	35.00
395	Willie Mays AS	30.00
396	Frank Robinson AS	18.00
397	John Roseboro AS	3.00
398	Don Drysdale AS	15.00
399	Warren Spahn AS	15.00
400	Elston Howard	7.00
401	AL & NL Homer Kings (Orlando Cepeda, Roger Maris)	20.00
402	Gino Cimoli	2.50
403	Chet Nichols	2.50
404	Tim Harkness	2.50
405	Jim Perry	3.00
406	Bob Taylor	2.50
407	Hank Aguirre	2.50
408	Gus Bell	3.00
409	Pirates Team	3.50
410	Al Smith	2.50
411	Danny O'Connell	2.50
412	Charlie James	2.50
413	Matty Alou	3.50
414	Joe Gaines	2.50
415	Bill Virdon	3.50
416	Bob Scheffing	2.50
417	Joe Azcue	2.50
418	Andy Carey	2.50
419	Bob Bruce	2.50
420	Gus Triandos	2.75
421	Ken MacKenzie	2.50
422	Steve Bilko	2.50

423	Rival League Relief Aces (Roy Face, Hoyt Wilhelm) ...	5.00
424	Al McBean	2.50
425	Carl Yastrzemski	200.00
426	Bob Farley	2.50
427	Jake Wood	2.50
428	Joe Hicks	2.50
429	Bill O'Dell	2.50
430	Tony Kubek	7.00
431	*Bob Rodgers*	3.00
432	Jim Pendleton	2.50
433	Jim Archer	2.50
434	Clay Dalrymple	2.50
435	Larry Sherry	2.50
436	Felix Mantilla	2.50
437	Ray Moore	2.50
438	Dick Brown	2.50
439	Jerry Buchek	2.50
440	Joe Jay	2.50
441	Checklist 430-506	5.00
442	Wes Stock	2.50
444	Ted Wills	2.50
446	Don Elston	2.50
447	Willie Kirkland	2.50
448	Joe Gibbon	2.50
449	Jerry Adair	2.50
450	Jim O'Toole	2.50
451	*Jose Tartabull*	2.75
452	Earl Averill	2.50
453	Cal McLish	2.50
454	Floyd Robinson	2.50
455	Luis Arroyo	2.75
456	Joe Amalfitano	2.50
457	Lou Clinton	2.50
458	Bob Buhl ("M" on cap)	2.50
458	Bob Buhl (plain cap)	50.00
459	Ed Bailey	2.50
460	Jim Bunning	8.00
461	*Ken Hubbs*	8.00
462	Willie Tasby ("W" on cap)	2.50
462	Willie Tasby (plain cap)	50.00
463	Hank Bauer	3.00
464	*Al Jackson*	3.50
465	Reds Team	4.00

320 Hank Aaron

466	Norm Cash AS	4.00
467	Chuck Schilling AS	3.00
468	Brooks Robinson AS	18.00
469	Luis Aparicio AS	13.00
470	Al Kaline AS	15.00
471	Mickey Mantle AS	70.00
472	Rocky Colavito AS	10.00
473	Elston Howard AS	10.00
474	Frank Lary AS	5.00
475	Whitey Ford AS	15.00
476	Orioles Team	3.50
477	Andre Rodgers	2.50
478	Don Zimmer	3.50
479	*Joel Horlen*	2.75
480	Harvey Kuenn	3.50
481	Vic Wertz	2.75
482	Sam Mele	2.50
483	Don McMahon	2.50
484	Dick Schofield	2.50
485	Pedro Ramos	2.50
486	Jim Gilliam	4.00
487	Jerry Lynch	2.50
488	Hal Brown	2.50
489	Julio Gotay	2.50
490	Clete Boyer	3.75
491	Leon Wagner	2.50
492	Hal Smith	2.50
493	Danny McDevitt	2.50
494	Sammy White	2.50
495	Don Cardwell	2.50
496	Wayne Causey	2.50
497	Ed Bouchee	2.50
498	Jim Donohue	2.50
499	Zoilo Versalles	2.75
500	Duke Snider	30.00
501	Claude Osteen	2.75
502	Hector Lopez	2.50
503	Danny Murtaugh	2.75
504	Eddie Bressoud	2.50
505	Juan Marichal	25.00
506	Charley Maxwell	2.50
507	Ernie Broglio	2.50
508	Gordy Coleman	2.50

387 Lou Brock

509	*Dave Giusti*	2.75
510	Jim Lemon	2.50
511	Bubba Phillips	2.50
512	Mike Fornieles	2.50
513	Whitey Herzog	4.00
514	Sherm Lollar	2.75
515	Stan Williams	2.50
516	Checklist 507-598	8.00
517	Dave Wickersham	2.50
518	Lee Maye	2.50
519	Bob Johnson	2.50
520	Bob Friend	3.00
521	Jacke Davis	2.50
522	Lindy McDaniel	2.50
523	Russ Nixon	12.00
524	Howie Nunn	12.00
525	George Thomas	12.00
526	Hal Woodeshick	12.00
527	*Dick McAuliffe*	13.00
528	Turk Lown	12.00
529	John Schaive	12.00
530	Bob Gibson	150.00
531	Bobby G. Smith	12.00
532	Dick Stigman	12.00
533	Charley Lau	13.00
534	Tony Gonzalez	12.00
535	Ed Roebuck	12.00
536	Dick Gernert	12.00
537	Indians Team	14.00
538	Jack Sanford	12.00
539	Billy Moran	12.00
540	Jim Landis	12.00
541	Don Nottebart	12.00
542	Dave Philley	12.00
543	Bob Allen	12.00
544	Willie McCovey	150.00
545	Hoyt Wilhelm	55.00
546	Moe Thacker	12.00
547	Don Ferrarese	12.00
548	Bobby Del Greco	12.00
549	Bill Rigney	12.00
550	Art Mahaffey	12.00
551	Harry Bright	12.00
552	Cubs Team	14.00

5 Sandy Koufax

553	Jim Coates	12.00
554	Bubba Morton	12.00
555	John Buzhardt	12.00
556	Al Spangler	12.00
557	Bob Anderson	12.00
558	John Goryl	12.00
559	Mike Higgins	12.00
560	Chuck Estrada	12.00
561	Gene Oliver	12.00
562	Bill Henry	12.00
563	Ken Aspromonte	12.00
564	Bob Grim	12.00
565	Jose Pagan	12.00
570	Bill Stafford	12.00
571	Billy Klaus	12.00
572	Bob Miller	12.00
573	Johnny Logan	12.50
574	Dean Stone	12.00
575	Red Schoendienst	25.00
576	Russ Kemmerer	12.00
577	Dave Nicholson	12.00
578	Jim Duffalo	12.00
579	Jim Schaffer	12.00
580	Bill Monbouquette	12.00

581	Mel Roach	12.00
582	Ron Piche	12.00
583	Larry Osborne	12.00
584	Twins Team	12.00
585	Glen Hobbie	12.00
586	Sammy Esposito	12.00
587	Frank Funk	12.00
588	Birdie Tebbets	12.00
589	Bob Turley	18.00
590	Curt Flood	18.00
591	Rookie Parade Pitchers (Sam McDowell, Ron Mischwitz, Art Quirk, Dick Radatz, Ron Taylor)	35.00
592	Rookie Parade Pitchers (Bo Belinsky, Joe Bonikowski, Jim Bouton, Dan Pfister, Dave Stenhouse)	45.00
593	Rookie Parade Pitchers (Craig Anderson, Jack Hamilton, Jack Lamabe, Bob Moorhead, Bob Veale)	18.00

594	Rookie Parade Catchers (Doug Camilli, Doc Edwards, Don Pavletich, Ken Retzer, Bob Uecker)	110.00
595	Rookie Parade Infielders (Ed Charles, Marlin Coughtry, Bob Sadowski, Felix Torres)	18.00
596	Rookie Parade Infielders (Bernie Allen, Phil Linz, Joe Pepitone, Rich Rollins)	40.00
597	Rookie Parade Infielders (Rod Kanehl, Jim McKnight, Denis Menke, Amado Samuel)	18.00
598	Rookie Parade Outfielders (Howie Goss, Jim Hickman, Manny Jimenez, Al Luplow, Ed Olivares)	75.00

1963 FLEER

Nearly three decades after its quiet debut, the 1963 Fleer set is finally gaining recognition from the collecting world. In 1963, Fleer challenged Topps in the "confectionary" department by issuing its cards with a cookie. Topps responded by hauling Fleer into court. No one knew whether or not the Philadelphia-based Fleer would have added to the 66-card issue in the absence of legal roadblocks. In any case, Fleer topped Topps by providing the first nationally distributed card of Maury Wills, the base-stealing star of the LA Dodgers. Wills, still upset that Topps had neglected him in his rookie days, seemed to enjoy sharing his fame with a rival company. Other stars in the set include Willie Mays, Carl Yastrzemski, Brooks Robinson, Sandy Koufax, Warren Spahn, Bob Gibson, and Roberto Clemente. However, the rarest cards in the set are for Joe Adcock, number 46, and an unnumbered checklist. The scarcity is supposedly due to short-printing of these two cards.

56 Roberto Clemente

		NR MT
Complete set		**$965.00**
Commons		**2.00**

1	Steve Barber	$4.00
2	Ron Hansen	2.00
3	Milt Pappas	3.00
4	Brooks Robinson	40.00
5	Willie Mays	125.00
6	Lou Clinton	2.00
7	Bill Monbouquette	2.00
8	Carl Yastrzemski	125.00
9	Ray Herbert	2.00
10	Jim Landis	2.50
11	Dick Donovan	2.00
12	Tito Francona	2.00
13	Jerry Kindall	2.00
14	Frank Lary	2.00
15	Dick Howser	3.50
16	Jerry Lumpe	2.00

17	Norm Siebern	2.00
18	Don Lee	2.00
19	Albie Pearson	2.50
20	Bob Rodgers	2.00
21	Leon Wagner	2.00
22	Jim Kaat	4.00
23	Vic Power	3.00
24	Rich Rollins	2.00
25	Bobby Richardson	6.00
26	Ralph Terry	3.50
29	Jimmy Piersall	3.50
32	Ron Santo	5.00
34	Vada Pinson	5.00
40	Tommy Davis	3.50
41	Don Drysdale	40.00
42	Sandy Koufax	140.00
43	Maury Wills	70.00
44	Frank Bolling	2.00
45	Warren Spahn	25.00
46	Joe Adcock	95.00

47	Roger Craig	4.00
48	Al Jackson	2.50
49	Rod Kanehl	2.00
50	Ruben Amaro	2.00
51	John Callison	2.50
52	Clay Dalrymple	2.00
53	Don Demeter	2.00
54	Art Mahaffey	2.00
55	"Smoky" Burgess	2.00
56	Roberto Clemente	150.00
57	Elroy Face	3.00
58	Vernon Law	3.00

46 Joe Adcock

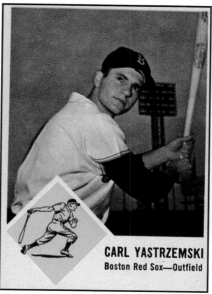

8 Carl Yastrzemski

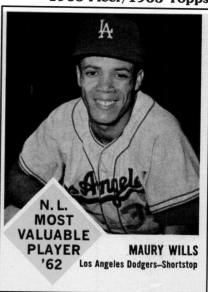

43 Maury Wills

59	Bill Mazeroski	5.00
60	Ken Boyer	5.00
61	Bob Gibson	38.00
62	Gene Oliver	2.00
63	Bill White	5.00
64	Orlando Cepeda	5.00
65	Jimmy Davenport	2.00
66	Billy O'Dell	3.00
—	Checklist 1-66	300.00

1963 TOPPS

This set of 576 cards is most remembered as the set in which Pete Rose made his premiere. His rookie card is far from glamorous, yet it is one of the most valuable cards of the 1960s. Rose shares card 537 with three other players: Pedro Gonzalez, Ken McMullen, and Al Weis. Only the players' heads are shown, reduced to the size of postage stamps. Aside from the rookie cards, the only specialty subsets in 1963 honor league leaders (marking the set's first 10 cards) and the 1962 World Series. The 1963 Topps set also features an ultrascarce series, from 447 to 506, which commands a premium.

	NR MT
Complete set	$4100.00
Commons 1-283	.70
Commons 284-446	2.00
Commons 447-506	8.00
Commons 507-576	5.00

1 NL Batting Ldrs (Hank Aaron, Tommy Davis, Stan Musial, Frank Robinson, Bill White) $40.00
2 AL Batting Ldrs (Chuck Hinton, Mickey Mantle, Floyd Robinson, Pete Runnels, Norm Siebern).... 20.00
3 NL HR Ldrs (Hank Aaron, Ernie Banks, Orlando Cepeda, Willie Mays, Frank Robinson)................. 8.00
4 AL HR Ldrs (Norm Cash, Rocky Colavito, Jim Gentile, Harmon Killebrew, Roger Maris, Leon Wagner) 4.00
5 NL ERA Ldrs (Don Drysdale, Bob Gibson, Sandy Koufax, Bob Purkey, Bob Shaw) 4.00
6 AL ERA Ldrs (Hank Aguirre, Dean Chance, Eddie Fisher, Whitey Ford, Robin Roberts).......... 3.50
7 NL Pitching Ldrs (Don Drysdale, Joe Jay, Art Mahaffey, Billy O'Dell, Bob Purkey, Jack Sanford) 3.50
8 AL Pitching Ldrs (Jim Bunning, Dick Donovan, Ray Herbert, Camilo Pascual, Ralph Terry) 3.00
9 NL SO Ldrs (Don Drysdale, Dick Farrell, Bob Gibson, Sandy Koufax, Billy O'Dell) 4.00
10 AL SO Ldrs (Jim Bunning, Jim Kaat, Camilo Pascual, Juan Pizarro, Ralph Terry) 3.00
11 Lee Walls .... .70
12 Steve Barber .... .70
13 Phillies Team....................... 2.25
14 Pedro Ramos .... .70
15 Ken Hubbs 2.00
16 Al Smith................................ .70
17 Ryne Duren 1.00
18 Bucs Blasters (Smoky Burgess, Bob Clemente, Bob Skinner, Dick Stuart).... 8.00
19 Pete Burnside....................... .70
20 Tony Kubek 6.00
21 Marty Keough....................... .70
22 Curt Simmons .... .75
23 Ed Lopat.............................. 1.00
24 Bob Bruce .... .70
25 Al Kaline 25.00
26 Ray Moore .... .70
27 Choo Choo Coleman.......... 1.00
28 Mike Fornieles...................... .70
29 1962 Rookie Stars (John Boozer, *Ray Culp*, *Sammy Ellis*, Jesse Gonder) 5.00

53

537 1963 Rookie Stars

64	Dick McAuliffe	.95
65	Jackie Brandt	.70
66	Mike Joyce	.70
67	Ed Charles	.70
68	Friendly Foes (Gil Hodges, Duke Snider)	6.50
69	Bud Zipfel	.70
70	Jim O'Toole	.70
71	*Bobby Wine*	.95
72	Johnny Romano	.70
73	Bobby Bragan	.85
74	*Denver LeMaster*	.90
75	Bob Allison	1.50
76	Earl Wilson	.70
77	Al Spangler	.70
78	Marv Throneberry	3.00
79	Checklist 1-88	2.50
80	Jim Gilliam	3.00
81	Jimmie Schaffer	.70
82	Ed Rakow	.70
83	Charley James	.70
84	Ron Kline	.70
85	Tom Haller	.85
86	Charley Maxwell	.70
87	Bob Veale	.90
88	Ron Hansen	.70
89	Dick Stigman	.70
90	Gordy Coleman	.70
91	Dallas Green	.90
92	Hector Lopez	1.00
93	Galen Cisco	.75
94	Bob Schmidt	.70
95	Larry Jackson	.70
96	Lou Clinton	.70
97	Bob Duliba	.70
98	George Thomas	.70
99	Jim Umbricht	.70
100	Joe Cunningham	1.00
101	Checklist 89-176 ("Checklist" in red on front)	3.00
101	Checklist 89-176 ("Checklist" in white on front)	6.00

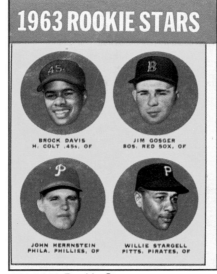

553 1963 Rookie Stars

29	1963 Rookie Stars (John Boozer, *Ray Culp, Sammy Ellis,* Jesse Gonder)	1.25
30	Harvey Kuenn	1.50
31	Cal Koonce	.70
33	Bob Belinsky	2.00
34	Dick Schofield	.70
35	John Buzhardt	.70
36	Jerry Kindall	.70
37	Jerry Lynch	.70
38	Bud Daley	.75
39	Angels Team	2.50
40	Vic Power	.70
41	Charlie Lau	1.00
42	Stan Williams	1.00
43	Veteran Masters (Casey Stengel, Gene Woodling)	4.00
44	Terry Fox	.70
45	Bob Aspromonte	.70
46	*Tommie Aaron*	1.50
47	Don Lock	.70
48	Birdie Tebbetts	.70
49	*Dal Maxvill*	1.50
50	*Bill Pierce	1.25
51	George Alusik	.70
52	Chuck Schilling	.70
53	Joe Moeller	.70
54	1962 Rookie Stars (Jack Cullen, *Dave DeBuschere,* Harry Fanok, Nelson Mathews)	6.50
55	1962 Rookie Stars (Jack Cullen, *Dave DeBuschere,* Harry Fanok, Nelson Mathews)	3.00
56	Bill Virdon	1.50
57	Billy Moran	.70
58	Bob Will	.70
59	Craig Anderson	.75
60	Elston Howard	6.00
61	Ernie Bowman	.70
62	Bob Hendley	.70
63	Reds Team	2.50

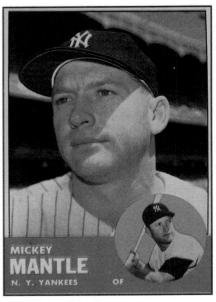

200 Mickey Mantle

103	Chuck Essegian	.70
104	Lew Krause	.70
105	Ron Fairly	1.00
106	Bob Bolin	.70
107	Jim Hickman	.90
108	Hoyt Wilhelm	9.00
109	Lee Maye	.70
110	Rich Rollins	.75
111	Al Jackson	.90
112	Dick Brown	.70
113	Don Landrum (photo is Ron Santo)	.90
114	Dan Osinski	.70
115	Carl Yastrzemski	75.00
116	Jim Brosnan	.90
117	Jacke Davis	.70
118	Sherm Lollar	.90
120	Roger Maris	40.00
121	Jim Hannan	.70
122	Julio Gotay	.70
123	Frank Howard	2.50
124	Dick Howser	1.50
125	Robin Roberts	6.00
126	Bob Uecker	30.00
127	Bill Tuttle	.70
128	Matty Alou	.90
129	Gary Bell	.70
130	Dick Groat	1.50
131	Senators Team	2.25
132	Jack Hamilton	.70
133	Gene Freese	.70
134	Bob Scheffing	.70
135	Richie Ashburn	4.50
136	Ike Delock	.70
137	Mack Jones	.70
138	Pride of NL (Willie Mays, Stan Musial)	25.00
139	Earl Averill	.70
140	Frank Lary	.90
141	*Manny Mota*	4.00
142	World Series Game 1 (Yanks' Ford Wins Series Opener)	3.50

143	World Series Game 2 (Sanford Flashes Shutout Magic)	2.25
144	World Series Game 3 (Maris Sparks Yankee Rally)	4.00
145	World Series Game 4 (Hiller Blasts Grand Slam)	2.25
146	World Series Game 5 (Tresh's Homer Defeats Giants)	3.00
147	World Series Game 6 (Pierce Stars In 3 Hit Victory)	3.00
148	World Series Game 7 (Yanks Celebrate As Terry Wins)	3.00
149	Marv Breeding	.70
150	Johnny Podres	2.00
151	Pirates Team	2.25
153	Hal Smith	.70
154	Walt Alston	4.00
155	Bill Stafford	1.00
156	Roy McMillan	.75
157	Diego Segui	1.00
158	1963 Rookie Stars (Rogelio Alvarez, Tommy Harper, Dave Roberts, Bob Saverine)	1.00
162	Twins Team	2.25
163	Don Larsen	1.00
165	Jim Kaat	5.00
166	Johnny Keane	.75
167	Jim Fregosi	1.50
169	1963 Rookie Stars (Dick Egan, Julio Navarro, Gaylord Perry, Tommie Sisk)	20.00
170	Joe Adcock	1.50
172	Gene Oliver	.70
173	Bomber's Best (Mickey Mantle, Bobby Richardson, Tom Tresh)	35.00

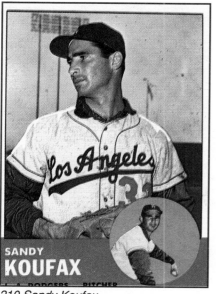

210 Sandy Koufax

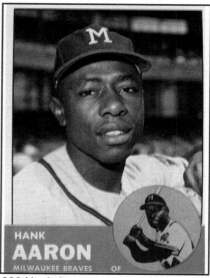

Willie
MAYS
S. F. GIANTS   OF

300 Willie Mays

175	Bob Buhl	.75
180	Bill Skowron	1.50
181	Sammy Esposito	.70
182	Albie Pearson	.70
183	Joe Pepitone	4.00
184	Vern Law	1.50
190	*Minnie Minoso	1.50
191	Checklist 177-264	3.00
194	Joe Nuxhall	.90
197	Roger Craig	2.00
200	Mickey Mantle	295.00
202	Red Sox Team	2.50
205	Luis Aparicio	6.00
206	Ray Washburn	.70
210	Sandy Koufax	125.00
215	Bob Skinner	.90
217	Joe Christopher	.90
218	*Tiger Twirlers (Jim Bunning, Frank Lary, Don Mossi)	2.00
220	Camilo Pascual	.90
221	Cookie Rojas	.90
222	Cubs Team	2.25
226	Julian Javier	.90
227	Jim Grant	.70
228	*1963 Rookie Stars (Max Alvis, Bob Bailey, Ed Kranepool, Pedro Oliva)	25.00
229	Willie Davis	1.50
230	Pete Runnels	.90
231	Eli Grba (photo is Ryne Duren)	.90
232	Frank Malzone	.90
233	Casey Stengel	12.00
239	Harvey Haddix	.90
240	Rocky Colavito	3.00
242	Power Plus (Hank Aaron, Ernie Banks)	15.00
245	Gil Hodges	12.00
247	Yankees Team	8.00
250	Stan Musial	100.00
252	Ron Santo	2.00

275	Ed Mathews	12.00
300	Willie Mays	125.00
301	Bill Fischer	2.00
302	Whitey Herzog	3.50
303	Earl Francis	2.00
312	Colt .45s Team	7.00
313	Ernie Broglio	2.00
317	Sam McDowell	3.00
318	Gene Mauch	2.00
320	Warren Spahn	25.00
324	1963 Rookie Stars (Vic Davalillo, Phil Roof, Pete Ward, George Williams)	2.50
335	Leon Wagner	2.50
337	Dodgers Team	8.00
340	Yogi Berra	80.00
347	Joe Torre	5.00
353	Billy Williams	20.00
360	Don Drysdale	20.00
363	Dick Radatz	2.25
364	Howie Goss	2.00
365	Jim Bunning	8.00
366	Tony Taylor	2.25
367	Tony Cloninger	2.00
368	Ed Bailey	2.00
369	Jim Lemon	2.00
370	Dick Donovan	2.00
371	Ron Kanehl	2.00
372	Don Lee	2.00
373	Jim Campbell	2.00
374	Claude Osteen	2.25
375	*Ken Boyer	2.00
376	Johnnie Wyatt	2.00
377	Orioles Team	3.50
378	Bill Henry	2.00
379	Bob Anderson	2.00
380	Ernie Banks	40.00
381	Frank Baumann	2.00
382	Ralph Houk	3.50
385	Art Mahaffey	2.00
386	1963 Rookie Stars (John Bateman, Larry Bearnarth, Ed Kirkpatrick, Garry Roggenburk)	2.25

HANK
AARON
MILWAUKEE BRAVES   OF

390 Hank Aaron

55

540 Bob Clemente

387	Al McBean	2.00
388	Jim Davenport	2.00
389	Frank Sullivan	2.00
390	Hank Aaron	125.00
391	Bill Dailey	2.00
392	Tribe Thumpers (Tito Francona, Johnny Romano)	2.25
393	Ken MacKenzie	2.25
394	*Tim McCarver	4.00
395	Don MacMahon	2.00
396	Joe Koppe	2.00
397	Athletics Team	3.50
398	*Boog Powell	5.00
399	Dick Ellsworth	2.00
400	Frank Robinson	45.00
401	Jim Bouton	8.00
402	Mickey Vernon	2.25
403	Ron Perranoski	2.25
404	Bob Oldis	2.00
405	Floyd Robinson	2.00
406	Howie Koplitz	2.00
407	1963 Rookie Stars (Larry Elliot, Frank Kostro, Chico Ruiz, Dick Simpson)	2.00
408	Billy Gardner	2.00
409	Roy Face	2.50
410	Earl Battey	2.25
411	Jim Constable	2.00
412	Dodgers' Big Three (Don Drysdale, Sandy Koufax, Johnny Podres)	25.00
413	Jerry Walker	2.00
414	Ty Cline	2.00
415	Bob Gibson	30.00
416	Alex Grammas	2.00
417	Giants Team	3.50
418	Johnny Orsino	2.00
419	Tracy Stallard	2.00
420	Bobby Richardson	8.00
421	Tom Morgan	2.00
422	Fred Hutchinson	2.25
423	Ed Hobaugh	2.00

424	Charley Smith	2.00
425	Smoky Burgess	2.25
426	Barry Latman	2.00
427	Bernie Allen	2.00
428	Carl Boles	2.00
429	Lou Burdette	3.00
430	Norm Siebern	2.25
431	Checklist 430-506 ("Checklist" in black on front)	7.00
432	Checklist 430-506 ("Checklist" in white on front)	4.50
433	Denis Menke	2.25
434	Johnny Callison	2.50
435	Woody Held	2.00
436	Tim Harkness	2.00
437	Bill Bruton	2.00
438	Wes Stock	2.00
439	Don Zimmer	2.75
440	Juan Marichal	20.00
441	Lee Thomas	2.00
442	J.C. Hartman	2.00
443	Jim Piersall	2.50
444	Jim Maloney	2.25
445	Norm Cash	2.25
446	Whitey Ford	30.00
447	Felix Mantilla	8.00
448	Jack Kralick	8.00
449	Jose Tartabull	8.00
450	Bob Friend	9.00
451	Indians Team	10.00
452	Barney Schultz	8.00
453	Jake Wood	8.00
454	Art Fowler	8.00
455	Ruben Amaro	8.00
456	Jim Coker	8.00
457	Tex Clevenger	8.00
458	Al Lopez	11.00
459	Dick LeMay	8.00
460	Del Crandall	9.00
461	Norm Bass	8.00
462	Wally Post	8.00
463	Joe Schaffernoth	8.00

250 Stan Musial

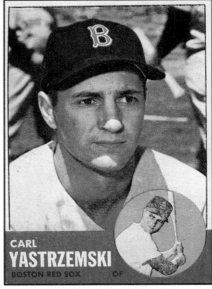

115 Carl Yastrzemski

464	Ken Aspromonte	8.00
465	Chuck Estrada	8.00
466	1963 Rookie Stars (Bill Freehan, Tony Martinez, Nate Oliver, Jerry Robinson)	25.00
467	Phil Ortega	8.00
468	Carroll Hardy	8.00
469	Jay Hook	8.00
470	Tom Tresh	20.00
471	Ken Retzer	8.00
472	Lou Brock	80.00
473	Mets Team	75.00
474	Jack Fisher	8.00
475	Gus Triandos	8.00
476	Frank Funk	8.00
477	Donn Clendenon	9.00
478	Paul Brown	8.00
479	Ed Brinkman	9.00
480	Bill Monbouquette	8.00
481	Bob Taylor	8.00
482	Felix Torres	8.00
483	Jim Owens	8.00
484	Dale Long	8.50
485	Jim Landis	8.00
486	Ray Sadecki	8.00
487	John Roseboro	9.00
488	Jerry Adair	8.00
489	Paul Toth	8.00
490	Willie McCovey	90.00
491	Harry Craft	8.00
492	Dave Wickersham	8.00
493	Walt Bond	8.00
494	Phil Regan	8.00
495	Frank Thomas	9.00
496	1963 Rookie Stars (Carl Bouldin, Steve Dalkowski, Fred Newman, Jack Smith)	9.00
497	Bennie Daniels	8.00
498	Eddie Kasko	8.00
499	J.C. Martin	8.00
500	Harmon Killebrew	90.00

400 Frank Robinson

501	Joe Azcue	8.00
502	Daryl Spencer	8.00
503	Braves Team	10.00
504	Bob Johnson	8.00
505	Curt Flood	12.00
506	Gene Green	9.00
507	Rolando Sheldon	5.00
508	Ted Savage	4.00
509	Checklist 509-576	12.00
510	Ken McBride	5.00
511	Charlie Neal	5.00
512	Cal McLish	5.00
513	Gary Geiger	5.00
514	Larry Osborne	5.00

515	Don Elston	5.00
516	Purnal Goldy	5.00
517	Hal Woodeshick	5.00
518	Don Blasingame	5.00
519	Claude Raymond	5.00
520	Orlando Cepeda	20.00
521	Dan Pfister	5.00
522	1963 Rookie Stars (Mel Nelson, Gary Peters, Art Quirk, Jim Roland)	5.00
523	Bill Kunkel	5.50
524	Cardinals Team	7.50
525	Nellie Fox	12.00
526	Dick Hall	5.00
527	Ed Sadowski	5.00
528	Carl Willey	5.00
529	Wes Covington	5.00
530	Don Mossi	5.00
531	Sam Mele	5.00
532	Steve Boros	5.00
533	Bobby Shantz	5.50
534	Ken Walters	5.00
535	Jim Perry	5.50
536	Norm Larker	5.00
537	1963 Rookie Stars (Pedro Gonzalez, *Ken McMullen, Pete Rose, Al Weis*)	650.00
538	George Brunet	5.00
539	Wayne Causey	5.00
540	Bob Clemente	125.00
541	Ron Moeller	5.00
542	Lou Klimlock	5.00
543	Russ Snyder	5.00
544	1963 Rookie Stars (Duke Carmel, Bill Haas, Dick Phillips, *Rusty Staub*)	35.00
545	Jose Pagan	5.00
546	Hal Reniff	5.00
547	Gus Bell	5.50

548	Tom Satriano	5.00
549	1963 Rookie Stars (*Marcelino Lopez*, Pete Lovrich, Elmo Plaskett, Paul Ratliff)	5.50
550	Duke Snider	60.00
551	Billy Klaus	5.00
552	Tigers Team	5.50
553	1963 Rookie Stars (Brock Davis, Jim Gosger, John Herrnstein, *Willie Stargell*)	225.00
554	Hank Fischer	5.00
555	John Blanchard	5.50
556	Al Worthington	5.00
557	Cuno Barragan	5.00
558	1963 Rookie Stars (Bill Faul, *Ron Hunt*, Bob Lipski, Al Moran)	5.75
559	Danny Murtaugh	5.50
560	Ray Herbert	5.00
561	Mike de la Hoz	5.00
562	1963 Rookie Stars (Randy Cardinal, *Dave McNally*, Don Rowe, Ken Rowe)	14.00
563	Mike McCormick	5.50
564	George Banks	5.00
565	Larry Sherry	5.00
566	Cliff Cook	5.00
567	Jim Duffalo	5.00
568	Bob Sadowski	5.00
569	Luis Arroyo	5.00
570	Frank Bolling	5.00
571	Johnny Klippstein	5.00
572	Jack Spring	5.00
573	Coot Veal	5.00
574	Hal Kolstad	5.00
575	Don Cardwell	5.00
576	Johnny Temple	5.50

1964 TOPPS

A simple but striking format highlighted Topps' 1964 set of 587 cards. Large photos and a lack of clutter made the cards especially attractive. For the first time ever, Topps grouped rookies by team, featuring two players per card. Phil Niekro, Richie Allen, Lou Piniella, and Tommy John are the most recognizable names found in the first-year cards, while Pete Rose and Mickey Mantle are the set's most valuable. One of the most unusual cards in the set is an In Memoriam card for Chicago Cubs second baseman Ken Hubbs, who was killed in a plane crash. On many card backs a baseball quiz could be answered by rubbing the question box with a coin.

	NR MT
Complete set	$2400.00
Commons (1-370)	.70
Commons (371-522)	1.00
Commons (523-587)	5.00

1	NL ERA Ldrs (Dick Ellsworth, Bob Friend, Sandy Koufax)	$10.00
2	AL ERA Ldrs (Camilo Pascual, Gary Peters, Juan Pizarro)	3.00
3	NL Pitching Ldrs (Sandy Koufax, Jim Maloney, Juan Marichal, Warren Spahn)	5.00
4	AL Pitching Ldrs (Jim Bouton, Whitey Ford, Camilo Pascual)	3.50

50 Mickey Mantle

125 Pete Rose

5 NL SO Ldrs (Don
   Drysdale, Sandy Koufax,
   Jim Maloney) **4.00**
6 AL SO Ldrs (Jim
   Bunning, Camilo Pascual,
   Dick Stigman) **3.00**
7 NL Batting Ldrs (Hank
   Aaron, Bob Clemente,
   Tommy Davis, Dick Groat) .. **5.00**
8 AL Batting Ldrs (Al
   Kaline, Rich Rollins,
   Carl Yastrzemski) **5.00**
9 NL HR Ldrs (Hank Aaron,
   Orlando Cepeda, Willie
   Mays, Willie McCovey) **5.00**
10 AL HR Ldrs (Bob
   Allison, Harmon Killebrew,
   Dick Stuart) **4.50**
11 NL RBI Ldrs (Hank Aaron,
   Ken Boyer, Bill White) **4.00**
12 AL RBI Ldrs (Al Kaline,
   Harmon Killebrew, Dick
   Stuart) **4.00**
13 Hoyt Wilhelm **8.00**
14 Dodgers Rookies (Dick
   Nen, Nick Willhite) .... **.70**
15 Zoilo Versalles...................... **.80**
16 John Boozer .... **.70**
17 Willie Kirkland....................... **.70**
18 Billy O'Dell .... **.70**
19 Don Wert .... **.70**
20 Bob Friend........................... **1.25**
21 Yogi Berra **30.00**
22 Jerry Adair .... **.70**
23 Chris Zachary .... **.70**
24 Carl Sawatski .... **.70**
25 Bill Monbouquette .... **.70**
26 Gino Cimoli.......................... **.70**
27 Mets Team **3.50**
28 Claude Osteen .... **.80**
29 Lou Brock **25.00**
30 Ron Perranoski .... **.80**
31 Dave Nicholson .... **.70**

32 Dean Chance **1.25**
33 Reds Rookies (Sammy
   Ellis, Mel Queen) .... **.80**
34 Jim Perry **1.25**
35 Ed Mathews **12.00**
36 Hal Reniff .... **.70**
37 Smoky Burgess **1.25**
38 *Jim Wynn.......................... **1.50**
39 Hank Aguirre .... **.70**
40 Dick Groat **1.50**
41 Friendly Foes (Willie
   McCovey, Leon Wagner) **3.00**
42 Moe Drabowsky .... **.70**
43 Roy Sievers.......................... **.90**
44 Duke Carmel .... **.80**
45 Milt Pappas .... **.90**
46 Ed Brinkman......................... **.80**
47 Giants Rookies (*Jesus
   Alou*, Ron Herbel) **1.25**
49 Bill Henry .... **.70**
50 Mickey Mantle **225.00**
51 Pete Richert .... **.70**
52 Chuck Hinton....................... **.70**
53 Denis Menke .... **.70**
54 Sam Mele .... **.70**
55 Ernie Banks **20.00**
56 Hal Brown........................... **.70**
57 Tim Harkness .... **.70**
58 Don Demeter....................... **.70**
59 Ernie Broglio .... **.70**
60 Frank Malzone .... **.80**
61 Angel Backstops (Bob
   Rodgers, Ed Sadowski)........ **.80**
62 Ted Savage .... **.70**
63 Johnny Orsino .... **.70**
64 Ted Abernathy .... **.70**
65 Felipe Alou **1.25**
66 Eddie Fisher .... **.70**
67 Tigers Team **3.50**
68 Willie Davis.......................... **1.50**
69 Clete Boyer **1.50**
70 Joe Torre............................ **2.50**
71 Jack Spring .... **.70**
72 Chico Cardenas .... **.70**

150 Willie Mays

210 Carl Yastrzemski

73 *Jimmie Hall*............................ **.80**
74 Pirates Rookies (Tom
   Butters, Bob Priddy) .... **.70**
75 Wayne Causey .... **.70**
76 Checklist 1-88 .... **3.00**
77 Jerry Walker .... **.70**
78 Merritt Ranew .... **.70**
79 Bob Heffner .... **.70**
80 Vada Pinson........................ **2.50**
81 All-Star Vets (Nellie
   Fox, Harmon Killebrew)....... **4.00**
82 Jim Davenport .... **.70**
83 Gus Triandos .... **.70**
84 Carl Willey .... **.70**
85 Pete Ward .... **.80**
86 Al Downing **1.50**
87 Cardinals Team **4.00**
88 John Roseboro .... **.80**
89 Boog Powell **2.50**
90 Earl Battey .... **.80**
91 Bob Bailey .... **.80**
92 Steve Ridzik .... **.70**
93 Gary Geiger .... **.70**
94 Braves Rookies (Jim
   Britton, Larry Maxie) .... **.70**
95 George Altman .... **.80**
96 Bob Buhl............................. **.80**
97 Jim Fregosi.......................... **1.25**
98 Bill Bruton .... **.80**
99 Al Stanek .... **.70**
100 Elston Howard..................... **5.00**
101 Walt Alston **3.00**
102 Checklist 89-176 .... **3.00**
103 *Curt Flood **2.00**
104 Art Mahaffey .... **.70**
105 Woody Held.......................... **.70**
106 Joe Nuxhall .... **.80**
107 White Sox Rookies
   (Bruce Howard, Frank
   Kreutzer) .... **.70**
108 John Wyatt .... **.70**
109 Rusty Staub......................... **5.00**
110 Albie Pearson .... **.70**

111	Don Elston	.70
112	Bob Tillman	.70
113	Grover Powell	.70
114	Don Lock	.70
116	*Twins Rookies (Tony Oliva, Jay Ward)	5.00
118	John Blanchard	1.00
120	Don Drysdale	15.00
121	Pete Runnels	.80
122	Don McMahon	.70
123	Jose Pagan	.70
124	Orlando Pena	.70
125	Pete Rose	150.00
128	*Mickey Lolich	8.00
132	Braves Team	2.25
134	Don Zimmer	1.50
135	John Callison	1.50
136	World Series Game 1 (Koufax Strikes Out 15)	5.00
137	World Series Game 2 (Davis Sparks Rally)	2.50
138	World Series Game 3 (L.A. Takes 3rd Straight)	2.50
139	World Series Game 4 (Sealing Yanks' Doom)	2.50
140	World Series Summary (The Dodgers Celebrate)	2.50
141	Danny Murtaugh	.80
145	Norm Siebern	.80
146	Indians Rookies (Tommy John, Bob Chance)	50.00
150	Willie Mays	75.00
151	Athletics Team	2.25
153	Dick Williams	1.50
155	Duke Snider	25.00
157	Gene Mauch	.90
160	Ken Boyer	4.00
161	Dave McNally	1.25
167	Senators Rookies (Mike Brumley, Lou Piniella)	17.00
169	Del Crandall	1.25
172	Indians Team	2.25
175	Billy Williams	8.00
180	Tommy Davis	1.50

200 Sandy Koufax

182	Sox Sockers (Chuck Schilling, Carl Yastrzemski)	7.00
188	Checklist 177-264	3.00
190	Bobby Richardson	4.50
200	Sandy Koufax	70.00
201	Orioles Rookies (Sam Bowens, Wally Bunker)	.80
204	Matty Alou	.90
205	Nellie Fox	4.00
207	Fred Hutchinson	.80
210	Carl Yastrzemski	70.00
213	Angels Team	2.25
219	Young Aces (Jim Bouton, Al Downing)	2.00
222	Bill Pierce	.90
225	Roger Maris	50.00
226	Colts Rookies (Gerald Grote, Larry Yellen)	1.25
230	Brooks Robinson	20.00
232	Al Lopez	3.00
235	Ron Hunt	.80
237	Cubs Team	2.25
240	*Bill White	1.50
242	*Harvey Kuenn	1.50
243	Phillies Rookies (Richie Allen, John Herrnstein)	8.00
244	*Tony LaRussa	5.00
246	Manny Mota	1.25
247	*Dave DeBusschere	2.00
250	Al Kaline	18.00
251	Choo Choo Coleman	.80
257	Giants Team	2.25
260	Frank Robinson	18.00
262	Cardinals Rookies (Harry Fanok, Mike Shannon)	1.50
265	Jim Bunning	5.00
267	Wilbur Wood	1.50
274	Checklist 265-352	3.00
280	Juan Marichal	15.00
281	Yankees Rookies (Jake Gibbs, Tom Metcalf)	1.00

440 Bob Clemente

283	Tommy McGraw	.80
285	Robin Roberts	15.00
287	Red Sox Rookies (Tony Conigliaro, Bill Spanswick)	12.00
290	*Bob Allison	.90
293	Phillies Team	2.25
295	*Roger Craig	1.50
300	Hank Aaron	65.00
306	*Giant Gunners (Orlando Cepeda, Willie Mays)	12.00
310	Jim Gilliam	3.00
318	Twins Team	2.25
320	Rocky Colavito	3.00
324	Casey Stengel	12.00
331	A.L. Bombers (Norm Cash, Al Kaline, Mickey Mantle, Roger Maris)	55.00
342	Willie Stargell	25.00
343	Senators Team	2.25
350	Willie McCovey	18.00
353	Wally Moon	.70
354	Dave Giusti	.70
355	Vic Power	.70
356	Reds Rookies (Bill McCool, Chico Ruiz,)	.70
357	Charley James	.70
358	Ron Kline	.70
359	Jim Schaffer	.70
360	Joe Pepitone	.70
361	Jay Hook	.70
362	Checklist 353-429	3.00
363	Dick McAuliffe	.80
364	Joe Gaines	.70
365	Cal McLish	.70
366	Nelson Mathews	.70
367	Fred Whitfield	.70
368	White Sox Rookies (Fritz Ackley, Don Buford)	.90
369	Jerry Zimmerman	.70
370	Hal Woodeshick	.70
371	Frank Howard	3.00
372	Howie Koplitz	1.00
373	Pirates Team	3.00

225 Roger Maris

331 A.L. Bombers

460	Bob Gibson	15.00
461	George Thomas	1.00
462	Birdie Tebbetts	1.00
463	Don Leppert	1.00
464	Dallas Green	1.25
465	Mike Hershberger	1.00
466	Athletics Rookies (*Dick Green*, Aurelio Monteagudo)	1.25
467	Bob Aspromonte	1.00
468	Gaylord Perry	25.00
469	Cubs Rookies (Fred Norman, Sterling Slaughter)	1.00
470	Jim Bouton	3.00
471	*Gates Brown*	1.25
472	Vern Law	1.50
473	Orioles Team	3.00
474	Larry Sherry	1.00
475	Ed Charles	1.00
476	Braves Rookies (*Rico Carty,* Dick Kelley)	1.25
477	Mike Joyce	.90
478	Dick Howser	2.00
479	Cardinals Rookies (Dave Bakenhaster, Johnny Lewis)	1.00
481	Chuck Schilling	1.00
482	Phillies Rookies (*Danny Cater,* John Briggs)	1.25
483	Fred Valentine	1.00
484	Bill Pleis	1.00
485	Tom Haller	1.25
486	Bob Kennedy	1.00
487	Mike McCormick	1.25
488	Yankees Rookies (Bob Meyer, Pete Mikkelsen)	1.50
489	Julio Navarro	1.00
490	Ron Fairly	1.50
491	Ed Rakow	1.00
492	Colts Rookies (Jim Beauchamp, Mike White)	1.00
493	Don Lee	1.00
494	Al Jackson	1.25

374	Bobby Bolin	1.00
375	Ron Santo	3.00
376	Dave Morehead	1.50
377	Bob Skinner	1.00
378	Braves Rookies (Jack Smith, *Woody Woodward*)	1.25
379	Tony Gonzalez	1.00
380	Whitey Ford	25.00
381	Bob Taylor	1.00
382	Wes Stock	1.00
383	Bill Rigney	1.00
384	Ron Hansen	1.00
385	Curt Simmons	1.25
386	Lenny Green	1.00
387	Terry Fox	1.00
388	Athletics Rookies (John O'Donoghue, George Williams)	1.00
389	Jim Umbricht	1.00
390	Orlando Cepeda	4.50
391	Sam McDowell	1.25
392	Jim Pagliaroni	1.00
393	Casey Teaches (Ed Kranepool, Casey Stengel)	3.00
394	Bob Miller	1.00
395	Tom Tresh	3.00
396	Dennis Bennett	1.00
397	Chuck Cottier	1.00
398	Mets Rookies (Bill Haas, Dick Smith)	1.25
399	Jackie Brandt	1.00
400	Warren Spahn	20.00
401	Charlie Maxwell	1.00
402	Tom Sturdivant	1.00
403	Reds Team	3.50
404	Tony Martinez	1.00
405	Ken McBride	1.00
406	Al Spangler	1.00
407	Bill Freehan	2.00
408	Cubs Rookies (Fred Burdette, Jim Stewart)	1.00
409	Bill Fischer	1.00
410	Dick Stuart	1.25
411	Lee Walls	1.00
412	Ray Culp	1.00
413	Johnny Keane	1.00
414	Jack Sanford	1.00

415	Tony Kubek	5.00
416	Lee Maye	1.00
417	Don Cardwell	1.00
418	Orioles Rookies (*Darold Knowles,* Les Narum)	1.25
419	*Ken Harrelson*	3.00
420	Jim Maloney	1.25
421	Camilo Carreon	1.00
422	Jack Fisher	1.25
423	Topps in NL (Hank Aaron, Willie Mays)	50.00
424	Dick Bertell	1.00
425	Norm Cash	2.50
426	Bob Rodgers	1.25
428	Red Sox Rookies (Archie Skeen, Pete Smith)	1.00
429	Tim McCarver	3.00
430	Juan Pizarro	1.00
431	George Alusik	1.00
432	Reuben Amaro	1.00
433	Yankees Team	8.00
434	Don Nottebart	1.00
435	Vic Davalillo	1.00
436	Charlie Neal	1.00
437	Ed Bailey	1.00
438	Checklist 430-506	4.00
439	Harvey Haddix	1.25
440	Bob Clemente	75.00
441	Bob Duliba	1.00
442	Pumpsie Green	1.25
443	Chuck Dressen	1.25
444	Larry Jackson	1.00
445	Bill Skowron	2.50
446	Julian Javier	1.25
447	Ted Bowsfield	1.00
448	Cookie Rojas	1.25
449	Deron Johnson	1.00
450	Steve Barber	1.00
451	Joe Amalfitano	1.00
452	Giants Rookies (Gil Garrido, *Jim Hart*)	1.25
454	Tommie Aaron	1.25
455	Bernie Allen	1.00
456	Dodgers Rookies (*Wes Parker,* John Werhas)	2.00
457	Jesse Gonder	1.00
458	Ralph Terry	2.00
459	Red Sox Rookies (Pete Charton, Dalton Jones)	1.00

21 Yogi Berra

495	Bill Virdon	2.00
496	White Sox Team	3.00
497	Jeoff Long	1.00
498	Dave Stenhouse	1.00
499	Indians Rookies (Chico Salmon, Gordon Seyfried)	1.00
500	Camilo Pascual	1.25
501	Bob Veale	1.25
502	Angels Rookies (*Bobby Knoop,* Bob Lee)	1.25
503	Earl Wilson	1.00
504	Claude Raymond	1.00
505	Stan Williams	1.50
506	Bobby Bragan	1.00
507	John Edwards	1.00
508	Diego Segui	1.00
509	Pirates Rookies (*Gene Alley,* Orlando McFarlane)	1.25
510	Lindy McDaniel	1.00
511	Lou Jackson	1.00
512	Tigers Rookies (Willie Horton, Joe Sparma)	3.00
513	Don Larsen	1.25
514	Jim Hickman	1.25
515	Johnny Romano	1.00
516	Twins Rookies (Jerry Arrigo, Dwight Siebler)	1.00
517	Checklist 507-587	4.50
518	Carl Bouldin	1.00
519	Charlie Smith	1.00
520	Jack Baldschun	1.00
521	Tom Satriano	1.00
522	Bobby Tiefenauer	1.00
523	Lou Burdette	7.00
524	Reds Rookies (Jim Dickson, Bobby Klaus)	5.00
527	Larry Bearnarth	5.00
528	Athletics Rookies (*Dave Duncan,* Tom Reynolds)	5.50
529	Al Dark	5.50
530	Leon Wagner	5.50
531	Dodgers Team	9.00
532	Twins Rookies (Bud Bloomfield, Joe Nossek)	5.00

342 Willie Stargell

230 Brooks Robinson

533	Johnny Klippstein	5.00
534	Gus Bell	5.50
535	Phil Regan	5.00
536	Mets Rookies (Larry Elliot, John Stephenson)	5.50
537	Dan Osinski	5.00
538	Minnie Minoso	7.00
539	Roy Face	6.00
540	Luis Aparicio	15.00
541	Braves Rookies (*Phil Niekro,* Phil Roof)	150.00
542	Don Mincher	5.50
543	Bob Uecker	45.00
544	Colts Rookies (Steve Hertz, Joe Hoerner)	5.00
545	Max Alvis	5.50
546	Joe Christopher	5.25
547	Gil Hodges	13.00
548	NL Rookies (Wayne Schurr, Paul Speckenbach)	5.00
549	Joe Moeller	5.00
550	Ken Hubbs	10.00
551	Billy Hoeft	5.00
552	Indians Rookies (Tom Kelley, *Sonny Siebert*)	5.50
553	Jim Brewer	5.00
556	Mets Rookies (Steve Dillon, Ron Locke)	5.50
561	Phillies Rookies (Dave Bennett, *Rick Wise*)	5.50
562	Pedro Ramos	5.00
563	Dal Maxvill	5.50
564	AL Rookies (Joe McCabe, Jerry McNertney)	5.00
565	Stu Miller	5.00
566	Ed Kranepool	6.00
567	Jim Kaat	9.00
568	NL Rookies (Phil Gagliano, Cap Peterson)	5.00
569	Fred Newman	5.00
570	Bill Mazeroski	7.00
571	Gene Conley	4.50

572	AL Rookies (Dick Egan, Dave Gray)	5.00
573	Jim Duffalo	5.00
574	Manny Jimenez	5.00
575	Tony Cloninger	5.50
576	Mets Rookies (Jerry Hinsley, Bill Wakefield)	5.50
577	Gordy Coleman	5.00
578	Glen Hobbie	5.00
579	Red Sox Team	6.00
580	Johnny Podres	7.00
581	Yankees Rookies (Pedro Gonzalez, Archie Moore)	6.00
582	Rod Kanehl	5.50
583	Tito Francona	5.50
585	Tony Taylor	5.00
586	Jim Piersall	7.00
587	Bennie Daniels	8.00

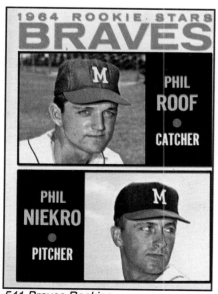

541 Braves Rookies

415 Tony Kubek

1965 TOPPS

Team logos returned to the front of the 1965 Topps set of 598 cards. Each 2 1/2-by 3 1/2-inch card also has a team pennant. Cartoons and year-by-year statistics are the main elements of card backs. A number of first-class players have rookie cards in the 1965 set. The most valuable of these rookie cards are those for Steve Carlton, Joe Morgan, Jim Hunter, and Tony Perez. For the first time since 1957, no multiplayer feature cards are included except rookie and league leader cards. An eight-card subset highlights the Cardinals World Series win over the Yankees. Noted baseball funnyman Bob Uecker (card number 519), a catcher who hit right-handed, tricked the photographer and posed as if a left-handed batter.

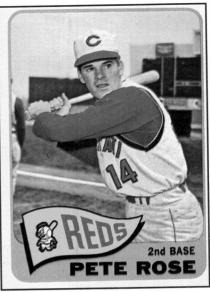

207 Pete Rose

		NR MT
Complete set		$2600.00
Commons (1-198)		.70
Commons (199-446)		.90
Commons (447-552)		1.25
Commons (553-598)		4.00

1	AL Batting Ldrs (Elston Howard, Tony Oliva, Brooks Robinson)	$8.00
2	NL Batting Ldrs (Hank Aaron, Rico Carty, Bob Clemente)	5.00
3	AL HR Ldrs (Harmon Killebrew, Mickey Mantle, Boog Powell)	15.00
4	NL HR Ldrs (Johnny Callison, Orlando Cepeda, Jim Hart, Willie Mays, Billy Williams)	4.50
5	AL RBI Ldrs (Harmon Killebrew, Mickey Mantle, Brooks Robinson, Dick Stuart)	15.00
6	NL RBI Ldrs (Ken Boyer, Willie Mays, Ron Santo)	4.50
7	AL ERA Ldrs (Dean Chance, Joel Horlen)	2.50
8	NL ERA Ldrs (Don Drysdale, Sandy Koufax)	4.50
9	AL Pitching Ldrs (Wally Bunker, Dean Chance, Gary Peters, Juan Pizarro, Dave Wickersham)	4.00
10	NL Pitching Ldrs (Larry Jackson, Juan Marichal, Ray Sadecki)	3.50
11	AL SO Ldrs (Dean Chance, Al Downing, Camilo Pascual)	2.50
12	NL SO Ldrs (Don Drysdale, Bob Gibson, Bob Veale)	4.00
13	Pedro Ramos	1.00
14	Len Gabrielson	.70
15	Robin Roberts	8.00
16	Colt .45s Rookies (*Sonny Jackson, Joe Morgan*)	150.00

350 Mickey Mantle

17	Johnny Romano	.70
18	Bill McCool	.70
19	Gates Brown	.80
20	*Jim Bunning	4.00
24	Twins Team	4.00
30	Jim Bouton	2.50
36	Bobby Wine	.80
43	Mike Shannon	.80
47	Tommy Harper	.80
49	Orioles Rookies (*Curt Blefary,* John Miller)	.90
50	Juan Marichal	8.00
55	Tony Conigliaro	2.50
57	Cardinals Team	2.50
62	*Jim Katt (Kaat)	5.00
64	Lou Burdette	2.00
65	Tony Kubek	4.50
67	Harvey Haddix	.90
68	Del Crandall	.90
69	Bill Virdon	1.25
70	Bill Skowron	1.25
74	Red Sox Rookies (*Rico Petrocelli,* Jerry Stephenson)	2.50
76	Sam McDowell	.90
79	Checklist 1-88	3.00

80	Turk Farrell	.80
91	Cubs Team	2.25
92	Dick Howser	1.25
94	Charlie Lau	.90
95	Bill Mazeroski	2.50
97	Pedro Gonzalez	.90
99	Gil Hodges	6.00
100	Ken Boyer	2.50
104	Checklist 89-176	3.00
107	Phillies Rookies (*Pat Corrales* Costen Shockley)	2.00
108	Don Mincher	.80
110	Ron Santo	1.50
114	Jim Hickman	.90
115	Bobby Richardson	4.50
116	Cardinals Rookies (Dave Dowling, *Bob Tolan*)	1.25
118	*Hal Lanier*	1.50
120	Frank Robinson	20.00
126	Dodgers Team	4.00
130	Al Kaline	20.00
131	Johnny Keane	1.50
132	World Series Game 1 (Cards Take Opener)	2.50
133	World Series Game 2 (Stottlemyre Wins)	3.00
134	World Series Game 3 (Mantle's Clutch HR)	18.00
135	World Series Game 4 (Boyer's Grand Slam)	2.50
136	World Series Game 5 (10th Inning Triumph)	2.50
137	World Series Game 6 (Bouton Wins Again)	2.50
138	World Series Game 7 (Gibson Wins Finale)	3.50
139	World Series Summary (The Cards Celebrate)	2.50
144	Ed Kranepool	.90
145	*Luis Tiant	7.00
150	Brooks Robinson	20.00
151	Athletics Team	2.25

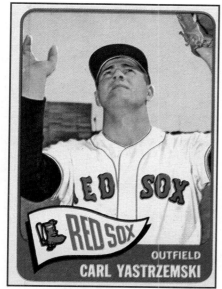

385 Carl Yastrzemski

170 Hank Aaron

300 Sandy Koufax

153	Norm Cash	2.00
155	Roger Maris	45.00
157	Zoilo Versalles	1.50
160	Bob Clemente	75.00
166	Indians Rookies (*Tommie Agee,* George Culver)	1.50
170	Hank Aaron	75.00
172	Jim Piersall	1.50
173	Tigers Team	3.25
176	Willie McCovey	20.00
180	Bob Allison	1.75
187	Casey Stengel	20.00
189	Checklist 177-264	3.00
193	Gaylord Perry	12.00
200	Joe Torre	2.50
201	Twins Rookies (*Cesar Tovar,* Sandy Valdespino)	1.00
202	Leo Burke	.90
203	Dallas Green	1.50
204	Russ Snyder	.90
205	Warren Spahn	20.00
206	Willie Horton	1.25
207	Pete Rose	150.00
208	*Tommy John	10.00
209	Pirates Team	2.50
210	Jim Fregosi	1.50
212	Ron Brand	.90
213	Jim Davenport	.90
214	Bob Purkey	.90
215	Pete Ward	.90
216	Al Worthington	.90
217	Walt Alston	3.50
218	Dick Schofield	.90
219	Bob Meyer	.90
220	Billy Williams	10.00
221	John Tsitouris	.90
222	Bob Tillman	.90
223	Dan Osinski	.90
224	Bob Chance	.90
225	Bob Belinsky	1.00
226	Yankees Rookies (Jake Gibbs, Elvio Jimenez)	1.25

227	Bobby Klaus	.90
228	Jack Sanford	.90
229	Lou Clinton	.90
230	Ray Sadecki	.90
231	Jerry Adair	.90
232	*Steve Blass*	1.00
233	Don Zimmer	1.50
234	White Sox Team	4.00
235	Chuck Hinton	.90
236	*Dennis McLain*	12.00
237	Bernie Allen	.90
238	Joe Moeller	.90
239	Doc Edwards	1.00
240	Bob Bruce	.90
241	Mack Jones	.90
242	George Brunet	.90
243	Reds Rookies (*Tommy Helms,* Ted Davidson)	1.00
244	Lindy McDaniel	.90
245	Joe Pepitone	3.00
246	Tom Butters	.90
247	Wally Moon	1.00
248	Gus Triandos	1.00
249	Dave McNally	1.25
250	Willie Mays	90.00
251	Billy Herman	2.00
252	Pete Richert	.90
253	Danny Cater	1.00
254	Roland Sheldon	1.25
255	Camilo Pascual	1.00
256	Tito Francona	1.00
257	*Jim Wynn	1.25
258	Larry Bearnarth	1.00
259	Tigers Rookies (*Jim Northrup,* Ray Oyler)	1.25
260	Don Drysdale	15.00
261	Duke Carmel	1.00
262	Bud Daley	.90
263	Marty Keough	.90
264	Bob Buhl	1.00
266	*Bert Campaneris*	3.00
267	Senators Team	2.50
268	Ken McBride	.90

269	Frank Bolling	.90
270	Milt Pappas	1.00
271	Don Wert	.90
272	Chuck Schilling	.90
273	Checklist 265-352	3.25
275	Dick Groat	1.75
276	Hoyt Wilhelm	10.00
277	Johnny Lewis	1.00
278	Ken Retzer	.90
279	Dick Tracewski	.90
280	Dick Stuart	1.00
281	Bill Stafford	1.25
282	Giants Rookies (Dick Estelle, *Masanori Murakami*)	1.25
283	Fred Whitfield	.90
284	Nick Willhite	.90
285	Ron Hunt	1.00
286	Athletics Rookies (Jim Dickson, Aurelio Monteagudo)	.90
288	Jack Hamilton	.90
289	Gordy Coleman	.90
290	Wally Bunker	.90
291	Jerry Lynch	.90
292	Larry Yellen	.90
293	Angels Team	2.50
294	Tim McCarver	2.75
295	Dick Radatz	1.00
296	Tony Taylor	1.00
297	*Dave DeBusschere	3.50
298	Jim Stewart	.90
299	Jerry Zimmerman	.90
300	Sandy Koufax	90.00
301	Birdie Tebbetts	.90
302	Al Stanek	.90
303	Johnny Orsino	.90
304	Dave Stenhouse	.90
305	Rico Carty	1.50
306	Bubba Phillips	.90
307	Barry Latman	.90
308	Mets Rookies (*Cleon Jones,* Tom Parsons)	1.25

1965 Topps

477 Cardinals Rookies

309	Steve Hamilton	1.25
310	Johnny Callison	1.50
311	Orlando Pena	.90
312	Joe Nuxhall	1.25
313	Jimmie Schaffer	.90
314	Sterling Slaughter	.90
315	Frank Malzone	1.25
316	Reds Team	2.75
318	Matty Alou	1.00
319	Ken McMullen	.90
320	Bob Gibson	20.00
321	Rusty Staub	3.50
322	Rick Wise	1.00
323	Hank Bauer	1.00
325	Donn Clendenon	1.00
330	Whitey Ford	20.00
331	Dodgers Rookies (Al Ferrara, John Purdin)	1.00
333	Tommie Reynolds	.90
334	Vic Roznovsky	.90
335	Mickey Lolich	3.50
336	Woody Held	.90
337	Mike Cuellar	1.50
338	Phillies Team	2.50
339	Ryne Duren	1.00
340	*Tony Oliva	3.50
342	Bob Rodgers	1.00
343	Mike McCormick	1.00
344	Wes Parker	1.00
345	Floyd Robinson	.90
346	Bobby Bragan	1.00
347	Roy Face	1.50
350	Mickey Mantle	350.00
351	Jim Perry	1.25
352	*Alex Johnson*	1.00
353	Jerry Lumpe	1.00
355	Vada Pinson	2.50
356	Bill Spanswick	.90
357	Carl Warwick	.90
358	Albie Pearson	.90
359	Ken Johnson	.90
360	Orlando Cepeda	5.00
361	Checklist 353-429	3.25
362	Don Schwall	.90
363	Bob Johnson	.90
364	Galen Cisco	1.00
365	Jim Gentile	1.00
366	Dan Schneider	.90
367	Leon Wagner	1.00

368	White Sox Rookies (*Ken Berry*, Joel Gibson)	1.00
369	Phil Linz	1.00
370	Tommy Davis	2.00
371	Frank Kreutzer	.90
372	Clay Dalrymple	.90
373	Curt Simmons	1.00
374	Angels Rookies (*Jose Cardenal*, Dick Simpson)	1.00
375	Dave Wickersham	.90
376	Jim Landis	.90
377	Willie Stargell	20.00
378	Chuck Estrada	.90
379	Giants Team	2.50
380	Rocky Colavito	3.00
381	Al Jackson	1.00
382	J.C. Martin	.90
383	Felipe Alou	1.00
384	Johnny Klippstein	.90
385	Carl Yastrzemski	90.00
386	Cubs Rookies (Paul Jaeckel, Fred Norman)	.90
387	Johnny Podres	2.00
388	John Blanchard	1.00
389	Don Larsen	1.25
390	Bill Freehan	1.50
391	Mel McGaha	.90
392	Bob Friend	1.50
393	Ed Kirkpatrick	.90
394	Jim Hannan	.90
395	Jim Hart	1.00

396	Frank Bertaina	.90
397	Jerry Buchek	.90
398	Reds Rookies (Dan Neville, *Art Shamsky*)	1.00
399	Ray Herbert	.90
400	Harmon Killebrew	15.00
401	Carl Willey	1.00
402	Joe Amalfitano	.90
403	Red Sox Team	3.00
405	John Roseboro	.90
406	Ralph Terry	1.00
407	Lee Maye	.90
408	Larry Sherry	.90
409	Astros Rookies (Jim Beauchamp, *Larry Dierker*)	.90
410	Luis Aparicio	9.00
411	Roger Craig	2.00
412	Bob Bailey	.90
413	Hal Reniff	.90
414	Al Lopez	3.00
415	*Curt Flood	1.50
416	Jim Brewer	.90
417	Ed Brinkman	1.00
418	Johnny Edwards	.90
419	Ruben Amaro	.90
420	Larry Jackson	.90
421	Twins Rookies (Gary Dotter, Jay Ward)	.90
422	Aubrey Gatewood	.90
423	Jesse Gonder	.90
424	Gary Bell	.90
425	Wayne Causey	.90
426	Braves Team	2.50
427	Bob Saverine	.90
428	Bob Shaw	.90
429	Don Demeter	.90
430	Gary Peters	1.00
431	Cardinals Rookies (*Nelson Briles,* Wayne Spiezio)	1.00
432	Jim Grant	.90
433	John Bateman	.90
434	Dave Morehead	.90
435	Willie Davis	1.50
436	Don Elston	.90
437	Chico Cardenas	.90
438	Harry Walker	1.00
439	Moe Drabowsky	.90
440	Tom Tresh	1.50
441	Denver Lemaster	.90

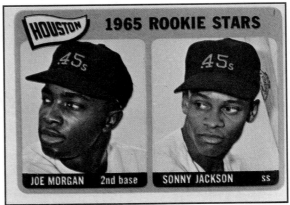

16 Colt .45s Rookies

160 Bob Clemente

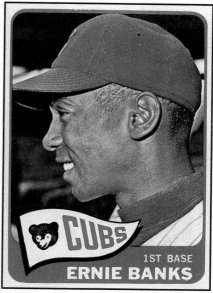

510 Ernie Banks

442	Vic Power	.90
443	Checklist 430-506	3.50
444	Bob Hendley	.90
445	Don Lock	.90
446	Art Mahaffey	.90
447	Julian Javier	1.50
448	Lee Stange	1.25
449	Mets Rookies (Jerry Hinsley, Gary Kroll)	1.50
450	Elston Howard	5.00
451	Jim Owens	1.25
452	Gary Geiger	1.25
453	Dodgers Rookies (*Willie Crawford*, John Werhas)	1.50
454	Ed Rakow	1.25
455	Norm Siebern	1.50
456	Bill Henry	1.25
457	Bob Kennedy	1.25
458	John Buzhardt	1.25
459	Frank Kostro	1.25
460	Richie Allen	7.00
461	Braves Rookies (Phil Niekro, *Clay Carroll*)	35.00
462	Lew Krausse (photo is Pete Lovrich)	1.50
463	Manny Mota	1.50
464	Ron Piche	1.25
465	Tom Haller	1.25
466	Senators Rookies (Pete Craig, Dick Nen)	1.25
467	Ray Washburn	1.25
468	Larry Brown	1.25
469	Don Nottebart	1.25
470	Yogi Berra	50.00
471	Billy Hoeft	1.25
472	Don Pavletich	1.25
473	Orioles Rookies (*Dave Johnson, Paul Blair*)	10.00
474	Cookie Rojas	1.25
475	Clete Boyer	3.00
477	Cardinals Rookies (Fritz Ackley, *Steve Carlton*)	300.00
478	Wilbur Wood	1.25

479	Ken Harrelson	2.75
480	Joel Horlen	1.25
481	Indians Team	3.00
482	Bob Priddy	1.25
483	George Smith	1.25
484	Ron Perranoski	1.50
485	Nellie Fox	6.00
486	Angels Rookies (Tom Egan, Pat Rogan)	1.25
487	Woody Woodward	1.50
488	Ted Wills	1.25
489	Gene Mauch	1.50
490	Earl Battey	1.50
491	Tracy Stallard	1.25
492	Gene Freese	1.25
493	Tigers Rookies (Bruce Brubaker, Bill Roman)	1.25
494	Jay Ritchie	1.25
495	Joe Christopher	1.25
496	Joe Cunningham	1.75
497	Giants Rookies (*Ken Henderson*, Jack Hiatt)	1.50
498	Gene Stephens	1.25
499	Stu Miller	1.25
500	Ed Mathews	20.00
501	Indians Rookies (Ralph Gagliano, Jim Rittwage)	1.25
502	Don Cardwell	1.25
503	Phil Gagliano	1.25
504	Jerry Grote	1.50
505	Ray Culp	1.25
506	Sam Mele	1.25
507	Sammy Ellis	1.25
508	Checklist 507-598	4.00
509	Red Sox Rookies (Bob Guindon, Gerry Vezendy)	1.25
510	Ernie Banks	60.00
511	Ron Locke	1.50
512	Cap Peterson	1.50
513	Yankees Team	10.00
514	Joe Azcue	1.25
515	Vern Law	2.00
516	Al Weis	1.25

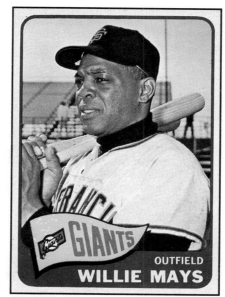

250 Willie Mays

517	Angels Rookies (Paul Schaal, Jack Warner)	1.25
518	Ken Rowe	1.25
519	Bob Uecker	45.00
520	Tony Cloninger	1.50
521	Phillies Rookies (Dave Bennett, Morrie Stevens)	1.25
523	Mike Brumley	4.00
524	Dave Giusti	4.00
525	Eddie Bressoud	4.00
526	Athletics Rookies (*Jim Hunter, Rene Lachemann, Skip Lockwood, Johnny Odom*)	135.00
527	Jeff Torborg	4.50
528	George Altman	4.00
529	Jerry Fosnow	4.00
530	Jim Maloney	4.50
531	Chuck Hiller	4.00
532	Hector Lopez	4.50
533	Mets Rookies (Jim Bethke, *Tug McGraw*, Dan Napolean, *Ron Swoboda*)	15.00
534	John Herrnstein	4.00
535	Jack Kralick	4.00
536	Andre Rodgers	4.00
537	Angels Rookies (Marcelino Lopez, *Rudy May*, Phil Roof)	5.00
538	Chuck Dressen	4.75
539	Herm Starrette	4.00
540	Lou Brock	50.00
541	White Sox Rookies (Greg Bollo, Bob Locker)	4.00
542	Lou Klimchock	4.00
543	Ed Connolly	4.00
544	Howie Reed	4.00
545	Jesus Alou	4.75
546	Indians Rookies (Ray Barker, Bill Davis, Mike Hedlund, Floyd Weaver)	4.00

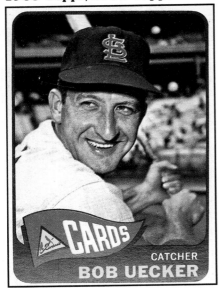

519 Bob Uecker

547	Jake Wood	4.00
548	Dick Stigman	4.00
549	Cubs Rookies (*Glenn Beckert,* Roberto Pena)	5.25
550	*Mel Stottlemyre*	15.00
551	Mets Team	12.00
552	Julio Gotay	4.00

553	Astros Rookies (Dan Coombs, Jack McClure, Gene Ratliff)	4.00
554	Chico Ruiz	4.00
555	Jack Baldschun	4.00
556	Red Schoendienst	7.00
557	Jose Santiago	4.00
558	Tommie Sisk	4.00
559	Ed Bailey	4.00
560	Boog Powell	6.00
561	*Dodgers Rookies (Dennis Daboll, *Mike Kekich, Jim Lefebvre,* Hector Valle)	5.00
562	Billy Moran	4.00
563	Julio Navarro	4.00
564	Mel Nelson	4.00
565	Ernie Broglio	4.00
566	Yankees Rookies (Gil Blanco, Art Lopez, Ross Moschitto)	5.00
567	Tommie Aaron	4.50
568	Ron Taylor	4.00
569	Gino Cimoli	4.00
570	Claude Osteen	4.50
571	Ossie Virgil	4.00
572	Orioles Team	6.00
573	Red Sox Rookies (*Jim Lonborg,* Gerry Moses, Mike Ryan, Bill Schlesinger)	8.00
574	Roy Sievers	4.50
575	Jose Pagan	4.00

576	Terry Fox	4.00
577	AL Rookies (Jim Buschhorn, Darold Knowles, Richie Scheinblum)	4.00
578	Camilo Carreon	4.00
579	Dick Smith	4.00
580	Jimmie Hall	4.00
581	NL Rookies (Kevin Collins, *Tony Perez,* Dave Ricketts)	80.00
582	Bob Schmidt	4.00
583	Wes Covington	4.00
584	Harry Bright	4.00
585	Hank Fischer	4.00
586	Tommy McGraw	4.00
587	Joe Sparma	4.00
588	Lenny Green	4.00
589	Giants Rookies (Frank Linzy, Bob Schroeder)	4.00
590	Johnnie Wyatt	4.00
591	Bob Skinner	4.25
592	Frank Bork	4.00
593	Tigers Rookies (Jackie Moore, John Sullivan)	4.00
594	Joe Gaines	4.00
595	Don Lee	4.00
596	Don Landrum	4.00
597	Twins Rookies (Joe Nossek, Dick Reese, John Sevcik)	4.50
598	Al Downing	10.00

1966 TOPPS

Topps unveiled no surprises in its 1966 set of 598 cards, although multiplayer cards reappeared. Well-known rookies who made their debuts in the 1966 Topps offering include Don Sutton, Ferguson Jenkins, Bobby Murcer, Jim Palmer, and George "Boomer" Scott. The set features two series that are tough to locate today: Cards numbering 447 to 522 are somewhat hard to find, while the high numbers from 523 through 598 constitute one of the scarcest series of the 1960s. Short supply and his probable election to the Hall of Fame explain the $275 value placed on Gaylord Perry's card, number 598.

598 Gaylord Perry

		NR MT
Complete set		**$3750.00**
Commons (1-110)		**.60**
Commons (111-446)		**.70**
Commons (447-522)		**4.50**
Commons (523-598)		**16.00**

1	Willie Mays	$200.00
28	Phil Niekro	10.00
30	Pete Rose	60.00
36	Jim Hunter	25.00
37	Billy Herman	1.50
50	Mickey Mantle	185.00
62	Merritt Ranew (with sold statement)	.60
62	Merritt Ranew (w/o sold statement)	15.00
70	Carl Yastrzemski	60.00
72	Tony Perez	8.00
76	Red Schoendienst	1.50
90	Luis Aparicio	9.00
91	Bob Uecker (with trade statement)	15.00
91	Bob Uecker (w/o trade statement)	80.00
92	Yankees Team	4.00
99	Buc Belters (Donn Clendenon, Willie Stargell)	3.50
100	Sandy Koufax	100.00
101	Checklist 89-176 (115 is Spahn)	7.00
101	Checklist 89-176 (115 is Henry)	3.00

126 Jim Palmer

70 Carl Yastrzemski

103	Dick Groat (with trade statement)	1.50
103	Dick Groat (w/o trade statement)	20.00
104	Alex Johnson (with trade statement)	.70
104	Alex Johnson (w/o trade statement)	15.00
110	Ernie Banks	25.00
111	Gary Peters	.80
112	Manny Mota	.90
113	Hank Aguirre	.70
114	Jim Gosger	.70
115	Bill Henry	.70
116	Walt Alston	2.50
117	Jake Gibbs	1.00
118	Mike McCormick	.80
119	Art Shamsky	.70
120	Harmon Killebrew	15.00
121	Ray Herbert	.70
122	Joe Gaines	.70
123	Pirates Rookies (Frank Bork, Jerry May)	.70
124	Tug McGraw	3.00
125	Lou Brock	20.00
126	*Jim Palmer*	225.00
127	Ken Berry	.70
128	Jim Landis	.70
129	Jack Kralick	.70
130	Joe Torre	2.25
131	Angels Team	2.25
132	Orlando Cepeda	3.50
133	Don McMahon	.70
134	Wes Parker	.85
135	Dave Morehead	.70
136	Woody Held	.70
137	Pat Corrales	1.00
138	Roger Repoz	1.00
139	Cubs Rookies (Byron Browne, Don Young)	.70
140	Jim Maloney	.70
141	Tom McCraw	.70
142	Don Dennis	.70

143	Jose Tartabull	.70
144	Don Schwall	.70
145	Bill Freehan	.90
146	George Altman	.70
147	Lum Harris	.70
148	Bob Johnson	.70
149	Dick Nen	.70
150	Rocky Colavito	2.50
151	Gary Wagner	.70
152	Frank Malzone	.80
153	Rico Carty	1.50
154	Chuck Hiller	.80
155	Marcelino Lopez	.70
156	DP Combo (Hal Lanier, Dick Schofield)	1.00
157	Rene Lachemann	.80
158	Jim Brewer	.70
159	Chico Ruiz	.70
160	Whitey Ford	20.00
161	Jerry Lumpe	.70
162	Lee Maye	.70
163	Tito Francona	.80
164	White Sox Rookies (Tommie Agee, Marv Staehle)	.90
165	Don Lock	.70
166	Chris Krug	.70
167	Boog Powell	2.50
168	Dan Osinski	.70
169	Duke Sims	.70
170	Cookie Rojas	.70
171	Nick Willhite	.70
172	Mets Team	3.00
173	Al Spangler	.70
174	Ron Taylor	.70
175	Bert Campaneris	1.50
176	Jim Davenport	.70
177	Hector Lopez	.90
178	Bob Tillman	.70
179	Cardinals Rookies (Dennis Aust, Bob Tolan)	.80
180	Vada Pinson	2.50
181	Al Worthington	.70
182	Jerry Lynch	.70

550 Willie McCovey

183	Checklist 177-264	2.50
184	Denis Menke	.75
185	Bob Buhl	.75
186	Ruben Amaro	.90
187	Chuck Dressen	.80
188	Al Luplow	.70
189	John Roseboro	.90
190	Jimmie Hall	.70
191	Darrell Sutherland	.70
192	Vic Power	.70
193	Dave McNally	1.00
194	Senators Team	2.25
195	Joe Morgan	40.00
197	Sonny Siebert	.80
198	*Mickey Stanley*	1.00
199	Chisox Clubbers (Floyd Robinson, Johnny Romano, Bill Skowron)	1.00
200	Ed Mathews	8.00
201	Jim Dickson	.70
202	Clay Dalrymple	.70
203	Jose Santiago	.70
204	Cubs Team	2.25
205	Tom Tresh	2.00
209	Tigers Rookies (Fritz Fisher, *John Hiller*)	1.35
210	Bill Mazeroski	2.25
212	Ed Kranepool	1.00
213	Fred Newman	1.00
214	Tommy Harper	.80
215	NL Batting Ldrs (Hank Aaron, Bob Clemente, Willie Mays)	8.00
216	AL Batting Ldrs (Vic Davalillo, Tony Oliva, Carl Yastrzemski)	4.00
217	NL HR Ldrs (Willie Mays, Willie McCovey, Billy Williams)	5.00
218	AL HR Ldrs (Norm Cash, Tony Conigliaro, Willie Horton)	2.50

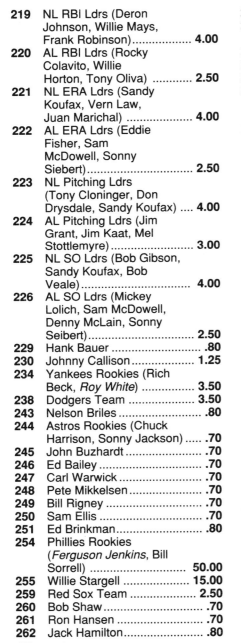

288 Dodgers Rookies

300 Bob Clemente

219	NL RBI Ldrs (Deron Johnson, Willie Mays, Frank Robinson)	4.00
220	AL RBI Ldrs (Rocky Colavito, Willie Horton, Tony Oliva)	2.50
221	NL ERA Ldrs (Sandy Koufax, Vern Law, Juan Marichal)	4.00
222	AL ERA Ldrs (Eddie Fisher, Sam McDowell, Sonny Siebert)	2.50
223	NL Pitching Ldrs (Tony Cloninger, Don Drysdale, Sandy Koufax)	4.00
224	AL Pitching Ldrs (Jim Grant, Jim Kaat, Mel Stottlemyre)	3.00
225	NL SO Ldrs (Bob Gibson, Sandy Koufax, Bob Veale)	4.00
226	AL SO Ldrs (Mickey Lolich, Sam McDowell, Denny McLain, Sonny Siebert)	2.50
229	Hank Bauer	.80
230	Johnny Callison	1.25
234	Yankees Rookies (Rich Beck, *Roy White*)	3.50
238	Dodgers Team	3.50
243	Nelson Briles	.80
244	Astros Rookies (Chuck Harrison, Sonny Jackson)	.70
245	John Buzhardt	.70
246	Ed Bailey	.70
247	Carl Warwick	.70
248	Pete Mikkelsen	.70
249	Bill Rigney	.70
250	Sam Ellis	.70
251	Ed Brinkman	.80
254	Phillies Rookies (*Ferguson Jenkins*, Bill Sorrell)	50.00
255	Willie Stargell	15.00
259	Red Sox Team	2.50
260	Bob Shaw	.70
261	Ron Hansen	.70
262	Jack Hamilton	.80

263	Tom Egan	.70
264	Twins Rookies (Andy Kosco, Ted Uhlaender)	.70
265	Stu Miller	.70
270	Claude Osteen	.80
271	Hal Lanier	1.00
273	Astro Aces (Bob Aspromonte, Rusty Staub)	1.50
275	Tim McCarver	2.50
276	Jim Bouton	2.50
277	George Thomas	.70
279	Checklist 265-352	4.00
280	Bobby Knoop	.70
281	Bruce Howard	.70
282	Johnny Lewis	.80
283	Jim Perry	1.00
284	Bobby Wine	.80
285	*Luis Tiant	2.50
286	Gary Geiger	.70
287	Jack Aker	.70
288	*Dodgers Rookies (*Bill Singer, Don Sutton*)	125.00
290	Ron Santo	2.00
293	Mike Shannon	.80
295	Jim Hart	.80
296	Johnny Keane	1.25
298	Rico Petrocelli	1.25
299	Lou Burdette	2.00
300	Bob Clemente	55.00

303	Indians Team	2.25
305	Camilo Pascual	.90
307	Clay Carroll	.80
310	Frank Robinson	25.00
315	Norm Cash	2.00
318	Harry Walker	.80
320	Bob Gibson	15.00
326	Braves Team	2.25
328	Jerry Grote	.90
330	Ron Fairly	.90
333	Senators Rookies (*Joe Coleman*, Jim French)	.90
338	Dal Maxvill	.80
339	Del Crandall	1.00
341	Wes Westrum	.90
344	Steve Blass	.80
345	Bob Allison	1.00
348	Orioles Team	3.75
350	Mel Stottlemyre	3.00
354	Smoky Burgess	1.00
355	Wade Blasingame	.70
356	Red Sox Rookies (Owen Johnson, Ken Sanders)	.70

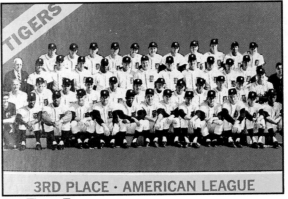

583 Tigers Team

357	Gerry Arrigo	.70
358	Charlie Smith	.70
359	Johnny Briggs	.70
360	Ron Hunt	.90
361	Tom Satriano	.70
362	Gates Brown	.70
363	Checklist 353-429	3.00
364	Nate Oliver	.70
365	Roger Maris	75.00
366	Wayne Causey	.70
367	Mel Nelson	.70
368	Charlie Lau	.90
369	Jim King	.70
370	Chico Cardenas	.70
371	Lee Stange	.70
372	*Harvey Kuenn	1.50
373	Giants Rookies (Dick Estelle, Jack Hiatt)	.70
374	Bob Locker	.70
375	Donn Clendenon	.80
376	Paul Schaal	.70
377	Turk Farrell	.70
378	Dick Tracewski	.70
379	Cardinals Team	2.25
380	Tony Conigliaro	2.25
381	Hank Fischer	.70
382	Phil Roof	.70
383	Jackie Brandt	.70
384	Al Downing	1.50
385	Ken Boyer	2.50
386	Gil Hodges	5.00
387	Howie Reed	.70
388	Don Mincher	.80
389	Jim O'Toole	.70
390	Brooks Robinson	15.00
391	Chuck Hinton	.70
392	Cubs Rookies (*Bill Hands, Randy Hundley*)	.90
393	George Brunet	.70
394	Ron Brand	.70
395	Len Gabrielson	.70
396	Jerry Stephenson	.70
397	*Bill White	1.00
398	Danny Cater	.70

580 Billy Williams

530 Robin Roberts

399	Ray Washburn	.70
400	Zoilo Versalles	.80
401	Ken McMullen	.70
402	Jim Hickman	.90
403	Fred Talbot	.70
404	Pirates Team	2.25
405	*Elston Howard	4.00
406	Joe Jay	.70
407	John Kennedy	.70
408	Lee Thomas	.70
409	Billy Hoeft	.70
410	Al Kaline	18.00
411	Gene Mauch	.90
412	Sam Bowens	.70
413	John Romano	.70
414	Dan Coombs	.70
415	Max Alvis	.70
416	Phil Ortega	.70
417	Angels Rookies (Jim McGlothlin, Ed Sukla)	.70
418	Phil Gagliano	.70
419	Mike Ryan	.70
420	Juan Marichal	8.00
421	Roy McMillan	.70
422	Ed Charles	.70
423	Ernie Broglio	.70
424	Reds Rookies (*Lee May*, Darrell Osteen)	2.25
425	Bob Veale	.80
426	White Sox Team	2.25
427	John Miller	.70
428	Sandy Alomar	.70
429	Bill Monbouquette	.70
430	Don Drysdale	12.00
431	Walt Bond	.70
432	Bob Heffner	.70
433	Alvin Dark	.80
434	Willie Kirkland	.70
435	Jim Bunning	6.00
436	Julian Javier	.75
437	Al Stanek	.70
438	Willie Smith	.70
439	Pedro Ramos	.75

440	Deron Johnson	.75
441	Tommie Sisk	.70
442	Orioles Rookies (Ed Barnowski, Eddie Watt)	.75
443	Bill Wakefield	.70
444	Checklist 430-506	5.00
445	*Jim Kaat	4.00
446	Mack Jones	.70
447	Dick Ellsworth (photo is Ken Hubbs)	4.50
448	Eddie Stanky	4.75
449	Joe Moeller	4.50
450	Tony Oliva	7.00
451	Barry Latman	4.50
452	Joe Azcue	4.50
453	Ron Kline	4.50
454	Jerry Buchek	4.50
455	Mickey Lolich	6.00
456	Red Sox Rookies (Darrell Brandon, Joe Foy)	4.50
457	Joe Gibbon	4.50
458	Manny Jiminez (Jimenez)	4.50
459	Bill McCool	4.50
460	Curt Blefary	4.50
461	Roy Face	5.50
462	Bob Rodgers	4.50
463	Phillies Team	6.00
464	Larry Bearnarth	4.50
465	Don Buford	4.50
466	Ken Johnson	4.50
467	Vic Roznovsky	4.50
468	Johnny Podres	6.00
469	Yankees Rookies (*Bobby Murcer*, Dooley Womack)	10.00
470	Sam McDowell	5.00
471	Bob Skinner	4.50
472	Terry Fox	4.50
473	Rich Rollins	4.50
474	Dick Schofield	4.50
475	Dick Radatz	4.75
476	Bobby Bragan	4.75
477	Steve Barber	4.50

540 Denny McLain

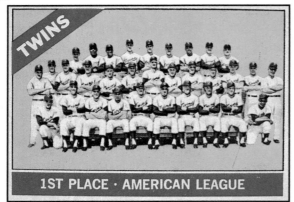

526 Twins Team

478	Tony Gonzalez	4.50	527	Julio Navarro	16.00
479	Jim Hannan	4.50	528	Jesse Gonder	21.00
480	Dick Stuart	4.75	529	White Sox Rookies (*Lee Elia*, Dennis Higgins, Bill Voss)	19.00
481	Bob Lee	4.50	530	Robin Roberts	31.00
482	Cubs Rookies (John Boccabella, Dave Dowling)	4.50	531	Joe Cunningham	17.00
483	Joe Nuxhall	4.75	532	Aurelio Monteagudo	16.00
484	Wes Covington	4.50	533	Jerry Adair	16.00
485	Bob Bailey	4.50	534	Mets Rookies (Dave Eilers, Rob Gardner)	19.00
486	Tommy John	16.00	535	Willie Davis	21.00
487	Al Ferrara	4.50	536	Dick Egan	16.00
488	George Banks	4.50	537	Herman Franks	16.00
489	Curt Simmons	4.75	538	Bob Allen	16.00
490	Bobby Richardson	13.00	539	Astros Rookies (Bill Heath, Carroll Sembera)	16.00
491	Dennis Bennett	4.50	540	Denny McLain	36.00
492	Athletics Team	6.00	541	Gene Oliver	16.00
493	Johnny Klippstein	4.50	542	George Smith	16.00
494	Gordon Coleman	4.50	543	Roger Craig	21.00
495	Dick McAuliffe	4.75	544	Cardinals Rookies (Joe Hoerner, George Kernek, Jimmy Williams)	21.00
496	Lindy McDaniel	4.50	545	Dick Green	21.00
497	Chris Cannizzaro	4.50	546	Dwight Siebler	16.00
498	Pirates Rookies (*Woody Fryman, Luke Walker*)	5.00	547	*Horace Clarke*	21.00
499	Wally Bunker	4.50	548	Gary Kroll	21.00
500	Hank Aaron	80.00	549	Senators Rookies (Al Closter, Casey Cox)	16.00
503	Steve Hamilton	4.50	550	Willie McCovey	95.00
504	Grady Hatton	4.50	551	Bob Purkey	21.00
505	Jose Cardenal	4.50	552	Birdie Tebbetts	16.00
506	Bo Belinsky	4.50	553	Major League Rookies (Pat Garrett, Jackie Warner)	16.00
508	*Steve Hargan*	4.75	554	Jim Northrup	19.00
509	Jake Wood	4.50	555	Ron Perranoski	19.00
510	Hoyt Wilhelm	15.00	556	Mel Queen	20.00
511	Giants Rookies (Bob Barton, *Tito Fuentes*)	4.75	557	Felix Mantilla	16.00
512	Dick Stigman	4.50	558	Red Sox Rookies (Guido Grilli, Pete Magrini, *George Scott*)	19.00
513	Camilo Carreon	4.50	559	Roberto Pena	16.00
514	Hal Woodeshick	4.50	560	Joel Horlen	16.00
515	Frank Howard	6.00	561	Choo Choo Coleman	21.00
517	Checklist 507-598	10.00	562	Russ Snyder	16.00
518	Braves Rookies (Herb Hippauf, Arnie Umbach)	4.50	563	Twins Rookies (Pete Cimino, Cesar Tovar)	19.00
520	Jim Wynn	5.50			
523	Bob Sadowski	16.00			
524	Giants Rookies (Ollie Brown, Don Mason)	21.00			
525	Gary Bell	16.00			
526	Twins Team	51.00			

564	Bob Chance	16.00
565	Jimmy Piersall	31.00
566	Mike Cuellar	19.00
567	Dick Howser	21.00
568	Athletics Rookies (Paul Lindblad, Ron Stone)	16.00
569	Orlando McFarlane	16.00
570	Art Mahaffey	20.00
571	Dave Roberts	16.00
572	Bob Priddy	16.00
573	Derrell Griffith	16.00
574	Mets Rookies (Bill Hepler, Bill Murphy)	19.00
575	Earl Wilson	16.00
576	Dave Nicholson	21.00
577	Jack Lamabe	16.00
578	Chi Chi Olivo	16.00
579	Orioles Rookies (Frank Bertaina, Gene Brabender, Dave Johnson)	21.00
580	Billy Williams	56.00
581	Tony Martinez	16.00
582	Garry Roggenburk	16.00
583	Tigers Team	100.00
584	Yankees Rookies (Frank Fernandez, *Fritz Peterson*)	19.00
585	Tony Taylor	16.00
586	Claude Raymond	16.00
587	Dick Bertell	16.00
588	Athletics Rookies (Chuck Dobson, Ken Suarez)	16.00
589	Lou Klimchock	16.00
590	Bill Skowron	31.00
591	NL Rookies (*Grant Jackson*, Bart Shirley)	21.00
592	Andre Rodgers	16.00
593	Doug Camilli	21.00
594	Chico Salmon	16.00
595	Larry Jackson	16.00
596	Astros Rookies (*Nate Colbert*, Greg Sims)	19.00
597	John Sullivan	16.00
598	Gaylord Perry	275.00

36 Jim Hunter

1967 TOPPS

Scarcity and attractiveness make the 1967 Topps set one of the hottest collectibles of the 1960s. The 609 cards in the set made it the largest produced by Topps as of the time of issue. The standard-sized cards feature large color photos with facsimile autographs (except for Milt Pappas, number 254, which lacks an autograph). Card backs are the first ever from Topps to utilize vertical backs. The set is highlighted by a 12-card subset of 1966 league leaders and a five-card series honoring the previous World Series. An ultrarare final series, from 534 through 609, makes completing the set a real challenge, especially since four key cards in the series (Tommy John, Brooks Robinson, and rookie cards of Tom Seaver and Rod Carew) together are valued at nearly $2000.

150 Mickey Mantle

		NR MT
Complete set		$4050.00
Commons (1-110)		.60
Commons (111-370)		.70
Commons (371-457)		.80
Commons (458-533)		3.00
Commons (534-609)		6.00

1	The Champs (Hank Bauer, Brooks Robinson, Frank Robinson)	$8.00
2	Jack Hamilton	.80
3	Duke Sims	.60
4	Hal Lanier	.80
5	Whitey Ford	12.00
6	Dick Simpson	.60
10	Matty Alou	.80
12	Dodgers Rookies (Jimmy Campanis, Bill Singer)	.70
15	Earl Battey	.70
20	*Orlando Cepeda	4.00
25	Elston Howard	3.00
26	Bob Priddy (with trade statement)	.60
26	Bob Priddy (w/o trade statement)	8.00
30	Al Kaline	15.00
33	Athletics Rookies (*Sal Bando,* Randy Schwartz)	1.75
35	Rico Carty	1.00
37	Rick Wise	.70
39	Curt Simmons	.80
42	Mets Team	3.00
44	Joe Nuxhall	.80
45	Roger Maris	45.00
48	Bill Freehan	.80
49	Roy Face	1.25
50	Tony Oliva	2.50
51	Astros Rookies (Dave Adlesh, Wes Bales)	.60
52	Dennis Higgins	.60
55	Don Drysdale	12.00
57	*Pat Jarvis*	.70
59	Ralph Terry	.80
60	Luis Aparicio	5.00
62	Checklist 1-109 (Frank Robinson)	3.00

600 Brooks Robinson

63	Cards' Clubbers (Lou Brock, Curt Flood)	5.00
65	Tom Haller	.70
66	Manny Mota	.80
68	Bob Buhl	.70
70	Ron Santo	1.75
71	Camilo Pascual	.70
72	Tigers Rookies (George Korince, John Matchick)	.70
73	Rusty Staub	3.00
75	George Scott	1.00
78	Pat Corrales	1.00
80	Jim Maloney	.70
81	Eddie Stanky	.70
85	Johnny Callison	.80
86	Mike McCormick (with trade statement)	.70
86	Mike McCormick (w/o trade statement)	9.00
88	Mickey Lolich	2.25
89	*Felix Millan*	.85
91	Johnny Lewis	.70
92	Ray Washburn	.65
93	Yankees Rookies (*Stan Bahnsen,* Bobby Murcer)	2.50

94	Ron Fairly	.80
95	Sonny Siebert	.70
97	Mike Cuellar	.80
98	Rich Rollins	.60
99	Lee Stange	.60
100	Frank Robinson	10.00
102	Phillies Team	6.00
103	Checklist 110-196 (Mickey Mantle)	8.00
105	Ken Boyer	2.00
106	Randy Hundley	.70
109	Tribe Thumpers (Rocky Colavito, Leon Wagner)	1.50
110	Jack Aker	.70
116	Herman Franks	.70
123	Pirates Rookies (Jim Price, Luke Walker)	.70
125	Moe Drabowsky	.70
131	Yankees Team	4.00
134	Gates Brown	.70
140	Willie Stargell	20.00
143	Sox Sockers (Don Buford, Pete Ward)	.80
146	Steve Carlton	75.00
150	Mickey Mantle	200.00
151	World Series Game 1 (Moe Mows Down 11)	2.00
152	World Series Game 2 (Palmer Blanks Dodgers)	3.50
153	World Series Game 3 (Blair's Homer Defeats L.A.)	2.00
154	World Series Game 4 (Orioles Win 4th Straight)	2.00
155	World Series Summary (The Winners Celebrate)	2.00
160	Willie Davis	1.25
161	Dick Williams	1.25
165	Cleon Jones	.80
166	Ed Mathews	8.00
167	Senators Rookies (Joe Coleman, Tim Cullen)	.70
169	Horace Clarke	1.00

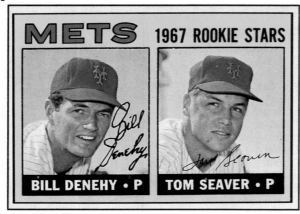

581 Mets Rookies

170	Dick McAuliffe	.80
173	Cardinals Team	3.00
174	Dick Radatz	.75
177	Tito Fuentes	.70
179	Braves Rookies (Cecil Upshaw, Chas. Vaughn)	.70
180	Curt Blefary	.70
185	*Ken Holtzman*	2.75
186	Mets Maulers (Ed Kranepool, Ron Swoboda)	1.50
188	Ken Harrelson	1.50
191	Checklist 197-283 (Willie Mays) (214 is Dick Kelley)	5.00
191	Checklist 197-283 (Willie Mays) (214 is Tom Kelley)	4.00
194	Bob Allison	.90
197	Ron Perranoski	.80
198	Chuck Hiller	.80
200	Willie Mays	55.00
201	Hal Reniff	.90
204	Orioles Rookies (Tom Phoebus, *Mike Epstein*)	.90
205	Dick Groat	1.50
210	Bob Gibson	10.00
211	Twins Team	2.00
213	*Jay Johnstone*	1.75
215	Ernie Banks	15.00
216	*Bengal Belters (Norm Cash, Al Kaline)	3.50
217	Rob Gardner	.80
218	Wes Parker	.85
219	Clay Carroll	.80
220	Jim Hart	.80
221	Woody Fryman	.80
222	Reds Rookies (Lee May, Darrell Osteen)	1.00
223	Mike Ryan	.70
225	Mel Stottlemyre	2.25
226	Julian Javier	.80
227	Paul Lindblad	.70
228	Gil Hodges	5.00
230	Boog Powell	2.50
232	Don Buford	.80
233	AL ERA Ldrs (Steve Hargan, Joel Horlen, Gary Peters)	2.00

234	NL ERA Ldrs (Mike Cuellar, Sandy Koufax, Juan Marichal)	4.00
235	AL Pitching Ldrs (Jim Kaat, Denny McLain, Earl Wilson)	2.50
236	NL Pitching Ldrs (Bob Gibson, Sandy Koufax, Juan Marichal, Gaylord Perry)	5.00
237	AL SO Ldrs (Jim Kaat, Sam McDowell, Earl Wilson)	2.50
238	NL SO Ldrs (Jim Bunning, Sandy Koufax, Bob Veale)	4.00
239	AL Batting Ldrs (Al Kaline, Tony Oliva, Frank Robinson)	4.00
240	NL Batting Ldrs (Felipe Alou, Matty Alou, Rico Carty)	2.00
241	AL RBI Ldrs (Harmon Killebrew, Boog Powell, Frank Robinson)	3.50
242	NL RBI Ldrs (Hank Aaron, Richie Allen, Bob Clemente)	5.00
243	AL HR Ldrs (Harmon Killebrew, Boog Powell, Frank Robinson)	3.50
244	NL HR Ldrs (Hank Aaron, Richie Allen, Willie Mays)	5.00
245	*Curt Flood	1.50
246	Jim Perry	1.00
247	Jerry Lumpe	.80
248	Gene Mauch	.80
250	Hank Aaron	75.00
251	Woody Held	.70
253	Indians Rookies (Bill Davis, Gus Gil)	.70
254	Milt Pappas	.80
255	Frank Howard	2.50
257	Charley Smith	.80
260	Jim Lefevbre	1.00
262	Athletics Team	2.00
264	Ron Swoboda	.80
265	Lou Burdette	1.50

266	Pitt Power (Donn Clendenon, Willie Stargell)	3.50
270	Zoilo Versalles	.80
272	Cubs Rookies (Bill Connors, Dave Dowling)	.75
278	Checklist 284-370 (Jim Kaat)	3.00
280	Tony Conigliaro	2.00
282	Johnny Odom	.80
283	Gene Alley	.80
284	Johnny Podres	2.00
285	Lou Brock	15.00
287	Mets Rookies (Greg Goossen, Bart Shirley)	.80
289	Tom Tresh	1.75
290	*Bill White	1.00
293	Ed Kirkpatrick	.70
294	Walt Alston	4.00
295	Sam McDowell	1.00
296	Glenn Beckert	.80
299	Norm Siebern	.80
300	*Jim Kaat	4.50
302	Orioles Team	2.00
306	*Bud Harrelson*	1.75
308	Al Downing	1.25
309	Hurlers Beware (Richie Allen, Johnny Callison)	2.00
310	Gary Peters	.80
311	Ed Brinkman	.80
312	Don Mincher	.80
314	Red Sox Rookies (*Mike Andrews, Reggie Smith*)	3.00
315	*Billy Williams	8.00
316	Jack Kralick	.70
326	Bob Uecker	20.00
327	Angels Team	2.00
328	Clete Boyer	.90
329	Charlie Lau	.80
330	Claude Osteen	.80
332	Jesus Alou	.75
334	*Twin Terrors (Bob Allison, Harmon Killebrew)	3.50
335	Bob Veale	.80

609 Tommy John

336	Joe Azcue	.70
337	Joe Morgan	15.00
338	Bob Locker	.70
339	Chico Ruiz	.70
340	Joe Pepitone	2.00
341	Giants Rookies (Dick Dietz, Billy Sorrell)	.80
342	Hank Fischer	.70
343	Tom Satriano	.70
344	Ossie Chavarria	.70
345	Stu Miller	.70
346	Jim Hickman	.80
347	Grady Hatton	.70
348	Tug McGraw	2.25
350	Joe Torre	2.00
351	Vern Law	1.25
354	Cubs Team	2.00
355	Carl Yastrzemski	90.00
356	Larry Jaster	.70
357	Bill Skowron	1.50
358	Ruben Amaro	1.00
359	Dick Ellsworth	.70
360	Leon Wagner	.80
361	Checklist 371-457 (Bob Clemente)	4.50
362	Darold Knowles	.70
363	Dave Johnson	2.00
364	Claude Raymond	.70
365	John Roseboro	.80
366	Andy Kosco	.70
367	Angels Rookies (Bill Kelso, Don Wallace)	.70
368	Jack Hiatt	.70
369	*Jim Hunter	8.00
370	Tommy Davis	1.50
371	Jim Lonborg	1.50
372	Mike de la Hoz	.80
373	White Sox Rookies (Duane Josephson, Fred Klages)	.80
374	Mel Queen	.80
375	Jake Gibbs	.90
376	Don Lock	.80
377	Luis Tiant	2.25

569 AL Rookies

475 Jim Palmer

378	Tigers Team	3.00
379	Jerry May	.80
380	Dean Chance	.90
381	Dick Schofield	.80
382	Dave McNally	1.00
383	Ken Henderson	.80
384	Cardinals Rookies (Jim Cosman, Dick Hughes)	.80
385	Jim Fregosi	1.25
386	Dick Selma	.85
387	Cap Peterson	.80
388	Arnold Earley	.80
389	Al Dark	.90
390	Jim Wynn	1.00
391	Wilbur Wood	.90
392	Tommy Harper	.90
393	Jim Bouton	2.25
394	Jake Wood	.80
395	Chris Short	.90
396	Atlanta Aces (Tony Cloninger, Denis Menke)	1.00
397	Willie Smith	.80
398	Jeff Torborg	.90
399	Al Worthington	.80
400	Bob Clemente	55.00
401	Jim Coates	.80
402	Phillies Rookies (Grant Jackson, Billy Wilson)	.80
403	Dick Nen	.80
404	Nelson Briles	.90
405	Russ Snyder	.80
406	Lee Elia	.90
407	Reds Team	2.50
408	Jim Northrup	.90
409	Ray Sadecki	.80
410	Lou Johnson	.80
411	Dick Howser	1.50
412	*Astros Rookies (Norm Miller, Doug Rader)	1.00
413	Jerry Grote	.90
417	Bob Bruce	.80
418	Sam Mele	.80
419	Don Kessinger	.90
420	Denny McLain	3.00
421	Dal Maxvill	.90
422	Hoyt Wilhelm	8.00
423	Fence Busters (Willie Mays, Willie McCovey)	12.00
424	Pedro Gonzalez	.80

425	Pete Mikkelsen	.80
426	Lou Clinton	.80
427	Ruben Gomez	.80
428	Dodgers Rookies (Tom Hutton, Gene Michael)	.95
429	Gary Roggenburk	.80
430	Pete Rose	75.00
431	Ted Uhlaender	.80
432	Jimmie Hall	.80
433	Al Luplow	.80
434	Eddie Fisher	.85
435	Mack Jones	.80
436	Pete Ward	.80
437	Senators Team	2.25
441	Jim Davenport	.80
442	Yankees Rookies (Bill Robinson, Joe Verbanic)	1.25
443	Tito Francona	.90
444	George Smith	.90
445	*Don Sutton	15.00
447	Bo Belinsky	1.00
448	Harry Walker	.90
450	Richie Allen	3.00
452	Ed Kranepool	1.00
453	Aurelio Monteagudo	.80
454	Checklist 458-533 (Juan Marichal)	4.50
455	Tommie Agee	.75
456	*Phil Niekro	7.00
458	Lee Thomas	3.00
459	Senators Rookies (Dick Bosman, Pete Craig)	4.00
460	Harmon Killebrew	60.00
461	Bob Miller	3.00
462	Bob Barton	3.00
463	Tribe Hill Aces (Sam McDowell, Sonny Siebert)	4.00
464	Dan Coombs	3.00
465	Willie Horton	4.00
466	Bobby Wine	3.00
467	Jim O'Toole	3.00
468	Ralph Houk	4.50
469	Len Gabrielson	3.00
470	Bob Shaw	3.00
471	Rene Lachemann	3.00
472	Pirates Rookies (John Gelnar, George Spriggs)	3.00
473	Jose Santiago	3.00
474	Bob Tolan	3.75

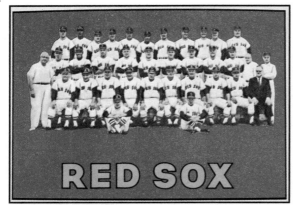

604 Red Sox Team

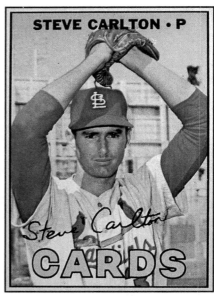

146 Steve Carlton

475	Jim Palmer	80.00
476	Tony Perez	70.00
477	Braves Team	4.75
478	Bob Humphreys	3.00
479	Gary Bell	3.00
480	Willie McCovey	15.00
481	Leo Durocher	5.00
482	Bill Monbouquette	3.25
483	Jim Landis	3.00
484	Jerry Adair	3.00
485	Tim McCarver	4.50
486	Twins Rookies (Rich Reese, Bill Whitby)	3.00
487	Tom Reynolds	3.00
488	Gerry Arrigo	3.00
489	Doug Clemens	3.00
490	Tony Cloninger	3.75
491	Sam Bowens	3.00
492	Pirates Team	4.75
493	Phil Ortega	3.00
494	Bill Rigney	3.00
495	Fritz Peterson	3.75
496	Orlando McFarlane	3.00
497	Ron Campbell	3.00
498	Larry Dierker	3.75
499	Indians Rookies (George Culver, Jose Vidal)	3.00
500	Juan Marichal	15.00
501	Jerry Zimmerman	3.00
502	Derrell Griffith	3.00
503	Dodgers Team	5.00
504	Orlando Martinez	3.00
505	Tommy Helms	3.00
506	Smoky Burgess	3.00
507	Orioles Rookies (Ed Barnowski, Larry Haney)	3.00
508	Dick Hall	3.00
509	Jim King	3.00
510	Bill Mazeroski	4.50
511	Don Wert	3.00
512	Red Schoendienst	6.00
513	Marcelino Lopez	3.00
514	John Werhas	3.00
515	Bert Campaneris	4.00
516	Giants Team	5.00
517	Fred Talbot	3.00
518	Denis Menke	3.00
519	Ted Davidson	3.00
520	Max Alvis	3.00

521	Bird Bombers (Curt Blefary, Boog Powell)	4.50
522	John Stephenson	3.00
523	Jim Merritt	3.00
524	Felix Mantilla	3.00
525	Ron Hunt	3.00
526	Tigers Rookies (Pat Dobson, George Korince)	3.75
527	Dennis Ribant	3.00
528	Rico Petrocelli	3.75
529	Gary Wagner	3.00
530	Felipe Alou	3.00
531	Checklist 534-609 (Brooks Robinson)	6.00
532	Jim Hicks	3.00
533	Jack Fisher	3.00
534	Hank Bauer	6.50
535	Donn Clendenon	6.50
536	Cubs Rookies (Joe Niekro, Paul Popovich)	30.00
537	Chuck Estrada	6.00
538	J.C. Martin	6.00
539	Dick Egan	6.00
540	Norm Cash	25.00
541	Joe Gibbon	6.00
542	Athletics Rookies (Rick Monday, Tony Pierce)	13.00
543	Dan Schneider	6.00
544	Indians Team	10.00
545	Jim Grant	6.00
546	Woody Woodward	6.00
547	Red Sox Rookies (Russ Gibson, Bill Rohr)	6.00
548	Tony Gonzalez	6.00
549	Jack Sanford	8.00
550	Vada Pinson	7.00
551	Doug Camili	6.00
552	Ted Savage	6.00
553	Yankees Rookies (Mike Hegan, Thad Tillotson)	16.00
554	Andre Rodgers	6.00
555	Don Cardwell	6.00
556	Al Weis	6.00
557	Al Ferrara	8.00
558	Orioles Rookies (Mark Belanger, Bill Dillman)	30.00
559	Dick Tracewski	6.00

560	Jim Bunning	42.00
561	Sandy Alomar	6.00
562	Steve Blass	7.00
563	Joe Adcock	19.00
564	Astros Rookies (Alonzo Harris, Aaron Pointer)	6.00
565	Lew Krausse	6.00
566	Gary Geiger	6.00
567	Steve Hamilton	7.00
568	John Sullivan	6.00
569	AL Rookies (Hank Allen, Rod Carew)	380.00
570	Maury Wills	76.00
571	Larry Sherry	7.00
572	Don Demeter	7.00
573	White Sox Team	16.00
574	Jerry Buchek	7.00
575	Dave Boswell	7.00

355 Carl Yastrzemski

576	NL Rookies (Norm Gigon, Ramon Hernandez)	19.00
577	Bill Short	6.00
578	John Boccabella	6.00
579	Bill Henry	6.00
580	Rocky Colavito	36.00
581	Mets Rookies (Bill Denehy, *Tom Seaver*)	1275.00
582	Jim Owens	6.00
583	Ray Barker	6.00
584	Jim Piersall	19.00
585	Wally Bunker	6.00
586	Manny Jimenez	6.00
587	NL Rookies (Don Shaw, Gary Sutherland)	16.00
588	Johnny Klippstein	6.00
589	Dave Ricketts	6.00
590	Pete Richert	6.00
591	Ty Cline	6.00

592	NL Rookies (Jim Shellenback, Ron Willis)	7.00
595	Cookie Rojas	6.00
596	Galen Cisco	6.00
597	Ted Abernathy	6.00
598	White Sox Rookies (Ed Stroud, Walt Williams)	7.50
599	Bob Duliba	6.00
600	Brooks Robinson	200.00
601	Bill Bryan	6.00
602	Juan Pizarro	6.00
603	Athletics Rookies (Tim Talton, Ramon Webster)	6.00
604	Red Sox Team	60.00
605	Mike Shannon	7.00
606	Ron Taylor	6.00
607	Mickey Stanley	7.00
608	Cubs Rookies (Rich Nye, John Upham)	7.00
609	Tommy John	100.00

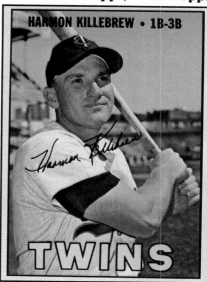

460 Harmon Killebrew

1968 TOPPS

Collectors think of the 1968 Topps issue of 598 cards as the "burlap sack" issue. That's because all the color photos appear on backgrounds of brown mesh. Card backs are still in a vertical format, but the cartoon now appears at the bottom, with year-by-year statistics in the middle. An All-Star subseries returned in 1968 that featured 20 players chosen by *The Sporting News*. Topps continued the practice of placing a small mug shot of a star like Orlando Cepeda or Juan Marichal on the usually bland checklists. Rookie cards of Nolan Ryan and Johnny Bench are by far the most valuable in the set, while Eddie Mathews and Roger Maris made the last card appearances of their careers in 1968.

45 Tom Seaver

		NR MT
Complete set		**$2700.00**
Commons (1-533)		**.60**
Commons (534-598)		**1.00**

1	NL Batting Ldrs (Matty Alou, Bob Clemente, Tony Gonzalez)	$8.00
2	AL Batting Ldrs (Al Kaline, Frank Robinson, Carl Yastrzemski)	4.00
3	NL RBI Ldrs (Hank Aaron, Orlando Cepeda, Bob Clemente)	4.00
4	AL RBI Ldrs (Harmon Killebrew, Frank Robinson, Carl Yastrzemski)	4.00
5	NL HR Ldrs (Hank Aaron, Willie McCovey, Ron Santo, Jim Wynn)	4.00
6	AL HR Ldrs (Frank Howard, Harmon Killebrew, Carl Yastrzemski)	4.00

7	NL ERA Ldrs (Jim Bunning, Phil Niekro, Chris Short)	2.50
8	AL ERA Ldrs (Joe Horlen, Gary Peters, Sonny Siebert)	1.50
9	NL Pitching Ldrs (Jim Bunning, Ferguson Jenkins, Mike McCormick, Claude Osteen)	2.50
10	AL Pitching Ldrs (Dean Chance, Jim Lonborg, Earl Wilson) ("Lonberg" on back)	3.50
10	AL Pitching Ldrs (Dean Chance, Jim Lonborg, Earl Wilson) ("Lonborg" on back)	1.50
11	NL SO Ldrs (Jim Bunning, Ferguson Jenkins, Gaylord Perry)	3.00
12	AL SO Ldrs (Dean Chance, Jim Lonborg, Sam McDowell)	1.50
13	Chuck Hartenstein	.60
14	Jerry McNertney	.60

15	Ron Hunt	.70
16	*Indians Rookies (Lou Piniella, Richie Scheinblum)	2.50
17	Dick Hall	.60
18	Mike Hershberger	.60
19	Juan Pizarro	.60
20	Brooks Robinson	13.00
21	Ron Davis	.60
22	Pat Dobson	.70
23	Chico Cardenas	.60
24	Bobby Locke	.60

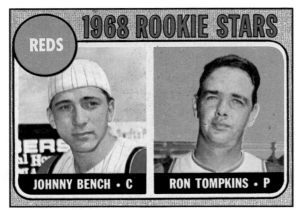

247 Reds Rookies

280 Mickey Mantle

25	Julian Javier	.70
26	Darrell Brandon	.60
27	Gil Hodges	6.00
28	Ted Uhlaender	.60
29	Joe Verbanic	.80
30	Joe Torre	2.00
31	Ed Stroud	.60
32	Joe Gibbon	.60
33	Pete Ward	.60
34	Al Ferrera	.60
35	Steve Hargan	.60
36	Pirates Rookies (Bob Moose, Bob Robertson)	1.00
37	Billy Williams	8.00
38	Tony Pierce	.60
39	Cookie Rojas	.60
40	Denny McLain	4.00
41	Julio Gotay	.60
42	Larry Haney	.60
43	Gary Bell	.60
44	Frank Kostro	.60
45	Tom Seaver	150.00
46	Dave Ricketts	.60
47	Ralph Houk	2.00
48	Ted Davidson	.60
49	Ed Brinkman (yellow team letters)	60.00
49	Ed Brinkman (white team letters)	.70
50	Willie Mays	40.00
51	Bob Locker	.60
52	Hawk Taylor	.60
53	Gene Alley	.65
54	Stan Williams	.60
55	Felipe Alou	1.00
56	Orioles Rookies (Dave Leonhard, Dave May)	.60
57	Dan Schneider	.60
58	Ed Mathews	7.00
59	Don Lock	.60
60	Ken Holtzman	1.00
61	Reggie Smith	1.50
62	Chuck Dobson	.60
63	Dick Henworthy	.60
64	Jim Merritt	.60
65	John Roseboro	.75
66	Casey Cox (yellow team letters)	60.00

66	Casey Cox (white team letters)	.60
67	Checklist 1-109 (Jim Kaat)	3.00
68	Ron Willis	.60
69	Tom Tresh	1.75
70	Bob Veale	.60
71	Vern Fuller	.60
72	Tommy John	5.00
73	Jim Hart	.90
74	Milt Pappas	.75
75	Don Mincher	.80
76	Braves Rookies (Jim Britton, *Ron Reed*)	1.00
77	*Don Wilson*	.90
78	Jim Northrup	.70
79	Ted Kubiak	.60
80	Rod Carew	75.00
81	Larry Jackson	.60
82	Sam Bowens	.60
84	Bob Tolan	.70
85	Gaylord Perry	6.00
86	Willie Stargell	8.00
87	Dick Williams	1.00
88	Phil Regan	.60
89	Jake Gibbs	.80
90	Vada Pinson	2.00
91	Jim Ollom	.60
92	Ed Kranepool	.80

93	Tony Cloninger	.80
94	Lee Maye	.60
96	Senators Rookies (Frank Coggins, Dick Nold)	.60
97	Tom Phoebus	.60
98	Gary Sutherland	.60
99	Rocky Colavito	2.25
100	Bob Gibson	10.00
101	Glenn Beckert	.90
102	Jose Cardenal	6.00
103	Don Sutton	6.00
104	Dick Dietz	.60
105	Al Downing	1.00
107	Checklist 110-196 (Juan Marichal)	3.50
109	Bert Campaneris	1.00
110	Hank Aaron	45.00
112	Woody Fryman	.70
113	Tigers Rookies (Tom Matchick, Daryl Patterson)	.60
114	Ron Swoboda	.90
115	Sam McDowell	.90
116	Ken McMullen	.60
117	Larry Jaster	.60

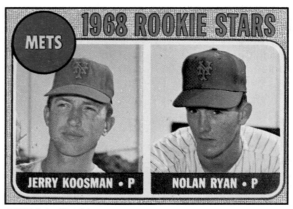

177 Mets Rookies

118	Mark Belanger	1.00
119	Ted Savage	.60
120	Mel Stottlemyre	2.00
121	Jimmie Hall	.60
122	Gene Mauch	.80
123	Jose Santiago	.60
124	Nate Oliver	.60
125	Joe Horlen	.65
126	Bobby Etheridge	.60
127	Paul Lindblad	.60
128	Astros Rookies (Tom Dukes, Alonzo Harris)	.60
129	Mickey Stanley	.65
130	Tony Perez	5.00
132	Bud Harrelson	1.00
133	Fred Whitfield	.60
134	Pat Jarvis	.60
135	Paul Blair	.60
136	Randy Hundley	.70
137	Twins Team	2.00
138	Ruben Amaro	.65
139	Chris Short	.80
140	Tony Conigliaro	2.00
141	Dal Maxvill	.75
142	White Sox Rookies (Buddy Bradford, Bill Voss)	.60
143	Pete Cimino	.60
144	Joe Morgan	10.00
145	Don Drysdale	8.00
146	Sal Bando	1.00
147	Frank Linzy	.60
148	Dave Bristol	.60
149	Bob Saverine	.60
150	Bob Clemente	45.00
151	World Series Game 1 (Brock Socks 4 Hits in Opener)	3.50
152	World Series Game 2 (Yaz Smashes 2 Homers)	5.00
153	World Series Game 3 (Briles Cools Off Boston)	2.00
154	World Series Game 4 (Gibson Hurls Shutout!)	3.50

80 Rod Carew

155	World Series Game 5 (Lonborg Wins Again!)	2.50
156	World Series Game 6 (Petrocelli Socks Two Homers)	2.50
157	World Series Game 7 (St. Louis Wins It!)	2.00
158	World Series Summary (The Cardinals Celebrate)	2.00
159	Don Kessinger	.90
160	Earl Wilson	.70
162	Cardinals Rookies (Hal Gilson, *Mike Torrez*)	1.00
163	Gene Brabender	.60
164	Ramon Webster	.60
165	*Tony Oliva	2.50
166	Claude Raymond	.60
167	Elston Howard	3.00
168	Dodgers Team	2.50
170	Jim Fregosi	1.00
175	Maury Wills	3.50
177	Mets Rookies (*Jerry Koosman, Nolan Ryan*)	1200.00
180	Curt Flood	1.50
190	*Bill White	1.00
192	Checklist 197-283 (Carl Yastrzemski)	5.00
195	Joe Pepitone	2.00
198	Roy Face	1.25
199	A's Rookies (Darrell Osteen, Roberto Rodriguez)	.60
200	Orlando Cepeda	4.00
201	Mike Marshall	1.75
205	Juan Marichal	8.00
208	Willie Davis	1.00
210	Gary Peters	.75
215	Jim Bunning	5.00
220	Harmon Killebrew	9.00
225	Richie Allen	2.25
228	Dodgers Rookies (Jack Billingham, Jim Fairey)	.80

66 Casey Cox

230	Pete Rose	50.00
233	George Scott	.90
235	Ron Santo	1.50
236	Tug McGraw	2.00
237	Alvin Dark	.90
240	Al Kaline	10.00
241	Felix Millan	.75
247	Reds Rookies (Johnny Bench, Ron Tompkins)	400.00
250	Carl Yastrzemski	35.00
257	Phil Niekro	5.00
280	Mickey Mantle	150.00
290	Willie McCovey	8.00
300	Rusty Staub	2.00
310	Luis Aparicio	5.00
321	*Leo Durocher	2.25
330	Roger Maris	25.00
334	Orioles Team	2.00
350	Hoyt Wilhelm	6.00
351	Bob Barton	.60
352	Jackie Hernandez	.60
353	Mack Jones	.60
354	Pete Richert	.60
355	Ernie Banks	10.00
356	Checklist 371-457 (Ken Holtzman)	2.50
357	Len Gabrielson	.60
358	Mike Epstein	.70
359	Joe Moeller	.60
360	Willie Horton	1.00
361	Harmon Killebrew AS	5.00
362	Orlando Cepeda AS	2.75
363	Rod Carew AS	8.00
364	Joe Morgan AS	3.00
365	Brooks Robinson AS	6.00
366	Ron Santo AS	2.00
367	Jim Fregosi AS	1.00
368	Gene Alley AS	1.00
369	Carl Yastrzemski AS	15.00
370	Hank Aaron AS	15.00
371	Tony Oliva AS	2.00
372	Lou Brock AS	5.00
373	Frank Robinson AS	5.00

408 Steve Carlton

490 Super Stars

374	Bob Clemente AS	15.00
375	Bill Freehan AS	1.00
376	Tim McCarver AS	1.50
377	Joe Horlen AS	1.00
378	Bob Gibson AS	5.00
379	Gary Peters AS	1.00
380	Ken Holtzman AS	1.00
381	Boog Powell	2.50
382	Ramon Hernandez	.60
383	Steve Whitaker	.65
384	Reds Rookies (Bill Henry, *Hal McRae*)	6.00
385	*Jim Hunter	5.00
386	Greg Goossen	.70
387	Joe Foy	.60
388	Ray Washburn	.60
389	*Jay Johnstone	.90
390	Bill Mazeroski	1.75
391	Bob Priddy	.60
392	Grady Hatton	.60
393	Jim Perry	1.00
394	Tommie Aaron	.90
395	Camilo Pascual	.80
396	Bobby Wine	.60
397	Vic Davalillo	.65
398	Jim Grant	.60
399	Ray Oyler	.60
400	Mike McCormick	.75
401	Mets Team	4.50
402	Mike Hegan	1.00
403	John Buzhardt	.60
404	Floyd Robinson	.60
405	Tommy Helms	.70
406	Dick Ellsworth	.60
407	Gary Kolb	.60
408	Steve Carlton	42.00
409	Orioles Rookies (Frank Peters, Ron Stone)	.60
410	*Ferguson Jenkins	3.50
411	Ron Hansen	.60
412	Clay Carroll	.70
413	Tommy McCraw	.60
414	Mickey Lolich	2.75
415	Johnny Callison	1.00
416	Bill Rigney	.60
417	Willie Crawford	.60
418	Eddie Fisher	.60
419	Jack Hiatt	.60
420	Cesar Tovar	.65

421	Ron Taylor	.60
422	Rene Lachemann	.60
423	Fred Gladding	.60
424	White Sox Team	2.00
425	Jim Maloney	.70
426	Hank Allen	.60
427	Dick Calmus	.60
428	Vic Roznovsky	.60
429	Tommie Sisk	.60
430	Rico Petrocelli	.90
431	Dooley Womack	.65
432	Indians Rookies (Bill Davis, Jose Vidal)	.60
433	Bob Rodgers	.85
434	Ricardo Joseph	.60
435	Ron Perranoski	.70
436	Hal Lanier	.75
437	Don Cardwell	.60
438	Lee Thomas	.60
439	Luman Harris	.60
440	Claude Osteen	.95
441	Alex Johnson	.60
442	Dick Bosman	.60
443	Joe Azcue	.60
444	Jack Fisher	.60
445	Mike Shannon	.70
446	Ron Kline	.60
447	Tigers Rookies (George Korince, Fred Lasher)	.60
448	Gary Wagner	.60
449	Gene Oliver	.60
450	Jim Kaat	4.00
451	Al Spangler	.60
452	Jesus Alou	.70
453	Sammy Ellis	.60
454	Checklist 458-533 (Frank Robinson)	4.00
455	Rico Carty	1.00
456	John O'Donoghue	.60
457	*Jim Lefevbre	.70
458	Lew Krausse	.60
459	Dick Simpson	.60
460	Jim Lonborg	1.00
461	Chuck Hiller	.60
462	Barry Moore	.60
463	Jimmie Schaffer	.60
464	Don McMahon	.60
465	Tommie Agee	.90
466	Bill Dillman	.60

467	Dick Howser	1.50
468	Larry Sherry	.60
469	Ty Cline	.60
470	Bill Freehan	1.00
471	Orlando Pena	.60
472	Walt Alston	2.50
473	Al Worthington	.60
474	Paul Schaal	.60
475	Joe Niekro	2.25
476	Woody Woodward	.70
477	Phillies Team	2.00
478	Dave McNally	1.00
479	Phil Gagliano	.60
480	Manager's Dream (Chico Cardenas, Bob Clemente, Tony Oliva)	15.00
481	John Wyatt	.60
482	Jose Pagan	.60
483	Darold Knowles	.60
484	Phil Roof	.60
485	Ken Berry	.60
486	Cal Koone	.60
487	Lee May	1.35
488	Dick Tracewski	.60
490	Super Stars (Harmon Killebrew, Willie Mays, Mickey Mantle	80.00
491	Denny LeMaster	.60
492	Jeff Torborg	.70
493	Jim McGlothlin	.60
494	Ray Sadecki	.60
495	Leon Wagner	.70
496	Steve Hamilton	.80
497	Cards Team	5.00
498	Bill Bryan	.70
499	Steve Blass	.70
500	Frank Robinson	10.00
501	John Odom	.70
502	Mike Andrews	.60
503	Al Jackson	.70
504	Russ Snyder	.60
505	Joe Sparma	.60
506	Clarence Jones	.60

230 Pete Rose

50 Willie Mays

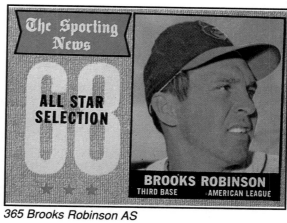

365 Brooks Robinson AS

507	Wade Blasingame	.60
508	Duke Sims	.60
509	Dennis Higgins	.60
510	Ron Fairly	.90
511	Bill Kelso	.60
512	Grant Jackson	.60
513	Hank Bauer	.95
514	Al McBean	.60
515	Russ Nixon	.60
516	Pete Mikkelsen	.60
517	Diego Segui	.65
518	Checklist 534-598	4.00
519	Jerry Stephenson	.60
520	Lou Brock	14.00
521	Don Shaw	.60
522	Wayne Causey	.60
523	John Tsitouris	.60
524	Andy Kosco	.70
525	Jim Davenport	.60
526	Bill Denehy	.60
527	Tito Francona	.70
528	Tigers Team	8.00
529	Bruce Von Hoff	.60

530	*Bird Belters (Brooks Robinson, Frank Robinson)	7.00
531	Chuck Hinton	.60
532	Luis Tiant	1.75
533	Wes Parker	.90
534	Bob Miller	1.00
535	Danny Cater	1.00
536	Bill Short	1.00
537	Norm Siebern	1.00
538	Manny Jimenez	1.00
539	Major League Rookies (Mike Ferraro, Jim Ray)	1.25
540	Nelson Briles	1.00
541	Sandy Alomar	1.00
542	John Boccabella	1.00
543	Bob Lee	1.00
544	Mayo Smith	1.00
545	Lindy McDaniel	1.00
546	Roy White	2.00
547	Dan Coombs	1.00
548	Bernie Allen	1.00
549	Orioles Rookies (Curt Motton, Roger Nelson)	1.00
550	Clete Boyer	1.25
551	Darrell Sutherland	1.00
552	Ed Kirkpatrick	1.00
553	Hank Aguirre	1.00
554	A's Team	3.00

555	Jose Tartabull	1.00
556	Dick Selma	1.00
557	Frank Quilici	1.00
558	John Edwards	1.00
559	Pirates Rookies (Carl Taylor, Luke Walker)	1.00
560	Paul Casanova	1.00
561	Lee Elia	1.00
562	Jim Bouton	2.50
563	Ed Charles	1.25
564	Eddie Stanky	1.25
565	Larry Dierker	1.00
566	Ken Harrelson	2.00
567	Clay Dalrymple	1.00
568	Willie Smith	1.00
569	NL Rookies (Ivan Murrell, Les Rohr)	1.25
570	Rick Reichardt	1.00
571	Tony LaRussa	1.75
572	Don Bosch	1.25
573	Joe Coleman	1.25
574	Reds Team	3.00
575	Jim Palmer	40.00
576	Dave Adlesh	1.00
577	Fred Talbot	1.25
578	Orlando Martinez	1.00
579	NL Rookies (Larry Hisle, Mike Lum)	2.00
580	Bob Bailey	1.00
581	Garry Roggenburk	1.00
582	Jerry Grote	1.25
583	Gates Brown	1.25
584	Larry Shepard	1.00
585	Wilbur Wood	1.25
586	Jim Pagliaroni	1.00
587	Roger Repoz	1.00
588	Dick Schofield	1.00
589	Twins Rookies (Ron Clark, Moe Ogler)	1.00
590	Tommy Harper	1.25
591	Dick Nen	1.00
592	John Bateman	1.00
593	Lee Stange	1.00
594	Phil Linz	1.25
595	Phil Ortega	1.00
596	Charlie Smith	1.00
597	Bill McCool	1.00
598	Jerry May	2.00

361 Harmon Killebrew AS

1969 TOPPS

Topps reached another record in terms of quantity with the release of its 664-card 1969 set. No team cards are included, however, and multiplayer feature cards appear for the last time. Other subsets include league statistical leaders, World Series cards, a *Sporting News* All-Star group, and rookie cards for Graig Nettles, Rollie Fingers, Reggie Jackson, and others. The 2¹/2- by 3¹/2-inch cards feature color photos on the front with the player name and position in a circle in the upper corner, printed in a variety of color combinations. Cards with white letters occur in the range of 440 through 511. They are scarce, expensive, and not included in the full set price. Card backs, now in a horizontal format, have black-and-pink printing on white cardboard, and feature lifetime stats, a brief bio, and a cartoon.

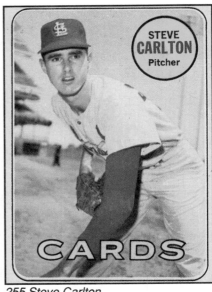

255 Steve Carlton

		NR MT
Complete set		**$1800.00**
Commons (1-218)		**.40**
Commons (219-327)		**.90**
Commons (328-512)		**.40**
Commons (513-664)		**.70**

190 Willie Mays

1	AL Batting Ldrs (Danny Cater, Tony Oliva, Carl Yastrzemski)	$7.00
2	NL Batting Ldrs (Felipe Alou, Matty Alou, Pete Rose)	4.00
3	AL RBI Ldrs (Ken Harrelson, Frank Howard, Jim Northrup)	2.00
4	NL RBI Ldrs (Willie McCovey, Ron Santo, Billy Williams)	3.50
5	AL HR Ldrs (Ken Harrelson, Willie Horton, Frank Howard)	2.00
6	NL HR Ldrs (Richie Allen, Ernie Banks, Willie McCovey)	3.50
7	AL ERA Ldrs (Sam McDowell, Dave McNally, Luis Tiant)	2.00
8	NL ERA Ldrs (Bobby Bolin, Bob Gibson, Bob Veale)	3.00
9	AL Pitching Ldrs (Denny McLain, Dave McNally, Mel Stottlemyre, Luis Tiant)	2.00
10	NL Pitching Ldrs (Bob Gibson, Fergie Jenkins, Juan Marichal)	3.50
11	AL SO Ldrs (Sam McDowell, Denny McLain, Luis Tiant)	2.00
12	NL SO Ldrs (Bob Gibson, Fergie Jenkins, Bill Singer)	3.00
13	Mickey Stanley	.50
14	Al McBean	.40
15	Boog Powell	2.50

16	Giants Rookies (Cesar Gutierrez, Rich Robertson)	.40
17	Mike Marshall	1.25
18	Dick Schofield	.40
19	Ken Suarez	.40
20	Ernie Banks	10.00
21	Jose Santiago	.40
22	Jesus Alou	.50
23	Lew Krausse	.40
24	Walt Alston	3.00
25	Roy White	1.00
26	Clay Carroll	.50
27	Bernie Allen	.40
28	Mike Ryan	.40
29	Dave Morehead	.40
30	Bob Allison	1.00
31	Mets Rookies (*Gary Gentry, Amos Otis*)	1.50
32	Sammy Ellis	.40
33	Wayne Causey	.40
34	Gary Peters	.50
35	*Joe Morgan	10.00

36	Luke Walker	.40
37	Curt Motton	.40
38	Zoilo Versalles	.50
39	Dick Hughes	.40
40	Mayo Smith	.40
41	Bob Barton	.40
42	Tommy Harper	1.00
43	Joe Niekro	1.25
44	Danny Cater	.40
45	Maury Wills	2.50
46	Fritz Peterson	.80
47	Paul Popovich (with helmet logo)	4.00
47	Paul Popovich (w/o helmet logo)	.40
49	Royals Rookies (Steve Jones, Eliseo Rodriquez) ("Rodriquez" on front)	6.00
49	Royals Rookies (Steve Jones, Eliseo Rodriguez) ("Rodriguez" on front)	.40
50	Bob Clemente	35.00
51	Woody Fryman	.50
53	Sonny Jackson	.40
54	Cisco Carlos	.40
55	Jerry Grote	1.00
56	Rich Reese	.40
57	Checklist 1-109 (Denny McLain)	3.00
58	Fred Gladding	.40
59	*Jay Johnstone	.70
60	Nelson Briles	.45
61	Jimmie Hall	.40
62	Chico Salmon	.40
63	Jim Hickman	.50
64	Bill Monbouquette	.50
65	Willie Davis	1.00
66	Orioles Rookies (Mike Adamson, *Merv Rettenmund*)	.70
67	Bill Stoneman	.40

68	Dave Duncan	.40
69	Steve Hamilton	.50
70	Tommy Helms	.50
71	Steve Whitaker	.40
72	Ron Taylor	.40
73	Johnny Briggs	.40
74	Preston Gomez	.40
75	Luis Aparicio	5.00
76	Norm Miller	.40
77	Ron Perranoski (with "LA" on cap)	4.50
77	Ron Perranoski (w/o "LA" on cap)	.40
79	Milt Pappas	.70
80	Norm Cash	1.75
81	Mel Queen	.40
82	Pirates Rookies (*Rich Hebner, Al Oliver*)	9.00
83	Mike Ferraro	.75
84	Bob Humphreys	.40
85	Lou Brock	8.00
86	Pete Richert	.40
87	Horace Clarke	.55
88	Rich Nye	.40
89	Russ Gibson	.40
90	Jerry Koosman	2.50
91	Al Dark	.75
92	Jack Billingham	.50
93	Joe Foy	.40
94	Hank Aguirre	.40
95	Johnny Bench	150.00
97	Buddy Bradford	.40
98	Dave Giusti	.40
99	Twins Rookies (Danny Morris, *Graig Nettles*) (with black loop above "Twins")	20.00
99	Twins Rookies (Danny Morris, *Graig Nettles*) (w/o black loop above "Twins")	12.00
100	Hank Aaron	40.00
101	Daryl Patterson	.40

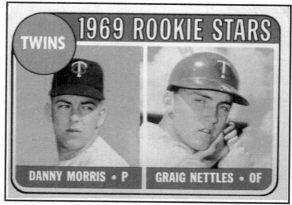

99 Twins Rookies

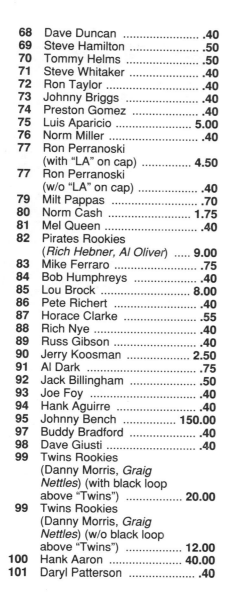

510 Rod Carew

102	Jim Davenport	.40
103	Roger Repoz	.40
104	Steve Blass	.50
105	Rick Monday	.85
106	Jim Hannan	.40
107	Checklist 110-218 (Bob Gibson) (161 is Jim Purdin)	3.00
107	Checklist 110-218 (Bob Gibson) (161 is John Purdin)	6.00
108	Tony Taylor	.40
109	Jim Lonborg	.90
110	Mike Shannon	.60
111	Johnny Morris	.70
112	J.C. Martin	.70
113	Dave May	.40
114	Yankees Rookies (Alan Closter, John Cumberland)	.70
115	Bill Hands	.40
117	Jim Fairey	.40
118	Stan Williams	.40
119	Doug Rader	.50
120	Pete Rose	35.00
121	Joe Grzenda	.40
122	Ron Fairly	.80
123	Wilbur Wood	.75
125	Ray Sadecki	.40
126	Dick Tracewski	.40
127	Kevin Collins	.50
128	Tommie Aaron	.70
129	Bill McCool	.40
130	Carl Yastrzemski	25.00
131	Chris Cannizzaro	.40
132	Dave Baldwin	.40
133	Johnny Callison	1.00
134	Jim Weaver	.40
135	Tommy Davis	1.50
136	Cards Rookies (Steve Huntz, Mike Torrez)	.50
137	Wally Bunker	.40
138	John Bateman	.40
140	*Jim Lefevbre	.50
142	Woody Woodward	.50
144	Bob Hendley	.60
145	Max Alvis	.50
146	Jim Perry	1.00
147	*Leo Durocher	2.25

150	Denny McLain	3.00
151	Clay Dalrymple (Phillies)	7.00
151	Clay Dalrymple (Orioles)	.40
153	Ed Brinkman	.50
156	Astros Rookies (Hal Gilson, Leon McFadden)	.40
157	Bob Rodgers	.70
160	Vada Pinson	2.00
162	World Series Game 1 (Gibson Fans 17; Sets New Record)	3.50
163	World Series Game 2 (Tiger Homers Deck the Cards)	2.50
164	World Series Game 3 (McCarver's Homer Puts St. Louis Ahead)	2.50
165	World Series Game 4 (Brock's Leadoff Homer Starts Cards' Romp)	3.50
166	World Series Game 5 (Kaline's Key Hit Sparks Tigers Rally)	3.50
167	World Series Game 6 (Tiger 10-Run Inning Ties Mark)	2.50
168	World Series Game 7 (Lolich Series Hero, Outduels Gibson)	2.75
169	World Series Summary (Tigers Celebrate Their Victory)	2.50
170	Frank Howard	2.00
175	*Jim Bunning	4.00
190	Willie Mays	40.00
200	Bob Gibson	12.00
208	Donn Clendenon (Expos)	7.00
208	Donn Clendenon (Houston)	.50
214	Checklist 219-327	2.50
216	Don Sutton	4.00
235	Jim Hunter	7.00
250	Frank Robinson	12.00
255	Steve Carlton	30.00
260	*Reggie Jackson*	450.00
270	Mickey Lolich	3.50
271	Larry Stahl	.90
272	Ed Stroud	.90

500 Mickey Mantle

383	Casey Cox	.40
384	Larry Shepard	.40
385	Orlando Cepeda	3.50
388	Tom McCraw	.40
390	Bill Freehan	.75
391	Ray Culp	.40
392	Bob Burda	.40
393	Gene Brabender	.40
394	*Pilots Rookies (Lou Piniella, Marv Staehle)	3.00
400	Don Drysdale	8.00
410	Al Kaline	10.00
411	Larry Dierker	.50
412	Checklist 426-512 (Mickey Mantle)	7.00
413	Roland Sheldon	.80
414	Duke Sims	.40
415	Ray Washburn	.40
416	Willie McCovey AS	3.50
417	Ken Harrelson AS	1.00
418	Tommy Helms AS	.70
419	Rod Carew AS	4.50
420	Ron Santo AS	1.00
421	Brooks Robinson AS	4.00
422	Don Kessinger AS	.70
423	Bert Campaneris AS	.80
424	Pete Rose AS	12.00
425	Carl Yastrzemski AS	6.00
426	*Curt Flood AS	1.00
427	Tony Oliva AS	1.50
428	Lou Brock AS	3.50
429	Willie Horton AS	.75
430	Johnny Bench AS	10.00
431	Bill Freehan AS	.70
432	Bob Gibson AS	3.50
433	Denny McLain AS	1.50
434	Jerry Koosman AS	1.00
435	Sam McDowell AS	.80
436	Gene Alley	.70
437	Luis Alcaraz	.40
439	White Sox Rookies (Ed Herrmann, Dan Lazar)	.40

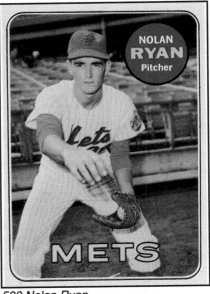

533 Nolan Ryan

440	Willie McCovey (last name in white)	90.00
440	Willie McCovey (last name in yellow)	20.00
441	Dennis Higgins (last name in white)	10.00
441	Dennis Higgins (last name in yellow)	.40
444	Joe Moeller (last name in white)	10.00
444	Joe Moeller (last name in yellow)	.40
445	Bobby Knoop	.40
446	Claude Raymond	.40
447	Ralph Houk (last name in white)	15.00
447	Ralph Houk (last name in yellow)	1.50
448	Bob Tolan	.50
449	Paul Lindblad	.40
450	Billy Williams	6.00
451	Rich Rollins (first name in white)	10.00
451	Rich Rollins (first name in yellow)	.80
452	Al Ferrera (first name in white)	10.00
452	Al Ferrera (first name in yellow)	.40
453	Mike Cuellar	.80
454	Phillies Rookies (Larry Colton, Don Money) (names in white)	10.00
454	Phillies Rookies (Larry Colton, Don Money) (names in yellow)	.80
456	Bud Harrelson	1.00
460	Joe Torre	1.75
461	Mike Epstein (last name in white)	10.00
461	Mike Epstein (last name in yellow)	.50
462	Red Schoendienst	1.00

273	Ron Willis	.90
274	Clyde King	.90
275	Vic Davalillo	.90
276	Gary Wagner	.90
277	Rod Hendricks	.90
278	Gary Geiger	.90
279	Roger Nelson	.90
280	Alex Johnson	.90
281	Ted Kubiak	.90
282	Pat Jarvis	.90
283	Sandy Alomar	.90
284	Expos Rookies (Jerry Robertson, Mike Wegener)	.90
285	Don Mincher	1.00
286	Dock Ellis	1.25
287	Jose Tartabull	.90
288	Ken Holtzman	1.00
289	Bart Shirley	.90
290	Jim Kaat	4.50
295	Tony Perez	4.50
296	Andy Messersmith	1.50
297	Deron Johnson	.90
298	Dave Nicholson	.90
299	Mark Belanger	.90
300	Felipe Alou	1.00
311	*Sparky Lyle	4.00
320	Dal Maxvill	1.00
321	Jim McAndrew	1.00
322	Jose Vidal	1.00
325	Jose Cardenal	1.00
330	Tony Conigliaro	1.50
355	Phil Niekro	5.00
370	Juan Marichal	7.00
375	Harmon Killebrew	12.00
376	Royals Rookies (Mike Fiore, Jim Rooker)	.50
377	Gary Bell	.75
378	Jose Herrera	.40
379	*Ken Boyer	1.75
380	Stan Bahnsen	.80
381	Ed Kranepool	.80
382	Pat Corrales	.75

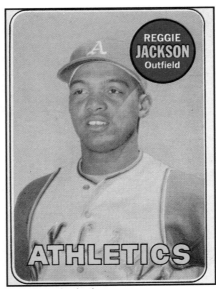

260 Reggie Jackson

464	Dave Marshall (last name in white)	10.00
464	Dave Marshall (last name in yellow)	.40
468	Pirates Rookies (Bruce Dal Canton, Bob Robertson) (names in white)	10.00
468	Pirates Rookies (Bruce Dal Canton, Bob Robertson) (names in yellow)	.40
469	Chico Ruiz	.40
470	Mel Stottlemyre (last name in white)	15.00
470	Mel Stottlemyre (last name in yellow)	1.50
471	Ted Savage (last name in white)	10.00
471	Ted Savage (last name in yellow)	.40
472	Jim Price	.40
473	Jose Arcia (first name in white)	10.00
473	Jose Arcia (first name in yellow)	.40
474	Tom Murphy	.40
475	Tim McCarver	1.50
476	Red Sox Rookies (*Ken Brett*, Gerry Moses) (names in white)	10.00
476	Red Sox Rookies (*Ken Brett*, Gerry Moses) (names in yellow)	.50
477	Jeff James	.40
478	Don Buford	.60
479	Richie Scheinblum	.40
480	Tom Seaver	90.00
481	*Bill Melton*	.80
482	Jim Gosger (first name in white)	10.00
482	Jim Gosger (first name in yellow)	.40
483	Ted Abernathy	.40

480 Tom Seaver

484	Joe Gordon	.50
485	Gaylord Perry (last name in white)	75.00
485	Gaylord Perry (last name in yellow)	10.00
486	Paul Casanova (last name in white)	10.00
486	Paul Casanova (last name in yellow)	.40
487	Denis Menke	.40
488	Joe Sparma	.40
489	Clete Boyer	.90
490	Matty Alou	1.00
491	Twins Rookies (Jerry Crider, George Mitterwald) (names in white)	10.00
491	Twins Rookies (Jerry Crider, George Mitterwald) (names in yellow)	.40
492	Tony Cloninger	.50
493	Wes Parker (last name in white)	10.00
493	Wes Parker (last name in yellow)	.70
495	Bert Campaneris	1.25
497	Julian Javier	.50
498	Juan Pizarro	.45
499	Astros Rookies (Don Bryant, Steve Shea)	.40
500	Mickey Mantle (last name in white)	500.00
500	Mickey Mantle (last name in yellow)	200.00
501	Tony Gonzalez (first name in white)	10.00
501	Tony Gonzales (first name in yellow)	.40
502	Minnie Rojas	.40
503	Larry Brown	.40
504	Checklist 513-588 (Brooks Robinson)	4.00
505	Bobby Bolin (last name in white)	10.00

505	Bobby Bolin (last name in yellow)	.40
506	Paul Blair	.50
507	Cookie Rojas	.40
508	Moe Drabowsky	.40
509	Manny Sanguillen	.50
510	Rod Carew	40.00
511	Diego Segui (first name in white)	10.00
511	Diego Segui (first name in yellow)	.80
512	Cleon Jones	.80
513	Camilo Pascual	.80
514	Mike Lum	.70
515	Dick Green	.70
516	Earl Weaver	3.50
517	Mike McCormick	.80
518	Fred Whitfield	.70
519	Yankees Rookies (Len Boehmer, Gerry Kenney)	1.00
520	Bob Veale	.80
521	George Thomas	.70
523	Bob Chance	.70
524	Expos Rookies (Jose Laboy, Floyd Wicker)	.70
525	Earl Wilson	.70
526	Hector Torres	.70
527	Al Lopez	3.00
528	Claude Osteen	.90
529	Ed Kirkpatrick	.70
530	Cesar Tovar	.70
531	Dick Farrell	.70
532	Bird Hill Aces (Mike Cuellar, Jim Hardin, Dave McNally, Tom Phoebus)	1.50
533	Nolan Ryan	300.00
534	Jerry McNertney	.70
535	Phil Regan	.70
536	Padres Rookies (Danny Breeden, *Dave Roberts*)	.80

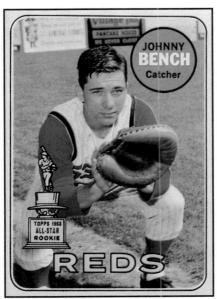

95 Johnny Bench

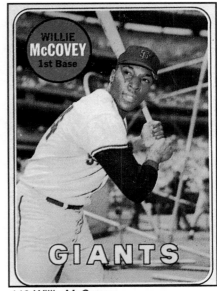

440 Willie McCovey

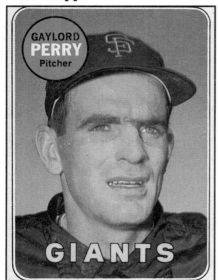

485 Gaylord Perry

537	Mike Paul	.70
538	Charlie Smith	.70
539	Ted Shows How (Mike Epstein, Ted Williams)	3.25
540	*Curt Flood	1.50
541	Joe Verbanic	.90
542	Bob Aspromonte	.70
543	Fred Newman	.70
544	Tigers Rookies (Mike Kilkenny, Ron Woods)	.70
545	Willie Stargell	10.00
546	Jim Nash	.70
547	Billy Martin	3.25
548	Bob Locker	.70
549	Ron Brand	.70
550	Brooks Robinson	12.00
551	Wayne Granger	.70
552	Dodgers Rookies (*Ted Sizemore, Bill Sudakis*)	.85
553	Ron Davis	.70
554	Frank Bertaina	.70
555	Jim Hart	.80
556	A's Stars (Sal Bando, Bert Campaneris, Danny Cater)	1.50
557	Frank Fernandez	1.00
558	*Tom Burgemeier*	.85
559	Cards Rookies (Joe Hague, Jim Hicks)	.70
560	Luis Tiant	1.50
561	Ron Clark	.70
562	*Bob Watson*	1.00
563	Marty Pattin	.90
564	Gil Hodges	6.00
565	Hoyt Wilhelm	6.00
566	Ron Hansen	.70
567	Pirates Rookies (Elvio Jimenez, Jim Shellenback)	.70

568	Cecil Upshaw	.70
569	Billy Harris	.70
570	Ron Santo	2.00
571	Cap Peterson	.70
572	*Giants Heroes (Juan Marichal, Willie McCovey)	7.00
573	Jim Palmer	25.00
574	George Scott	.90
575	Bill Singer	.90
576	Phillies Rookies (Ron Stone, Bill Wilson)	.70
577	Mike Hegan	1.00
578	Don Bosch	.70
579	*Dave Nelson*	.80
580	Jim Northrup	.80
581	Gary Nolan	.70
582	Checklist 589-664 (Tony Oliva)	3.00
583	*Clyde Wright*	.80
585	Ron Swoboda	.80
586	Tim Cullen	.70
587	*Joe Rudi*	2.00
588	*Bill White	1.00
589	Joe Pepitone	2.00
590	Rico Carty	1.00
591	Mike Hedlund	.70
592	Padres Rookies (Rafael Robles, Al Santorini)	.70
593	Don Nottebart	.70
594	Dooley Womack	.70
595	Lee Maye	.70
596	Chuck Hartenstein	.70
597	AL Rookies (Larry Burchart, *Rollie Fingers,* Bob Floyd)	50.00
598	Ruben Amaro	.80
599	John Boozer	.70
600	*Tony Oliva	2.25
601	Tug McGraw	2.00
602	Cubs Rookies (Alec Distaso, Jim Qualls, Don Young)	.75

100 Hank Aaron

35 Joe Morgan

603	Joe Keough	.70
604	Bobby Etheridge	.70
605	Dick Ellsworth	.70
606	Gene Mauch	.90
607	Dick Bosman	.80
608	Dick Simpson	.70
609	Phil Gagliano	.70
610	Jim Hardin	.70
611	Braves Rookies (Bob Didier, Walt Hriniak, Gary Neibauer)	.70
612	Jack Aker	.70
613	Jim Beauchamp	.70
614	Astros Rookies (Tom Griffin, Skip Guinn)	.70
615	Len Gabrielson	.70
616	Don McMahon	.70
617	Jesse Gander	.70
618	Ramon Webster	.70
619	Royals Rookies (Bill Butler, *Pat Kelly,* Juan Rios)	.80
620	Dean Chance	.80
621	Bill Voss	.70
622	Dan Osinski	.70
623	Hank Allen	.70
624	NL Rookies (Darrel Chaney, Duffy Dyer, Terry Harmon)	.80
625	Mack Jones	.70
626	Gene Michael	.70
627	George Stone	.70
628	Red Sox Rookies (*Bill Conigliaro,* Syd O'Brien, Fred Wenz)	.90
629	Jack Hamilton	.70
630	*Bobby Bonds*	9.00
631	John Kennedy	.70
632	Jon Warden	.70
633	Harry Walker	.80
634	Andy Etchebarren	.70
635	George Culver	.70
636	Woodie Held	.70

637	Padres Rookies (Jerry DaVanon, *Clay Kirby*, Frank Reberger)	.75
638	Ed Sprague	.70
639	Barry Moore	.70
640	Fergie Jenkins	3.50
641	NL Rookies (Bobby Darwin, Tommy Dean, John Miller)	.75
642	John Hiller	.80
643	Billy Cowan	.80
644	Chuck Hinton	.70
645	George Brunet	.70

646	Expos Rookies (Dan McGinn, *Carl Morton*)	.90
647	Dave Wickersham	.70
648	Bobby Wine	.70
649	Al Jackson	.80
650	*Ted Williams	7.00
651	Gus Gil	.90
653	*Aurelio Rodriguez* (photo is team batboy Leonard Garcia)	1.50
654	White Sox Rookies (*Carlos May*, Rich Morales, Don Secrist)	.90

655	Mike Hershberger	.70
656	Dan Schneider	.70
657	Bobby Murcer	2.25
658	AL Rookies (Bill Burbach, Tom Hall, Jim Miles)	1.00
659	Johnny Podres	1.75
660	Reggie Smith	2.00
661	Royals Rookies (Dick Drago, Bob Oliver, George Spriggs)	.80
663	Dick Radatz	.90
664	Ron Hunt	2.00

1970 TOPPS

Team cards returned in 1970 with Topps' largest set to date of 720 cards. Card number 1 features a team photo of the new World Champion Mets, who make additional appearances in subsets highlighting the World Series and the first League Championship Series. Statistical leaders are grouped together, as are All-Star cards, which will not appear again until 1982. Backs of the 2½- by 3½-inch cards feature blue-and-yellow printing on white cardboard with yearly stats, brief bios, and a cartoon. Fronts show crisp color photos with team names in the upper corners and player names in script in the lower gray border. This set is a popular starting point for the modern collector.

660 Johnny Bench

	NR MT
Complete set	$1500.00
Commons (1-546)	.30
Commons (547-633)	.80
Commons (634-720)	2.00

1	World Champions (Mets Team)	$10.00
2	Diego Segui	.60
3	Darrel Chaney	.30
4	Tom Egan	.30
5	Wes Parker	.40
6	Grant Jackson	.30
7	Indians Rookies (Gary Boyd, Russ Nagelson)	.30
8	Jose Martinez	.30
9	Checklist 1-132	2.50
10	Carl Yastrzemski	25.00
11	Nate Colbert	.30
12	John Hiller	.40
13	Jack Hiatt	.30
14	Hank Allen	.30
15	Larry Dierker	.40
16	Charlie Metro	.30
17	Hoyt Wilhelm	4.00
21	Athletics Rookies (*Vida Blue*, Gene Tenace)	3.00
22	Ray Washburn	.30
23	Bill Robinson	.50
24	Dick Selma	.30
25	Cesar Tovar	.30
26	Tug McGraw	1.25

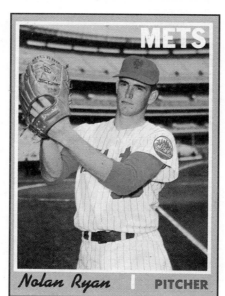

712 Nolan Ryan

27	Chuck Hinton	.30
28	Billy Wilson	.30
29	Sandy Alomar	.30
30	Matty Alou	.80
31	Marty Pattin	.50
32	Harry Walker	.40
33	Don Wert	.30
34	Willie Crawford	.30
36	Reds Rookies (Danny Breeden, *Bernie Carbo*)	.50

40	Rich Allen	1.50
45	Dave Johnson	1.00
50	Tommie Agee	.50
53	John Kennedy	.50
54	Jeff Torborg	.40
55	John Odom	.40
56	Phillies Rookies (Joe Lis, Scott Reid)	.30
57	Pat Kelly	.30
58	Dave Marshall	.30
59	Dick Ellsworth	.30
60	*Jim Wynn	.60
61	NL Batting Ldrs (Bob Clemente, Cleon Jones, Pete Rose)	5.00
62	AL Batting Ldrs (Rod Carew, Tony Oliva, Reggie Smith)	2.50
63	NL RBI Ldrs (Willie McCovey, Tony Perez, Ron Santo)	2.50

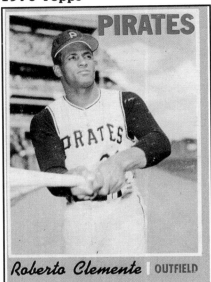

350 Roberto Clemente

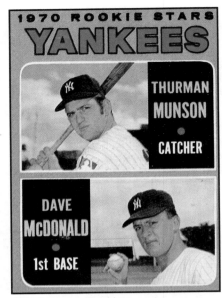

189 Yankees Rookies

97	Joe Moeller	.30
98	Gates Brown	.30
99	Bobby Pfeil	.30
100	Mel Stottlemyre	1.00
102	Joe Rudi	.80
103	Frank Reberger	.30
104	Gerry Moses	.30
105	Tony Gonzalez	.30
106	Darold Knowles	.30
107	Bobby Etheridge	.30
108	Tom Burgmeier	.30
109	Expos Rookies (Garry Jestadt, Carl Morton)	.40
110	Bob Moose	.30
111	Mike Hegan	.50
112	Dave Nelson	.30
113	Jim Ray	.30
114	Gene Michael	.45
115	Alex Johnson	.40
116	*Sparky Lyle	1.00
117	Don Young	.30
118	George Mitterwald	.30
119	Chuck Taylor	.30
120	Sal Bando	.80
121	Orioles Rookies (Fred Beene, *Terry Crowley*)	.90
122	George Stone	.30
124	Larry Jaster	.30
125	Deron Johnson	.30
126	Marty Martinez	.30
127	Joe Coleman	.40
128	Checklist 133-263	2.75
129	Jimmie Price	.30
130	Ollie Brown	.30
131	Dodgers Rookies (Ray Lamb, Bob Stinson)	.30
132	Jim McGlothlin	.30
133	Clay Carroll	.40
134	Danny Walton	.40
135	Dick Dietz	.30
136	Steve Hargan	.30
137	Art Shamsky	.30
138	Joe Foy	.30

64	AL RBI Ldrs (Reggie Jackson, Harmon Killebrew, Boog Powell)	2.50
65	NL HR Ldrs (Hank Aaron, Lee May, Willie McCovey)	3.00
66	AL HR Ldrs (Frank Howard, Reggie Jackson, Harmon Killebrew)	2.50
67	NL ERA Ldrs (Steve Carlton, Bob Gibson, Juan Marichal)	3.00
68	AL ERA Ldrs (Dick Bosman, Mike Cuellar, Jim Palmer)	2.00
69	NL Pitching Ldrs (Fergie Jenkins, Juan Marichal, Phil Niekro, Tom Seaver)	2.50
70	AL Pitching Ldrs (Dave Boswell, Mike Cuellar, Dennis McLain, Dave McNally, Jim Perry, Mel Stottlemyre)	2.50
71	NL SO Ldrs (Bob Gibson, Fergie Jenkins, Bill Singer)	2.50
72	AL SO Ldrs (Mickey Lolich, Sam McDowell, Andy Messersmith)	2.00
73	Wayne Granger	.30
74	Angels Rookies (Greg Washburn, Wally Wolf)	.30
75	Jim Kaat	2.50
80	Don Kessinger	.40
82	Frank Fernandez	.40
85	Max Alvis	.30
87	Steve Renko	.30
88	Pilots Rookies (Dick Baney, Miguel Fuentes)	.50
90	Tim McCarver	1.00
94	Fred Patek	.40
96	Cards Rookies (Leron Lee, *Jerry Reuss*)	1.75

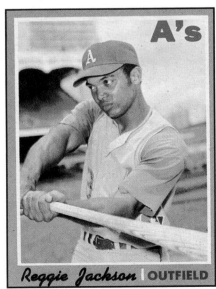

140 Reggie Jackson

139	Rich Nye	.30
140	Reggie Jackson	80.00
141	Pirates Rookies (*Dave Cash*, Johnny Jeter)	.50
142	Fritz Peterson	.50
143	Phil Gagliano	.40
144	Ray Culp	.30
145	Rico Carty	.80
146	Danny Murphy	.30
147	Angel Hermoso	.30
148	Earl Weaver	1.50
149	Billy Champion	.30
150	Harmon Killebrew	6.00
151	Dave Roberts	.30
152	Ike Brown	.30
153	Gary Gentry	.30
154	Senators Rookies (Jan Dukes, Jim Miles)	.30
155	Denis Menke	.30
156	Eddie Fisher	.30
157	Manny Mota	.40
158	Jerry McNertney	.50
159	Tommy Helms	.40
160	Phil Niekro	3.50
161	Richie Scheinblum	.30
162	Jerry Johnson	.30
163	Syd O'Brien	.30
164	Ty Cline	.30
165	Ed Kirkpatrick	.30
166	Al Oliver	2.00
167	Bill Burbach	.30
168	Dave Watkins	.30
169	Tom Hall	.30
170	Billy Williams	4.50
172	Braves Rookies (*Ralph Garr*, Garry Hill)	1.00
173	Jim Hicks	.30
174	Ted Sizemore	.30
175	Dick Bosman	.35
176	Jim Hart	.40
177	Jim Northrup	.45
178	Denny Lemaster	.30
179	Ivan Murrell	.30

180	Tommy John	2.75
181	*Sparky Anderson	1.25
183	Jerry Grote	.45
184	Ray Fosse	.45
185	Don Mincher	.50
186	Rick Joseph	.30
187	Mike Hedlund	.30
188	Manny Sanguillen	.40
189	Yankees Rookies (*Thurman Munson*, Dave McDonald)	70.00
190	Joe Torre	1.25
191	Vicente Romo	.30
192	Jim Qualls	.30
193	Mike Wegener	.30
194	Chuck Manuel	.30
195	NL Playoff Game 1 (Seaver Wins Opener!)	3.00
196	NL Playoff Game 2 (Mets Show Muscle!)	1.75
197	NL Playoff Game 3 (Ryan Saves the Day!)	3.00
198	NL Playoffs Summary (We're Number One!)	1.75
199	AL Playoff Game 1 (Orioles Win A Squeaker!)	1.50
200	AL Playoff Game 2 (Powell Scores Winning Run!)	1.75
201	AL Playoff Game 3 (Birds Wrap it Up!)	1.50
202	AL Playoffs Summary (Sweep Twins in Three!)	1.50
203	Rudy May	.40
204	Len Gabrielson	.30
205	Bert Campaneris	.80
206	Clete Boyer	.85
207	Tigers Rookies (Norman McRae, Bob Reed)	.30
208	Fred Gladding	.30
209	Ken Suarez	.30
210	Juan Marichal	8.00
211	*Ted Williams	7.00

600 Willie Mays

212	Al Santorina	.30
213	Andy Etchebarren	.30
214	Ken Boswell	.30
215	Reggie Smith	.65
216	Chuck Hartenstein	.30
217	Ron Hansen	.30
218	Ron Stone	.30
219	Jerry Kenney	.30
220	Steve Carlton	18.00
222	Jim Rooker	.30
225	Lee May	.60
226	Ron Perranoski	.40
227	Astros Rookies (*John Mayberry*, Bob Watkins)	.30
228	Aurelio Rodriguez	.40
229	Rich Robertson	.30
230	Brooks Robinson	10.00
240	Fergie Jenkins	2.50
242	Walter Alston	1.75
244	Checklist 264-372	2.75
248	Jesus Alou	.45
250	Willie McCovey	6.00
251	Dick Schofield	.30
252	Lowell Palmer	.30
253	Ron Woods	.50
254	Camilo Pascual	.50
255	*Jim Spencer*	.50
256	Vic Davalillo	.40
257	Dennis Higgins	.30
258	Paul Popovich	.30
259	Tommie Reynolds	.30
260	Claude Osteen	.50
261	Curt Motton	.30
262	Padres Rookies (Jerry Morales, Jim Williams)	.30
263	Duane Josephson	.30
264	Rich Hebner	.40
265	Randy Hundley	.40
266	Wally Bunker	.30
267	Twins Rookies (Herman Hill, Paul Ratliff)	.30
268	Claude Raymond	.30
269	Cesar Gutierrez	.30
270	Chris Short	.40
271	Greg Goossen	.40
272	Hector Torres	.30
273	Ralph Houk	1.00
274	Gerry Arrigo	.30
275	Duke Sims	.30

278	Tommie Aaron	.40
279	*Bill Lee*	.50
280	Donn Clendenon	.40
285	Paul Blair	.40
286	Dodgers Rookies (*Bill Buckner*, Jack Jenkins)	5.00
290	Rod Carew	15.00
300	Tom Seaver	55.00
304	*Bill Russell*	1.50
305	World Series Game 1 (Buford Belts Leadoff Homer!)	1.75
306	World Series Game 2 (Clendenon's Homer Breaks Ice!)	1.75
307	World Series Game 3 (Agee's Catch Saves the Day!)	1.75
308	World Series Game 4 (Martin's Bunt Ends Deadlock!)	1.75
309	World Series Game 5 (Koosman Shuts the Door!)	1.75
310	World Series Summary (Mets Whoop it Up!)	1.75
311	Dick Green	.30
312	Mike Torrez	.30
313	Mayo Smith	.30
314	Bill McCool	.30
315	Luis Aparicio	4.50
330	Lou Brock	6.00
336	Del Unser	.30
337	Mike McCormick	.40
338	Paul Schaal	.30
339	Johnny Edwards	.30
340	Tony Conigliaro	1.25
341	Bill Sudakis	.30
342	Wilbur Wood	.40
343	Checklist 373-459 (red bat on front)	3.50
343	Checklist 373-459 (brown bat on front)	3.00
344	Marcelino Lopez	.30
345	Al Ferrera	.30
346	*Red Schoendienst	.75
347	Russ Snyder	.30
348	Mets Rookies (Jesse Hudson, Mike Jorgensen)	.40

1 World Champions

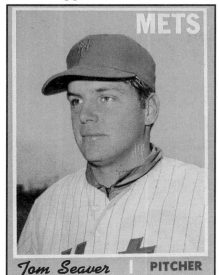

300 Tom Seaver

349	Steve Hamilton	.40
350	Roberto Clemente	45.00
351	Tom Murphy	.30
352	Bob Barton	.30
353	Stan Williams	.30
354	Amos Otis	.50
355	Doug Rader	.30
356	Fred Lasher	.30
357	Bob Burda	.30
358	Pedro Borbon	.50
359	Phil Roof	.40
360	*Curt Flood	1.00
361	Ray Jarvis	.30
362	Joe Hague	.30
363	Tom Shopay	.30
364	Dan McGinn	.30
365	Zoilo Versalles	.40
366	Barry Moore	.30
367	Mike Lum	.30
368	Ed Herrmann	.30
369	Alan Foster	.30
370	Tommy Harper	.70
373	Roy White	1.00
375	Johnny Callison	.80
378	Jim Davenport	.30
380	Tony Perez	3.00
387	Orioles Team	1.50
394	Gil Hodges	4.00
403	Jim Bunning	3.25
407	Bob Watson	.40
409	Bob Tolan	.40
410	Boog Powell	2.00
411	Dodgers Team	1.50
416	Joe Verbanic	.40
418	John Donaldson	.40
419	Ron Taylor	.30
420	Ken McMullen	.30
421	Pat Dobson	.40
422	Royals Team	1.25
427	Fred Norman	.30
430	Andy Messersmith	.50
449	Jim Palmer	15.00
450	Willie McCovey AS	3.50

451	*Boog Powell AS	1.00
452	Felix Millan AS	.50
453	Rod Carew AS	4.00
454	Ron Santo AS	.85
455	Brooks Robinson AS	3.50
456	Don Kessinger AS	.50
457	Rico Petrocelli AS	.50
458	Pete Rose AS	8.00
459	Reggie Jackson AS	8.00
460	Matty Alou AS	.75
461	Carl Yastrzemski AS	5.00
462	Hank Aaron AS	5.50
463	Frank Robinson AS	3.50
464	Johnny Bench AS	5.00
465	Bill Freehan AS	.50
466	Juan Marichal AS	3.00
467	Denny McLain AS	.80
468	Jerry Koosman AS	.60
469	Sam McDowell AS	.60
470	Willie Stargell	7.00
471	Chris Zachary	.30
472	Braves Team	1.25
473	Don Bryant	.50
474	Dick Kelley	.30
475	Dick McAuliffe	.40
476	Don Shaw	.30
477	Orioles Rookies (Roger Freed, Al Severinsen)	.30
478	Bob Heise	.30
479	Dick Woodson	.30
480	Glenn Beckert	.40
481	Jose Tartabull	.30
482	Tom Hilgendorf	.30
483	Gail Hopkins	.30
484	Gary Nolan	.30
485	*Jay Johnstone	.50
486	Terry Harmon	.30
487	Cisco Carlos	.30
488	J.C. Martin	.30
489	Eddie Kasko	.30
490	Bill Singer	.40
491	Graig Nettles	4.00

630 Ernie Banks

150 Harmon Killebrew

492	Astros Rookies (Keith Lampard, Scipio Spinks)	.30
493	Lindy McDaniel	.50
494	Larry Stahl	.30
495	Dave Morehead	.30
496	Steve Whitaker	.30
497	Eddie Watt	.30
498	Al Weis	.30
499	Skip Lockwood	.50
500	Hank Aaron	35.00
501	White Sox Team	1.25
502	Rollie Fingers	4.00
503	Dal Maxvill	.40
504	Don Pavletich	.30
505	Ken Holtzman	.40
506	Ed Stroud	.30
507	Pat Corrales	.50
508	Joe Niekro	.70
509	Expos Team	1.25
510	*Tony Oliva	1.75
511	Joe Hoerner	.30
512	Billy Harris	.30
513	Preston Gomez	.30
514	Steve Hovley	.50
515	Don Wilson	.30
516	Yankees Rookies (John Ellis, Jim Lyttle)	.50
517	Joe Gibbon	.30
518	Bill Melton	.40
519	Don McMahon	.30
520	Willie Horton	.75
521	Cal Koonce	.30
522	Angels Team	1.25
523	Jose Pena	.30
524	Alvin Dark	.60
525	Jerry Adair	.30
526	Ron Herbel	.30
527	Don Bosch	.30
528	Elrod Hendricks	.30
529	Bob Aspromonte	.30
530	Bob Gibson	8.00
531	Ron Clark	.30
532	Danny Murtaugh	.50

533	Buzz Stephen	.50
534	Twins Team	1.50
535	Andy Kosco	.30
536	Mike Kekich	.50
537	Joe Morgan	8.00
538	Bob Humphreys	.30
539	*Phillies Rookies (Larry Bowa, Dennis Doyle)	3.00
540	Gary Peters	.40
541	Bill Heath	.30
542	Checklist 547-633	3.00
543	Clyde Wright	.30
544	Reds Team	1.25
545	Ken Harrelson	1.25
546	Ron Reed	.40
547	Rick Monday	1.00
548	Howie Reed	.80
549	Cardinals Team	1.75
550	Frank Howard	2.25
551	Dock Ellis	.90
552	Royals Rookies (Don O'Riley, Dennis Paepke, Fred Rico)	.80
553	*Jim Lefebvre	.90
560	Gaylord Perry	7.00
565	Jim Hunter	7.00
580	Pete Rose	90.00
590	Mike Cuellar	.90
593	Cubs Team	1.75
595	Maury Wills	2.50
600	Willie Mays	45.00
601	Pete Richert	.80
602	Ted Savage	.80
603	Ray Oyler	.80
604	Clarence Gaston	.80
605	Rick Wise	.90
606	Chico Ruiz	.80
607	Gary Waslewski	.80
608	Pirates Team	1.75
609	Buck Martinez	.90
610	Jerry Koosman	1.25
611	Norm Cash	1.50

640 Al Kaline

500 Hank Aaron image — Braves, Hank Aaron, OUTFIELD

500 Hank Aaron

612	Jim Hickman	.90
613	Dave Baldwin	.90
614	Mike Shannon	.90
615	Mark Belanger	.90
616	Jim Merritt	.80
617	Jim French	.80
618	Billy Wynne	.80
619	Norm Miller	.80
620	Jim Perry	1.00
621	Braves Rookies (Darrell Evans, Rick Kester, Mike McQueen)	10.00
622	Don Sutton	4.50
623	Horace Clarke	.90
624	Clyde King	.80
625	Dean Chance	.90
626	Dave Ricketts	.80
627	Gary Wagner	.80
628	Wayne Garrett	.80
629	Merv Rettenmund	.90
630	Ernie Banks	15.00
631	Athletics Team	1.75
632	Gary Sutherland	.80
633	Roger Nelson	.80
634	Bud Harrelson	2.25
635	Bob Allison	2.25
636	Jim Stewart	1.75
637	Indians Team	3.00
638	Frank Bertaina	1.75
639	Dave Campbell	1.75
640	Al Kaline	25.00
641	Al McBean	1.75
642	Angels Rookies (Greg Garrett, Gordon Lund, Jarvis Tatum)	1.75
643	Jose Pagan	1.75
644	Gerry Nyman	1.75
645	Don Money	1.75
646	Jim Britton	1.75
647	Tom Matchick	1.75
648	Larry Haney	1.75
649	Jimmie Hall	1.75
650	Sam McDowell	2.50

651	Jim Gosger	1.75
652	Rich Rollins	2.00
653	Moe Drabowsky	1.75
654	NL Rookies (Boots Day, Oscar Gamble, Angel Mangual)	2.50
655	John Roseboro	2.00
656	Jim Hardin	1.75
657	Padres Team	3.00
658	Ken Tatum	1.75
659	Pete Ward	2.00
660	Johnny Bench	150.00
661	Jerry Robertson	1.75
662	Frank Lucchesi	1.75
663	Tito Francona	2.00
664	Bob Robertson	1.75
665	Jim Lonborg	2.25
666	Adolfo Phillips	1.75
667	Bob Meyer	2.00
668	Bob Tillman	1.75
669	White Sox Rookies (Bart Johnson, Dan Lazar, Mickey Scott)	1.75
670	Ron Santo	3.00
671	Jim Campanis	1.75
672	Leon McFadden	1.75
673	Ted Uhlaender	1.75
674	Dave Leonhard	1.75
675	Jose Cardenal	2.00
676	Senators Team	3.00
677	Woodie Fryman	2.00
678	Dave Duncan	1.75
679	Ray Sadecki	1.75
680	Rico Petrocelli	2.00
681	Bob Garibaldi	1.75
682	Dalton Jones	1.75
683	Reds Rookies (Vern Geishert, Hal McRae, Wayne Simpson)	2.50
684	Jack Fisher	1.75
685	Tom Haller	2.00
686	Jackie Hernandez	1.75
687	Bob Priddy	1.75

10 Carl Yastrzemski

688	Ted Kubiak	2.00
689	Frank Tepedino	2.00
690	Ron Fairly	2.00
691	Joe Grzenda	1.75
692	Duffy Dyer	1.75
693	Bob Johnson	1.75
694	Gary Ross	1.75
695	Bobby Knoop	1.75
696	Giants Team	3.00
697	Jim Hannan	1.75
698	Tom Tresh	2.25
699	Hank Aguirre	1.75
700	Frank Robinson	30.00

701	Jack Billingham	1.75
702	AL Rookies (Bob Johnson, Ron Klimkowski, Bill Zepp)	2.00
703	Lou Marone	1.75
704	Frank Baker	1.75
705	Tony Cloninger	2.00
706	John McNamara	2.25
707	Kevin Collins	1.75
708	Jose Santiago	1.75
709	Mike Fiore	1.75
710	Felix Millan	1.75

711	Ed Brinkman	2.00
712	Nolan Ryan	300.00
713	Pilots Team	12.00
714	Al Spangler	1.75
715	Mickey Lolich	5.00
716	Cards Rookies (Sam Campisi, *Reggie Cleveland*, Santiago Guzman)	2.00
717	Tom Phoebus	1.75
718	Ed Spiezio	1.75
719	Jim Roland	2.00
720	Rick Reichardt	4.00

1971 TOPPS

Although Topps' 752-card set for 1971 makes a strong artistic statement, the black borders have proven difficult for collectors to maintain in mint condition. On the front, the team name appears in bold print across the top of the 2¹/2- by 3¹/2-inch cards, with the player name and position in smaller print just below. Facsimile autographs are superimposed at the bottom. Gray card backs with green-and-black printing were the first to feature player photos in a black-and-white inset. Brief player bios are rounded out with lifetime and 1970 stats, first pro and major league games, and abbreviated personal facts. Subsets include statistical leaders; league playoffs; World Series; and rookies, such as Steve Garvey, Ted Simmons, and Dave Concepcion.

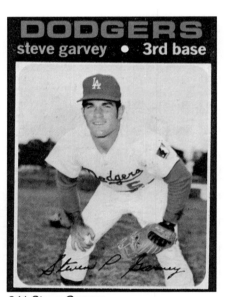
341 Steve Garvey

		NR MT
Complete set		$1600.00
Commons (1-523)		.35
Commons (524-643)		.80
Commons (644-752)		2.25

1	World Champions (Orioles Team)	$5.00
2	Dock Ellis	.50
5	Thurman Munson	20.00
9	George Scott	.50
10	Claude Osteen	.50
11	*Elliott Maddox*	.50
12	Johnny Callison	.60
13	White Sox Rookies (Charlie Brinkman, Dick Moloney)	.35
14	*Dave Concepcion*	5.00
16	*Ken Singleton*	1.75
20	Reggie Jackson	50.00
26	*Bert Blyleven*	50.00
27	Pirates Rookies (Fred Cambria, Gene Clines)	.35
30	Phil Niekro	3.25
35	Lou Piniella	1.25
38	*Jim Colborn*	.40
39	Tigers Rookies (Gene Lamont, *Lerrin LaGrow*)	.40
45	Jim Hunter	3.75
50	Willie McCovey	6.00

513 Nolan Ryan

52	Braves Rookies (Oscar Brown, *Earl Williams*)	.40
54	Checklist 1-132	2.50
55	Steve Carlton	15.00
59	Gene Mauch	.60
61	AL Batting Ldrs (Alex Johnson, Tony Oliva, Carl Yastrzemski)	2.25

62	NL Batting Ldrs (Rico Carty, Manny Sanguillen, Joe Torre)	1.25
63	AL RBI Ldrs (Tony Conigliaro, Frank Howard, Boog Powell)	1.25
64	NL RBI Ldrs (Johnny Bench, Tony Perez, Billy Williams)	2.25
65	AL HR Ldrs (Frank Howard, Harmon Killebrew, Carl Yastrzemski)	2.25
66	NL HR Ldrs (Johnny Bench, Tony Perez, Billy Williams)	2.25
67	AL ERA Ldrs (Jim Palmer, Diego Segui, Clyde Wright)	1.25
68	NL ERA Ldrs (Tom Seaver, Wayne Simpson, Luke Walker)	1.50

69	AL Pitching Ldrs (Mike Cuellar, Dave McNally, Jim Perry) **1.25**
70	NL Pitching Ldrs (Bob Gibson, Fergie Jenkins, Gaylord Perry) **2.00**
71	AL SO Ldrs (Bob Johnson, Mickey Lolich, Sam McDowell) **1.25**
72	NL SO Ldrs (Bob Gibson, Fergie Jenkins, Tom Seaver) **2.25**
74	Twins Rookies (Pete Hamm, Jim Nettles) .... **.35**
83	Mets Rookies (Randy Bobb, *Tim Foli*) .... **.50**
90	Joe Pepitone .... **.70**
91	Bob Lemon **1.50**
93	Senators Rookies (Norm McRae, Denny Riddleberger) .... **.35**
95	Luis Tiant **1.50**
100	Pete Rose **55.00**
102	Astros Rookies (*Ken Forsch*, Larry Howard) .... **.50**
105	Tony Conigliaro **1.50**
110	Bill Mazeroski **1.50**
111	Yankees Rookies (Loyd Colson, Bobby Mitchell) .... **.40**
112	Manny Mota .... **.60**
117	*Ted Simmons* **8.00**
120	Willie Horton .... **.60**
121	1971 Rookie Stars (Jim Dunegan, Roe Skidmore) ..... **.35**
123	Checklist 133-263 (Card number on right) **2.50**
123	Checklist 133-263 (Card number centered) **3.50**
124	Don Gullett .... **.70**
133	Mickey Lolich **1.50**
135	Rick Monday .... **.50**
138	Phillies Rookies (Joe Lis, *Willie Montanez*) .... **.50**

570 Jim Palmer

140	Gaylord Perry **4.00**
146	Ralph Houk .... **.80**
148	John Mayberry .... **.50**
150	Sam McDowell .... **.70**
151	Tommy Davis .... **.70**
152	Angels Rookies (Lloyd Allen, Winston Llenas) .... **.35**
158	Jerry Reuss **1.00**
160	Tom Seaver **25.00**
161	Coins Checklist **2.50**
164	Reds Rookies (Frank Duffy, *Milt Wilcox*) ..... **.60**
170	Mike Cuellar .... **.60**
174	*Dave LaRoche* .... **.50**
176	Red Sox Rookies (Doug Griffin, Bob Montgomery) ..... **.35**
177	Hal McRae .... **.70**
180	Al Kaline **12.00**
181	Hal Lanier .... **.60**
183	Gil Hodges **4.00**
184	Stan Bahnsen .... **.50**
188	Dodgers Rookies (Mike Strahler, *Bob Valentine*) **1.75**
193	*Bob Grich* **1.75**
195	AL Playoff Game 1 (Powell Muscles Twins!) **1.25**
196	AL Playoff Game 2 (McNally Makes it Two Straight!) **1.25**
197	AL Playoff Game 3 (Palmer Mows 'Em Down!) **1.75**
198	AL Playoffs Summary (A Team Effort!) **1.25**
199	NL Playoff Game 1 (Cline Pinch-Triple Decides It!) **1.25**
200	NL Playoff Game 2 (Tolan Scores For Third Time!) **1.25**
201	NL Playoff Game 3 (Cline Scores Winning Run!) **1.25**

202	NL Playoff Summary (World Series Bound!) **1.25**
203	*Larry Gura* .... **.70**
204	Brewers Rookies (George Kopacz, Bernie Smith) .... **.35**
205	Gerry Moses .... **.35**
206	Checklist 264-393 (orange helmet) **2.50**
206	Checklist 264-393 (red helmet) **2.50**
208	Billy Martin **2.00**
210	Rod Carew **19.00**
216	Cards Rookies (Reggie Cleveland, Luis Melendez) .... **.35**
220	*Ron Santo .... **.80**
226	Bill Russell .... **.60**
230	Willie Stargell **6.00**
231	Indians Rookies (Vince Colbert, *John Lowenstein*) .... **.50**
233	Larry Bowa **1.75**
237	*Cesar Cedeno* **1.25**
239	Red Schoendienst .... **.60**
245	Jim Kaat **2.50**
247	Royals Rookies (Jerry Cram, *Paul Splittorff*) .... **.75**
248	Hoyt Wilhelm **4.00**
250	Johnny Bench **45.00**
262	Padres Rookies (Dave Robinson, Jim Williams) .... **.35**
264	Joe Morgan **5.00**
268	Phillies Team **1.25**
270	Rico Carty .... **.70**
272	Tommy Helms .... **.40**
275	Vada Pinson **1.50**
276	Giants Rookies (Mike Davison, *George Foster*) **4.00**
278	Jerry Grote .... **.50**
280	*Fergie Jenkins **3.00**
285	Sal Bando .... **.60**
289	White Sox Team **1.25**

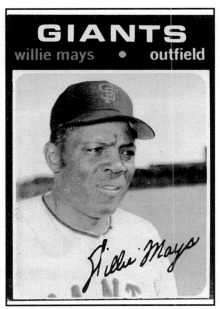

600 Willie Mays

26 Bert Blyleven

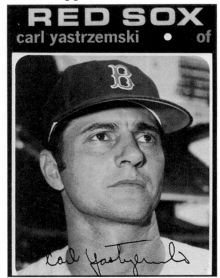

530 Carl Yastrzemski

290	Tony Oliva	1.50
292	Jay Johnstone	.60
293	Pat Corrales	.50
295	Bobby Bonds	1.25
300	Brooks Robinson	10.00
305	Reggie Smith	.60
308	Cards Team	1.25
315	Ron Fairly	.50
317	Athletics Rookies (Jim Driscoll, Angel Mangual)	.35
318	Rudy May	.40
320	Dave McNally	.50
322	Jim Beauchamp	.35
323	Billy Champion	.35
324	Graig Nettles	2.50
325	Juan Marichal	5.00
326	Richie Scheinblum	.35
327	World Series Game 1 (Powell Homers to Opposite Field!)	1.25
328	World Series Game 2 (Buford Goes 2-For 4!)	1.25
329	World Series Game 3 (F. Robinson Shows Muscle!)	2.00
330	World Series Game 4 (Reds Stay Alive!)	1.25
331	World Series Game 5 (B. Robinson Commits Robbery!)	2.00
332	World Series Summary (Clinching Performance!)	1.25
333	Clay Kirby	.35
334	Roberto Pena	.35
335	Jerry Koosman	1.00
336	Tigers Team	1.75
337	Jesus Alou	.40
338	Gene Tenace	.50
339	Wayne Simpson	.35
340	Rico Petrocelli	.50
341	*Steve Garvey*	75.00
342	Frank Tepedino	.40

343	Pirates Rookies (Ed Acosta, *Milt May*)	.40
344	Ellie Rodriguez	.35
345	Joe Horlen	.35
346	Lum Harris	.35
347	Ted Uhlaender	.35
348	Fred Norman	.35
349	Rich Reese	.35
350	Billy Williams	4.50
351	Jim Shellenback	.35
352	Denny Doyle	.35
354	Don McMahon	.35
355	Bud Harrelson	.40
356	Bob Locker	.35
357	Reds Team	1.50
358	Danny Cater	.40
359	Ron Reed	.40
360	Jim Fregosi	.80
361	Don Sutton	3.50
362	Orioles Rookies (Mike Adamson, Roger Freed)	.35
363	Mike Nagy	.35
364	Tommy Dean	.35
365	Bob Johnson	.35
366	Ron Stone	.35
367	Dalton Jones	.35
368	Bob Veale	.40
369	Checklist 394-523 (orange helmet)	2.50
369	Checklist 394-523 (red helmet, black line over ear)	2.50
369	Checklist 394-523 (red helmet, no line)	2.50
370	Joe Torre	2.50
371	Jack Hiatt	.35
372	Lew Krausse	.35
373	Tom McCraw	.35
374	Clete Boyer	.50
375	Steve Hargan	.35
376	Expos Rookies (Clyde Mashore, Ernie McAnally)	.35

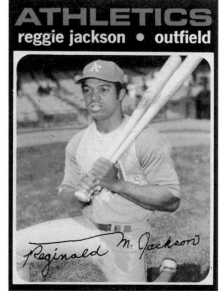

20 Reggie Jackson

250 Johnny Bench

377	Greg Garrett	.35
378	Tito Fuentes	.35
379	Wayne Granger	.35
380	*Ted Williams	5.00
381	Fred Gladding	.35
382	Jake Gibbs	.40
383	Rod Gaspar	.35
384	Rollie Fingers	2.50
385	Maury Wills	1.25
386	Red Sox Team	1.50
387	Ron Herbel	.35
388	Al Oliver	1.75
389	Ed Brinkman	.40
390	Glenn Beckert	.45
391	Twins Rookies (Steve Brye, Cotton Nash)	.35
392	Grant Jackson	.35
393	Merv Rettenmund	.40
394	Clay Carroll	.40
395	Roy White	.70
396	Dick Schofield	.35
397	Alvin Dark	.50
398	Howie Reed	.35
399	Jim French	.35
400	Hank Aaron	30.00
401	Tom Murphy	.35
402	Dodgers Team	1.50
403	Joe Coleman	.40
404	Astros Rookies (Buddy Harris, Roger Metzger)	.35
405	Leo Cardenas	.35
406	Ray Sadecki	.35
407	Joe Rudi	.60
408	Rafael Robles	.35
409	Don Pavletich	.35
410	Ken Holtzman	.40
411	George Spriggs	.35
412	Jerry Johnson	.35
413	Pat Kelly	.35
414	Woodie Fryman	.40
415	Mike Hegan	.35
416	Gene Alley	.35
417	Dick Hall	.35

418	Adolfo Phillips	.35
419	Ron Hansen	.40
420	Jim Merritt	.35
421	John Stephenson	.35
422	Frank Bertaina	.35
423	Tigers Rookies (Tim Marting, Dennis Saunders)	.35
424	Roberto Rodriquez (Rodriguez)	.35
425	Doug Rader	.35
426	Chris Cannizzaro	.35
427	Bernie Allen	.35
428	Jim McAndrew	.35
429	Chuck Hinton	.35
430	Wes Parker	.40
431	Tom Burgmeier	.35
432	Bob Didier	.35
433	Skip Lockwood	.35
434	Gary Sutherland	.35
435	Jose Cardenal	.40
436	Wilbur Wood	.50
437	Danny Murtaugh	.45
438	Mike McCormick	.50
439	Phillies Rookies (*Greg Luzinski,* Scott Reid)	2.00
440	Bert Campaneris	.75
441	Milt Pappas	.40
442	Angels Team	1.25
443	Rich Robertson	.35
444	Jimmie Price	.35
446	Bobby Bolin	.35
447	*Cesar Geronimo*	.60
448	Dave Roberts	.35
449	Brant Alyea	.35
450	Bob Gibson	8.00
451	Joe Keough	.35
452	John Boccabella	.35
453	Terry Crowley	.35
454	Mike Paul	.35
455	Don Kessinger	.40
456	Bob Meyer	.35
457	Willie Smith	.35
458	White Sox Rookies (Dave Lemonds, Ron Lolich)	.35
459	*Jim Lefebvre	.40
460	Fritz Peterson	.50
461	Jim Hart	.40
462	Senators Team	1.75

463	Tom Kelley	.35
464	Aurelio Rodriguez	.40
465	Tim McCarver	.85
466	Ken Berry	.35
467	Al Santorini	.35
468	Frank Fernandez	.35
469	Bob Aspromonte	.35
470	Bob Oliver	.35
471	Tom Griffin	.35
472	Ken Rudolph	.35
473	Gary Wagner	.35
474	Jim Fairey	.35
475	Ron Perranoski	.35
476	Dal Maxvill	.40
477	Earl Weaver	1.00
478	Bernie Carbo	.40
479	Dennis Higgins	.35
480	Manny Sanguillen	.40
481	Daryl Patterson	.35
482	Padres Team	1.25
483	Gene Michael	.45
484	Don Wilson	.35
485	Ken McMullen	.35
486	Steve Huntz	.35
487	Paul Schaal	.35
488	Jerry Stephenson	.35
489	Luis Alvarado	.35
490	Deron Johnson	.35
491	Jim Hardin	.35
492	Ken Boswell	.35
493	Dave May	.35
494	Braves Rookies (Ralph Garr, Rick Kester)	.50
495	Felipe Alou	.65
496	Woody Woodward	.40
497	Horacio Pina	.35
498	John Kennedy	.35
499	Checklist 524-643	2.50
500	Jim Perry	.60
501	Andy Etchebarren	.35
502	Cubs Team	1.25
503	Gates Brown	.40
504	Ken Wright	.35
505	Ollie Brown	.35
506	Bobby Knoop	.35
507	George Stone	.35
508	Roger Repoz	.35
509	Jim Grant	.35
510	Ken Harrelson	1.25

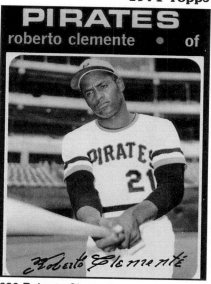

630 Roberto Clemente

511	Chris Short	.40
512	Red Sox Rookies (Mike Garman, Dick Mills)	.35
513	Nolan Ryan	95.00
514	Ron Woods	.35
515	Carl Morton	.35
516	Ted Kubiak	.35
517	Charlie Fox	.35
518	Joe Grzenda	.35
519	Willie Crawford	.35
520	Tommy John	3.00
521	Leron Lee	.35
522	Twins Team	1.25
523	John Odom	.40
524	Mickey Stanley	.90
525	Ernie Banks	15.00
526	Ray Jarvis	.80
527	Cleon Jones	.90
528	Wally Bunker	.80
529	NL Rookies (Bill Buckner, Enzo Hernandez, Marty Perez)	2.50
530	Carl Yastrzemski	50.00
531	Mike Torrez	.90
532	Bill Rigney	.80
533	Mike Ryan	.80
534	Luke Walker	.80
535	*Curt Flood	1.75
536	Claude Raymond	.80
537	Tom Egan	.80
538	Angel Bravo	.80
539	Larry Brown	.80
540	Larry Dierker	.80
541	Bob Burda	.80
542	Bob Miller	.80
543	Yankees Team	2.75
544	Vida Blue	2.50
545	Dick Dietz	.80
546	John Matias	.80
547	Pat Dobson	.90
548	Don Mason	.80
549	Jim Brewer	.80
550	Harmon Killebrew	12.00

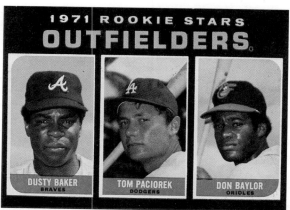

709 Major League Rookies

400 Hank Aaron

551	Frank Linzy	.80
552	Buddy Bradford	.80
553	Kevin Collins	.80
554	Lowell Palmer	.80
555	Walt Williams	.80
556	Jim McGlothlin	.80
557	Tom Satriano	.80
558	Hector Torres	.80
559	AL Rookies (Terry Cox, Bill Gogolewski, Gary Jones)	.90
560	Rusty Staub	2.25
561	Syd O'Brien	.80
562	Dave Giusti	.80
563	Giants Team	2.00
564	Al Fitzmorris	.80
565	Jim Wynn	1.00
566	Tim Cullen	.80
567	Walt Alston	2.50
568	Sal Campisi	.80
569	Ivan Murrell	.80
570	Jim Palmer	10.00
571	Ted Sizemore	.80
572	Jerry Kenney	.90
573	Ed Kranepool	1.00
574	Jim Bunning	4.00
575	Bill Freehan	1.00
576	Cubs Rookies (Brock Davis, Adrian Garrett, Garry Jestadt)	.80
577	Jim Lonborg	1.00
578	Ron Hunt	.90
579	Marty Pattin	.80
580	Tony Perez	4.00
581	Roger Nelson	.80
582	Dave Cash	.80
583	Ron Cook	.80
584	Indians Team	2.00
585	Willie Davis	2.25
586	Dick Woodson	.80
587	Sonny Jackson	.80
588	Tom Bradley	.80
589	Bob Barton	.80

590	Alex Johnson	.80
591	Jackie Brown	.80
592	Randy Hundley	.80
593	Jack Aker	.80
594	*Cards Rookies (Bob Chlupsa, Al Hrabosky, Bob Stinson)	2.25
595	Dave Johnson	1.75
596	Mike Jorgensen	.80
597	Ken Suarez	.80
598	Rick Wise	.90
599	Norm Cash	2.00
600	Willie Mays	60.00
601	Ken Tatum	.80
602	Marv Martinez	.80
603	Pirates Team	3.00
604	John Gelnor	.80
605	Orlando Cepeda	3.50
606	Chuck Taylor	.80
607	Paul Ratliff	.80
608	Mike Wegener	.80
609	*Leo Durocher	2.25
610	Amos Otis	1.00
611	Tom Phoebus	.80
612	Indians Rookies (Lou Camilli, Ted Ford, Steve Mingori)	.80
613	Pedro Borbon	.90
614	Billy Cowan	.80
615	Mel Stottlemyre	1.75
616	Larry Hisle	.90
617	Clay Dalrymple	.80
618	Tug McGraw	2.25
619	Checklist 644-752	4.00
620	Frank Howard	2.25
621	Ron Bryant	.80
622	Joe Lahoud	.80
623	Pat Jarvis	.80
624	Athletics Team	2.00
625	Lou Brock	10.00
626	Freddie Patek	.90
627	Steve Hamilton	.80
628	John Bateman	.80

160 Tom Seaver

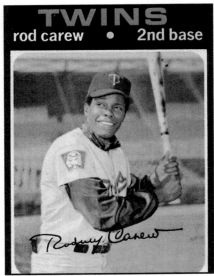

210 Rod Carew

629	John Hiller	.90
630	Roberto Clemente	35.00
631	Eddie Fisher	.80
632	Darrel Chaney	.80
633	AL Rookies (Bobby Brooks, Pete Koegel, Scott Northey)	.80
634	Phil Regan	.80
635	Bobby Mercer	2.00
636	Denny Lemaster	.80
637	Dave Bristol	.80
638	Stan Williams	.80
639	Tom Haller	.80
640	Frank Robinson	15.00
641	Mets Team	3.50
642	Jim Roland	.80
643	Rick Reichardt	.80
644	Jim Stewart	2.25
645	Jim Maloney	2.50
646	Bobby Floyd	2.25
647	Juan Pizarro	2.25
648	Mets Rookies (Rich Folkers, Ted Martinez, Jon Matlack)	3.50
649	*Sparky Lyle	3.00
650	Rich Allen	6.00
651	Jerry Robertson	2.25
652	Braves Team	3.25
653	Russ Snyder	2.25
654	Don Shaw	2.25
655	Mike Epstein	2.50
656	Gerry Nyman	2.25
657	Jose Azcue	2.25
658	Paul Lindblad	2.25
659	Byron Browne	2.25
660	Ray Culp	2.25
661	Chuck Tanner	3.00
662	Mike Hedlund	2.25
663	Marv Staehle	2.25
664	Major League Rookies (Archie Reynolds, Bob Reynolds, Ken Reynolds)	2.25

665	Ron Swoboda	2.25
666	Gene Brabender	2.25
667	Pete Ward	2.25
668	Gary Neibauer	2.25
669	Ike Brown	2.25
670	Bill Hands	2.25
671	Bill Voss	2.25
672	Ed Crosby	2.25
673	Gerry Janeski	2.25
674	Expos Team	3.25
675	Dave Boswell	2.25
676	Tommie Reynolds	2.25
677	Jack DiLauro	2.25
678	George Thomas	2.25
679	Dan O'Riley	2.25
680	Don Mincher	2.25
681	Bill Butler	2.25
682	Terry Harmon	2.25
683	Bill Burbach	2.25
684	Curt Motton	2.25
685	Moe Drabowsky	2.25
686	Chico Ruiz	2.25
687	Ron Taylor	2.25
688	*Sparky Anderson	3.50
689	Frank Baker	2.25
690	Bob Moose	2.25
691	Bob Heise	2.25
692	AL Rookies (Hal Haydel, Rogelio Moret, Wayne Twitchell)	2.25
693	Jose Pena	2.25
694	Rick Renick	2.25
695	Joe Niekro	3.25
696	Jerry Morales	2.25
697	Rickey Clark	2.25
698	Brewers Team	3.25
699	Jim Britton	2.25
700	Boog Powell	4.00
701	Bob Garibaldi	2.25
702	Milt Ramirez	2.25
703	Mike Kekich	2.25

704	J.C. Martin	2.25
705	Dick Selma	2.25
706	Joe Foy	2.25
707	Fred Lasher	2.25
708	Russ Nagelson	2.25
709	Major League Rookies (Dusty Baker, Tom Paciorek, Don Baylor)	30.00
710	Sonny Siebert	2.25
711	Larry Stahl	2.25
712	Jose Martinez	2.25
713	Mike Marshall	2.75
714	Dick Williams	2.75
715	Horace Clarke	2.50
716	Dave Leonhard	2.25
717	Tommie Aaron	2.50
718	Billy Wynne	2.25
719	Jerry May	2.25
720	Matty Alou	2.75
721	John Morris	2.25
722	Astros Team	3.25
723	Vicente Romo	2.25
724	Tom Tischinski	2.25
725	Gary Gentry	2.25
726	Paul Popovich	2.25
727	Ray Lamb	2.25
728	NL Rookies (Keith Lampard, Wayne Redmond, Bernie Williams)	2.25
729	Dick Billings	2.25
730	Jim Rooker	2.25
731	Jim Qualls	2.25
732	Bob Reed	2.25
733	Lee Maye	2.25
734	Rob Gardner	2.25
735	Mike Shannon	2.50
736	Mel Queen	2.25
737	Preston Gomez	2.25
738	Russ Gibson	2.25
739	Barry Lersch	2.25

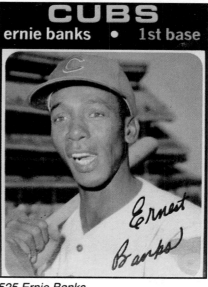

525 Ernie Banks

740	Luis Aparicio	15.00
741	Skip Guinn	2.25
742	Royals Team	2.25
743	John O'Donoghue	2.25
744	Chuck Manuel	2.25
745	Sandy Alomar	2.25
746	Andy Kosco	2.25
747	NL Rookies (Balor Moore, Al Severinsen, Scipio Spinks)	2.25
748	John Purdin	2.25
749	Ken Szotkiewicz	2.25
750	Denny McLain	6.00
751	Al Weis	2.25
752	Dick Drago	2.25

1972 TOPPS

Topps released a 787-card set in 1972, larger than any previous edition. Card fronts exhibit a wild design of various border colors, along with cartoonlike team headings. A number of subsets account for the increase of 35 cards over 1971. There is a seven-card series of traded players that includes Steve Carlton, Joe Morgan, and Frank Robinson. Eight cards display black-and-white boyhood photos of players. Thirty-four players are depicted both on standard and "in-action" cards (the latter indicated by "IA" on the card list). A high-number series (657-787) is hard to locate, while cards of Pete Rose, Steve Garvey, and Rod Carew are the most valuable.

	NR MT
Complete set	$1500.00
Commons (1-394)	.25
Commons (395-525)	.30
Commons (526-656)	.70
Commons (657-787)	2.25

1	World Champions (Pirates Team)	$4.00
4	Checklist 1-132	2.25
11	Bobby Valentine	.60
18	Juan Pizarro (green under "C" and "S")	3.50
21	Braves Team	.90

28	Twins Rookies (Steve Brye, Bob Gebhard, Hal Haydel)	.25
29	Bill Bonham (green under "C" and "S")	3.50
30	Rico Petrocelli	.50
31	Cleon Jones	.30
32	Cleon Jones IA	.30
33	Billy Martin	1.50
34	Billy Martin IA	.80
35	Jerry Johnson	.25
36	Jerry Johnson IA	.25
37	Carl Yastrzemski	12.00
38	Carl Yastrzemski IA	8.00
39	Bob Barton	.25
40	Bob Barton IA	.25
41	Tommy Davis	.60
42	Tommy Davis IA	.30
43	Rick Wise	.30

695 Rod Carew

90	AL HR Ldrs (Norm Cash, Reggie Jackson, Bill Melton) **1.75**
91	NL ERA Ldrs (Dave Roberts, Tom Seaver, Don Wilson) **1.75**
92	AL ERA Ldrs (Vida Blue, Jim Palmer, Wilbur Wood) **1.50**
93	NL Pitching Ldrs (Steve Carlton, Al Downing, Fergie Jenkins, Tom Seaver) **2.00**
94	AL Pitching Ldrs (Vida Blue, Mickey Lolich, Wilbur Wood) **1.25**
95	NL SO Ldrs (Fergie Jenkins, Tom Seaver, Bill Stoneman) **1.75**
96	AL SO Ldrs (Vida Blue, Joe Coleman, Mickey Lolich) **1.25**
98	Chuck Tanner .... **.50**
99	*Ross Grimsley* .... **.60**
100	Frank Robinson **4.00**
101	Astros Rookies (Ray Busse, Bill Grief, J.R. Richard) **1.00**
103	Checklist 133-263 .... **2.25**
104	*Toby Harrah* **1.00**
106	Brewers Team .... **.90**
107	*Jose Cruz* **1.75**
112	Greg Luzinski .... **.80**
114	Bill Buckner **1.25**
115	Jim Fregosi .... **.70**
117	Cleo James (green under "C" and "S") **3.50**
117	Cleo James (yellow under "C" and "S") .... **.25**
120	Bill Freehan .... **.60**
124	Yankees Rookies (Alan Closter, Roger Hambright, Rusty Torres) ..... **.30**

44	Rick Wise IA .... **.25**
45	Glenn Beckert (green under "C" and "S") **3.50**
45	Glenn Beckert (yellow under "C" and "S") .... **.40**
46	Glenn Beckert IA .... **.30**
47	John Ellis .... **.30**
48	John Ellis IA .... **.30**
49	Willie Mays **18.00**
50	Willie Mays IA **9.00**
51	Harmon Killebrew **4.00**
52	*Harmon Killebrew IA **2.00**
53	Bud Harrelson .... **.40**
53	Bud Harrelson IA .... **.30**
59	*Fred Stanley* .... **.40**
61	Cubs Rookies (Gene Hiser, *Burt Hooton*, Earl Stephenson) **1.00**
65	Cesar Cedeno .... **.80**
67	Red Schoendienst .... **.50**
70	Mike Cuellar .... **.50**
71	Angels Team .... **.90**
72	Bruce Kison .... **.80**
75	Bert Campaneris .... **.60**
79	Red Sox Rookies (*Cecil Cooper, Carlton Fisk,* Mike Garman) **85.00**
80	Tony Perez **2.00**
85	NL Batting Ldrs (Glenn Beckert, Ralph Garr, Joe Torre) **1.25**
86	AL Batting Ldrs (Bobby Murcer, Tony Oliva, Merv Rettenmund) **1.25**
87	NL RBI Ldrs (Hank Aaron, Willie Stargell, Joe Torre) **2.25**
88	AL RBI Ldrs (Harmon Killebrew, Frank Robinson, Reggie Smith) **2.25**
89	NL HR Ldrs (Hank Aaron, Lee May, Willie Stargell) **2.25**

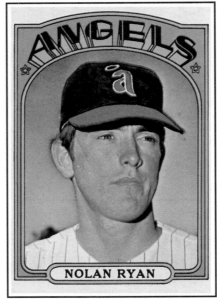

595 Nolan Ryan

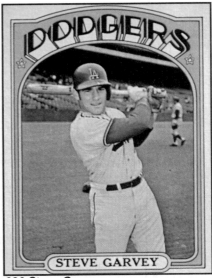

686 Steve Garvey

130	Bob Gibson **5.00**
132	Joe Morgan **4.00**
135	Vada Pinson .... **.80**
137	Dick Williams .... **.50**
139	Tim McCarver .... **.80**
141	Mets Rookies (Buzz Capra, Jon Matlack, Leroy Stanton) .... **.40**
142	*Chris Chambliss* **1.25**
145	Don Kessinger .... **.40**
147	*Dave Kingman* **3.50**
150	Norm Cash .... **.70**
154	Ted Simmons **1.50**
156	Twins Team .... **.90**
157	Don Gullett .... **.40**
160	Andy Messersmith .... **.40**
162	Brewers Rookies (Jerry Bell, *Darrell Porter,* Bob Reynolds) (Bell & Porter photos reversed) **1.00**
163	Tug McGraw .... **.80**
164	Tug McGraw IA .... **.40**
165	*Chris Speier* .... **.80**
166	*Chris Speier* IA .... **.40**
167	Deron Johnson .... **.25**
168	Deron Johnson IA .... **.25**
169	Vida Blue .... **.80**
170	Vida Blue IA .... **.40**
171	Darrell Evans **1.50**
172	Darrell Evans IA .... **.80**
173	Clay Kirby .... **.25**
174	Clay Kirby IA .... **.25**
175	Tom Haller .... **.30**
176	Tom Haller IA .... **.25**
177	Paul Schaal .... **.25**
178	Paul Schaal IA .... **.25**
179	Dock Ellis .... **.30**
180	Dock Ellis IA .... **.25**
181	Ed Kranepool .... **.40**
182	Ed Kranepool IA .... **.30**
183	Bill Melton .... **.30**
184	Bill Melton IA .... **.25**
185	Ron Bryant .... **.25**

560 Pete Rose IA

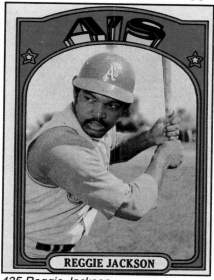

435 Reggie Jackson

253	Sandy Alomar	.25
256	George Foster	1.50
259	Sparky Lyle	.70
260	Ralph Garr	.40
262	Padres Team	.90
263	Felipe Alou	.50
264	Tommy John	2.00
267	Dave Concepcion	1.75
270	Jim Palmer	5.00
272	*Mickey Rivers*	1.00
276	Gene Mauch	.50
280	Willie McCovey	5.00
282	Astros Team	.90
285	Gaylord Perry	4.00
291	Hal McRae	.60
292	Hal McRae IA	.30
293	Danny Frisella	.25
294	Danny Frisella IA	.25
295	Dick Dietz	.25
296	Dick Dietz IA	.25
297	Claude Osteen	.40
298	Claude Osteen IA	.30
299	Hank Aaron	23.00
300	Hank Aaron IA	11.00
301	George Mitterwald	.25
302	George Mitterwald IA	.25
303	Joe Pepitone	.50
304	Joe Pepitone IA	.30
305	Ken Boswell	.25
306	Ken Boswell IA	.25
307	Steve Renko	.25
308	Steve Renko IA	.25
309	Roberto Clemente	23.00
310	Roberto Clemente IA	11.00
311	Clay Carroll	.30
312	Clay Carroll IA	.25
313	Luis Aparicio	3.00
314	Luis Aparicio IA	1.50
316	Cardinals Rookies (*Jim Bibby,* Santiago Guzman, Jorge Roque)	.50
323	Earl Weaver	.80
325	Mel Stottlemyre	.80

186	Ron Bryant IA	.25
191	*Jeff Burroughs*	.80
192	Cubs Team	.90
193	Kurt Bevacqua	.40
195	Orlando Cepeda	2.00
198	Dodgers Rookies (*Charlie Hough,* Bob O'Brien, Mike Strahler)	2.25
200	Lou Brock	4.00
203	*Ron Blomberg*	.50
206	Dal Maxvill	.30
208	Milt Pappas	.40
209	Joe Rudi	.60
210	Denny McLain	1.25
213	Angels Rookies (Art Kusnyer, Billy Parker, Tom Silverio)	.25
216	Joe Niekro	.50
219	*Rennie Stennett*	.40
220	Jim Perry	.60
221	NL Playoffs (Bucs Champs!)	1.25
222	AL Playoffs (Orioles Champs!)	1.25
223	World Series Game 1	1.25
224	World Series Game 2	1.25
225	World Series Game 3	1.25
226	World Series Game 4	1.50
227	World Series Game 5	1.25
228	World Series Game 6	1.25
229	World Series Game 7	1.25
230	World Series Summary (Series Celebration)	1.25
233	*Jay Johnstone	.40
237	Yankees Team	1.25
240	Rich Allen	1.75
241	Rollie Fingers	2.50
245	Tommie Agee	.30
250	Boog Powell	1.25
251	Checklist 264-394 (small print on front)	2.25
251	Checklist 264-394 (large print on front)	2.25

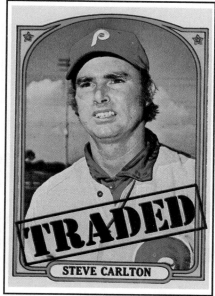

751 Steve Carlton Traded

327	*Steve Stone*	1.00
328	Red Sox Team	1.00
330	Jim Hunter	3.50
338	Bob Grich	.70
340	Roy White	.70
341	Boyhood Photo (*Joe Torre*)	.50
347	Boyhood Photo (*Tom Seaver*)	2.00
395	Matty Alou	.60
396	Paul Lindblad	.30
397	Phillies Team	.90
398	Larry Hisle	.40
399	Milt Wilcox	.40
400	Tony Oliva	1.50
401	Jim Nash	.30
402	Bobby Heise	.30
403	John Cumberland	.30
404	Jeff Torborg	.40
405	Ron Fairly	.50
406	*George Hendrick*	1.00
407	Chuck Taylor	.30
408	Jim Northrup	.40
409	Frank Baker	.40
410	*Fergie Jenkins	2.00
411	Bob Montgomery	.30
412	Dick Kelley	.30
413	White Sox Rookies (Don Eddy, Dave Lemonds)	.30
414	Bob Miller	.30
415	Cookie Rojas	.30
416	Johnny Edwards	.30
417	Tom Hall	.30
418	Tom Shopay	.30
419	Jim Spencer	.30
420	Steve Carlton	15.00
421	Ellie Rodriguez	.30
422	Ray Lamb	.30
423	Oscar Gamble	.40
424	Bill Gogolewski	.30
425	Ken Singleton	.70
426	Ken Singleton IA	.40
427	Tito Fuentes	.30

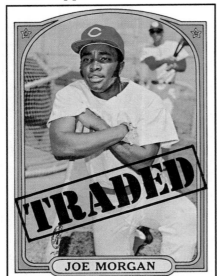

752 Joe Morgan Traded

428	Tito Fuentes IA	.30
429	Bob Robertson	.30
430	Bob Robertson IA	.30
431	Clarence Gaston	.30
432	Clarence Gaston IA	.30
433	Johnny Bench	25.00
434	Johnny Bench IA	10.00
435	Reggie Jackson	25.00
436	Reggie Jackson IA	13.00
437	Maury Wills	1.50
438	Maury Wills IA	.70
439	Billy Williams	3.50
440	Billy Williams IA	1.75
441	Thurman Munson	15.00
442	Thurman Munson IA	8.00
443	Ken Henderson	.30
444	Ken Henderson IA	.30
445	Tom Seaver	25.00
446	Tom Seaver IA	9.00
447	Willie Stargell	4.00
448	Willie Stargell IA	2.00
449	Bob Lemon	.90
450	Mickey Lolich	1.25
451	Tony LaRussa	.60
452	Ed Herrmann	.30
453	Barry Lersch	.30
454	A's Team	2.00
455	Tommy Harper	.40
456	Mark Belanger	.40
457	Padres Rookies (Darcy Fast, Mike Ivie, *Derrel Thomas*)	.40
458	Aurelio Monteagudo	.30
459	Rick Renick	.30
460	Al Downing	.40
461	Tim Cullen	.30
462	Rickey Clark	.30
463	Bernie Carbo	.30
464	Jim Roland	.30
465	Gil Hodges	3.00
466	Norm Miller	.30
467	Steve Kline	.30
468	Richie Scheinblum	.30

469	Ron Herbel	.30
470	Ray Fosse	.30
471	Luke Walker	.30
472	Phil Gagliano	.30
473	Dan McGinn	.30
474	Orioles Rookies (Don Baylor, Roric Harrison, Johnny Oates)	3.50
475	Gary Nolan	.30
476	Lee Richard	.30
477	Tom Phoebus	.30
478	Checklist 526-656	2.25
479	Don Shaw	.30
480	Lee May	.60
481	Billy Conigliaro	.30
482	Joe Hoerner	.30
483	Ken Suarez	.30
484	Lum Harris	.30
485	Phil Regan	.30
486	John Lowenstein	.30
487	Tigers Team	1.50
488	Mike Nagy	.30
489	Expos Rookies (Terry Humphrey, Keith Lampard)	.30
490	Dave McNally	.50
491	Boyhood Photo (Lou Piniella)	.60
492	Boyhood Photo (Mel Stottlemyre)	.40
493	Boyhood Photo (Bob Bailey)	.30
494	Boyhood Photo (Willie Horton)	.40
495	Boyhood Photo (Bill Melton)	.30
496	Boyhood Photo (Bud Harrelson)	.40
497	Boyhood Photo (Jim Perry)	.40
498	Boyhood Photo (Brooks Robinson)	2.00
499	Vicente Romo	.30

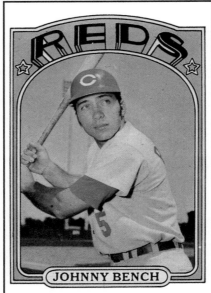

433 Johnny Bench

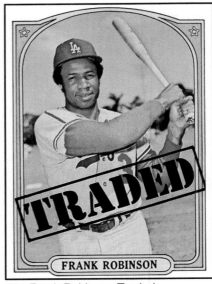

754 Frank Robinson Traded

500	Joe Torre	1.25
501	Pete Hamm	.30
502	Jackie Hernandez	.30
503	Gary Peters	.30
504	Ed Spiezio	.30
505	Mike Marshall	.50
506	Indians Rookies (Terry Ley, Jim Moyer, *Dick Tidrow*)	.60
507	Fred Gladding	.30
508	Ellie Hendricks	.30
509	Don McMahon	.30
510	*Ted Williams	5.00
511	Tony Taylor	.30
512	Paul Popovich	.30
513	Lindy McDaniel	.40
514	Ted Sizemore	.30
515	*Bert Blyleven	3.25
516	Oscar Brown	.30
517	Ken Brett	.40
518	Wayne Garrett	.30
519	Ted Abernathy	.30
520	Larry Bowa	1.25
521	Alan Foster	.30
522	Dodgers Team	1.25
523	Chuck Dobson	.30
524	Reds Rookies (Ed Armbrister, Mel Behney)	.30
525	Carlos May	.40
526	Bob Bailey	.70
527	Dave Leonhard	.70
528	Ron Stone	.70
529	Dave Nelson	.70
530	Don Sutton	3.50
531	Freddie Patek	1.25
532	Fred Kendall	.70
533	Ralph Houk	1.25
534	Jim Hickman	.80
535	Ed Brinkman	.80
536	Doug Rader	.70
537	Bob Locker	.70
538	Charlie Sands	.70

539	*Terry Forster*	1.25
540	Felix Millan	.70
541	Roger Repoz	.70
542	Jack Billingham	.70
543	Duane Josephson	.70
544	Ted Martinez	.70
545	Wayne Granger	.70
546	Joe Hague	.70
547	Indians Team	1.50
548	Frank Reberger	.70
549	Dave May	.70
550	Brooks Robinson	12.00
551	Ollie Brown	.70
552	Ollie Brown IA	.70
553	Wilbur Wood	.90
554	Wilbur Wood IA	.80
555	Ron Santo	1.50
556	Ron Santo IA	.80
557	John Odom	.70
558	John Odom IA	.70
559	Pete Rose	65.00
560	Pete Rose IA	35.00
561	Leo Cardenas	.70
562	Leo Cardenas IA	.70
563	Ray Sadecki	.70
564	Ray Sadecki IA	.70
565	Reggie Smith	.90
566	Reggie Smith IA	.80
567	Juan Marichal	6.00
568	Juan Marichal IA	3.00
569	Ed Kirkpatrick	.70
570	Ed Kirkpatrick IA	.70
571	Nate Colbert	.70
572	Nate Colbert IA	.70
573	Fritz Peterson	.75
574	Fritz Peterson IA	.75
575	Al Oliver	2.00
576	*Leo Durocher	1.25
577	Mike Paul	.70
578	Billy Grabarkewitz	.70
579	*Doyle Alexander*	2.50
580	Lou Piniella	1.75
581	Wade Blasingame	.70

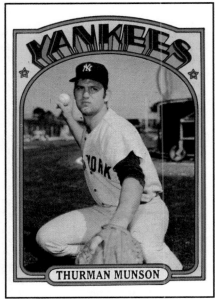

441 Thurman Munson

37 Carl Yastrzemski

582	Expos Team	2.25
583	Darold Knowles	.70
584	Jerry McNertney	.75
585	George Scott	.80
586	Denis Menke	.70
587	Billy Wilson	.70
588	Jim Holt	.70
589	Hal Lanier	1.00
590	Graig Nettles	2.50
591	Paul Casanova	.70
592	Lew Krausse	.70
593	Rich Morales	.70
594	Jim Beauchamp	.70
595	Nolan Ryan	70.00
596	Manny Mota	.90
597	Jim Magnuson	.80
599	Billy Champion	.70
600	Al Kaline	12.00
601	George Stone	.70
602	Dave Bristol	.70
603	Jim Ray	.70
604	Checklist 657-787	4.00
605	Nelson Briles	.70
606	Luis Melendez	.70
607	Frank Duffy	.70
608	Mike Corkins	.70
609	Tom Grieve	.70
610	Bill Stoneman	.70
611	Rich Reese	.70
612	Joe Decker	.70
613	Mike Ferraro	.70
614	Ted Uhlaender	.70
615	Steve Hargan	.70
616	*Joe Ferguson*	.80
617	Royals Team	2.25
618	Rich Robertson	.70
619	Rich McKinney	.70
620	*Phil Niekro	4.50
621	Commissioners Award	.90
622	MVP Award	.90
623	Cy Young Award	.90
624	Minor League Player of the Year Award	.90

625	Rookie of the Year Award	.90
626	Babe Ruth Award	.90
627	Moe Drabowsky	.70
628	Terry Crowley	.70
629	Paul Doyle	.70
630	Rich Hebner	.80
631	John Strohmayer	.70
632	Mike Hegan	.70
633	Jack Hiatt	.70
634	Dick Woodson	.70
635	Don Money	.80
636	Bill Lee	.90
637	Preston Gomez	.70
638	Ken Wright	.70
639	J.C. Martin	.70
640	Joe Coleman	.80
641	Mike Lum	.70
642	Denny Riddleberger	.70
643	Russ Gibson	.70
644	Bernie Allen	.80
645	Jim Maloney	.80
646	Chico Salmon	.70
647	Bob Moose	.70
648	Jim Lyttle	.70
649	Pete Richert	.70
650	Sal Bando	1.00
651	Reds Team	2.00
652	Marcelino Lopez	.70
653	Jim Fairey	.70
654	Horacio Pina	.70
655	Jerry Grote	.80
656	Rudy May	.80
657	Bobby Wine	2.25
658	Steve Dunning	2.25
659	Bob Aspromonte	2.25
660	Paul Blair	2.50
661	Bill Virdon	2.25
662	Stan Bahnsen	2.25
663	Fran Healy	2.25
664	Bobby Knoop	2.25
665	Chris Short	2.25
666	Hector Torres	2.25
667	Ray Newman	2.25

310 Roberto Clemente IA

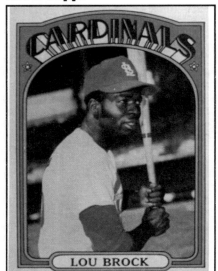

200 Lou Brock

710	Jim Kaat IA	3.25
711	Bobby Bonds	3.75
712	Bobby Bonds IA	2.50
713	Gene Michael	2.50
714	Gene Michael IA	2.50
715	Mike Epstein	2.50
716	Jesus Alou	2.50
717	Bruce Dal Canton	2.25
718	Del Rice	2.25
719	Cesar Geronimo	2.50
720	Sam McDowell	3.00
721	Eddie Leon	2.25
722	Bill Sudakis	2.25
723	Al Santorini	2.25
724	AL Rookies (John Curtis, Rich Hinton, Mickey Scott)	2.50
725	Dick McAuliffe	2.50
726	Dick Selma	2.25
727	Jose Laboy	2.25
728	Gail Hopkins	2.25
729	Bob Veale	2.50
730	Rick Monday	2.75
731	Orioles Team	2.25
732	George Culver	2.25
733	Jim Hart	2.50
734	Bob Burda	2.25
735	Diego Segui	2.25
736	Bill Russell	3.00
737	*Lenny Randle*	2.50
738	Jim Merritt	2.25
739	Don Mason	2.25
740	Rico Carty	3.25
741	Major League Rookies (Tom Hutton, *Rick Miller, John Milner*)	2.50
742	Jim Rooker	2.25
743	Cesar Gutierrez	2.25
744	*Jim Slaton*	2.50
745	Julian Javier	2.50
746	Lowell Palmer	2.25
747	Jim Stewart	2.25
748	Phil Hennigan	2.25

330 Jim Hunter

668	Rangers Team	3.25
669	Willie Crawford	2.25
670	Ken Holtzman	2.75
671	Donn Clendenon	2.50
672	Archie Reynolds	2.25
673	Dave Marshall	2.25
674	John Kennedy	2.25
675	Pat Jarvis	2.25
676	Danny Cater	2.25
677	Ivan Murrell	2.25
678	Steve Luebber	2.25
679	Astros Rookies (Bob Fenwick, Bob Stinson)	2.25
680	Dave Johnson	3.50
681	Bobby Pfeil	2.25
682	Mike McCormick	2.50
683	Steve Hovley	2.25
684	Hal Breeden	2.25
685	Joe Horlen	2.25
686	Steve Garvey	65.00
687	Del Unser	2.25
688	Cardinals Team	3.25
689	Eddie Fisher	2.25
690	Willie Montanez	2.50
691	Curt Blefary	2.25
692	Curt Blefary IA	2.25
693	Alan Gallagher	2.25
694	Alan Gallagher IA	2.25
695	Rod Carew	80.00
696	Rod Carew IA	35.00
697	Jerry Koosman	4.50
698	Jerry Koosman IA	2.50
699	Bobby Murcer	4.00
700	Bobby Murcer IA	2.50
701	Jose Pagan	2.25
702	Jose Pagan IA	2.25
703	Doug Griffin	2.25
704	Doug Griffin IA	2.25
705	Pat Corrales	2.50
706	Pat Corrales IA	2.25
707	Tim Foli	2.25
708	Tim Foli IA	2.25
709	Jim Kaat	6.75

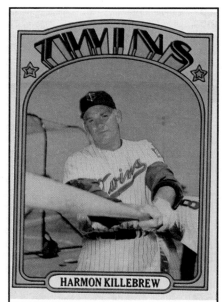

51 Harmon Killebrew

749	Walter Alston	5.00
750	Willie Horton	2.75
751	Steve Carlton Traded	35.00
752	Joe Morgan Traded	25.00
753	Denny McLain Traded	6.00
754	Frank Robinson Traded	23.00
755	Jim Fregosi	2.75
756	Rick Wise Traded	2.75
757	Jose Cardenal Traded	2.50
758	Gil Garrido	2.25
759	Chris Cannizzaro	2.25
760	Bill Mazeroski	3.75
761	Major League Rookies (*Ron Cey, Ben Oglivie,* Bernie Williams)	13.00
762	Wayne Simpson	2.25
763	Ron Hansen	2.25
764	Dusty Baker	3.00
765	Ken McMullen	2.25
766	Steve Hamilton	2.25
767	Tom McCraw	2.25
768	Denny Doyle	2.25
769	Jack Aker	2.50
770	Jim Wynn	2.75
771	Giants Team	3.25
772	Ken Tatum	2.25
773	Ron Brand	2.25
774	Luis Alvarado	2.25
775	Jerry Reuss	3.50
776	Bill Voss	2.25
777	Hoyt Wilhelm	10.00
778	Twins Rookies (Vic Albury, *Rick Dempsey,* Jim Strickland)	3.25
779	Tony Cloninger	2.50
780	Dick Green	2.25
781	Jim McAndrew	2.25
782	Larry Stahl	2.25
783	Les Cain	2.25
784	Ken Aspromonte	2.25
785	Vic Davalillo	2.25
786	Chuck Brinkman	2.25
787	Ron Reed	4.50

1973 TOPPS

Topps marked the end of an era with its 1973 edition: It was the last time a major set was issued one series at a time throughout the summer. Card fronts contain a small silhouetted figure depicting each player's position—an unusual design element. Card backs have a vertical format once again, and retain the basic elements of cartoons, brief biographies, and year-by-year stats. The 660-card set is noted for odd-looking manager cards. These cards include tiny black-and-white portraits of team coaches along with pictures of each team skipper. They can be found with different backgrounds surrounding the photos of the coaches, although the variations have little difference in value. Without question the most popular card in the set is number 615, titled Rookie Third Basemen, which shows Ron Cey and future Hall of Famer Mike Schmidt. It currently fetches prices approaching $400.

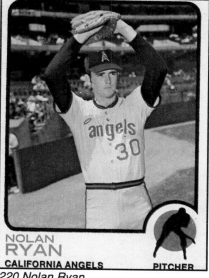

220 Nolan Ryan

		NR MT
Complete set		$1100.00
Commons (1-396)		.25
Commons (397-528)		.40
Commons (529-660)		1.25

1	All Time HR Ldrs (Babe Ruth, Hank Aaron, Willie Mays)	$15.00
2	Rich Hebner	.30
3	Jim Lonborg	.30
5	Ed Brinkman	.30
7	Rangers Team	.90
10	Don Sutton	2.00
11	Chris Chambliss	.70
12	Padres Mgr./Coaches (Dave Garcia, Johnny Podres, Bob Skinner, Whitey Wietelmann, Don Zimmer)	.40
13	George Hendrick	.70
15	Ralph Garr	.30
23	Dave Kingman	1.25
25	Roy White	.40
26	Pirates Team	1.00
28	Hal McRae	.50
30	Tug McGraw	.60
31	*Buddy Bell*	3.50
35	Willie Davis	.50
40	Reggie Smith	.50
43	*Randy Moffitt*	.30
44	Rick Monday	.40
45	Ellie Rodriguez (photo is Paul Ratliff)	.25
49	Twins Mgr./Coaches (Vern Morgan, Frank Quilici, Bob Rodgers, Ralph Rowe, Al Worthington)	.30
50	Roberto Clemente	25.00
54	Checklist 1-132	2.00
55	Jon Matlack	.40
59	*Steve Yeager*	.60
60	Ken Holtzman	.40
61	Batting Ldrs (Rod Carew, Billy Williams)	1.75
62	HR Ldrs (Dick Allen, Johnny Bench)	1.50

63	RBI Ldrs (Dick Allen, Johnny Bench)	1.50
64	SB Ldrs (Lou Brock, Bert Campaneris)	1.25
65	ERA Ldrs (Steve Carlton, Luis Tiant)	1.25
66	Victory Ldrs (Steve Carlton, Gaylord Perry, Wilbur Wood)	1.25
67	SO Ldrs (Steve Carlton, Nolan Ryan)	2.50
68	Leading Firemen (Clay Carroll, Sparky Lyle)	.80
70	Milt Pappas	.40
75	Vada Pinson	.80
80	Tony Oliva	1.50
81	Cubs Mgr./Coaches (Hank Aguirre, Ernie Banks, Larry Jansen, Whitey Lockman, Pete Reiser)	.55
84	Rollie Fingers	1.50
85	Ted Simmons	1.25
90	Brooks Robinson	5.00

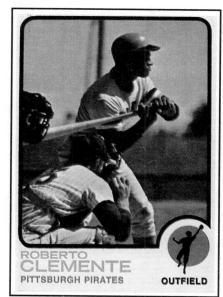

50 Roberto Clemente

91	Dodgers Team	1.00
100	Hank Aaron	22.00
108	Bill Russell	.40
109	Doyle Alexander	1.00
115	Ron Santo	.80
116	Yankees Mgr./Coaches (Jim Hegan, Ralph Houk, Elston Howard, Dick Howser, Jim Turner)	.75
118	John Mayberry	.40
119	Larry Bowa	.80
125	Ron Fairly	.40
127	Brewers Team	.90
129	Terry Forster	.40
130	Pete Rose	20.00
131	Red Sox Mgr./Coaches (Doug Camilli, Eddie Kasko, Don Lenhardt, Eddie Popowski, Lee Stange)	.40
133	Dave Roberts	.25
136	Orioles Mgr./Coaches (George Bamberger, Jim Frey, Billy Hunter, George Staller, Earl Weaver)	.75
140	Lou Piniella	.80
142	Thurman Munson	6.00
145	Bobby Bonds	.70
148	*Dave Goltz*	.60
150	Wilbur Wood	.40
153	Al Hrabosky	.40
155	Sal Bando	.70
158	Astros Team	.90
160	Jim Palmer	8.00
165	Luis Aparicio	3.00
167	Steve Stone	.50
170	Harmon Killebrew	3.50
174	*Rich Gossage*	5.00
175	Frank Robinson	5.00
179	A's Mgr./Coaches (Jerry Adair, Vern Hoscheit, Irv Noren, Wes Stock, Dick Williams)	.60
180	*Fergie Jenkins*	1.50

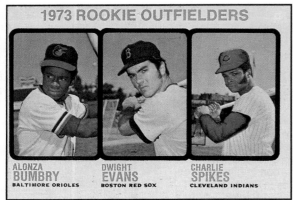

614 Rookie Outfielders

255 Reggie Jackson

182	*Mike Caldwell*	.50
184	Jerry Koosman	.50
185	*Jim Wynn	.40
189	Greg Luzinski	.70
190	Bob Gibson	3.50
191	Tigers Team	1.25
193	Carlton Fisk	10.00
194	*Jorge Orta*	.50
199	*Bert Blyleven	1.50
200	Billy Williams	3.00
201	AL Playoffs (Hendrick Scores Winning Run!)	1.00
202	NL Playoffs (Foster's Run Decides It!)	1.00
203	World Series Game 1 (Tenace the Menace)	1.00
204	World Series Game 2 (A's Make It Two Straight)	1.00
205	World Series Game 3 (Reds Win Squeaker)	1.00
206	World Series Game 4 (Tenace Singles In Ninth)	1.00
207	World Series Game 5 (Odom Out At Plate)	1.00
208	World Series Game 6 (Reds' Slugging Ties Series)	1.00
209	World Series Game 7 (Campy Starts Winning Rally)	1.00
210	World Series Summary (World Champions)	1.00
213	Steve Garvey	10.00
215	Dusty Baker	.50
216	Toby Harrah	.40
219	Cardinals Team	.90
220	Nolan Ryan	35.00
225	Al Oliver	1.25
230	Joe Morgan	5.00
232	Ken Singleton	.40
234	*Bill North*	.50
235	Jim Hunter	3.00
237	Braves Mgr./Coaches (Lew Burdette, Jim Busby, Roy Hartsfield, Eddie Mathews, Ken Silvestri)	1.25
240	Bobby Murcer	.60
243	Angels Team	.90

245	Carl Yastrzemski	15.00
252	Giants Mgr./Coaches (Joe Amalfitano, Charlie Fox, Andy Gilbert, Don McMahon, John McNamara)	.40
255	Reggie Jackson	20.00
257	Mets Mgr./Coaches (Yogi Berra, Roy McMillan, Joe Pignatano, Rube Walker, Eddie Yost)	1.50
258	Tommy John	1.75
264	Checklist 133-264	2.00
265	Gene Michael	.40
269	Tim McCarver	.70
270	Luis Tiant	.25
275	Tony Perez	1.25
278	Orioles Team	.90
280	Al Kaline	5.00
290	Cesar Cedeno	.40
292	Jose Cruz	.80
295	Bert Campaneris	.60
296	Reds Mgr./Coaches (Sparky Anderson, Alex Grammas, Ted Kluszewski, George Scherger, Larry Shepard)	.70
297	Walt Williams	.25
298	Ron Bryant	.25
299	Ted Ford	.25
300	Steve Carlton	10.00
301	Billy Grabarkewitz	.25
302	Terry Crowley	.25
303	Nelson Briles	.25
304	Duke Sims	.25
305	Willie Mays	20.00
306	Tom Burgmeier	.25
307	Boots Day	.25
308	Skip Lockwood	.25
309	Paul Popovich	.25
310	Dick Allen	.80
311	Joe Decker	.25
312	Oscar Brown	.25
313	Jim Ray	.25
314	Ron Swoboda	.25
315	John Odom	.25
316	Padres Team	.90
317	Danny Cater	.25
318	Jim McGlothlin	.25
319	Jim Spencer	.25

320	Lou Brock	3.50
321	Rich Hinton	.25
322	*Garry Maddox*	.80
323	Tigers Mgr./Coaches (Art Fowler, Billy Martin, Joe Schultz, Charlie Silvera, Dick Tracewski)	1.00
324	Al Downing	.25
325	Boog Powell	1.00
326	Darrell Brandon	.25
327	John Lowenstein	.25
328	Bill Bonham	.25
329	Ed Kranepool	.30
330	Rod Carew	10.00
331	Carl Morton	.25
332	*John Felske*	.30
333	Gene Clines	.25
334	Freddie Patek	.25
335	Bob Tolan	.25
336	Tom Bradley	.25
337	Dave Duncan	.25
338	Checklist 265-396	2.00
339	Dick Tidrow	.30
340	Nate Colbert	.30
341	Boyhood Photo (Jim Palmer)	1.50
342	Boyhood Photo (Sam McDowell)	.40
343	Boyhood Photo (Bobby Murcer)	.40
344	Boyhood Photo (Jim Hunter)	1.50
345	Boyhood Photo (Chris Speier)	.30
346	Boyhood Photo (Gaylord Perry)	1.50
347	Royals Team	.90
348	Rennie Stennett	.30
349	Dick McAuliffe	.30
350	Tom Seaver	15.00
351	Jimmy Stewart	.25
352	*Don Stanhouse*	.40
353	Steve Brye	.30

ALLTIME HOME RUN LEADERS

BABE RUTH

714

HANK AARON 673

WILLIE MAYS 654

1 All Time HR Ldrs

1973 ROOKIE THIRD BASEMEN

RON CEY
LOS ANGELES DODGERS

JOHN HILTON
SAN DIEGO PADRES

MIKE SCHMIDT
PHILADELPHIA PHILLIES

615 Rookie Third Basemen

354	Billy Parker	.25
355	Mike Marshall	.40
356	White Sox Mgr./Coaches (Joe Lonnett, Jim Maloney, Al Monchak, Johnny Sain, Chuck Tanner)	.50
357	Ross Grimsley	.30
358	Jim Nettles	.25
359	Cecil Upshaw	.25
360	Joe Rudi (photo is Gene Tenace)	.40
361	Fran Healy	.25
362	Eddie Watt	.25
363	Jackie Hernandez	.25
364	Rick Wise	.30
365	Rico Petrocelli	.30
366	Brock Davis	.25
367	Burt Hooton	.40
368	Bill Buckner	.75
369	Lerrin LaGrow	.25
370	Willie Stargell	3.50
371	Mike Kekich	.25
372	Oscar Gamble	.30
373	Clyde Wright	.30
374	Darrell Evans	.75
375	Larry Dierker	.30
376	Frank Duffy	.25
377	Expos Mgr./Coaches (Dave Bristol, Larry Doby, Gene Mauch, Cal McLish, Jerry Zimmerman)	.50
378	Lenny Randle	.25
379	Cy Acosta	.25
380	Johnny Bench	15.00
381	Vicente Romo	.25
382	Mike Hegan	.25
383	Diego Segui	.25
384	*Don Baylor	1.00
385	Jim Perry	.50
386	Don Money	.30
387	Jim Barr	.25
388	Ben Oglivie	.50
389	Mets Team	2.00

390	*Mickey Lolich	.70
391	Lee Lacy	.80
392	Dick Drago	.25
393	Jose Cardenal	.30
394	*Sparky Lyle	.70
395	Roger Metzger	.25
396	Grant Jackson	.25
397	Dave Cash	.40
398	Rich Hand	.40
399	George Foster	1.50
400	Gaylord Perry	3.00
401	Clyde Mashore	.40
402	Jack Hiatt	.40
403	Sonny Jackson	.40
404	Chuck Brinkman	.40
405	Cesar Tovar	.40
406	Paul Lindblad	.40
407	Felix Millan	.40
408	Jim Colborn	.40
409	Ivan Murrell	.40
410	Willie McCovey	5.00
411	Ray Corbin	.40
412	Manny Mota	.60
413	Tom Timmermann	.40

STEVE CARLTON
PHILADELPHIA PHILLIES

PITCHER

300 Steve Carlton

414	Ken Rudolph	.40
415	Marty Pattin	.40
416	Paul Schaal	.40
417	Scipio Spinks	.40
418	Bobby Grich	.60
419	Casey Cox	.40
420	Tommie Agee	.50
421	Angels Mgr./Coaches (Tom Morgan, Salty Parker, Jimmie Reese, John Roseboro, Bobby Winkles)	.45
422	Bob Robertson	.40
423	Johnny Jeter	.40
424	Denny Doyle	.40
425	Alex Johnson	.40
426	Dave LaRoche	.40
427	Rick Auerbach	.40
428	Wayne Simpson	.40
429	Jim Fairey	.40
430	Vida Blue	.80
431	Gerry Moses	.40
432	Dan Frisella	.40
433	Willie Horton	.60
434	Giants Team	1.00
435	Rico Carty	.60
436	Jim McAndrew	.40
437	John Kennedy	.40
438	Enzo Hernandez	.40
439	Eddie Fisher	.40
440	Glenn Beckert	.50
441	Gail Hopkins	.40
442	Dick Dietz	.40
443	Danny Thompson	.45
444	Ken Brett	.50
445	Ken Berry	.40
446	Jerry Reuss	.60
447	Joe Hague	.40
448	John Hiller	.45
449	Indians Mgr./Coaches (Ken Aspromonte, Rocky Colavito, Joe Lutz, Warren Spahn)	.60
450	Joe Torre	1.00
451	John Vuckovich	.40
452	Paul Casanova	.40
453	Checklist 397-528	2.25
454	Tom Haller	.45
455	Bill Melton	.45
456	Dick Green	.40

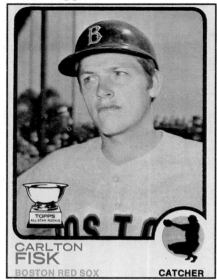

193 Carlton Fisk

457	John Strohmayer	.40
458	Jim Mason	.40
459	Jimmy Howarth	.40
460	Bill Freehan	.65
461	Mike Corkins	.40
462	Ron Blomberg	.45
463	Ken Tatum	.40
464	Cubs Team	1.25
465	Dave Giusti	.45
466	Jose Arcia	.40
467	Mike Ryan	.40
468	Tom Griffin	.40
469	Dan Monzon	.40
470	Mike Cuellar	.65
471	Hit Ldr (Ty Cobb)	3.00
472	Grand Slam Ldr (Lou Gehrig)	3.00
473	Total Base Ldr (Hank Aaron)	3.00
474	RBI Ldr (Babe Ruth)	5.00
475	Batting Ldr (Ty Cobb)	3.00
476	Shutout Ldr (Walter Johnson)	1.25
477	Victory Ldr (Cy Young)	1.25
478	SO Ldr (Walter Johnson)	1.25
479	Hal Lanier	.60
480	Juan Marichal	3.50
481	White Sox Team	1.25
482	*Rick Reuschel	6.00
483	Dal Maxvill	.45
484	Ernie McAnally	.40
485	Norm Cash	.85
486	Phillies Mgr./Coaches (Carroll Berringer, Billy DeMars, Danny Ozark, Ray Rippelmeyer, Bobby Wine)	.65
487	Bruce Dal Canton	.40
488	Dave Campbell	.40
489	Jeff Burroughs	.65
490	Claude Osteen	.65
491	Bob Montgomery	.40
492	Pedro Borbon	.45

493	Duffy Dyer	.40
494	Rich Morales	.40
495	Tommy Helms	.45
496	Ray Lamb	.40
497	Cardinals Mgr./Coaches (Vern Benson, George Kissell, Red Schoendienst, Barney Schultz)	.90
498	Graig Nettles	2.50
499	Bob Moose	.40
500	A's Team	2.00
501	Larry Gura	.50
502	Bobby Valentine	.65
503	*Phil Niekro	3.00
504	Earl Williams	.40
505	Bob Bailey	.40
506	Bart Johnson	.40
507	Darrel Chaney	.40
508	Gates Brown	.40
509	Jim Nash	.40
510	Amos Otis	.60
511	Sam McDowell	.65
512	Dalton Jones	.40
513	Dave Marshall	.40
514	Jerry Kenney	.40
515	Andy Messersmith	.50
516	Danny Walton	.40
517	Pirates Mgr./Coaches (Don Leppert, Bill Mazeroski, Dave Ricketts, Bill Virdon, Mel Wright)	.70
518	Bob Veale	.45
519	John Edwards	.40
520	Mel Stottlemyre	.65
521	Braves Team	1.20
522	Leo Cardenas	.40
523	Wayne Granger	.40
524	Gene Tenace	.40
525	Jim Fregosi	.65
526	Ollie Brown	.40
527	Dan McGinn	.40
528	Paul Blair	.50
529	Milt May	1.25

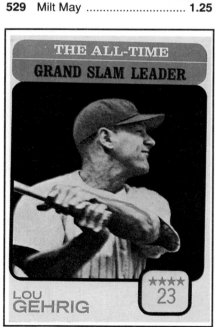

472 Grand Slam Leader

THE ALL-TIME **HIT LEADER**

TY COBB ★★★★ 4,191

471 Hit Leader

530	Jim Kaat	3.25
531	Ron Woods	1.25
532	Steve Mingori	1.25
533	Larry Stahl	1.25
534	Dave Lemonds	1.25
535	John Callison	1.50
536	Phillies Team	2.50
538	Jim Hart	1.50
539	Tom Murphy	1.25
540	Cleon Jones	1.50
541	Bob Bolin	1.25
542	Pat Corrales	1.50
543	Alan Foster	1.25
544	Von Joshua	1.25
545	Orlando Cepeda	3.50
546	Jim York	1.25
548	Don Durham	1.25
549	Rangers Mgr./Coaches (Chuck Estrada, Whitey Herzog, Chuck Hiller, Jackie Moore)	2.00
550	Dave Johnson	3.00
551	Mike Kilkenny	1.25
552	J.C. Martin	1.25
553	Mickey Scott	1.25
554	Dave Concepcion	2.50
555	Bill Hands	1.25
556	Yankees Team	4.00
557	Bernie Williams	1.25
558	Jerry May	1.25
559	Barry Lersch	1.25
560	Frank Howard	2.25
561	Jim Geddes	1.25
562	Wayne Garrett	1.25
563	Larry Haney	1.25
564	Mike Thompson	1.25
565	Jim Hickman	1.50
567	Bob Fenwick	1.25
568	Ray Newman	1.25
569	Dodgers Mgr./Coaches (Red Adams, Walt Alston, Monty Basgall, Jim Gillam, Tom Lasorda)	3.00

570	Bill Singer	1.50
571	Rusty Torres	1.50
572	Gary Sutherland	1.25
573	Fred Beene	1.25
574	Bob Didier	1.25
575	Dock Ellis	1.25
576	Expos Team	2.50
577	*Eric Soderholm*	1.50
578	Ken Wright	1.25
579	Tom Grieve	1.25
580	Joe Pepitone	2.00
581	Steve Kealey	1.25
582	Darrell Porter	1.75
583	Bill Greif	1.25
584	Chris Arnold	1.25
585	Joe Niekro	2.00
586	Bill Sudakis	1.50
587	Rich McKinney	1.25
588	Checklist 529-660	10.00
589	Ken Forsch	1.25
590	Deron Johnson	1.25
591	Mike Hedlund	1.25
592	John Boccabella	1.25
593	Royals Mgr./Coaches (Galen Cisco, Harry Dunlop, Charlie Lau, Jack McKeon)	1.50
594	Vic Harris	1.25
595	Don Gullett	1.50
596	Red Sox Team	2.75
597	Mickey Rivers	1.75
598	Phil Roof	1.25
599	Ed Crosby	1.25
600	Dave McNally	1.75
601	Rookie Catchers (George Pena, Sergio Robles, Rick Stelmaszek)	1.25
602	Rookie Pitchers (Mel Behney, Ralph Garcia, *Doug Rau*)	1.50
603	Rookie Third Basemen (Terry Hughes, Bill McNulty, *Ken Reitz*)	1.50

165 Luis Aparicio

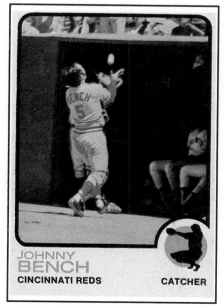

350 Tom Seaver

604	Rookie Pitchers (Jesse Jefferson, Dennis O'Toole, Bob Strampe)	1.25
605	Rookie First Basemen (Pat Bourque, *Enos Cabell*, Gonzalo Marquez)	1.75
606	Rookie Outfielders (*Gary Matthews,* Tom Paciorek, Jorge Roque)	2.25
607	Rookie Shortstops (Ray Busse, Pepe Frias, Mario Guerrero)	1.25
608	Rookie Pitchers (*Steve Busby,* Dick Colpaert, *George Medich*)	1.50
609	Rookie Second Basemen (Larvell Blanks, Pedro Garcia, *Dave Lopes*)	2.25
610	*Rookie Pitchers (Jimmy Freeman, Charlie Hough, Hank Webb)	1.75
611	Rookie Outfielders (Rich Coggins, Jim Wohlford, Richie Zisk)	1.50
612	Rookie Pitchers (Steve Lawson, Bob Reynolds, Brent Strom)	1.25
613	Rookie Catchers (*Bob Boone,* Mike Ivie, Skip Jutze)	25.00
614	Rookie Outfielders (*Alonza Bumbry, Dwight Evans,* Charlie Spikes)	50.00
615	Rookie Third Basemen (Ron Cey, Dave Hilton, *Mike Schmidt*)	400.00
616	Rookie Pitchers (Norm Angelini, Steve Blateric, Mike Garman)	1.50
617	Rich Chiles	1.25
618	Andy Etchebarren	1.25
619	Billy Wilson	1.25
620	Tommy Harper	1.50

621	Joe Ferguson	1.25
622	Larry Hisle	1.50
623	Steve Renko	1.25
624	Astros Mgr./Coaches (Leo Durocher, Preston Gomez, Grady Hatton, Hub Kittle, Jim Owens)	2.25
625	Angel Mangual	1.25
627	Luis Alvarado	1.25
628	Jim Slaton	1.25
629	Indians Team	2.50
630	Denny McLain	3.00
631	Tom Matchick	1.25
632	Dick Selma	1.25
633	Ike Brown	1.25
635	Gene Alley	1.25
636	Rick Clark	1.25
637	Norm Miller	1.25
638	Ken Reynolds	1.25
639	Willie Crawford	1.25
640	Dick Bosman	1.35
641	Reds Team	2.75
642	Jose Laboy	1.25
643	Al Fitzmorris	1.25
644	Jack Heidemann	1.25
645	Bob Locker	1.25
646	Brewers Mgr./Coaches (Del Crandall, Harvey Kuenn, Joe Nossek, Bob Shaw, Jim Walton)	1.50
647	George Stone	1.25
648	Tom Egan	1.25
650	Felipe Alou	1.85
651	Don Carrithers	1.25
652	Ted Kubiak	1.25
653	Joe Hoerner	1.25
654	Twins Team	2.50
655	Clay Kirby	1.25
656	John Ellis	1.25
657	Bob Johnson	1.25
658	Elliott Maddox	1.50
659	Jose Pagan	1.50
660	Fred Scherman	2.50

380 Johnny Bench

1974 TOPPS

For the first time, instead of issuing cards by series—the traditional way—Topps issued all 660 cards at one time. That allowed collectors the chance to acquire any card number at any time instead of having to wait and piece together a collection of different 132-card series throughout the summer. Because everyone guessed, falsely, that the San Diego Padres would be moved to Washington, D.C., Topps changed 15 Padres cards to read "Washington, Nat'l League." When the team stayed in San Diego, Topps quickly changed the cards, but not in time to prevent the release of many that contained the error. This was also the time that Hank Aaron was just two homers short of breaking Babe Ruth's career record, and Aaron is featured on the first six cards of the 1974 set. His previous cards were reproduced in miniature in the six-card series.

456 Dave Winfield

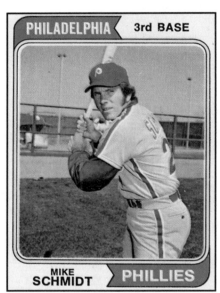
283 Mike Schmidt

		NR MT
Complete set		**$450.00**
Commons		**.20**

1	Hank Aaron	$30.00
2	Aaron Special 1954-57	3.00
3	Aaron Special 1958-61	3.00
4	Aaron Special 1962-65	3.00
5	Aaron Special 1966-69	3.00
6	Aaron Special 1970-73	3.00
7	Jim Hunter	3.00
9	Mickey Lolich	.60
10	Johnny Bench	12.00
11	Jim Bibby	.25
12	Dave May	.20
15	Joe Torre	.80
16	Orioles Team	.80
19	Gerry Moses	.25
20	Nolan Ryan	25.00
24	John Hiller	.25
25	Ken Singleton	.30
26	*Bill Campbell*	.40
27	George Scott	.30
28	Manny Sanguillen	.25
29	Phil Niekro	2.00
30	Bobby Bonds	.50
31	Astros Mgr./Coaches (Roger Craig, Preston Gomez, Grady Hatton, Hub Kittle, Bob Lillis)	.25
32	Johnny Grubb (Washington)	3.50
32	Johnny Grubb (San Diego)	.25
35	Gaylord Perry	2.25
36	Cardinals Team	2.25
37	Dave Sells	.20
38	Don Kessinger	.25
40	Jim Palmer	5.00
41	Bobby Floyd	.20
42	Claude Osteen	.30
43	*Jim Wynn	.30
44	Mel Stottlemyre	.40
45	Dave Johnson	.75
47	*Dick Ruthven*	.25
50	Rod Carew	6.00
52	Al Oliver	1.00
53	Fred Kendall (Washington)	3.50

53	Fred Kendall (San Diego)	.25
54	*Elias Sosa*	.25
55	Frank Robinson	3.50
56	Mets Team	1.00
59	Ross Grimsley	.25
60	Lou Brock	3.50
61	Luis Aparicio	2.50
65	Amos Otis	.30
66	*Sparky Lyle	.50
70	Dick Allen	.80
72	Aurelio Rodriguez	.25
73	Mike Marshall	.75
74	Twins Team	.80
76	Mickey Rivers	.30
77	Rich Troedson (Washington)	3.50
77	Rich Troedson (San Diego)	.25
78	Giants Mgr./Coaches (Joe Amalfitano, Charlie Fox, Andy Gilbert, Don McMahon, John McNamara)	.25

79	Gene Tenace	.35
80	Tom Seaver	10.00
81	Frank Duffy	.20
82	Dave Giusti	.20
83	Orlando Cepeda	1.00
84	Rick Wise	.25
85	*Joe Morgan	2.75
86	Joe Ferguson	.20
87	Fergie Jenkins	1.25
88	Freddie Patek	.20
89	Jackie Brown	.20
90	Bobby Murcer	.40
91	Ken Forsch	.25
92	Paul Blair	.25
93	Rod Gilbreath	.20
94	Tigers Team	.90
95	Steve Carlton	12.00
96	*Jerry Hairston*	.35
97	Bob Bailey	.20
98	*Bert Blyleven	1.00
99	Brewers Mgr./Coaches (Del Crandall, Harvey Kuenn, Joe Nossek, Jim Walton, Al Widmar)	.25
100	Willie Stargell	3.00
101	Bobby Valentine	.30
102	Bill Greif (Washington)	3.50
102	Bill Greif (San Diego)	.25
103	Sal Bando	.45
104	Ron Bryant	.20
105	*Carlton Fisk	2.00
106	Harry Parker	.20
107	Alex Johnson	.20
108	Al Hrabosky	.30
109	Bob Grich	.40
110	Billy Williams	2.75
111	Clay Carroll	.25
112	Dave Lopes	.45
113	Dick Drago	.20
114	Angels Team	.80
115	Willie Horton	.30
116	Jerry Reuss	.30
117	Ron Blomberg	.25

252 Dave Parker

130 Reggie Jackson

118	Bill Lee	.25
119	Phillies Mgr./Coaches (Carroll Beringer, Bill DeMars, Danny Ozark, Ray Ripplemeyer, Bobby Wine)	.25
120	Wilbur Wood	.30
121	Larry Lintz	.20
122	Jim Holt	.20
123	Nelson Briles	.20
125	Nate Colbert (Washington)	3.50
125	Nate Colbert (San Diego)	.30
126	Checklist 1-132	1.50
127	Tom Paciorek	.25
128	John Ellis	.20
129	Chris Speier	.25
130	Reggie Jackson	14.00
131	*Bob Boone	.50
132	Felix Millan	.25
133	David Clyde	.30
134	Denis Menke	.25
135	Roy White	.40
136	Rick Reuschel	.85
137	Al Bumbry	.25
138	Ed Brinkman	.25
139	Aurelio Monteagudo	.20
140	Darrell Evans	.60
141	Pat Bourque	.20
142	Pedro Garcia	.20
143	Dick Woodson	.20
144	Dodgers Mgr./Coaches (Red Adams, Walter Alston, Monty Basgall, Jim Gilliam, Tom Lasorda)	1.50
145	Dock Ellis	.25
146	Ron Fairly	.30
147	Bart Johnson	.20
148	Dave Hilton (Washington)	3.50
148	Dave Hilton (San Diego)	.25

149	Mac Scarce	.20
150	John Mayberry	.30
151	Diego Segui	.20
152	Oscar Gamble	.30
153	Jon Matlack	.30
154	Astros Team	.80
155	Bert Campaneris	.40
156	Randy Moffitt	.20
157	Vic Harris	.20
158	Jack Billingham	.20
159	Jim Ray Hart	.25
160	Brooks Robinson	3.50
161	Ray Burris	.40
162	Bill Freehan	.40
163	Ken Berry	.20
164	Tom House	.20
165	Willie Davis	.40
166	Royals Mgr./Coaches (Galen Cisco, Harry Dunlop, Charlie Lau, Jack McKeon)	.25
167	Luis Tiant	.50
168	Danny Thompson	.25
169	Steve Rogers	.75
170	Bill Melton	.25
171	Eduardo Rodriguez	.20
172	Gene Clines	.20
173	Randy Jones (Washington)	4.50
173	Randy Jones (San Diego)	.50
174	Bill Robinson	.20
175	Reggie Cleveland	.20
176	John Lowenstein	.20
177	Dave Roberts	.20
178	Garry Maddox	.40
179	Mets Mgr./Coaches (Yogi Berra, Roy McMillan, Joe Pignatano, Rube Walker, Eddie Yost)	1.25
180	Ken Holtzman	.30
181	Cesar Geronimo	.25
182	Lindy McDaniel	.20
183	Johnny Oates	.20

250 Willie McCovey

184	Rangers Team	.80
185	Jose Cardenal	.25
187	Don Baylor	.75
188	Rudy Meoli	.20
189	Jim Brewer	.20
190	Tony Oliva	.80
191	Al Fitzmorris	.20
192	Mario Guerrero	.20
193	Tom Walker	.20
194	Darrell Porter	.30
195	Carlos May	.25
196	Jim Fregosi	.40
197	Vicente Romo (Washington)	3.50
197	Vicente Romo (San Diego)	.25
198	Dave Cash	.20
199	Mike Kekich	.20
200	Cesar Cedeno	.40
201	Batting Ldrs (Rod Carew, Pete Rose)	3.00
202	HR Ldrs (Reggie Jackson, Willie Stargell)	2.25
203	RBI Ldrs (Reggie Jackson, Willie Stargell)	2.00
204	SB Ldrs (Lou Brock, Tommy Harper)	1.25
205	Victory Ldrs (Ron Bryant, Wilbur Wood)	.50
206	ERA Ldrs (Jim Palmer, Tom Seaver)	2.00
207	SO Ldrs (Nolan Ryan, Tom Seaver)	2.00
208	Leading Firemen (John Hiller, Mike Marshall)	.85
210	Bill Singer	.25
211	Cubs Team	.85
212	Rollie Fingers	1.50
213	Dave Rader	.20
215	Al Kaline	3.50
216	Ray Sadecki	.20
217	Tim Foli	.20
220	Don Sutton	2.00

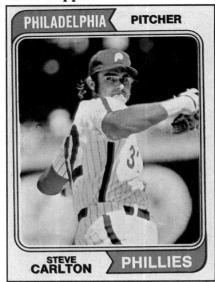

95 Steve Carlton

221	White Sox Mgr./Coaches (Joe Lonnett, Jim Mahoney, Alex Monchak, Johnny Sain, Chuck Tanner)	.35
222	Ramon Hernandez	.20
223	Jeff Burroughs	.50
224	Roger Metzger	.20
225	Paul Splittorff	.25
226	Washington Nat'l. Team	7.00
226	Padres Team	1.00
229	Fritz Peterson	.30
230	Tony Perez	1.25
235	Dave McNally	.30
236	*Cardinals Mgr./Coaches (Vern Benson, George Kissell, Johnny Lewis, Red Schoendienst, Barney Schultz)	.30
237	Ken Brett	.25
238	Fran Healy	.20
239	Bill Russell	.30
240	Joe Coleman	.25
241	Glenn Beckert (Washington)	4.00
241	Glenn Beckert (San Diego)	.30
243	Bob Oliver	.20
244	Carl Morton	.20
245	Cleon Jones	.25
246	A's Team	1.25
247	Rick Miller	.20
248	Tom Hall	.20
250	Willie McCovey (Washington)	25.00
250	Willie McCovey (San Diego)	4.00
251	Graig Nettles	1.50
252	*Dave Parker*	30.00
253	John Boccabella	.20
255	Larry Bowa	.40
257	Buddy Bell	1.25
258	Jerry Morales	.20
259	Bob Reynolds	.20

260	Ted Simmons	.80
261	Jerry Bell	.20
263	Checklist 133-264	1.50
264	Joe Rudi	.40
265	Tug McGraw	.60
266	Jim Northrup	.25
267	Andy Messersmith	.30
270	Ron Santo	.50
271	Bill Hands	.20
273	Checklist 265-396	1.50
274	Fred Beene	.25
275	Ron Hunt	.25
277	Gary Nolan	.20
278	Cookie Rojas	.20
279	Jim Crawford	.20
280	Carl Yastrzemski	9.00
281	Giants Team	.80
282	Doyle Alexander	.40
283	Mike Schmidt	75.00
284	Dave Duncan	.20
285	Reggie Smith	.40
286	Tony Muser	.20
287	Clay Kirby	.20
288	*Gorman Thomas*	1.00
289	Rick Auerbach	.20
290	Vida Blue	.60
291	Don Hahn	.20
292	Chuck Seelbach	.20
293	Milt May	.20
294	Steve Foucault	.20
295	Rick Monday	.35
296	Ray Corbin	.20
297	Hal Breeden	.20
298	Roric Harrison	.20
299	Gene Michael	.30
300	Pete Rose	20.00
301	Bob Montgomery	.20
302	Rudy May	.25
303	George Hendrick	.30
304	Don Wilson	.20
305	Tito Fuentes	.20
306	Orioles Mgr./Coaches (George Bamberger, Jim Frey, Billy Hunter, George Staller, Earl Weaver)	.75
307	Luis Melendez	.20
308	Bruce Dal Canton	.20
309	Dave Roberts (Washington)	3.50

309	Dave Roberts (San Diego)	.25
310	Terry Forster	.30
311	Jerry Grote	.25
312	Deron Johnson	.20
313	Barry Lersch	.20
314	Brewers Team	.80
315	Ron Cey	.60
316	Jim Perry	.45
317	Richie Zisk	.30
318	Jim Merritt	.20
319	Randy Hundley	.20
320	Dusty Baker	.40
321	Steve Braun	.20
322	Ernie McAnally	.20
323	Richie Scheinblum	.20
324	Steve Kline	.25
325	Tommy Harper	.25
326	Reds Mgr./Coaches (Sparky Anderson, Alex Grammas, Ted Kluszewski, George Scherger, Larry Shepard)	.50
327	Tom Timmermann	.20
328	Skip Jutze	.20
329	Mark Belanger	.30
330	Juan Marichal	2.75
331	AS Catchers (Johnny Bench, Carlton Fisk)	2.00
332	AS First Basemen (Hank Aaron, Dick Allen)	2.00
333	AS Second Basemen (Rod Carew, Joe Morgan)	2.00
334	AS Third Basemen (Brooks Robinson, Ron Santo)	1.50
335	AS Shortstops (Bert Campaneris, Chris Speier)	.45
336	AS Left Fielders (Bobby Murcer, Pete Rose)	2.50
337	AS Center Fielders (Cesar Cedeno, Amos Otis)	.40
338	AS Right Fielders (Reggie Jackson, Billy Williams)	2.00
339	AS Pitchers (Jim Hunter, Rick Wise)	.80
340	Thurman Munson	4.00

226 Washington Nat'l. Team

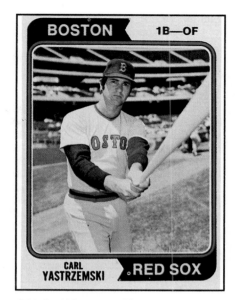

280 Carl Yastrzemski

55 Frank Robinson

340 Thurman Munson

341	Dan Driessen	.80
342	Jim Lonborg	.30
343	Royals Team	.80
344	Mike Caldwell	.25
345	Bill North	.25
346	Ron Reed	.25
347	Sandy Alomar	.20
348	Pete Richert	.20
349	John Vukovich	.20
350	Bob Gibson	3.00
351	*Dwight Evans	3.50
352	Bill Stoneman	.20
353	Rich Coggins	.20
354	Cubs Mgr./Coaches (Hank Aguirre, Whitey Lockman, Jim Marshall, J.C. Martin, Al Spangler)	.25
355	Dave Nelson	.20
356	Jerry Koosman	.40
357	Buddy Bradford	.20
358	Dal Maxvill	.25
359	Brent Strom	.20
360	Greg Luzinski	.70
361	Don Carrithers	.20
363	Yankees Team	1.25
364	Clarence Gaston (Washington)	3.50
364	Clarence Gaston (San Diego)	.25
365	Steve Busby	.25
366	Larry Hisle	.25
367	Norm Cash	.50
368	Manny Mota	.40
370	Bob Watson	.25
376	Jorge Orta	.25
378	Burt Hooton	.30
379	Rangers Mgr./Coaches (Art Fowler, Frank Lucchesi, Billy Martin, Jackie Moore, Charlie Silvera)	.85
380	Bud Harrelson	.25
383	Phillies Team	.80
384	Chris Chambliss	.40

385	Don Gullett	.25
386	Gary Matthews	.60
387	Rich Morales (Washington)	3.50
387	Rich Morales (San Diego)	.25
390	Lou Piniella	.70
396	Tommy Davis	.40
398	Duke Sims	.25
400	Harmon Killebrew	3.00
403	Red Sox Mgr./Coaches (Don Bryant, Darrell Johnson, Eddie Popowski, Lee Stange, Don Zimmer)	.25
408	Charlie Hough	.40
413	Don Money	.25
414	Checklist 397-528	1.50
416	White Sox Team	.80
423	Fred Stanley	.25
430	Matty Alou	.40
431	Gene Garber	.50
435	Dave Concepcion	.70
440	Jim Kaat	1.25
444	Vic Davalillo	.25
445	George Medich	.25
450	Rich Hebner	.25
451	Tommy John	1.50
456	Dave Winfield	60.00
459	Reds Team	.90
460	Boog Powell	.95
461	John Odom	.25
463	Pat Dobson	.20
464	Jose Cruz	.80
470	AL Playoffs	2.00
471	NL Playoffs	.80
472	World Series Game 1	.80
473	World Series Game 2	2.00
474	World Series Game 3	.80
475	World Series Game 4	.80
476	World Series Game 5	.80
477	World Series Game 6	2.00
478	World Series Game 7	.80
479	World Series Summary	.80

483	Braves Team	.80
485	Felipe Alou	.40
486	Steve Stone	.40
489	Pirates Mgr./Coaches (Don Leppert, Bill Mazeroski, Danny Murtaugh, Don Osborn, Bob Skinner)	.35
490	*Vada Pinson	.70
495	Dick McAuliffe	.25
498	Pat Corrales	.35
500	Lee May	.35
504	Joe Niekro	.40
505	Bill Buckner	.50
508	Expos Team	.80
511	Toby Harrah	.30
515	Willie Montanez	.25
517	Mike Hegan	.25
520	Tim McCarver	.60
522	J.R. Richard	.30
523	Cecil Cooper	1.50
529	Horace Clarke	.25
530	Mickey Stanley	.25
531	Expos Mgr./Coaches (Dave Bristol, Larry Doby, Gene Mauch, Cal McLish, Jerry Zimmerman)	.40
532	Skip Lockwood	.20
533	Mike Phillips	.20
534	Eddie Watt	.20
535	Bob Tolan	.25
536	Duffy Dyer	.20
537	Steve Mingori	.20
538	Cesar Tovar	.20
539	Lloyd Allen	.20
540	Bob Robertson	.20
541	Indians Team	.80
542	Rich Gossage	2.00
543	Danny Cater	.20
544	Ron Schueler	.20
545	Billy Conigliaro	.20
546	Mike Corkins	.20
547	Glenn Borgmann	.20
548	Sonny Siebert	.20

549	Mike Jorgensen	.20
550	Sam McDowell	.40
551	Von Joshua	.20
555	Woodie Fryman	.30
556	Dave Campbell	.25
560	Mike Cuellar	.35
561	Ed Kranepool	.30
563	Hal McRae	.40
565	Milt Wilcox	.25
567	Red Sox Team	.90
568	Mike Torrez	.25
569	Rick Dempsey	.30
570	Ralph Garr	.30
575	Steve Garvey	14.00
578	Ralph Houk	.40
582	*Bucky Dent*	1.00
585	Merv Rettenmund	.25
587	*Larry Christensen*	.40
588	Hal Lanier	.40
593	Steve Yeager	.25
595	Steve Blass	.25

596 Rookie Pitchers
(*Wayne Garland,* Fred
Holdsworth, *Mark Littell,*
Dick Pole) .... .35

597 Rookie Shortstops
(Dave Chalk, John Gamble,
Pete Mackanin, *Manny
Trillo*) .... .80

598 Rookie Outfielders
(Dave Augustine, *Ken Griffey,*
Steve Ontiveros, Jim
Tyrone) 5.00

599 Rookie Pitchers
(Ron Diorio, Dave
Freisleben, Frank Riccelli,
Greg Shanahan) (Freisleben
with Washington) .... .80

599 Rookie Pitchers
(Ron Diorio, Dave
Freisleben, Frank Riccelli,
Greg Shanahan) (Freisleben
with San Diego—
large print) 3.50

599 Rookie Pitchers
(Ron Diorio, Dave Freisleben,
Frank Riccelli, Greg
Shanahan) (Freisleben with
San Diego—small print) 6.00

600 Rookie Infielders
(Ron Cash, Jim Cox,
Bill Madlock, Reggie
Sanders) 3.00

601 *Rookie Outfielders
(Ed Armbrister, Rich Bladt,
Brian Downing, Bake
McBride) 2.00

603 Rookie Catchers
(Barry Foote, Tom
Lundstedt, *Charlie Moore,*
Sergio Robles) .... .30

604 *Rookie Infielders
(Terry Hughes, John Knox,
*Andy Thornton, Frank
White*) 4.00

605 Rookie Pitchers
(Vic Albury, Ken Frailing,
Kevin Kobel, *Frank
Tanana*) 1.50

606 Rookie Outfielders
(Jim Fuller, Wilbur Howard,
Tommy Smith, Otto Velez) ... .25

607 Rookie Shortstops
(Leo Foster, Tom
Heintzelman, Dave Rosello,
Frank Taveras) .... .25

608 Rookie Pitchers
(Bob Apodaco, Dick Baney,
John D'Acquisto, Mike
Wallace) 2.50

608 Rookie Pitchers
(Bob Apodaca, Dick Baney,
John D'Adquisto, Mike
Wallace) .... .25

609	Rico Petrocelli	.30
610	Dave Kingman	.90
616	Larry Gura	.25
620	Al Downing	.25
621	Bernie Carbo	.20
622	Phil Gagliano	.20
626	Pirates Team	.80
627	Carl Taylor	.20
629	Rusty Staub	.70
630	Tommie Agee	.25

634 Braves Mgr./Coaches
(Jim Busby, Eddie Mathews,
Connie Ryan, Ken Silvestri,
Herm Starrette) .... .95

636	Dave Goltz	.25
637	Checklist 529-660	1.50
638	Ken Sanders	.20
640	Milt Pappas	.40
643	Dodgers Team	.95
644	Wayne Granger	.25
646	George Foster	1.25
647	*Juan Beniquez*	.75
650	Mike Epstein	.25
651	Leron Lee	.20

654 Jesus Alou
(no position listed) 5.00

654	Jesus Alou (outfield)	.40
658	Lee Lacy	.30
659	Joe Lis	.20
660	Larry Dierker	.50

1975 TOPPS

Although all 660 cards in the 1975 Topps set were issued at once, collectors found that the first 132 cards (from the first of five printing sheets) were produced in a somewhat smaller quantity. Each card front uses three colors, two for the border and one for the bold team name at the top. A large subset of 24 cards features the American and National League MVPs since 1951, pictured in miniature versions of the Topps cards from their award-winning seasons. Rookie cards show four players, grouped by position. Famous rookies include Robin Yount, George Brett, Jim Rice, Gary Carter, Fred Lynn, and Keith Hernandez. Topps also test-marketed this set in a smaller format with cards measuring 2¼ by 3⅛ inches.

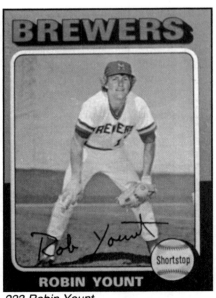

223 Robin Yount

	NR MT
Complete set	**$650.00**
Commons (1-132)	**.30**
Commons (133-660)	**.20**
Complete Mini set	**1250.00**
Mini commons	**.45**

1 '74 Highlights
(Hank Aaron) $21.00

2 '74 Highlights
(Lou Brock) 2.00

3 '74 Highlights
(Bob Gibson) 1.75

4 '74 Highlights
(Al Kaline) 1.75

5 '74 Highlights
(Nolan Ryan) 6.00

6 '74 Highlights
(Mike Marshall) .... .40

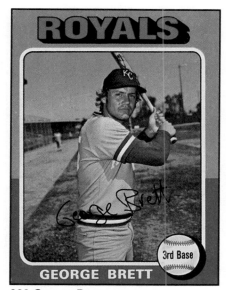

228 George Brett

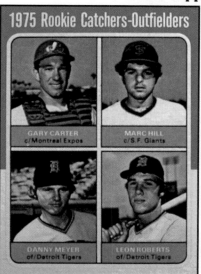

620 Rookie Catchers-Outfielders

7	'74 Highlights (Dick Bosman, Steve Busby, Nolan Ryan)	1.00
8	Rogelio Moret	.30
9	Frank Tepedino	.30
10	Willie Davis	.35
11	Bill Melton	.35
12	David Clyde	.35
13	Gene Locklear	.30
14	Milt Wilcox	.35
15	Jose Cardenal	.35
16	Frank Tanana	.40
17	Dave Concepcion	.60
18	Tigers Team (Ralph Houk)	.90
19	Jerry Koosman	.40
20	Thurman Munson	6.00
21	Rollie Fingers	1.50
22	Dave Cash	.30
23	Bill Russell	.35
24	Al Fitzmorris	.30
25	Lee May	.40
26	Dave McNally	.35
27	Ken Reitz	.30
28	Tom Murphy	.30
29	Dave Parker	5.00
30	*Bert Blyleven	.30
31	Dave Rader	.30
32	Reggie Cleveland	.30
33	Dusty Baker	.40
34	Steve Renko	.30
35	Ron Santo	.50
36	Joe Lovitto	.30
37	Dave Freisleben	.30
38	Buddy Bell	.80
39	Andy Thornton	.70
40	Bill Singer	.35
41	Cesar Geronimo	.35
42	Joe Coleman	.35
43	Cleon Jones	.35
44	Pat Dobson	.35
45	Joe Rudi	.40
46	Phillies Team (Danny Ozark)	.80

47	Tommy John	1.25
48	Freddie Patek	.30
49	Larry Dierker	.30
50	Brooks Robinson	3.50
51	Bob Forsch	.80
52	Darrell Porter	.35
53	Dave Giusti	.30
54	Eric Soderholm	.30
55	Bobby Bonds	.50
56	Rick Wise	.35
57	Dave Johnson	.80
58	Chuck Taylor	.30
59	Ken Henderson	.30
60	Fergie Jenkins	1.25
61	Dave Winfield	13.00
62	Fritz Peterson	.30
63	Steve Swisher	.30
64	Dave Chalk	.30
65	Don Gullett	.35
66	Willie Horton	.35
67	Tug McGraw	.50
68	Ron Blomberg	.35
69	John Odom	.35
70	Mike Schmidt	50.00
71	Charlie Hough	.35
72	Royals Team (Jack McKeon)	.80
73	J.R. Richard	.35
74	Mark Belanger	.35
75	Ted Simmons	.70
76	Ed Sprague	.30
77	Richie Zisk	.35
78	Ray Corbin	.30
79	Gary Matthews	.40
80	Carlton Fisk	2.00
81	Ron Reed	.35
82	Pat Kelly	.30
83	Jim Merritt	.30
84	Enzo Hernandez	.30
85	Bill Bonham	.30
86	Joe Lis	.30
87	George Foster	1.25
88	Tom Egan	.30
89	Jim Ray	.30

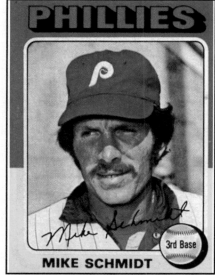

70 Mike Schmidt

90	Rusty Staub	.60
91	Dick Green	.30
92	Cecil Upshaw	.35
93	Dave Lopes	.40
94	Jim Lonborg	.35
95	John Mayberry	.35
96	Mike Cosgrove	.30
97	Earl Williams	.30
98	Rich Folkers	.30
99	Mike Hegan	.30
100	Willie Stargell	2.50
101	Expos Team (Gene Mauch)	2.50
102	Joe Decker	.30
103	Rick Miller	.30
104	Bill Madlock	1.25
105	Buzz Capra	.30
106	Mike Hargrove	.40
107	Jim Barr	.30
108	Tom Hall	.30
109	George Hendrick	.35
110	Wilbur Wood	.35
111	Wayne Garrett	.30
112	Larry Hardy	.30
113	Elliott Maddox	.30
114	Dick Lange	.30
115	Joe Ferguson	.30
116	Lerrin LaGrow	.30
117	Orioles Team (Earl Weaver)	1.00
118	Mike Anderson	.30
119	Tommy Helms	.30
120	Steve Busby (photo is Fran Healy)	.35
121	Bill North	.30
122	Al Hrabosky	.30
123	Johnny Briggs	.35
124	Jerry Reuss	.40
125	Ken Singleton	.40
126	Checklist 1-132	1.50
127	Glen Borgmann	.30
128	Bill Lee	.35
129	Rick Monday	.35

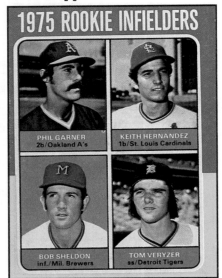

1975 ROOKIE INFIELDERS

PHIL GARNER
2b/Oakland A's

KEITH HERNANDEZ
1b/St. Louis Cardinals

BOB SHELDON
inf./Mil. Brewers

TOM VERYZER
ss/Detroit Tigers

623 Rookie Infielders

130	Phil Niekro	**2.00**
131	Toby Harrah	.35
132	Randy Moffitt	.30
133	Dan Driessen	.30
136	Jim Mason	.25
137	Terry Forster	.30
140	Steve Garvey	**6.00**
141	Mickey Stanley	.25
143	*Cliff Johnson*	.40
145	Ken Holtzman	.30
146	Padres Team (John McNamara)	.80
150	Bob Gibson	**2.50**
156	Dave Kingman	.90
158	Jerry Grote	.25
160	Graig Nettles	**1.50**
166	Woody Fryman	.25
170	Bert Campaneris	.40
172	Red Sox Team (Darrell Johnson)	**1.25**
173	Steve Rogers	.30
174	Bake McBride	.25
175	Don Money	.25
180	Joe Morgan	**3.00**
183	Mel Stottlemyre	.40
185	Steve Carlton	**6.00**
189	1951—MVPs (Yogi Berra, Roy Campanella)	**1.50**
190	1952—MVPs (Hank Sauer, Bobby Shantz)	.40
191	1953—MVPs (Roy Campanella, Al Rosen)	.90
192	1954—MVPs (Yogi Berra, Willie Mays)	**1.50**
193	1955—MVPs (Yogi Berra, Roy Campanella)	**1.50**
194	1956—MVPs (Mickey Mantle, Don Newcombe)	**6.00**

195	1957—MVPs (Hank Aaron, Mickey Mantle)	**7.00**
196	1958—MVPs (Ernie Banks, Jackie Jensen)	.90
197	1959—MVPs (Ernie Banks, Nellie Fox)	.90
198	1960—MVPs (Dick Groat, Roger Maris)	**1.25**
199	1961—MVPs (Roger Maris, Frank Robinson)	**1.50**
200	1962—MVPs (Mickey Mantle, Maury Wills)	**5.00**
201	1963—MVPs (Elston Howard, Sandy Koufax)	**1.50**
202	1964—MVPs (Ken Boyer, Brooks Robinson)	**1.25**
203	1965—MVPs (Willie Mays, Zoilo Versalles)	**1.25**
204	1966—MVPs (Bob Clemente, Frank Robinson)	**1.50**
205	1967—MVPs (Orlando Cepeda, Carl Yastrzemski)	**1.25**
206	1968—MVPs (Bob Gibson, Denny McLain)	**1.25**
207	1969—MVPs (Harmon Killebrew, Willie McCovey)	**1.50**
208	1970—MVPs (Johnny Bench, Boog Powell)	**1.25**
209	1971—MVPs (Vida Blue, Joe Torre)	**1.25**

A'S

Outfield

REGGIE JACKSON

300 Reggie Jackson

RED SOX

OF-1B

CARL YASTRZEMSKI

280 Carl Yastrzemski

210	1972—MVPs (Rich Allen, Johnny Bench)	**1.25**
211	1973—MVPs (Reggie Jackson, Pete Rose)	**4.00**
212	1974—MVPs (Jeff Burroughs, Steve Garvey)	.90
213	Oscar Gamble	.25
215	Bobby Valentine	.30
216	Giants Team (Wes Westrum)	.30
217	Lou Piniella	.70
220	Don Sutton	**1.50**
221	Aurelio Rodriquez (Rodriguez)	.25
223	*Robin Yount*	**150.00**
225	Bob Grich	.40
226	Bill Campbell	.25
227	Bob Watson	.25
228	*George Brett*	**100.00**
230	*Jim Hunter	**2.00**
236	Angels Team (Dick Williams)	.80
239	George Stone	.20
240	Garry Maddox	.25
241	Dick Tidrow	.20
242	Jay Johnstone	.25
244	Bill Buckner	**1.25**
245	*Mickey Lolich	.50
246	*Cardinals Team (Red Schoendienst)	.80
247	Enos Cabell	.25
248	Randy Jones	.25
249	Danny Thompson	.25
250	Ken Brett	.25
252	Fred Scherman	.20
253	Jesus Alou	.25
254	Mike Torrez	.25
255	*Dwight Evans	**1.50**
257	Checklist 133-264	**1.50**
260	Johnny Bench	**7.00**

263	Jim Perry	.40
266	Sandy Alomar	.25
268	Hal McRae	.40
270	Ron Fairly	.30
275	Paul Blair	.25
276	White Sox Team (Chuck Tanner)	.80
280	Carl Yastrzemski	8.00
284	Ken Griffey	.70
290	Jon Matlack	.25
291	Bill Sudakis	.25
294	*Geoff Zahn*	.40
295	*Vada Pinson	.60
299	Bucky Dent	.40
300	Reggie Jackson	15.00
302	*Rick Burleson*	.50
304	Pirates Team (Danny Murtaugh)	.85
306	Batting Ldrs (Rod Carew, Ralph Garr)	.80
307	HR Ldrs (Dick Allen, Mike Schmidt)	.90
308	RBI Ldrs (Johnny Bench, Jeff Burroughs)	.90
309	SB Ldrs (Lou Brock, Bill North)	.80
310	Victory Ldrs (Jim Hunter, Fergie Jenkins, Andy Messersmith, Phil Niekro)	.80
311	ERA Ldrs (Buzz Capra, Jim Hunter)	.50
312	SO Ldrs (Steve Carlton, Nolan Ryan)	1.75
313	Leading Firemen (Terry Forster, Mike Marshall)	.50
315	Don Kessinger	.25
320	Pete Rose	23.00
321	Rudy May	.25
324	Ed Kranepool	.30

140 Steve Garvey

325	Tony Oliva	.80
330	Mike Marshall	.30
331	Indians Team (Frank Robinson)	.90
334	*Greg Gross*	.30
335	Jim Palmer	3.50
339	Jim Fregosi	.40
340	Paul Splittorff	.25
344	Ben Oglivie	.30
345	Clay Carroll	.25
350	Bobby Murcer	.40
351	*Bob Boone	.40
356	Rico Petrocelli	.30
357	Ken Forsch	.25
358	Al Bumbry	.25
360	George Scott	.30
361	Dodgers Team (Walter Alston)	1.00
370	Tom Seaver	8.00
375	Roy White	.40
380	Sal Bando	.40
382	Don Baylor	.60
384	Brewers Team (Del Crandall)	.75
385	Dock Ellis	.25
386	Checklist 265-396	1.50
388	Steve Stone	.30
390	Ron Cey	.40
392	Bruce Bochte	.40
395	Bud Harrelson	.25
397	Bill Freehan	.40
400	Dick Allen	.80
401	Mike Wallace	.25
402	Bob Tolan	.25
407	*Herb Washington*	.30
410	Mike Cueller (Cuellar)	.40
414	Manny Mota	.30
415	John Hiller	.25
419	Dave Goltz	.25
420	Larry Bowa	.40
421	Mets Team (Yogi Berra)	1.00
422	Brian Downing	.30
426	George Medich	.25

429	*Jim Dwyer*	.30
430	*Luis Tiant	.50
437	*Al Cowens*	.40
439	Ed Brinkman	.25
440	Andy Messersmith	.30
443	Twins Team (Frank Quilici)	.80
444	Gene Garber	.25
450	Willie McCovey	3.00
451	Rick Dempsey	.40
453	Claude Osteen	.30
458	Ross Grimsley	.25
459	AL Championships	.80
460	NL Championships	.80
461	World Series Game 1	1.50
462	World Series Game 2	.80
463	World Series Game 3	1.00
464	World Series Game 4	.80
465	World Series Game 5	.80
466	World Series Summary	.80
470	Jeff Burroughs	.30
475	Darrell Evans	.60
477	Tom Hutton	.20
478	Tom Burgmeier	.20
479	Ken Boswell	.20
480	Carlos May	.25
481	*Will McEnaney*	.25
482	Tom McCraw	.20
483	Steve Ontiveros	.20
484	Glenn Beckert	.30
485	Sparky Lyle	.40
486	Ray Fosse	.20
487	Astros Team (Preston Gomez)	.80
488	Bill Travers	.20
489	Cecil Cooper	1.00
490	Reggie Smith	.30
491	Doyle Alexander	.40
492	Rich Hebner	.25
493	Don Stanhouse	.20
494	*Pete LaCock*	.25
495	Nelson Briles	.20
496	Pepe Frias	.20

20 Thurman Munson

185 Steve Carlton

200 1962—MVPs

497	Jim Nettles	.20
498	Al Downing	.25
499	Marty Perez	.20
500	Nolan Ryan	22.00
501	Bill Robinson	.20
502	Pat Bourque	.20
503	Fred Stanley	.20
504	Buddy Bradford	.25
505	Chris Speier	.25
506	Leron Lee	.20
507	Tom Carroll	.20
508	Bob Hansen	.20
509	Dave Hilton	.20
510	Vida Blue	.50
511	Rangers Team (Billy Martin)	.90
512	Larry Milbourne	.20
513	Dick Pole	.20
514	Jose Cruz	.50
515	Manny Sanguillen	.25
516	Don Hood	.20
517	Checklist 397-528	1.25
518	Leo Cardenas	.20
519	Jim Todd	.20
520	Amos Otis	.30
521	Dennis Blair	.20
522	Gary Sutherland	.20
523	Tom Paciorek	.25
524	John Doherty	.20
525	Tom House	.20
526	Larry Hisle	.20
527	Mac Scarce	.20
528	Eddie Leon	.20
529	Gary Thomasson	.20
530	Gaylord Perry	2.25
531	Reds Team (Sparky Anderson)	.90
532	Gorman Thomas	.60
533	Rudy Meoli	.20
534	Alex Johnson	.20
535	Gene Tenace	.25
536	Bob Moose	.20
537	Tommy Harper	.20
538	Duffy Dyer	.20
539	Jesse Jefferson	.20
540	Lou Brock	3.00
541	Roger Metzger	.20
542	Pete Broberg	.20
543	Larry Biittner	.20

544	Steve Mingori	.20
545	Billy Williams	2.25
546	John Knox	.20
547	Von Joshua	.20
548	Charlie Sands	.20
549	Bill Butler	.20
550	Ralph Garr	.25
551	Larry Christensen	.20
552	Jack Brohamer	.20
553	John Boccabella	.20
554	*Rich Gossage	1.25
555	Al Oliver	.80
556	Tim Johnson	.20
557	Larry Gura	.20
558	Dave Roberts	.20
559	Bob Montgomery	.20
560	Tony Perez	.20
561	A's Team (Alvin Dark)	.90
562	Gary Nolan	.20
563	Wilbur Howard	.20
564	Tommy Davis	.40
565	Joe Torre	.75
566	Ray Burris	.20
567	*Jim Sundberg*	.75
568	Dale Murray	.20
569	Frank White	.20
570	*Jim Wynn	.40
571	Dave Lemanczyk	.20
572	Roger Nelson	.20
573	Orlando Pena	.20
574	Tony Taylor	.20
575	Gene Clines	.20
576	Phil Roof	.20
577	John Morris	.20
578	Dave Tomlin	.20
579	Skip Pitlock	.20
580	Frank Robinson	3.00
581	Darrel Chaney	.20
582	Eduardo Rodriguez	.20
583	Andy Etchebarren	.20
584	Mike Garman	.20
585	Chris Chambliss	.40
586	Tim McCarver	.60
587	Chris Ward	.20
588	Rick Auerbach	.20
589	Braves Team (Clyde King)	.40
590	Cesar Cedeno	.40
591	Glenn Abbott	.20
592	Balor Moore	.20

593	Gene Lamont	.20
594	Jim Fuller	.20
595	Joe Niekro	.40
596	Ollie Brown	.20
598	Bruce Kison	.20
599	Nate Colbert	.20
600	Rod Carew	5.00
601	Juan Beniquez	.30
602	John Vukovich	.20
603	Lew Krausse	.20
604	Oscar Zamora	.20
605	John Ellis	.20
606	Bruce Miller	.20
607	Jim Holt	.20
608	Gene Michael	.30
610	Ron Hunt	.25
611	Yankees Team (Bill Virdon)	1.25
612	Terry Hughes	.20
613	Bill Parsons	.20
614	Rookie Pitchers (Jack Kucek, Dyar Miller, Vern Ruhle, Paul Siebert)	.20
615	Rookie Pitchers (Pat Darcy, *Dennis Leonard, Tom Underwood,* Hank Webb)	.60
616	Rookie Outfielders (Dave Augustine, Pepe Mangual, *Jim Rice,* John Scott)	35.00
617	Rookie Infielders (Mike Cubbage, *Doug DeCinces,* Reggie Sanders, Manny Trillo)	1.50
618	Rookie Pitchers (*Jaime Easterly,* Tom Johnson, *Scott McGregor, Rick Rhoden*)	2.25
619	Rookie Outfielders (Benny Ayala, Nyls Nyman, Tommy Smith, Jerry Turner)	.20

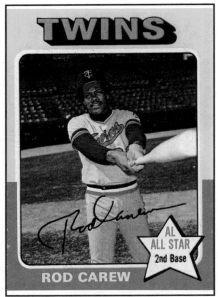

600 Rod Carew

620	Rookie Catchers-Outfielders (*Gary Carter*, Marc Hill, Danny Meyer, Leon Roberts)	35.00
621	Rookie Pitchers (*John Denny, Rawly Eastwick, Jim Kern,* Juan Veintidos)	.60
622	Rookie Outfielders (Ed Armbrister, *Fred Lynn,* Tom Poquette, Terry Whitfield)	12.00
623	Rookie Infielders (*Phil Garner, Keith Hernandez,* Bob Sheldon, Tom Veryzer)	20.00
624	Rookie Pitchers (Doug Konieczny, *Gary Lavelle,* Jim Otten, Eddie Solomon)	.30
625	Boog Powell	.75
626	Larry Haney	.20
627	Tom Walker	.20
628	*Ron LeFlore*	.80
629	Joe Hoerner	.20
630	Greg Luzinski	.75
631	Lee Lacy	.25

632	Morris Nettles	.20
633	Paul Casanova	.20
634	Cy Acosta	.20
635	Chuck Dobson	.20
636	Charlie Moore	.20
637	Ted Martinez	.20
638	Cubs Team (Jim Marshall)	.80
639	Steve Kline	.20
640	Harmon Killebrew	2.50
641	Jim Northrup	.25
642	Mike Phillips	.20
643	Brent Strom	.20
644	Bill Fahey	.20
645	Danny Cater	.20
646	Checklist 529-660	1.50
647	*Claudell Washington*	2.25
648	Dave Pagan	.20
649	Jack Heidemann	.20
650	Dave May	.20
651	John Morlan	.20
652	Lindy McDaniel	.20
653	Lee Richards	.20
654	Jerry Terrell	.20
655	Rico Carty	.40
656	Bill Plummer	.20
657	Bob Oliver	.20
658	Vic Harris	.20

370 Tom Seaver

659	Bob Apodaca	.20
660	Hank Aaron	20.00

1976 TOPPS

Topps introduced a new design concept with its 1976 set, offering 660 cards which stress quality photos instead of gaudy borders. A large, clear photo appears on each card, complemented by just two color strips on the card bottom that show the player name and team. Horizontal card backs have a simpler design and are easier to read than those of many earlier sets. One interesting subset in 1976 contains ten All-Time All-Stars selected by *The Sporting News.* Another shows five players (Bob Boone, Buddy Bell, Joe Coleman, Mike Hegan, and Roy Smalley) with their fathers, who were all major-leaguers themselves in their day. Later in the season Topps issued 43 "traded" cards which show players as members of the new teams to which they had been traded. This group of cards is not considered part of the major set, however, and sells, as a subset, for $9.00.

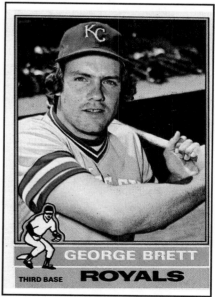

19 George Brett

		NR MT
Complete set		**$350.00**
Commons		**.15**

1	'75 Record Breaker (Hank Aaron)	$12.00
2	'75 Record Breaker (Bobby Bonds)	.40
3	'75 Record Breaker (Mickey Lolich)	.35
4	'75 Record Breaker (Dave Lopes)	.35
5	'75 Record Breaker (Tom Seaver)	1.50
6	'75 Record Breaker (Rennie Stennett)	.30
10	Lou Brock	2.50

12	Richie Zisk	.20
14	Gene Garber	.20
15	George Scott	.25
17	Yankees Team (Billy Martin)	1.25
19	George Brett	30.00
20	Bob Watson	.20
22	Bill Russell	.20
23	Brian Downing	.25
24	Cesar Geronimo	.20
25	Mike Torrez	.20
26	Andy Thornton	.25
28	Dusty Baker	.25
29	Rick Burleson	.30
30	*John Montefusco*	.35
35	Tony Oliva	.60
37	John Hiller	.20

38	Garry Maddox	.20
40	Dave Kingman	.80
41	*Tippy Martinez*	.40
43	Paul Splittorff	.20
45	Boog Powell	.65
46	Dodgers Team (Walter Alston)	1.00

316 Robin Yount

110	Carlos May	.20
111	Danny Thompson	.20
112	*Kent Tekulve*	.90
114	Jay Johnstone	.25
115	Ken Holtzman	.25
118	Red Sox Team (Darrell Johnson)	.90
119	Checklist 1-132	1.25
120	Rusty Staub	.35
123	Walt Williams	.20
124	Doug Rau	.15
125	Don Baylor	.50
128	Ken Griffey	.35
130	Luis Tiant	.40
131	Bill Stein	.20
132	Don Hood	.15
133	Gary Matthews	.25
134	Mike Ivie	.15
135	Bake McBride	.25
136	Dave Goltz	.20
139	Gorman Thomas	.30
140	Vida Blue	.40
141	*Larry Parrish*	.80
142	Dick Drago	.15
143	Jerry Grote	.20
145	Larry Bowa	.35
146	George Medich	.20
147	Astros Team (Bill Virdon)	.80
149	Tommy Davis	.30
150	Steve Garvey	4.50
154	Bucky Dent	.30
156	Rico Carty	.25
158	Ken Reitz	.15
160	Dave Winfield	6.00
162	Jack Pierce	.15
163	Jim Slaton	.15
165	Gene Tenace	.20
166	Skip Lockwood	.15
167	Freddie Patek	.15
169	Graig Nettles	1.00
170	Rick Wise	.20
171	Gregg Gross	.15
172	Rangers Team (Frank Luccesi)	.80

480 Mike Schmidt

330 Nolan Ryan

48	Dave Concepcion	.40
50	Fred Lynn	2.00
55	Gaylord Perry	2.00
57	Phil Garner	.30
58	Ron Reed	.20
59	Larry Hisle	.20
60	Jerry Reuss	.30
61	Ron LeFlore	.30
64	Jerry Koosman	.30
65	Chris Chambliss	.30
66	Father & Son (Buddy Bell, Gus Bell)	.50
67	Father & Son (Bob Boone, Ray Boone)	.40
68	Father & Son (Joe Coleman, Joe Coleman, Jr.)	.20
69	Father & Son (Jim Hegan, Mike Hegan)	.20
70	Father & Son (Roy Smalley, Roy Smalley, Jr.)	.25
71	Steve Rogers	.20
72	Hal McRae	.25
73	Orioles Team (Earl Weaver)	.80
74	Oscar Gamble	.20
75	Larry Dierker	.20
78	Cecil Cooper	1.00
80	Jim Kaat	1.00
81	Darrell Evans	.50
85	Mickey Rivers	.25
86	Mike Tyson	.15
88	Duffy Dyer	.15
89	Vern Ruhle	.15
90	Sal Bando	.30
91	Tom Hutton	.15
93	Mike Phillips	.15
94	Jim Dwyer	.25
95	Brooks Robinson	2.75
96	Doug Bird	.15
98	*Dennis Eckersley*	7.00
100	Jim Hunter	2.00
104	Reds Team (Sparky Anderson)	1.00

174	Charlie Hough	.25
175	Ken Singleton	.30
176	Dick Lange	.15
177	Marty Perez	.15
178	Tom Buskey	.15
179	George Foster	1.00
180	Rich Gossage	1.25
181	Willie Montanez	.20
184	Bill Greif	.15
185	Dave Parker	4.00
186	Tom Walker	.15
189	Claudell Washington	.40
190	Jon Matlack	.25
191	NL Batting Ldrs (Bill Madlock, Manny Sanguillen, Ted Simmons)	.60
192	AL Batting Ldrs (Rod Carew, Fred Lynn, Thurman Munson)	1.50
193	NL HR Ldrs (Dave Kingman, Greg Luzinski, Mike Schmidt)	1.25
194	AL HR Ldrs (Reggie Jackson, John Mayberry, George Scott)	1.25
195	NL RBI Ldrs (Johnny Bench, Greg Luzinski, Tony Perez)	1.25
196	AL RBI Ldrs (Fred Lynn, John Mayberry, George Scott)	.60
197	NL SB Ldrs (Lou Brock, Dave Lopes, Joe Morgan)	.90
198	AL SB Ldrs (Amos Otis, Mickey Rivers, Claudell Washington)	.50
199	NL Victory Ldrs (Randy Jones, Andy Messersmith, Tom Seaver)	.80
200	AL Victory Ldrs (Vida Blue, Jim Hunter, Jim Palmer)	.90

201	NL ERA Ldrs (Randy Jones, Andy Messersmith, Tom Seaver) .... .80
202	AL ERA Ldrs (Dennis Eckersley, Jim Hunter, Jim Palmer) .... .90
203	NL SO Ldrs (Andy Messersmith, John Montefusco, Tom Seaver) .... .80
204	AL SO Ldrs (Bert Blyleven, Gaylord Perry, Frank Tanana) .... .70
205	Major League Leading Firemen (Rich Gossage, Al Hrabosky) .... .50
206	Manny Trillo .... .20
209	Alan Ashby .... .35
210	Lee May .... .25
211	Clay Carroll .... .20
215	Reggie Smith .... .25
216	Expos Team (Karl Kuehl) .... .80
220	Manny Sanguillen .... .20
225	Roy White .... .25
226	Jim Sundberg .... .25
229	*Jerry Remy* .... .30
230	Carl Yastrzemski 7.00
235	*Bert Blyleven 1.00
236	Royals Team (Whitey Herzog) .... .90
240	Pete Rose 20.00
248	Dick Tidrow .... .20
249	Cliff Johnson .... .20
250	Fergie Jenkins 1.00
251	Rick Monday .... .30
253	Bill Buckner .... .50
257	Ross Grimsley .... .20
260	Steve Busby .... .20
262	Checklist 133-264 .... 1.50
263	*Lyman Bostock* .... .80
265	Willie Davis .... .30
267	Aurelio Rodriguez .... .20
270	Willie Stargell 3.00

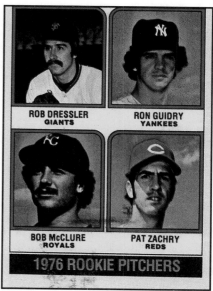

500 Reggie Jackson

271	Jim Lonborg .... .20
272	Rick Dempsey .... .25
273	Joe Niekro .... .30
274	Tommy Harper .... .20
275	*Rick Manning* .... .40
277	Cubs Team (Jim Marshall) .... .80
280	Burt Hooton .... .20
285	Mike Cuellar .... .25
290	Ted Simmons .... .60
296	Pat Dobson .... .20
300	Johnny Bench 6.00
302	Rick Miller .... .15
304	Angels Team (Dick Williams) .... .80
305	Andy Messersmith .... .25
307	Al Bumbry .... .20
308	Jim Barr .... .15
309	Bill Melton .... .20
310	Randy Jones .... .30
311	Cookie Rojas .... .15
313	*Dan Ford* .... .25
314	Ed Kranepool .... .25
315	Al Hrabosky .... .25
316	*Robin Yount 30.00
317	*John Candelaria* .... .30
318	*Bob Boone .... .30
319	Larry Gura .... .20
320	Willie Horton .... .25
321	Jose Cruz .... .35
325	Tony Perez .... .80
330	Nolan Ryan 19.00
331	Padres Team (John McNamara) .... .80
334	Dennis Leonard .... .25
335	Bob Grich .... .25
337	Bud Harrelson .... .20
339	John Denny .... .25
340	*Jim Rice 8.00
341	All Time AS (Lou Gehrig) 3.00
342	All Time AS (Rogers Hornsby) 1.25

441 Gary Carter

343	All Time AS (Pie Traynor) .... .80
344	All Time AS (Honus Wagner) 1.25
345	All Time AS (Babe Ruth) 5.00
346	All Time AS (Ty Cobb) 3.00
347	All Time AS (Ted Williams) 3.00
348	All Time AS (Mickey Cochrane) .... .80
349	All Time AS (Walter Johnson) 1.25
350	All Time AS (Lefty Grove) 1.00
353	*Sixto Lezcano* .... .30
354	Ron Blomberg .... .20
355	Steve Carlton 5.00
357	Ken Forsch .... .20
358	Buddy Bell .... .50
359	Rick Reuschel .... .30
360	Jeff Burroughs .... .20
361	Tigers Team (Ralph Houk) 1.00
363	*Dave Collins* .... .60
365	*Carlton Fisk 1.25
366	Bobby Valentine .... .30
368	Wilbur Wood .... .25
369	Frank White .... .30
370	Ron Cey .... .40
375	Ron Fairly .... .25
376	Rich Hebner .... .20
378	Steve Stone .... .25
380	Bobby Bonds .... .35
384	Phillies Team (Danny Ozark) .... .80
385	Mickey Lolich .... .40
390	Don Gullett .... .20
392	Checklist 265-396 .... 1.50
395	*Jim Wynn .... .30
396	Bill Lee .... .20
397	Tim Foli .... .15
400	Rod Carew 5.00

599 Rookie Pitchers

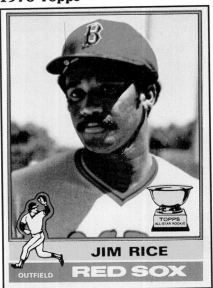

340 Jim Rice

405	Rollie Fingers	1.25
406	Ed Herrmann	.15
408	Charlie Spikes	.15
410	Ralph Garr	.20
411	Bill Singer	.20
412	Toby Harrah	.25
413	Pete Varney	.15
414	Wayne Garland	.15
415	*Vada Pinson	.50
416	Tommy John	1.25
417	Gene Clines	.15
418	Jose Morales	.15
419	Reggie Cleveland	.15
420	*Joe Morgan	4.00
421	A's Team	.80
422	Johnny Grubb	.15
423	Ed Halicki	.15
424	Phil Roof	.15
425	Rennie Stennett	.15
426	Bob Forsch	.25
427	Kurt Bevacqua	.20
428	Jim Crawford	.15
429	Fred Stanley	.20
430	Jose Cardenal	.20
431	Dick Ruthven	.20
432	Tom Veryzer	.15
433	Rick Waits	.15
434	Morris Nettles	.15
435	Phil Niekro	2.00
436	Bill Fahey	.15
437	Terry Forster	.25
438	Doug DeCinces	.50
439	Rick Rhoden	.60
440	John Mayberry	.25
441	Gary Carter	15.00
442	Hank Webb	.15
443	Giants Team	.80
444	Gary Nolan	.15
445	Rico Petrocelli	.25
446	Larry Haney	.15
447	Gene Locklear	.15
448	Tom Johnson	.15
449	Bob Robertson	.15

450	Jim Palmer	4.00
451	Buddy Bradford	.15
452	Tom Hausman	.15
453	Lou Piniella	.65
454	Tom Griffin	.15
455	Dick Allen	.50
456	Joe Coleman	.20
457	Ed Crosby	.15
458	Earl Williams	.15
459	Jim Brewer	.15
460	Cesar Cedeno	.30
461	NL & AL Championships	.80
462	1975 World Series	.80
463	Steve Hargan	.15
464	Ken Henderson	.15
465	Mike Marshall	.30
466	Bob Stinson	.15
467	Woodie Fryman	.20
468	Jesus Alou	.20
469	Rawly Eastwick	.20
470	Bobby Murcer	.35
471	Jim Burton	.15
472	Bob Davis	.15
473	Paul Blair	.25
474	Ray Corbin	.15
475	Joe Rudi	.30
476	Bob Moose	.15
477	Indians Team (Frank Robinson)	.80
478	Lynn McGlothlen	.15
479	Bobby Mitchell	.15
480	Mike Schmidt	25.00
481	Rudy May	.25
482	Tim Hosley	.15
483	Mickey Stanley	.20
484	Eric Raich	.15
485	Mike Hargrove	.20
486	Bruce Dal Canton	.15
487	Leron Lee	.15
488	Claude Osteen	.20
489	Skip Jutze	.15
490	Frank Tanana	.30
491	Terry Crowley	.15
492	Marty Pattin	.15

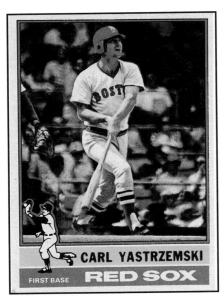

230 Carl Yastrzemski

160 Dave Winfield

493	Derrel Thomas	.15
494	Craig Swan	.15
495	Nate Colbert	.15
496	Juan Beniquez	.20
497	Joe McIntosh	.15
498	Glenn Borgmann	.15
499	Mario Guerrero	.15
500	Reggie Jackson	10.00
501	Billy Champion	.15
502	Tim McCarver	.50
503	Elliott Maddox	.15
504	Pirates Team (Danny Murtaugh)	.90
505	Mark Belanger	.20
506	George Mitterwald	.15
507	Raye Bare	.15
508	Duane Kuiper	.20
509	Bill Hands	.15
510	Amos Otis	.25
511	Jamie Easterly	.15
512	Ellie Rodriguez	.15
513	Bart Johnson	.15
514	Dan Driessen	.30
515	Steve Yeager	.15
516	Wayne Granger	.15
517	John Milner	.15
518	Doug Flynn	.20
519	Steve Brye	.15
520	Willie McCovey	2.50
521	Jim Colborn	.15
522	Ted Sizemore	.20
523	Bob Montgomery	.15
524	Pete Falcone	.15
525	Billy Williams	2.25
526	Checklist 397-528	2.25
527	Mike Anderson	.15
528	Dock Ellis	.20
529	Deron Johnson	.15
530	Don Sutton	1.50
531	Mets Team (Joe Frazier)	.90
532	Milt May	.15
533	Lee Richard	.15

534	Stan Bahnsen	.15
535	Dave Nelson	.15
536	Mike Thompson	.15
537	Tony Muser	.15
538	Pat Darcy	.15
539	John Balaz	.15
540	Bill Freehan	.25
541	Steve Mingori	.15
542	Keith Hernandez	6.00
543	Wayne Twitchell	.15
544	Pepe Frias	.15
545	Sparky Lyle	.35
546	Dave Rosello	.15
547	Roric Harrison	.15
548	Manny Mota	.15
549	Randy Tate	.15
550	Hank Aaron	15.00
551	Jerry DaVanon	.15
552	Terry Humphrey	.15
553	Randy Moffitt	.15
554	Ray Fosse	.15
555	Dyar Miller	.15
556	Twins Team (Gene Mauch)	.80
557	Dan Spillner	.15
558	Clarence Gaston	.15
559	Clyde Wright	.15
560	Jorge Orta	.15
561	Tom Carroll	.15
562	Adrian Garrett	.15
563	Larry Demery	.15
564	Bubble Gum Blowing Champ (Kurt Bevacqua)	.30
565	Tug McGraw	.35
566	Ken McMullen	.15
567	George Stone	.15
568	Rob Andrews	.15
569	Nelson Briles	.15
570	George Hendrick	.20
571	Don DeMola	.15
572	Rich Coggins	.15
573	Bill Travers	.15
574	Don Kessinger	.20
575	*Dwight Evans	1.00

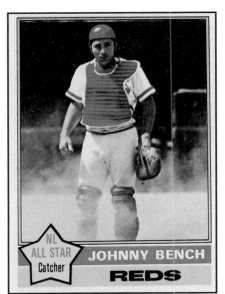

300 Johnny Bench

577	Marc Hill	.15
578	Ted Kubiak	.15
579	Clay Kirby	.15
580	Bert Campaneris	.30
581	*Cardinals Team (Red Schoendienst)	.80
582	Mike Kekich	.15
583	Tommy Helms	.15
584	Stan Wall	.15
585	Joe Torre	.50
586	Ron Schueler	.15
588	Kevin Kobel	.15
589	Rookie Pitchers (Santo Alcala, *Mike Flanagan*, Joe Pactwa, Pablo Torrealba)	1.50
590	Rookie Outfielders (Henry Cruz, *Chet Lemon*, *Ellis Valentine*, Terry Whitfield)	1.00
591	Rookie Pitchers (Steve Grilli, Craig Mitchell, Jose Sosa, George Throop)	.15
592	Rookie Infielders (Dave McKay, *Willie Randolph*, *Jerry Royster*, Roy Staiger)	5.00
593	Rookie Pitchers (Larry Anderson, Ken Crosby, Mark Littell, *Butch Metzger*)	.25
594	Rookie Catchers and Outfielders (Andy Merchant, Ed Ott, Royle Stillman, Jerry White)	.20
595	Rookie Pitchers (Steve Barr, Art DeFillipis, Randy Lerch, Sid Monge)	.15
596	Rookie Infielders (Lamar Johnson, *Johnny LeMaster*, Jerry Manuel, *Craig Reynolds*)	.45

650 Thurman Munson

597	Rookie Pitchers (*Don Aase*, Jack Kucek, Frank LaCorte, Mike Pazik)	.50
598	Rookie Outfielders (Hector Cruz, *Jamie Quirk*, Jerry Turner, Joe Wallis)	.20
599	Rookie Pitchers (Rob Dressler, *Ron Guidry*, *Bob McClure*, Pat Zachry)	10.00
600	Tom Seaver	8.00
601	Ken Rudolph	.15
602	Doug Konieczny	.15
603	Jim Holt	.15
604	Joe Lovitto	.15
605	Al Downing	.20
606	Brewers Team (Alex Grammas)	.80
607	Rich Hinton	.15
608	Vic Correll	.15
609	Fred Norman	.15
610	Greg Luzinski	.45
611	Rick Folkers	.15
612	Joe Lahoud	.15
613	Tim Johnson	.15
614	Fernando Arroyo	.15
615	Mike Cubbage	.15
616	Buck Martinez	.15
617	Darold Knowles	.15
619	Bill Butler	.15
620	Al Oliver	.70
621	Tom Hall	.15
622	Rick Auerbach	.15
623	Bob Allietta	.15
624	Tony Taylor	.15
625	J.R. Richard	.25
626	Bob Sheldon	.15
627	Bill Plummer	.15
628	John D'Acquisto	.15
629	Sandy Alomar	.15
630	Chris Speier	.20
631	Braves Team (Dave Bristol)	.80

98 Dennis Eckersley

632	Rogelio Moret .... .15	642	Dennis Blair .... .15
633	*John Stearns* .... .30	643	Checklist 529-660 .... 1.50
634	Larry Christenson .... .15	644	Tom Bradley .... .15
635	Jim Fregosi .... .25	645	Darrell Porter .... .20
636	Joe Decker .... .15	646	John Lowenstein .... .15
637	Bruce Bochte .... .20	647	Ramon Hernandez .... .15
638	Doyle Alexander .... .30	648	Al Cowens .... .20
639	Fred Kendall .... .15	649	Dave Roberts .... .15
640	Bill Madlock 1.00	650	Thurman Munson 5.00
641	Tom Paciorek .... .20	651	John Odom .... .20

652	Ed Armbrister .... .15
653	*Mike Norris* .... .30
654	Doug Griffin .... .15
655	Mike Vail .... .15
656	White Sox Team (Chuck Tanner) .... .80
657	*Roy Smalley* .... .40
658	Jerry Johnson .... .15
659	Ben Oglivie .... .25
660	Dave Lopes .... .60

1977 TOPPS

The 1977 Topps set of 660 cards continued to offer superior photos, but few major surprises in subject matter were introduced. An eight-card set of league leaders opens the 1977 issue, while a smaller set acknowledges the record-setting 1976 performances of George Brett, Minnie Minoso, Jose Morales, and Nolan Ryan. A unique four-card novelty series entitled Big League Brothers is a 1977 highlight. It features Rick and Paul Reuschel (wrongly identified on their card), George and Ken Brett, Bob and Ken Forsch, and Lee and Carlos May. The hottest cards are from the multi-player rookie card subset: Dale Murphy (identified as a catcher), Andre Dawson, and Jack Clark. The set also contains the last regular-issue card of Brooks Robinson, who retired in 1977.

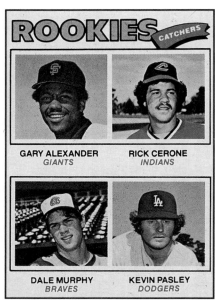

476 Rookie Catchers

		NR MT
Complete set		**$335.00**
Commons		**.15**

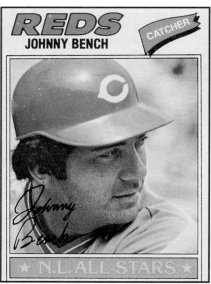

70 Johnny Bench

1	Batting Ldrs (George Brett, Bill Madlock)	$2.50
2	HR Ldrs (Graig Nettles, Mike Schmidt)	1.25
3	RBI Ldrs (George Foster, Lee May)	.50
4	SB Ldrs (Dave Lopes, Bill North)	.30
5	Victory Ldrs (Randy Jones, Jim Palmer)	.80
6	SO Ldrs (Nolan Ryan, Tom Seaver)	3.00
7	ERA Ldrs (John Denny, Mark Fidrych)	.30
8	Leading Firemen (Bill Campbell, Rawly Eastwick)	.30
9	Doug Rader	.15
10	Reggie Jackson	10.00
11	Rob Dressler	.15
12	Larry Haney	.15
13	Luis Gomez	.15
14	Tommy Smith	.15
15	Don Gullett	.20
16	Bob Jones	.15
17	Steve Stone	.25
18	Indians Team (Frank Robinson)	.85
19	John D'Acquisto	.15
20	Graig Nettles	.90
21	Ken Forsch	.20
22	Bill Freehan	.25
23	Dan Driessen	.25
24	Carl Morton	.15

25	*Dwight Evans	1.75
26	Ray Sadecki	.15
27	Bill Buckner	.35
28	Woodie Fryman	.20
29	Bucky Dent	.25
30	Greg Luzinski	.45
31	Jim Todd	.15
32	Checklist 1-132	1.25
33	Wayne Garland	.15
34	Angels Team (Norm Sherry)	.70
35	Rennie Stennett	.15
36	John Ellis	.15
37	Steve Hargan	.15

38	Craig Kusick	.15
39	Tom Griffin	.15
40	Bobby Murcer	.30
41	Jim Kern	.15
42	Jose Cruz	.35
43	Ray Bare	.15
44	Bud Harrelson	.20
45	Rawly Eastwick	.15
46	Buck Martinez	.15
47	Lynn McGlothlen	.15
48	Tom Paciorek	.15
49	Grant Jackson	.15
50	Ron Cey	.35
51	Brewers Team (Alex Grammas)	.70
52	Ellis Valentine	.20
53	Paul Mitchell	.15
54	Sandy Alomar	.20
55	Jeff Burroughs	.25
56	Rudy May	.20
57	Marc Hill	.15
58	Chet Lemon	.30
59	Larry Christenson	.15
60	Jim Rice	5.00
61	Manny Sanguillen	.15
62	Eric Raich	.15

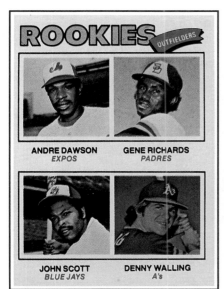

473 Rookie Outfielders

63	Tito Fuentes	.15
64	Larry Biittner	.15
65	Skip Lockwood	.15
66	Roy Smalley	.15
67	*Joaquin Andujar*	.60
68	Bruce Bochte	.20
69	Jim Crawford	.15
70	Johnny Bench	7.00
71	Dock Ellis	.20
72	Mike Anderson	.15
73	Charlie Williams	.15
74	A's Team (Jack McKeon)	.70
75	Dennis Leonard	.20
76	Tim Foli	.15
77	Dyar Miller	.15
78	Bob Davis	.15
79	Don Money	.15
80	Andy Messersmith	.15
81	Juan Beniquez	.20
82	Jim Rooker	.15
83	Kevin Bell	.15
84	Ollie Brown	.15
85	Duane Kuiper	.15
86	Pat Zachry	.15
87	Glenn Borgmann	.15
88	Stan Wall	.15
89	*Butch Hobson*	.20
90	Cesar Cedeno	.25
91	John Verhoeven	.15
92	Dave Rosello	.15
93	Tom Poquette	.15
94	Craig Swan	.15
95	Keith Hernandez	3.00
96	Lou Piniella	.40
97	Dave Heaverlo	.15
98	Milt May	.15
99	Tom Hausman	.15
100	*Joe Morgan	2.50
104	*Omar Moreno*	.25
106	Mike Flanagan	.35
107	Bill Melton	.20
110	Steve Carlton	5.00
111	Rico Petrocelli	.25

113	Blue Jays Mgr./Coaches (Roy Hartsfield, Don Leppert, Bob Miller, Jackie Moore, Harry Warner)	.25
115	Rick Manning	.20
116	Joe Niekro	.30
117	Frank White	.25
119	John Stearns	.20
120	Rod Carew	5.00
122	Ben Oglivie	.20
123	Fred Stanley	.15
127	Ron Fairly	.25
128	*Tommy John	1.25
130	Al Oliver	.60
133	Ralph Garr	.20
134	Padres Team (John McNamara)	.70
135	Mark Belanger	.20
136	*Jerry Mumphrey*	.40
140	Mike Schmidt	20.00
144	*Bruce Sutter*	2.25
146	Dusty Baker	.20
148	Fran Healy	.20
150	Tom Seaver	5.00
152	*Gaylord Perry	1.75
155	Joe Rudi	.20
157	Ken Brett	.20
161	*Garry Templeton*	.80
162	Mike Cuellar	.20
164	Tug McGraw	.30
165	Jim Wynn	.25
170	*Thurman Munson	5.00
175	*Butch Wynegar*	.40
180	Dave Lopes	.25
183	Cardinals Team (Vern Rapp)	.70
185	Sixto Lezcano	.20
187	Dick Pole	.15
188	Bob Tolan	.20
189	Rick Dempsey	.15
193	Larry Gura	.20
194	Gary Matthews	.25
195	Ed Figueroa	.20

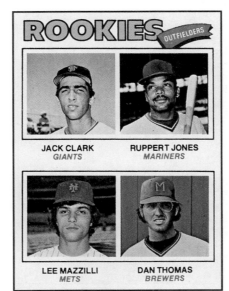

488 Rookie Outfielders

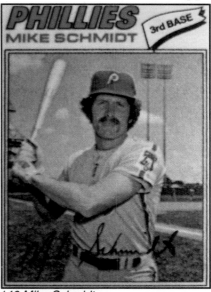

140 Mike Schmidt

196	Len Randle	.15
197	Ed Ott	.15
198	Wilbur Wood	.20
199	Pepe Frias	.15
200	Frank Tanana	.30
201	Ed Kranepool	.25
206	Boog Powell	.50
208	Checklist 133-264	1.25
210	Fred Lynn	1.50
211	Giants Team (Joe Altobelli)	.70
212	Jim Mason	.15
213	Maximino Leon	.15
214	Darrell Porter	.20
215	Butch Metzger	.15
216	Doug DeCinces	.25
217	Tom Underwood	.15
218	*John Wathan*	.60
219	Joe Coleman	.20
220	Chris Chambliss	.35
221	Bob Bailey	.15
222	Francisco Barrios	.15
223	Earl Williams	.15
224	Rusty Torres	.15
225	Bob Apodaca	.15
226	Leroy Stanton	.15
227	*Joe Sambito*	.25
228	Twins Team (Gene Mauch)	.80
229	Don Kessinger	.20
230	Vida Blue	.40
231	Record Breaker (George Brett)	2.00
232	Record Breaker (Minnie Minoso)	.35
233	Record Breaker (Jose Morales)	.20
234	Record Breaker (Nolan Ryan)	4.00
235	Cecil Cooper	.65
236	Tom Buskey	.15
237	Gene Clines	.15
238	Tippy Martinez	.15
239	Bill Plummer	.15

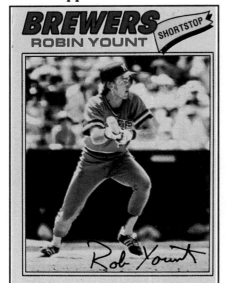

635 Robin Yount

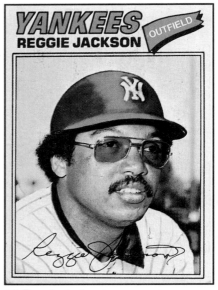

10 Reggie Jackson

279	Joe Wallis	.15
280	Jim Hunter	2.00
281	Roy Staiger	.15
282	Sid Monge	.15
283	Jerry DaVanon	.15
284	Mike Norris	.20
285	Brooks Robinson	2.50
286	Johnny Grubb	.15
287	Reds Team (Sparky Anderson)	.85
288	Bob Montgomery	.15
289	Gene Garber	.20
290	Amos Otis	.20
291	*Jason Thompson*	.35
292	Rogelio Moret	.15
293	Jack Brohamer	.15
294	George Medich	.15
295	Gary Carter	6.00
296	Don Hood	.15
297	Ken Reitz	.15
298	Charlie Hough	.25
299	Otto Velez	.15
300	Jerry Koosman	.35
301	Toby Harrah	.25
302	Mike Garman	.20
303	Gene Tenace	.25
304	Jim Hughes	.15
305	Mickey Rivers	.25
306	Rick Waits	.15
307	Gary Sutherland	.15
308	Gene Pentz	.15
309	Red Sox Team (Don Zimmer)	.75
310	Larry Bowa	.30
311	Vern Ruhle	.15
312	Rob Belloir	.15
313	Paul Blair	.20
314	Steve Mingori	.15
315	Dave Chalk	.15
316	Steve Rogers	.20
317	Kurt Bevacqua	.15
318	Duffy Dyer	.15
319	*Rich Gossage	1.00
320	Ken Griffey	.30

240	Ron LeFlore	.25
241	Dave Tomlin	.15
242	Ken Henderson	.15
243	Ron Reed	.20
244	John Mayberry	.20
245	Rick Rhoden	.30
246	Mike Vail	.15
247	Chris Knapp	.15
248	Wilbur Howard	.15
249	Pete Redfern	.15
250	Bill Madlock	.40
251	Tony Muser	.15
252	Dale Murray	.15
253	John Hale	.15
254	Doyle Alexander	.30
255	George Scott	.20
256	Joe Hoerner	.15
257	Mike Miley	.15
258	*Luis Tiant	.35
259	Mets Team (Joe Frazier)	.80
260	J.R. Richard	.25
261	Phil Garner	.20
262	Al Cowens	.15
263	Mike Marshall	.25
264	Tom Hutton	.15
265	*Mark Fidrych*	.75
266	Derrel Thomas	.15
267	Ray Fosse	.15
268	Rick Sawyer	.15
269	Joe Lis	.15
270	Dave Parker	3.00
271	Terry Forster	.20
272	Lee Lacy	.15
273	Eric Soderholm	.15
274	Don Stanhouse	.15
275	Mike Hargrove	.20
276	AL Championship (Chambliss' Dramatic Homer Decides It)	.70
277	NL Championship (Reds Sweep Phillies 3 In Row)	.70
278	Danny Frisella	.15

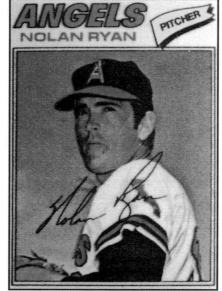

650 Nolan Ryan

321	Dave Goltz	.20
322	Bill Russell	.20
323	Larry Lintz	.15
324	John Curtis	.15
325	Mike Ivie	.15
326	Jesse Jefferson	.15
327	Astros Team (Bill Virdon)	.70
328	Tommy Boggs	.15
329	Ron Hodges	.15
330	George Hendrick	.20
331	Jim Colborn	.15
332	Elliott Maddox	.20
333	Paul Reuschel	.15
334	Bill Stein	.15
335	Bill Robinson	.20
336	Denny Doyle	.15
337	Ron Schueler	.15
338	Dave Duncan	.15
339	Adrian Devine	.15
340	Hal McRae	.30
341	Joe Kerrigan	.15
342	Jerry Remy	.15
343	Ed Halicki	.15
344	Brian Downing	.25
345	Reggie Smith	.25
346	Bill Singer	.20
347	George Foster	1.25
348	Brent Strom	.15
349	Jim Holt	.15
350	Larry Dierker	.20
351	Jim Sundberg	.20
352	Mike Phillips	.15
353	Stan Thomas	.15
354	Pirates Team (Chuck Tanner)	.80
355	Lou Brock	2.50
356	Checklist 265-396	1.25
357	*Tim McCarver	.40
358	Tom House	.15
359	Willie Randolph	.85
360	Rick Monday	.25
361	Eduardo Rodriguez	.15
362	Tommy Davis	.30

363	Dave Roberts	.15
364	Vic Correll	.15
365	Mike Torrez	.20
366	Ted Sizemore	.15
367	Dave Hamilton	.15
368	Mike Jorgensen	.15
369	Terry Humphrey	.15
370	John Montefusco	.20
371	Royals Team (Whitey Herzog)	.80
372	Rich Folkers	.15
373	Bert Campaneris	.30
374	*Kent Tekulve	.30
375	Larry Hisle	.20
376	Nino Espinosa	.15
377	Dave McKay	.15
378	Jim Umbarger	.15
379	Larry Cox	.15
380	Lee May	.25
381	Bob Forsch	.20
382	Charlie Moore	.15
383	Stan Bahnsen	.15
384	Darrel Chaney	.15
385	Dave LaRoche	.15
386	Manny Mota	.25
387	Yankees Team (Billy Martin)	1.25
388	Terry Harmon	.15
389	Ken Kravec	.15
390	Dave Winfield	4.00
391	Dan Warthen	.15
392	Phil Roof	.15
393	John Lowenstein	.15
394	Bill Laxton	.15
395	Manny Trillo	.20
396	Tom Murphy	.15
397	*Larry Herndon*	.40
398	Tom Burgmeier	.15
399	Bruce Boisclair	.15
400	Steve Garvey	3.50
401	Mickey Scott	.15
402	Tommy Helms	.15
403	Tom Grieve	.15
404	Eric Rasmussen	.15

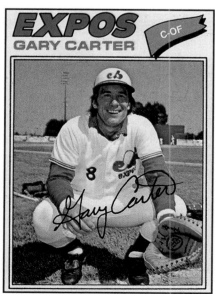

295 Gary Carter

405	Claudell Washington	.25
406	Tim Johnson	.15
407	Dave Freisleben	.15
408	Cesar Tovar	.15
409	Pete Broberg	.15
410	Willie Montanez	.15
411	World Series Games 1 & 2	.70
412	World Series Games 3 & 4	.70
413	World Series Summary	1.00
414	Tommy Harper	.20
415	Jay Johnstone	.20
416	Chuck Hartenstein	.15
417	Wayne Garrett	.15
418	White Sox Team (Bob Lemon)	.80
419	Steve Swisher	.15
420	Rusty Staub	.35
421	Doug Rau	.15
422	Freddie Patek	.15
423	Gary Lavelle	.15
424	Steve Brye	.15
425	Joe Torre	.40
426	Dick Drago	.15
427	Dave Rader	.15
428	Rangers Team (Frank Lucchesi)	.80
429	Ken Boswell	.15
430	Fergie Jenkins	.85
431	Dave Collins	.25
432	Buzz Capra	.15
433	Turn Back The Clock (Nate Colbert)	.20
434	Turn Back The Clock (Carl Yastrzemski)	2.00
435	Turn Back The Clock (Maury Wills)	.35
436	Turn Back The Clock (Bob Keegan)	.20
437	Turn Back The Clock (Ralph Kiner)	.50
438	Marty Perez	.15
439	Gorman Thomas	.25
440	Jon Matlack	.20

480 Carl Yastrzemski

441	Larvell Blanks	.15
442	Braves Team (Dave Bristol)	.70
443	Lamar Johnson	.15
444	Wayne Twitchell	.15
445	Ken Singleton	.25
446	Bill Bonham	.15
450	Pete Rose	9.00
451	Checklist 397-528	1.25
455	Rick Wise	.20
460	Willie Stargell	2.50
461	Dick Tidrow	.20
462	Don Baylor	.35
465	Rico Carty	.25
467	Phillies Team (Danny Ozark)	.70
470	Ted Simmons	.60
472	Rookie Pitchers (Don Aase, Bob McClure, Gil Patterson, David Wehrmeister)	.25
473	Rookie Outfielders (*Andre Dawson,* Gene Richards, John Scott, *Denny Walling*)	38.00
475	Rookie Pitchers (Chris Batton, Rick Camp, Scott McGregor, Manny Sarmiento)	.30
476	Rookie Catchers (Gary Alexander, *Rick Cerone, Dale Murphy,* Kevin Pasley)	65.00
477	Rookie Infielders (Doug Ault, *Rich Dauer,* Orlando Gonzalez, Phil Mankowski)	.25
479	Rookie Outfielders (Brian Asselstine, *Wayne Gross,* Sam Mejias, Alvis Woods)	.25
480	Carl Yastrzemski	5.00
483	Richie Zisk	.20
484	Burt Hooton	.20

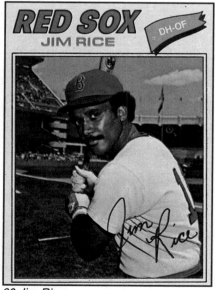

60 Jim Rice

123

485	Roy White .... .30	
488	Rookie Outfielders (*Jack Clark, Ruppert Jones, Lee Mazzilli*, Dan Thomas) 27.00	
489	Rookie Pitchers (*Len Barker*, Randy Lerch, *Greg Minton*, Mike Overy) .... .40	
490	Rookie Shortstops (*Billy Almon*, Mickey Klutts, Tommy McMillan, Mark Wagner) .... .25	
491	Rookie Pitchers (Mike Dupree, *Denny Martinez*, Craig Mitchell, Bob Sykes) 1.00	
492	Rookie Outfielders (*Tony Armas, Steve Kemp*, Carlos Lopez, Gary Woods) 1.25	
493	Rookie Pitchers (*Mike Krukow*, Jim Otten, Gary Wheelock, Mike Willis) .... .70	
494	Rookie Infielders (Juan Bernhardt, Mike Champion, *Jim Gantner, Bump Wills*) .... .50	
495	Al Hrabosky .... .20	
497	Clay Carroll .... .20	
498	Sal Bando .... .25	
500	Dave Kingman .... .60	
503	Bill Lee .... .20	
504	Dodgers Team (Tom Lasorda) 1.00	
505	Oscar Gamble .... .20	
510	John Candelaria .... .80	
517	*Pete Vuckovich* .... .50	

518	Cubs Team (Herman Franks) .... .70
520	Garry Maddox .... .20
521	Bob Grich .... .25
523	*Rollie Fingers 1.00
525	*Dennis Eckersley 1.50
526	Larry Parrish .... .35
530	Rick Reuschel .... .30
531	Lyman Bostock .... .25
533	Mickey Stanley .... .20
534	Paul Splittorff .... .20
535	Cesar Geronimo .... .20
540	Bob Watson .... .20
541	John Denny .... .20
543	Ron Blomberg .... .20
545	*Bob Boone .... .25
546	Orioles Team (Earl Weaver) .... .80
547	*Willie McCovey 2.00
548	*Joel Youngblood* .... .30
550	Randy Jones .... .20
555	Dan Ford .... .20
560	Dave Concepcion .... .35
562	Checklist 529-660 .... 1.25
564	Alan Ashby .... .20
565	Mickey Lolich .... .50
567	Enos Cabell .... .20
568	Carlos May .... .20
569	Jim Lonborg .... .20
570	Bobby Bonds .... .35
571	Darrell Evans .... .40
574	Aurelio Rodriguez .... .20
578	Bob Randall .... .15
580	George Brett 13.00
585	Rick Burleson .... .20
590	Buddy Bell .... .30
595	John Hiller .... .20
596	*Jerry Martin* .... .25

597	Mariners Mgr./Coaches (Don Bryant, Jim Busby, Darrell Johnson, Vada Pinson, Wes Stock) .... .25
598	*Sparky Lyle .... .35
600	*Jim Palmer 3.00
603	Willie Davis .... .25
608	Roy Howell .... .15
609	Jim Barr .... .15
610	Jose Cardenal .... .20
615	Phil Niekro 1.50
618	Pat Dobson .... .20
620	Don Sutton 1.50
621	Tigers Team (Ralph Houk) .... .80
625	Ken Holtzman .... .25
626	Al Bumbry .... .20
629	Bobby Valentine .... .25
630	Bert Blyleven .... .80
631	Big League Brothers (George Brett, Ken Brett) ... 1.75
632	Big League Brothers (Bob Forsch, Ken Forsch) ..... .30
633	Big League Brothers (Carlos May, Lee May) .... .30
634	Big League Brothers (Paul Reuschel, Rick Reuschel) (names reversed) .... .30
635	Robin Yount 20.00
638	*Jim Kaat .... .80
640	Carlton Fisk 1.25
645	Jerry Reuss .... .25
647	Expos Team (Dick Williams) .... .80
650	Nolan Ryan 18.00
655	Tony Perez .... .80
656	Ron Guidry 2.75
660	Willie Horton .... .40

1978 TOPPS

The 1978 Topps set grew to 726 cards—the biggest since 1972. The simply designed cards use an extra-large photo and a minimal border. All Stars from 1977 are honored with a small red, white, and blue shield in the upper right-hand corner of their cards. Card backs contain a small box that features baseball situations such as a home run or ground out; this allows two people to play a simulated baseball game. Because Topps increased the set size, it needed to print 11 cards twice on each 132-card sheet. Although this increased the availability of those cards, prices for them have seen little fluctuation.

		NR MT
Complete set		**$250.00**
Commons		**.12**

1	Record Breaker (Lou Brock) $2.00	
2	Record Breaker (Sparky Lyle) .... .25	
3	Record Breaker (Willie McCovey) .... .70	
4	Record Breaker (Brooks Robinson) .... .90	

5	Record Breaker (Pete Rose) 2.00
6	Record Breaker (Nolan Ryan) 2.50
7	Record Breaker (Reggie Jackson) 1.50
8	Mike Sadek .... .12
9	Doug DeCinces .... .25
10	Phil Niekro 1.25
11	Rick Manning .... .12
12	Don Aase .... .15
13	Art Howe .... .12

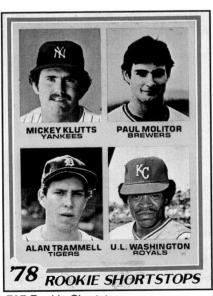

'78 ROOKIE SHORTSTOPS

MICKEY KLUTTS YANKEES · PAUL MOLITOR BREWERS · ALAN TRAMMELL TIGERS · U.L. WASHINGTON ROYALS

707 Rookie Shortstops

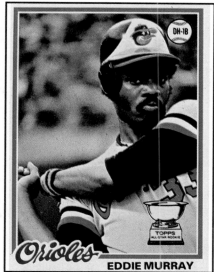

36 Eddie Murray

15	Tony Perez	.25
16	Roy White	.20
17	Mike Krukow	.20
18	Bob Grich	.25
19	Darrell Porter	.20
20	Pete Rose	3.50
21	Steve Kemp	.20
22	Charlie Hough	.25
25	Jon Matlack	.20
28	Ed Ott	.12
30	George Hendrick	.20
32	Garry Templeton	.25
34	Willie McCovey	2.00
35	*Sparky Lyle	.30
36	*Eddie Murray*	36.00
39	*Floyd Bannister*	1.00
40	Carl Yastrzemski	3.00
41	Burt Hooton	.20
44	Toby Harrah	.20
45	Mark Fidrych	.25
48	Don Baylor	.35
49	Ed Kranepool	.20
50	Rick Reuschel	.25
52	Jim Lonborg	.20
56	Randy Jones	.20
58	Bob Forsch	.20
60	Thurman Munson	2.50
62	Jim Barr	.20
65	Ken Singleton	.25
66	White Sox Team	.50
67	Claudell Washington	.25
70	Rich Gossage	.70
72	Andre Dawson	6.00
74	Checklist 1-121	.90
80	Ken Griffey	.25
82	Giants Team	.50
84	Kent Tekulve	.25
85	Ron Fairly	.20
89	Ken Clay	.15
90	Larry Bowa	.30
96	Orioles Team	.50
99	*Willie Hernandez*	.65
100	George Brett	5.00

101	Sid Monge	.12
104	Lee Lacy	.12
109	Joe Torre	.30
110	Richie Zisk	.20
111	Mike Tyson	.12
112	Astros Team	.50
114	Paul Blair	.20
119	Denny Martinez	.25
120	Gary Carter	3.00
122	Dennis Eckersley	1.00
123	Manny Trillo	.20
124	*Dave Rozema*	.25
125	George Scott	.20
127	Chet Lemon	.20
128	Bill Russell	.20
130	Jeff Burroughs	.20
131	Bert Blyleven	.60
132	Enos Cabell	.20
134	*Steve Henderson*	.25
135	Ron Guidry	.90
140	Rollie Fingers	.75
141	Ruppert Jones	.20
142	John Montefusco	.20
143	Keith Hernandez	2.50
145	Rick Monday	.20
146	Doyle Alexander	.30
147	Lee Mazilli	.20
148	Andre Thornton	.25
150	Bobby Bonds	.35
152	*Ivan DeJesus*	.20
153	Steve Stone	.25
154	Cecil Cooper	.20
156	Andy Messersmith	.20
158	Joaquin Andujar	.25
159	Lou Piniella	.35
160	Jim Palmer	3.00
161	*Bob Boone	.25
168	Reggie Smith	.25
170	Lou Brock	2.00
172	Mike Hargrove	.20
173	Robin Yount	9.00
176	Milt May	.12
179	Dick Tidrow	.20

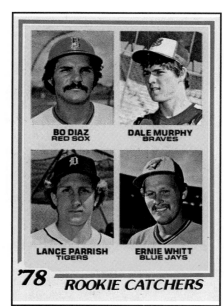

'78 ROOKIE CATCHERS

708 Rookie Catchers

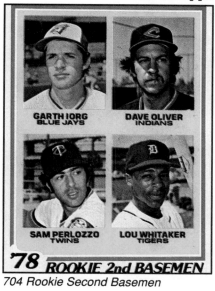

'78 ROOKIE 2nd BASEMEN

704 Rookie Second Basemen

180	Dave Concepcion	.35
181	Ken Forsch	.20
183	Doug Bird	.12
184	Checklist 122-242	.90
185	Ellis Valentine	.25
186	*Bob Stanley*	.25
188	Al Bumbry	.20
189	Tom Lasorda	.25
190	John Candelaria	.25
192	Padres Team	.50
195	Larry Dierker	.20
200	Reggie Jackson	4.00
201	Batting Ldrs (Rod Carew, Dave Parker)	.80
202	HR Ldrs (George Foster, Jim Rice)	.25
203	RBI Ldrs (George Foster, Larry Hisle)	.25
205	Victory Ldrs (Steve Carlton, Dave Goltz, Dennis Leonard, Jim Palmer)	.65
206	SO Ldrs (Phil Niekro, Nolan Ryan)	.35
208	Leading Firemen (Bill Campbell, Rollie Fingers)	.35
211	*Earl Weaver	.20
214	Angels Team	.50
215	Darrell Evans	.35
221	Chris Speier	.15
224	Jerry Tabb	.12
230	Al Hrabosky	.20
232	Mickey Stanley	.20
233	Dick Pole	.12
235	*Tim McCarver	.35
237	Rich Dauer	.12
238	Juan Beniquez	.20
239	Dyar Miller	.12
240	Gene Tenace	.20
241	Pete Vuckovich	.20
244	Expos Team	.20

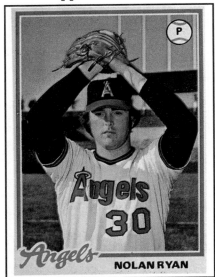

400 Nolan Ryan

331	Mark Littell	.12
333	Jim Todd	.12
334	John Stearns	.12
335	Bucky Dent	.30
336	Steve Busby	.20
337	Tom Grieve	.12
338	Dave Heaverlo	.12
339	Mario Guerrero	.12
340	Bake McBride	.12
341	Mike Flanagan	.25
342	Aurelio Rodriguez	.20
343	John Wathan	.12
344	Sam Ewing	.12
345	Luis Tiant	.35
346	Larry Biittner	.12
347	Terry Forster	.20
348	Del Unser	.12
349	Rick Camp	.12
350	Steve Garvey	2.75
351	Jeff Torborg	.20
352	Tony Scott	.12
353	Doug Bair	.12
354	Cesar Geronimo	.20
355	Bill Travers	.12
356	Mets Team	.75
357	Tom Poquette	.12
358	Mark Lemongello	.12
359	Marc Hill	.12
360	Mike Schmidt	8.00
361	Chris Knapp	.12
362	Dave May	.12
363	Bob Randall	.12
364	Jerry Turner	.12
365	Ed Figueroa	.20
366	Larry Milbourne	.12
367	Rick Dempsey	.20
368	Balor Moore	.12
369	Tim Nordbrook	.12
370	Rusty Staub	.35
371	Ray Burris	.12
372	Brian Asselstine	.12
373	Jim Willoughby	.12
374	Jose Morales	.12
375	Tommy John	.90

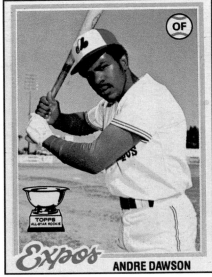

72 Andre Dawson

245	Rick Burleson	.20
246	Dan Driessen	.20
250	Graig Nettles	.30
253	Jim Kern	.12
254	Dave Collins	.20
255	Jerry Reuss	.20
258	John Hiller	.20
259	Dodgers Team	.80
260	Bert Campaneris	.25
262	Rudy May	.12
265	Sal Bando	.12
266	*Bob Shirley*	.20
267	Doug Ault	.12
270	Carlton Fisk	1.50
275	Dan Ford	.12
279	Bill Virdon	.20
280	Buddy Bell	.30
282	Yankees Team	1.00
286	Ben Oglivie	.20
289	Checklist 243-363	.90
290	Willie Horton	.20
291	Gary Ross	.12
294	Larry Parrish	.25
295	Bill Lee	.20
298	Tony Armas	.25
299	Whitey Herzog	.30
300	*Joe Morgan	2.00
302	Cubs Team	.50
303	Sam Hinds	.12
305	Rico Carty	.20
306	Joe Niekro	.25
309	Cliff Johnson	.20
310	Don Sutton	1.25
311	Jose Baez	.12
315	Mark Belanger	.20
316	Henry Cruz	.12
317	Dave Johnson	.30
320	Fred Lynn	.90
324	Vern Rapp	.12
325	Bruce Sutter	.70
326	Mike Lum	.12
328	Brewers Team	.50
330	Bob Watson	.20

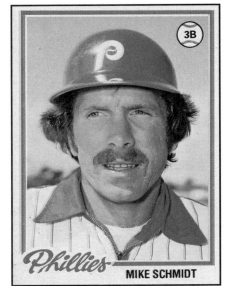

360 Mike Schmidt

376	Jim Wohlford	.12
377	Manny Sarmiento	.12
378	Bobby Winkles	.12
379	Skip Lockwood	.12
380	Ted Simmons	.40
381	Phillies Team	.70
382	Joe Lahoud	.12
383	Mario Mendoza	.12
384	Jack Clark	3.25
385	Tito Fuentes	.12
386	Bob Gorinski	.12
387	Ken Holtzman	.25
388	Bill Fahey	.12
389	Julio Gonzalez	.12
390	Oscar Gamble	.20
391	Larry Haney	.12
392	Billy Almon	.12
393	Tippy Martinez	.12
394	Roy Howell	.12
395	Jim Hughes	.12
397	Greg Gross	.15
398	Don Hood	.12
399	Pete Mackanin	.12
400	Nolan Ryan	10.00
401	Sparky Anderson	.30
402	Dave Campbell	.12
403	Bud Harrelson	.20
404	Tigers Team	.60
405	Rawly Eastwick	.12
406	Mike Jorgensen	.12
407	Odell Jones	.12
408	Joe Zdeb	.12
409	Ron Schueler	.12
410	Bill Madlock	.50
411	AL Championships (Yankees Rally To Defeat Royals)	.70
412	NL Championships (Dodgers Overpower Phillies In Four)	.50
413	World Series (Reggie & Yankees Reign Supreme)	1.25

414	Darold Knowles	.12
415	Ray Fosse	.12
416	Jack Brohamer	.12
417	Mike Garman	.12
418	Tony Muser	.12
419	Jerry Garvin	.12
420	Greg Luzinski	.35
421	Junior Moore	.12
422	Steve Braun	.12
423	Dave Rosello	.12
424	Red Sox Team	.70
425	Steve Rogers	.12
426	Fred Kendall	.12
427	*Mario Soto*	.40
428	Joel Youngblood	.20
429	Mike Barlow	.12
430	Al Oliver	.40
431	Butch Metzger	.12
432	Terry Bulling	.12
433	Fernando Gonzalez	.12
434	Mike Norris	.12
435	Checklist 364-484	.90
436	Vic Harris	.12
437	Bo McLaughlin	.12
438	John Ellis	.12
439	Ken Kravec	.12
440	Dave Lopes	.25
441	Larry Gura	.12
442	Elliott Maddox	.12
443	Darrel Chaney	.12
444	Roy Hartsfield	.12
445	Mike Ivie	.12
446	Tug McGraw	.35
447	Leroy Stanton	.12
448	Bill Castro	.12
449	Tim Blackwell	.12
450	Tom Seaver	4.00
451	Twins Team	.50
452	Jerry Mumphrey	.20
453	Doug Flynn	.12
454	Dave LaRoche	.12
455	Bill Robinson	.12
456	Vern Ruhle	.12
457	Bob Bailey	.12

530 Dave Winfield

458	Jeff Newman	.12
459	Charlie Spikes	.12
460	Jim Hunter	1.75
461	Rob Andrews	.12
462	Rogelio Moret	.12
463	Kevin Bell	.12
464	Jerry Grote	.20
465	Hal McRae	.30
466	Dennis Blair	.12
467	Alvin Dark	.20
468	*Warren Cromartie*	.20
469	Rick Cerone	.20
470	J.R. Richard	.25
471	Roy Smalley	.20
472	Ron Reed	.20
473	Bill Buckner	.30
474	Jim Slaton	.12
475	Gary Matthews	.20
476	Bill Stein	.12
477	Doug Capilla	.12
478	Jerry Remy	.12
479	Cardinals Team	.50
480	Ron LeFlore	.25
481	Jackson Todd	.12
482	Rick Miller	.12
483	Ken Macha	.12
484	Jim Norris	.12
485	Chris Chambliss	.30
486	John Curtis	.12
487	Jim Tyrone	.12
488	Dan Spillner	.12
489	Rudy Meoli	.12
490	Amos Otis	.20
491	Scott McGregor	.20
492	Jim Sundberg	.20
493	Steve Renko	.12
494	Chuck Tanner	.20
495	Dave Cash	.12
496	*Jim Clancy*	.30
497	Glenn Adams	.12
498	Joe Sambito	.12
499	Mariners Team	.50
500	George Foster	.70

200 Reggie Jackson

501	Dave Roberts	.12
502	Pat Rockett	.12
503	Ike Hampton	.12
504	Roger Freed	.12
505	Felix Millan	.12
506	Ron Blomberg	.12
507	Willie Crawford	.12
508	Johnny Oates	.12
509	Brent Strom	.12
510	Willie Stargell	2.00
511	Frank Duffy	.12
512	Larry Herndon	.20
513	Barry Foote	.12
514	Rob Sperring	.12
515	Tim Corcoran	.12
516	Gary Beare	.12
517	Andres Mora	.12
518	Tommy Boggs	.12
519	Brian Downing	.25
520	Larry Hisle	.20
521	Steve Staggs	.12
522	Dick Williams	.20
523	*Donnie Moore*	.25
524	Bernie Carbo	.12
525	Jerry Terrell	.12
526	Reds Team	.60
527	Vic Correll	.12
528	Rob Picciolo	.12
529	Paul Hartzell	.12
530	Dave Winfield	4.50
531	Tom Underwood	.12
532	Skip Jutze	.12
533	Sandy Alomar	.12
534	Wilbur Howard	.12
535	Checklist 485-605	.90
536	Roric Harrison	.12
537	Bruce Bochte	.20
538	Johnnie LeMaster	.12
539	Vic Davalillo	.12
540	Steve Carlton	3.00
541	Larry Cox	.12
542	Tim Johnson	.12
543	Larry Harlow	.12
544	Len Randle	.12

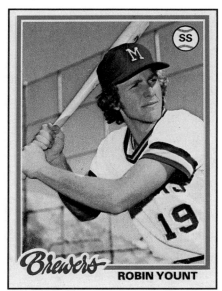

173 Robin Yount

127

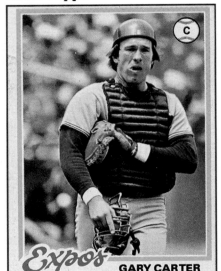

120 Gary Carter

545	Bill Campbell	.12
546	Ted Martinez	.12
547	John Scott	.12
548	Billy Hunter	.12
549	Joe Kerrigan	.12
550	John Mayberry	.20
551	Braves Team	.50
552	Francisco Barrios	.12
553	*Terry Puhl*	.35
554	Joe Coleman	.20
555	Butch Wynegar	.20
556	Ed Armbrister	.12
557	Tony Solaita	.12
558	Paul Mitchell	.12
559	Phil Mankowski	.12
560	Dave Parker	2.00
561	Charlie Williams	.12
562	Glenn Burke	.12
563	Dave Rader	.12
564	Mick Kelleher	.12
565	Jerry Koosman	.25
566	Merv Rettenmund	.12
567	Dick Drago	.12
568	Tom Hutton	.12
569	*Lary Sorensen*	.20
570	Dave Kingman	.60
571	Buck Martinez	.12
572	Rick Wise	.20
573	Luis Gomez	.12
574	Bob Lemon	.30
575	Pat Dobson	.20
576	Sam Mejias	.12
577	A's Team	.50
578	Buzz Capra	.12
579	*Rance Mulliniks*	.35
580	Rod Carew	3.00
581	Lynn McGlothen	.12
582	Fran Healy	.15
583	George Medich	.12
584	John Hale	.12
585	Woodie Fryman	.12
586	Ed Goodson	.12
587	John Urrea	.12

588	Jim Mason	.12
589	*Bob Knepper*	1.00
590	Bobby Murcer	.30
591	George Zeber	.15
592	Bob Apodaca	.12
593	Dave Skaggs	.12
594	Dave Freisleben	.12
595	Sixto Lezcano	.12
596	Gary Wheelock	.12
597	Steve Dillard	.12
598	Eddie Solomon	.12
599	Gary Woods	.12
600	Frank Tanana	.25
601	Gene Mauch	.25
602	Eric Soderholm	.12
605	Rick Rhoden	.25
606	Pirates Team	.50
608	Johnny Grubb	.12
609	John Denny	.12
610	Garry Maddox	.20
611	Pat Scanlon	.12
613	Marty Perez	.12
614	Joe Wallis	.12
615	Clay Carroll	.20
616	Pat Kelly	.12
617	Joe Nolan	.12
618	Tommy Helms	.12
619	*Thad Bosley*	.20
620	Willie Randolph	.30
621	Craig Swan	.12
622	Champ Summers	.12
624	Gary Alexander	.12
625	Jose Cruz	.25
626	Blue Jays Team	.25
627	Dave Johnson	.12
628	Ralph Garr	.20
629	Don Stanhouse	.12
630	Ron Cey	.25
631	Danny Ozark	.20
632	Rowland Office	.12
633	Tom Veryzer	.12
634	Len Barker	.20
635	Joe Rudi	.25
636	Jim Bibby	.12

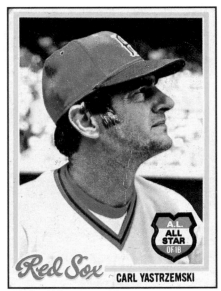

40 Carl Yastrzemski

60 Thurman Munson

637	Duffy Dyer	.12
638	Paul Splittorff	.20
639	Gene Clines	.12
640	Lee May	.12
641	Doug Rau	.12
642	Denny Doyle	.12
643	Tom House	.12
644	Jim Dwyer	.12
645	Mike Torrez	.20
646	Rick Auerbach	.12
647	Steve Dunning	.12
649	*Moose Haas*	.25
650	Cesar Cedeno	.25
651	Doug Rader	.12
652	Checklist 606-726	.90
653	Ron Hodges	.12
654	Pepe Frias	.12
655	Lyman Bostock	.20
656	Dave Garcia	.12
657	Bombo Rivera	.12
658	Manny Sanguillen	.20
659	Rangers Team	.50
660	Jason Thompson	.20
661	Grant Jackson	.12
662	Paul Dade	.12
663	Paul Reuschel	.12
664	Fred Stanley	.15
665	Dennis Leonard	.25
666	Billy Smith	.12
667	Jeff Byrd	.12
668	Dusty Baker	.25
670	Jim Rice	3.50
672	Don Kessinger	.20
673	Steve Brye	.12
674	*Ray Knight*	.90
675	Jay Johnstone	.20
677	Ed Herrmann	.20
680	Vida Blue	.30
682	Ken Brett	.20
684	Ralph Houk	.20
686	Gaylord Perry	1.75
687	*Julio Cruz*	.25
689	Indians Team	.50

690	Mickey Rivers	.25
691	Ross Grimsley	.20
692	Ken Reitz	.20
695	Dwight Evans	1.00
700	Johnny Bench	3.50
701	Rookie Pitchers (*Tom Hume*, Larry Landreth, *Steve McCatty*, Bruce Taylor)	.25
702	Rookie Catchers (Bill Nahorodny, Kevin Pasley, Rick Sweet, Don Werner)	.12
703	Rookie Pitchers (*Larry Andersen*, Tim Jones, Mickey Mahler, *Jack Morris*)	8.00
704	Rookie Second Basemen (*Garth Iorg*, Dave Oliver, Sam Perlozzo, *Lou Whitaker*)	13.00
705	Rookie Outfielders (*Dave Bergman*, Miguel Dilone, *Clint Hurdle*, Willie Norwood)	.25
706	Rookie First Basemen (Wayne Cage, Ted Cox, *Pat Putnam, Dave Revering*)	.20
707	Rookie Shortstops (Mickey Klutts, *Paul Molitor, Alan Trammell, U.L Washington*)	45.00
708	Rookie Catchers (*Bo Diaz*, Dale Murphy, *Lance Parrish*, Ernie *Whitt*)	27.00
709	Rookie Pitchers (Steve Burke, *Matt Keough*, Lance Rautzhan, Dan Schatzeder)	.25
710	Rookie Outfielders (Dell Alston, Rick Bosetti, *Mike Easler*, Keith Smith)	.50
712	Bobby Valentine	.25
715	Jim Kaat	.60
720	Fergie Jenkins	.60
721	Billy Martin	.70
724	Royals Team	.70
726	Wilbur Wood	.40

1979 TOPPS

Although Topps kept supplying collectors with attractive cards in 1979, few innovations were included in the 726-card set. For the first time, rookie prospect cards are arranged by team, with each card featuring three black-and-white photos of promising young players. Ozzie Smith led the rookie parade in 1979, and today his card is also the most valuable of the entire set. Other rookies include Bob Welch, Lonnie Smith, Pedro Guerrero, Carney Lansford, and Kevin Bass. In early print runs Texas Rangers shortstop Bump Wills was mistakenly identified as a member of the Toronto Blue Jays, probably due to the letter "T" on his cap. Many collectors believe that the correct card is scarcer.

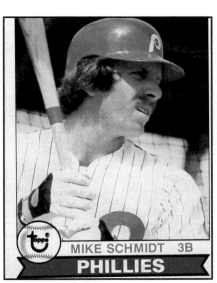

610 Mike Schmidt

		NR MT
Complete set		**$175.00**
Commons		**.12**
1	Batting Ldrs (Rod Carew, Dave Parker)	$1.50
2	HR Ldrs (George Foster, Jim Rice)	.50
3	RBI Ldrs (George Foster, Jim Rice)	.50
4	SB Ldrs (Ron LeFlore, Omar Moreno)	.25
5	Victory Ldrs (Ron Guidry, Gaylord Perry)	.50
6	SO Ldrs (J.R. Richard, Nolan Ryan)	.50
7	ERA Ldrs (Ron Guidry, Craig Swan)	.25
8	Leading Firemen (Rollie Fingers, Rich Gossage)	.40
10	Lee May	.20
15	Ross Grimsley	.20
16	Fred Stanley	.15
17	Donnie Moore	.20
20	Joe Morgan	.40
23	Terry Forster	.20

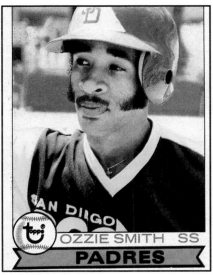

116 Ozzie Smith

24	Paul Molitor	4.00
25	Steve Carlton	3.00
27	Dave Goltz	.20
30	Dave Winfield	2.50
35	Ed Figueroa	.20
39	Dale Murphy	8.00
40	Dennis Eckersley	.35

41	Twins Team (Gene Mauch)	.50
45	Al Hrabosky	.20
50	Steve Garvey	1.25
55	Willie Stargell	2.00
58	Bob Randall	.15
60	Mickey Rivers	.20
61	Bo Diaz	.20
65	Mark Belanger	.20
66	Tigers Team (Les Moss)	.60
70	John Candelaria	.25
71	Brian Downing	.20
74	*Shane Rawley*	.70
80	Jason Thompson	.20
82	Mets Team (Joe Torre)	.60
85	Gary Matthews	.20
89	Dick Tidrow	.20

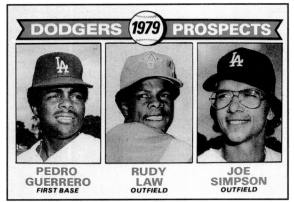

719 Dodgers Prospects

90	*Bob Boone	.25
95	Robin Yount	6.00
96	Indians Team (Jeff Torborg)	.50
99	John Wathan	.20
100	Tom Seaver	2.00
107	Jesus Alou	.20
110	Vida Blue	.30
112	Phillies Team (Danny Ozark)	.50
114	Cliff Johnson	.20
115	Nolan Ryan	9.00
116	Ozzie Smith	36.00
118	Bud Harrelson	.20
120	Jim Sundberg	.20
121	Checklist 1-121	.25
123	Lou Whitaker	3.00
125	Rick Burleson	.20
131	Jim Clancy	.25
135	Bobby Murcer	.25
136	Jim Kaat	.60
140	Don Gullett	.20
145	Rick Rhoden	.25
151	John Hiller	.20
152	Rick Cerone	.20
155	*Dwight Evans	.80
159	Roy White	.20
160	Mike Flanagan	.30
164	Mickey Lolich	.40
170	Don Sutton	1.25
175	George Hendrick	.20
176	Aurelio Rodriguez	.20
177	Ron Reed	.20
180	Larry Hisle	.20
183	Paul Splittorff	.20
185	Mike Torrez	.20
189	Eddie Whitson	.50
190	Ron Cey	.25
192	Cardinals Team (Ken Boyer)	.50
194	Randy Jones	.20
195	Bill Madlock	.40
200	Johnny Bench	1.50
201	Record Breaker (Mike Edwards)	.12
202	Record Breaker (Ron Guidry)	.35
203	Record Breaker (J.R. Richard)	.20

204	Record Breaker (Pete Rose)	1.50
205	Record Breaker (John Stearns)	.12
206	Record Breaker (Sammy Stewart)	.12
210	Larry Bowa	.30
211	Denny Martinez	.20
212	Carney Lansford	5.00
214	Red Sox Team (Don Zimmer)	.60
215	Willie McCovey	1.50
216	Wilbur Wood	.20
218	Dennis Leonard	.20
219	Roy Smalley	.20
220	Cesar Geronimo	.20
223	Kent Tekulve	.25
225	Rich Gossage	.70
227	Steve Stone	.20
230	Bob Forsch	.20
234	Toby Harrah	.20
239	Willie Horton	.20
240	Rick Reuschel	.25
241	Checklist 122-242	.25
244	Pirates Team (Chuck Tanner)	.80
245	Jeff Burroughs	.20
250	Willie Randolph	.30
251	Jack Morris	2.00
253	Rick Wise	.20
255	Tommy John	.80
259	Reds Team (Sparky Anderson)	.60
260	Richie Zisk	.20
263	Oscar Gamble	.20
264	Don Robinson	.50
267	Joe Rudi	.20
269	Woodie Fryman	.20
278	Andy Messersmith	.25
280	Andre Thornton	.25
282	Blue Jays Team (Roy Hartsfield)	.50
285	Bobby Bonds	.30
288	Milt Wilcox	.20
289	Jose Cruz	.25
290	Dave Lopes	.25
300	Rod Carew	2.50
302	Braves Team (Bobby Cox)	.50

306	Floyd Bannister	.30
308	Bert Blyleven	.60
309	Ralph Garr	.20
310	Thurman Munson	2.25
315	Jon Matlack	.20
316	Milt May	.12
317	Jose Cardenal	.12
318	Bob Welch	2.50
319	Wayne Garrett	.12
320	Carl Yastrzemski	2.50
321	Gaylord Perry	1.50
322	Danny Goodwin	.12
323	Lynn McGlothen	.12
324	Mike Tyson	.12
325	Cecil Cooper	.40
326	Pedro Borbon	.12
327	Art Howe	.12
328	A's Team (Jack McKeon)	.50
329	Joe Coleman	.20
330	George Brett	3.00
331	Mickey Mahler	.12
332	Gary Alexander	.12
333	Chet Lemon	.20
334	Craig Swan	.12
335	Chris Chambliss	.25
336	Bobby Thompson	.12
337	John Montague	.12
338	Vic Harris	.12
339	Ron Jackson	.12
340	Jim Palmer	1.50
341	Willie Upshaw	.40
342	Dave Roberts	.12
343	Ed Glynn	.12
344	Jerry Royster	.12
345	Tug McGraw	.30
346	Bill Buckner	.30
347	Doug Rau	.12
348	Andre Dawson	4.00
349	Jim Wright	.12
350	Garry Templeton	.20
351	Wayne Nordhagen	.12
352	Steve Renko	.12
353	Checklist 243-363	.60

95 Robin Yount

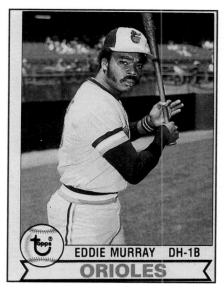

640 Eddie Murray

358 Alan Trammell

393	Scott McGregor	.20
394	Randy Stein	.12
395	Dave Cash	.20
396	Bill Plummer	.12
397	Sergio Ferrer	.12
398	Ivan DeJesus	.12
399	David Clyde	.12
400	Jim Rice	2.50
401	Ray Knight	.25
402	Paul Hartzell	.12
403	Tim Foli	.12
404	White Sox Team (Don Kessinger)	.50
405	Butch Wynegar	.20
406	Joe Wallis	.12
407	Pete Vuckovich	.20
408	Charlie Moore	.12
409	*Willie Wilson*	1.25
410	Darrell Evans	.30
411	Hits Record Holders (Ty Cobb, Dick Sisler)	.70
412	RBI Record Holders (Hank Aaron, Hack Wilson)	.70
413	HR Record Holders (Hank Aaron, Roger Maris)	1.00
414	Batting Average Record Holders (Ty Cobb, Rogers Hornsby)	.70
415	SB Record Holder (Lou Brock)	.70
416	Wins Record Holders (Jack Chesbro, Cy Young)	.40
417	SO Record Holders (Walter Johnson, Nolan Ryan)	.40
418	ERA Record Holders (Walter Johnson, Dutch Leonard)	.20
419	Dick Ruthven	.12
420	Ken Griffey	.25
421	Doug DeCinces	.25
422	Ruppert Jones	.12

348 Andre Dawson

354	Bill Bonham	.12
355	Lee Mazzilli	.20
356	Giants Team (Joe Altobelli)	.50
357	Jerry Augustine	.12
358	Alan Trammell	4.00
359	Dan Spillner	.12
360	Amos Otis	.20
361	Tom Dixon	.12
362	Mike Cubbage	.12
363	Craig Skok	.12
364	Gene Richards	.12
365	*Sparky Lyle	.30
366	Juan Bernhardt	.12
367	Dave Skaggs	.12
368	Don Aase	.20
369	Bump Wills (Blue Jays)	3.00
369	Bump Wills (Rangers)	3.50
370	Dave Kingman	.35
371	Jeff Holly	.12
372	Lamar Johnson	.12
374	Ed Herrmann	.12
375	Bill Campbell	.12
376	Gorman Thomas	.20
377	Paul Moskau	.12
378	Rob Picciolo	.12
379	Dale Murray	.12
380	John Mayberry	.20
381	Astros Team (Bill Virdon)	.50
382	Jerry Martin	.12
383	Phil Garner	.20
384	Tommy Boggs	.12
385	Dan Ford	.12
386	Francisco Barrios	.12
387	Gary Thomasson	.12
388	Jack Billingham	.12
389	Joe Zdeb	.12
390	Rollie Fingers	.70
391	Al Oliver	.40
392	Doug Ault	.12

423	Bob Montgomery	.12
424	Angels Team (Jim Fregosi)	.60
425	Rick Manning	.12
426	Chris Speier	.20
427	Andy Replogle	.12
428	Bobby Valentine	.25
429	John Urrea	.12
430	Dave Parker	1.50
431	Glenn Borgmann	.12
432	Dave Heaverlo	.12
433	Larry Biittner	.12
434	Ken Clay	.12
435	Gene Tenace	.20
436	Hector Cruz	.12
437	Rick Williams	.12
438	Horace Speed	.12
439	Frank White	.25
440	Rusty Staub	.30
441	Lee Lacy	.12
442	Doyle Alexander	.25
443	Bruce Bochte	.12
444	*Aurelio Lopez*	.20
445	Steve Henderson	.12
446	Jim Lonborg	.20
447	Manny Sanguillen	.12
448	Moose Haas	.12
449	Bombo Rivera	.12
450	Dave Concepcion	.30
451	Royals Team (Whitey Herzog)	.60
452	Jerry Morales	.12
453	Chris Knapp	.12
454	Len Randle	.12
455	Bill Lee	.12
456	Chuck Baker	.12
457	Bruce Sutter	.75
458	Jim Essian	.12
459	Sid Monge	.12
460	Graig Nettles	.50
461	Jim Barr	.12
462	Otto Velez	.12
463	Steve Comer	.12

330 George Brett

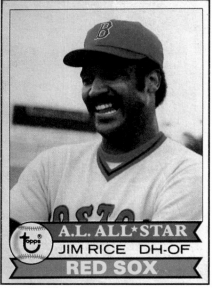

400 Jim Rice

504	Larry McWilliams	.20
505	Ed Kranepool	.20
506	John D'Acquisto	.12
507	Tony Armas	.20
508	Charlie Hough	.20
509	Mario Mendoza	.12
510	Ted Simmons	.45
511	Paul Reuschel	.12
512	Jack Clark	1.50
513	Dave Johnson	.30
514	Mike Proly	.12
515	Enos Cabell	.12
516	Champ Summers	.12
517	Al Bumbry	.15
518	Jim Umbarger	.12
519	Ben Oglivie	.20
520	Gary Carter	2.50
521	Sam Ewing	.12
522	Ken Holtzman	.20
523	John Milner	.15
524	Tom Burgmeier	.12
525	Freddie Patek	.12
526	Dodgers Team (Tom Lasorda)	.65
527	Lerrin LaGrow	.12
528	Wayne Gross	.12
529	Brian Asselstine	.12
530	Frank Tanana	.25
531	Fernando Gonzalez	.12
532	Buddy Schultz	.12
533	Leroy Stanton	.12
534	Ken Forsch	.12
535	Ellis Valentine	.12
536	Jerry Reuss	.20
537	Tom Veryzer	.12
538	Mike Ivie	.12
539	John Ellis	.20
540	Greg Luzinski	.30
541	Jim Slaton	.12
542	Rick Bosetti	.12
543	Kiko Garcia	.12
544	Fergie Jenkins	.40
545	John Stearns	.12
546	Bill Russell	.20

464	Joe Nolan	.12
465	Reggie Smith	.25
466	Mark Littell	.12
467	Don Kessinger	.12
468	Stan Bahnsen	.12
469	Lance Parrish	3.00
470	Garry Maddox	.12
471	Joaquin Andujar	.20
472	Craig Kusick	.12
473	Dave Roberts	.12
474	Dick Davis	.12
475	Dan Driessen	.20
476	Tom Poquette	.12
477	Bob Grich	.25
478	Juan Beniquez	.15
479	Padres Team (Roger Craig)	.50
480	Fred Lynn	.70
481	Skip Lockwood	.12
482	Craig Reynolds	.12
483	Checklist 364-484	.25
484	Rick Waits	.12
485	Bucky Dent	.25
486	Bob Knepper	.20
487	Miguel Dilone	.12
488	Bob Owchinko	.12
489	Larry Cox (photo is Dave Rader)	.12
490	Al Cowens	.12
491	Tippy Martinez	.12
492	Bob Bailor	.12
493	Larry Christenson	.12
494	Jerry White	.12
495	Tony Perez	.60
496	Barry Bonnell	.12
497	Glenn Abbott	.12
498	Rich Chiles	.12
499	Rangers Team (Pat Corrales)	.50
500	Ron Guidry	.90
501	Junior Kennedy	.12
502	Steve Braun	.12
503	Terry Humphrey	.12

25 Steve Carlton

547	Clint Hurdle	.12
548	Enrique Romo	.12
549	Bob Bailey	.12
550	Sal Bando	.20
551	Cubs Team (Herman Franks)	.50
552	Jose Morales	.12
553	Denny Walling	.12
554	Matt Keough	.12
555	Biff Pocoroba	.12
556	Mike Lum	.12
557	Ken Brett	.20
558	*Jay Johnstone	.20
559	Greg Pryor	.12
560	John Montefusco	.12
561	Ed Ott	.12
562	Dusty Baker	.25
563	Roy Thomas	.12
564	Jerry Turner	.12
565	Rico Carty	.25
566	Nino Espinosa	.12
567	Rich Hebner	.12
568	Carlos Lopez	.12
569	Bob Sykes	.12
570	Cesar Cedeno	.25
571	Darrell Porter	.20
572	Rod Gilbreath	.12
573	Jim Kern	.12
574	Claudell Washington	.20
575	Luis Tiant	.30
576	Mike Parrott	.12
577	Brewers Team (George Bamberger)	.50
578	Pete Broberg	.12
579	Gregg Gross	.12
580	Ron Fairly	.20
581	Darold Knowles	.12
582	Paul Blair	.20
583	Julio Cruz	.12
584	Jim Rooker	.12
585	Hal McRae	.25
586	*Bob Horner*	1.00
587	Ken Reitz	.12

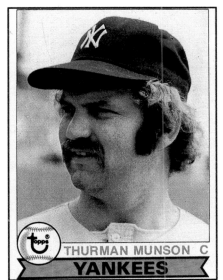

310 Thurman Munson

100 Tom Seaver

629	Gene Garber	.12
630	Bake McBride	.12
631	Jorge Orta	.12
632	Don Kirkwood	.12
633	Rob Wilfong	.12
634	Paul Lindblad	.12
635	Don Baylor	.50
636	Wayne Garland	.12
637	Bill Robinson	.12
638	Al Fitzmorris	.12
639	Manny Trillo	.20
640	Eddie Murray	5.00
641	*Bobby Castillo*	.12
642	Wilbur Howard	.12
643	Tom Hausman	.12
644	Manny Mota	.20
645	George Scott	.20
646	Rick Sweet	.12
647	Bob Lacey	.12
648	Lou Piniella	.35
649	John Curtis	.12
650	Pete Rose	4.50
651	Mike Caldwell	.12
652	Stan Papi	.12
653	Warren Brusstar	.12
654	Rick Miller	.12
655	Jerry Koosman	.30
656	Hosken Powell	.12
657	George Medich	.12
658	Taylor Duncan	.12
659	Mariners Team (Darrell Johnson)	.50
660	Ron LeFlore	.12
661	Bruce Kison	.12
662	Kevin Bell	.12
663	Mike Vail	.12
664	Doug Bird	.12
665	Lou Brock	1.50
666	Rich Dauer	.12
667	Don Hood	.12
668	Bill North	.12
669	Checklist 606-726	.60
670	*Jim Hunter	.70
671	Joe Ferguson	.12

588	Tom Murphy	.12
589	Terry Whitfield	.12
590	J.R. Richard	.20
591	Mike Hargrove	.20
592	Mike Krukow	.20
593	Rick Dempsey	.15
594	Bob Shirley	.12
595	Phil Niekro	1.25
596	Jim Wohlford	.12
597	Bob Stanley	.20
598	Mark Wagner	.12
599	Jim Spencer	.20
600	George Foster	.60
601	Dave LaRoche	.12
602	Checklist 485-605	.60
603	Rudy May	.12
604	Jeff Newman	.12
605	Rick Monday	.12
606	Expos Team (Dick Williams)	.55
607	Omar Moreno	.12
608	Dave McKay	.12
609	Silvio Martinez	.12
610	Mike Schmidt	8.00
611	Jim Norris	.12
612	*Rick Honeycutt*	.30
613	Mike Edwards	.12
614	Willie Hernandez	.20
615	Ken Singleton	.20
616	Billy Almon	.12
617	Terry Puhl	.12
618	Jerry Remy	.12
619	*Ken Landreaux*	.20
620	Bert Campaneris	.25
621	Pat Zachry	.12
622	Dave Collins	.20
623	Bob McClure	.12
624	Larry Herndon	.20
625	Mark Fidrych	.25
626	Yankees Team (Bob Lemon)	.85
627	Gary Serum	.12
628	Del Unser	.12

212 Carney Lansford

672	Ed Halicki	.12
673	Tom Hutton	.12
674	Dave Tomlin	.12
675	Tim McCarver	.30
676	Johnny Sutton	.12
677	Larry Parrish	.25
679	Derrel Thomas	.12
680	Carlton Fisk	1.00
681	*John Henry Johnson*	.12
683	Dan Meyer	.12
684	Jamie Easterly	.12
685	Sixto Lezcano	.12
686	Ron Schueler	.12
687	Rennie Stennett	.12
688	Mike Willis	.12
689	Orioles Team (Earl Weaver)	.70
690	Buddy Bell	.12
691	Dock Ellis	.12
692	Mickey Stanley	.20
693	Dave Rader	.12
694	Burt Hooton	.20
695	Keith Hernandez	2.00
696	Andy Hassler	.12
697	Dave Bergman	.12
698	Bill Stein	.12
699	Hal Dues	.12
700	Reggie Jackson	2.00
701	Orioles Prospects (Mark Corey, John Flinn, *Sammy Stewart*)	.20
702	Red Sox Prospects (Joel Finch, Garry Hancock, Allen Ripley)	.12
703	Angels Prospects (Jim Anderson, Dave Frost, Bob Slater)	.12
704	White Sox Prospects (Ross Baumgarten, Mike Colbern, *Mike Squires*)	.20
705	Indians Prospects (*Alfredo Griffin*, Tim Norrid, Dave Oliver)	.70

706 Tigers Prospects
(Dave Stegman, Dave Tobik,
Kip Young) .... .20
707 Royals Prospects
(Randy Bass, Jim Gaudet,
Randy McGilberry) .... .15
708 Brewers Prospects
(*Kevin Bass, Eddie
Romero,* Ned Yost) **1.25**
709 Twins Prospects
(Sam Perlozzo, Rick Sofield,
Kevin Stanfield) .... .12
710 Yankees Prospects
(Brian Doyle, *Mike Heath,*
Dave Rajsich) .... .35
711 A's Prospects
(*Dwayne Murphy,* Bruce
Robinson, Alan Wirth) .... .50
712 Mariners Prospects
(Bud Anderson, Greg
Biercevicz, Byron
McLaughlin) .... .12

713 Rangers Prospects
(*Danny Darwin,* Pat
Putnam, *Billy Sample*) .... .45
714 Blue Jays Prospects
(Victor Cruz, Pat Kelly,
Ernie Whitt) .... .25
715 Braves Prospects
(*Bruce Benedict, Glenn
Hubbard,* Larry
Whisenton) .... .40
716 Cubs Prospects
(Dave Geisel, Karl Pagel,
Scot Thompson) .... .12
717 Reds Prospects
(*Mike LaCoss, Ron Oester,
Harry Spilman*) .... .40
718 Astros Prospects
(Bruce Bochy, Mike Fischlin,
Don Pisker) .... .12
719 Dodgers Prospects
(*Pedro Guerrero, Rudy Law,*
Joe Simpson) **11.00**

720 Expos Prospects
(Jerry Fry, Jerry Pirtle,
Scott Sanderson) .... .30
721 Mets Prospects
(*Juan Berenguer,*
Dwight Bernard, Dan
Norman) .... .30
722 Phillies Prospects
(*Jim Morrison, Lonnie Smith,*
Jim Wright) **2.00**
723 Pirates Prospects
(*Dale Berra,* Eugenio Cotes,
Ben Wiltbank) .... .25
724 Cardinals Prospects
(Tom Bruno, *George Frazier,
Terry Kennedy*) .... .60
725 Padres Prospects
(Jim Beswick, Steve Mura,
Broderick Perkins) .... .12
726 Giants Prospects
(Greg Johnston, Joe Strain,
John Tamargo) .... .25

1980 TOPPS

Topps began the new decade with another 726-card issue. The Topps logo, which diminishes the appeal of the 1979 set, was dropped from the front of the 2 1/2- by 3 1/2-inch cards. Another improvement in 1980 involves the Future Stars cards. Top names include Mike Scott and Jesse Orosco of the Mets, Tom Herr of the Cardinals, Dickie Thon of the Astros, and Dan Quisenberry of the Royals. This subset is arranged by team, with three players to a card, but, unlike the preceding year, all the mug shots are in color. Some of the most important rookie cards in the main set are not found in the Future Stars subset. Rookies getting individual cards include Rickey Henderson, Rick Sutcliffe, and Dave Stieb. Future Stars are indicated with "FS" on the following lists.

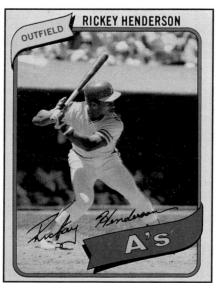

482 Rickey Henderson

		MINT
Complete set		**$180.00**
Commons		**.12**

1	1979 Highlights (Lou Brock, Carl Yastrzemski) ..	**$1.50**
2	1979 Highlights (Willie McCovey)	.80
3	1979 Highlights (Manny Mota)	.20
4	1979 Highlights (Pete Rose)	**2.00**
5	1979 Highlights (Garry Templeton)	.20
6	1979 Highlights (Del Unser)	.12
10	Denny Martinez	.12
16	Jerry Narron	.12
17	Bruce Sutter	.45
25	Lee Mazzilli	.20
30	Vida Blue	.30
31	Jay Johnstone	.20
35	Luis Tiant	.30
40	Carlton Fisk	.95
41	Rangers Team (Pat Corrales)	.50

42	*Dave Palmer*	.40
45	Frank White	.25
46	Rico Carty	.20
50	J.R. Richard	.20
53	Ben Oglivie	.20
55	Bill Madlock	.40
56	Bobby Valentine	.20
57	Pete Vuckovich	.15
60	Bucky Dent	.25
62	Mike Ivie	.12
63	Bob Stanley	.20
65	Al Bumbry	.15
66	Royals Team (Jim Frey)	.60
67	Doyle Alexander	.25
70	Gary Carter	**2.00**
73	Dave Collins	.20
75	Bill Russell	.20
77	*Dave Stieb*	**3.50**
80	Ron LeFlore	.20
82	Astros Team (Bill Virdon)	.50
83	*Steve Trout*	.30
85	Ted Simmons	.40
88	Ken Landreaux	.20
89	Don Hood	.12

90	Manny Trillo	.20
91	Rick Dempsey	.15
92	Rick Rhoden	.20
94	*Neil Allen*	.25
95	Cecil Cooper	.25
96	A's Team (Jim Marshall)	.50
97	Bill Lee	.20
100	Johnny Bench	**3.00**
103	*Bill Caudill*	.20
104	Manny Mota	.20
105	Frank Tanana	.20
106	*Jeff Leonard*	**1.00**
108	Bob Horner	.40

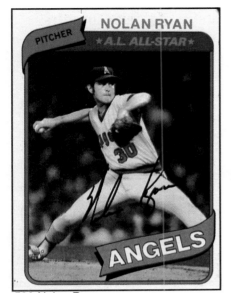

580 Nolan Ryan

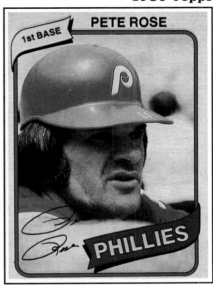

540 Pete Rose

110	Fred Lynn	.35
111	Bob Knepper	.15
112	White Sox Team (Tony LaRussa)	.55
115	*Sparky Lyle	.25
120	Greg Luzinski	.20
121	Checklist 1-121	.50
125	Tony Perez	.50
130	Amos Otis	.20
135	Bill Buckner	.20
137	*John Castino*	.20
139	*Dane Iorg*	.20
140	Rich Gossage	.60
145	Darrell Evans	.20
146	Bob Welch	.50
150	Jason Thompson	.20
157	Willie Wilson	.15
160	Eddie Murray	3.00
167	Jack Clark	1.00
170	Burt Hooton	.20
174	Ray Knight	.20
175	Rick Reuschel	.20
178	*Tim McCarver	.30
179	*Ron Davis*	.25
185	Hal McRae	.25
190	Buddy Bell	.25
192	Braves Team (Bobby Cox)	.50
193	Dave Goltz	.20
194	Mike Easler	.20
195	John Montefusco	.15
196	Lance Parrish	1.50
199	Mike LaCoss	.20
200	Jim Rice	2.00
201	Batting Ldrs (Keith Hernandez, Fred Lynn)	.50
202	HR Ldrs (Dave Kingman, Gorman Thomas)	.25
203	RBI Ldrs (Don Baylor, Dave Winfield)	.50

204	SB Ldrs (Omar Moreno, Willie Wilson)	.20
205	Victory Ldrs (Mike Flanagan, Joe Niekro, Phil Niekro)	.40
206	SO Ldrs (J.R. Richard, Nolan Ryan)	.50
207	ERA Ldrs (Ron Guidry, J.R. Richard)	.25
210	Steve Carlton	3.00
214	Angels Team (Jim Fregosi)	.50
220	Dave Concepcion	.25
222	*Ron Hassey*	.30
225	Lou Piniella	.30
230	Dave Winfield	2.00
232	Alan Trammell	2.00
235	Andre Dawson	3.00
240	Dave Kingman	.40
241	Checklist 122-242	.50
244	Cardinals Team (Ken Boyer)	.50
245	Phil Niekro	.90
246	Tim Foli	.12
249	Jim Clancy	.20
250	Jim Kaat	.50
254	Paul Dade	.12
255	Dusty Baker	.20
257	Larry Herndon	.15
259	Mets Team (Joe Torre)	.55
260	Al Oliver	.35
265	Robin Yount	5.00
270	Mike Schmidt	2.00
271	Dick Drago	.12
272	Ralph Garr	.20
274	Dale Murphy	5.00
275	Jerry Koosman	.25
278	Jim Spencer	.15
280	Gaylord Perry	.90

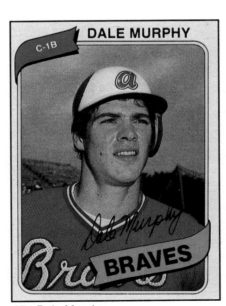

274 Dale Murphy

281	Paul Blair	.20
282	Mariners Team (Darrell Johnson)	.50
283	John Ellis	.12
285	Don Baylor	.35
290	Steve Garvey	2.00
298	Ken Holtzman	.20
300	Ron Guidry	.70
302	Dodgers Team (Tom Lasorda)	.65
303	Bill Castro	.12
304	Butch Wynegar	.20
305	Randy Jones	.20
307	Rick Honeycutt	.20
308	Mike Hargrove	.20
310	Dave Parker	1.00
314	*Tim Stoddard*	.20
315	Steve Kemp	.25
318	Jerry Reuss	.20
320	Dennis Eckersley	.25
321	Keith Hernandez	1.50
322	Claudell Washington	.20
325	Dan Driessen	.20
327	Ray Fosse	.12
328	Twins Team (Gene Mauch)	.50
335	Willie McCovey	1.50
337	Carney Lansford	.30
340	Ken Singleton	.20
341	Jim Essian	.12
342	Odell Jones	.12
343	Mike Vail	.12
344	Randy Lerch	.12
345	Larry Parrish	.12
346	Buddy Solomon	.12
347	*Harry Chappas*	.20
348	Checklist 243-363	.50
349	Jack Brohamer	.12
350	George Hendrick	.20
351	Bob Davis	.12
352	Dan Briggs	.12
353	Andy Hassler	.12
354	Rick Auerbach	.12

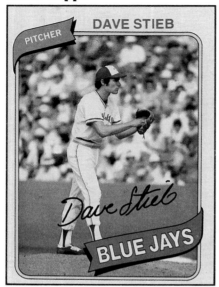

PITCHER
DAVE STIEB

BLUE JAYS

77 Dave Stieb

355	Gary Matthews	.20
356	Padres Team (Jerry Coleman)	.50
357	Bob McClure	.12
358	Lou Whitaker	1.25
359	Randy Moffitt	.12
360	Darrell Porter	.15
361	Wayne Garland	.12
362	Danny Goodwin	.12
363	Wayne Gross	.12
364	Ray Burris	.12
365	Bobby Murcer	.25
366	Rob Dressler	.12
367	Billy Smith	.12
368	*Willie Aikens*	.20
369	Jim Kern	.12
370	Cesar Cedeno	.25
371	Jack Morris	1.00
372	Joel Youngblood	.12
373	*Dan Petry*	.30
374	Jim Gantner	.15
375	Ross Grimsley	.12
376	Gary Allenson	.12
377	Junior Kennedy	.12
378	Jerry Mumphrey	.12
379	Kevin Bell	.12
380	Garry Maddox	.15
381	Cubs Team (Preston Gomez)	.50
382	Dave Freisleben	.12
383	Ed Ott	.12
384	Joey McLaughlin	.12
385	Enos Cabell	.12
386	Darrell Jackson	.12
387	Fred Stanley (name in yellow)	3.00
387	Fred Stanley (name in red)	.15
389	Pete LaCock	.12
390	Fergie Jenkins	.45
391	Tony Armas	.15
392	Milt Wilcox	.12
393	Ozzie Smith	4.50

394	Reggie Cleveland	.12
395	Ellis Valentine	.12
396	Dan Meyer	.12
397	Roy Thomas	.12
398	Barry Foote	.12
399	Mike Proly	.12
400	George Foster	.50
401	Pete Falcone	.12
402	Merv Rettenmund	.12
403	Pete Redfern	.12
404	Orioles Team (Earl Weaver)	.60
405	*Dwight Evans	.65
406	Paul Molitor	1.50
407	Tony Solaita	.12
408	Bill North	.12
409	Paul Splittorff	.20
410	Bobby Bonds	.25
411	Frank LaCorte	.12
412	Thad Bosley	.12
413	Allen Ripley	.12
414	George Scott	.20
415	Bill Atkinson	.12
416	*Tom Brookens*	.35
417	Craig Chamberlain	.12
418	Roger Freed	.12
419	Vic Correll	.12
420	Butch Hobson	.12
421	Doug Bird	.12
422	Larry Milbourne	.12
423	Dave Frost	.12
424	Yankees Team (Dick Howser)	.75
425	Mark Belanger	.20
426	Grant Jackson	.12
427	Tom Hutton	.12
428	Pat Zachry	.12
429	Duane Kuiper	.12
430	Larry Hisle	.12
431	Mike Krukow	.20
432	Willie Norwood	.12
433	Rich Gale	.12
434	Johnnie LeMaster	.12
435	Don Gullett	.20

3rd BASE
GEORGE BRETT
★ A.L. ALL-STAR ★

ROYALS

450 George Brett

PITCHER
RICK SUTCLIFFE

DODGERS

544 Rick Sutcliffe

436	Billy Almon	.12
437	Joe Niekro	.20
438	Dave Revering	.12
439	Mike Phillips	.12
440	Don Sutton	.90
441	Eric Soderholm	.12
442	Jorge Orta	.12
443	Mike Parrott	.12
444	Alvis Woods	.12
445	Mark Fidrych	.20
446	Duffy Dyer	.12
447	Nino Espinosa	.12
448	Jim Wohlford	.12
449	Doug Bair	.12
450	George Brett	3.50
451	Indians Team (Dave Garcia)	.50
452	Steve Dillard	.12
453	Mike Bascik	.12
454	Tom Donohue	.12
455	Mike Torrez	.20
456	Frank Taveras	.12
457	Bert Blyleven	.50
458	Billy Sample	.12
459	*Mickey Lolich	.12
460	Willie Randolph	.25
461	Dwayne Murphy	.12
462	Mike Sadek	.12
463	Jerry Royster	.12
464	John Denny	.12
465	Rick Monday	.20
466	Mike Squires	.12
467	Jesse Jefferson	.12
468	Aurelio Rodriguez	.20
469	Randy Niemann	.12
470	*Bob Boone	.20
471	Hosken Powell	.12
472	Willie Hernandez	.20
473	Bump Wills	.12
474	Steve Busby	.12
475	Cesar Geronimo	.12
476	Bob Shirley	.12
477	Buck Martinez	.12

478	Gil Flores	.12
479	Expos Team (Dick Williams)	.50
480	Bob Watson	.20
481	Tom Paciorek	.12
482	*Rickey Henderson*	85.00
483	Bo Diaz	.15
484	Checklist 364-484	.50
485	Mickey Rivers	.20
486	Mike Tyson	.12
487	Wayne Nordhagen	.12
488	Roy Howell	.12
489	Preston Hanna	.12
490	Lee May	.20
491	Steve Mura	.12
492	Todd Cruz	.12
493	Jerry Martin	.12
494	Craig Minetto	.12
495	Bake McBride	.12
496	Silvio Martinez	.12
497	Jim Mason	.12
498	Danny Darwin	.20
499	Giants Team (Dave Bristol)	.50
500	Tom Seaver	2.00
501	Rennie Stennett	.12
502	Rich Wortham	.12
503	Mike Cubbage	.12
504	Gene Garber	.12
505	Bert Campaneris	.20
506	Tom Buskey	.12
507	Leon Roberts	.12
508	U.L. Washington	.12
509	Ed Glynn	.12
510	Ron Cey	.25
511	Eric Wilkins	.12
512	Jose Cardenal	.12
513	Tom Dixon	.12
514	Steve Ontiveros	.12
515	Mike Caldwell	.12
516	Hector Cruz	.12
517	Don Stanhouse	.12
518	Nelson Norman	.12
519	Steve Nicosia	.12

![STEVE CARLTON — PITCHER ★N.L. ALL-STAR★ — PHILLIES]

210 Steve Carlton

520	Steve Rogers	.20
521	Ken Brett	.12
522	Jim Morrison	.12
523	Ken Henderson	.12
524	Jim Wright	.12
525	Clint Hurdle	.12
526	Phillies Team (Dallas Green)	.70
527	Doug Rau	.12
528	Adrian Devine	.12
529	Jim Barr	.12
530	Jim Sundberg	.12
531	Eric Rasmussen	.12
532	Willie Horton	.20
533	Checklist 485-605	.50
534	Andre Thornton	.25
535	Bob Forsch	.20
536	Lee Lacy	.12
537	*Alex Trevino*	.20
538	Joe Strain	.12
539	Rudy May	.12
540	Pete Rose	5.00
541	Miguel Dilone	.12
542	Joe Coleman	.12
543	Pat Kelly	.12
544	*Rick Sutcliffe*	3.00
545	Jeff Burroughs	.20
546	Rick Langford	.12
547	John Wathan	.20
548	Dave Rajsich	.12
549	Larry Wolfe	.12
550	Ken Griffey	.25
551	Pirates Team (Chuck Tanner)	.50
552	Bill Nahorodny	.12
553	Dick Davis	.12
554	Art Howe	.12
555	Ed Figueroa	.20
556	Joe Rudi	.20
557	Mark Lee	.12
558	Alfredo Griffin	.25
559	Dale Murray	.12
560	Dave Lopes	.25

561	Eddie Whitson	.20
562	Joe Wallis	.12
563	Will McEnaney	.12
564	Rick Manning	.12
565	Dennis Leonard	.20
566	Bud Harrelson	.20
567	Skip Lockwood	.12
568	*Gary Roenicke*	.25
569	Terry Kennedy	.25
570	Roy Smalley	.20
571	Joe Sambito	.12
572	Jerry Morales	.12
573	Kent Tekulve	.20
574	Scot Thompson	.12
575	Ken Kravec	.12
576	Jim Dwyer	.12
577	Blue Jays Team (Bobby Mattick)	.50
578	Scott Sanderson	.20
579	Charlie Moore	.12
580	Nolan Ryan	7.50
581	Bob Bailor	.12
582	Brian Doyle	.20
583	Bob Stinson	.12
584	Kurt Bevacqua	.12
585	Al Hrabosky	.20
586	Mitchell Page	.12
587	Garry Templeton	.20
588	Greg Minton	.12
589	Chet Lemon	.20
590	Jim Palmer	2.00
591	Rick Cerone	.12
592	Jon Matlack	.20
593	Jesus Alou	.12
594	Dick Tidrow	.12
595	Don Money	.12
596	Rick Matula	.12
597	Tom Poquette	.12
598	Fred Kendall	.12
599	Mike Norris	.12
600	Reggie Jackson	2.50
601	Buddy Schultz	.12
602	Brian Downing	.20
603	Jack Billingham	.12

![EDDIE MURRAY — 1st BASE — ORIOLES]

160 Eddie Murray

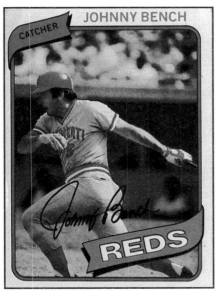

100 Johnny Bench

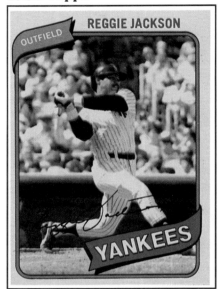

600 Reggie Jackson

604	Glenn Adams	.12
605	Terry Forster	.20
606	Reds Team	
	(John McNamara)	.50
607	Woodie Fryman	.20
608	Alan Bannister	.12
609	Ron Reed	.20
610	Willie Stargell	1.50
611	Jerry Garvin	.12
612	Cliff Johnson	.12
613	Randy Stein	.12
614	John Hiller	.20
615	Doug DeCinces	.20
616	Gene Richards	.12
617	Joaquin Andujar	.20
618	Bob Montgomery	.12
619	Sergio Ferrer	.12
620	Richie Zisk	.20
621	Bob Grich	.20
622	Mario Soto	.20
623	Gorman Thomas	.20
624	Lerrin LaGrow	.12
625	Chris Chambliss	.25
626	Tigers Team	
	(Sparky Anderson)	.65
627	Pedro Borbon	.12
628	Doug Capilla	.12
630	Larry Bowa	.25
631	Mark Littell	.12
632	Barry Bonnell	.12
633	Bob Apodaca	.12
634	Glenn Borgmann	.12
635	John Candelaria	.20
636	Toby Harrah	.20
638	*Mark Clear*	.25
639	Larry Biittner	.12
640	Mike Flanagan	.25
641	Ed Kranepool	.20
642	Ken Forsch	.15
643	John Mayberry	.20
644	Charlie Hough	.20
645	Rick Burleson	.20
646	Checklist 606-726	.50

647	Milt May	.12
648	Roy White	.20
649	Tom Griffin	.12
650	*Joe Morgan	1.50
651	*Rollie Fingers	.50
652	Mario Mendoza	.12
653	Stan Bahnsen	.12
655	Tug McGraw	.25
657	Dave Edwards	.12
658	Chris Knapp	.12
659	Brewers Team	
	(George Bamberger)	.50
660	Rusty Staub	.30
661	Orioles FS	
	(Mark Corey, Dave Ford, Wayne Krenchicki)	.12
662	Red Sox FS	
	(Joel Finch, Mike O'Berry, Chuck Rainey)	.12
663	Angels FS	
	(Ralph Botting, Bob Clark, *Dickie Thon*)	.35
664	White Sox FS	
	(Mike Colbern, *Guy Hoffman,* Dewey Robinson)	.15
665	Indians FS	
	(Larry Andersen, Bobby Cuellar, Sandy Wihtol)	.12
666	Tigers FS	
	(Mike Chris, Al Greene, Bruce Robbins)	.12
667	*Royals FS	
	(Renie Martin, Bill Paschall, *Dan Quisenberry*)	2.00
668	Brewers FS	
	(Danny Boitano, Willie Mueller, Lenn Sakata)	.12
669	Twins FS	
	(Dan Graham, Rick Sofield, *Gary Ward*)	.35
670	Yankees FS	
	(Bobby Brown, Brad Gulden, Darryl Jones)	.15

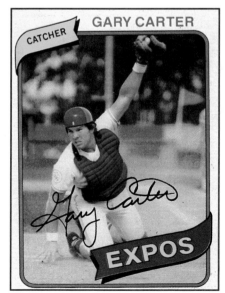

70 Gary Carter

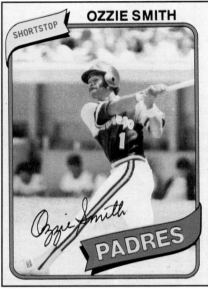

393 Ozzie Smith

671	*A's FS	
	(Derek Bryant, Brian Kingman, *Mike Morgan*)	.20
672	Mariners FS	
	(Charlie Beamon, Rodney Craig, Rafael Vasquez)	.12
673	Rangers FS	
	(Brian Allard, Jerry Don Gleaton, Greg Mahlberg)	.12
674	Blue Jays FS	
	(Butch Edge, Pat Kelly, Ted Wilborn)	.12
675	Braves FS	
	(Bruce Benedict, Larry Bradford, Eddie Miller)	.15
676	Cubs FS	
	(Dave Geisel, Steve Macko, Karl Pagel)	.12
677	Reds FS	
	(Art DeFreites, *Frank Pastore,* Harry Spilman)	.15
678	Astros FS	
	(Reggie Baldwin, Alan Knicely, *Pete Ladd*)	.12
679	*Dodgers FS	
	(Joe Beckwith, *Mickey Hatcher,* Dave Patterson)	.50
680	Expos FS	
	(*Tony Bernazard,* Randy Miller, John Tamargo)	.25
681	Mets FS	
	(Dan Norman, *Jesse Orosco, Mike Scott*)	10.00
682	Phillies FS	
	(Ramon Aviles, *Dickie Noles,* Kevin Saucier)	.20
683	Pirates FS	
	(Dorian Boyland, Alberto Lois, Harry Saferight)	.12
684	Cardinals FS	
	(George Frazier, *Tom Herr,* Dan O'Brien)	.65

685	Padres FS (Tim Flannery, Brian Greer, Jim Wilhelm) .... .12	695	Reggie Smith .... .25
686	Giants FS (Greg Johnston, Dennis Littlejohn, Phil Nastu) .... .12	696	Julio Gonzalez .... .12
		697	David Clyde .... .12
		698	Oscar Gamble .... .20
		699	Floyd Bannister .... .20
687	Mike Heath .... .12	700	*Rod Carew 1.50
688	Steve Stone .... .12	701	*Ken Oberkfell* .... .30
689	Red Sox Team (Don Zimmer) .... .60	702	Ed Farmer .... .12
		703	Otto Velez .... .12
690	Tommy John .... .60	704	Gene Tenace .... .20
691	Ivan DeJesus .... .12	705	Freddie Patek .... .12
692	Rawly Eastwick ...... .12	706	Tippy Martinez .... .12
693	Craig Kusick .... .12	707	Elliott Maddox .... .12
694	Jim Rooker .... .12	708	Bob Tolan .... .12
		709	Pat Underwood .... .12

710	Graig Nettles .... .35
712	Rodney Scott .... .12
713	Terry Whitfield .... .12
714	Fred Norman .... .12
715	Sal Bando .... .20
717	Mickey Klutts .... .12
718	Greg Gross .... .12
719	Don Robinson .... .20
720	Carl Yastrzemski 1.35
721	Paul Hartzell .... .12
722	Jose Cruz .... .20
723	Shane Rawley .... .12
724	Jerry White .... .12
725	Rick Wise .... .20
726	Steve Yeager .... .12

1981 DONRUSS

Donruss joined Topps and Fleer in the baseball card market in 1981 with a set of 605 cards. In the past, Donruss had marketed its bubble gum products only with card sets unrelated to sports. And from the looks of their initial product, it is obvious that Donruss had little experience with baseball cards. To begin with, the set was printed on ultra-thin cardboard, which makes the cards more susceptible to damage. The color reproductions are of poor quality, and the set is filled with factual and photographic errors (38 of which were corrected). Few of the errors add significant value to the affected cards. Donruss did acknowledge the popularity of superstars George Brett, Mike Schmidt, Pete Rose, Reggie Jackson, and Steve Garvey, all of whom appear more than once in the set.

251 Pete Rose

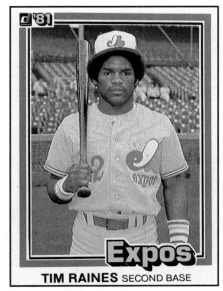

538 Tim Raines

		MINT
Complete set		**$38.00**
Commons		**.06**

1	Ozzie Smith	$.50
2	Rollie Fingers	.25
3	Rick Wise	.08
5	Alan Trammell	.40
6	Tom Brookens	.08
7	Duffy Dyer	.10
8	Mark Fidrych	.08
11	Mike Schmidt	2.00
12	Willie Stargell	.50
13	Tim Foli	.06
18	Joe Morgan	.50
22	Manny Trillo	.08
23	*Dave Smith*	.25
25	Bump Wills	.06
26	John Ellis	.10
27	Jim Kern	.06
28	Richie Zisk	.08
29	John Mayberry	.08
32	Al Woods	.06
33	Steve Carlton	.85
34	Lee Mazzilli	.06
37	Mike Scott	.75
44	Ron Reed	.08
49	Rod Carew	.60
50	Bert Campaneris	.08
51	Tom Donahue (incorrect spelling)	1.00
51	Tom Donohue (correct spelling)	.10

52	Dave Frost	.06
54	Dan Ford	.06
55	Garry Maddox	.10
56	Steve Garvey	.60
57	Bill Russell	.08
58	Don Sutton	.30
59	Reggie Smith	.10
60	Rick Monday	.10

61	Ray Knight	.08
62	Johnny Bench	.85
63	Mario Soto	.08
65	George Foster	.15
66	Jeff Burroughs	.08
67	Keith Hernandez	.35
68	Tom Herr	.10
69	Bob Forsch	.08
71	Bobby Bonds	.15
72	Rennie Stennett	.10
73	Joe Strain	.06
77	Gene Garber	.06
80	Ron Hassey	.06
82	*Joe Charboneau*	.15
83	Cecil Cooper	.10
84	Sal Bando	.10
85	Moose Haas	.06
87	Larry Hisle	.10
88	Luis Gomez	.06
89	Larry Parrish	.10
90	Gary Carter	.35

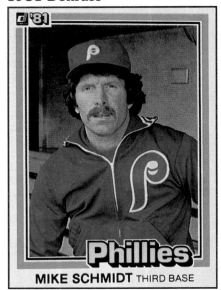

MIKE SCHMIDT THIRD BASE

11 Mike Schmidt

91	*Bill Gullickson*	.10
94	Carl Yastrzemski	.80
96	Dennis Eckersley	.12
97	Tom Burgmeier	.10
99	Bob Horner	.10
100	George Brett	.80
102	Dennis Leonard	.08
103	Renie Martin	.06
104	Amos Otis	.08
105	Graig Nettles	.15
107	Tommy John	.20
109	Lou Piniella	.15
111	Bobby Murcer	.10
112	Eddie Murray	.70
113	Rick Dempsey	.08
114	Scott McGregor	.08
115	Ken Singleton	.10
119	Rickey Henderson	4.50
120	Mike Heath	.06
121	Dave Cash	.06
122	Randy Jones	.08
127	Jack Morris	.30
128	Dan Petry	.08
131	Pete Rose	1.50
132	Willie Stargell	.40
134	Jim Bibby	.06
135	Bert Blyleven	.12
136	Dave Parker	.30
140	J.R. Richard	.10
141	Ken Forsch	.06
142	Larry Bowa	.15
145	Buddy Bell	.12
146	Ferguson Jenkins	.20
148	John Grubb	.06
149	Alfredo Griffin	.08
151	*Paul Mirabella* (FC)	.10
152	Rick Bosetti	.06
156	*Jeff Reardon*	.70
160	Lamarr Hoyt (LaMarr)	.10
162	Thad Bosley	.06
163	Julio Cruz	.06

164	Del Unser	.10
167	Shane Rawley	.08
168	Joe Simpson	.06
169	Rod Carew	.60
170	Fred Patek	.06
171	Frank Tanana	.10
173	Chris Knapp	.06
174	Joe Rudi	.10
175	Greg Luzinski	.15
176	Steve Garvey	.50
178	Bob Welch	.15
179	Dusty Baker	.10
180	Rudy Law	.06
181	Dave Concepcion	.15
182	Johnny Bench	.50
184	Ken Griffey	.08
187	Garry Templeton	.10
189	Pete Vukovich	.08
190	John Urrea	.06
192	Darrell Evans	.12
193	Milt May	.06
194	Bob Knepper	.08
196	Larry Herndon	.08
198	Andre Thornton	.08
201	Rick Waits	.06
202	Rick Manning	.06
203	Paul Molitor	.25
208	Bruce Benedict	.08
211	Bill Lee	.12
212	Andre Dawson	.50
214	Carl Yastrzemski	1.00
215	Jerry Remy	.06
216	Mike Torrez	.08
218	Fred Lynn	.20
219	Chris Chambliss	.10
220	Willie Aikens	.08
221	John Wathan	.08
222	Dan Quisenberry	.15
223	Willie Wilson	.15
224	Clint Hurdle	.08
225	Bob Watson	.08
226	Jim Spencer	.06
227	Ron Guidry	.25
228	Reggie Jackson	.75

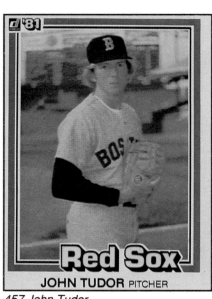

JOHN TUDOR PITCHER

457 John Tudor

DALE MURPHY OUTFIELD

437 Dale Murphy

229	Oscar Gamble	.08
230	Jeff Cox	.06
231	Luis Tiant	.12
233	Dan Graham	.06
234	Mike Flanagan	.10
235	John Lowenstein	.06
237	Wayne Gross	.06
238	Rick Langford	.06
239	Tony Armas	.10
240	Bob Lacy (incorrect spelling)	1.00
240	Bob Lacey (correct spelling)	.10
241	Gene Tenace	.08
243	Gary Lucas	.08
246	Stan Papi	.06
247	Milt Wilcox	.06
249	Steve Kemp	.10
251	Pete Rose	2.00
252	Bill Madlock	.15
253	Dale Berra	.06
254	Kent Tekulve	.10
258	Art Howe	.06
259	Alan Ashby	.06
260	Nolan Ryan	2.25
261	Vern Ruhle (photo is Ken Forsch)	1.25
261	Vern Ruhle (correct photo)	.10
262	Bob Boone	.10
263	Cesar Cedeno	.10
264	Jeff Leonard	.15
266	Jon Matlack	.08
269	*Damaso Garcia*	.10
273	Tug McGraw	.10
275	Pat Zachry	.06
276	Neil Allen	.08
279	*Britt Burns*	.10
280	*Rich Dotson*	.35
283	Ted Cox	.06
284	Sparky Lyle	.10
285	Larry Cox	.06
286	Floyd Bannister	.10

289	Bobby Grich	.10
290	Dickie Thon	.08
294	Rick Miller	.06
295	Lonnie Smith	.10
296	Ron Cey	.12
297	Steve Yeager	.06
299	Manny Mota	.10
300	Jay Johnstone	.10
301	Dan Driessen	.08
302	Joe Nolan	.06
306	Gary Mathews (incorrect spelling)	1.25
306	Gary Matthews (correct spelling)	.15
307	Ken Reitz	.06
308	Ted Simmons	.12
312	Mike Ivie	.06
314	Gary LaVelle (Lavelle)	.06
315	Jack Clark	.25
317	Rick Matula	.06
318	Toby Harrah	.08
319	Dwane Kuiper (incorrect spelling)	1.00
319	Duane Kuiper (correct spelling)	.10
320	Len Barker	.06
322	Dell Alston	.06
323	Robin Yount	1.25
326	Gorman Thomas	.15
327	Bob Rodgers	.08
328	Phil Niekro	.30
330	Steve Rodgers (incorrect spelling)	1.00
330	Steve Rogers (correct spelling)	.10
331	Woodie Fryman	.10
334	Tony Perez	.20
335	Carlton Fisk	.40
336	Dick Drago	.06
338	Jim Rice	.50
340	Frank White	.10
342	Paul Spittorff (incorrect spelling)	1.00

EDDIE MURRAY FIRST BASE

112 Eddie Murray

342	Paul Splittorff (correct spelling)	.15
345	Willie Randolph	.10
346	Rick Cerone	.06
347	Rich Gossage	.20
348	Reggie Jackson	.85
351	*Yogi Berra	.15
352	Doug Decinces (DeCinces)	.10
353	Jim Palmer	.75
355	Al Bumbry	.08
356	Earl Weaver	.10
357	Bob Picciolo (incorrect spelling)	1.00
357	Rob Picciolo (correct spelling)	.10
359	Dwayne Murphy	.06
362	Steve Mura	.06
364	Dave Winfield	.50
365	Lou Whitaker	.30
366	Lance Parrish	.35
369	Al Cowens	.06
370	Sparky Anderson	.10
371	Pete Rose	1.00
374	John Candelaria	.06
376	Lee Lacy	.06
377	John Milner	.06
379	Luis Pujois (incorrect spelling)	1.00
379	Luis Pujols (correct spelling)	.10
380	Joe Niekro	.15
381	Joaquin Andujar	.10
382	*Keith Moreland*	.35
383	Jose Cruz	.12
384	Bill Virdon	.06
385	Jim Sundberg	.08
386	Doc Medich	.06
387	Al Oliver	.15
389	Bob Bailor	.06
390	Ernie Whitt	.08
392	Roy Howell	.06
393	*Bob Walk*	.20

399	Marvis Foley	.06
400	Steve Trout	.06
402	Tony Larussa (LaRussa)	.08
404	Bake McBride	.06
406	Rob Dressler	.06
408	Tom Paciorek	.06
409	Carney Lansford	.10
410	Brian Downing	.10
411	Don Aase	.06
412	Jim Barr	.06
413	Don Baylor	.10
414	Jim Fregosi	.08
415	Dallas Green	.08
416	Dave Lopes	.10
417	Jerry Reuss	.10
418	Rick Sutcliffe	.15
420	Tommy LaSorda (Lasorda)	.15
421	*Charlie Leibrandt*	.25
422	Tom Seaver	.65
423	Ron Oester	.06
425	Tom Seaver	.50
426	Bobby Cox	.06
427	*Leon Durham*	.25
428	Terry Kennedy	.08
430	George Hendrick	.08
431	Red Schoendienst	.10
433	Vida Blue	.10
434	John Montefusco	.08
436	Dave Bristol	.06
437	Dale Murphy	.90
439	Jorge Orta	.06
442	Dave Garcia	.06
443	Don Money	.06
444	Buck Martinez (photo backward)	1.00
444	Buck Martinez (photo correct)	.10
446	Ben Oglivie	.08
447	Jim Slaton	.06
448	Doyle Alexander	.10
451	Dave Palmer	.06
453	Dick Williams	.06

REGGIE JACKSON OUTFIELD

228 Reggie Jackson

STEVE GARVEY FIRST BASE

56 Steve Garvey

537 Best Hitters

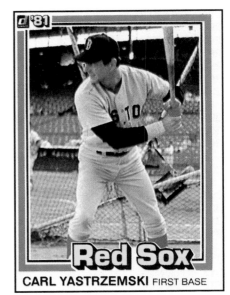

Red Sox

CARL YASTRZEMSKI FIRST BASE

214 Carl Yastrzemski

454	Rick Burleson	.08
456	Bob Stanley	.06
457	*John Tudor*	1.00
458	*Dwight Evans	.15
459	Glenn Hubbard	.08
461	Larry Gura	.08
462	Rich Gale	.06
463	Hal McRae	.10
464	Jim Frey	.06
465	Bucky Dent	.10
467	Ron Davis	.06
468	Reggie Jackson	.75
469	Bobby Brown	.06
470	*Mike Davis*	.25
471	Gaylord Perry	.30
472	Mark Belanger	.08
473	Jim Palmer	.45
474	Sammy Stewart	.06
475	Tim Stoddard	.06
476	Steve Stone	.08
477	Jeff Newman	.06
479	Bill Martin	.15
480	Mitchell Page	.06
481	Cy Young 1980 (Steve Carlton)	.35
482	Bill Buckner	.10
483	Ivan DeJesus	.10
484	Cliff Johnson	.06
485	Lenny Randle	.06
487	Roy Smalley	.06
488	John Castino	.06
489	Ron Jackson	.06
490	Dave Roberts	.10
491	MVP (George Brett)	.60
493	Rob Wilfong	.06
496	Mickey Rivers	.08
498	Mike Sadek	.06
501	Dave Roberts	.06
502	Steve Dillard	.06
503	Jim Essian	.06
505	Darrell Porter	.06
506	Joe Torre	.08
508	Bill Travers	.06
510	Bob McClure	.06
511	*Steve Howe*	.10
512	Dave Rader	.06
514	Kiko Garcia	.06
516	Willie Norwood	.10
517	Bo Diaz	.06

518	Juan Beniquez	.06
520	Jim Tracy	.06
521	Carlos Lezcano	.06
524	Ray Burris	.10
526	Mickey Hatcher	.08
527	John Goryl	.06
528	Dick Davis	.06
530	Sal Butera	.06
531	Jerry Koosman	.10
532	Jeff Zahn (Geoff)	.10
533	Dennis Martinez	.08
535	Steve Macko	.06
536	Jim Kaat	.15
537	Best Hitters (George Brett, Rod Carew)	1.25
538	Tim Raines	5.00
539	Keith Smith	.06
540	Ken Macha	.06
541	Burt Hooton	.08
543	Bill Stein	.06
545	Bob Pate	.06
548	Pete Redfern	.06
550	Al Hrabosky	.08
551	Dick Tidrow	.06

NOLAN RYAN PITCHER

260 Nolan Ryan

553	Dave Kingman	.15
554	Mike Vail	.10
555	Jerry Martin	.10
556	Jesus Figueroa	.10
560	*Bruce Sutter	.15
561	Rick Reuschel	.10
563	Bob Owchinko	.10
566	Glen Adams (incorrect spelling)	1.00
566	Glenn Adams (correct spelling)	.10
569	*Danny Ainge*	.25
570	Bobby Mattick	.06
571	Joe LeFebvre (Lefebvre)	.06
572	Bobby Clark	.06
573	Dennis Lamp	.06
574	Randy Lerch	.06
575	*Mookie Wilson*	.60
576	Ron LeFlore	.08
577	Jim Dwyer	.06
578	Bill Castro	.06
579	Greg Minton	.06
580	Mark Littell	.08
582	Dave Stieb	.20
583	Ken Oberkfell	.06
584	Larry Bradford	.06
585	Fred Stanley	.06
586	Bill Caudill	.06
587	Doug Capilla	.06
589	Willie Hernandez	.10
590	MVP (Mike Schmidt)	.80
591	Cy Young 1980 (Steve Stone)	.08
593	Bombo Rivera	.06
594	Gary Ward	.08
595	Dave Edwards	.10
596	Mike Proly	.06
597	Tommy Boggs	.06
598	Gregg Gross	.06
599	Elias Sosa	.06
600	Pat Kelly	.06

1981 FLEER

A 1980 Pennsylvania court ruling allowed Fleer to break the virtual monopoly held by Topps and produce its own set of baseball cards. This legal victory permitted the Philadelphia company to make independent contracts with major league baseball and the Players Association—a right that had been held exclusively by Topps since 1964. The Fleer set of 660 cards is not first-rate, however, with photographic quality a notch below the standard established by Topps. It is also marred by 40 different errors, although the error cards were corrected in two subsequent press runs and aren't collected by most hobbyists, who stop with 660 cards. The only notable exception is Graig Nettles' card, number 87. In early press runs his name appears on the back as "Craig," but the corrected version is far more common than the card with the error.

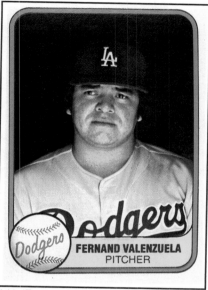

140 (Fernando) Valenzuela

Complete set
MINT

Complete set (without variations)	$40.00
Commons	.06

1	Pete Rose	$1.75
2	Larry Bowa	.15
3	Manny Trillo	.08
4	Bob Boone	.10
5	Mike Schmidt (batting)	1.00
5	Mike Schmidt (portrait)	1.25
6	Steve Carlton ("Lefty" on front)	1.00
6	Steve Carlton ("Pitcher of the Year" on front, date "1066" on back)	.60
6	Steve Carlton ("Pitcher of the Year" on front, date "1966" on back)	2.00
7	Tug McGraw ("Game Saver" on front)	.50
7	Tug McGraw ("Pitcher" on front)	.12
10	Greg Luzinski	.15
13	*Keith Moreland*	.35
14	*Bob Walk*	.25
15	Lonnie Smith	.10
17	Sparky Lyle	.10
18	Greg Gross	.06
19	Garry Maddox	.10
24	Kevin Saucier ("Ken Saucier" on back)	.15
24	Kevin Saucier ("Kevin Saucier" on back)	.75
26	Del Unser	.06
27	Tim McCarver	.15
28	George Brett (batting)	1.25
28	George Brett (portrait)	.90
29	Willie Wilson (batting)	.10
29	Willie Wilson (portrait)	.65
31	Dan Quisenberry	.15
32	Amos Otis (batting)	.50

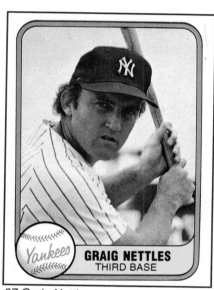

87 Graig Nettles

32	Amos Otis (portrait)	.10
33	Steve Busby	.08
36	Darrell Porter	.08
38	Larry Gura	.06
40	Rich Gale	.06
41	Hal McRae	.15
42	Dennis Leonard	.08
44	Frank White	.15
46	John Wathan	.08
51	Art Howe	.06
52	Ken Forsch	.06
53	Vern Ruhle	.06
54	Joe Niekro	.15
56	J.R. Richard	.10
57	*Nolan Ryan	2.00
59	Cesar Cedeno	.12
60	Jose Cruz	.12
61	Bill Virdon	.06
63	Joaquin Andujar	.10
64	Alan Ashby	.06
67	Jeff Leonard	.12
68	Luis Pujols	.06

69	Bruce Bochy	.06
71	*Dave Smith*	.25
72	*Danny Heep*	.10
78	*Joe Morgan	.30
79	Reggie Jackson (batting)	.75
79	Reggie Jackson (portrait)	1.00
80	Bucky Dent	.10
81	Tommy John	.20
82	*Luis Tiant	.12
85	Lou Piniella	.12
87	Graig Nettles ("Craig" on back)	12.00
87	Graig Nettles ("Graig" on back)	.30
88	Ron Guidry	.25
89	Rich Gossage	.20
91	*Gaylord Perry	.30
93	Bob Watson	.10
94	Bobby Murcer	.10
98	Oscar Gamble	.10
109	Willie Randolph	.10
110	Steve Garvey	.50
111	Reggie Smith	.10
112	Don Sutton	.30
113	Burt Hooton	.08
114	Davy Lopes (Davey) (with fingerlike mark on back)	1.00
114	Davy Lopes (Davey) (w/o mark on back)	.10
115	Dusty Baker	.10
116	Tom Lasorda	.10
117	Bill Russell	.10
119	Terry Forster	.06
120	Robert Welch ("Bob Welch" on back)	.20
120	Robert Welch ("Robert Welch" on back)	1.00
122	Rick Monday	.10

143

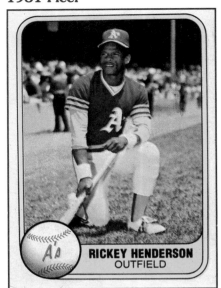

574 Rickey Henderson

125	Rick Sutcliffe	.15
126	Ron Cey (with fingerlike mark on back)	1.00
126	Ron Cey (w/o mark on back)	.10
127	Dave Goltz	.10
128	Jay Johnstone	.08
130	Gary Weiss	.06
131	*Mike Scioscia*	.65
132	Vic Davalillo	.08
133	Doug Rau	.06
135	Mickey Matcher	.08
136	*Steve Howe*	.08
139	Rudy Law	.06
140	*Fernand Valenzuela* (Fernando)	4.50
141	Manny Mota	.08
142	Gary Carter	.45
143	Steve Rogers	.08
145	Andre Dawson	.40
146	Larry Parrish	.10
150	*Bill Gullickson*	.15
154	Ron LeFlore	.08
155	Rodney Scott	.06
157	Bill Lee	.08
158	Fred Norman	.06
159	Woodie Fryman	.08
160	Dave Palmer	.06
161	Jerry White	.06
165	*Charlie Lea*	.10
167	Ken Macha	.06
169	Jim Palmer	.40
171	Mike Flanagan	.10
172	Al Bumbry	.06
173	Doug DeCinces	.10
174	Scott McGregor	.08
175	Mark Belanger	.08
177	Rick Dempsey (with fingerlike mark on front)	1.00
177	Rick Dempsey (w/o mark on front)	.10
178	Earl Weaver	.10

180	Dennis Martinez	.08
183	Lee May	.08
184	Eddie Murray	.75
185	Benny Ayala	.06
188	Ken Singleton	.10
189	Dan Graham	.06
192	Dave Ford	.06
195	Doug DeCinces	.10
196	Johnny Bench	.75
197	Dave Concepcion	.15
198	Ray Knight	.10
199	Ken Griffey	.12
200	Tom Seaver	.75
201	Dave Collins	.08
202	George Foster	.20
205	Dan Driessen	.08
206	Hector Cruz	.06
208	*Charlie Leibrandt*	.30
210	*Joe Price*	.08
211	Tom Hume	.06
213	Doug Bair	.06
214	Mario Soto	.08
215	Bill Bonham (with fingerlike mark on back)	1.00
215	Bill Bonham (w/o mark on back)	.10
216	George Foster ("Slugger" on front)	.20
216	George Foster ("Outfield" on front)	.20
219	Sam Mejias	.06
221	Carl Yastrzemski	.80
222	Jim Rice	.50
223	Fred Lynn	.20
224	Carlton Fisk	.50
225	Rick Burleson	.08
226	Dennis Eckersley	.15
227	Butch Hobson	.06
230	Don Zimmer	.06
231	Steve Renko	.06
232	*Dwight Evans	.15
233	Mike Torrez	.08
238	Jerry Remy	.06

346 Harold Baines

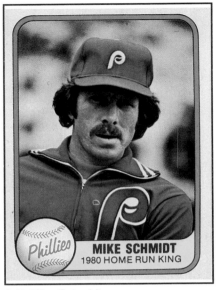

640 Mike Schmidt

239	Dick Drago	.06
241	Tony Perez	.20
242	Phil Niekro	.30
243	Dale Murphy	.90
244	Bob Horner	.15
245	Jeff Burroughs	.08
247	Bob Cox	.06
251	Gary Matthews (with fingerlike mark on back)	1.00
251	Gary Matthews (w/o mark on back)	.12
252	Chris Chambliss	.08
253	Luis Gomez	.06
255	Doyle Alexander	.10
258	Mike Lum	.06
260	Glenn Hubbard	.08
261	Tommy Boggs	.06
262	Al Hrabosky	.08
263	Rick Matula	.06
266	*Rafael Ramirez*	.20
268	*Rod Carew	.60
269	Bobby Grich	.10
270	Carney Lansford	.10
271	Don Baylor	.10
272	Joe Rudi	.10
274	Jim Fregosi	.08
275	Dave Frost	.06
276	Frank Tanana	.10
277	Dickie Thon	.08
279	Rick Miller	.06
280	Bert Campaneris	.10
282	Brian Downing	.10
283	Fred Patek	.06
286	Don Aase	.06
287	Jim Barr	.06
289	Larry Harlow	.06
290	Andy Hassler	.06
291	Dave Kingman	.15
292	Bill Buckner	.10
293	Rick Reuschel	.12
294	Bruce Sutter	.10
299	Dick Tidrow	.06

300	Randy Martz	.06
301	Lenny Randle	.06
303	Cliff Johnson	.06
305	Dennis Lamp	.06
306	Bill Caudill	.06
308	Jim Tracy	.06
310	Willie Hernandez	.10
311	Mike Vail	.06
312	Mike Krukow	.12
313	Barry Foote	.06
314	Larry Biittner	.06
315	Mike Tyson	.06
316	Lee Mazzilli	.06
317	John Stearns	.06
318	Alex Trevino	.06
319	Craig Swan	.06
322	Neil Allen	.08
323	Mark Bomback	.06
325	Joe Torre	.06
326	Elliott Maddox	.06
327	Pete Falcone	.06
328	Ray Burris	.06
329	Claudell Washington	.06
330	Doug Flynn	.06
332	Bill Almon	.06
335	*Jeff Reardon*	.75
336	*Wally Backman*	.25
337	Dan Norman	.06
339	Ed Farmer	.06
341	Todd Cruz	.06
342	*Britt Burns* (with fingerlike mark on front)	1.00
342	*Britt Burns* (w/o mark on front)	.20
343	Kevin Bell	.06
344	*Tony LaRussa	.08
346	*Harold Baines*	2.50
349	Mike Squires	.06
350	Lamar Johnson	.06
351	Rickey Henderson	4.00
353	Thad Bosley	.06
354	Chet Lemon	.08
355	Bruce Kimm	.06

356	*Richard Dotson*	.35
357	Jim Morrison	.06
358	Mike Proly	.06
359	Greg Pryor	.06
360	Dave Parker	.30
361	Omar Moreno	.06
362	Kent Tekulve	.15
363	Willie Stargell	.40
364	Phil Garner	.08
365	Ed Ott	.06
366	Don Robinson	.08
367	Chuck Tanner	.08
369	Dale Berra	.06
370	Jim Bibby	.06
371	Steve Nicosia	.06
372	Mike Easler	.08
373	Bill Robinson	.06
374	Lee Lacy	.06
375	John Candelaria	.10
377	Rick Rhoden	.10
379	Tim Foli	.06
380	*Rod Scurry*	.08
381	Bill Madlock	.12
382	Kurt Bevacqua (negative reversed, backward "P" on cap)	.15
382	Kurt Bevacqua (correct photo)	.70
383	Bert Blyleven	.15
384	Eddie Solomon	.06
385	Enrique Romo	.06
386	John Milner	.06
388	Jorge Orta	.06
389	Toby Harrah	.06
390	Tom Veryzer	.06
391	Miguel Dilone	.06
392	Dan Spillner	.06
393	Jack Brohamer	.06
394	Wayne Garland	.06
395	Sid Monge	.06
396	Rick Waits	.06
397	*Joe Charboneau*	.10
398	Gary Alexander	.06

399	Jerry Dybzinski	.06
400	Mike Stanton	.06
401	Mike Paxton	.06
402	Gary Gray	.06
403	Rick Manning	.06
404	Bo Diaz	.06
406	Ross Grimsley	.06
407	Victor Cruz	.06
408	Len Barker	.08
409	Bob Bailor	.06
410	Otto Velez	.06
411	Ernie Whitt	.08
412	Jim Clancy	.08
413	Barry Bonnell	.06
414	Dave Stieb	.20
415	*Damaso Garcia*	.10
416	John Mayberry	.08
418	*Dan Ainge*	.30
419	Jesse Jefferson ("Blue Jays" on back)	.50
419	Jesse Jefferson ("Pirates" on back)	.10
420	Joey McLaughlin	.06
421	*Lloyd Moseby*	.75
422	Al Woods	.06
423	Garth Iorg	.06
424	Doug Ault	.06
425	*Ken Schrom*	.08
426	Mike Willis	.06
427	Steve Braun	.06
428	Bob Davis	.06
429	Jerry Garvin	.06
430	Alfredo Griffin	.08
432	Vida Blue	.12
433	Jack Clark	.25
434	*Willie McCovey	.40
435	Mike Ivie	.06
436	Darrell Evans ("Darrel" on front)	.15
436	Darrell Evans ("Darrell" correct on front)	.75
437	Terry Whitfield	.06
438	Rennie Stennett	.06
439	John Montefusco	.08

481 Kirk Gibson

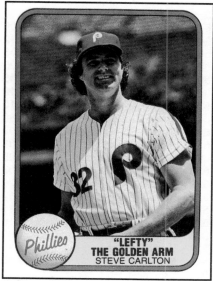

6 Steve Carlton

655 George Brett

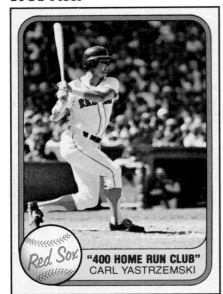

638 Carl Yastrzemski

440	Jim Wohlford	.06
441	Bill North	.06
442	Milt May	.06
443	Max Venable	.06
444	Ed Whitson	.06
445	*Al Holland*	.08
447	Bob Knepper	.06
448	Gary Lavelle	.06
449	Greg Minton	.06
450	Johnnie LeMaster	.06
451	Larry Herndon	.08
452	Rich Murray	.06
453	Joe Pettini	.06
454	Allen Ripley	.06
455	Dennis Littlejohn	.06
456	Tom Griffin	.06
457	Alan Hargesheimer	.06
458	Joe Strain	.06
459	Steve Kemp	.08
460	Sparky Anderson	.10
461	Alan Trammell	.40
462	Mark Fidrych	.08
463	Lou Whitaker	.30
465	Milt Wilcox	.06
466	Champ Summers	.06
467	Lance Parrish	.35
468	Dan Petry	.08
469	Pat Underwood	.06
470	Rick Peters	.06
471	Al Cowens	.06
472	John Wockenfuss	.06
473	Tom Brookens	.08
474	Richie Hebner	.06
475	Jack Morris	.35
476	Jim Lentine	.06
477	Bruce Robbins	.06
478	Mark Wagner	.06
480	Stan Papi ("Pitcher" on front)	.15
480	Stan Papi ("Shortstop" on front)	.70
481	*Kirk Gibson*	4.00
482	Dan Schatzeder	.06

483	Amos Otis	.15
484	Dave Winfield	.50
485	Rollie Fingers	.25
486	Gene Richards	.06
487	Randy Jones	.08
488	Ozzie Smith	.40
489	Gene Tenace	.08
492	Dave Cash	.06
493	Tim Flannery (negative reversed, batting right)	.15
493	Tim Flannery (correct photo, batting left)	.70
494	Jerry Mumphrey	.06
495	Bob Shirley	.06
496	Steve Mura	.06
498	Broderick Perkins	.06
499	Barry Evans	.06
500	Chuck Baker	.06
501	*Luis Salazar*	.15
502	Gary Lucas	.08
503	Mike Armstrong	.06
504	Jerry Turner	.06
506	Willy Montanez (Willie)	.06
507	Gorman Thomas	.10
508	Ben Oglivie	.08
509	Larry Hisle	.08
510	Sal Bando	.10
511	Robin Yount	1.25
514	Jerry Augustine (photo is Billy Travers)	.15
514	Billy Travers (correct name and photo)	.75
515	Paul Molitor	.20
516	Moose Haas	.06
517	Bill Castro	.06
518	Jim Slaton	.06
522	Jim Gantner	.08
524	Don Money	.08
528	Ted Simmons	.15
529	Garry Templeton	.10
530	Ken Reitz	.06

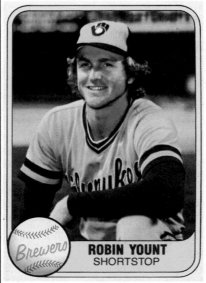

511 Robin Yount

57 Nolan Ryan

531	Tony Scott	.06
536	Jim Kaat	.15
537	Bob Forsch	.08
539	*Terry Landrum*	.10
540	*Leon Durham*	.25
541	Terry Kennedy	.08
542	George Hendrick	.08
543	Dane Iorg	.06
544	Mark Littell (photo is Jeff Little)	.08
545	Keith Hernandez	.40
547	Pete Vuckovich (photo is Don Hood)	.15
547	Don Hood (correct name and photo)	.70
548	Bobby Bonds	.10
550	Tom Herr	.10
552	Jerry Koosman	.10
560	Pete Redfern	.06
570	Sal Butera	.06
574	Rickey Henderson	3.00
575	Tony Armas	.10
578	Bob Lacey	.06
581	Billy Martin	.12
583	Mike Heath	.06
586	*Mike Davis*	.25
590	Dwayne Murphy	.08
595	Maury Wills	.10
599	Floyd Bannister	.10
606	Steve Garvey	.50
617	Mickey Rivers	.08
619	Jim Sundberg	.08
620	Richie Zisk	.08
621	Jon Matlack	.08
622	Ferguson Jenkins	.20
625	Buddy Bell	.12
626	Al Oliver	.15
629	Rusty Staub	.10
638	Carl Yastrzemski	1.00
639	Cecil Cooper	.12
640	Mike Schmidt	2.00
641	Checklist 1-50	.15
642	Checklist 51-109	.06

643	Checklist 110-168	.06
644	Checklist 169-220	.10
645	Triple Threat (Larry Bowa, Pete Rose, Mike Schmidt) (with number on back)	2.00
645	Triple Threat (Larry Bowa, Pete Rose, Mike Schmidt) (w/o number on back)	1.00

646	Checklist 221-267	.06
647	Checklist 268-315	.06
648	Checklist 316-359	.06
649	Checklist 360-408	.06
650	Reggie Jackson	2.50
651	Checklist 409-458	.06
652	Checklist 459-506	.10
653	Willie Wilson	1.00
654	Checklist 507-550	.10
655	George Brett	3.00

1981 Fleer/1981 Topps

656	Checklist 551-593	.10
657	Tug McGraw	1.00
658	Checklist 594-637	.06
659	Checklist 640-660	.10
660	Steve Carlton	1.00

1981 TOPPS

The 1981 Topps set contains 726 cards, but because it was printed in six sheets of 132 cards each, 66 cards were printed twice. This happened because each sheet had one row of 11 cards that was printed a second time, making such cards twice as common as the others. Among the double-printed cards are those for Mike Schmidt and Rich Dotson. The 1981 set marks the last appearance of team cards with the manager's photo in the upper right. Once again, three Future Stars from each team share a card. At the time this set was released, and for the first time in years, Topps was facing major competition in the baseball card market.

261 Rickey Henderson

		MINT
Complete set		**$95.00**
Commons		**.08**

1	Batting Ldrs (George Brett, Bill Buckner)	$ .70
2	HR Ldrs (Reggie Jackson, Ben Oglivie, Mike Schmidt)	.40
3	RBI Ldrs (Cecil Cooper, Mike Schmidt)	.30
4	SB Ldrs (Rickey Henderson, Ron LeFlore)	.25
5	Victory Ldrs (Steve Carlton, Steve Stone)	.20
6	SO Ldrs (Len Barker, Steve Carlton)	.20
7	ERA Ldrs (Rudy May, Don Sutton)	.15
8	Leading Firemen (Rollie Fingers, Tom Hume, Dan Quisenberry)	.10
9	Pete LaCock	.08
10	Mike Flanagan	.10
11	Jim Wohlford	.08
12	Mark Clear	.08
13	*Joe Charboneau*	.15
14	*John Tudor*	1.25
15	Larry Parrish	.12
16	Ron Davis	.08
17	Cliff Johnson	.08
18	Glenn Adams	.08
19	Jim Clancy	.08
20	Jeff Burroughs	.10
21	Ron Oester	.08
22	Danny Darwin	.08
23	Alex Trevino	.08
24	Don Stanhouse	.08

25	Sixto Lezcano	.08
26	U.L. Washington.	.08
27	Champ Summers	.08
28	Enrique Romo	.08
29	Gene Tenace	.10
30	Jack Clark	.50
31	Checklist 1-121	.10
32	Ken Oberkfell	.08
34	Aurelio Rodriguez	.08
35	Mitchell Page	.08
36	Ed Farmer	.08
37	Gary Roenicke	.08
38	Win Remmerswaal	.08
39	Tom Veryzer	.08
40	Tug McGraw	.20
41	Rangers FS (Bob Babcock, John Butcher, Jerry Don Gleaton)	.10
42	Jerry White	.08

43	Jose Morales	.08
45	Enos Cabell	.08
46	Rick Bosetti	.08
47	Ken Brett	.10
48	Dave Skaggs	.08

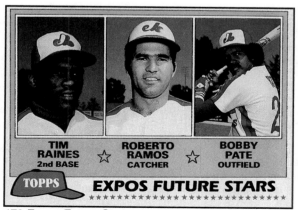

479 Expos Future Stars

147

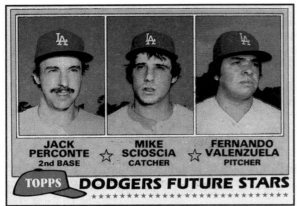

302 Dodgers Future Stars

49	Bob Shirley	.08
50	Dave Lopes	.10
51	Bill Robinson	.08
52	Hector Cruz	.08
53	Kevin Saucier	.08
54	Ivan DeJesus	.08
55	Mike Norris	.08
56	Buck Martinez	.08
57	Dave Roberts	.08
58	Joel Youngblood	.08
59	Dan Petry	.08
60	Willie Randolph	.10
61	Butch Wynegar	.08
62	Joe Pettini	.08
64	Brian Asselstine	.08
65	Scott McGregor	.10
67	Ken Kravec	.08
68	Matt Alexander	.08
69	Ed Halicki	.08
70	Al Oliver	.15
71	Hal Dues	.08
72	Barry Evans	.08
73	Doug Bair	.08
74	Mike Hargrove	.08
75	Reggie Smith	.15
76	Mario Mendoza	.08
77	Mike Barlow	.08
78	Steve Dillard	.08
79	Bruce Robbins	.08
80	Rusty Staub	.15
81	Dave Stapleton	.08
83	Mike Proly	.08
84	Johnnie LeMaster	.08
85	Mike Caldwell	.08
86	Wayne Gross	.08
87	Rick Camp	.08
88	Joe Lefebvre	.08
90	Bake McBride	.08
91	Tim Stoddard	.08
92	Mike Easler	.08
93	Ed Glynn	.08
94	Harry Spilman	.08
95	Jim Sundberg	.10
96	A's FS (Dave Beard, *Ernie Camacho,* Pat Dempsey)	.12
97	Chris Speier	.08
98	Clint Hurdle	.08
99	Eric Wilkins	.08

100	Rod Carew	1.50
101	Benny Ayala	.08
102	Dave Tobik	.08
103	Jerry Martin	.08
104	Terry Forster	.10
105	Jose Cruz	.15
106	Don Money	.08
107	Rich Wortham	.08
108	Bruce Benedict	.08
109	Mike Scott	1.00
110	Carl Yastrzemski	2.00
111	Greg Minton	.08
113	Mike Phillips	.08
114	Tom Underwood	.08
115	Roy Smalley	.08
116	Joe Simpson	.08
117	Pete Falcone	.08
118	Kurt Bevacqua	.08
119	Tippy Martinez	.08
120	Larry Bowa	.20
121	Larry Harlow	.08
122	John Denny	.08
123	Al Cowens	.08
124	Jerry Garvin	.08
125	Andre Dawson	.90
126	*Charlie Leibrandt*	.40
127	Rudy Law	.08
128	Gary Allenson	.08
129	Art Howe	.08
130	Larry Gura	.08
131	*Keith Moreland*	.45
132	Tommy Boggs	.08
133	Jeff Cox	.08
134	Steve Mura	.08
135	Gorman Thomas	.10
136	Doug Capilla	.08
137	Hosken Powell	.08
138	Richard Dotson	.25
139	Oscar Gamble	.10
140	Bob Forsch	.10
141	Miguel Dilone	.08
143	Dan Meyer	.08
144	Allen Ripley	.08
145	Mickey Rivers	.08
146	Bobby Castillo	.08
147	Dale Berra	.08
148	Randy Niemann	.08
149	Joe Nolan	.08
150	Mark Fidrych	.10

151	Claudell Washington	.12
152	John Urrea	.08
153	Tom Poquette	.08
154	Rick Langford	.08
155	Chris Chambliss	.08
156	Bob McClure	.08
157	John Wathan	.10
158	Fergie Jenkins	.35
159	Brian Doyle	.08
160	Garry Maddox	.10
161	Dan Graham	.08
162	Doug Corbett	.08
163	Billy Almon	.08
164	*Lamarr Hoyt* (LaMarr)	.15
166	Floyd Bannister	.12
167	Terry Whitfield	.08
168	Don Robinson	.10
169	John Mayberry	.10
170	Ross Grimsley	.08
171	Gene Richards	.08
172	Gary Woods	.08
173	Bump Wills	.08
174	Doug Rau	.08
175	Dave Collins	.10
176	Mike Krukow	.10
177	Rick Peters	.08
178	Jim Essian	.08
179	Rudy May	.08
180	Pete Rose	3.50
181	Elias Sosa	.08
182	Bob Grich	.12
183	Dick Davis	.08
184	Jim Dwyer	.08
185	Dennis Leonard	.10
186	Wayne Nordhagen	.08
187	Mike Parrott	.08
188	Doug DeCinces	.12
189	Craig Swan	.08
190	Cesar Cedeno	.10
191	Rick Sutcliffe	.40
192	Braves FS (*Terry Harper,* Ed Miller, *Rafael Ramirez*)	.25

315 Kirk Gibson

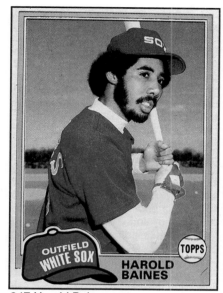

347 Harold Baines

193	Pete Vuckovich	.10
194	*Rod Scurry*	.10
195	Rich Murray	.08
196	Duffy Dyer	.08
197	Jim Kern	.08
198	Jerry Dybzinski	.08
199	Chuck Rainey	.08
200	George Foster	.25
201	Record Breaker (Johnny Bench)	.40
202	Record Breaker (Steve Carlton)	.40
203	Record Breaker (Bill Gullickson)	.08
204	Record Breaker (Ron LeFlore, Rodney Scott)	.10
205	Record Breaker (Pete Rose)	.80
206	Record Breaker (Mike Schmidt)	.50
207	Record Breaker (Ozzie Smith)	.20
208	Record Breaker (Willie Wilson)	.20
209	Dickie Thon	.10
210	Jim Palmer	1.50
211	Derrel Thomas	.08
212	Steve Nicosia	.08
213	*Al Holland*	.10
215	Larry Hisle	.10
216	John Henry Johnson	.08
217	Rich Hebner	.08
218	Paul Splittorff	.10
219	Ken Landreaux	.08
220	Tom Seaver	1.50
221	Bob Davis	.08
222	Jorge Orta	.08
223	Roy Lee Jackson	.08
224	Pat Zachry	.08
225	Ruppert Jones	.08
226	Manny Sanguillen	.08

227	Fred Martinez	.08
228	Tom Paciorek	.08
229	Rollie Fingers	.60
230	George Hendrick	.08
231	Joe Beckwith	.08
232	Mickey Klutts	.08
233	Skip Lockwood	.08
234	Lou Whitaker	.60
235	Scott Sanderson	.08
237	Charlie Moore	.08
238	Willie Hernandez	.10
239	Rick Miller	.08
240	Nolan Ryan	3.25
241	Checklist 122-242	.08
242	Chet Lemon	.10
243	Sal Butera	.08
244	Cardinals FS (*Tito Landrum,* Al Olmsted, Andy Rincon)	.15
245	Ed Figueroa	.08
246	Ed Ott	.08
247	Glenn Hubbard	.08
248	Joey McLaughlin	.08
249	Larry Cox	.08
250	Ron Guidry	.50
251	Tom Brookens	.08
252	Victor Cruz	.08
253	Dave Bergman	.08
254	Ozzie Smith	2.00
255	Mark Littell	.10
256	Bombo Rivera	.08
257	Rennie Stennett	.08
258	*Joe Price*	.10
259	*Mets FS (Juan Berenguer, *Hubie Brooks, Mookie Wilson*)	2.50
260	Ron Cey	.15
261	Rickey Henderson	9.50
262	Sammy Stewart	.08
263	Brian Downing	.12
264	Jim Norris	.08
265	John Candelaria	.12
266	Tom Herr	.10

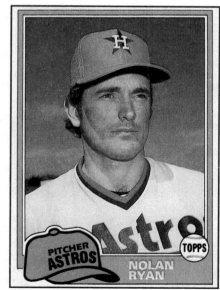

240 Nolan Ryan

700 George Brett

267	Stan Bahnsen	.08
268	Jerry Royster	.08
270	Greg Luzinski	.12
271	Bill Castro	.08
272	Bruce Kimm	.08
273	Stan Papi	.08
274	Craig Chamberlain	.08
275	*Dwight Evans	.25
276	Dan Spillner	.08
277	Alfredo Griffin	.10
278	Rick Sofield	.08
279	Bob Knepper	.08
280	Ken Griffey	.10
281	Fred Stanley	.08
283	Billy Sample	.08
284	Brian Kingman	.08
285	Jerry Turner	.08
286	Dave Frost	.08
287	Lenn Sakata	.08
288	Bob Clark	.08
289	Mickey Hatcher	.10
290	*Bob Boone	.08
291	Aurelio Lopez	.08
292	Mike Squires	.08
293	*Charlie Lea*	.15
294	Mike Tyson	.08
295	Hal McRae	.15
296	Bill Nahorodny	.08
298	Buddy Solomon	.08
299	Elliott Maddox	.08
300	Paul Molitor	.40
301	Matt Keough	.08
302	Dodgers FS (Jack Perconte, *Mike Scioscia, Fernando Valenzuela*)	6.50
303	Johnny Oates	.08
304	John Castino	.08
305	Ken Clay	.08
306	Juan Beniquez	.08
307	Gene Garber	.08
308	Rick Manning	.08

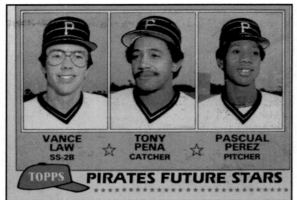

551 Pirates Future Stars

309	Luis Salazar	.15
310	Vida Blue	.10
311	Freddie Patek	.08
312	Rick Rhoden	.10
313	Luis Pujols	.08
314	Rich Dauer	.08
315	Kirk Gibson	6.00
316	Craig Minetto	.08
317	Lonnie Smith	.08
319	Rowland Office	.08
320	Tom Burgmeier	.08
321	Leon Durham	.20
322	Neil Allen	.08
323	Jim Morrison	.08
324	Mike Willis	.08
325	Ray Knight	.12
326	Biff Pocoroba	.08
327	Moose Haas	.08
328	Twins FS (Dave Engle, Greg Johnston, Gary Ward)	.12
330	Frank White	.12
331	Dennis Lamp	.08
332	Lee Lacy	.08
333	Sid Monge	.08
334	Dane Iorg	.08
335	Rick Cerone	.08
336	Eddie Whitson	.10
337	Lynn Jones	.08
338	Checklist 243-363	.08
339	John Ellis	.08
340	Bruce Kison	.08
341	Dwayne Murphy	.08
342	Eric Rasmussen	.08
343	Frank Taveras	.08
344	Byron McLaughlin	.08
345	Warren Cromartie	.08
346	Larry Christenson	.08
347	Harold Baines	4.00
348	Bob Sykes	.08
349	Glenn Hoffman	.08
350	J.R. Richard	.10
351	Otto Velez	.08
352	Dick Tidrow	.08
353	Terry Kennedy	.08
354	Mario Soto	.08
355	Bob Horner	.20
357	Jim Slaton	.08
358	Mark Wagner	.08

359	Tom Hausman	.08
360	Willie Wilson	.25
361	Joe Strain	.08
362	Bo Diaz	.08
363	Geoff Zahn	.08
364	Mike Davis	.25
365	Graig Nettles	.12
366	Mike Ramsey	.08
367	Denny Martinez	.08
368	Leon Roberts	.08
369	Frank Tanana	.12
370	Dave Winfield	1.00
371	Charlie Hough	.15
372	Jay Johnstone	.10
373	Pat Underwood	.08
374	Tom Hutton	.08
375	Dave Concepcion	.20
376	Ron Reed	.08
378	Dave Rader	.08
380	Willie Stargell	1.00
382	Paul Mirabella (FC)	.12
384	Mike Sadek	.08
387	Phil Niekro	.70
392	Lance Parrish	.70
394	Woodie Fryman	.10
397	Julio Cruz	.08
399	*Orioles FS (Mike Boddicker, Mark Corey, Floyd Rayford)	1.75
400	Reggie Jackson	2.00
401	AL Championships (Royals Sweep Yankees)	.50
402	NL Championships (Phillies Squeak Past Astros)	.40
403	World Series (Phillies Beat Royals in 6)	.25
404	World Series Summary (Phillies Win First World Series)	.25
407	Ernie Whitt	.10
409	Larry Herndon	.08
410	Bert Campaneris	.10
411	Terry Puhl	.08
412	Britt Burns	.12
413	Tony Bernazard	.10
415	Ben Oglivie	.10
420	Keith Hernandez	.80
422	Dan Ford	.08

423	Shane Rawley	.08
425	Al Bumbry	.10
430	Jim Bibby	.08
432	Len Barker	.08
438	John Montefusco	.08
440	Jerry Reuss	.12
441	Ken Reitz	.08
444	Garth Iorg	.08
446	Checklist 364-484	.25
450	Dave Kingman	.10
451	Indians FS (Chris Bando, Tom Brennan, Sandy Wihtol)	.12
455	Rick Burleson	.10
456	*Jeff Reardon	1.25
457	Mike Lum	.08
458	Randy Jones	.10
460	Rich Gossage	.40
463	Milt May	.08
465	Bill Russell	.10
467	Dave Stieb	.40
469	Jeff Leonard	.15
470	Manny Trillo	.10
471	Mike Vail	.08
475	Buddy Bell	.15
476	Jerry Koosman	.12
479	Expos FS (Bobby Pate, Tim Raines, Roberto Ramos)	10.00
480	Carlton Fisk	.90
482	Jim Gantner	.10
485	Garry Templeton	.10
488	Damaso Garcia	.12
489	John Littlefield (photo is Mark Riggins)	.08
490	Eddie Murray	1.50
493	Dan Quisenberry	.20
494	Bob Walk	.50
495	Dusty Baker	.10
500	Jim Rice	1.00
504	Dale Murphy	2.50
510	Lee Mazzilli	.08
515	Robin Yount	1.00
517	Richie Zisk	.10

110 Carl Yastrzemski

254 Ozzie Smith

525	Mike Torrez	.08
528	Gary Matthews	.12
530	Steve Garvey	1.50
534	*Dave Smith*	.40
540	Mike Schmidt	2.00
548	Dave Goltz	.08
550	Tommy John	.50
551	*Pirates FS (*Vance Law, Tony Pena, Pascual Perez*)	2.75
554	Bert Blyleven	.25
555	Cecil Cooper	.20
560	Joe Morgan	.75
562	Checklist 485-605	.25
563	Jim Kaat	.30
565	Burt Hooton	.10
570	Ken Singleton	.10
572	Jack Morris	.60
573	Phil Garner	.10
575	Tony Perez	.35
577	Blue Jays FS (Luis Leal, Brian Milner, *Ken Schrom*)	.20
578	*Bill Gullickson*	.20
580	Don Baylor	.15
582	Gaylord Perry	.70
585	Amos Otis	.10
590	Bruce Sutter	.25
593	Steve Kemp	.10
600	Johnny Bench	1.50
605	Don Sutton	.70
610	Darrell Porter	.10
615	Rick Dempsey	.10
616	Rick Wise	.10
620	Dennis Eckersley	.20
623	Sal Bando	.10
624	Bob Welch	.20
625	Bill Buckner	.15
627	Luis Tiant	.20
629	Tony Armas	.12
630	Steve Carlton	1.25
633	Bill Lee	.10
635	Bobby Bonds	.15

636	Al Hrabosky	.10
638	Checklist 606-726	.15
639	Carney Lansford	.15
640	Dave Parker	.60
641	Mark Belanger	.10
643	*Lloyd Moseby*	.90
645	Rick Reuschel	.15
648	Darrell Evans	.25
650	Bucky Dent	.12
651	Pedro Guerrero	1.25
655	Dan Driessen	.10
656	Jon Matlack	.10
659	Brewers FS (John Flinn, Ed Romero, Ned Yost)	.08
660	Gary Carter	1.00
661	Orioles Team (Earl Weaver)	.30
662	Red Sox Team (Ralph Houk)	.30
663	Angels Team (Jim Fregosi)	.25
664	White Sox Team (Tony LaRussa)	.25
665	Indians Team (Dave Garcia)	.25
666	Tigers Team (Sparky Anderson)	.25
667	Royals Team (Jim Frey)	.25
668	Brewers Team (Bob Rodgers)	.25
669	Twins Team (John Goryl)	.25
670	Yankees Team (Gene Michael)	.25
671	A's Team (Billy Martin)	.30
672	Mariners Team (Maury Wills)	.25
673	Rangers Team (Don Zimmer)	.25
674	Blue Jays Team (Bobby Mattick)	.25

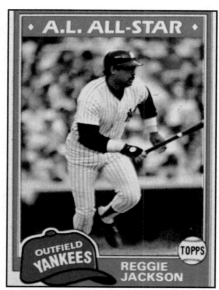

400 Reggie Jackson

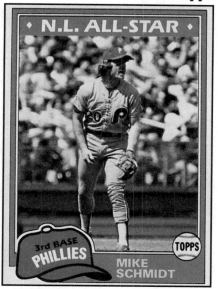

540 Mike Schmidt

675	Braves Team (Bobby Cox)	.25
676	Cubs Team (Joe Amalfitano)	.25
677	Reds Team (John McNamara)	.25
678	Astros Team (Bill Virdon)	.25
679	Dodgers Team (Tom Lasorda)	.35
680	Expos Team (Dick Williams)	.25
681	Mets Team (Joe Torre)	.25
682	Phillies Team (Dallas Green)	.25
683	Pirates Team (Chuck Tanner)	.25
684	Cardinals Team (Whitey Herzog)	.30
685	Padres Team (Frank Howard)	.25
686	Giants Team (Dave Bristol)	.25
689	Red Sox FS (*Bruce Hurst,* Keith MacWhorter, *Reid Nichols*)	2.75
693	Steve Howe	.10
696	Alan Ashby	.12
700	George Brett	2.50
701	Joe Rudi	.12
705	Ted Simmons	.25
708	Doyle Alexander	.10
709	Alan Trammell	.30
715	Bill Madlock	.25
719	Sparky Lyle	.12
720	Fred Lynn	.35
721	Toby Harrah	.10
722	Joe Niekro	.12
724	Lou Piniella	.20
725	Steve Rogers	.10
726	Rick Monday	.25

1981 TOPPS TRADED

Faced with its only competition in the baseball card market since 1963, Topps scrambled for a competitive edge in 1981. The company found that edge in its Traded set. Unlike later years when Traded sets had a "T" designation following the card numbers and featured different color printing on the back, the 1981 Topps Traded series is a genuine extension of the 726-card regular issue. As a result, many collectors think of the extension set as the "high numbers" for 1981. Topps sold the issue in the form of a complete boxed set, and only to hobby dealers. The initial price of this 132-card edition was around nine dollars, which made the cost per card about seven cents. In comparison, cards in the major set that year cost only about two cents each.

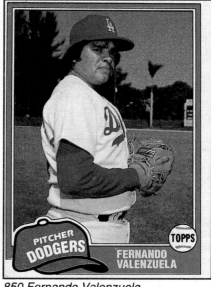

850 Fernando Valenzuela

		MINT
Complete set		**$32.00**
Commons		.10

727	Danny Ainge (FC)	$ .60
728	Doyle Alexander	.20
729	Gary Alexander	.10
730	Billy Almon	.10
731	Joaquin Andujar	.15
732	Bob Bailor	.10
735	Tony Bernazard	.10
737	Doug Bird	.10
738	Bert Blyleven	.50
740	Bobby Bonds	.20
741	Rick Bosetti	.10
742	Hubie Brooks	1.50
743	Rick Burleson	.15
744	Ray Burris	.10
745	Jeff Burroughs	.15
746	Enos Cabell	.10
747	Ken Clay	.10
748	Mark Clear	.10
749	Larry Cox	.10
750	Hector Cruz	.10
751	Victor Cruz	.10
753	Dick Davis	.10
754	Brian Doyle	.10
755	Dick Drago	.10
756	Leon Durham	.25
757	Jim Dwyer	.10
758	Dave Edwards	.10
759	Jim Essian	.10
760	Bill Fahey	.10
761	Rollie Fingers	1.00
762	Carlton Fisk	1.75
763	Barry Foote	.10
764	Ken Forsch	.10
765	Kiko Garcia	.10
766	Cesar Geronimo	.10
768	Mickey Hatcher	.15
770	Marc Hill	.10
771	Butch Hobson	.10
772	Rick Honeycutt	.10
773	Roy Howell	.10
774	Mike Ivie	.10
776	Cliff Johnson	.10

816 Tim Raines

777	Randy Jones	.15
780	Terry Kennedy	.20
781	Dave Kingman	.40
782	Bob Knepper	.10
784	Bob Lacey	.10
785	Dennis Lamp	.10
788	Carney Lansford	.25
789	Dave LaRoche	.10
791	Ron LeFlore	.15
793	Sixto Lezcano	.10
795	Mike Lum	.10
796	Greg Luzinski	.25
797	Fred Lynn	.50
800	Gary Matthews	.20
803	Rick Miller	.10
805	Jerry Morales	.10
806	Jose Morales	.10
807	*Joe Morgan	2.00
809	Gene Nelson (FC)	.30
810	Ed Ott	.10
811	Bob Owchinko	.10

812	Gaylord Perry	1.25
814	Darrell Porter	.15
815	Mike Proly	.10
816	Tim Raines	8.00
818	Doug Rau	.10
819	Jeff Reardon	.50
820	Ken Reitz	.10
821	Steve Renko	.10
822	Rick Reuschel	.25
824	Dave Roberts	.10
825	Leon Roberts	.10
826	Joe Rudi	.20
827	Kevin Saucier	.10
828	Tony Scott	.10
829	Bob Shirley	.10
830	Ted Simmons	.40
835	Rusty Staub	.35
838	Bruce Sutter	.50
839	Don Sutton	1.25
840	Steve Swisher	.10
841	Frank Tanana	.20
842	Gene Tenace	.10
844	Dickie Thon	.10
845	Bill Travers	.10
847	John Urrea	.10
848	Mike Vail	.10
849	Ellis Valentine	.10
850	Fernando Valenzuela	4.50
851	Pete Vuckovich	.10
852	Mark Wagner	.10
853	Bob Walk	.10
854	Claudell Washington	.10
855	Dave Winfield	2.75
857	Richie Zisk	.15

1982 DONRUSS

The Memphis company showed a number of improvements in its second full set of baseball cards. There were marked upgrades in the quality of photography and reproduction, as well as statistical content, but the 1982 Donruss set was not distributed in gum packs. Due to a federal court ruling that Topps held the exclusive right to market baseball cards with confectionary products, Donruss created a 63-piece Babe Ruth puzzle as a substitute. Each wax pack contained three puzzle pieces. The new set was increased to 660 cards, and contains the first series of paintings, called Diamond Kings, that depict one star from each team. These are shown in the lists that follow with the abbreviation "DK" following the player name. Rookie cards of Cal Ripken, Jr., Steve Sax, and Kent Hrbek also enrich the set.

405 Cal Ripken, Jr.

54 Jorge Bell

		MINT
Complete set		**$38.00**
Commons		**.06**

1	Pete Rose (DK)	$1.50
2	Gary Carter (DK)	.50
3	Steve Garvey (DK)	.50
4	Vida Blue (DK)	.15
5	Alan Trammel (DK) (incorrect spelling)	1.50
5	Alan Trammell (DK) (correct spelling)	.40
6	Len Barker (DK)	.08
7	*Dwight Evans (DK)	.15
8	Rod Carew (DK)	.50
9	George Hendrick (DK)	.10
10	Phil Niekro (DK)	.35
11	Richie Zisk (DK)	.08
12	Dave Parker (DK)	.30
13	Nolan Ryan (DK)	1.00
14	Ivan DeJesus (DK)	.08
15	George Brett (DK)	.75
16	Tom Seaver (DK)	.50
17	Dave Kingman (DK)	.15
18	Dave Winfield (DK)	.50
19	Mike Norris (DK)	.10
20	Carlton Fisk (DK)	.25
21	Ozzie Smith (DK)	.25
22	Roy Smalley (DK)	.08
23	Buddy Bell (DK)	.10
24	Ken Singleton (DK)	.10
25	John Mayberry (DK)	.08
26	Gorman Thomas (DK)	.10
27	Earl Weaver	.10
28	Rollie Fingers	.20
29	Sparky Anderson	.10
30	Dennis Eckersley	.12
31	Dave Winfield	.50
32	Burt Hooton	.08
34	George Brett	.75
36	Steve Rogers	.08
40	George Hendrick	.08
42	Steve Carlton	.50
46	Jack Clark	.25
47	Chris Chambliss	.08
49	Lee Mazzilli	.08
52	Dave Stieb	.10
54	*Jorge Bell* (FC)	8.00

56	Rusty Staub	.10
58	Claudell Washington (FC)	.10
63	Larry Bowa	.15
68	Woodie Fryman	.10
70	Amos Otis	.08
72	Toby Harrah	.08
73	*Dave Righetti* (FC)	2.00
74	Carl Yastrzemski	.85
75	Bob Welch	.12
76	Alan Trammel (incorrect spelling)	1.25
76	Alan Trammell (correct spelling)	.40
77	Rick Dempsey	.08
78	Paul Molitor	.20
82	Carney Lansford	.10
84	Steve Garvey	.50
86	John Wathan	.08
88	Andre Dawson	.35
90	Bobby Grich	.10
91	Bob Forsch	.08
94	Ozzie Smith	.20
95	Dave Parker	.30

96	Doyle Alexander	.10
97	Al Hrabosky	.08
100	Floyd Bannister	.10
101	Alfredo Griffin	.08
103	Mario Soto	.08
105	Ken Singleton	.10
106	Ted Simmons	.10
107	Jack Morris	.30
108	Bob Watson	.08
109	*Dwight Evans	.15
110	Tom Lasorda	.10
111	Bert Blyleven	.15
112	Dan Quisenberry	.15
113	Rickey Henderson	2.25
114	Gary Carter	.35
115	Brian Downing	.10
116	Al Oliver	.15
118	Cesar Cedeno	.10
119	Keith Moreland	.08
121	Terry Kennedy	.08
124	Tony Pena (FC)	.20
127	Richie Zisk	.08
128	*Mike Scott	.15
129	Lloyd Moseby (FC)	.20
132	Gorman Thomas	.10
133	Dan Petry	.08
135	Lou Piniella	.10
136	Pedro Guerrero	.40
137	Len Barker	.08
140	*Tim Wallach* (FC)	1.50
141	Gene Mauch	.08
148	Tom Seaver	.65
151	Leon Durham	.08
152	Gene Tenace	.08
153	Al Bumbry	.06
157	Rick Reuschel	.10
158	Steve Howe	.08

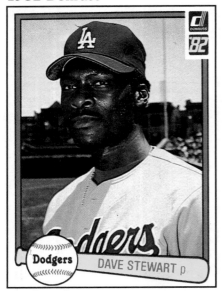

410 Dave Stewart

162	Bill Gullickson	.08
165	Ron LeFlore	.08
167	Joe Niekro	.10
168	Pete Rose	1.00
169	Dave Collins	.08
170	Rick Wise	.08
172	Larry Herndon	.08
173	Bob Horner	.15
175	Mookie Wilson	.10
182	Dave Kingman	.15
189	*Sparky Lyle	.10
190	Whitey Herzog	.08
191	Dave Smith	.10
193	Greg Luzinski	.15
194	Bill Lee	.08
196	Hal McRae	.12
200	Jim Rice	.35
209	Bucky Dent	.10
210	Ron Cey	.10
214	Tim Raines	1.00
215	Jon Matlack	.08
216	Rod Carew	.50
217	*Jim Kaat	.15
221	Mike Easler	.08
222	Vida Blue	.10
225	Jody Davis (FC)	.25
231	Jim Palmer	.40
232	Bob Rodgers	.08
235	Mike Torrez	.08
237	Von Hayes (FC)	1.00
239	Dwayne Murphy	.08
242	Mickey Rivers	.08
244	Jose Cruz	.10
245	Manny Trillo	.08
248	Dan Driessen	.08
252	Lee Smith (FC)	.75
258	Cecil Cooper	.10
260	John Tudor	.15
262	Jay Johnstone	.08
263	Bo Diaz	.08
264	Dennis Leonard	.08
268	Jim Sundberg	.08
274	George Foster	.20

275	Brett Butler (FC)	.85
278	Keith Hernandez	.40
279	Doug DeCinces	.10
281	Lance Parrish	.35
282	Ralph Houk	.08
283	Rich Gossage	.20
284	Jerry Reuss	.10
286	Frank White	.10
291	Chet Lemon	.08
294	Mike Schmidt	1.00
297	John Candelaria	.10
299	Dale Murphy	.90
306	John Mayberry	.08
311	Kent Tekulve	.08
312	*Joe Morgan	.45
319	Tony LaRussa	.08
320	Charlie Lea	.08
324	Andre Thornton	.10
326	Frank Tanana	.10
327	Davey Lopes	.10
329	Mike Flanagan	.10
331	Scott McGregor	.08
335	Graig Nettles	.15
336	Dusty Baker	.10
340	Warren Cromartie	.06
341	Steve Comer	.06
342	Rick Burleson	.08
343	John Martin	.06
344	Craig Reynolds	.06
345	Mike Proly	.06
346	Ruppert Jones	.06
347	Omar Moreno	.06
348	Greg Minton	.06
349	Rick Mahler (FC)	.15
350	Alex Trevino	.06
351	Mike Krukow	.08
352	Shane Rawley (photo is Jim Anderson, shaking hands)	1.25
352	Shane Rawley (Shane Rawley, kneeling)	.15
353	Garth Iorg	.06
354	Pete Mackanin	.06

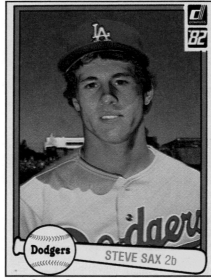

624 Steve Sax

557 Kent Hrbek

355	Paul Moskau	.06
356	Richard Dotson	.08
357	Steve Stone	.08
358	Larry Hisle	.08
359	Aurelio Lopez	.08
360	Oscar Gamble	.08
361	Tom Burgmeier	.06
362	Terry Forster	.08
363	Joe Charboneau	.08
364	Ken Brett	.08
365	Tony Armas	.10
366	Chris Speier	.06
367	Fred Lynn	.20
368	Buddy Bell	.12
369	Jim Essian	.06
370	Terry Puhl	.06
371	Greg Gross	.06
372	*Bruce Sutter	.15
373	Joe Lefebvre	.06
374	Ray Knight	.10
375	Bruce Benedict	.06
376	Tim Foli	.06
377	Al Holland	.06
378	Ken Kravec	.06
379	Jeff Burroughs	.06
380	Pete Falcone	.06
381	Ernie Whitt	.08
382	Brad Havens	.06
383	Terry Crowley	.06
384	Don Money	.06
385	Dan Schatzeder	.06
386	Gary Allenson	.06
387	Yogi Berra	.15
388	Ken Landreaux	.06
389	Mike Hargrove	.06
390	Darryl Motley	.06
391	Dave McKay	.06
392	Stan Bahnsen	.06
393	Ken Forsch	.06
394	Mario Mendoza	.06
395	Jim Morrison	.06
396	Mike Ivie	.06
397	Broderick Perkins	.06

398	Darrell Evans	.15
399	Ron Reed	.08
400	Johnny Bench	.65
401	*Steve Bedrosian* (FC)	.80
402	Bill Robinson	.06
403	Bill Buckner	.12
404	Ken Oberkfell	.06
405	*Cal Ripken, Jr.* (FC)	9.00
406	Jim Gantner	.08
407	Kirk Gibson (FC)	1.50
408	Tony Perez	.20
409	Tommy John	.20
410	*Dave Stewart* (FC)	3.50
411	Dan Spillner	.06
412	Willie Aikens	.06
413	Mike Heath	.06
414	Ray Burris	.06
415	Leon Roberts	.06
416	*Mike Witt* (FC)	.75
417	Bobby Molinaro	.06
418	Steve Braun	.06
419	Nolan Ryan	.85
420	Tug McGraw	.12
421	Dave Concepcion	.12
422	Juan Eichelberger (photo is Gary Lucas)	1.25
422	Juan Eichelberger (correct photo)	.15
423	Rick Rhoden	.10
424	Frank Robinson	.12
425	Eddie Miller	.06
426	Bill Caudill	.06
427	Doug Flynn	.06
428	*Larry Anderson* (Andersen) (FC)	.10
429	Al Williams	.06
430	Jerry Garvin	.06
431	Glenn Adams	.06
432	Barry Bonnell	.06
433	Jerry Narron	.06
434	John Stearns	.06
435	Mike Tyson	.06
436	Glenn Hubbard	.06

73 Dave Righetti

437	Eddie Solomon	.06
438	Jeff Leonard	.10
439	Randy Bass	.06
440	Mike LaCoss	.06
441	Gary Matthews	.10
442	Mark Littell	.06
443	Don Sutton	.30
444	John Harris	.06
445	*Vada Pinson	.08
446	Elias Sosa	.06
447	Charlie Hough	.10
448	Willie Wilson	.15
449	Fred Stanley	.06
450	Tom Veryzer	.06
451	Ron Davis	.06
452	Mark Clear	.06
453	Bill Russell	.08
454	Lou Whitaker	.45
455	Dan Graham	.06
456	Reggie Cleveland	.06
457	Sammy Stewart	.06
458	Pete Vuckovich	.08
459	John Wockenfuss	.06
460	Glenn Hoffman	.06
461	Willie Randolph	.10
462	Fernando Valenzuela (FC)	.75
463	Ron Hassey	.06
464	Paul Splittorff	.06
465	Rob Picciolo	.06
466	Larry Parrish	.10
467	Johnny Grubb	.06
468	Dan Ford	.06
469	Silvio Martinez	.06
470	Kiko Garcia	.06
471	*Bob Boone	.10
472	Luis Salazar	.08
473	Randy Niemann	.06
474	Tom Griffin	.06
475	Phil Niekro	.30
476	Hubie Brooks (FC)	.25
477	Dick Tidrow	.06
479	Damaso Garcia	.06
480	Mickey Hatcher	.08

481	Joe Price	.06
482	Ed Farmer	.06
483	Eddie Murray	.65
484	Ben Oglivie	.08
485	Kevin Saucier	.06
486	Bobby Murcer	.10
487	Bill Campbell	.06
488	Reggie Smith	.10
489	Wayne Garland	.06
490	Jim Wright	.06
491	*Billy Martin	.12
492	Jim Fanning	.06
493	Don Baylor	.12
494	Rick Honeycutt	.06
495	Carlton Fisk	.50
496	Denny Walling	.06
497	Bake McBride	.06
498	Darrell Porter	.08
499	Gene Richards	.06
500	Ron Oester	.06
501	*Ken Dayley* (FC)	.15
502	Jason Thompson	.06
503	Milt May	.06
504	Doug Bird	.06
505	Bruce Bochte	.06
506	Neil Allen	.06
507	Joey McLaughlin	.06
508	Butch Wynegar	.06
509	Gary Roenicke	.06
510	Robin Yount	1.50
511	Dave Tobik	.06
512	*Rich Gedman* (FC)	.25
513	*Gene Nelson* (FC)	.10
514	Rick Monday	.10
515	Miguel Dilone	.06
516	Clint Hurdle	.06
517	Jeff Newman	.06
518	Grant Jackson	.06
519	Andy Hassler	.06
520	Pat Putnam	.06
521	Greg Pryor	.06
522	Tony Scott	.06
523	Steve Mura	.06

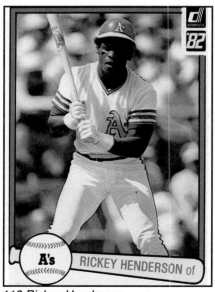

113 Rickey Henderson

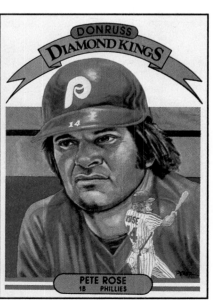

1 Pete Rose (DK)

155

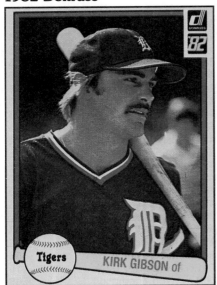

407 Kirk Gibson

524	Johnnie LeMaster	.06
525	Dick Ruthven	.06
527	Larry McWilliams	.06
528	*Johnny Ray* (FC)	.75
529	*Pat Tabler* (FC)	.60
530	Tom Herr	.10
531	San Diego Chicken (with trademark symbol on front)	1.25
531	San Diego Chicken (w/o trademark symbol)	.50
532	Sal Butera	.06
533	Mike Griffin	.06
534	Kelvin Moore	.06
535	Reggie Jackson	.65
536	Ed Romero	.06
537	Derrel Thomas	.06
540	*Bob Ojeda* (FC)	.40
541	Roy Lee Jackson	.06
542	Lynn Jones	.06
543	Gaylord Perry	.35
544	Phil Garner (photo is backward)	1.25
544	Phil Garner (correct photo)	.15
545	Garry Templeton	.10
546	Rafael Ramirez (FC)	.10
547	Jeff Reardon	.20
548	Ron Guidry	.25
549	*Tim Laudner* (FC)	.15
550	John Henry Johnson	.06
551	Chris Bando	.06
552	Bobby Brown	.06
553	Larry Bradford	.06
554	*Scott Fletcher* (FC)	.30
555	Jerry Royster	.06
556	Shooty Babbitt	.06
557	*Kent Hrbek* (FC)	3.00
558	Yankee Winners (Ron Guidry, Tommy John)	.15
559	Mark Bomback	.06
561	Buck Martinez	.06
562	*Mike Marshall* (FC)	1.50
563	Rennie Stennett	.06

564	Steve Crawford	.06
565	Bob Babcock	.06
566	Johnny Podres	.08
568	Harold Baines (FC)	.75
569	Dave LaRoche	.06
570	Lee May	.08
571	Gary Ward (FC)	.10
572	John Denny	.06
573	Roy Smalley	.06
574	*Bob Brenly* (FC)	.20
575	Bronx Bombers (Reggie Jackson, Dave Winfield)	.45
577	Butch Hobson	.06
578	Harvey Kuenn	.08
579	Cal Ripken, Sr.	.08
580	Juan Berenguer	.08
581	Benny Ayala	.06
582	Vance Law (FC)	.15
583	*Rich Leach* (FC)	.10
584	George Frazier	.06
585	Phillies Finest (Pete Rose, Mike Schmidt)	.75
586	Joe Rudi	.10
587	Juan Beniquez	.06
588	*Luis DeLeon* (FC)	.08
589	Craig Swan	.06
591	Billy Gardner	.06
592	Sal Bando	.08
593	Bert Campaneris	.10
594	Steve Kemp	.08
595	Randy Lerch (Braves)	1.25
595	Randy Lerch (Brewers)	.08
597	Dave Ford	.06
598	Mike Scioscia (FC)	.20
599	John Lowenstein	.06
600	Rene Lachmann (Lachemann)	.06
601	Mick Kelleher	.06
602	Ron Jackson	.06
603	Jerry Koosman	.10
604	Dave Goltz	.08
605	Ellis Valentine	.06
606	*Lonnie Smith	.08

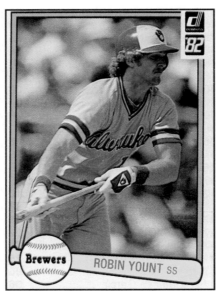

510 Robin Yount

13 Nolan Ryan (DK)

607	Joaquin Andujar	.08
610	Bob Bonner	.06
611	Jim Dwyer	.06
612	Terry Bulling	.06
613	Joel Youngblood	.06
614	Larry Milbourne	.06
615	Phil Roof (Gene)	.06
617	Dave Rosello	.06
619	Dennis Lamp	.06
620	Sid Monge	.06
621	Jerry White	.06
622	*Luis Aguayo* (FC)	.10
623	Jamie Easterly	.06
624	*Steve Sax* (FC)	3.00
625	Dave Roberts	.06
626	Rick Bosetti	.06
627	Terry Francona (FC)	.10
628	*Pride of the Reds (Johnny Bench, Tom Seaver)	.35
629	Paul Mirabella	.06
630	Rance Mulliniks	.06
631	Kevin Hickey	.06
633	Dave Geisel	.06
634	Ken Griffey	.10
635	Bob Lemon	.10
636	Orlando Sanchez	.06
637	Bill Almon	.06
638	*Danny Ainge	.12
639	Willie Stargell	.45
640	Bob Sykes	.06
641	Ed Lynch	.06
642	John Ellis	.06
643	Fergie Jenkins	.15
645	Julio Gonzales	.06
646	Jesse Orosco (FC)	.20
648	Tommy Davis	.08
650	Felipe Alou	.08
651	Harvey Haddix	.08
652	Willie Upshaw (FC)	.15
653	Bill Madlock	.15
—	Checklist 1-26 Diamond Kings (5 spelled Trammell)	.08

1982 FLEER

After a triumphant debut into the baseball card world in 1981, Fleer's 1982 set of 660 cards paled in comparison. It featured many fuzzy photographs and was full of errors, only some of which were corrected. Some skeptics feel that the company purposely botched many cards just to sell more product. The hottest error card is number 576, which (due to a flipped negative) shows righty John Littlefield pitching left-handed, while Cal Ripken, Jr., is the set's biggest rookie-card draw. Due to a court ruling in favor of Topps, Fleer was prevented from issuing bubble gum in wax packs. The company distributed team logo stickers instead, which aren't considered collectibles by most hobbyists.

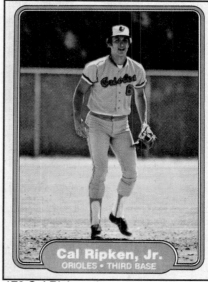

176 Cal Ripken, Jr.

438 Al Hrabosky

		MINT
Complete set		**$39.00**
Commons		**.06**

1	Dusty Baker	$ .10
2	Robert Castillo	.06
3	Ron Cey	.10
4	Terry Forster	.08
5	Steve Garvey	.50
6	Dave Goltz	.08
7	Pedro Guerrero (FC)	.75
8	Burt Hooton	.08
9	Steve Howe	.08
10	Jay Johnstone	.10
11	Ken Landreaux	.06
12	Davey Lopes	.10
13	*Mike Marshall* (FC)	1.50
14	Bobby Mitchell	.06
15	Rick Monday	.10
16	*Tom Niedenfuer* (FC)	.20
17	*Ted Power* (FC)	.20
18	Jerry Reuss	.10
19	Ron Roenicke	.06
20	Bill Russell	.08
21	*Steve Sax* (FC)	3.00
22	Mike Scioscia	.08
23	Reggie Smith	.10
24	*Dave Stewart* (FC)	3.00
25	Rick Sutcliffe	.15
26	Derrel Thomas	.06
27	Fernando Valenzuela	.60
28	Bob Welch	.15
29	Steve Yeager	.06
30	Bobby Brown	.06
31	Rick Cerone	.06
32	Ron Davis	.06
33	Bucky Dent	.10
34	Barry Foote	.06
35	George Frazier	.06
36	Oscar Gamble	.08
37	Rich Gossage	.20
38	Ron Guidry	.25
39	Reggie Jackson	.60
40	Tommy John	.20
41	Rudy May	.06
42	Larry Milbourne	.06
43	Jerry Mumphrey	.06
44	Bobby Murcer	.10
45	*Gene Nelson*	.12
46	Graig Nettles	.15

47	Johnny Oates	.06
48	Lou Piniella	.15
49	Willie Randolph	.10
50	Rick Reuschel	.10
51	Dave Revering	.06
52	*Dave Righetti* (FC)	2.25
53	Aurelio Rodriguez	.08
54	Bob Watson	.08
55	Dennis Werth	.06
56	Dave Winfield	.50
57	Johnny Bench	.60
58	Bruce Berenyi	.06
59	Larry Biittner	.06
60	Scott Brown	.06
61	Dave Collins	.08
62	Geoff Combe	.06
63	Dave Concepcion	.10
64	Dan Driessen	.08
65	Joe Edelen	.06
66	George Foster	.20
67	Ken Griffey	.15
68	Paul Householder	.06
69	Tom Hume	.06
70	Junior Kennedy	.06
71	Ray Knight	.10

72	Mike LaCoss	.06
73	Rafael Landestoy	.06
74	Charlie Leibrandt	.10
75	Sam Mejias	.06
76	Paul Moskau	.06
77	Joe Nolan	.06
78	Mike O'Berry	.06
79	Ron Oester	.06
80	Frank Pastore	.06
81	Joe Price	.06
82	Tom Seaver	.60
83	Mario Soto	.08
84	Mike Vail	.06
85	Tony Armas	.10
86	Shooty Babitt	.06
87	Dave Beard	.06
88	Rick Bosetti	.06
89	Keith Drumright	.06
90	Wayne Gross	.06
91	Mike Heath	.06
92	Rickey Henderson	1.00
93	Cliff Johnson	.06
94	Jeff Jones	.06
95	Matt Keough	.06
96	Brian Kingman	.06
97	Mickey Klutts	.06
98	Rick Langford	.06
99	Steve McCatty	.06
100	Dave McKay	.06
101	Dwayne Murphy	.06
102	Jeff Newman	.06
103	Mike Norris	.06
104	Bob Owchinko	.06
105	Mitchell Page	.06
106	Rob Picciolo	.06
107	Jim Spencer	.06
108	Fred Stanley	.06

609 Jorge Bell

109	Tom Underwood	.06
110	Joaquin Andujar	.06
111	Steve Braun	.06
112	Bob Forsch	.08
113	George Hendrick	.08
114	Keith Hernandez	.40
115	Tom Herr	.10
116	Dane Iorg	.06
117	*Jim Kaat	.20
118	Tito Landrum	.06
119	Sixto Lezcano	.06
120	Mark Littell	.08
121	John Martin	.06
122	Silvio Martinez	.06
123	Ken Oberkfell	.06
124	Darrell Porter	.08
125	Mike Ramsey	.06
126	Orlando Sanchez	.06
127	Bob Shirley	.06
128	Lary Sorensen	.06
129	*Bruce Sutter	.15
130	Bob Sykes	.06
131	Garry Templeton	.10
132	Gene Tenace	.08
133	Jerry Augustine	.08
134	Sal Bando	.08
135	Mark Brouhard	.06
136	Mike Caldwell	.06
137	Reggie Cleveland	.06
138	Cecil Cooper	.15
139	Jamie Easterly	.06
140	Marshall Edwards	.06
141	*Rollie Fingers	.25
142	Jim Gantner	.08
143	Moose Haas	.06
144	Larry Hisle	.06
145	Roy Howell	.06
146	Rickey Keeton	.06
147	Randy Lerch	.06
148	Paul Molitor	.25
149	Don Money	.06
150	Charlie Moore	.06
151	Ben Oglivie	.08

152	Ted Simmons	.15
153	Jim Slaton	.06
154	Gorman Thomas	.10
155	Robin Yount	1.25
156	Pete Vukovich	.08
157	Benny Ayala	.06
158	Mark Belanger	.08
159	Al Bumbry	.06
160	Terry Crowley	.06
161	Rich Dauer	.06
162	Doug DeCinces	.10
163	Rick Dempsey	.08
164	Jim Dwyer	.06
165	Mike Flanagan	.08
166	Dave Ford	.06
167	Dan Graham	.06
168	Wayne Krenchicki	.06
169	John Lowenstein	.06
170	Dennis Martinez	.08
171	Tippy Martinez	.06
172	Scott McGregor	.06
173	Jose Morales	.06
174	Eddie Murray	.60
175	Jim Palmer	.40
176	*Cal Ripken, Jr.* (FC)	9.00
177	Gary Roenicke	.06
178	Lenn Sakata	.06
179	Ken Singleton	.10
180	Sammy Stewart	.06
181	Tim Stoddard	.06
182	Steve Stone	.08
183	Stan Bahnsen	.06
184	Ray Burris	.06
185	Gary Carter	.35
186	Warren Cromartie	.06
187	Andre Dawson	.35
188	*Terry Francona* (FC)	.10
189	Woodie Fryman	.08
190	Bill Gullickson	.06
191	Grant Jackson	.06
192	Wallace Johnson	.06
193	Charlie Lea	.08
194	Bill Lee	.08

21 Steve Sax

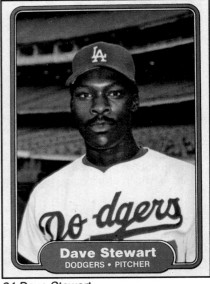

24 Dave Stewart

195	Jerry Manuel	.06
196	Brad Mills	.06
197	John Milner	.06
198	Rowland Office	.06
199	David Palmer	.06
200	Larry Parrish	.10
201	Mike Phillips	.06
202	Tim Raines	1.00
203	Bobby Ramos	.06
204	Jeff Reardon	.20
205	Steve Rogers	.08
206	Scott Sanderson	.06
207	Rodney Scott (photo of Tim Raines)	.10
208	Elias Sosa	.06
209	Chris Speier	.06
210	*Tim Wallach* (FC)	1.50
211	Jerry White	.06
212	Alan Ashby	.06
213	Cesar Cedeno	.12
214	Jose Cruz	.15
215	Kiko Garcia	.06
216	Phil Garner	.08
217	Danny Heep	.06
218	Art Howe	.06
219	Bob Knepper	.06
220	Frank LaCorte	.06
221	Joe Niekro	.15
222	Joe Pittman	.06
223	Terry Puhl	.06
224	Luis Pujols	.06
225	Craig Reynolds	.06
226	J.R. Richard	.10
227	Dave Roberts	.06
228	Vern Ruhle	.06
229	Nolan Ryan	2.00
230	Joe Sambito	.06
231	Tony Scott	.06
232	Dave Smith	.10
233	Harry Spilman	.06
234	Don Sutton	.30
235	Dickie Thon	.08
236	Denny Walling	.08

237	Gary Woods	.06
238	*Luis Aguayo* (FC)	.10
239	Ramos Aviles	.06
240	*Bob Boone	.10
241	Larry Bowa	.15
242	Warren Brusstar	.06
243	Steve Carlton	.50
244	Larry Christenson	.06
245	Dick Davis	.06
247	Greg Gross	.08
248	*Sparky Lyle	.10
249	Garry Maddox	.10
250	Bake McBride	.06
251	Tug McGraw	.15
252	Keith Moreland	.06
253	Dickie Noles	.06
254	Mike Proly	.06
255	Ron Reed	.06
256	Pete Rose	1.00
257	Dick Ruthven	.06
258	Mike Schmidt	1.50
259	Lonnie Smith	.10
260	Manny Trillo	.08
261	Del Unser	.06
262	George Vukovich	.06
263	Tom Brookens	.08
264	George Capuzzello	.06
265	Marty Castillo	.06
266	Al Cowens	.06
267	Kirk Gibson	.75
268	Richie Hebner	.06
269	Ron Jackson	.06
270	Lynn Jones	.06
271	Steve Kemp	.10
272	*Rick Leach* (FC)	.10
273	Aurelio Lopez	.06
274	Jack Morris	.30
275	Kevin Saucier	.06
276	Lance Parrish	.35
277	Rick Peters	.06
278	Dan Petry	.06
279	David Rozema	.06
280	Stan Papi	.06

![Mike Marshall card]

13 Mike Marshall

281	Dan Schatzeder	.06
282	Champ Summers	.06
283	Alan Trammell	.40
284	Lou Whitaker	.06
285	Milt Wilcox	.06
286	John Wockenfuss	.06
287	Gary Allenson	.06
288	Tom Burgmeier	.06
289	Bill Campbell	.06
290	Mark Clear	.06
291	Steve Crawford	.06
292	Dennis Eckersley	.15
293	*Dwight Evans	.20
294	*Rich Gedman* (FC)	.20
295	Garry Hancock	.06
296	Glenn Hoffman	.06
297	Bruce Hurst (FC)	.35
298	Carney Lansford	.10
299	Rick Miller	.06
300	Reid Nichols	.06
301	*Bob Ojeda* (FC)	.35
302	Tony Perez	.25
303	Chuck Rainey	.06
304	Jerry Remy	.06
305	Jim Rice	.40
306	Joe Rudi	.10
307	Bob Stanley	.06
308	Dave Stapleton	.08
309	Frank Tanana	.10
310	Mike Torrez	.10
311	John Tudor (FC)	.25
312	Carl Yastrzemski	.85
313	Buddy Bell	.12
314	Steve Comer	.06
315	Danny Darwin	.06
316	John Ellis	.06
317	John Grubb	.06
318	Rick Honeycutt	.06
319	Charlie Hough	.10
320	Ferguson Jenkins	.15
321	John Henry Johnson	.06
322	Jim Kern	.06
323	Jon Matlack	.08

324	Doc Medich	.06
325	Mario Mendoza	.06
326	Al Oliver	.15
327	Pat Putnam	.06
328	Mickey Rivers	.08
329	Leon Roberts	.06
330	Billy Sample	.06
331	Bill Stein	.06
332	Jim Sundberg	.08
333	Mark Wagner	.06
334	Bump Wills	.06
335	Bill Almon	.06
336	Harold Baines	.35
337	Ross Baumgarten	.06
338	Tony Bernazard	.06
339	Britt Burns	.06
340	Richard Dotson	.08
341	Jim Essian	.06
342	Ed Farmer	.06
343	Carlton Fisk	.40
344	Kevin Hickey	.06
345	Lamarr Hoyt (LaMarr)	.06
346	Lamar Johnson	.06
347	Jerry Koosman	.06
348	Rusty Kuntz	.06
349	Dennis Lamp	.06
350	Ron LeFlore	.08
351	Chet Lemon	.08
352	Greg Luzinski	.15
353	Bob Molinaro	.06
354	Jim Morrison	.06
355	Wayne Nordhagen	.06
356	Greg Pryor	.06
357	Mike Squires	.06
358	Steve Trout	.06
359	Alan Bannister	.06
360	Len Barker	.08
361	Bert Blyleven	.12
362	Joe Charboneau	.08
363	John Denny	.06
364	Bo Diaz	.08
365	Miguel Dilone	.06
366	Jerry Dybzinski	.06

![Dave Righetti card]

52 Dave Righetti

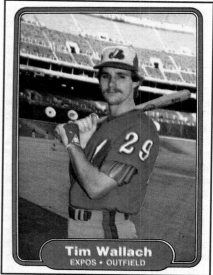

210 Tim Wallach

258 Mike Schmidt

367	Wayne Garland	.06
368	Mike Hargrove	.06
369	Toby Harrah	.08
370	Ron Hassey	.06
371	*Von Hayes* (FC)	1.00
372	Pat Kelly	.06
373	Duane Kuiper	.06
374	Rick Manning	.06
375	Sid Monge	.06
376	Jorge Orta	.06
377	Dave Rosello	.06
378	Dan Spillner	.06
379	Mike Stanton	.06
380	Andre Thornton	.10
381	Tom Veryzer	.06
382	Rick Waits	.06
383	Doyle Alexander	.10
384	Vida Blue	.12
385	Fred Breining	.06
386	Enos Cabell	.06
387	Jack Clark	.25
388	Darrell Evans	.15
389	Tom Griffin	.06
390	Larry Herndon	.08
391	Al Holland	.06
392	Gary Lavelle	.06
393	Johnnie LeMaster	.06
394	Jerry Martin	.06
395	Milt May	.06
396	Greg Minton	.06
397	*Joe Morgan	.50
398	Joe Pettini	.06
399	Alan Ripley	.06
400	Billy Smith	.06
402	Ed Whitson	.06
404	Willie Aikens	.06
405	George Brett	.75
406	Ken Brett	.08
407	Dave Chalk	.06
408	Rich Gale	.06
409	Cesar Geronimo	.06
410	Larry Gura	.06
411	Clint Hurdle	.06

412	Mike Jones	.06
413	Dennis Leonard	.08
415	Lee May	.08
416	Hal McRae	.15
419	Amos Otis	.10
420	Ken Phelps (FC)	.50
422	Dan Quisenberry	.15
425	John Wathan	.08
426	*Frank White	.10
427	Willie Wilson	.10
436	Bob Horner	.10
437	Glenn Hubbard	.08
438	Al Hrabosky (All Hrabosky, 5'1" on back)	20.00
438	Al Hrabosky (Al Hrabosky, 5'1" on back)	1.25
438	Al Hrabosky (Al Hrabosky, 5'10" on back)	.35
440	*Rick Mahler* (FC)	.20
443	Dale Murphy	.90
444	Phil Niekro	.30
445	Gaylord Perry	.30
451	Don Baylor	.15
453	Rick Burleson	.08
454	Bert Campaneris	.10
455	Rod Carew	.50
457	Brian Downing	.10
461	Bobby Grich	.10
468	Fred Lynn	.20
473	*Mike Witt* (FC)	.65
484	Vance Law (FC)	.15
485	Bill Madlock	.15
489	Dave Parker	.30
490	Tony Pena (FC)	.25
491	Pascual Perez (FC)	.15
492	*Johnny Ray* (FC)	.75
493	Rick Rhoden	.10
499	Willie Stargell	.40
500	Kent Tekulve	.10
504	Floyd Bannister	.10
517	Shane Rawley	.08
522	Hubie Brooks (FC)	.25
530	Dave Kingman	.15

155 Robin Yount

27 Fernando Valenzuela

532	Mike Marshall	.10
535	Mike Scott (FC)	.50
536	Rusty Staub	.10
542	Mookie Wilson (FC)	.15
555	Darrell Jackson (black cap on front)	1.00
555	Darrell Jackson (red cap, no emblem)	.25
555	Darrell Jackson (red cap with emblem)	.10
576	John Littlefield (pitching left-handed)	150.00
576	John Littlefield (correct photo)	.08
588	Bobby Bonds	.10
589	Bill Buckner	.12
592	*Jody Davis* (FC)	.20
603	*Lee Smith* (FC)	.65
608	Danny Ainge	.12
609	*Jorge Bell* (FC)	8.00
621	Lloyd Moseby	.12
622	Dave Stieb	.12
624	Willie Upshaw (FC)	.15
626	Ernie Whitt	.08
628	1981 AS Game	.10
629	AS Infielders (Bucky Dent, Frank White)	.10
630	Big Red Machine (Dave Concepcion, Dan Driessen, George Foster)	.15
631	Top NL Relief Pitcher (Bruce Sutter)	.15
632	Steve and Carlton (Steve Carlton, Carlton Fisk)	.25
633	3000th Game, May 25, 1981 (Carl Yastrzemski)	.35
634	Dynamic Duo (Johnny Bench, Tom Seaver)	.35
635	West Meets East (Gary Carter, Fernando Valenzuela)	.30

| 636 | NL SO King (Fernando Valenzuela) .50 | 640 | Pete & Re-Pete (Pete Rose, Pete Rose Jr.) **1.50** | 644 | Most Saves 1981 AL (Rollie Fingers) .15 |

636 NL SO King (Fernando Valenzuela) .... .50

637 '81 HR King (Mike Schmidt) . .50

638 NL All Stars (Gary Carter, Dave Parker) .... .25

639 Perfect Game (Len Barker, Bo Diaz) .... .08

640 Pete & Re-Pete (Pete Rose, Pete Rose Jr.) **1.50**

641 Phillies' Finest (Steve Carlton, Mike Schmidt, Lonnie Smith) .... .50

643 1981 Most Hits, Most Runs (Rickey Henderson) .... .35

644 Most Saves 1981 AL (Rollie Fingers) .... .15

645 Most 1981 Wins (Tom Seaver) .... .25

646 Yankee Powerhouse (Reggie Jackson, Dave Winfield) .... .65

1982 TOPPS

Topps produced its largest set ever—792 cards—in 1982. This eliminated double-printing, and allowed the new, larger set to be printed with an equal number of cards per press sheet (in six 132-card sheets). Collectors later found that the hobby was no longer flooded with certain cards. The 1982 set has a mediocre design with indistinct blue-and-green printing on card backs. Two variations in the 1982 set are hard to locate: George Foster All-Star, number 342, is found with and without the facsimile autograph, while Pascual Perez, number 383, sometimes does not have the word "Pitcher" printed at the lower left.

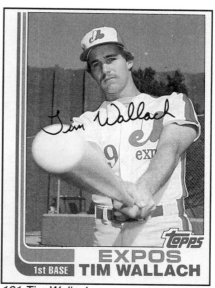

191 Tim Wallach

		MINT
Complete set		**$92.00**
Commons		.08

1 1981 Highlight (Steve Carlton) .... $ .50

2 1981 Highlight (Ron Davis) .... .08

3 1981 Highlight (Tim Raines) .... .30

4 1981 Highlight (Pete Rose) .... .70

5 1981 Highlight (Nolan Ryan) .... .30

6 1981 Highlight (Fernando Valenzuela) .... .30

9 Ron Guidry .... .35

10 Ron Guidry IA .... .15

14 Steve Howe .... .10

17 Darrell Evans .... .25

19 Ernie Whitt .... .10

20 Garry Maddox .... .10

21 Orioles FS (Bob Bonner, *Cal Ripken* (FC), Jeff Schneider) **16.00**

27 Tom Herr .... .10

29 Dwayne Murphy .... .10

30 Tom Seaver .... .70

31 Tom Seaver IA .... .30

36 Rangers Ldrs (George Medich, Al Oliver) .... .12

39 Lou Whitaker .... .40

40 Dave Parker .... .35

41 Dave Parker IA .... .15

47 Jeff Leonard .... .15

50 Buddy Bell .... .15

51 Cubs FS (*Jay Howell* (FC), Carlos Lezcano, Ty Waller) .... .40

52 *Larry Andersen* (FC) .... .10

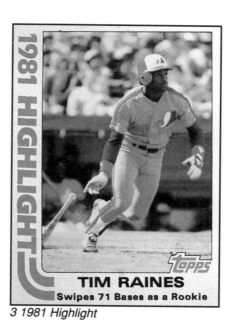

3 1981 Highlight

55 Rick Burleson .... .10

59 *Rich Gedman* (FC) .... .50

60 Tony Armas .... .12

65 Terry Kennedy .... .10

66 Astros Ldrs (Art Howe, Nolan Ryan) .... .25

70 Tim Raines 1.75

75 Tommy John .... .35

80 Jim Palmer .... .60

81 Jim Palmer IA .... .30

82 Bob Welch .... .20

83 Yankees FS (*Steve Balboni* (FC), Andy McGaffigan (FC), *Andre Robertson* (FC)) .... .50

90 Nolan Ryan 2.25

91 Carney Lansford .... .10

93 Larry Hisle .... .10

95 Ozzie Smith .... .40

96 Royals Ldrs (George Brett, Larry Gura) ... .35

100 Mike Schmidt 1.50

101 Mike Schmidt IA .... .70

105 Kirk Gibson 1.25

110 Carlton Fisk .... .50

111 Carlton Fisk IA .... .15

115 Gaylord Perry .... .40

118 Expos FS (*Terry Francona*, Brad Mills, Bryn Smith (FC)) .... .25

125 *Danny Ainge .... .20

126 Braves Ldrs (Rick Mahler, Claudell Washington) .... .10

127 Lonnie Smith .... .10

129 Checklist 1-132 .... .12

132 Lee May .... .10

138 Tony Pena .... .20

140 Ron LeFlore .... .10

141 Indians FS (Chris Bando, Tom Brennan, *Von Hayes* (FC)) 1.50

21 Orioles Future Stars

143	Mookie Wilson	.10
145	Bob Horner	.20
150	Ted Simmons	.20
156	A's Ldrs (Rickey Henderson, Steve McCatty)	.25
158	Brian Downing	.10
160	Luis Tiant	.15
161	Batting Ldrs (Carney Lansford, Bill Madlock)	.20
162	HR Ldrs (Tony Armas, Dwight Evans, Bobby Grich, Eddie Murray, Mike Schmidt)	.35
163	RBI Ldrs (Eddie Murray, Mike Schmidt)	.40
164	SB Ldrs (Rickey Henderson, Tim Raines)	.35
165	Victory Ldrs (Denny Martinez, Steve McCatty, Jack Morris, Tom Seaver, Pete Vuckovich)	.20
166	SO Ldrs (Len Barker, Fernando Valenzuela)	.20
167	ERA Ldrs (Steve McCatty, Nolan Ryan)	.20
168	Leading Relievers (Rollie Fingers, Bruce Sutter)	.20
169	Charlie Leibrandt	.10
171	Giants FS (*Bob Brenly* (FC), *Chili Davis* (FC), Bob Tufts)	1.25
172	Bill Gullickson	.10
179	Steve Garvey	.85
180	Steve Garvey IA	.40
185	Phil Niekro	.50
186	Cardinals Ldrs (Bob Forsch, Keith Hernandez)	.25
190	J.R. Richard	.12
191	*Tim Wallach* (FC)	2.00
195	Paul Molitor	.25
196	Willie Upshaw	.10
197	Shane Rawley	.10
200	George Brett	1.50
201	George Brett IA	.75
203	Blue Jays FS (*Jesse Barfield* (FC), Brian Milner, Boomer Wells)	5.00

208	Bobby Murcer	.15
210	Keith Hernandez	.60
211	Dan Petry	.10
213	Dave Stewart (FC)	3.00
215	Mike Krukow	.10
216	White Sox Ldrs (Dennis Lamp, Chet Lemon)	.10
220	Manny Trillo	.10
223	Lloyd Moseby	.20
225	Mike Torrez	.10
226	Checklist 133-264	.12
230	Willie Wilson	.20
231	*Phillies FS (*Mark Davis* (FC), *Bob Dernier* (FC), *Ozzie Virgil*)	1.50
239	Jon Matlack	.10
240	Bucky Dent	.10
241	Bucky Dent IA	.10
246	Mets Ldrs (Hubie Brooks, Mike Scott)	.20
247	Pedro Guerrero	.75
250	Tug McGraw	.15
251	Fred Lynn	.30
252	Fred Lynn IA	.15
254	*Jorge Bell* (FC)	10.00
255	Tony Perez	.30
256	Tony Perez IA	.15
260	Bruce Sutter	.20
261	Tigers FS (Howard Bailey, Marty Castillo, Dave Rucker)	.08
264	Dan Quisenberry	.20
265	Al Bumbry	.10
266	Rick Leach	.10
270	Rusty Staub	.15
274	*Bob Ojeda* (FC)	.60
275	Bob Watson	.10
276	Angels Ldrs (Rod Carew, Ken Forsch)	.25
279	Bill Russell	.10
280	Ben Oglivie	.10
284	Bob Grich	.15
285	*Sparky Lyle	.12
288	Garry Templeton	.10
290	Ken Singleton	.10
291	Pirates FS (Vance Law, Bob Long, *Johnny Ray* (FC))	1.00

296	Bob Walk	.10
300	Reggie Jackson	1.00
301	Reggie Jackson IA	.50
305	Don Sutton	.50
306	Don Sutton IA	.25
311	Dodgers Ldrs (Dusty Baker, Burt Hooton)	.12
320	Chris Chambliss	.10
321	Chris Chambliss IA	.10
323	Bill Lee	.10
325	Jose Cruz	.15
332	Don Robinson	.10
333	Brewers FS (*Frank DiPino*, Marshall Edwards, Chuck Porter)	.12
334	Aurelio Rodriguez	.10
335	Jim Sundberg	.10
336	Mariners Ldrs (Glenn Abbott, Tom Paciorek)	.10
337	Pete Rose AS	.85
338	Dave Lopes AS	.12
339	Mike Schmidt AS	.60
340	Dave Concepcion AS	.12
341	Andre Dawson AS	.25
342	George Foster AS (with autograph)	.40
342	George Foster AS (w/o autograph)	2.25
343	Dave Parker AS	.20
344	Gary Carter AS	.35
345	Fernando Valenzuela AS	.35
346	Tom Seaver AS	.35
347	Bruce Sutter AS	.12
351	Reds FS (Scott Brown, Geoff Combe, Paul Householder)	.08
355	*Dwight Evans	.25
360	Len Barker	.10
361	Rafael Landestoy	.08
362	Jim Wright	.08
363	Bob Molinaro	.08
364	Doyle Alexander	.10
365	Bill Madlock	.20

254 Jorge Bell

366	Padres Ldrs (Juan Eichelberger, Luis Salazar)	.10
367	Jim Kaat	.25
368	Alex Trevino	.08
369	Champ Summers	.08
370	Mike Norris	.08
371	Jerry Don Gleaton	.08
372	Luis Gomez	.08
373	Gene Nelson	.15
374	Tim Blackwell	.08
375	Dusty Baker	.10
376	Chris Welsh	.08
377	Kiko Garcia	.08
378	Mike Caldwell	.08
379	Rob Wilfong	.08
380	Dave Stieb	.25
381	*Red Sox FS (Bruce Hurst, Dave Schmidt, Julio Valdez)	.25
382	Joe Simpson	.08
383	Pascual Perez (with position on front)	.12
383	Pascual Perez (w/o position on front)	35.00
384	Keith Moreland	.10
385	Ken Forsch	.08
386	Jerry White	.08
387	Tom Veryzer	.08
388	Joe Rudi	.10
389	George Vukovich	.08
390	Eddie Murray	1.25
391	Dave Tobik	.08
392	Rick Bosetti	.08
393	Al Hrabosky	.10
394	Checklist 265-396	.12
395	Omar Moreno	.08
396	Twins Ldrs (Fernando Arroyo, John Castino)	.10
397	Ken Brett	.10
398	Mike Squires	.08
399	Pat Zachry	.08
400	Johnny Bench	.90
401	Johnny Bench IA	.45
402	Bill Stein	.08
403	Jim Tracy	.08
404	Dickie Thon	.10
405	Rick Reuschel	.15
406	Al Holland	.08

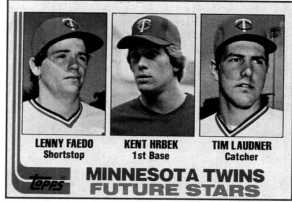

766 Twins Future Stars

407	Danny Boone	.08
408	Ed Romero	.08
409	Don Cooper	.08
410	Ron Cey	.15
411	Ron Cey IA	.10
412	Luis Leal	.08
413	Dan Meyer	.08
414	Elias Sosa	.08
415	Don Baylor	.15
416	Marty Bystrom	.08
417	Pat Kelly	.08
418	Rangers FS (John Butcher, Bobby Johnson, Dave Schmidt (FC))	.20
419	Steve Stone	.10
420	George Hendrick	.10
421	Mark Clear	.08
422	Cliff Johnson	.08
423	Stan Papi	.08
424	Bruce Benedict	.08
425	John Candelaria	.10
426	Orioles Ldrs (Eddie Murray, Sammy Stewart)	.35
427	Ron Oester	.08
428	Lamarr Hoyt (LaMarr)	.08
429	John Wathan	.10
430	Vida Blue	.15
431	Vida Blue IA	.10
432	*Mike Scott	.25

433	Alan Ashby	.08
434	Joe Lefebvre	.08
435	Robin Yount	2.00
436	Joe Strain	.08
437	Juan Berenguer	.08
438	Pete Mackanin	.08
439	Dave Righetti (FC)	2.50
440	Jeff Burroughs	.10
441	Astros FS (Danny Heep, Billy Smith, Bobby Sprowl)	.08
442	Bruce Kison	.08
443	Mark Wagner	.08
444	Terry Forster	.08
445	Larry Parrish	.10
446	Wayne Garland	.08
447	Darrell Porter	.10
448	Darrell Porter IA	.10
449	Luis Aguayo (FC)	.12
450	Jack Morris	.50
451	Ed Miller	.08
452	Lee Smith (FC)	1.00
453	Art Howe	.08
454	Rick Langford	.08
455	Tom Burgmeier	.08
456	Cubs Ldrs (Bill Buckner, Randy Martz)	.15
457	Tim Stoddard	.08
458	Willie Montanez	.08
459	Bruce Berenyi	.08
460	Jack Clark	.30
461	Rich Dotson	.12
462	Dave Chalk	.08
463	Jim Kern	.08
464	Juan Bonilla	.08
465	Lee Mazzilli	.10
466	Randy Lerch	.08
467	Mickey Hatcher	.10
468	Floyd Bannister	.12
469	Ed Ott	.08
470	John Mayberry	.10
471	Royals FS (Atlee Hammaker, Mike Jones, Darryl Motley)	.25
472	Oscar Gamble	.10
473	Mike Stanton	.08
474	Ken Oberkfell	.08
475	Alan Trammell	.50
476	Brian Kingman	.08

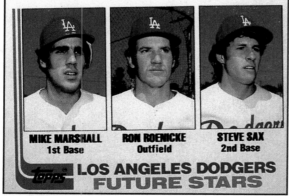

681 Dodgers Future Stars

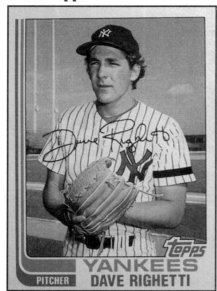

439 Dave Righetti

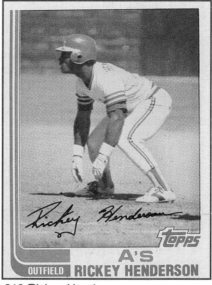

610 Rickey Henderson

516	Larry Bowa IA	.12
517	Mark Brouhard	.08
518	Garth Iorg	.08
519	Glenn Adams	.08
520	Mike Flanagan	.10
521	Billy Almon	.08
522	Chuck Rainey	.08
523	Gary Gray	.08
524	Tom Hausman	.08
525	Ray Knight	.08
526	Expos Ldrs (Warren Cromartie, Bill Gullickson)	.10
527	John Henry Johnson	.08
528	Matt Alexander	.08
529	Allen Ripley	.08
530	Dickie Noles	.08
531	A's FS (Rich Bordi, Mark Budaska, Kelvin Moore)	.08
532	Toby Harrah	.10
533	Joaquin Andujar	.10
534	Dave McKay	.08
535	Lance Parrish	.50
536	Rafael Ramirez	.10
537	Doug Capilla	.08
538	Lou Piniella	.15
539	Vern Ruhle	.08
540	Andre Dawson	.50
541	Barry Evans	.08
542	Ned Yost	.08
543	Bill Robinson	.08
544	Larry Christenson	.08
545	Reggie Smith	.15
546	Reggie Smith IA	.10
547	Rod Carew AS	.35
548	Willie Randolph AS	.12
549	George Brett AS	.60
550	Bucky Dent AS	.12
551	Reggie Jackson AS	.50
552	Ken Singleton AS	.12
553	Dave Winfield AS	.40
554	Carlton Fisk AS	.20

477	Steve Yeager	.08
478	Ray Searage	.08
479	Rowland Office	.08
480	Steve Carlton	.85
481	Steve Carlton IA	.40
482	Glenn Hubbard	.10
483	Gary Woods	.08
484	Ivan DeJesus	.08
485	Kent Tekulve	.10
486	Yankees Ldrs (Tommy John, Jerry Mumphrey)	.20
487	Bob McClure	.08
488	Ron Jackson	.08
489	Rick Dempsey	.10
490	Dennis Eckersley	.12
491	Checklist 397-528	.12
492	Joe Price	.08
493	Chet Lemon	.10
494	Hubie Brooks	.20
495	Dennis Leonard	.10
496	Johnny Grubb	.08
497	Jim Anderson	.08
498	Dave Bergman	.08
499	Paul Mirabella	.08
500	Rod Carew	.80
501	Rod Carew IA	.40
502	Braves FS (*Steve Bedrosian* (FC), Brett Butler (FC), Larry Owen)	2.50
503	Julio Gonzalez	.08
504	Rick Peters	.08
505	Graig Nettles	.25
506	Graig Nettles IA	.12
507	Terry Harper	.08
508	*Jody Davis* (FC)	.40
509	Harry Spilman	.08
510	Fernando Valenzuela	1.50
511	Ruppert Jones	.08
512	Jerry Dybzinski	.08
513	Rick Rhoden	.10
514	Joe Ferguson	.08
515	Larry Bowa	.20

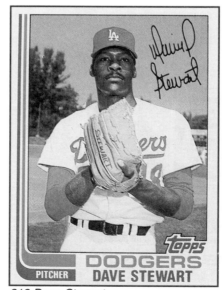

213 Dave Stewart

555	Scott McGregor AS	.12
556	Jack Morris AS	.20
557	Rich Gossage AS	.20
558	John Tudor	.30
559	Indians Ldrs (Bert Blyleven, Mike Hargrove)	.15
560	Doug Corbett	.08
561	Cardinals FS (Glenn Brummer, Luis DeLeon, Gene Roof)	.08
562	Mike O'Berry	.08
563	Ross Baumgarten	.08
564	Doug DeCinces	.15
565	Jackson Todd	.08
566	Mike Jorgensen	.08
567	Bob Babcock	.08
568	Joe Pettini	.08
569	Willie Randolph	.15
570	Willie Randolph IA	.10
571	Glenn Abbott	.08
572	Juan Beniquez	.08
573	Rick Waits	.08
574	Mike Ramsey	.08
575	Al Cowens	.08
576	Giants Ldrs (Vida Blue, Milt May)	.15
577	Rick Monday	.10
578	Shooty Babitt	.08
579	*Rick Mahler* (FC)	.25
580	Bobby Bonds	.15
581	Ron Reed	.10
582	Luis Pujols	.08
583	Tippy Martinez	.08
584	Hosken Powell	.08
585	Rollie Fingers	.35
586	Rollie Fingers IA	.15
587	Tim Lollar	.08
588	Dale Berra	.08
589	Dave Stapleton	.08
590	Al Oliver	.20
591	Al Oliver IA	.10
592	Craig Swan	.08
593	Billy Smith	.08

594 Renie Martin .... .08
595 Dave Collins .... .10
596 Damaso Garcia .... .08
597 Wayne Nordhagen .... .08
598 Bob Galasso .... .08
599 White Sox FS (Jay
    Loviglio, Reggie Patterson,
    Leo Sutherland) .... .08
600 Dave Winfield .... .65
601 Sid Monge .... .08
602 Freddie Patek .... .08
603 Rich Hebner .... .08
604 Orlando Sanchez .... .08
605 Steve Rogers .... .10
606 Blue Jays Ldrs (John
    Mayberry, Dave Stieb) .... .15
607 Leon Durham .... .10
608 Jerry Royster .... .08
609 Rick Sutcliffe .... .25
610 Rickey Henderson 3.50
611 Joe Niekro .... .20
612 Gary Ward .... .08
613 Jim Gantner .... .08
614 Juan Eichelberger .... .08
615 *Bob Boone .... .12
616 Bob Boone IA .... .10
617 Scott McGregor .... .10
618 Tim Foli .... .08
619 Bill Campbell .... .08
620 Ken Griffey .... .15
621 Ken Griffey IA .... .10
622 Dennis Lamp .... .08
623 Mets FS (Ron Gardenhire,
    Terry Leach (FC),
    Tim Leary (FC)) .... .90
624 Fergie Jenkins .... .25
625 Hal McRae .... .15
626 Randy Jones .... .10
627 Enos Cabell .... .08
628 Bill Travers .... .08
629 Johnny Wockenfuss .... .08
630 Joe Charboneau .... .10
631 Gene Tenace .... .10

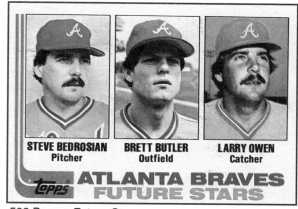

502 Braves Future Stars

632 Bryan Clark .... .08
633 Mitchell Page .... .08
634 Checklist 529-660 .... .12
635 Ron Davis .... .10
636 Phillies Ldrs (Steve
    Carlton, Pete Rose) .... .50
637 Rick Camp .... .08
638 John Milner .... .08
639 Ken Kravec .... .08
640 Cesar Cedeno .... .15
641 Steve Mura .... .08
642 Mike Scioscia .... .10
643 Pete Vuckovich .... .10
644 John Castino .... .08
645 Frank White .... .10
646 Frank White IA .... .10
647 Warren Brusstar .... .08
648 Jose Morales .... .08
649 Ken Clay .... .08
650 Carl Yastrzemski 1.25
651 Carl Yastrzemski IA .... .60
652 Steve Nicosia .... .08
653 Angels FS (Tom
    Brunansky (FC), Luis
    Sanchez, Daryl Sconiers) ... 2.25
654 Jim Morrison .... .08
655 Joel Youngblood .... .08
656 Eddie Whitson .... .08
657 Tom Poquette .... .08
658 Tito Landrum .... .08
659 Fred Martinez .... .08
660 Dave Concepcion .... .15
661 Dave Concepcion IA .... .10
662 Luis Salazar .... .08
663 Hector Cruz .... .08
664 Dan Spillner .... .08
665 Jim Clancy .... .10
666 Tigers Ldrs (Steve Kemp,
    Dan Petry) .... .15
667 Jeff Reardon .... .25
668 Dale Murphy 2.00
669 Larry Milbourne .... .08
670 Steve Kemp .... .12
671 Mike Davis .... .10
672 Bob Knepper .... .08
673 Keith Drumright .... .08
674 Dave Goltz .... .08
675 Cecil Cooper .... .10

676 Sal Butera .... .08
677 Alfredo Griffin .... .08
678 Tom Paciorek .... .08
679 Sammy Stewart .... .08
680 Gary Matthews .... .12
681 Dodgers FS
    (Mike Marshall (FC),
    Ron Roenicke, Steve
    Sax (FC)) 4.00
682 Jesse Jefferson .... .08
683 Phil Garner .... .10
684 Harold Baines .... .75
685 Bert Blyleven .... .20
686 Gary Allenson .... .08
687 Greg Minton .... .08
688 Leon Roberts .... .08
689 Lary Sorensen .... .08
690 Dave Kingman .... .20
691 Dan Schatzeder .... .08
692 Wayne Gross .... .08
693 Cesar Geronimo .... .08
694 Dave Wehrmeister .... .08
695 Warren Cromartie .... .08
696 Pirates Ldrs (Bill
    Madlock, Buddy Solomon) ... .15
697 John Montefusco .... .10
698 Tony Scott .... .08
699 Dick Tidrow .... .08
700 George Foster .... .25
701 George Foster IA .... .12
702 Steve Renko .... .08
703 Brewers Ldrs (Cecil
    Cooper, Pete Vuckovich) ..... .15
704 Mickey Rivers .... .10
705 Mickey Rivers IA .... .10
706 Barry Foote .... .08
707 Mark Bomback .... .08
708 Gene Richards .... .08
709 Don Money .... .08
710 Jerry Reuss .... .10
711 Mariners FS (Dave Edler,
    Dave Henderson (FC),
    Reggie Walton) 1.25
712 Denny Martinez .... .08
713 Del Unser .... .08
714 Jerry Koosman .... .12
715 Willie Stargell .... .75
716 Willie Stargell IA .... .30

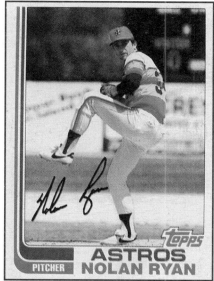

90 Nolan Ryan

165

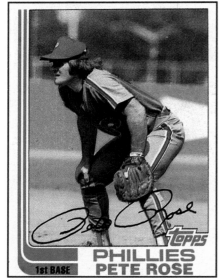

780 Pete Rose

717	Rick Miller	.08
718	Charlie Hough	.10
719	Jerry Narron	.08
720	Greg Luzinski	.20
721	Greg Luzinski IA	.12
722	Jerry Martin	.08
723	Junior Kennedy	.08
724	Dave Rosello	.08
725	Amos Otis	.10
726	Amos Otis IA	.10

727	Sixto Lezcano	.08
728	Aurelio Lopez	.08
729	Jim Spencer	.08
730	Gary Carter	.70
731	Padres FS (Mike Armstrong, Doug Gwosdz, Fred Kuhaulua)	.08
732	Mike Lum	.08
733	Larry McWilliams	.08
734	Mike Ivie	.08
735	Rudy May	.08
736	Jerry Turner	.08
737	Reggie Cleveland	.08
738	Dave Engle	.08
739	Joey McLaughlin	.08
740	Dave Lopes	.12
741	Dave Lopes IA	.10
742	Dick Drago	.08
743	John Stearns	.08
744	*Mike Witt*	1.00
745	Bake McBride	.08
746	Andre Thornton	.10
747	John Lowenstein	.08
748	Marc Hill	.08
749	Bob Shirley	.08
750	Jim Rice	.85
751	Rick Honeycutt	.08
752	Lee Lacy	.08
753	Tom Brookens	.08
754	*Joe Morgan	.50
755	Joe Morgan IA	.20
756	Reds Ldrs (Ken Griffey, Tom Seaver)	.30
757	Tom Underwood	.08
758	Claudell Washington	.10
759	Paul Splittorff	.08

760	Bill Buckner	.15
761	Dave Smith	.12
762	Mike Phillips	.08
763	Tom Hume	.08
764	Steve Swisher	.08
765	Gorman Thomas	.10
766	Twins FS (Lenny Faedo, *Kent Hrbek* (FC), *Tim Laudner* (FC))	5.00
767	Roy Smalley	.08
768	Jerry Garvin	.08
769	Richie Zisk	.10
770	Rich Gossage	.35
771	Rich Gossage IA	.15
772	Bert Campaneris	.10
773	John Denny	.08
774	Jay Johnstone	.10
775	Bob Forsch	.10
776	Mark Belanger	.10
777	Tom Griffin	.08
778	Kevin Hickey	.08
780	Pete Rose	2.25
781	Pete Rose IA	1.00
783	*Greg Harris* (FC)	.15
784	Milt Wilcox	.08
785	Dan Driessen	.10
786	Red Sox Batting and Pitching Ldrs (Carney Lansford, Mike Torrez)	.12
787	Fred Stanley	.08
788	Woodie Fryman	.10
789	Checklist 661-792	.12
790	Larry Gura	.08
791	Bobby Brown	.08
792	Frank Tanana	.15

1982 TOPPS TRADED

Like it or not, Topps Traded cards returned again in 1982. The company found that sufficient positive response could make the "extension" set into an annual affair. In addition, the Traded set deflected criticism for the failure of Topps to include rookies and traded players in their larger set of the same year, which they issued earlier than ever before. Topps added a "T" suffix to each card in the alphabetized set to distinguish it from the year's earlier issue (the "T" has been omitted from the following lists). Once again, the Traded cards were available only from hobby dealers in boxed, complete sets. Noteworthy cards include the first solo Topps' card of Cal Ripken, Jr., along with the first picture of Ozzie Smith in a Cardinals uniform.

		MINT
Complete set		**$41.00**
Commons		**.10**

1	Doyle Alexander	$ .20
2	Jesse Barfield	2.25
3	Ross Baumgarten	.10
4	Steve Bedrosian	.85
5	Mark Belanger	.15
6	Kurt Bevacqua	.10
7	Tim Blackwell	.10
8	Vida Blue	.25
9	Bob Boone	.20
10	Larry Bowa	.25
11	Dan Briggs	.10
12	Bobby Brown	.10

13	Tom Brunansky	1.75
14	Jeff Burroughs	.15
15	Enos Cabell	.10
16	Bill Campbell	.10
17	Bobby Castillo	.10
18	Bill Caudill	.10
19	Cesar Cedeno	.20
20	Dave Collins	.15
21	Doug Corbett	.10
22	Al Cowens	.10
23	Chili Davis	1.50
24	Dick Davis	.10
25	Ron Davis	.10
26	Doug DeCinces	.20
27	Ivan DeJesus	.10
28	Bob Dernier	.20
29	Bo Diaz	.15
30	Roger Erickson	.10
31	Jim Essian	.10
32	Ed Farmer	.10
33	Doug Flynn	.10

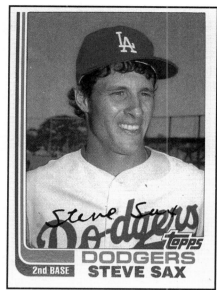

103 Steve Sax

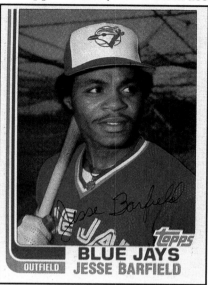

2 Jesse Barfield

47	Reggie Jackson	3.00
48	Ron Jackson	.10
49	*Fergie Jenkins	.40
50	Lamar Johnson	.10
51	Randy Johnson	.10
52	Jay Johnstone	.15
53	Mick Kelleher	.10
54	Steve Kemp	.15
55	Junior Kennedy	.10
56	Jim Kern	.10
57	Ray Knight	.20
58	Wayne Krenchicki	.10
59	Mike Krukow	.15
60	Duane Kuiper	.10
61	Mike LaCoss	.10
62	Chet Lemon	.15
63	Sixto Lezcano	.10
64	Dave Lopes	.15
65	Jerry Martin	.10
66	Renie Martin	.10
67	John Mayberry	.15
68	Lee Mazzilli	.15
69	Bake McBride	.10
70	Dan Meyer	.10
71	Larry Milbourne	.10
72	Eddie Milner (FC)	.20
73	Sid Monge	.10
74	Jose Morales	.10
75	Keith Moreland	.20
83	Al Oliver	.35
86	Larry Parrish	.20
88	Gaylord Perry	1.50
94	Charlie Puleo (FC)	.15
95	Shane Rawley	.20
96	Johnny Ray	.80
98	Cal Ripken	14.00
101	Aurelio Rodriguez	.15
102	Joe Rudi	.20
103	Steve Sax	5.00

34	Tim Foli	.10
35	Dan Ford	.10
36	George Foster	.40
37	Dave Frost	.10
38	Rich Gale	.10
39	Ron Gardenhire	.10
40	Ken Griffey	.25
41	Greg Harris	.15
42	Von Hayes	1.50
43	Larry Herndon	.15
44	Kent Hrbek	5.00
45	Mike Ivie	.10
46	Grant Jackson	.10

106	Eric Show (FC)	.70
107	Roy Smalley	.15
108	Lonnie Smith	.15
109	Ozzie Smith	6.00
110	Reggie Smith	.20
116	Rick Sutcliffe	.50
117	Frank Tanana	.20
119	Garry Templeton	.20
122	Ed Vande Berg (FC)	.15
125	Bob Watson	.15
127	Eddie Whitson	.15
131	Butch Wynegar	.15
132	Checklist 1-132	.10

1983 DONRUSS

Donruss had few innovations to offer in its third year of baseball card production. Card backs retain the same format as the previous year, although a different yellow ink was used. Fronts again display a large photo along with a baseball bat graphic with the player name and position. A 63-piece Ty Cobb puzzle replaced the Babe Ruth puzzle of 1982, and the set was distributed in wax packs, three pieces per package. The final card of the numbered set shows the entire puzzle. For the first time, Donruss sold complete boxed sets to dealers on a wholesale basis. Rookie cards of Wade Boggs, Tony Gwynn, and Ryne Sandberg are the most popular cards in the set.

		MINT
Complete set		$67.00
Commons		.06

1	Fernando Valenzuela (DK)	$ .40
2	Rollie Fingers (DK)	.20
3	Reggie Jackson (DK)	.50
4	Jim Palmer (DK)	.40

5	Jack Morris (DK)	.25
6	George Foster (DK)	.20
7	Jim Sundberg (DK)	.08
8	Willie Stargell (DK)	.40
9	Dave Stieb (DK)	.10
10	Joe Niekro (DK)	.08
11	Rickey Henderson (DK)	.60
12	Dale Murphy (DK)	.80
13	Toby Harrah (DK)	.08

14	Bill Buckner (DK)	.15
15	Willie Wilson (DK)	.15
16	Steve Carlton (DK)	.40
17	Ron Guidry (DK)	.25
18	Steve Rogers (DK)	.08
19	Kent Hrbek (DK)	.40
20	Keith Hernandez (DK)	.40
21	Floyd Bannister (DK)	.08
22	Johnny Bench (DK)	.40
23	Britt Burns (DK)	.08
24	Joe Morgan (DK)	.30
25	Carl Yastrzemski (DK)	.80
26	Terry Kennedy (DK)	.08
31	Ron Guidry	.25
32	Burt Hooton	.08
34	Vida Blue	.10
35	Rickey Henderson	.60
39	Jerry Koosman	.10
40	Bruce Sutter	.15
41	Jose Cruz	.10
42	Pete Rose	1.00

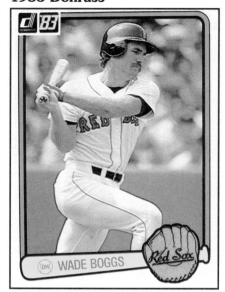

586 Wade Boggs

122	Tom Seaver	.50
123	Chris Chambliss	.08
126	*Mel Hall* (FC)	.40
128	*Charlie Puleo* (FC)	.10
134	Bruce Hurst (FC)	.25
136	Tom LaSorda (Lasorda)	.10
140	Al Oliver	.15
143	Harold Baines	.15
145	Garry Templeton	.10
147	Bo Diaz	.08
148	Dave Concepcion	.10
152	Keith Hernandez	.40
156	Rich Gedman	.06
157	Rich Gossage	.20
158	Jerry Reuss	.08
161	Dwayne Murphy	.06
162	Woodie Fryman	.08
168	Mike Schmidt	.85
169	*Eddie Milner* (FC)	.10
171	Don Robinson	.08
173	Steve Bedrosian	.12
174	Willie Hernandez	.10
177	Tim Laudner	.08
179	Kent Hrbek	1.25
180	Alfredo Griffin	.08
183	Jody Davis	.06
184	Glenn Hubbard	.06
189	Bob Dernier (FC)	.08
190	*Willie McGee* (FC)	1.25
191	Dickie Thon	.08
192	*Bob Boone	.10
194	Jeff Reardon	.10
195	Jon Matlack	.08
196	*Don Slaught* (FC)	.10
199	Dave Righetti	.25
207	Alan Trammell	.40
208	Jim Rice	.40
210	Bill Russell	.08
211	Andre Thornton	.10
215	Buddy Bell	.10
216	Doug DeCinces	.08
217	Tom Herr	.10
219	Steve Carlton	.50

43	Cesar Cedeno	.10
47	Dale Murphy	.85
49	Hubie Brooks	.10
50	Floyd Bannister	.08
53	*Gary Gaetti* (FC)	4.00
56	Mookie Wilson	.10
58	Bob Horner	.15
59	Tony Pena	.10
63	Garry Maddox	.10
64	Bob Forsch	.08
69	Charlie Hough	.10
70	Dan Quisenberry	.15
71	Tony Armas	.10
72	Rick Sutcliffe	.10
73	Steve Balboni (FC)	.06
77	Jim Palmer	.50
78	Rollie Fingers	.20
83	Graig Nettles	.15
84	Ron Cey	.10
88	Byrn Smith (first name incorrect)	.90
88	Bryn Smith (correct name)	.15
90	Rod Carew	.50
91	Lonnie Smith	.10
92	Bob Knepper	.08
97	Phil Niekro	.30
99	Bill Buckner	.12
100	*Ed VandeBerg* (Vande Berg) (FC)	.10
101	Jim Clancy	.08
104	Carlton Fisk	.30
105	Mike Flanagan	.10
106	Cecil Cooper	.10
107	Jack Morris	.25
108	Mike Morgan (FC)	.10
110	Pedro Guerrero	.25
111	Len Barker	.08
112	Willie Wilson	.10
115	Reggie Jackson	.50
117	Vance Law	.08
118	Nolan Ryan	1.50
119	Mike Kurkow	.08
120	Ozzie Smith	.20

598 Tony Gwynn

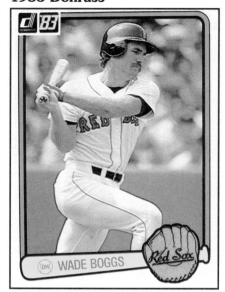

277 Ryne Sandberg

220	Terry Kennedy	.08
221	Mike Easler	.08
222	Jack Clark	.25
231	Dennis Martinez	.08
232	Jim Gantner	.06
234	Dave Collins	.08
238	Hal McRae	.10
241	Fred Lynn	.20
248	Mario Soto	.08
249	Claudell Washington	.08
250	Rick Rhoden	.10
251	Darrell Evans	.12
257	Ken Singleton	.10
258	Robin Yount	.50
260	Bob Ojeda	.08
261	Bobby Murcer	.10
262	*Candy Maldonado* (FC)	.35
269	Steve Kemp	.10
270	Phil Garner	.08
274	Dan Dreissen	.08
277	*Ryne Sandberg* (FC)	11.00
279	Cal Ripken	1.00
283	Willie Randolph	.10
284	Fernando Valenzuela	.30
287	Joe Rudi	.08
294	Manny Trillo	.08
295	Greg Harris (FC)	.08
297	Kent Tekulve	.08
298	Atlee Hammaker (FC)	.10
300	Fergie Jenkins	.15
301	Dave Kingman	.15
304	Ernie Whitt	.08
307	Gaylord Perry	.30
309	Keith Moreland	.08
311	Bill Madlock	.12
316	Joaquin Andujar	.08
318	Rick Burleson	.08
319	Richard Dotson	.08
320	Steve Rogers	.08
321	Dave Schmidt (FC)	.10
322	*Bud Black* (FC)	.20
323	Jeff Burroughs	.08
324	Von Hayes	.15

326	Carl Yastrzemski	.75
328	*Howard Johnson* (FC)	10.00
329	Rick Dempsey	.08
330	Jim Slaton	.08
332	Ted Simmons	.10
333	Lou Whitaker	.45
335	Lou Piniella	.10
336	Steve Sax	.35
337	Toby Harrah	.08
338	George Brett	.75
339	Davey Lopes	.10
340	Gary Carter	.40
342	*Jim Kaat	.15
347	Omar Moreno	.06
348	Charles Davis (FC)	.08
349	Tommy Boggs	.06
350	Rusty Staub	.10
351	Bump Wills	.06
353	*Jim Gott* (FC)	.15
354	Terry Felton	.06
355	Jim Kern	.06
356	Bill Almon	.06
357	Tippy Martinez	.06
358	Roy Howell	.06
359	Dan Petry	.08
360	Jerry Mumphrey	.06
361	Mark Clear	.06
362	Mike Marshall	.15
363	Lary Sorensen	.06
364	Amos Otis	.08
365	Rick Langford	.06
366	Brad Mills	.06
367	Brian Downing	.10
368	Mike Richardt	.06
369	Aurelio Rodriguez	.08
370	*Dave Smith	.08
371	Tug McGraw	.12
372	Doug Bair	.06
373	Ruppert Jones	.06
374	Alex Trevino	.06
375	Ken Dayley	.06
376	Rod Scurry	.06
377	Bob Brenly (FC)	.08

382 Frank Viola

378	Scot Thompson	.06
379	Julio Cruz	.06
380	John Stearns	.06
381	Dale Murray	.06
382	*Frank Viola* (FC)	5.00
383	Al Bumbry	.08
384	Ben Oglivie	.08
385	Dave Tobik	.06
386	Bob Stanley	.06
387	Andre Robertson	.06
388	Jorge Orta	.06
389	Ed Whitson	.06
390	Don Hood	.06
391	Tom Underwood	.06
392	Tim Wallach	.20
393	Steve Renko	.06
394	Mickey Rivers	.08
395	Greg Luzinski	.10
396	Art Howe	.06
397	Alan Wiggins	.06
398	Jim Barr	.06
399	Ivan DeJesus	.06
400	*Tom Lawless* (FC)	.08
401	Bob Walk	.08
402	Jimmy Smith	.06
403	Lee Smith	.15
404	George Hendrick	.08
405	Eddie Murray	.60
406	Marshall Edwards	.06
407	Lance Parrish	.35
408	Carney Lansford	.08
409	Dave Winfield	.40
410	Bob Welch	.10
411	Larry Milbourne	.08
412	Dennis Leonard	.08
413	Dan Meyer	.06
414	Charlie Lea	.06
415	Rick Honeycutt	.06
416	Mike Witt	.15
417	Steve Trout	.06
418	Glenn Brummer	.06
419	Denny Walling	.06
420	Gary Matthews	.10

421	Charlie Liebrandt (Leibrandt)	.08
422	Juan Eichelberger	.06
423	*Matt Guante* (FC)	.15
425	Jerry Royster	.06
426	Dickie Noles	.06
427	George Foster	.15
428	*Mike Moore* (FC)	.90
429	Gary Ward	.08
430	Barry Bonnell	.06
431	Ron Washington	.06
432	Rance Mulliniks	.06
433	Mike Stanton	.06
434	Jesse Orosco	.10
435	Larry Bowa	.12
436	Biff Pocoroba	.06
437	Johnny Ray	.12
438	Joe Morgan	.35
439	*Eric Show* (FC)	.25
440	Larry Biittner	.06
441	Greg Gross	.06
442	Gene Tenace	.08
443	Danny Heep	.06
444	Bobby Clark	.06
445	Kevin Hickey	.06
446	Scott Sanderson	.06
447	Frank Tanana	.10
448	Cesar Geronimo	.06
449	Jimmy Sexton	.06
450	Mike Hargrove	.06
451	Doyle Alexander	.08
452	*Dwight Evans	.15
453	Terry Forster	.08
454	Tom Brookens	.08
455	Rich Dauer	.06
456	Rob Picciolo	.06
457	Terry Crowley	.06
458	Ned Yost	.06
459	Kirk Gibson	.35
460	Reid Nichols	.06
461	Oscar Gamble	.08
462	Dusty Baker	.08
463	Jack Perconte	.06

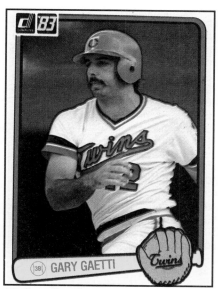

53 Gary Gaetti

328 Howard Johnson

525 Julio Franco

190 Willie McGee

507	Dave Stieb	.15
508	Al Williams	.06
509	Dan Ford	.06
510	Gorman Thomas	.10
511	Chet Lemon	.08
512	Mike Torrez	.08
513	Shane Rawley	.06
514	Mark Belanger	.08
515	Rodney Craig	.06
516	Onix Concepcion	.06
517	Mike Heath	.06
518	Andre Dawson	.35
519	Luis Sanchez	.06
520	Terry Bogener	.06
521	Rudy Law	.06
522	Ray Knight	.10
523	Joe Lefebvre	.06
524	Jim Wohlford	.06
525	*Julio Franco* (FC)	**4.00**
526	Ron Oester	.06
527	Rick Mahler	.06
528	Steve Nicosia	.06
529	Junior Kennedy	.06
530	Whitey Herzog	.10
531	Don Sutton (blue frame around photo)	**1.00**
531	Don Sutton (green frame around photo)	.30
532	Mark Brouhard	.06
533	Sparky Anderson	.10
534	Roger LaFrancois	.06
535	George Frazier	.06
536	Tom Niedenfuer	.08
537	Ed Glynn	.06
538	Lee May	.08
539	Bob Kearney	.06
540	Tim Raines	.35
541	Paul Mirabella	.06
542	Luis Tiant	.12
543	Ron LeFlore	.08
544	*Dave LaPoint* (FC)	.25
545	Randy Moffitt	.06
546	Luis Aguayo	.06

464	Frank White	.10
465	Mickey Klutts	.06
466	Warren Cromartie	.06
467	Larry Parrish	.10
468	Bobby Grich	.10
469	Dane Iorg	.06
470	Joe Niekro	.12
471	Ed Farmer	.06
472	Tim Flannery	.06
473	Dave Parker	.30
474	Jeff Leonard	.08
475	Al Hrabosky	.10
476	Ron Hodges	.06
477	Leon Durham	.08
478	Jim Essian	.06
479	Roy Lee Jackson	.06
480	Brad Havens	.06
481	Joe Price	.06
482	Tony Bernazard	.06
483	Scott McGregor	.08
484	Paul Molitor	.20
485	Mike Ivie	.06
486	Ken Griffey	.10
487	Dennis Eckersley	.10
488	Steve Garvey	.40
489	Mike Fischlin	.06
490	U.L. Washington	.06
491	Steve McCatty	.06
492	Roy Johnson	.06
493	Don Baylor	.10
494	Bobby Johnson	.06
495	Mike Squires	.06
496	Bert Roberge	.06
497	Dick Ruthven	.06
498	Tito Landrum	.06
499	Sixto Lezcano	.06
500	Johnny Bench	.40
501	Larry Whisenton	.06
502	Manny Sarmiento	.06
503	Fred Breining	.06
504	Bill Campbell	.06
505	Todd Cruz	.06
506	Bob Bailor	.06

118 Nolan Ryan

547	Brad Lesley	.06
548	Luis Salazar	.06
549	John Candelaria	.10
550	Dave Bergman	.06
551	Bob Watson	.08
552	Pat Tabler	.06
553	Brent Gaff	.06
554	Al Cowens	.06
555	Tom Brunansky (FC)	.25
556	Lloyd Moseby	.10
557	Pascual Perez (FC) (Twins)	.90
557	Pascual Perez (FC) (Braves)	.15
558	Willie Upshaw	.08
559	Richie Zisk	.08
560	Pat Zachry	.06
561	Jay Johnstone	.06
562	Carlos Diaz	.06
563	John Tudor	.10
564	Frank Robinson	.12
565	Dave Edwards	.06
566	Paul Householder	.06
567	Ron Reed	.06
568	Mike Ramsey	.06
569	Kiko Garcia	.06
570	Tommy John	.20
571	Tony LaRussa	.10
572	Joel Youngblood	.06
573	*Wayne Tolleson* (FC)	.12
574	Keith Creel	.06
575	Billy Martin	.15
576	Jerry Dybzinski	.06
577	Rick Cerone	.06
578	Tony Perez	.20
579	*Greg Brock* (FC)	.25
580	*Glen Wilson* (Glenn) (FC)	.35
581	Tim Stoddard	.06
582	Bob McClure	.06
583	Jim Dwyer	.06
584	Ed Romero	.06
585	Larry Hearndon	.06
586	*Wade Boggs* (FC)	**19.00**

587	Jay Howell (FC)	.15
588	*Dave Stewart	.15
589	Bert Blyleven	.15
590	Dick Howser	.06
591	Wayne Gross	.06
592	Terry Francona	.06
593	Don Werner	.06
594	Bill Stein	.06
595	Jesse Barfield (FC)	.60
596	Bobby Molinaro	.06
597	Mike Vail	.06
598	*Tony Gwynn* (FC)	13.00
599	Gary Rajsich	.06
600	Jerry Ujdur	.06
601	Cliff Johnson	.06
602	Jerry White	.06
603	Bryan Clark	.06
604	Joe Ferguson	.06
605	Guy Sularz	.06
606	Ozzie Virgil	.08
607	Terry Harper (FC)	.08
608	Harvey Kuenn	.08
609	Jim Sundberg	.08
610	Willie Stargell	.40
611	Reggie Smith	.10
612	Rob Wilfong	.06

613	Niekro Brothers (Joe Niekro, Phil Niekro)	.15
614	Lee Elia	.06
615	Mickey Hatcher	.08
616	Jerry Hairston	.06
617	John Martin	.06
618	Wally Backman (FC)	.15
619	*Storm Davis* (FC)	.50
620	Alan Knicely	.06
621	John Stuper	.06
622	Matt Sinatro	.06
623	*Gene Petralli* (FC)	.15
624	Duane Walker	.06
625	Dick Williams	.06
626	Pat Corrales	.06
627	Vern Ruhle	.06
628	Joe Torre	.08
629	Anthony Jackson	.06
630	Steve Howe	.06
631	Gary Woods	.06
632	Lamarr Hoyt (LaMarr)	.06
633	Steve Swisher	.06
634	Terry Leach (FC)	.10
635	Jeff Newman	.06
636	Brett Butler	.10
637	Gary Gray	.06

638	Lee Mazzilli	.08
639	Ron Jackson (A's)	18.00
639	Ron Jackson (Angels)	.20
640	Juan Beniquez	.06
641	Dave Rucker	.06
642	Luis Pujols	.06
643	Rick Monday	.10
644	Hosken Powell	.06
645	*San Diego Chicken	.20
646	Dave Engle	.06
647	Dick Davis	.06
648	MVPs (Vida Blue, Joe Morgan, Frank Robinson)	.15
649	Al Chambers	.06
650	Jesus Vega	.06
651	Jeff Jones	.06
652	Marvis Foley	.06
653	Ty Cobb puzzle	.06
—	Dick Perez/Diamond King	.08
—	Checklist 27-130	.06
—	Checklist 131-234	.06
—	Checklist 235-338	.06
—	Checklist 339-442	.06
—	Checklist 443-546	.06
—	Checklist 547-653	.06

1983 FLEER

After errors and variations plagued Fleer's first two offerings, the company rebounded in 1983 with a nearly perfect set of baseball cards. The 660-card edition is arranged by team, beginning with the 1982 World Champion St. Louis Cardinals, and then alphabetically by player within each team. For the first time since the 1971 Topps set, Fleer cards feature a black-and-white shot of each player on the back of his card. The biggest sellers in this edition include rookie cards of Wade Boggs, Ryne Sandberg, and Tony Gwynn. On the other hand, the rookie card for Ron Kittle, which originally sold for more than $2.50, has dropped to a modest 85 cents today. Because Fleer flooded the market with unsold cards at season's end, this set is still plentiful today.

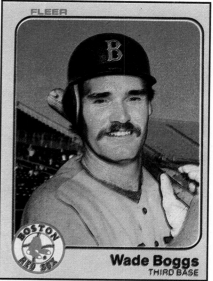

179 Wade Boggs

		MINT
Complete set		$65.00
Commons		.06

2	Doug Bair	$ .06
3	Steve Braun	.06
5	Bob Forsch	.08
6	David Green	.06
8	Keith Hernandez	.40
9	Tom Herr	.10
10	Dane Iorg	.06
11	Jim Kaat	.15
12	Jeff Lahti	.06
14	*Dave LaPoint* (FC)	.25
15	*Willie McGee* (FC)	1.25
16	Steve Mura	.06
18	Darrell Porter	.08
19	Mike Ramsey	.06
20	Gene Roof	.06
21	Lonnie Smith	.08
22	Ozzie Smith	.20

23	John Stuper	.06
24	Bruce Sutter	.15
25	Gene Tenace	.08
26	Jerry Augustine	.06
29	Mike Caldwell	.06
30	Cecil Cooper	.10
31	Jamie Easterly	.06
33	Rollie Fingers	.20
36	Roy Howell	.06
37	Peter Ladd	.06
39	Doc Medich	.06
40	Paul Molitor	.20
41	Don Money	.06
44	Ed Romero	.06
45	Ted Simmons	.15
46	Jim Slaton	.06
47	Don Sutton	.30
48	Gorman Thomas	.10
50	Ned Yost	.06
51	Robin Yount	.50
54	Al Bumbry	.06

56	*Storm Davis* (FC)	.50
57	Rich Dauer	.06
59	Jim Dwyer	.06
60	Mike Flanagan	.08
61	Dan Ford	.06
62	Glenn Gulliver	.06
67	Eddie Murray	.65
68	Joe Nolan	.06

171

360 Tony Gwynn

69	Jim Palmer	.50
70	Cal Ripken Jr.	1.50
73	Ken Singleton	.10
75	Tim Stoddard	.06
76	Don Aase	.06
77	Don Baylor	.15
79	*Bob Boone	.10
81	Rod Carew	.50
82	Bobby Clark	.06
84	John Curtis	.06
85	Doug DeCinces	.10
86	Brian Downing	.10
88	Tim Foli	.06
89	Ken Forsch	.06
90	Dave Goltz	.08
91	Bobby Grich	.10
93	Reggie Jackson	.50
94	Ron Jackson	.06
95	Tommy John	.20
96	Bruce Kison	.06
97	Fred Lynn	.20
98	Ed Ott	.06
99	Steve Renko	.06
101	Rob Wilfong	.06
102	Mike Witt	.10
103	Geoff Zahn	.06
104	Willie Aikens	.06
106	Vida Blue	.10
107	*Bud Black* (FC)	.20
108	George Brett	.75
109	Bill Castro	.06
111	Dave Frost	.06
113	Larry Gura	.06
115	Don Hood	.06
117	Jerry Martin	.06
118	Lee May	.08
119	Hal McRae	.10
120	Amos Otis	.08
121	Greg Pryor	.06
122	Dan Quisenberry	.15
123	*Don Slaught* (FC)	.20
126	John Wathan	.08
127	Frank White	.10

128	Willie Wilson	.15
129	Steve Bedrosian (FC)	.35
132	Brett Butler (FC)	.15
133	Rick Camp	.06
134	Chris Chambliss	.08
135	Ken Dayley (FC)	.10
136	Gene Garber	.06
137	Terry Harper	.06
138	Bob Horner	.20
139	Glenn Hubbard	.08
140	Rufino Linares	.06
141	Rick Mahler	.08
142	Dale Murphy	.90
143	Phil Niekro	.30
144	Pascual Perez	.08
147	Jerry Royster	.06
148	Ken Smith	.06
149	Bob Walk	.06
151	Bob Watson	.08
155	Steve Carlton	.50
159	Bob Dernier	.10
160	Bo Diaz	.08
163	Mike Krukow	.08
164	Garry Maddox	.10
165	Gary Matthews	.10
166	Tug McGraw	.12
171	Pete Rose	1.00
173	Mike Schmidt	.85
175	Ozzie Virgil (FC)	.10
177	Gary Allenson	.06
178	Luis Aponte	.06
179	*Wade Boggs* (FC)	19.00
181	Mark Clear	.06
182	Dennis Eckersley	.15
183	*Dwight Evans	.15
184	Rich Gedman	.06
185	Glenn Hoffman	.06
186	Bruce Hearst	.10
187	Carney Lansford	.08
188	Rick Miller	.06
190	Bob Ojeda	.08
191	Tony Perez	.20
193	Jerry Remy	.06

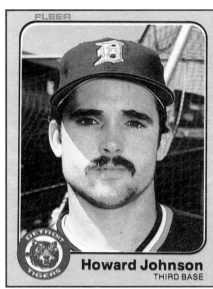

332 Howard Johnson

507 Ryne Sandberg

194	Jim Rice	.40
195	Bob Stanley	.06
197	Mike Torrez	.08
198	John Tudor	.10
199	Julio Valdez	.06
200	Carl Yastrzemski	.75
201	Dusty Baker	.10
202	Joe Beckwith	.06
203	*Greg Brock* (FC)	.25
204	Ron Cey	.10
205	Terry Forster	.08
206	Steve Garvey	.40
207	Pedro Guerrero	.25
208	Burt Hooton	.08
209	Steve Howe	.08
211	Mike Marshall	.15
212	*Candy Maldonado* (FC)	.50
213	Rick Monday	.10
215	Jorge Orta	.06
216	Jerry Reuss	.10
219	Bill Russell	.08
220	Steve Sax	.35
222	*Dave Stewart	.15
223	Derrel Thomas	.06
224	Fernando Valenzuela	.25
225	Bob Welch	.10
226	Ricky Wright	.06
227	Steve Yeager	.06
228	Bill Almon	.06
229	Harold Baines	.15
232	Britt Burns	.06
233	Richard Dotson	.10
235	Carlton Fisk	.30
236	Jerry Hairston	.06
237	Kevin Hickey	.06
238	LaMarr Hoyt	.06
239	Steve Kemp	.10
240	Jim Kern	.06
241	*Ron Kittle* (FC)	.85
242	Jerry Koosman	.10
243	Dennis Lamp	.06
245	Vance Law	.06
246	Ron LeFlore	.10

247	Greg Luzinski	.10
250	Mike Squires	.06
251	Steve Trout	.06
252	Jim Barr	.06
253	Dave Bergman	.06
254	Fred Breining	.06
255	Bob Brenly (FC)	.08
256	Jack Clark	.25
257	Chili Davis (FC)	.20
258	Darrell Evans	.10
259	Alan Fowlkes	.06
260	Rich Gale	.06
261	Atlee Hammaker (FC)	.10
262	Al Holland	.06
263	Duane Kuiper	.06
264	Bill Laskey	.06
265	Gary Lavalle	.06
267	Renie Martin	.06
268	Milt May	.06
269	Greg Minton	.06
270	Joe Morgan	.40
271	Tom O'Malley	.06
272	Reggie Smith	.10
273	Guy Sularz	.06
275	Max Venable	.06
276	Jim Wohlford	.06
277	Ray Burris	.06
278	Gary Carter	.35
280	Andre Dawson	.35
281	Terry Francona	.06
282	Doug Flynn	.06
283	Woody Fryman	.08
286	Charlie Lea	.06
287	Randy Lerch	.06
288	Brad Mills	.06
289	Dan Norman	.06
290	Al Oliver	.15
291	David Palmer	.06
292	Tim Raines	.35
293	Jeff Reardon	.12
294	Steve Rogers	.08
297	Bryn Smith	.08
298	Chris Speier	.06

613 Gary Gaetti

Gary Gaetti
THIRD BASE

299	Tim Wallach	.20
300	Jerry White	.06
303	Dale Berra	.06
304	John Candelaria	.10
305	Dick Davis	.06
306	Mike Easler	.06
307	Rich Hebner	.06
308	Lee Lacy	.06
309	Bill Madlock	.10
311	John Milner	.06
312	Omar Morino	.06
313	Jim Morrison	.06
314	Steve Nicosia	.06
315	Dave Parker	.30
316	Tony Pena	.10
317	Johnny Ray	.10
318	Rick Rhoden	.08
320	Enrique Romo	.06
322	Rod Scurry	.06
323	Jim Smith	.06
324	Willie Stargell	.40
326	Kent Tukulve	.08
327	Tom Brookens	.08
328	Enos Cabell	.08
329	Kirk Gibson	.40
330	Larry Herndon	.06
331	Mike Ivie	.06
332	*Howard Johnson*	10.00
333	Lynn Jones	.06
334	Rick Leach	.06
335	Chet Lemon	.08
336	Jack Morris	.25
337	Lance Parrish	.35
339	Dan Petry	.08
340	Dave Rozema	.06
341	Dave Rucker	.06
342	Elias Sosa	.06
343	Dave Tobik	.06
344	Alan Trammell	.40
345	Jerry Turner	.06
348	Lou Whitaker	.45
349	Milt Wilcox	.06
350	*Glenn Wilson* (FC)	.45

625 Frank Viola

Frank Viola
PITCHER

353	Juan Bonilla	.06
354	Floyd Chiffer	.06
355	Luis DeLeon	.06
356	*Dave Dravecky* (FC)	.25
357	Dave Edwards	.06
359	Tim Flannery	.06
360	*Tony Gwynn* (FC)	13.00
361	Ruppert Jones	.06
362	Terry Kennedy	.08
365	Tim Lollar	.06
366	Gary Lucas	.06
369	Joe Pittman	.06
370	Gene Richards	.06
371	Luis Salazar	.06
372	*Eric Show* (FC)	.25
373	Garry Templeton	.10
374	Chris Welsh	.06
375	Alan Wiggins	.06
376	Rick Cerone	.06
377	Dave Collins	.08
378	Roger Erickson	.06
379	George Frazier	.06
380	Oscar Gamble	.08
381	Goose Gossage	.20
382	Ken Griffey	.10
383	Ron Guidry	.25
384	Dave LaRoche	.06
385	Rudy May	.06
386	John Mayberry	.08
387	Lee Mazzilli	.08
388	Mike Morgan (FC)	.10
390	Bobby Murcer	.10
391	Graig Nettles	.15
392	Lou Piniella	.10
393	Willie Randolph	.10
394	Shane Rawley	.06
395	Dave Righetti	.25
396	Andre Robertson	.06
397	Roy Smalley	.06
398	Dave Winfield	.40
399	Butch Wynegar	.06
400	Chris Bando	.06
401	Alan Bannister	.06

70 Cal Ripken Jr.

Cal Ripken Jr.
SHORTSTOP

15 Willie McGee

402	Len Barker	.06
403	Tom Brennan	.06
404	*Carmelo Castillo* (FC)	.10
405	Miguel Dilone	.06
406	Jerry Dybzinski	.06
407	Mike Fischlin	.06
409	Mike Hargrove	.06
410	Toby Harrah	.08
411	Ron Hassey	.06
412	Von Hayes	.15
413	Rick Manning	.06
414	Bake McBride	.06
415	Larry Milbourne	.06
417	Jack Perconte	.06
419	Dan Spillner	.06
420	Rick Sutcliffe	.12
421	Andre Thornton	.10
422	Rick Waits	.06
423	Eddie Whitson	.06
424	Jesse Barfield (FC)	.60
425	Barry Bonnell	.06
426	Jim Clancy	.08
427	Damaso Garcia	.06
428	Jerry Garvin	.06
429	Alfredo Griffin	.08
430	Garth Iorg	.06
432	Luis Leal	.06
433	Buck Martinez	.06
435	Lloyd Moseby	.12
437	Dale Murray	.06
439	*Gene Petralli* (FC)	.15
440	Hosken Powell	.06
441	Dave Stieb	.12
442	Willie Upshaw	.08
443	Ernie Whitt	.08
444	Al Woods	.06
445	Alan Ashby	.06
446	Jose Cruz	.10
447	Kiko Garcia	.06
448	Phil Garner	.08
449	Danny Heep	.06
450	Art Howe	.06
451	Bob Knepper	.06

452	Alan Knicely	.06
453	Ray Knight	.10
455	Mike LaCoss	.06
456	Randy Moffitt	.06
457	Joe Niekro	.10
458	Terry Puhl	.06
460	Craig Reynolds	.06
461	Bert Roberge	.06
462	Vern Ruhle	.06
463	Nolan Ryan	1.25
464	Joe Sambito	.06
465	Tony Scott	.06
466	Dave Smith	.08
467	Harry Spilman	.06
468	Dickie Thon	.06
469	Denny Walling	.06
471	Floyd Bannister	.10
472	Jim Beattie	.06
473	Bruce Bochte	.06
475	Bill Caudill	.06
476	Bryan Clark	.06
477	Al Cowens	.06
478	Julio Cruz	.06
479	Todd Cruz	.06
480	Gary Gray	.06
481	Dave Henderson (FC)	.20
482	*Mike Moore* (FC)	1.25
483	Gaylord Perry	.30
484	Dave Revering	.06
485	Joe Simpson	.06
486	Mike Stanton	.06
487	Rick Sweet	.06
488	*Ed Vande Berg* (FC)	.10
489	Richie Zisk	.08
490	Doug Bird	.06
491	Larry Bowa	.12
492	Bill Buckner	.12
493	Bill Campbell	.06
494	Jody Davis	.08
495	Leon Durham	.08
497	Willie Hernandez	.08
498	*Ferguson Jenkins	.15
499	*Jay Johnstone	.08

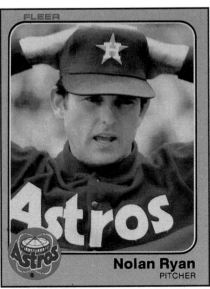

463 Nolan Ryan

482 Mike Moore

501	Randy Martz	.06
502	Jerry Morales	.06
504	Dickie Noles	.06
505	Mike Proly	.06
506	Allen Ripley	.06
507	*Ryne Sandberg* (FC)	10.00
508	Lee Smith	.15
509	Pat Tabler (FC)	.15
510	Dick Tidrow	.06
511	Bump Wills	.06
512	Gary Woods	.06
513	Tony Armas	.10
514	Dave Beard	.06
515	Jeff Burroughs	.08
517	Wayne Gross	.06
518	Mike Heath	.06
519	Rickey Henderson	.60
520	Cliff Johnson	.06
521	Matt Keough	.06
522	Brian Kingman	.06
523	Rick Langford	.06
524	Davey Lopes	.06
525	Steve McCatty	.06
526	Dave McKay	.06
527	Dan Meyer	.06
529	Jeff Newman	.06
530	Mike Norris	.06
532	Joe Rudi	.10
533	Jimmy Sexton	.06
534	Fred Stanley	.06
536	Neil Allen	.06
538	Bob Bailor	.06
539	Hubie Brooks	.12
540	Carlos Diaz	.06
541	Pete Falcone	.06
542	George Foster	.15
544	Brian Giles	.06
545	Ron Hodges	.06
546	Randy Jones	.08
548	Dave Kingman	.15
549	Ed Lynch	.06
550	Jesse Orosco (FC)	.15
551	Rick Ownbey	.06

552	Charlie Puleo (FC)	.10
553	Gary Rajsich	.06
554	*Mike Scott	.15
555	Rusty Staub	.10
556	John Stearns	.06
557	Craig Swan	.06
558	Ellis Valentine	.06
559	Tom Veryzer	.06
560	Mookie Wilson	.10
561	Pat Zachry	.06
562	Buddy Bell	.12
563	John Butcher	.06
564	Steve Comer	.06
565	Danny Darwin	.06
566	Bucky Dent	.10
567	John Grubb	.06
569	Dave Hostetler	.06
570	Charlie Hough	.10
572	Jon Matlack	.08
574	Larry Parrish	.10
576	Mickey Rivers	.08
578	Dave Schmidt (FC)	.10

580	Jim Sundberg	.08
581	Frank Tanana	.10
584	Johnny Bench	.40
587	Cesar Cedeno	.10
588	Dave Concepcion	.10
589	Dan Driessen	.08
590	Greg Harris (FC)	.08
597	Eddie Milner (FC)	.10
600	Joe Price	.06
601	Tom Seaver	.50
603	Mario Soto	.08
607	Tom Brunansky (FC)	.25
610	Ron Davis	.06
613	Gary Gaetti (FC)	4.00
614	Mickey Hatcher	.08
616	Kent Hrbek (FC)	.75
618	Tim Laudner (FC)	.08
625	Frank Viola (FC)	5.00
629	Red Sox AS (Mark Clear, Dennis Eckersley, Carl Yastrzemski)	.25

631	Pride of Venezuela (Dave Concepcion, Manny Trillo)	.10
632	AS Infielders (Buddy Bell, Robin Yount)	.15
633	Mr. Vet and Mr. Rookie (Kent Hrbek, Dave Winfield)	.25
634	Fountain of Youth (Pete Rose, Willie Stargell)	.40
637	Base Stealers' Threat (Gary Carter, Bo Diaz)	.15
638	AS Catchers (Gary Carter, Carlton Fisk)	.20
639	The Silver Shoe (Rickey Henderson)	.30
640	HR Threats (Reggie Jackson, Ben Oglivie)	.25
646	Speed and Power (RIckey Henderson)	.30

1983 TOPPS

Topps reached back 20 years for the design of this 726-card set. Like the 1963 set which it resembles, the 1983 edition features a large color photograph of the player with a small round portrait in a lower corner. This design works best when the portrait is contrasted with an action shot. Due to the popularity of the fall Traded sets, Topps omitted all rookie cards from its standard edition. One of the most appealing subsets of the decade came in 1983. Super Veteran cards use a then-and-now theme which displays a contemporary 1983 pose along with a vintage shot from early in the player's career. Pete Rose, Rod Carew, Reggie Jackson, and Carl Yastrzemski highlight this series. The value given for the complete set is somewhat misleading, however, since a single card, the Wade Boggs rookie card (498), by itself accounts for nearly a third of the price of the entire set.

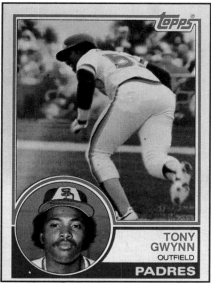
482 Tony Gwynn

		MINT
Complete set		**$100.00**
Commons		**.08**

1	Record Breaker (Tony Armas)	$ .12
2	Record Breaker (Rickey Henderson)	.35
4	Record Breaker (Lance Parrish)	.20
7	Gene Richards	.08
8	Steve Balboni	.08
10	Gorman Thomas	.10
13	Larry Herndon	.08
15	Ron Cey	.10
17	Kent Tekulve	.08
18	Super Vet (Kent Tekulve)	.10
19	Oscar Gamble	.10
20	Carlton Fisk	.40
21	Orioles Ldrs (Eddie Murray, Jim Palmer)	.35
24	Steve Mura	.08
25	Hal McRae	.15

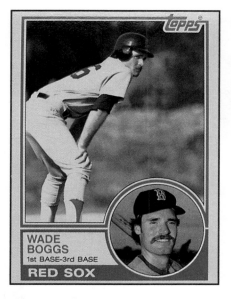
498 Wade Boggs

29	Randy Jones	.10
30	Jim Rice	.70
35	Rollie Fingers	.30
36	Super Vet (Rollie Fingers)	.15
37	Darrell Johnson	.08
38	Tim Flannery	.08
39	Terry Puhl	.08
40	Fernando Valenzuela	.50
43	Bob Dernier	.08
44	Don Robinson	.10

83 Ryne Sandberg

45	John Mayberry	.10
46	Richard Dotson	.12
47	Dave McKay	.08
49	*Willie McGee* (FC)	2.00
50	Bob Horner	.20
51	Cubs Ldrs (Leon Durham, Fergie Jenkins)	.15
53	Mike Witt	.30
54	Jim Maler	.08
55	Mookie Wilson	.12
58	Al Holland	.08
60	Johnny Bench	.60
61	Super Vet (Johnny Bench)	.15
62	Bob McClure	.08
63	Rick Monday	.10
64	Bill Stein	.08
65	Jack Morris	.35
66	Bob Lillis	.08
67	Sal Butera	.08
68	*Eric Show*	.25
69	Lee Lacy	.08
70	Steve Carlton	.65
71	Super Vet (Steve Carlton)	.25
72	Tom Paciorek	.08
73	Allen Ripley	.08
75	Amos Otis	.10
76	Rick Mahler	.10
77	Hosken Powell	.08
78	Bill Caudill	.08
79	Mick Kelleher	.08
80	George Foster	.20
81	Yankees Ldrs (Jerry Mumphrey, Dave Righetti)	.15
82	Bruce Hurst	.15
83	*Ryne Sandberg* (FC)	12.00
84	Milt May	.08
85	Ken Singleton	.10
86	Tom Hume	.08
87	Joe Rudi	.10
88	Jim Gantner	.08
90	Jerry Reuss	.10
95	Alan Trammell	.50
96	Dick Howser	.08

98	Vance Law	.08
100	Pete Rose	2.00
101	Super Vet (Pete Rose)	.80
102	Dave Beard	.08
103	Darrell Porter	.08
104	Bob Walk	.08
105	Don Baylor	.15
109	Luis Leal	.08
110	Ken Griffey	.10
111	Expos Ldrs (Al Oliver, Steve Rogers)	.15
112	Bob Shirley	.08
114	Jim Slaton	.08
115	Chili Davis	.08
116	Dave Schmidt	.08
118	Chris Welsh	.08
120	Len Barker	.08
121	Mickey Hatcher	.08
122	Jimmy Smith	.08
124	Marc Hill	.08
125	Leon Durham	.08
126	Joe Torre	.10
127	Preston Hanna	.08
128	Mike Ramsey	.08
129	Checklist 1-132	.12
130	Dave Stieb	.20
131	Ed Ott	.08
132	Todd Cruz	.08
133	Jim Barr	.08
134	Hubie Brooks	.15
135	*Dwight Evans	.25
136	Willie Aikens	.08
137	Woodie Fryman	.08
138	Rick Dempsey	.08
140	Willie Randolph	.10
141	Indians Ldrs (Toby Harrah, Rick Sutcliffe)	.15
142	Mike Caldwell	.08
143	Joe Pettini	.08
144	Mark Wagner	.08
145	Don Sutton	.40
146	Super Vet (Don Sutton)	.20
147	Rick Leach	.08

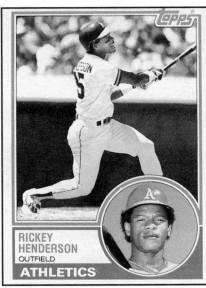

180 Rickey Henderson

586 Frank Viola

148	Dave Roberts	.08
149	Johnny Ray	.08
150	Bruce Sutter	.20
151	Super Vet (Bruce Sutter)	.15
152	Jay Johnstone	.10
153	Jerry Koosman	.10
155	Dan Quisenberry	.20
156	Billy Martin	.12
157	Steve Bedrosian	.25
158	Rob Wilfong	.10
159	Mike Stanton	.08
160	Dave Kingman	.15
161	Super Vet (Dave Kingman)	.10
162	Mark Clear	.08
163	Cal Ripken	3.00
164	Dave Palmer	.08
165	Dan Driessen	.08
166	John Pacella	.08
167	Mark Brouhard	.08
168	Juan Eichelberger	.08
169	Doug Flynn	.08
170	Steve Howe	.10
171	Giants Ldrs (Bill Laskey, Joe Morgan)	.15
172	Vern Ruhle	.08
173	Jim Morrison	.08
174	Jerry Ujdur	.08
175	Bo Diaz	.08
176	Dave Righetti	.35
177	Harold Baines	.25
178	Luis Tiant	.15
179	Super Vet (Luis Tiant)	.10
180	Rickey Henderson	2.00
181	Terry Felton	.08
182	Mike Fischlin	.08
183	*Ed Vande Berg*	.10
184	Bob Clark	.08
185	Tim Lollar	.08
186	Whitey Herzog	.10
187	Terry Leach	.08
188	Rick Miller	.08
189	Dan Schatzeder	.08

190	Cecil Cooper	.15
191	Joe Price	.08
192	Floyd Rayford	.08
193	Harry Spilman	.08
195	Bob Stoddard	.08
196	Bill Fahey	.08
197	*Jim Eisenreich* (FC)	.15
200	Rod Carew	.75
201	Super Vet (Rod Carew)	.35
202	Blue Jays Ldrs (Damaso Garcia, Dave Stieb)	.15
203	Mike Morgan	.15
204	Junior Kennedy	.08
205	Dave Parker	.35
206	Ken Oberkfell	.08
207	Rick Camp	.08
208	Dan Meyer	.08
209	*Mike Moore* (FC)	2.00
210	Jack Clark	.30
211	John Denny	.08
212	John Stearns	.08
214	Jerry White	.08
215	Mario Soto	.08
216	Tony LaRussa	.10
217	Tim Stoddard	.08
218	Roy Howell	.08
220	Dusty Baker	.10
221	Joe Niekro	.10
222	Damaso Garcia	.08
224	Mickey Rivers	.10
225	Enos Cabell	.08
226	Enrique Romo	.08
227	Chris Bando	.08
228	Joaquin Andujar	.08
229	Phillies Ldrs (Steve Carlton, Bo Diaz)	.15
230	Fergie Jenkins	.25
231	Super Vet (Fergie Jenkins)	.10
232	Tom Brunansky	.30
233	Wayne Gross	.08
235	Claudell Washington	.10
236	Steve Renko	.08

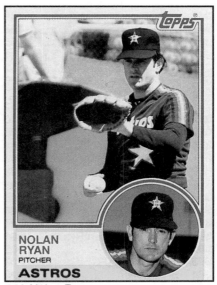

163 Cal Ripken

237	Dan Norman	.08
238	*Bud Black* (FC)	.20
239	Dave Stapleton	.08
240	Rich Gossage	.25
241	Super Vet (Rich Gossage)	.15
242	Joe Nolan	.08
243	Duane Walker	.08
244	Dwight Bernard	.08
245	Steve Sax	.35
246	George Bamberger	.08
247	Dave Smith	.10
248	Bake McBride	.08
249	Checklist 133-264	.12
250	Bill Buckner	.15
251	*Alan Wiggins* (FC)	.08
252	Luis Aguayo	.08
253	Larry McWilliams	.08
254	Rick Cerone	.08
255	Gene Garber	.08
256	Super Vet (Gene Garber)	.08
257	Jesse Barfield	.50
258	Manny Castillo	.08
259	Jeff Jones	.08
260	Steve Kemp	.10
261	Tigers Ldrs (Larry Herndon, Dan Petry)	.10
262	Ron Jackson	.08
263	Renie Martin	.08
264	Jamie Quirk	.08
266	Paul Boris	.08
268	*Storm Davis* (FC)	.75
269	Ron Oester	.08
270	Dennis Eckersley	.20
271	Ed Romero	.08
272	Frank Tanana	.10
273	Mark Belanger	.10
274	Terry Kennedy	.10
275	Ray Knight	.10
276	Gene Mauch	.10
278	Kevin Hickey	.08
279	Gregg Gross	.08
280	*Bert Blyleven	.20
282	Reggie Smith	.15

283	Super Vet (Reggie Smith)	.10
285	Lance Parrish	.45
286	Rick Langford	.08
287	Bobby Brown	.08
288	*Joe Cowley* (FC)	.10
289	Jerry Dybzinski	.08
290	Jeff Reardon	.15
291	Pirates Ldrs (John Candelaria, Bill Madlock)	.15
292	Craig Swan	.08
293	Glenn Gulliver	.08
294	Dave Engle	.08
295	Jerry Remy	.08
296	Greg Harris	.08
297	Ned Yost	.08
298	Floyd Chiffer	.08
299	George Wright	.08
300	Mike Schmidt	2.00
301	Super Vet (Mike Schmidt)	.65
302	Ernie Whitt	.10
303	Miguel Dilone	.08
304	Dave Rucker	.08
305	Larry Bowa	.15
306	Tom Lasorda	.10
307	Lou Piniella	.15
308	Jesus Vega	.08
309	Jeff Leonard	.10
310	Greg Luzinski	.15
311	Glenn Brummer	.08
312	Brian Kingman	.08
313	Gary Gray	.08
314	Ken Dayley (FC)	.15
315	Rick Burleson	.08
316	Paul Splittorff	.08
317	Gary Rajsich	.08
318	John Tudor	.15
319	Lenn Sakata	.08
320	Steve Rogers	.10
321	Brewers Ldrs (Pete Vuckovich, Robin Yount)	.15
322	Dave Van Gorder	.08
323	Luis DeLeon	.08
324	Mike Marshall	.25

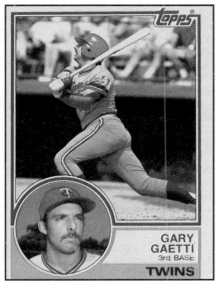

431 Gary Gaetti

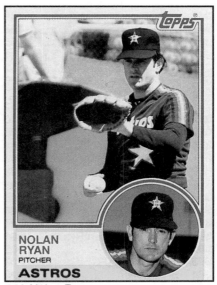

360 Nolan Ryan

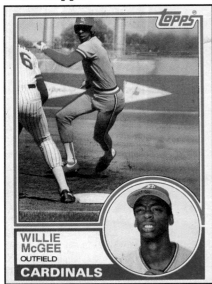

49 Willie McGee

325	Von Hayes	.20
326	Garth Iorg	.08
327	Bobby Castillo	.08
328	Craig Reynolds	.08
329	Randy Niemann	.08
330	Buddy Bell	.15
331	Mike Krukow	.10
332	*Glenn Wilson* (FC)	.25
333	Dave LaRoche	.08
334	Super Vet (Dave LaRoche)	.08
335	Steve Henderson	.08
336	Rene Lachemann	.08
337	Tito Landrum	.08
338	Bob Owchinko	.08
339	Terry Harper	.08
340	Larry Gura	.08
341	Doug DeCinces	.10
342	Atlee Hammaker	.08
343	Bob Bailor	.08
344	Roger LaFrancois	.08
345	Jim Clancy	.08
346	Joe Pittman	.08
347	Sammy Stewart	.08
348	Alan Bannister	.08
349	Checklist 265-396	.12
350	Robin Yount	.50
351	Reds Ldrs (Cesar Cedeno, Mario Soto)	.12
352	Mike Scioscia	.10
353	Steve Comer	.08
354	Randy Johnson	.08
355	Jim Bibby	.08
356	Gary Woods	.08
357	*Len Matuszek* (FC)	.08
358	Jerry Garvin	.08
359	Dave Collins	.08
360	Nolan Ryan	2.50
361	Super Vet (Nolan Ryan)	.35
362	Bill Almon	.08
363	*John Stuper* (FC)	.08
364	Brett Butler	.20
365	Dave Lopes	.12

366	Dick Williams	.08
367	Bud Anderson	.08
368	Richie Zisk	.10
369	Jesse Orosco	.15
370	Gary Carter	.50
371	Mike Richardt	.08
372	Terry Crowley	.08
373	Kevin Saucier	.08
374	Wayne Krenchicki	.08
375	Pete Vuckovich	.08
376	Ken Landreaux	.08
377	Lee May	.10
378	Super Vet (Lee May)	.08
379	Guy Sularz	.08
380	Ron Davis	.08
381	Red Sox Ldrs (Jim Rice, Bob Stanley)	.15
382	Bob Knepper	.08
383	Ozzie Virgil	.10
384	*Dave Dravecky* (FC)	.25
385	Mike Easler	.10
386	Rod Carew AS	.35
387	Bob Grich AS	.15
388	George Brett AS	.50
389	Robin Yount AS	.25
390	Reggie Jackson AS	.50
391	Rickey Henderson AS	.40
392	Fred Lynn AS	.15
393	Carlton Fisk AS	.15
394	Pete Vuckovich AS	.10
395	Larry Gura AS	.08
396	Dan Quisenberry AS	.15
397	Pete Rose AS	.75
398	Manny Trillo AS	.10
399	Mike Schmidt AS	.60
400	Dave Concepcion AS	.50
401	Dale Murphy AS	.75
402	Andre Dawson AS	.20
403	Tim Raines AS	.35
404	Gary Carter AS	.35
405	Steve Rogers AS	.10
406	Steve Carlton AS	.35
407	Bruce Sutter AS	.15

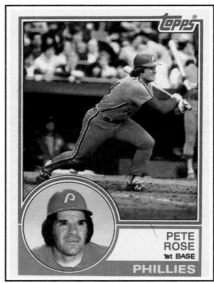

100 Pete Rose

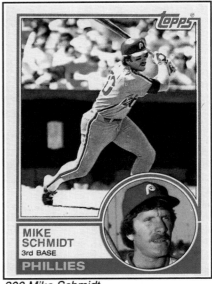

300 Mike Schmidt

408	Rudy May	.08
409	Marvis Foley	.08
410	Phil Niekro	.40
411	Super Vet (Phil Niekro)	.20
412	Rangers Ldrs (Buddy Bell, Charlie Hough)	.15
413	Matt Keough	.08
414	Julio Cruz	.08
415	Bob Forsch	.08
416	Joe Ferguson	.08
417	Tom Hausman	.08
418	Greg Pryor	.08
419	Steve Crawford	.08
420	Al Oliver	.20
421	Super Vet (Al Oliver)	.10
422	George Cappuzzello	.08
423	*Tom Lawless* (FC)	.10
424	Jerry Augustine	.08
425	Pedro Guerrero	.35
426	Earl Weaver	.10
427	Roy Lee Jackson	.08
428	Champ Summers	.08
429	Eddie Whitson	.08
430	Kirk Gibson	.50
431	*Gary Gaetti* (FC)	5.00
432	Porfirio Altamirano	.08
433	Dale Berra	.08
434	Dennis Lamp	.08
435	Tony Armas	.10
436	Bill Campbell	.08
437	Rick Sweet	.08
438	*Dave LaPoint* (FC)	.20
439	Rafael Ramirez	.08
440	Ron Guidry	.25
441	Astros Ldrs (Ray Knight, Joe Niekro)	.10
442	Brian Downing	.10
443	Don Hood	.08
444	Wally Backman (FC)	.20
445	Mike Flanagan	.10
446	Reid Nichols	.08
447	Bryn Smith	.10
448	Darrell Evans	.20

449	Eddie Milner	.12
450	Ted Simmons	.20
451	Super Vet (Ted Simmons)	.12
452	Lloyd Moseby	.20
453	Lamar Johnson	.08
454	Bob Welch	.15
455	Sixto Lezcano	.08
456	Lee Elia	.08
457	Milt Wilcox	.08
458	Ron Washington	.08
459	Ed Farmer	.08
460	Roy Smalley	.08
461	Steve Trout	.08
462	Steve Nicosia	.08
463	Gaylord Perry	.40
464	Super Vet (Gaylord Perry)	.25
465	Lonnie Smith	.08
466	Tom Underwood	.08
467	Rufino Linares	.08
468	Dave Goltz	.08
469	Ron Gardenhire	.08
470	Greg Minton	.08
471	Royals Ldrs (Vida Blue, Willie Wilson)	.15
472	Gary Allenson	.08
473	John Lowenstein	.08
474	Ray Burris	.08
475	Cesar Cedeno	.10
476	Rob Picciolo	.08
477	Tom Niedenfuer (FC)	.15
478	Phil Garner	.10
479	Charlie Hough	.12
480	Toby Harrah	.08
481	Scot Thompson	.08
482	Tony Gwynn (FC)	20.00
483	Lynn Jones	.08
484	Dick Ruthven	.08
485	Omar Moreno	.08
486	Clyde King	.08
487	Jerry Hairston	.08
488	Alfredo Griffin	.08
489	Tom Herr	.10
490	Jim Palmer	.50

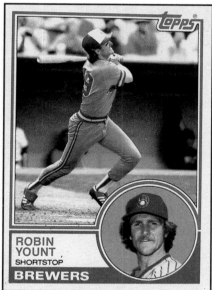

600 George Brett

491	Super Vet (Jim Palmer)	.20
492	Paul Serna	.08
493	Steve McCatty	.08
494	Bob Brenly	.08
495	Warren Cromartie	.08
496	Tom Veryzer	.08
497	Rick Sutcliffe	.10
498	Wade Boggs (FC)	35.00
499	Jeff Little	.08
500	Reggie Jackson	.75
501	Super Vet (Reggie Jackson)	.35
502	Braves Ldrs (Dale Murphy, Phil Niekro)	.50
503	Moose Haas	.08
504	Don Werner	.08
505	Garry Templeton	.08
506	Jim Gott (FC)	.08
507	Tony Scott	.08
509	Lou Whitaker	.40
510	Tug McGraw	.15
511	Super Vet (Tug McGraw)	.10
512	Doyle Alexander	.20
513	Fred Stanley	.10
514	Rudy Law	.08
515	Gene Tenace	.08
517	Gary Ward	.10
520	Fred Lynn	.25
525	Frank White	.12
526	Checklist 397-528	.12
529	Tim Laudner	.08
530	Eddie Murray	.80
531	Athletics Ldrs (Rickey Henderson, Rick Langford)	.25
532	*Dave Stewart	.10
540	Ozzie Smith	.30
542	Jody Davis	.08
545	Floyd Bannister	.10
549	Charlie Puleo	.08
550	Carl Yastrzemski	.80
551	Super Vet (Carl Yastrzemski)	.40

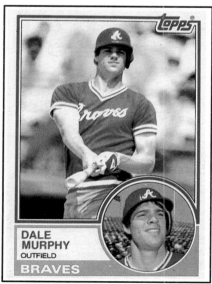

760 Dale Murphy

552	Tim Wallach	.10
561	Cardinals Ldrs (Joaquin Andujar, Lonnie Smith)	.15
565	Bucky Dent	.12
568	Willie Hernandez	.10
570	Vida Blue	.15
576	Frank Robinson	.10
580	Tom Seaver	.75
581	Super Vet (Tom Seaver)	.35
585	Jose Cruz	.15
586	Frank Viola (FC)	7.00
590	Tony Pena	.10
591	White Sox Ldrs (LaMarr Hoyt, Greg Luzinski)	.15
592	Shane Rawley	.08
595	Tim Raines	.50
600	George Brett	1.00
602	Rich Gedman	.08
603	*Joe Morgan	.40
604	*Super Vet (Joe Morgan)	.20
610	Steve Garvey	.75
615	Garry Maddox	.10
621	Mets Ldrs (Craig Swan, Mookie Wilson)	.12
630	Paul Molitor	.30
635	Graig Nettles	.20
636	Super Vet (Graig Nettles)	.12
640	Andre Thornton	.12
642	Checklist 529-660	.12
645	Bill Madlock	.15
650	George Hendrick	.10
651	Angels Ldrs (Rod Carew, Mike Witt)	.25
654	Bob Ojeda	.10
666	Sparky Anderson	.10
672	*Jim Kaat	.20
673	Super Vet (Jim Kaat)	.12
679	*Mike Scott	.20
680	Andre Dawson	.40
681	Dodgers Ldrs (Pedro Guerrero, Fernando Valenzuela)	.25

350 Robin Yount

690	Kent Hrbek	.50
693	*Sparky Lyle	.12
694	Super Vet (Sparky Lyle)	.10
700	Keith Hernandez	.50
701	Batting Ldrs (Al Oliver, Willie Wilson)	.15
702	HR Ldrs (Reggie Jackson, Dave Kingman, Gorman Thomas)	.35
703	RBI Ldrs (Hal McRae, Dale Murphy, Al Oliver)	.25
704	SB Ldrs (Rickey Henderson, Tim Raines)	.30
705	Victory Ldrs (Steve Carlton, LaMarr Hoyt)	.20
706	SO Ldrs (Floyd Bannister, Steve Carlton)	.20
707	ERA Ldrs (Steve Rogers, Rick Sutcliffe)	.12

708	Leading Firemen (Dan Quisenberry, Bruce Sutter)	.15
710	Willie Wilson	.20
711	Mariners Ldrs (Jim Beattie, Bruce Bochte)	.12
715	Tony Perez	.25
716	Super Vet (Tony Perez)	.15
720	Dave Concepcion	.10
726	Harvey Kuenn	.10
727	Chet Lemon	.10
732	Dave Henderson	.08
735	Tommy John	.25
736	Super Vet (Tommy John)	.15
737	Mitchell Page	.08
740	Rusty Staub	.15
741	Super Vet (Rusty Staub)	.10
742	Padres Ldrs (Terry Kennedy, Tim Lollar)	.12
743	Mike Torrez	.10
745	Scott McGregor	.10
746	John Wathan	.10

749	Jon Matlack	.10
750	Ben Oglivie	.10
755	John Candelaria	.10
760	Dale Murphy	1.50
765	*Bob Boone	.15
769	Checklist 661-792	.12
770	Dave Winfield	.50
771	Twins Ldrs (Bobby Castillo, Kent Hrbek)	.20
773	Larry Hisle	.10
775	Burt Hooton	.10
776	Larry Parrish	.10
778	Rich Hebner	.10
780	Gary Matthews	.10
781	Rick Rhoden	.12
782	Bobby Murcer	.12
783	Super Vet (Bobby Murcer)	.10
785	Dennis Leonard	.10
786	Ralph Houk	.10
788	Dane Lorg	.10
790	Bob Grich	.10
792	Chris Chambliss	.10

1983 TOPPS TRADED

Don't let the price of the complete set of the 1983 Topps Traded issue fool you. Three fourths of the estimated value is found in one card: the first-card issue of New York Mets superstar Darryl Strawberry, number 108. Other newcomers featured in this late-season series include John Shelby, Bill Doran, Greg Brock, Julio Franco, Ron Kittle, and Mel Hall. Steve Garvey, now dressed as a Padre, heads the class of veteran players in new uniforms. Because these cards were sold only through hobby dealers, many of whom were skeptical about the set's selling power, fewer sets than usual were produced and distributed to the public.

34 Julio Franco

		MINT
Complete set		**$89.00**
Commons		**.10**

1	Neil Allen	$ .10
2	Bill Almon	.10
3	Joe Altobelli	.10
4	Tony Armas	.20
5	Doug Bair	.10
6	Steve Baker	.10
7	Floyd Bannister	.20
8	Don Baylor	.30
9	Tony Bernazard	.10
10	Larry Biittner	.10
11	Dann Bilardello	.10
12	Doug Bird	.10
14	Greg Brock (FC)	.40
16	Tom Burgmeier	.10
17	Randy Bush (FC)	.25
18	Bert Campaneris	.20
19	Ron Cey	.25
20	Chris Codiroli (FC)	.15
21	Dave Collins	.15

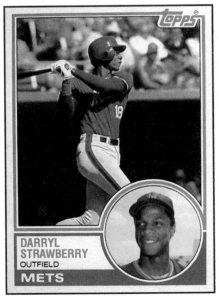

108 Darryl Strawberry

22	Terry Crowley	.10
23	Julio Cruz	.10
24	Mike Davis	.15
25	Frank DiPino	.10
26	Bill Doran (FC)	.90
27	Jerry Dybzinski	.10
28	Jamie Easterly	.10
29	Juan Eichelberger	.10
30	Jim Essian	.10
31	Pete Falcone	.10

180

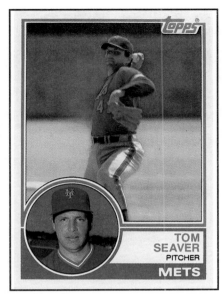

101 Tom Seaver

33	Terry Forster	.10
34	Julio Franco (FC)	4.00
35	Rich Gale	.10

36	Kiko Garcia	.10
37	Steve Garvey	2.00
39	Mel Hall (FC)	.90
40	Von Hayes	.50
41	Danny Heep	.10
42	Steve Henderson	.10
43	Keith Hernandez	1.00
44	Leo Hernandez	.10
45	Willie Hernandez	.25
46	Al Holland	.10
47	Frank Howard	.15
48	Bobby Johnson	.10
53	Steve Kemp	.15
55	Ron Kittle (FC)	.60
58	Mike Krukow	.15
60	Carney Lansford	.25
66	*Billy Martin	.20
67	Lee Mazzilli	.15
69	Craig McMurtry (FC)	.25
77	*Joe Morgan	1.75
81	Pete O'Brien (FC)	2.00
83	Alejandro Pena (FC)	.60
84	Pascual Perez	.20
85	Tony Perez	.60
87	Tony Phillips (FC)	.20
94	Gary Redus (FC)	.40
97	Aurelio Rodriguez	.15
100	*Mike Scott	.50
101	Tom Seaver	2.25

102	John Shelby (FC)	.40
103	Bob Shirley	.10
104	Joe Simpson	.10
105	Doug Sisk (FC)	.15
106	Mike Smithson (FC)	.20
107	Elias Sosa	.10
108	Darryl Strawberry (FC)	65.00
109	Tom Tellman	.10
110	Gene Tenace	.10
111	Gorman Thomas	.15
112	Dick Tidrow	.10
113	Dave Tobik	.10
114	Wayne Tolleson (FC)	.15
115	Mike Torrez	.15
116	Manny Trillo	.15
117	Steve Trout	.10
118	Lee Tunnell (FC)	.15
119	Mike Vail	.10
120	Ellis Valentine	.10
121	Tom Veryzer	.10
122	George Vukovich	.10
124	Greg Walker (FC)	1.00
126	Len Whitehouse	.10
127	Eddie Whitson	.15
128	Jim Wohlford	.10
129	Matt Young (FC)	.20
130	Joel Youngblood	.10
131	Pat Zachry	.10
132	Checklist 1-132	.10

1984 DONRUSS

The combination of a limited print run and the presence of several flashy rookies made the 1984 Donruss set the most expensive regular-season issue of the decade. For starters, nearly one fourth of the current estimated value can be traced to the incredible demand for the first-year card for Don Mattingly. Darryl Strawberry is another very popular rookie. Ironically, neither Strawberry nor Mattingly was included in Rated Rookies, the 20-card subset which highlights outstanding prospects. Two unnumbered cards for Living Legends were distributed only in wax packs: Johnny Bench and Carl Yastrzemski are featured on one; Rollie Fingers and Gaylord Perry on the other.

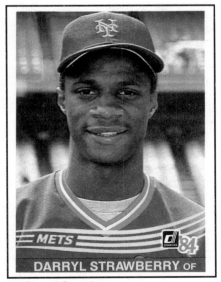

68 Darryl Strawberry

		MINT
Complete set		**$305.00**
Commons		**.10**

1	Robin Yount (DK)	$ .80
2	Dave Concepcion (DK)	.30
3	Dwayne Murphy (DK)	.25
4	John Castino (DK)	.20
5	Leon Durham (DK)	.25
6	Rusty Staub (DK)	.30
7	Jack Clark (DK)	.40
8	Dave Dravecky (DK)	.25
9	Al Oliver (DK)	.35
10	Dave Righetti (DK)	.40
11	Hal McRae (DK)	.30
12	Ray Knight (DK)	.25
13	Bruce Sutter (DK)	.35
14	Bob Horner (DK)	.40
15	Lance Parrish (DK)	.60

16	Matt Young (DK)	.25
17	Fred Lynn (DK)	.35
18	Ron Kittle (DK)	.35
19	Jim Clancy (DK)	.25
20	Bill Madlock (DK)	.30
21	Larry Parrish (DK)	.30
22	Eddie Murray (DK)	1.25
23	Mike Schimdt (DK)	1.25
24	Pedro Guerrero (DK)	.50
25	Andre Thornton (DK)	.30
26	Wade Boggs (DK)	3.75
29	Mike Stenhouse (RR) (number 29 on back)	8.00
29	Mike Stenhouse (RR) (no number on back)	.15
30	*Ron Darling* (RR) (FC) (number 30 on back)	20.00
30	*Ron Darling* (RR) (FC) (no number on back)	6.00

31	*Dion James* (RR) (FC)	.40
32	*Tony Fernandez* (RR) (FC)	8.00
34	*Kevin McReynolds* (RR) (FC)	12.00

181

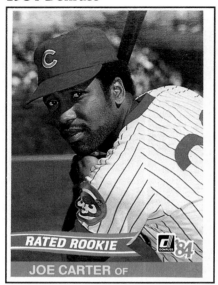

41 Joe Carter

35	Dick Schofield (RR) (FC)	.40
37	Tim Teufel (RR) (FC)	.40
39	Greg Gagne (RR) (FC)	.50
41	Joe Carter (RR) (FC)	16.00
44	Sid Fernandez (RR) (FC)	6.00
47	Eddie Murray	1.25
48	Robin Yount	2.00
49	Lance Parrish	.50
50	Jim Rice	.95
51	Dave Winfield	.95
52	Fernando Valenzuela	.75
53	George Brett	1.50
54	Rickey Henderson	3.00
55	Gary Carter	.75
56	Buddy Bell	.20
57	Reggie Jackson	1.25
58	Harold Baines	.25
59	Ozzie Smith	.25
60	Nolan Ryan	3.50
61	Pete Rose	2.50
62	Ron Oester	.10
63	Steve Garvey	.90
64	Jason Thompson	.10
65	Jack Clark	.35
66	Dale Murphy	1.50
67	Leon Durham	.10
68	Darryl Strawberry (FC)	36.00
69	Richie Zisk	.10
70	Kent Hrbek	.65
71	Dave Stieb	.25
72	Ken Schrom	.10
73	George Bell	1.75
74	John Moses	.15
75	Ed Lynch	.10
79	Jim Barr	.10
81	Tom Foley	.10
83	Andy Van Slyke (FC)	4.00
84	Bob Lillis	.10
85	Rick Adams	.10
87	Bob James	.10
89	Ed Romero	.10
90	John Grubb	.10
92	Juan Espino	.10

93	Candy Maldonado	.20
94	Andre Thornton	.20
96	Don Hill (FC)	.20
97	Andre Dawson	.60
98	Frank Tanana	.15
100	Larry Gura	.10
103	Dave Righetti	.40
104	Steve Sax	.30
105	Dan Petry	.10
106	Cal Ripken	1.50
107	Paul Molitor	.35
108	Fred Lynn	.35
109	Neil Allen	.10
110	Joe Niekro	.20
111	Steve Carlton	1.00
113	Bill Madlock	.20
114	Chili Davis	.15
115	Jim Gantner	.10
116	Tom Seaver	1.00
117	Bill Buckner	.20
118	Bill Caudill	.10
119	Jim Clancy	.10
120	John Castino	.10
121	Dave Concepcion	.15
122	Greg Luzinski	.15
123	Mike Boddicker (FC)	.20
124	Pete Ladd	.10
127	Ed Jurak	.10
129	Bert Blyleven	.30
130	Bud Black	.10
133	Ron Jackson	.10
134	Tom Henke (FC)	.95
136	Mike Scott	.30
137	Bo Diaz	.10
139	Sid Monge	.10
140	Rich Gale	.10
141	Brett Butler	.15
142	Brian Harper	.10
143	John Rabb	.10
144	Gary Woods	.10
145	Pat Putnam	.10
146	Jim Acker (FC)	.15
148	Todd Cruz	.10

151 Wade Boggs

RATED ROOKIE — KEVIN McREYNOLDS OF

34 Kevin McReynolds

149	Tom Tellmann	.10
151	Wade Boggs	12.00
152	Don Baylor	.20
153	Bob Welch	.20
154	Alan Bannister	.10
155	Willie Aikens	.10
157	Bryan Little	.10
158	*Bob Boone	.15
161	Mike Madden	.10
162	Luis DeLeon	.10
163	Willie Hernandez	.15
164	Frank Pastore	.10
165	Rick Camp	.10
166	Lee Mazzilli	.12
168	Bob Forsch	.12
169	Mike Flanagan	.15
171	Chet Lemon	.12
172	Jerry Remy	.10
173	Ron Guidry	.35
174	Pedro Guerrero	.50
175	Willie Wilson	.25
176	Carney Lansford	.20
177	Al Oliver	.30
179	Bobby Grich	.20
180	Richard Dotson	.20
182	Jose Cruz	.15
183	Mike Schmidt	4.00
184	Gary Redus (FC)	.30
185	Garry Templeton	.15
186	Tony Pena	.15
187	Greg Minton	.10
188	Phil Niekro	.50
189	Ferguson Jenkins	.35
190	Mookie Wilson	.15
191	Jim Beattie	.10
192	Gary Ward	.10
193	Jesse Barfield	.40
194	Pete Filson	.10
196	Rick Sweet	.10
197	Jesse Orosco	.15
198	Steve Lake (FC)	.10
199	Ken Dayley	.10
201	Mark Davis (FC)	.25

202	Tim Flannery	.10
203	Bill Scherrer	.10
204	Al Holland	.10
208	Juan Agosto (FC)	.20
209	Bobby Ramos	.10
210	Al Bumbry	.12
212	Howard Bailey	.10
213	Bruce Hurst	.25
214	Bob Shirley	.10
215	Pat Zachry	.10
216	Julio Franco	.25
218	Dave Beard	.10
219	Steve Rogers	.15
221	Mike Smithson (FC)	.20
222	Frank White	.20
223	Mike Heath	.10
224	Chris Bando	.10
225	Roy Smalley	.10
226	Dusty Baker	.20
227	Lou Whitaker	.65
229	Ben Oglivie	.10
230	Doug DeCinces	.15
231	Lonnie Smith	.12
232	Ray Knight	.15
233	Gary Matthews	.20
234	Juan Bonilla	.10
235	Rod Scurry	.10
237	Mike Caldwell	.10
238	Keith Hernandez	.80
239	Larry Bowa	.25
242	Tom Brunansky	.35
243	Dan Driessen	.12
244	Ron Kittle (FC)	.30
245	Tim Stoddard	.10
246	Bob Gibson	.10
247	Marty Castillo	.10
248	Don Mattingly (FC)	72.00
249	Jeff Newman	.10
250	Alejandro Pena (FC)	.40
251	Toby Harrah	.12
254	Doug Flynn	.10
256	Odell Jones	.10
257	Rudy Law	.10

324 Tony Gwynn

260	Dave Rucker	.10
261	Ruppert Jones	.10
262	Jeff Jones	.10
263	Gerald Perry (FC)	1.75
264	Gene Tenace	.12
266	Dickie Noles	.10
267	Jamie Allen	.10
268	Jim Gott	.15
269	Ron Davis	.10
271	Ned Yost	.10
272	Dave Rozema	.10
274	Lou Piniella	.20
275	Jose Morales	.10
276	Brod Perkins	.10
277	Butch Davis	.10
278	Tony Phillips (FC)	.25
279	Jeff Reardon	.25
280	Ken Forsch	.10
281	Pete O'Brien (FC)	1.50
282	Tom Paciorek	.10
284	Tim Lollar	.10
285	Greg Gross	.10
286	Alex Trevino	.10
287	Gene Garber	.10
288	Dave Parker	.50
289	Lee Smith	.20
291	John Shelby (FC)	.35
293	Alan Trammell	.60
294	Tony Armas	.20
296	Greg Brock	.15
297	Hal McRae	.20
298	Mike Davis	.12
299	Tim Raines	.80
300	Bucky Dent	.15
301	Tommy John	.40
302	Carlton Fisk	.50
303	Darrell Porter	.12
304	Dickie Thon	.10
305	Garry Maddox	.12
306	Cesar Cedeno	.20
307	Gary Lucas	.10
308	Johnny Ray	.20
311	Ryne Sandberg	4.50

312	George Foster	.30
313	Spike Owen (FC)	.30
314	Gary Gaetti	.90
315	Willie Upshaw	.12
316	Al Williams	.10
317	Jorge Orta	.10
319	Junior Ortiz (FC)	.12
320	Mike Proly	.10
324	Tony Gwynn	6.00
326	Ozzie Virgil	.10
327	Jeff Lahti	.10
329	Rob Wilfong	.10
330	Marc Hill	.10
331	Ray Burris	.10
333	Chuck Porter	.10
335	Gary Allenson	.10
336	Bob Meacham (FC)	.15
337	Joe Beckwith	.10
338	Rick Sutcliffe	.25
341	Scott Sanderson	.10
342	Larry Biittner	.10
343	Dave Stewart	.12
344	Darryl Motley	.10
348	Mike Marshall	.20
350	Rich Dauer	.10
351	Cecil Cooper	.20
352	Rod Carew	.90
353	Willie McGee	.40
354	Phil Garner	.10
355	Joe Morgan	.60
357	John Candelaria	.20
358	Bill Laskey	.10
360	Dave Kingman	.25
361	Ron Cey	.20
362	Matt Young (FC)	.20
363	Lloyd Moseby	.20
364	Frank Viola	1.50
366	Floyd Bannister	.20
367	Dan Ford	.10
368	Moose Haas	.10
369	Doug Bair	.10
371	Luis Aponte	.10
372	Jack Fimple	.10

Living Legends

32 Tony Fernandez

183

311 Ryne Sandberg

373	Neal Heaton (FC)	.20
374	Greg Pryor	.10
375	Wayne Gross	.10
376	Charlie Lea	.10
377	Steve Lubratich	.10
378	Jon Matlack	.12
379	Julio Cruz	.10
381	Kevin Gross (FC)	.40
382	Mike Ramsey	.10
384	Kelly Paris	.10
385	Pete Falcone	.10
386	Milt May	.10
388	Craig Lefferts (FC)	.25
390	Randy Moffitt	.10
393	Tom Candiotti (FC)	.30
395	*Dwight Evans	.30
396	Goose Gossage	.40
397	Derrel Thomas	.10
399	Leon Roberts	.10
400	Davey Lopes	.15
402	Geoff Zahn	.10
403	Billy Sample	.10
406	Eric Show	.15
407	John Denny	.10
410	Kent Tekulve	.12
411	Mel Hall	.20
412	John Stuper	.10
414	Don Sutton	.50
415	Jack Morris	.50
416	John Tudor	.20
417	Willie Randolph	.20
418	Jerry Reuss	.15
421	Tim Wallach	.25
422	Larry Parrish	.20
423	Brian Downing	.20
424	Britt Burns	.10
425	David Green	.10
428	Mario Soto	.12
429	Gene Richards	.10
430	Dale Berra	.10
431	Darrell Evans	.25
433	Jody Davis	.10
434	Danny Heep	.10

435	Ed Nunez (FC)	.25
437	Ernie Whitt	.12
438	Scott Ulger	.10
439	Doyle Alexander	.15
443	Len Barker	.12
444	Mike Easler	.12
445	Renie Martin	.10
446	Dennis Rasmussen (FC)	.70
447	Ted Power (FC)	.15
448	Charlie Hudson (FC)	.25
449	Danny Cox (FC)	.70
450	Kevin Bass (FC)	.30
451	Daryl Sconiers	.10
452	Scott Fletcher	.12
453	Bryn Smith	.10
454	Jim Dwyer	.10
455	Rob Picciolo	.10
456	Enos Cabell	.10
457	Dennis "Oil Can" Boyd (FC)	.50
458	Butch Wynegar	.10
459	Burt Hooton	.12
460	Ron Hassey	.10
461	Danny Jackson (FC)	3.00
462	Bob Kearney	.10
463	Terry Francona	.10
464	Wayne Tolleson	.10
465	Mickey Rivers	.12
466	John Wathan	.12
467	Bill Almon	.10
469	Steve Kemp	.15
471	Milt Wilcox	.10
472	Tippy Martinez	.10
473	Ted Simmons	.20
474	Tim Foli	.10
476	Terry Puhl	.10
477	Von Hayes	.25
478	Bobby Brown	.10
479	Lee Lacy	.10
481	Jim Slaton	.10
482	Mike Fitzgerald (FC)	.20
485	Luis Leal	.10
489	Joe Nolan	.10
491	Mike Laga (FC)	.12

60 Nolan Ryan

602 Nick Esasky

492	Rick Cerone	.10
497	Keith Atherton (FC)	.25
498	Chris Welsh	.10
499	Bruce Kison	.10
500	Bob Johnson	.10
501	Jerry Koosman	.15
503	Tony Perez	.40
506	Joe Price	.10
507	Pascual Perez	.15
508	Marvell Wynne (FC)	.25
509	Mike Krukow	.12
510	Dick Ruthven	.10
511	Al Cowens	.10
513	Randy Bush (FC)	.20
515	Bill Schroeder (FC)	.25
517	Mike Brown	.10
518	Graig Nettles	.35
519	Dave Sax	.10
523	Chris Speier	.10
524	Bobby Clark	.10
526	Dennis Lamp	.10
527	Tony Scott	.10
528	Ed Whitson	.10
529	Ron Reed	.10
530	Charlie Puleo	.10
531	Jerry Royster	.10
533	Steve Trout	.10
534	Bruce Sutter	.30
535	Bob Horner	.40
536	Pat Tabler	.15
538	Bob Ojeda	.10
539	Alan Ashby	.10
540	Jay Johnstone	.10
541	Bob Dernier	.10
542	Brook Jacoby (FC)	1.50
544	Danny Darwin	.10
545	Kiko Garcia	.10
546	Vance Law	.10
547	Tug McGraw	.20
548	Dave Smith	.12
550	Tom Hume	.10
551	Dave Dravecky	.15
552	Rick Rhoden	.15

553	Duane Kuiper	.10
554	Rusty Staub	.20
556	Mike Torrez	.12
557	Dave Henderson	.20
561	Garth Iorg	.10
562	Bryan Clark	.10
563	Brian Giles	.10
564	Vern Ruhle	.10
565	Steve Bedrosian	.20
567	Jeff Leonard	.15
569	*Jeff Russell* (FC)	.25
571	Dane Iorg	.10
576	Jim Palmer	.70
579	Rich Gedman	.10
580	*Bill Doran* (FC)	1.25
583	Dan Quisenberry	.15
585	Storm Davis	.15
587	Bill Russell	.12
588	Pat Sheridan (FC)	.20
593	Kirk Gibson	.65
594	Scott McGregor	.12
595	Bob Bailor	.10
596	Tom Herr	.20
597	Luis Sanchez	.10

598	Dave Engle	.10
599	*Craig McMurtry* (FC)	.15
600	Carlos Diaz	.10
601	Tom O'Malley	.10
602	*Nick Esasky* (FC)	3.50
603	Ron Hodges	.10
607	Hubie Brooks	.20
609	*Greg Walker* (FC)	.60
610	Ken Singleton	.20
611	Mark Clear	.10
612	Buck Martinez	.10
613	Ken Griffey	.15
614	Reid Nichols	.10
615	*Doug Sisk* (FC)	.12
616	Bob Brenly	.10
618	Glenn Wilson	.12
619	Bob Stoddard	.10
621	*Mike Young* (FC)	.20
623	*Carmelo Martinez* (FC)	.30
625	Runnin' Reds (David Green, Willie McGee, Lonnie Smith, Ozzie Smith)	.30
626	Rudy May	.10

627	Matt Keough	.10
628	*Jose DeLeon* (FC)	.90
629	Jim Essian	.10
630	*Darnell Coles* (FC)	.35
631	Mike Warren	.10
632	Del Crandall	.10
634	Mike Moore	.12
636	Ricky Nelson	.10
638	Charlie Hough	.15
639	Dennis Eckersley	.35
640	*Walt Terrell* (FC)	.40
642	Dave Anderson (FC)	.20
643	*Jose Oquendo* (FC)	.25
644	Bob Stanley	.10
645	Dave Geisel	.10
646	*Scott Garrelts* (FC)	.75
647	*Gary Pettis* (FC)	.45
648	Duke Snider puzzle card	.10
650	Dave Collins	.12
651	*San Diego Chicken	.25
—	Living Legends (Rollie Fingers, Gaylord Perry)	2.75
—	Living Legends (Johnny Bench, Carl Yastrzemski)	5.00

1984 FLEER

One of the finest Fleer sets ever offered was the 660-card edition of 1984. The design is simple and clean, with large, unobstructed photos and no glaring errors or variations. Along with the traditional action shots and portraits, some of the zaniest cards of the decade surfaced in 1984. For example, Jay Johnstone posed wearing an umbrella hat (495), while Glenn Hubbard is shown with a boa constrictor draped around his shoulders (182). Card 638 commemorates George Brett's illegal bat coated with pine tar. As usual, the Fleer cards are arranged by team, with players listed alphabetically within each team.

131 Don Mattingly

		MINT
Complete set		**$125.00**
Commons		**.08**

1	Mike Boddicker (FC)	$ .35
2	Al Bumbry	.10
5	Storm Davis	.15
6	Rick Dempsey	.10
8	Mike Flanagan	.12
11	Dennis Martinez	.10
13	Scott McGregor	.10
14	Eddie Murray	.60
16	Jim Palmer	.40
17	Cal Ripken Jr.	.90
20	*John Shelby* (FC)	.25
21	Ken Singleton	.12
25	Steve Carlton	.50
29	Bo Diaz	.10
32	*Kevin Gross* (FC)	.25
33	Von Hayes	.15
34	Willie Hernandez	.10
36	*Charles Hudson* (FC)	.15
39	Garry Maddox	.10
40	Gary Matthews	.12

42	Tug McGraw	.12
43	Joe Morgan	.40
44	Tony Perez	.20
45	Ron Reed	.08
46	Pete Rose	1.00
47	*Juan Samuel* (FC)	3.50
48	Mike Schmidt	.85
49	Ozzie Virgil	.08
50	*Juan Agosto* (FC)	.15
51	Harold Baines	.25
52	Floyd Bannister	.12
54	Britt Burns	.08
55	Julio Cruz	.08
56	Richard Dotson	.10
58	Carlton Fisk	.20
59	Scott Fletcher (FC)	.15
61	Kevin Hickey	.08
62	Marc Hill	.08
64	Ron Kittle	.15
65	Jerry Koosman	.12
66	Dennis Lamp	.08
67	Rudy Law	.08
68	Vance Law	.10
69	Greg Luzinski	.12

71	Mike Squires	.08
72	Dick Tidrow	.08
73	*Greg Walker* (FC)	.45
74	Glenn Abbott	.08
76	Doug Bair	.08
78	Tom Brookens	.08
79	Enos Cabell	.08
80	Kirk Gibson	.40
81	John Grub	.08
82	Larry Herndon	.10

185

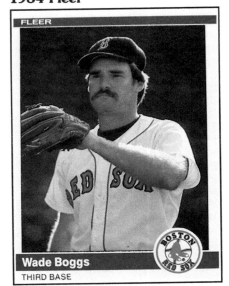

Wade Boggs
THIRD BASE

392 Wade Boggs

84	Rick Leach	.08
85	Chet Lemon	.10
87	Jack Morris	.30
88	Lance Parrish	.35
89	Dan Petry	.10
91	Alan Trammell	.40
92	Lou Whitaker	.40
93	Milt Wilcox	.08
94	Glenn Wilson	.10
96	Dusty Baker	.10
98	Greg Brock	.12
100	Pedro Guerrero	.35
102	Burt Hooton	.10
103	Steve Howe	.12
105	Mike Marshall	.15
106	Rick Monday	.10
107	Jose Morales	.08
109	*Alejandro Pena* (FC)	.30
110	Jerry Reuss	.12
111	Bill Russell	.10
112	Steve Sax	.20
115	Fernando Valenzuela	.40
116	Bob Welch	.15
117	Steve Yeager	.08
118	Pat Zachry	.08
119	Don Baylor	.15
121	Rick Cerone	.08
122	*Ray Fontenot* (FC)	.10
124	Oscar Gamble	.10
125	Goose Gossage	.25
126	Ken Griffey	.12
127	Ron Guidry	.30
128	Jay Howell (FC)	.15
129	Steve Kemp	.10
131	*Don Mattingly* (FC)	45.00
135	Graig Nettles	.20
136	Lou Piniella	.15
137	Willie Randolph	.12
138	Shane Rawley	.08
139	Dave Righetti	.25
143	Dave Winfield	.40
145	*Jim Acker* (FC)	.12
146	Doyle Alexander	.12

147	Jesse Barfield	.25
148	Jorge Bell	1.00
150	Jim Clancy	.10
151	Dave Collins	.10
152	*Tony Fernandez* (FC)	6.00
155	Jim Gott (FC)	.10
156	Alfredo Griffin	.10
157	Garth Iorg	.08
160	Luis Leal	.08
164	Lloyd Moseby	.12
166	Jorge Orta	.08
167	Dave Stieb	.15
168	Willie Upshaw	.10
169	Ernie Whitt	.10
170	Len Barker	.10
171	Steve Bedrosian	.12
173	Brett Butler	.10
174	Rick Camp	.08
175	Chris Chambliss	.10
176	Ken Dayley	.08
178	Terry Forster	.10
179	Gene Garber	.08
181	Bob Horner	.20
182	Glenn Hubbard	.10
184	Craig McMurtry (FC)	.12
185	Donnie Moore (FC)	.10
186	Dale Murphy	1.00
187	Phil Niekro	.30
188	Pascual Perez	.10
191	Jerry Royster	.08
192	Claudell Washington	.10
193	Bob Watson	.10
196	Mike Caldwell	.08
197	*Tom Candiotti* (FC)	.50
198	Cecil Cooper	.15
199	Rollie Fingers	.25
200	Jim Gantner	.10
201	Bob Gibson	.08
202	Moose Haas	.08
203	Roy Howell	.08
204	Pete Ladd	.08
207	Paul Molitor	.20
208	Don Money	.08
210	Ben Oglivie	.10

Kevin McReynolds
OUTFIELD

307 Kevin McReynolds

FLEER

Tony Fernandez
SHORTSTOP

152 Tony Fernandez

212	Ed Romero	.08
213	Ted Simmons	.15
214	Jim Slaton	.08
215	Don Sutton	.30
218	Ned Yost	.08
219	Robin Yount	.50
220	Alan Ashby	.08
221	Kevin Bass (FC)	.20
222	Jose Cruz	.12
223	*Bill Dawley* (FC)	.10
225	*Bill Doran* (FC)	.75
226	Phil Garner	.10
227	Art Howe	.08
229	Ray Knight	.12
231	Mike LaCoss	.08
232	Mike Madden	.08
235	Terry Puhl	.08
236	Luis Pujois	.08
237	Craig Reynolds	.08
238	Vern Ruhle	.08
239	Nolan Ryan	.75
240	Mike Scott	.20
241	Tony Scott	.08
242	Dave Smith	.10
243	Dickie Thon	.10
244	Denny Walling	.08
245	Dale Berra	.08
246	Jim Bibby	.08
247	John Candelaria	.12
248	*Jose DeLeon* (FC)	.50
249	Mike Easler	.10
250	Cecilio Guante (FC)	.10
251	Richie Hebner	.08
252	Lee Lacy	.08
253	Bill Madlock	.12
254	Milt May	.08
255	Lee Mazzilli	.10
257	Jim Morrison	.08
258	Dave Parker	.30
259	Tony Pena	.12
260	Johnny Ray	.12
261	Rick Rhoden	.12
262	Don Robinson	.10

264	Rod Scurry	.08
265	Kent Tekulve	.10
266	Gene Tenace	.10
268	*Lee Tunnell* (FC)	.10
269	*Marvell Wynne* (FC)	.20
270	Ray Burris	.08
271	Gary Carter	.40
273	Andre Dawson	.35
274	Doug Flynn	.08
276	Bill Gullickson	.08
277	Bob James	.08
278	Charlie Lea	.08
279	Bryan Little	.08
280	Al Oliver	.20
281	Tim Raines	.40
282	Bobby Ramos	.08
283	Jeff Reardon	.15
284	Steve Rogers	.10
286	Dan Schatzeder	.08
287	Bryn Smith	.08
288	Chris Speier	.08
289	Manny Trillo	.10
290	Mike Vail	.08
291	Tim Wallach	.15
292	Chris Welsh	.08
293	Jim Wohlford	.08
294	Kurt Bevacqua	.08
295	Juan Bonilla	.08
296	Bobby Brown	.08
297	Luis DeLeon	.08
298	Dave Dravecky	.10
299	Tim Flannery	.08
300	Steve Garvey	.50
301	Tony Gwynn	3.00
302	*Andy Hawkins* (FC)	.50
303	Ruppert Jones	.08
304	Terry Kennedy	.10
305	Tim Lollar	.08
306	Gary Lucas	.08
307	*Kevin McReynolds* (FC)	7.00
308	Sid Monge	.08
309	Mario Ramirez	.08
310	Gene Richards	.08
311	Luis Salazar	.08

47 Juan Samuel

312	Eric Show	.12
313	Elias Sosa	.08
314	Garry Templeton	.12
315	*Mark Thurmond* (FC)	.10
316	Ed Whitson	.10
317	Alan Wiggins	.08
318	Neil Allen	.08
320	Steve Braun	.08
322	Bob Forsch	.10
323	David Green	.08
324	George Hendrick	.10
325	Tom Herr	.12
326	Dane Iorg	.08
327	Jeff Lahti	.08
328	Dave LaPoint	.10
329	Willie McGee	.35
330	Ken Oberkfell	.08
331	Darrell Porter	.10
332	Jamie Quirk	.08
333	Mike Ramsey	.08
334	Floyd Rayford	.08
335	Lonnie Smith	.10
336	Ozzie Smith	.20
338	Bruce Sutter	.20
339	*Andy Van Slyke* (FC)	3.00
341	Willie Aikens	.08
343	Bud Black	.10
344	George Brett	.75
346	Keith Creel	.08
347	Larry Gura	.08
348	Don Hood	.08
350	Hal McRae	.12
351	Amos Otis	.12
352	Gaylord Perry	.30
353	Greg Pryor	.08
354	Dan Quisenberry	.12
355	Steve Renko	.08
356	Leon Roberts	.08
357	*Pat Sheridan* (FC)	.15
358	Joe Simpson	.08
359	Don Slaught	.08
362	John Wathan	.10
363	Frank White	.12

468 Nick Esasky

364	Willie Wilson	.15
365	Jim Barr	.08
366	Dave Bergman	.08
367	Fred Breining	.08
368	Bob Brenly	.08
369	Jack Clark	.25
370	Chili Davis	.12
371	Mark Davis (FC)	.12
372	Darrell Evans	.15
373	Atlee Hammaker	.08
374	Mike Krukow	.10
375	Duane Kuiper	.08
376	Bill Laskey	.08
377	Gary Lavelle	.08
379	Jeff Leonard	.12
380	Randy Lerch	.08
381	Renie Martin	.08
383	Greg Minton	.08
384	Tom O'Malley	.08
385	Max Venable	.08
386	Brad Wellman	.08
389	Luis Aponte	.08
390	Tony Armas	.12
391	Doug Bird	.08
392	Wade Boggs	8.00
393	*Dennis Boyd* (FC)	.35
394	Mike Brown	.08
395	Mark Clear	.08
396	Dennis Eckersley	.15
397	*Dwight Evans	.20
398	Rich Gedman	.10
399	Glenn Hoffman	.08
400	Bruce Hurst	.15
402	Ed Jurak	.08
403	Rick Miller	.08
404	Jeff Newman	.08
405	Reid Nichols	.08
406	Bob Ojeda	.10
407	Jerry Remy	.08
408	Jim Rice	.40
411	John Tudor	.10
412	Carl Yastrzemski	.85
413	Buddy Bell	.12
415	John Butcher	.08

504 Ryne Sandberg

187

542 Julio Franco

417	Bucky Dent	.12
418	Dave Hostetler	.08
419	Charlie Hough	.12
421	Odell Jones	.08
422	Jon Matlack	.10
423	*Pete O'Brien* (FC)	1.00
424	Larry Parrish	.12
425	Mickey Rivers	.10
426	Billy Sample	.08
427	Dave Schmidt	.08
428	*Mike Smithson* (FC)	.15
429	Bill Stein	.08
430	Dave Stewart	.15
431	Jim Sundberg	.10
432	Frank Tanana	.12
433	Dave Tobik	.08
434	Wayne Tolleson (FC)	.10
435	George Wright	.08
436	Bill Almon	.08
437	*Keith Atherton* (FC)	.20
438	Dave Beard	.08
440	Jeff Burroughs	.10
442	*Tim Conroy* (FC)	.12
443	Mike Davis	.10
444	Wayne Gross	.08
445	Garry Hancock	.08
446	Mike Heath	.08
447	Rickey Henderson	1.00
448	*Don Hill* (FC)	.10
450	Bill Krueger	.08
451	Rick Langford	.08
452	Carney Lansford	.12
453	Davey Lopes	.10
455	Dan Meyer	.08
456	Dwayne Murphy	.08
457	Mike Norris	.08
458	Ricky Peters	.08
459	*Tony Phillips* (FC)	.15
461	Mike Warren	.08
462	Johnny Bench	.40
465	Cesar Cedeno	.12
466	Dave Concepcion	.15
467	Dan Driessen	.10

468	*Nick Esasky* (FC)	3.00
469	Rich Gale	.08
470	Ben Hayes	.08
472	Tom Hume	.08
478	Ted Power	.10
479	Joe Price	.08
481	*Gary Redus* (FC)	.25
483	Mario Soto	.10
486	Larry Bowa	.15
488	Bill Buckner	.15
490	Ron Cey	.12
491	Jody Davis	.10
492	Leon Durham	.08
493	Mel Hall (FC)	.20
494	Ferguson Jenkins	.20
495	*Jay Johnstone	.10
496	*Craig Lefferts* (FC)	.25
497	*Carmelo Martinez* (FC)	.25
500	Dickie Noles	.08
501	Mike Proly	.08
503	Dick Ruthven	.08
504	Ryne Sandberg	3.00
505	Lee Smith	.15
506	Steve Trout	.08
507	Gary Woods	.08
509	*Bob Boone	.10
511	Rod Carew	.50
512	Bobby Clark	.08
513	John Curtis	.08
514	Doug DeCinces	.12
515	Brian Downing	.12
516	Tim Foli	.08
517	Ken Forsch	.08
518	Bobby Grich	.12
520	Reggie Jackson	.60
521	Ron Jackson	.08
522	Tommy John	.25
523	Bruce Kison	.08
525	Fred Lynn	.25
526	*Gary Pettis* (FC)	.25
527	Luis Sanchez	.08
530	Rob Wilfong	.08
531	Mike Witt	.15
532	Geoff Zahn	.08

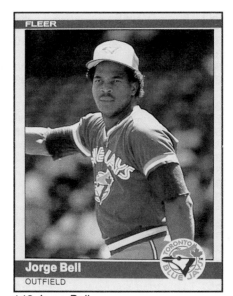

148 Jorge Bell

186 Dale Murphy

533	Bud Anderson	.08
534	Chris Bando	.08
536	Bert Blyleven	.20
540	Jim Essian	.08
542	Julio Franco (FC)	2.00
544	Toby Harrah	.10
545	Ron Hassey	.08
546	*Neal Heaton* (FC)	.15
550	Dan Spillner	.08
551	Rick Sutcliffe	.15
552	Pat Tabler	.10
553	Gorman Thomas	.10
554	Andre Thornton	.12
556	Darrell Brown	.08
557	Tom Brunansky	.20
558	*Randy Bush* (FC)	.15
560	John Castino	.08
561	Ron Davis	.08
562	Dave Engle	.08
564	Pete Filson	.08
565	Gary Gaetti	.60
567	Kent Hrbek	.40
568	Rusty Kuntz	.08
572	Ken Schrom	.08
573	Ray Smith	.08
574	*Tim Teufel* (FC)	.25
575	Frank Viola	.80
576	Gary Ward	.10
580	Bob Bailor	.08
582	Hubie Brooks	.15
583	Carlos Diaz	.08
584	George Foster	.20
585	Brian Giles	.08
586	Danny Heep	.08
587	Keith Hernandez	.35
588	Ron Hodges	.08
589	Scott Holman	.08
590	Dave Kingman	.15
591	Ed Lynch	.08
592	*Jose Oquendo* (FC)	.20
593	Jesse Orosco	.10
594	*Junior Ortiz* (FC)	.10
595	Tom Seaver	.50

596	*Doug Sisk* (FC)	.10
597	Rusty Staub	.12
598	John Stearns	.08
599	*Darryl Strawberry* (FC)	27.00
600	Craig Swan	.08
601	*Walt Terrell* (FC)	.30
602	Mike Torrez	.10
603	Mookie Wilson	.12
604	Jamie Allen	.08
605	Jim Beattie	.08
608	Bill Caudill	.08
609	Bryan Clark	.08
610	Al Cowens	.08
611	Dave Henderson	.12
614	Mike Moore	.15
616	*Spike Owen* (FC)	.20
617	Pat Putnam	.08
619	Mike Stanton	.08
621	Rick Sweet	.08
622	Roy Thomas	.08
624	*Matt Young* (FC)	.15

625	Richie Zisk	.10
626	'83 AS Game Record Breaker (Fred Lynn)	.12
627	'83 AS Game Record Breaker (Manny Trillo)	.10
628	NL Ironman (Steve Garvey)	.20
629	AL Batting Runner-up (Rod Carew)	.25
631	Letting Go of the Raines (Tim Raines)	.20
633	AS Second Base (Steve Sax)	.15
634	AS Shortstop (Dickie Thon)	.10
635	Ace Firemen (Tippy Martinez, Dan Quisenberry)	.10
636	Reds Reunited (Joe Morgan, Tony Perez, Pete Rose)	.50

1984 Fleer/1984 Fleer Update

637	Backstop Stars (Bob Boone, Lance Parrish)	.15
638	The Pine Tar Incident, 7/24/83 (George Brett, Gaylord Perry)	.30
639	1983 No-Hitters (Bob Forsch, Dave Righetti, Mike Warren)	.10
640	Retiring Superstars (Johnny Bench, Carl Yastrzemski)	.35
641	Going Out in Style (Gaylord Perry)	.15
642	300 Club & Strikeout Record (Steve Carlton)	.20
643	The Managers (Joe Altobelli, Paul Owens)	.10
644	The MVP (Rick Dempsey)	.10
645	The Rookie Winner (Mike Boddicker) (FC)	.12

1984 FLEER UPDATE

After Topps enjoyed free rein over the fall card market for three years with its Traded set, Fleer decided to try for a piece of the action. It duplicated the marketing formula used by Topps in precise detail by designing its own 132-card Update set. Fleer used the same front and back design as the standard 1984 set but added the letter "U" to each card number (it has been omitted from the following list, however). The company published 131 player cards and a checklist, though the checklist seems unnecessary since the cards were sold only as complete boxed sets through hobby dealers. Because Fleer's ability to compete with the Topps Traded set seemed questionable during the first year, some hobby dealers were hesitant to stock the Fleer Update sets. This accounts for the relative scarcity of these cards.

		MINT
Complete set		**$485.00**
Commons		**.15**

3	Mark Bailey (FC)	$ .20
5	Dusty Baker	.30
6	Steve Balboni (FC)	.40
8	Marty Barrett (FC)	3.50
15	Phil Bradley (FC)	4.00
18	Bill Buckner	.50
19	Ray Burris	.15
21	Brett Butler	.30
22	Enos Cabell	.15
24	Bill Caudill	.15
25	Bobby Clark	.15
27	Roger Clemens (FC)	95.00
28	Jaime Cocanower	.15
29	Ron Darling (FC)	12.00
30	Alvin Davis (FC)	12.00
33	Mike Easler	.20
34	Dennis Eckersley	.75
36	Darrell Evans	.50

37	Mike Fitzgerald (FC)	.20
38	Tim Foli	.15
39	John Franco (FC)	7.00
41	Rich Gale	.15
43	Dwight Gooden (FC)	85.00
44	*Goose Gossage	1.00
46	Mark Gubicza (FC)	11.00
48	Toby Harrah	.15
49	Ron Hassey	.15
51	Willie Hernandez	.40
52	Ed Hodge	.15
53	Ricky Horton (FC)	.65
54	Art Howe	.15
55	Dane Iorg	.15
56	Brook Jacoby (FC)	2.25
57	Dion James (FC)	.35
58	Mike Jeffcoat (FC)	.15
61	Jimmy Key (FC)	6.00
62	Dave Kingman	.75
63	Brad Komminsk (FC)	.15
64	Jerry Koosman	.50
66	Rusty Kuntz	.15

93 Kirby Puckett

68	Dennis Lamp	.15
69	Tito Landrum	.15
70	Mark Langston (FC)	30.00
71	Rick Leach	.15
72	Craig Lefferts (FC)	.25
73	Gary Lucas	.15
74	Jerry Martin	.15
75	Carmelo Martinez	.25
76	Mike Mason (FC)	.20
77	Gary Matthews	.30

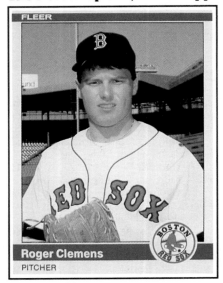

27 Roger Clemens

80	Joe Morgan	4.00
81	Darryl Motley	.15
82	Graig Nettles	1.50
83	Phil Niekro	2.50
84	Ken Oberkfell	.15
85	Al Oliver	.75
86	Jorge Orta	.15
87	Amos Otis	.30
89	Dave Parker	2.00
90	Jack Perconte	.25
91	Tony Perez	1.50
92	Gerald Perry (FC)	3.00
93	Kirby Puckett (FC)	150.00
94	Shane Rawley	.35
95	Floyd Rayford	.20
96	Ron Reed	.25
97	R.J. Reynolds (FC)	.90
98	Gene Richards	.20
99	Jose Rijo (FC)	2.50
100	Jeff Robinson (FC)	1.00
101	Ron Romanick (FC)	.15
102	Pete Rose	25.00
103	Bret Saberhagen	42.00

104	Scott Sanderson	.25
105	Dick Schofield (FC)	.40
106	Tom Seaver	10.00
108	Mike Smithson	.20
109	Lary Sorensen	.15
110	Tim Stoddard	.15
111	Jeff Stone (FC)	.20
113	Jim Sundberg	.20
114	Rick Sutcliffe	.75
115	Craig Swan	.15
116	Derrel Thomas	.15
117	Gorman Thomas	.20
119	Manny Trillo	.20
120	John Tudor	.60
122	Mike Vail	.15
123	Tom Waddell (FC)	.15
124	Gary Ward	.15
125	Terry Whitfield	.15
126	Curtis Wilkerson	.15
127	Frank Williams (FC)	.35
128	Glenn Wilson	.35
130	Ned Yost	.15
131	Mike Young (FC)	.50

1984 TOPPS

Despite retaining the general format of the 1983 design, the 1984 Topps set was not an immediate hit with collectors. All the single-player cards show a large action photo with a smaller portrait on the front. The first six cards of this 792-card edition highlight events of the previous season, such as Steve Carlton winning his 300th game and becoming the all-time strikeout king; Dave Righetti, Bob Forsch, and Mike Warren pitching no-hitters; and Rickey Henderson stealing 100 bases three seasons in a row. Recognition is also given to Johnny Bench, Gaylord Perry, and Carl Yastrzemski on their retirement. For the second year in a row, no team rookie or Future Stars cards were included.

8 Don Mattingly

		MINT
Complete set		**$115.00**
Commons		**.08**

1	1983 Highlight (Steve Carlton)	$ .30
2	1983 Highlight (Rickey Henderson)	.30
3	1983 Highlight (Dan Quisenberry)	.10
4	1983 Highlight (Steve Carlton, Gaylord Perry, Nolan Ryan)	.30
5	1983 Highlight (Bob Forsch, Dave Righetti, Mike Warren)	.30
6	1983 Highlight (Johnny Bench, Gaylord Perry, Carl Yastrzemski)	.40
7	Gary Lucas	.08
8	*Don Mattingly* (FC)	32.00
9	Jim Gott	.08
10	Robin Yount	.50
11	Twins Ldrs (Kent Hrbek, Ken Schrom)	.08

12	Billy Sample	.08
14	Tom Brookens	.08
15	Burt Hooton	.08
16	Omar Moreno	.08
17	John Denny	.08
18	Dale Berra	.08
19	*Ray Fontenot* (FC)	.10
20	Greg Luzinski	.12
21	Joe Altobelli	.08
22	Bryan Clark	.08
23	Keith Moreland	.08
24	John Martin	.08
25	Glenn Hubbard	.10
27	Daryl Sconiers	.08
28	Frank Viola	.75
29	Danny Heep	.08
30	Wade Boggs	8.00
32	Bobby Ramos	.08
33	Tom Burgmeier	.08
35	Don Sutton	.30
36	Denny Walling	.08
37	Rangers Ldrs (Buddy Bell, Rick Honeycutt)	.12
38	Luis DeLeon	.08
39	Garth Iorg	.08

40	Dusty Baker	.08
41	Tony Bernazard	.08
42	Johnny Grubb	.08
43	Ron Reed	.08
45	Jerry Mumphrey	.08
46	Ray Smith	.08
47	Rudy Law	.08
48	Julio Franco (FC)	2.00
49	John Stuper	.08
50	Chris Chambliss	.08
51	Jim Frey	.08
52	Paul Splittorff	.08

DARRYL
STRAWBERRY OF

182 Darryl Strawberry

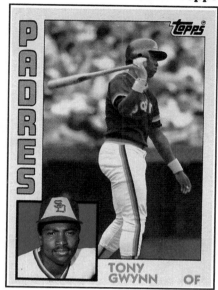

TONY
GWYNN OF

251 Tony Gwynn

98	Steve Nicosia	.08
99	*Craig Lefferts* (FC)	.20
100	Reggie Jackson	.60
101	Portfirio Altamirano	.08
102	Ken Oberkfell	.08
103	Dwayne Murphy	.08
105	Tony Armas	.08
106	Tim Stoddard	.08
107	Ned Yost	.08
108	Randy Moffitt	.08
109	Brad Wellman	.08
110	Ron Guidry	.25
111	Bill Virdon	.08
112	Tom Niedenfuer	.08
113	Kelly Paris	.08
114	Checklist 1-132	.12
115	Andre Thornton	.10
116	George Bjorkman	.08
117	Tom Veryzer	.08
118	Charlie Hough	.08
120	Keith Hernandez	.40
121	*Pat Sheridan* (FC)	.15
122	*Cecilio Guante* (FC)	.10
123	Butch Wynegar	.08
124	Damaso Garcia	.08
125	Britt Burns	.08
126	Braves Ldrs (Craig McMurtry, Dale Murphy)	.25
127	Mike Madden	.08
128	Rick Manning	.08
130	Ozzie Smith	.20
131	Batting Ldrs (Wade Boggs, Bill Madlock)	.50
132	HR Ldrs (Jim Rice, Mike Schmidt)	.50
133	RBI Ldrs (Cecil Cooper, Dale Murphy, Jim Rice)	.40
134	SB Ldrs (Rickey Henderson, Tim Raines)	.30
135	Victory Ldrs (John Denny, LaMarr Hoyt)	.10
136	SO Ldrs (Steve Carlton, Jack Morris)	.25

53	Juan Beniquez	.08
54	Jesse Orosco	.10
55	Dave Concepcion	.10
56	Gary Allenson	.08
57	Dan Schatzeder	.08
59	Sammy Stewart	.08
60	Paul Molitor	.20
61	*Chris Codiroli*	.10
62	Dave Hostetler	.08
63	Ed Vande Berg	.08
64	Mike Scioscia	.08
65	Kirk Gibson	.40
66	Astros Ldrs (Jose Cruz, Nolan Ryan)	.25
67	Gary Ward	.08
68	Luis Salazar	.08
70	Gary Matthews	.12
71	Leo Hernandez	.08
72	Mike Squires	.08
73	Jody Davis	.08
74	Jerry Martin	.08
75	Bob Forsch	.08
76	Alfredo Griffin	.08
77	Brett Butler	.10
78	Mike Torrez	.10
79	Rob Wilfong	.08
80	Steve Rogers	.10
81	Billy Martin	.12
83	Richie Zisk	.10
84	Lenny Faedo	.08
85	Atlee Hammaker	.08
86	*John Shelby* (FC)	.20
88	Rob Picciolo	.08
89	*Mike Smithson* (FC)	.15
90	Pedro Guerrero	.35
91	Dan Spillner	.08
92	Lloyd Moseby	.12
93	Bob Knepper	.10
94	Mario Ramirez	.08
95	Aurelio Lopez	.08
96	Royals Ldrs (Larry Gura, Hal McRae)	.10
97	LaMarr Hoyt	.08

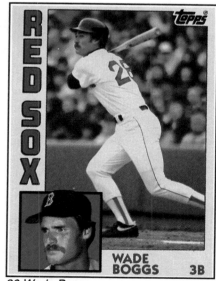

WADE
BOGGS 3B

30 Wade Boggs

137	ERA Ldrs (Atlee Hammaker, Rick Honeycutt)	.10
138	Leading Firemen (Al Holland, Dan Quisenberry)	.12
139	Bert Campaneris	.12
140	Storm Davis	.12
141	Pat Corrales	.08
142	Rich Gale	.08
143	Jose Morales	.08
145	Gary Lavelle	.08
146	Ed Romero	.08
147	Dan Petry	.08
148	Joe Lefebvre	.08
149	Jon Matlack	.10
150	Dale Murphy	1.00
151	Steve Trout	.08
152	Glenn Brummer	.08
153	Dick Tidrow	.08
154	Dave Henderson	.12
155	Frank White	.12
156	Athletics Ldrs (Tim Conroy, Rickey Henderson)	.25
157	Gary Gaetti	.75
158	John Curtis	.08
160	Mario Soto	.10
161	*Junior Ortiz* (FC)	.10
162	Bob Ojeda	.10
163	Lorenzo Gray	.08
164	Scott Sanderson	.08
165	Ken Singleton	.12
166	Jamie Nelson	.08
168	Juan Bonilla	.08
169	Larry Parrish	.12
170	Jerry Reuss	.10
171	Frank Robinson	.12
172	Frank DiPino	.08
173	*Marvell Wynne* (FC)	.20
174	Juan Berenguer	.08
175	Graig Nettles	.20
176	Lee Smith	.15
177	Jerry Hairston	.08
178	Bill Krueger	.08
179	Buck Martinez	.08

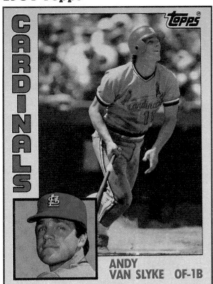

206 Andy Van Slyke

180	Manny Trillo	.10
181	Roy Thomas	.08
182	*Darryl Strawberry*	16.00
183	Al Williams	.08
185	Sixto Lezcano	.08
186	Cardinals Ldrs (Lonnie Smith, John Stuper)	.10
187	Luis Aponte	.08
188	Bryan Little	.08
189	*Tim Conroy* (FC)	.12
190	Ben Oglivie	.10
191	Mike Boddicker	.25
192	*Nick Esasky* (FC)	2.00
193	Darrell Brown	.08
194	Domingo Ramos	.08
195	Jack Morris	.30
196	Don Slaught (FC)	.12
197	Garry Hancock	.08
198	*Bill Doran*	.60
199	Willie Hernandez	.10
200	Andre Dawson	.35
201	Bruce Kison	.08
202	Bobby Cox	.08
204	*Bobby Meacham* (FC)	.12
205	Greg Minton	.08
206	*Andy Van Slyke* (FC)	2.50
207	Donnie Moore	.08
208	*Jose Oquendo* (FC)	.15
209	Manny Sarmiento	.08
210	Joe Morgan	.30
211	Rick Sweet	.08
212	Broderick Perkins	.08
213	Bruce Hurst	.15
215	Tippy Martinez	.08
216	White Sox Ldrs (Richard Dotson, Carlton Fisk)	.15
217	Alan Ashby	.08
218	Rick Waits	.08
219	Joe Simpson	.08
220	Fernando Valenzuela	.40
221	Cliff Johnson	.08
222	Rick Honeycutt	.10

223	Wayne Krenchicki	.08
224	Sid Monge	.08
225	Lee Mazzilli	.08
226	Juan Eichelberger	.08
227	Steve Braun	.08
229	Paul Owens	.08
230	Rickey Henderson	.60
231	Gary Woods	.08
232	Tim Wallach	.15
233	Checklist 133-264	.12
234	Rafael Ramirez	.08
235	*Matt Young*	.10
236	Ellis Valentine	.08
237	John Castino	.08
238	Reid Nichols	.08
239	Jay Howell	.10
240	Eddie Murray	.60
241	Billy Almon	.08
242	Alex Trevino	.08
243	Pete Ladd	.08
244	Candy Maldonado (FC)	.25
245	Rick Sutcliffe	.15
246	Mets Ldrs (Tom Seaver, Mookie Wilson)	.25
248	*Bill Dawley* (FC)	.08
249	Jay Johnstone	.10
250	Bill Madlock	.15
251	Tony Gwynn	3.25
252	Larry Christenson	.08
253	Jim Wohlford	.08
254	Shane Rawley	.08
256	Dave Geisel	.08
257	Julio Cruz	.08
258	Luis Sanchez	.08
259	Sparky Anderson	.12
260	Scott McGregor	.10
261	Bobby Brown	.08
262	*Tom Candiotti* (FC)	.25
264	Doug Frobel	.08
265	*Donnie Hill* (FC)	.12
267	*Carmelo Martinez* (FC)	.25
268	Jack O'Connor	.08
269	Aurelio Rodriguez	.08

596 Ryne Sandberg

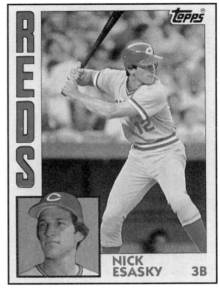

192 Nick Esasky

270	*Jeff Russell* (FC)	.25
271	Moose Haas	.08
272	Rick Dempsey	.08
273	Charlie Puleo	.08
274	Rick Monday	.10
275	Len Matuszek	.08
276	Angels Ldrs (Rod Carew, Geoff Zahn)	.20
277	Eddie Whitson	.08
278	Jorge Bell	1.00
279	Ivan DeJesus	.10
280	Floyd Bannister	.10
281	Larry Milbourne	.08
283	Larry Biittner	.08
284	Howard Bailey	.08
285	Darrell Porter	.08
286	Lary Sorensen	.08
288	Jim Beattie	.08
289	Randy Johnson	.08
290	Dave Dravecky	.10
291	Chuck Tanner	.08
295	Mike Flanagan	.12
300	Pete Rose	2.00
306	Dodgers Ldrs (Pedro Guerrero, Bob Welch)	.15
309	*Tony Phillips*	.12
310	Willie McGee	.35
311	Jerry Koosman	.12
315	Bob Grich	.10
324	*Alejandro Pena*	.25
329	Pat Tabler (FC)	.08
330	John Candelaria	.15
331	Bucky Dent	.12
332	*Kevin Gross* (FC)	.25
335	Don Baylor	.08
340	Hal McRae	.15
345	Kent Hrbek	.40
350	George Foster	.20
352	Dave Stewart	.65
357	Ron Cey	.10
359	*Jim Acker* (FC)	.10
360	Willie Randolph	.10
364	Scott Fletcher (FC)	.15

365	Steve Bedrosian	.10
366	Padres Ldrs (Dave Dravecky, Terry Kennedy)	.12
368	Hubie Brooks	.15
370	Tim Raines	.40
376	*Dave Anderson* (FC)	.10
380	Steve Garvey	.50
381	Ralph Houk	.10
384	*Lee Tunnell*	.10
385	Tony Perez	.20
386	George Hendrick AS	.10
387	Johnny Ray AS	.10
388	Mike Schmidt AS	.35
389	Ozzie Smith AS	.15
390	Tim Raines AS	.25
391	Dale Murphy AS	.35
392	Andre Dawson AS	.20
393	Gary Carter AS	.30
394	Steve Rogers AS	.10
395	Steve Carlton AS	.25
396	Jesse Orosco AS	.10
397	Eddie Murray AS	.35
398	Lou Whitaker AS	.20
399	George Brett AS	.35
400	Cal Ripken AS	.35
401	Jim Rice AS	.30
402	Dave Winfield AS	.30
403	Lloyd Moseby AS	.12
404	Ted Simmons AS	.15
405	LaMarr Hoyt AS	.10
406	Ron Guidry AS	.20
407	Dan Quisenberry AS	.15
408	Lou Piniella	.15
409	*Juan Agosto* (FC)	.15
410	Claudell Washington	.10
413	*Spike Owen* (FC)	.15
415	Tommy John	.15
420	Cecil Cooper	.10
422	Jose Cruz	.10
426	Orioles Ldrs (Mike Boddicker, Cal Ripken)	.25
429	*Randy Bush*	.15
430	Rusty Staub	.12

278 Jorge Bell

432	*Charlie Hudson* (FC)	.12
434	Harold Baines	.25
447	Tom Brunansky	.20
450	Gary Carter	.40
456	Cubs Ldrs (Fergie Jenkins, Keith Moreland)	.15
460	Dave Winfield	.40
465	Mookie Wilson	.12
470	Nolan Ryan	1.50
475	*Gary Redus*	.20
479	Frank Tanana	.10
480	Ron Kittle (FC)	.20
481	*Mark Thurmond* (FC)	.10
483	Fergie Jenkins	.20
485	Rick Rhoden	.10
486	Yankees Ldrs (Don Baylor, Ron Guidry)	.15
488	Jesse Barfield	.20
490	Cal Ripken	.65
494	Chili Davis	.12
495	Rollie Fingers	.25
498	Rich Gedman	.10
499	Mike Witt	.10
500	George Brett	.75
504	Mickey Rivers	.10
505	Pete Vuckovich	.10
508	Mel Hall	.15
510	Alan Trammell	.40
512	Oscar Gamble	.10
515	Gorman Thomas	.10
516	Expos Ldrs (Charlie Lea, Al Oliver)	.12
517	John Moses	.10
518	*Greg Walker*	.45
520	Bob Boone	.10
525	Willie Wilson	.15
529	*Keith Atherton* (FC)	.15
532	Eric Show	.10
534	*Pete O'Brien*	1.00
537	Johnny Ray	.10
538	Kevin Bass	.15
540	George Hendrick	.10
543	Craig McMurtry	.12

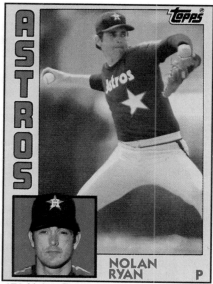
470 Nolan Ryan

545	Bill Buckner	.15
546	Indians Ldrs (Mike Hargrove, Lary Sorensen)	.10
547	Mike Moore	.15
549	*Walt Terrell*	.50
550	Jim Rice	.45
554	Ted Power (FC)	.10
555	Greg Brock	.10
558	Mike Davis	.10
559	Mike Scott	.20
560	Carlton Fisk	.35
561	Whitey Herzog	.10
563	Glenn Wilson	.10
565	Leon Durham	.08
570	Dan Quisenberry	.12
573	Dave Kingman	.15
574	Brian Downing	.12
575	Jim Clancy	.10
576	Giants Ldrs (Atlee Hammaker, Jeff Leonard)	.10
580	Lonnie Smith	.10
581	*Jose DeLeon* (FC)	.65
586	Joe Niekro	.10
587	Von Hayes	.15
589	Mike Easler	.08
590	Dave Stieb	.15
591	Tony LaRussa	.10
595	Jeff Reardon	.15
596	Ryne Sandberg	2.50
599	*Doug Sisk*	.10
600	Rod Carew	.50
601	John Tudor	.10
606	Blue Jays Ldrs (Lloyd Moseby, Dave Stieb)	.15
610	Steve Sax	.25
611	Chet Lemon	.10
614	Len Barker	.10
615	Garry Templeton	.10
620	Al Oliver	.20
621	Frank Howard	.10
625	Larry Gura	.10
627	Dave LaPoint	.08
630	Ted Simmons	.15

391 Dale Murphy AS

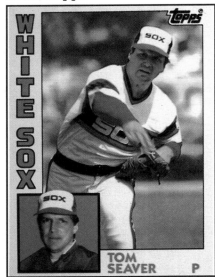

740 Tom Seaver

631	Denny Martinez	.08
633	Mike Krukow	.10
634	Mike Marshall	.15
635	Dave Righetti	.25
637	Phillies Ldrs (John Denny, Gary Matthews)	.10
640	Lance Parrish	.35
645	Tony Pena	.15
649	Tom Herr	.10
650	Phil Niekro	.30
655	Amos Otis	.10
663	Johnnie LeMaster	.08
664	Dave Stegman	.08
665	Buddy Bell	.15
666	Tigers Ldrs (Jack Morris, Lou Whitaker)	.15
667	Vance Law	.10
668	Larry McWilliams	.08
669	Dave Lopes	.10
670	Rich Gossage	.25
671	Jamie Quirk	.08
672	Ricky Nelson	.08
673	Mike Walters	.08
674	Tim Flannery	.08
675	Pascual Perez	.10
677	Doyle Alexander	.10
678	Chris Speier	.08
679	Art Howe	.08
680	Fred Lynn	.25
681	Tom Lasorda	.10
683	*Marty Barrett* (FC)	1.00
684	Bob Shirley	.08
685	Willie Aikens	.08
686	Joe Price	.08
687	Roy Howell	.08
689	Mike Fischlin	.08
690	Jack Clark	.25
691	*Steve Lake* (FC)	.10
692	Dickie Thon	.10
694	Mike Stanton	.08
695	Lou Whitaker	.40
696	Pirates Ldrs (Bill Madlock, Rick Rhoden)	.15

697	Dale Murray	.08
698	Marc Hill	.08
699	Dave Rucker	.08
700	Mike Schmidt	.85
701	NL Active Career Batting Ldrs (Bill Madlock, Dave Parker, Pete Rose)	.35
702	NL Active Career Hit Ldrs (Tony Perez, Pete Rose, Rusty Staub)	.35
703	NL Active Career HR Ldrs (Dave Kingman, Tony Perez, Mike Schmidt)	.30
704	NL Active Career RBI Ldrs (Al Oliver, Tony Perez, Rusty Staub)	.15
705	NL Active Career SB Ldrs (Larry Bowa, Cesar Cedeno, Joe Morgan)	.12
706	NL Active Career Victory Ldrs (Steve Carlton, Fergie Jenkins, Tom Seaver)	.35
707	NL Active Career SO Ldrs (Steve Carlton, Nolan Ryan, Tom Seaver)	.35
708	NL Active Career ERA Ldrs (Steve Carlton, Steve Rogers, Tom Seaver)	.25
709	NL Active Career Save Ldrs (Gene Garber, Tug McGraw, Bruce Sutter)	.12
710	AL Active Career Batting Ldrs (George Brett, Rod Carew, Cecil Cooper)	.30
711	AL Active Career Hit Ldrs (Bert Campaneris, Rod Carew, Reggie Jackson)	.30
712	AL Active Career HR Ldrs (Reggie Jackson, Greg Luzinski, Graig Nettles)	.20
713	AL Active Career RBI Ldrs (Reggie Jackson, Graig Nettles, Ted Simmons)	.20

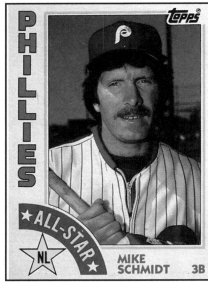

388 Mike Schmidt AS

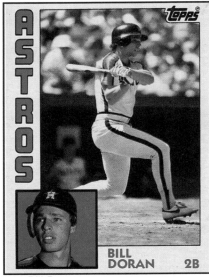

198 Bill Doran

714	AL Active Career SB Ldrs (Bert Campaneris, Dave Lopes, Omar Moreno)	.10
715	AL Active Career Victory Ldrs (Tommy John, Jim Palmer, Don Sutton)	.25
716	AL Active Career SO Ldrs (Bert Blyleven, Jerry Koosman, Don Sutton)	.15
717	AL Active Career ERA Ldrs (Rollie Fingers, Ron Guidry, Jim Palmer)	.15
718	AL Active Career Save Ldrs (Rollie Fingers, Rich Gossage, Dan Quisenberry)	.15
719	Andy Hassler	.08
720	*Dwight Evans	.20
721	Del Crandall	.08
722	Bob Welch	.08
724	Eric Rasmussen	.08
725	Cesar Cedeno	.12
726	Brewers Ldrs (Moose Haas, Ted Simmons)	.12
727	Joel Youngblood	.08
728	Tug McGraw	.12
729	Gene Tenace	.10
730	Bruce Sutter	.20
731	Lynn Jones	.08
732	Terry Crowley	.08
734	Odell Jones	.08
735	Rick Burleson	.10
736	Dick Ruthven	.08
737	Jim Essian	.08
738	*Bill Schroeder* (FC)	.15
739	Bob Watson	.10
740	Tom Seaver	.75
741	Wayne Gross	.08
742	Dick Williams	.08
743	Don Hood	.08
744	Jamie Allen	.08
745	Dennis Eckersley	.15
746	Mickey Hatcher	.08
747	Pat Zachry	.08

748	Jeff Leonard	.10	764	Mike Hargrove	.08	
750	*Jim Palmer	.50	765	Ken Forsch	.08	
751	Charlie Moore	.08	766	Mike Vail	.08	
753	Doug Gwosdz	.08	767	Carney Lansford	.10	
754	Kent Tekulve	.10	768	Champ Summers	.08	
755	Garry Maddox	.10	769	Bill Caudill	.08	
756	Reds Ldrs (Ron Oester, Mario Soto)	.10	770	Ken Griffey	.12	
757	Larry Bowa	.15	772	Jim Slaton	.08	
758	Bill Stein	.08	773	Todd Cruz	.08	
759	Richard Dotson	.10	774	Tom Gorman	.08	
760	Bob Horner	.15	775	Dave Parker	.30	
761	John Montefusco	.08	776	Craig Reynolds	.08	
763	Craig Swan	.08	777	Tom Paciorek	.08	
			778	*Andy Hawkins* (FC)	.50	

1984 Topps/1984 Topps Traded

779	Jim Sundberg	.10
780	Steve Carlton	.50
782	Steve Balboni	.08
783	Luis Leal	.08
784	Leon Roberts	.08
785	Joaquin Andujar	.10
786	Red Sox Ldrs (Wade Boggs, Bob Ojeda)	.30
787	Bill Campbell	.08
788	Milt May	.08
789	Bert Blyleven	.20
790	Doug DeCinces	.10
791	Terry Forster	.10
792	Bill Russell	.10

1984 TOPPS TRADED

During its fourth year, the Topps Traded set reached a new high in popularity. Although the issue was still distributed only through hobby dealers in complete sets, the players in the 132-card set are illustrious: Dwight Gooden's debut with Topps came in this series, along with cards for future Hall-of-Famers Tom Seaver, Pete Rose, and Joe Morgan. However, by the time the set was released in late September, Rose was no longer an Expo, which made his card outdated. Topps continued the practice of adding a "T" suffix to each card number so collectors could easily distinguish between Traded cards and the regular cards issued earlier in the season (though it has been omitted from the following lists).

104 Bret Saberhagen

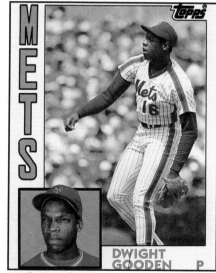

42 Dwight Gooden

		MINT
Complete set		**$115.00**
Commons		**.10**

5	Dusty Baker	$ .20
6	Steve Balboni	.20
13	Yogi Berra	.20
15	Phil Bradley (FC)	2.00
17	Bill Buckner	.25
20	Brett Butler	.20
27	Ron Darling (FC)	6.00
28	Alvin Davis (FC)	7.50
30	Jeff Dedmon (FC)	.15
33	Mike Easler	.15
34	Dennis Eckersley	.30
36	Darrell Evans	.25
37	Mike Fitzgerald (FC)	.15
41	Barbaro Garbey	.15
42	Dwight Gooden (FC)	45.00
43	Rich Gossage	.40
45	Mark Gubicza (FC)	6.00
47	Mel Hall	.20
48	Toby Harrah	.15
51	Willie Hernandez	.30
52	Ricky Horton (FC)	.40
55	Brook Jacoby (FC)	1.50
56	Mike Jeffcoat (FC)	.15
57	Dave Johnson	.15
59	Ruppert Jones	.10
61	Bob Kearney	.10

62	Jimmy Key (FC)	3.00
63	Dave Kingman	.45
64	Jerry Koosman	.25
65	Wayne Krenchicki	.10
66	Rusty Kuntz	.10

67	Rene Lachemann	.10
68	Frank LaCorte	.10
69	Dennis Lamp	.10
70	Mark Langston (FC)	18.00
71	Rick Leach	.10
72	Craig Lefferts	.15
75	Carmelo Martinez	.25
76	Mike Mason (FC)	.15
77	Gary Matthews	.25
78	Andy McGaffigan	.10
79	Larry Milbourne	.10
80	Sid Monge	.10
82	Joe Morgan	2.00
83	Graig Nettles	.50
84	Phil Niekro	1.00
85	Ken Oberkfell	.10
86	Mike O'Berry	.10

87	Al Oliver	.35
88	Jorge Orta	.10
89	Amos Otis	.15
90	Dave Parker	.90
91	Tony Perez	.65
92	Gerald Perry (FC)	1.25
93	Gary Pettis (FC)	.25
94	Rob Picciolo	.10
96	Floyd Rayford	.10
97	Randy Ready (FC)	.20
98	Ron Reed	.15
99	Gene Richards	.10
100	Jose Rijo (FC)	1.50
101	Jeff Robinson (FC)	.50

102	Ron Romanick (FC)	.20
103	Pete Rose	7.00
104	Bret Saberhagen (FC)	27.00
105	Juan Samuel (FC)	2.50
106	Scott Sanderson	.10
107	Dick Schofield (FC)	.35
108	Tom Seaver	3.50
110	Mike Smithson	.10
111	Lary Sorensen	.10
112	Tim Stoddard	.10
113	Champ Summers	.10
114	Jim Sundberg	.15
115	Rick Sutcliffe	.50
116	Craig Swan	.10

117	Tim Teufel	.30
118	Derrel Thomas	.10
119	Gorman Thomas	.20
120	Alex Trevino	.10
121	Manny Trillo	.15
122	John Tudor	.25
123	Tom Underwood	.10
125	Tom Waddell	.10
127	Curt Wilkerson	.10
128	Frank Williams (FC)	.20
129	Glenn Wilson	.25
130	Johnny Wockenfuss	.10
131	Ned Yost	.10
132	Checklist 1-132	.10

1985 DONRUSS

For the second straight year, a limited print run made Donruss the hottest collectible of 1985. By mid-spring, wax packs were virtually impossible to find on store shelves. Factory-collated sets were ransomed off by lucky dealers. All this despite two major errors. Card number 424, meant to picture Tom Seaver, wound up with a photo of Floyd Bannister by mistake. The goof was enormous, since Bannister is shown pitching left-handed, while Seaver throws with his right hand. In addition, Terry Pendleton's card front originally gave his name as "Jeff." In both cases the corrections were available only in wax packs. Don Mattingly's card and rookie appearances by Kirby Puckett and Eric Davis highlight the set.

438 Kirby Puckett

		MINT
Complete set		**$160.00**
Commons		**.08**

1	Ryne Sandberg (DK)	$ .60
7	Don Mattingly (DK)	6.00
14	Cal Ripken, Jr. (DK)	.60
15	Jim Rice (DK)	.50
18	Alvin Davis (DK) (FC)	.60
23	Juan Samuel (DK) (FC)	.40
25	Tony Gwynn (DK)	.50
27	*Danny Tartabull* (RR) (FC)	6.00
36	*Larry Sheets* (RR) (FC)	.50
38	*Calvin Schiraldi* (RR) (FC)	.30
39	*Shawon Dunston* (RR) (FC)	3.50
41	*Billy Hatcher* (RR) (FC)	.85
45	*Jim Traber* (RR) (FC)	.30
47	Eddie Murray	.60
48	Robin Yount	.90
49	Lance Parrish	.30
50	Jim Rice	.50
51	Dave Winfield	.50
52	Fernando Valenzuela	.35
53	George Brett	.75
55	Gary Carter	.40
57	Reggie Jackson	.60
60	Nolan Ryan	2.00
61	Mike Schmidt	2.00
62	Dave Parker	.50
63	Tony Gwynn	1.50
66	Dale Murphy	.80

67	Ryne Sandberg	.90
68	Keith Hernandez	.40
69	*Alvin Davis* (FC)	4.25
70	Kent Hrbek	.30
74	Jack Perconte	.10
75	Jesse Orosco	.10
76	Jody Davis	.10
77	Bob Horner	.15
79	Joel Youngblood	.08
80	Alan Wiggins	.08
81	Ron Oester	.08
82	Ozzie Virgil	.08
83	*Ricky Horton* (FC)	.35
84	Bill Doran	.12
85	Rod Carew	.50
86	LaMarr Hoyt	.08
87	Tim Wallach	.15
88	Mike Flanagan	.12
90	Chet Lemon	.10
91	Bob Stanley	.08
92	Willie Randolph	.12
93	Bill Russell	.10
94	Julio Franco	.15
95	Dan Quisenberry	.12
96	Bill Caudill	.08
98	Danny Darwin	.08
100	Bud Black	.08
101	Tony Phillips	.10
103	Jay Howell	.10
104	Burt Hooton	.10
105	Milt Wilcox	.08
106	Rich Dauer	.06
107	Don Sutton	.35

108	Mike Witt	.10
109	Bruce Sutter	.15
110	Enos Cabell	.08
111	John Denny	.08
112	Dave Dravecky	.08
113	Marvell Wynne	.08
115	Chuck Porter	.08
116	John Gibbons	.08
118	Darnell Coles	.08
119	Dennis Lamp	.08
120	Ron Davis	.08
121	Nick Esasky	.10
122	Vance Law	.10
124	Bill Schroeder	.08
126	Bobby Meacham	.08
127	Marty Barrett (FC)	.35
128	*R.J. Reynolds* (FC)	.30
130	Jorge Orta	.08
133	Fred Lynn	.25
134	Bobby Jones	.08
136	Kevin Bass	.10

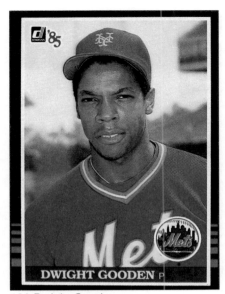

190 Dwight Gooden

137	Garry Maddox	.10
138	Dave LaPoint	.08
139	Kevin McReynolds	1.00
142	Rod Scurry	.08
143	Greg Minton	.08
144	Tim Stoddard	.08
146	George Bell	.50
147	Dave Meier	.08
154	Brook Jacoby	.15
156	Tim Conroy	.08
157	Joe Hesketh (FC)	.08
158	Brian Downing	.15
160	Marc Hill	.08
161	Phil Garner	.10
162	Jerry Davis	.08
164	John Franco (FC)	2.00
165	Len Barker	.10
168	Tito Landrum	.08
169	Cal Ripken	.60
170	Cecil Cooper	.15
171	Alan Trammell	.40
172	Wade Boggs	6.00
173	Don Baylor	.15
174	Pedro Guerrero	.30
175	Frank White	.12
176	Rickey Henderson	.60
177	Charlie Lea	.08
178	Pete O'Brien	.20
179	Doug DeCinces	.12
180	Ron Kittle	.12
182	Joe Niekro	.12
183	Juan Samuel (FC)	.60
184	Mario Soto	.10
185	Goose Gossage	.25
186	Johnny Ray	.15
187	Bob Brenly	.08
189	Leon Durham	.08
190	Dwight Gooden (FC)	15.00
191	Barry Bonnell	.08
192	Tim Teufel	.12
193	Dave Stieb	.15
195	Jesse Barfield	.25
196	Al Cowens	.08

197	Hubie Brooks	.12
198	Steve Trout	.08
200	Bill Madlock	.15
201	Jeff Robinson (FC)	.35
202	Eric Show	.10
203	Dave Concepcion	.15
205	Neil Allen	.08
207	Mike Brown	.08
208	Carlton Fisk	.40
209	Bryn Smith	.08
211	Dion James	.10
213	Mike Easler	.08
214	Ron Guidry	.30
216	Brett Butler	.12
217	Larry Gura	.08
218	Ray Burris	.08
219	Steve Rogers	.10
220	Frank Tanana	.12
221	Ned Yost	.08
222	Bret Saberhagen	10.00
223	Mike Davis	.10
224	Bert Blyleven	.15
225	Steve Kemp	.10
226	Jerry Reuss	.10
227	Darrell Evans	.15
230	*Bob Boone	.10
231	Lonnie Smith	.10
233	Jerry Koosman	.12
234	Graig Nettles	.20
235	John Tudor	.12
236	John Rabb	.08
239	Gary Matthews	.12
240	Jim Presley (FC)	.75
241	Dave Collins	.10
242	Gary Gaetti	.30
244	Rudy Law	.08
246	Tom Tellman	.08
247	Howard Johnson	1.75
249	Tony Armas	.12
251	Mike Jeffcoat (FC)	.10
252	Dane Iorg	.08
254	Pete Rose	1.25
255	Don Aase	.08

273 Roger Clemens

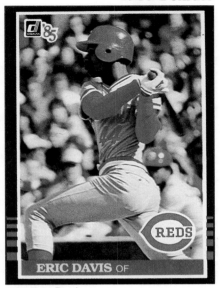

325 Eric Davis

257	Britt Burns	.08
258	Mike Scott	.20
260	Dave Rucker	.08
262	Jay Tibbs (FC)	.20
264	Don Robinson	.10
265	Gary Lavelle	.08
267	Matt Young	.10
268	Ernie Whitt	.10
270	Ken Dixon (FC)	.10
271	Peter Ladd	.08
273	Roger Clemens (FC)	16.00
274	Rick Cerone	.08
275	Dave Anderson	.08
277	Greg Pryor	.08
278	Mike Warren	.08
279	Bob James	.08
280	Bobby Grich	.12
281	Mike Mason (FC)	.12
282	Ron Reed	.08
283	Alan Ashby	.08
285	Joe Lefebvre	.08
286	Ted Power	.08
288	Lee Tunnell	.08
289	Rich Bordi	.08
292	Rollie Fingers	.25
293	Lou Whitaker	.40
294	*Dwight Evans	.15
295	Don Mattingly	17.00
296	Mike Marshall	.15
297	Willie Wilson	.12
298	Mike Heath	.08
299	Tim Raines	.50
300	Larry Parrish	.12
301	Geoff Zahn	.08
302	Rich Dotson	.10
303	David Green	.08
304	Jose Cruz	.12
305	Steve Carlton	.50
306	Gary Redus	.08
307	Steve Garvey	.50
308	Jose DeLeon	.15
309	Randy Lerch	.08
311	Lee Smith	.15

581 Orel Hershiser

312	Darryl Strawberry	**4.00**
313	Jim Beattie	.08
314	John Butcher	.08
316	Mike Smithson	.08
317	Luis Leal	.08
318	Ken Phelps (FC)	.25
319	Wally Backman	.10
320	Ron Cey	.12
323	*Frank Williams* (FC)	.20
324	Tim Lollar	.08
325	*Eric Davis* (FC)	**21.00**
326	Von Hayes	.15
327	Andy Van Slyke	.40
328	Craig Reynolds	.08
329	Dick Schofield	.10
330	Scott Fletcher	.10
331	Jeff Reardon	.15
332	Rick Dempsey	.10
333	Ben Oglivie	.10
334	Dan Petry	.10
336	Dave Righetti	.25
338	Mel Hall	.10
342	Gary Ward	.10
343	Dave Stewart	.15
344	*Mark Gubicza* (FC)	**2.00**
345	Carney Lansford	.12
346	Jerry Willard	.08
347	Ken Griffey	.08
348	*Franklin Stubbs* (FC)	.30
349	Aurelio Lopez	.08
350	Al Bumbry	.10
351	Charlie Moore	.08
352	Luis Sanchez	.08
353	Darrell Porter	.10
354	Bill Dawley	.08
357	Cecilio Guante	.08
358	Jeff Leonard	.10
359	Paul Molitor	.20
361	Larry Bowa	.12
362	Bob Kearney	.08
363	Garth Iorg	.08
364	Tom Brunansky	.15
365	Brad Gulden	.08

366	Greg Walker	.12
367	Mike Young	.10
368	Rick Waits	.08
369	Doug Bair	.08
371	Bob Ojeda	.10
372	Bob Welch	.15
373	Neal Heaton	.08
374	Danny Jackson (photo is Steve Farr)	.85
375	Donnie Hill	.08
377	Bruce Kison	.08
380	Vern Ruhle	.08
381	Tim Cocoran	.08
382	Kurt Kepshire	.08
383	Bobby Brown	.08
385	Rick Mahler	.08
387	Bill Laskey	.08
388	Thad Bosley	.08
390	Tony Fernandez	.50
393	Bob Gibson	.08
394	Marty Castillo	.08
397	Bob Bailor	.08
398	Mike Hargrove	.08
401	Razor Shines	.08
402	Rob Wilfong	.08
403	Tom Henke	.10
404	Al Jones	.08
406	Luis DeLeon	.08
407	Greg Gross	.08
408	Tom Hume	.08
409	Rick Camp	.08
410	Milt May	.08
411	*Henry Cotto* (FC)	.20
414	Ted Simmons	.15
415	Jack Morris	.30
416	Bill Buckner	.15
418	Steve Sax	.25
421	Andre Dawson	.30
422	Charlie Hough	.10
423	Tommy John	.25
424	Tom Seaver (photo is Floyd Bannister, throwing left)	.80

222 Bret Saberhagen

557 Mark Langston

424	Tom Seaver (correct photo, throwing right)	**7.00**
425	Tom Herr	.10
426	Terry Puhl	.08
427	Al Holland	.08
428	Eddie Milner	.08
429	Terry Kennedy	.08
430	John Candelaria	.12
431	Manny Trillo	.10
433	Rick Sutcliffe	.15
434	Ron Darling	.75
435	Spike Owen	.10
436	Frank Viola	.25
437	Lloyd Moseby	.12
438	*Kirby Puckett* (FC)	**25.00**
439	Jim Clancy	.10
440	Mike Moore	.15
441	Doug Sisk	.08
442	Dennis Eckersley	.15
443	Gerald Perry	.15
444	Dale Berra	.08
445	Dusty Baker	.10
446	Ed Whitson	.08
447	Cesar Cedeno	.12
448	*Rick Schu* (FC)	.20
449	Joaquin Andujar	.10
450	*Mark Bailey* (FC)	.12
451	*Ron Romanick* (FC)	.12
452	Julio Cruz	.08
453	Miguel Dilone	.08
454	Storm Davis	.12
456	Barbaro Garbey	.08
457	Rick Gedman	.08
458	Phil Niekro	.30
460	Pat Tabler	.08
461	Darryl Motley	.08
463	Doug Flynn	.08
464	Billy Sample	.08
465	Mickey Rivers	.10
466	John Wathan	.10
467	Bill Krueger	.08
468	Andre Thornton	.12

469	Rex Hudler	.10
470	*Sid Bream* (FC)	.50
471	Kirk Gibson	.40
472	John Shelby	.10
473	Moose Haas	.08
474	Doug Corbett	.08
475	Willie McGee	.35
476	Bob Knepper	.08
477	Kevin Gross	.12
479	Kent Tekulve	.10
480	Chili Davis	.12
481	Bobby Clark	.08
482	Mookie Wilson	.12
483	Dave Owen	.08
484	Ed Nunez	.08
486	Ken Schrom	.08
487	Jeff Russell	.12
488	Tom Paciorek	.08
489	Dan Ford	.08
490	Mike Caldwell	.08
491	Scottie Earl	.08
492	*Jose Rijo* (FC)	.75
493	Bruce Hurst	.15
495	Mike Fischlin	.08
496	Don Slaught	.08
498	Gary Lucas	.08
499	Gary Pettis	.10
500	Marvis Foley	.08
501	Mike Squires	.08
502	*Jim Pankovitz* (FC)	.08
503	Luis Aguayo	.08
504	Ralph Citarella	.08
505	Bruce Bochy	.08
508	Lee Lacy	.08
510	Bob Dernier	.08
512	Cliff Johnson	.08
515	Ed Romero	.08
516	Rusty Kuntz	.08
517	Rick Miller	.08
518	Dennis Rasmussen	.15
519	Steve Yeager	.08
520	Chris Bando	.08
521	U.L. Washington	.08

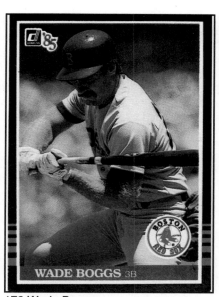
172 Wade Boggs

522	*Curt Young* (FC)	.40
523	Angel Salazar	.08
524	Curt Kaufman	.08
525	Odell Jones	.08
526	Juan Agosto	.08
528	Andy Hawkins	.12
529	Sixto Lezcano	.08
534	*Jeff Pendleton* (FC) (first name incorrect)	.85
534	*Terry Pendleton* (FC) (correct name)	3.00
535	Vic Rodriguez	.08
536	Bob McClure	.08
538	Mark Clear	.08
539	*Mike Pagliarulo* (FC)	.75
540	Terry Whitfield	.08
545	Jim Slaton	.08
546	Greg Luzinski	.12
547	*Mark Salas* (FC)	.15
548	Dave Smith	.10
552	Rick Rhoden	.10
553	Mark Davis	.15
554	*Jeff Dedmon* (FC)	.15
555	Gary Woods	.08
556	Danny Heep	.08
557	*Mark Langston* (FC)	7.00
559	*Jimmy Key* (FC)	1.50
560	Rick Lysander	.08
561	Doyle Alexander	.12
562	Mike Stanton	.08
563	Sid Fernandez	.50
565	Alex Trevino	.08
566	Brian Harper	.08
567	*Dan Gladden* (FC)	.40
568	Luis Salazar	.08
569	Tom Foley	.08
571	Danny Cox	.12
572	Joe Sambito	.08
574	Joel Skinner	.08
575	*Randy St. Claire* (FC)	.15
577	Roy Howell	.08
578	John Grubb	.08
579	Ed Jurak	.08

581	*Orel Hershiser* (FC)	11.00
584	*Joe Morgan	.30
586	Dave Schmidt	.08
588	Hal McRae	.12
592	*Ken Howell* (FC)	.20
596	*Tom Nieto* (FC)	.12
597	Walt Terrell	.10
598	Al Oliver	.15
599	Shane Rawley	.08
601	*Mark Grant* (FC)	.15
603	George Foster	.15
604	Davey Lopes	.10
609	Glenn Wilson	.10
610	*Rafael Santana* (FC)	.20
614	*Al Nipper* (FC) (photo is Mike Brown)	.20
615	Gene Nelson	.08
616	Joe Carter	1.50
617	Ray Knight	.12
623	Ed Lynch	.08
624	*Jeff Stone* (FC)	.15
628	Steve Bedrosian	.12
630	Mike Krukow	.10
631	*Phil Bradley* (FC)	.95
634	*Tom Browning* (FC)	2.00
637	*Dan Pasqua* (FC)	.75
640	*Mike Jones* (last line of highlights starts "spent some...")	1.25
640	*Mike Jones* (last line of highlights starts "Was 11-7...")	.10
641	Pete Rose	1.25
648	*John Russell* (FC)	.20
649	*Ron Robinson* (FC)	.25
651	Two for the Title (Don Mattingly, Dave Winfield) (player names in yellow)	4.00
651	Two for the Title (player names in white)	7.00
652	Tim Laudner	.08
653	*Steve Farr* (FC)	.35

27 Danny Tartabull

312 Darryl Strawberry

1985 FLEER

Other than its distinctive numbering system, the 1985 Fleer set of 660 cards has little that is noteworthy when compared to similar offerings from Donruss and Topps. Following Fleer tradition, the set is arranged by team, ranking the clubs by their 1984 results. Thus, the World Champion Detroit Tigers appear first, followed by the San Diego Padres, and then the rest of the teams in order, based on their winning percentages. Players are listed alphabetically within each team. A large, unobstructed color photo highlights the front of all single-player cards, while card backs, despite a small black-and-white portrait, are plain and boring. Rookies are grouped as Major League Prospects, two players to a card. Shawon Dunston, Danny Tartabull, and Glenn Davis top this group.

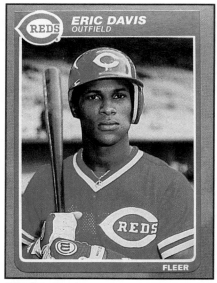

533 Eric Davis

286 Kirby Puckett

		MINT
Complete set		**$120.00**
Commons		**.06**

1	Doug Bair	$ .06
6	Darrell Evans	.12
7	Barbaro Garbey	.06
8	Kirk Gibson	.35
9	John Grubb	.06
11	Larry Herndon	.06
12	Howard Johnson	1.75
14	Rusty Kuntz	.06
15	Chet Lemon	.08
16	Aurelio Lopez	.06
17	Sid Monge	.06
18	Jack Morris	.25
19	Lance Parrish	.30
20	Dan Petry	.08
23	Alan Trammell	.35
24	Lou Whitaker	.35
25	Milt Wilcox	.06
27	*Greg Booker* (FC)	.15
28	Bobby Brown	.06
29	Luis DeLeon	.06
31	Tim Flannery	.06
32	Steve Garvey	.40
33	Goose Gossage	.20
34	Tony Gwynn	1.75
35	Greg Harris	.06
36	Andy Hawkins	.08
37	Terry Kennedy	.08
38	Craig Lefferts	.08
41	Kevin McReynolds	1.00
42	Graig Nettles	.15
44	Eric Show	.08
45	Garry Templeton	.08
47	Ed Whitson	.06
49	Rich Bordi	.06
50	Larry Bowa	.12
52	Ron Cey	.10
53	*Henry Cotto* (FC)	.15
54	Jody Davis	.08
56	Leon Durham	.06
57	Dennis Eckersley	.12
60	Dave Lopes	.08
61	Gary Matthews	.10
63	Rick Reuschel	.10
65	Ryne Sandberg	.50
67	Lee Smith	.10

69	Rick Sutcliffe	.12
70	Steve Trout	.06
71	Gary Woods	.06
74	Hubie Brooks	.10
76	Ron Darling	1.25
77	Sid Fernandez (FC)	1.00
79	George Foster	.15
80	Brent Gaff	.06
82	*Dwight Gooden*	11.00
83	Tom Gorman	.06
84	Danny Heep	.06
85	Keith Hernandez	.30
86	Ray Knight	.10
87	Ed Lynch	.06
90	*Rafael Santana* (FC)	.20
91	Doug Sisk	.06
92	Rusty Staub	.12
93	Darryl Strawberry	4.00
94	Walt Terrell	.08
95	Mookie Wilson	.10
96	Jim Acker	.06
97	Willie Aikens	.06
98	Doyle Alexander	.10
99	Jesse Barfield	.25

100	George Bell	.50
101	Jim Clancy	.06
103	Tony Fernandez	.40
104	Damaso Garcia	.06
105	Jim Gott	.06
107	Garth Iorg	.06
110	*Jimmy Key*	1.00
112	Rick Leach	.06
113	Luis Leal	.06
115	Lloyd Moseby	.10
117	Dave Stieb	.15
119	Ernie Whitt	.08
121	Don Baylor	.12
123	Rick Cerone	.06
126	Tim Foli	.06
128	Ken Griffey	.10
129	Ron Guidry	.25
130	Toby Harrah	.08
131	Jay Howell	.08
132	Steve Kemp	.08
133	Don Mattingly	13.00
137	Dale Murray	.06
138	Phil Niekro	.25
139	*Mike Pagliarulo* (FC)	.90
140	Willie Randolph	.10
141	Dennis Rasmussen (FC)	.35
142	Dave Righetti	.25
143	*Jose Rijo*	.50
145	Bob Shirley	.06
146	Dave Winfield	.35
149	Tony Armas	.10
150	Marty Barrett	.20
151	Wade Boggs	4.00
152	Dennis Boyd	.10
153	Bill Buckner	.12
154	Mark Clear	.06
155	*Roger Clemens*	12.50
157	Mike Easler	.08
158	*Dwight Evans	.12
159	Rich Gedman	.06
161	Bruce Hurst	.15
163	Rick Miller	.06
165	Al Nipper (FC)	.15

166	Bob Ojeda	.10
167	Jerry Remy	.06
168	Jim Rice	.35
169	Bob Stanley	.06
170	Mike Boddicker	.15
171	Al Bumbry	.08
172	Todd Cruz	.06
173	Rich Dauer	.06
174	Storm Davis	.10
176	Jim Dwyer	.06
178	Dan Ford	.06
179	Wayne Gross	.06
184	Eddie Murray	.50
185	Joe Nolan	.06
187	Cal Ripken, Jr.	.50
195	Mike Young	.08
198	Bud Black	.06
199	George Brett	.50
201	*Mark Gubicza*	2.00
202	Larry Gura	.06
204	Dane Iorg	.06
205	Danny Jackson (FC)	.90
207	Hal McRae	.10
209	Jorge Orta	.06
210	Greg Pryor	.06
212	*Bret Saberhagen*	8.50
214	Don Slaught	.06
216	John Wathan	.08
217	Frank White	.10
218	Willie Wilson	.10
219	Neil Allen	.06
221	Steve Braun	.06
222	Danny Cox (FC)	.25
223	Bob Forsch	.08
224	David Green	.06
226	Tom Herr	.10
227	*Ricky Horton*	.30
228	Art Howe	.06
230	Kurt Kepshire	.06
231	Jeff Lahti	.06
233	Dave LaPoint	.08
234	Willie McGee	.30
235	*Tom Nieto* (FC)	.10

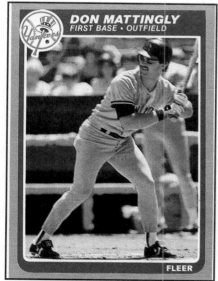

133 Don Mattingly

236	*Terry Pendleton* (FC)	.75
237	Darrell Porter	.08
238	Dave Rucker	.06
239	Lonnie Smith	.08
240	Ozzie Smith	.15
241	Bruce Sutter	.12
242	Andy Van Slyke	.35
245	Bill Campbell	.06
246	Steve Carlton	.40
249	John Denny	.06
250	Bo Diaz	.08
251	Greg Gross	.06
252	Kevin Gross	.08
253	Von Hayes	.15
254	Al Holland	.06
259	Garry Maddox	.10
261	Tug McGraw	.12
262	Al Oliver	.12
263	Shane Rawley	.06
264	Juan Samuel	.30
265	Mike Schmidt	1.00
266	*Jeff Stone*	.12
268	Glenn Wilson	.08
270	Darrell Brown	.06
271	Tom Brunansky	.12
272	Randy Bush	.08
273	John Butcher	.06
275	Ron Davis	.06
276	Dave Engle	.06
277	Pete Filson	.06
278	Gary Gaetti	.25
280	Ed Hodge	.06
281	Kent Hrbek	.25
283	Tim Laudner	.06
285	Dave Meier	.06
286	*Kirby Puckett*	21.00
287	Pat Putnam	.06
288	Ken Schrom	.06
290	Tim Teufel	.08
291	Frank Viola	.20
293	Don Aase	.06
295	*Bob Boone	.08
296	Mike Brown	.06
297	Rod Carew	.40
298	Doug Corbett	.06
300	Brian Downing	.10
301	Ken Forsch	.08
302	Bobby Grich	.10
303	Reggie Jackson	.40

304	Tommy John	.20
306	Bruce Kison	.06
307	Fred Lynn	.20
311	Dick Schofield	.10
313	Jim Slaton	.06
316	Mike Witt	.12
317	Geoff Zahn	.06
318	Len Barker	.08
319	Steve Bedrosian	.12
321	Rick Camp	.06
323	*Jeff Dedmon* (FC)	.12
324	Terry Forster	.08
325	Gene Garber	.06
326	*Albert Hall* (FC)	.15
327	Terry Harper	.06
328	Bob Horner	.15
330	Randy Johnson	.06
332	Rick Mahler	.06
333	Craig McMurtry	.06
334	Donnie Moore	.06
335	Dale Murphy	.60
337	Pascual Perez	.10
338	Gerald Perry	.20
340	Jerry Royster	.06
341	Alex Trevino	.06
343	Alan Ashby	.06
344	*Mark Bailey*	.10
345	Kevin Bass	.10
346	Enos Cabell	.06
347	Jose Cruz	.10
348	Bill Dawley	.06
350	Bill Doran	.12
351	Phil Garner	.08
353	Mike LaCoss	.06
355	Joe Niekro	.10
356	Terry Puhl	.06
358	Vern Ruhle	.06
359	Nolan Ryan	.90
360	Joe Sambito	.06
361	*Mike Scott	.15
362	Dave Smith	.08
364	Dickie Thon	.08
367	Bob Bailor	.06
368	Greg Brock	.08
369	Carlos Diaz	.06
370	Pedro Guerrero	.25
371	*Orel Hershiser* (FC)	10.00
373	Burt Hooton	.08
374	*Ken Howell* (FC)	.15

652 Major League Prospect

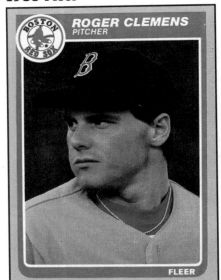

155 Roger Clemens

426	Donnie Hill	.06
427	Dave Kingman	.15
428	Bill Krueger	.06
429	Carney Lansford	.10
430	Steve McCatty	.06
431	*Joe Morgan	.35
432	Dwayne Murphy	.08
433	Tony Phillips	.08
434	Lary Sorensen	.06
435	Mike Warren	.06
436	*Curt Young* (FC)	.35
437	Luis Aponte	.06
438	Chris Bando	.06
439	Tony Bernazard	.06
440	Bert Blyleven	.15
441	Brett Butler	.10
442	Ernie Camacho	.06
443	Joe Carter (FC)	3.50
445	Jamie Easterly	.06
446	*Steve Farr* (FC)	.30
447	Mike Fischlin	.06
448	Julio Franco	.15
449	Mel Hall	.08
450	Mike Hargrove	.06
451	Neal Heaton	.06
452	Brook Jacoby	.30
453	*Mike Jeffcoat* (FC)	.08
454	*Don Schulze* (FC)	.08
455	Roy Smith	.06
456	Pat Tabler	.08
457	Andre Thornton	.10
459	Tom Waddell	.06
460	Jerry Willard	.06
461	Dale Berra	.06
462	John Candelaria	.10
463	Jose DeLeon	.12
464	Doug Frobel	.06
465	Cecilio Guante	.06
466	Brian Harper	.06
467	Lee Lacy	.06
468	Bill Madlock	.12
469	Lee Mazzilli	.08
471	Jim Morrison	.06

212 Bret Saberhagen

376	Candy Maldonado	.10
377	Mike Marshall	.15
380	Jerry Reuss	.08
381	*R.J. Reynolds*	.25
383	Bill Russell	.08
384	Steve Sax	.25
386	*Franklin Stubbs* (FC)	.25
387	Fernando Valenzuela	.35
388	Bob Welch	.12
390	Steve Yeager	.06
391	Pat Zachry	.06
393	Gary Carter	.35
394	Andre Dawson	.35
395	Miguel Dilone	.06
396	Dan Driessen	.08
397	Doug Flynn	.06
398	Terry Francona	.06
399	Bill Gullickson	.06
400	Bob James	.06
401	Charlie Lea	.06
402	Bryan Little	.06
403	Gary Lucas	.06
404	David Palmer	.06
405	Tim Raines	.35
406	Mike Ramsey	.06
407	Jeff Reardon	.12
408	Steve Rogers	.08
410	Bryn Smith	.08
411	Mike Stenhouse	.06
412	Tim.Wallach	.12
413	Jim Wohlford	.06
414	Bill Almon	.06
415	Keith Atherton	.06
416	Bruce Bochte	.06
417	Tom Burgmeier	.06
418	Ray Burris	.06
419	Bill Caudill	.06
420	Chris Codiroli	.06
421	Tim Conroy	.06
422	Mike Davis	.08
423	Jim Essian	.06
424	Mike Heath	.06
425	Rickey Henderson	.75

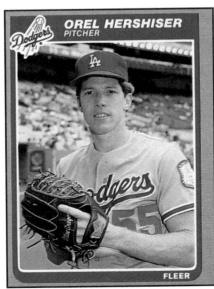

371 Orel Hershiser

472	Tony Pena	.10
473	Johnny Ray	.12
474	Rick Rhoden	.10
475	Don Robinson	.08
476	Rod Scurry	.06
477	Kent Tekulve	.08
478	Jason Thompson	.06
479	John Tudor	.10
480	Lee Tunnell	.06
481	Marvell Wynne	.06
483	Dave Beard	.06
484	Jim Beattie	.06
485	Barry Bonnell	.06
486	*Phil Bradley*	.95
487	Al Cowens	.06
488	*Alvin Davis*	3.25
489	Dave Henderson	.10
491	Bob Kearney	.06
492	*Mark Langston*	4.00
493	Larry Milbourne	.06
494	Paul Mirabella	.06
495	Mike Moore	.15
496	Edwin Nunez (FC)	.08
497	Spike Owen	.08
498	Jack Perconte	.06
499	Ken Phelps	.10
500	*Jim Presley* (FC)	.75
501	Mike Stanton	.06
502	Bob Stoddard	.06
503	Gorman Thomas	.08
505	Matt Young	.08
506	Juan Agosto	.06
507	Harold Baines	.15
508	Floyd Bannister	.10
509	Britt Burns	.06
510	Julio Cruz	.06
511	Richard Dotson	.10
513	Carlton Fisk	.35
514	Scott Fletcher	.08
515	Jerry Hairston	.06
516	Marc Hill	.06
517	LaMarr Hoyt	.08
518	Ron Kittle	.10

519	Rudy Law	.06
520	Vance Law	.08
521	Greg Luzinski	.10
522	Gene Nelson	.06
523	Tom Paciorek	.06
524	Ron Reed	.06
525	Bert Roberge	.06
526	Tom Seaver	.50
527	Roy Smalley	.06
528	Dan Spillner	.06
529	Mike Squires	.06
530	Greg Walker	.12
531	Cesar Cedeno	.10
532	Dave Concepcion	.12
533	*Eric Davis* (FC)	**18.50**
534	*Nick Esasky	.15
535	Tom Foley	.06
536	*John Franco*	**1.00**
537	Brad Gulden	.06
538	Tom Hume	.06
541	Eddie Milner	.06
542	Ron Oester	.06
543	Bob Owchinko	.06
544	Dave Parker	.25
545	Frank Pastore	.06
546	Tony Perez	.15
547	Ted Power	.06
548	Joe Price	.06
549	Gary Redus	.08
550	Pete Rose	**1.00**
551	Jeff Russell (FC)	.15
552	Mario Soto	.08
553	*Jay Tibbs* (FC)	.15
554	Duane Walker	.06
555	Alan Bannister	.06
556	Buddy Bell	.12
557	Danny Darwin	.06
558	Charlie Hough	.10
559	Bobby Jones	.06
560	Odell Jones	.06
561	*Jeff Kunkel* (FC)	.10
562	*Mike Mason*	.10
563	Pete O'Brien	.12

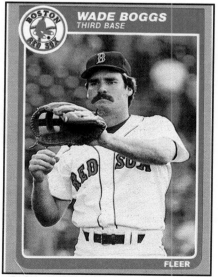

151 Wade Boggs

647 Major League Prospect

564	Larry Parrish	.10
565	Mickey Rivers	.08
566	Billy Sample	.06
567	Dave Schmidt	.06
568	Donnie Scott	.06
569	Dave Stewart	.15
570	Frank Tanana	.10
572	Gary Ward	.08
574	George Wright	.06
575	Ned Yost	.06
576	Mark Brouhard	.06
578	Bobby Clark	.06
580	Cecil Cooper	.15
581	Rollie Fingers	.20
584	Dion James	.20
585	Pete Ladd	.06
588	Paul Molitor	.15
590	Ben Oglivie	.08
591	Chuck Porter	.06
592	*Randy Ready* (FC)	.20
593	Ed Romero	.06
594	Bill Schroeder (FC)	.10
596	Ted Simmons	.12
597	Jim Sundberg	.08
598	Don Sutton	.30
600	Rick Waits	.06
601	Robin Yount	.75
602	Dusty Baker	.06
603	Bob Brenly	.06
604	Jack Clark	.20
605	Chili Davis	.10
606	Mark Davis	.10
607	*Dan Gladden* (FC)	.50
609	Mike Krukow	.08
611	Bob Lacy	.06
612	Bill Laskey	.06
615	Jeff Leonard	.10
616	Randy Lerch	.06
617	Greg Minton	.06
620	*Jeff Robinson*	.30
622	Manny Trillo	.08
624	*Frank Williams*	.15
626	Ripken-in-Action (Cal Ripken)	.30
627	Schmidt-in-Action (Mike Schmidt)	.30
629	AL Pitcher's Nightmare (Rickey Henderson, Dave Winfield)	.35

630	NL Pitcher's Nightmare (Ryne Sandberg, Mike Schmidt)	.30
631	NL All Stars (Gary Carter, Steve Garvey, Ozzie Smith, Darryl Strawberry)	.30
632	All-Star Game Winning Battery (Gary Carter, Charlie Lea)	.15
633	NL Pennant Clinchers (Steve Garvey, Goose Gossage)	.20
634	NL Rookie Phenoms (Dwight Gooden, Juan Samuel)	**1.00**
639	500th Homer (Reggie Jackson)	.30
641	Father and Son (Cal Ripken, Sr. and Jr.)	.30
643	1984's Two Perfect Games and One No Hitter (Jack Morris, David Palmer, Mike Witt)	.15
645	Major League Prospect (*Kelly Gruber* (FC), *Randy O'Neal* (FC))	**2.00**
646	Major League Prospect (*Jose Roman, Joel Skinner* (FC))	.12
647	Major League Prospect (*Steve Kiefer, Danny Tartabull* (FC))	**5.00**
648	Major League Prospect (*Rob Deer, Alejandro Sanchez* (FC))	**1.50**
649	Major League Prospect (*Shawon Dunston* (FC), *Bill Hatcher* (FC))	**3.00**
650	Major League Prospect (*Mike Bielecki, Ron Robinson* (FC))	.35
651	Major League Prospect (*Zane Smith, Paul Zuvella* (FC))	.35
652	Major League Prospect (*Glenn Davis* (FC), *Joe Hesketh* (FC))	**11.00**
653	Major League Prospect (*Steve Jeltz, John Russell* (FC))	.20

1985 FLEER UPDATE

54 Teddy Higuera

Because hobbyists were just beginning to realize how scarce the 1984 Fleer Update was, collectors gobbled up a massive quantity of the 1985 edition. The 132-card set, issued near the close of the 1985 baseball season, lacked the big names present in the initial fall offering from Fleer. This, combined with the abundance of sets available in the hobby today, has kept prices of the boxed sets low. Except for the "U" prefix of the card number on the back (omitted from the following list), there is nothing to distinguish the Updates from the regular 1985 Fleer cards. Many unknown rookies appear in the 1985 Fleer Update because Fleer, unlike Topps, agreed with the Major League Players Association to print cards for all of its members.

28 Vince Coleman

		MINT
Complete set		**$18.00**
Commons		**.10**

1	Don Aase	$.15
3	Dusty Baker	.15
4	Dale Berra	.10
5	Karl Best	.15
6	Tim Birtsas (FC)	.20
7	Vida Blue	.20
8	Rich Bordi	.10
9	Daryl Boston (FC)	.20
10	Hubie Brooks	.20
11	Chris Brown (FC)	.25
12	Tom Browning (FC)	1.25
14	Tim Burke (FC)	.45
15	Ray Burris	.10
16	Jeff Burroughs	.15
17	Ivan Calderon (FC)	.60
18	Jeff Calhoun	.20
19	Bill Campbell	.10
20	Don Carman (FC)	.35
21	Gary Carter	.85
24	Rick Cerone	.10
25	Jack Clark	.35
26	Pat Clements (FC)	.20
27	Stewart Cliburn (FC)	.15
28	Vince Coleman (FC)	4.00
29	Dave Collins	.15
30	Fritz Connally	.15
31	Henry Cotto (FC)	.20
32	Danny Darwin	.15
33	Darren Daulton (FC)	.20
34	Jerry Davis	.15
35	Brian Dayett	.15
36	Ken Dixon (FC)	.10
38	Mariano Duncan (FC)	.20
39	Bob Fallon	.15
40	Brian Fisher (FC)	.40
43	Greg Gagne (FC)	.35
44	Oscar Gamble	.15
45	Jim Gott	.15
47	Alfredo Griffin	.15
48	Ozzie Guillen (FC)	.85
49	Toby Harrah	.15
50	Ron Hassey	.10

51	Rickey Henderson	2.00
53	George Hendrick	.15
54	Teddy Higuera (FC)	2.50
56	Burt Hooton	.15
57	Jay Howell	.15
58	LaMarr Hoyt	.15
59	Tim Hulett (FC)	.20
60	Bob James	.10
62	Howard Johnson	2.25
64	Steve Kemp	.15
66	Mike LaCoss	.15
67	Lee Lacy	.15
68	Dave LaPoint	.15
70	Vance Law	.15
71	Manny Lee (FC)	.20
74	Urbano Lugo (FC)	.15
75	Fred Lynn	.25
76	Steve Lyons (FC)	.15
78	Ron Mathis (FC)	.10
80	Oddibe McDowell (FC)	.75
81	Roger McDowell (FC)	1.00

83	Ron Musselman	.10
84	Al Oliver	.25
85	Joe Orsulak (FC)	.20
86	Dan Pasqua (FC)	.50
87	Chris Pittaro (FC)	.10
88	Rick Reuschel	.20
89	Earnie Riles (FC)	.15
90	Jerry Royster	.10
92	Dave Rucker	.10
93	Vern Ruhle	.10
94	Mark Salas (FC)	.15
95	Luis Salazar	.10
96	Joe Sambito	.10
97	Billy Sample	.10
98	Alex Sanchez	.10
99	Calvin Schiraldi (FC)	.25
100	Rick Schu (FC)	.20
101	Larry Sheets (FC)	.50
102	Ron Shepherd	.15
103	Nelson Simmons (FC)	.10
105	Roy Smalley	.15
106	Lonnie Smith	.15
107	Nate Snell (FC)	.10
109	Chris Speier	.10
110	Mike Stenhouse	.10
111	Tim Stoddard	.10
113	Jim Sundberg	.15
114	Bruce Sutter	.25
115	Don Sutton	1.00
116	Bruce Tanner (FC)	.10
117	Kent Tekulve	.15
118	Walt Terrell	.15
119	Mickey Tettleton (FC)	1.00
120	Rich Thompson	.10
121	Louis Thornton (FC)	.10
123	John Tudor	.30
124	Jose Uribe (FC)	.25
125	Dave Valle (FC)	.20
126	Dave Von Ohlen	.10
128	U.L. Washington	.10
129	Ed Whitson	.10
130	Herm Winningham (FC)	.15
131	Rich Yett (FC)	.15

1985 TOPPS

For the first time in its history, Topps added amateur players to its annual set. The 792-card set includes a 16-card subset that features members of the U.S. Olympic baseball team. Each player—as well as head coach Rod Dedeaux—is shown wearing his Olympic uniform on what would come to be known as "pre-rookie" cards. Mark McGwire and Cory Snyder are the top names in this group. Notable regular rookies in the 1985 set include Kirby Puckett, Eric Davis, Roger Clemens, Dwight Gooden, Orel Hershiser, Bret Saberhagen, Mark Langston, Alvin Davis, Mark Gubicza, and Terry Pendleton. Other specialty cards include a dozen "#1 Draft Pick" cards.

536 Kirby Puckett

		MINT
Complete set		**$110.00**
Commons		**.06**

1	Record Breaker (Carlton Fisk)	$ .15
2	Record Breaker (Steve Garvey)	.20
3	Record Breaker (Dwight Gooden)	1.00
4	Record Breaker (Cliff Johnson)	.08
5	Record Breaker (Joe Morgan)	.15
6	Record Breaker (Pete Rose)	.60
7	Record Breaker (Nolan Ryan)	.30
8	Record Breaker (Juan Samuel) (FC)	.20
9	Record Breaker (Bruce Sutter)	.12
10	Record Breaker (Don Sutton)	.20
15	Jerry Koosman	.10
17	Mike Scott	.15
23	*Bret Saberhagen*	4.00
24	Jesse Barfield	.25
25	Steve Bedrosian	.12
30	Cal Ripken	.50
35	Graig Nettles	.15
40	Phil Niekro	.25
48	Tony Fernandez (FC)	1.25
50	John Candelaria	.10
54	Cesar Cedeno	.10
55	Frank Tanana	.10
65	Bill Buckner	.10
67	*Rafael Santana* (FC)	.15
68	Von Hayes	.10
69	*Jim Winn* (FC)	.10
70	Don Baylor	.15
72	Rick Sutcliffe	.12
80	Keith Hernandez	.30
85	Mike Marshall	.15
90	Rich Gossage	.20
93	*Don Schulze* (FC)	.10
95	Jose Cruz	.12
96	Johnny Ray	.10
100	George Brett	.50
105	Ron Kittle	.10

401 1984 US Baseball Team

108	Darnell Coles (FC)	.15
113	Tom Herr	.10
115	Rickey Henderson	.75
116	Dennis Boyd (FC)	.15
122	Tom Brunansky	.12
127	*Mark Gubicza*	.90
130	Al Oliver	.12
131	Father-Son (Buddy Bell, Gus Bell)	.12
132	Father-Son (Dale Berra, Yogi Berra)	.20
133	Father-Son (Bob Boone, Ray Boone)	.12
134	Father-Son (Terry Francona, Tito Francona)	.08
135	Father-Son (Bob Kennedy, Terry Kennedy)	.08
136	Father-Son (Bill Kunkel, Jeff Kunkel)	.08
137	Father-Son (Vance Law, Vern Law)	.10
138	Father-Son (Dick Schofield, Dick Schofield)	.08
139	Father-Son (Bob Skinner, Joel Skinner)	.08

140	Father-Son (Roy Smalley, Roy Smalley)	.08
141	Father-Son (Dave Stenhouse, Mike Stenhouse)	.08
142	Father-Son (Dizzy Trout, Steve Trout)	.08
143	Father-Son (Ossie Virgil, Ozzie Virgil)	.08
145	*Alvin Davis*	2.00
150	Jim Rice	.35
155	Yogi Berra	.12
157	Tug McGraw	.10
160	Lance Parrish	.20
162	*Benny Distefano* (FC)	.10
163	Dennis Eckersley	.15
170	George Foster	.15
173	Mike Young (FC)	.12
175	Dave Parker	.25
179	Tommy John	.20
180	Dave Winfield	.35
181	*Roger Clemens* (FC)	10.00
184	Carmen Castillo (FC)	.10
190	Rusty Staub	.12
192	Howard Johnson (FC)	4.00
193	*Jimmy Key*	1.00
196	Pete O'Brien	.12
200	Reggie Jackson	.40
202	Gorman Thomas	.10
210	Gary Matthews	.10
214	John Tudor	.10
218	Doyle Alexander	.10
219	Gerald Perry	.20
220	Fred Lynn	.20
222	Hubie Brooks	.10
225	Mike Boddicker	.10
228	Dion James (FC)	.20
230	Gary Carter	.35
235	Garry Maddox	.10
237	Julio Franco	.50
238	*Jose Rijo*	.40
239	Tim Teufel	.10
240	Dave Stieb	.12
243	Barbaro Garbey	.10

627 Eric Davis

304	Gary Gaetti	.25
305	Dale Berra	.06
306	Rick Reuschel	.10
309	Mike Witt	.10
317	*Jack Lazorko* (FC)	.10
318	Ted Simmons	.10
320	Dale Murphy	.60
321	*Ricky Horton*	.30
326	Kevin Bass	.10
327	Brook Jacoby	.30
333	Willie Hernandez	.10
340	Robin Yount	.65
342	Ted Power	.65
343	Bill Russell	.08
344	Dave Henderson	.10
345	Charlie Lea	.06
346	*Terry Pendleton* (FC)	.75
347	Rick Langford	.08
348	*Bob Boone	.10
349	Domingo Ramos	.06
350	Wade Boggs	3.50
351	Juan Agosto	.06
352	*Joe Morgan	.30
353	Julio Solano	.06
354	Andre Robertson	.06
355	Bert Blyleven	.12
356	Dave Meier	.08
357	Rich Bordi	.08
358	Tony Pena	.12
359	Pat Sheridan	.08
360	Steve Carlton	.40
361	Alfredo Griffin	.08
362	Craig McMurtry	.08
363	Ron Hodges	.06
364	Richard Dotson	.10
365	Danny Ozark	.06
366	Todd Cruz	.06
367	Keefe Cato	.06
368	Dave Bergman	.06
369	*R.J. Reynolds* (FC)	.25
370	Bruce Sutter	.12
371	Mickey Rivers	.08
372	Roy Howell	.08
373	Mike Moore	.10

665 Don Mattingly

245	Chili Davis	.10
249	Harold Baines	.15
253	*Sid Bream* (FC)	.35
260	Dave Righetti	.20
262	*Greg Booker* (FC)	.10
265	Juan Samuel (FC)	.50
266	Frank Viola	.20
267	*Henry Cotto* (FC)	.15
269	*Doug Baker* (FC)	.10
270	Dan Quisenberry	.15
271	1968 #1 Draft Pick (Tim Foli)	.08
272	1969 #1 Draft Pick (Jeff Burrroughs)	.08
273	1974 #1 Draft Pick (Bill Almon)	.08
274	1976 #1 Draft Pick (Floyd Bannister)	.08
275	1977 #1 Draft Pick (Harold Baines)	.15
276	1978 #1 Draft Pick (Bob Horner)	.15
277	1979 #1 Draft Pick (Al Chambers)	.08
278	1980 #1 Draft Pick (Darryl Strawberry)	1.25
279	1981 #1 Draft Pick (Mike Moore)	.08
280	1982 #1 Draft Pick (Shawon Dunston) (FC)	2.00
281	1983 #1 Draft Pick (Tim Belcher) (FC)	2.00
282	1984 #1 Draft Pick (Shawn Abner) (FC)	.60
288	*Jeff Kunkel* (FC)	.10
290	Cecil Cooper	.10
291	Bob Welch	.10
293	*Curt Young* (FC)	.35
294	*Tom Nieto* (FC)	.10
295	Joe Niekro	.06
298	Marty Barrett	.15
300	Rod Carew	.40
303	*Mike Jeffcoat*	.08

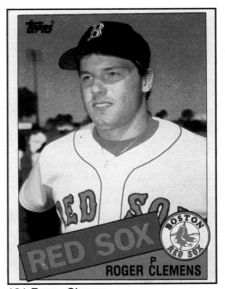

181 Roger Clemens

374	Brian Downing	.10
375	Jeff Reardon	.12
376	Jeff Newman	.08
377	Checklist 265-396	.06
378	Alan Wiggins	.06
379	Charles Hudson	.08
380	Ken Griffey	.08
381	Roy Smith	.06
382	Denny Walling	.06
383	Rick Lysander	.06
384	Jody Davis	.08
385	Jose DeLeon	.15
386	*Dan Gladden* (FC)	.25
387	*Buddy Biancalana* (FC)	.12
388	Bert Roberge	.08
389	1984 US Baseball Team (Rod Dedeaux) (FC)	.06
390	1984 US Baseball Team (Sid Akins) (FC)	.10
391	1984 US Baseball Team (Flavio Alfaro) (FC)	.06
392	1984 US Baseball Team (Don August) (FC)	.40
393	1984 US Baseball Team (Scott Bankhead) (FC)	.80
394	1984 US Baseball Team (Bob Caffrey) (FC)	.08
395	1984 US Baseball Team (Mike Dunne) (FC)	.50
396	1984 US Baseball Team (Gary Green) (FC)	.08
397	1984 US Baseball Team (John Hoover) (FC)	.06
398	1984 US Baseball Team (Shane Mack) (FC)	.50
399	1984 US Baseball Team (John Marzano) (FC)	.60
400	1984 US Baseball Team (Oddibe McDowell) (FC)	1.00
401	1984 US Baseball Team (Mark McGwire) (FC)	19.00
402	1984 US Baseball Team (Pat Pacillo) (FC)	.25

403	1984 US Baseball Team (Cory Snyder) (FC)	5.50
404	1984 US Baseball Team (Billy Swift) (FC)	.30
405	Tom Veryzer	.06
406	Len Whitehouse	.06
407	Bobby Ramos	.06
408	Sid Monge	.06
409	Brad Wellman	.06
410	Bob Horner	.20
411	Bobby Cox	.06
412	Bud Black	.06
413	Vance Law	.08
414	Gary Ward	.08
415	Ron Darling	1.25
416	Wayne Gross	.06
417	*John Franco* (FC)	1.00
418	Ken Landreaux	.08
419	Mike Caldwell	.08
420	Andre Dawson	.30
421	Dave Rucker	.08
422	Carney Lansford	.10
423	Barry Bonnell	.08
424	*Al Nipper* (FC)	.12
425	Mike Hargrove	.06
426	Vern Ruhle	.06
427	Mario Ramirez	.06
428	Larry Andersen	.06
429	Rick Cerone	.06
430	Ron Davis	.06
431	U.L. Washington	.06
432	Thad Bosley	.06
433	Jim Morrison	.06
434	Gene Richards	.06
435	Dan Petry	.06
436	Willie Aikens	.08
437	Al Jones	.06
438	Joe Torre	.08
439	Junior Ortiz	.06
440	Fernando Valenzuela	.30
441	Duane Walker	.06
442	Ken Forsch	.06
443	George Wright	.06
444	Tony Phillips	.10

493 Orel Hershiser

445	Tippy Martinez	.06
446	Jim Sundberg	.08
447	Jeff Lahti	.06
448	Derrel Thomas	.06
449	*Phil Bradley*	.85
450	Steve Garvey	.40
451	Bruce Hurst	.12
452	John Castino	.06
453	Tom Waddell	.06
454	Glenn Wilson	.08
455	Bob Knepper	.08
456	Tim Foli	.06
457	Cecilio Guante	.06
458	Randy Johnson	.06
459	Charlie Leibrandt	.06
460	Ryne Sandberg	.65
461	Marty Castillo	.06
462	Gary Lavelle	.06
463	Dave Collins	.08
464	*Mike Mason* (FC)	.08
465	Bob Grich	.10
466	Tony LaRussa	.10
467	Ed Lynch	.06
468	Wayne Krenchicki	.06
469	Sammy Stewart	.06
470	Steve Sax	.25
471	Pete Ladd	.06
472	Jim Essian	.06
473	Tim Wallach	.12
474	Kurt Kepshire	.06
475	Andre Thornton	.10
476	*Jeff Stone* (FC)	.12
477	Bob Ojeda	.10
478	Kurt Bevacqua	.06
479	Mike Madden	.06
480	Lou Whitaker	.25
481	Dale Murray	.08
482	Harry Spilman	.06
483	Mike Smithson	.06
484	Larry Bowa	.10
485	Matt Young	.06
487	*Frank Williams*	.15

488	Joel Skinner (FC)	.08
489	Bryan Clark	.06
490	Jason Thompson	.06
491	Rick Camp	.06
492	Dave Johnson	.08
493	*Orel Hershiser* (FC)	7.00
494	Rich Dauer	.06
495	Mario Soto	.08
496	Donnie Scott	.06
497	Gary Pettis	.15
498	Ed Romero	.06
499	Danny Cox (FC)	.20
500	Mike Schmidt	.65
501	Dan Schatzeder	.06
502	Rick Miller	.06
503	Tim Conroy	.06
504	Jerry Willard	.06
505	Jim Beattie	.06
506	*Franklin Stubbs* (FC)	.25
507	Ray Fontenot	.06
508	John Shelby	.08
509	Milt May	.06
510	Kent Hrbek	.25
511	Lee Smith	.15
512	Tom Brookens	.06
513	Lynn Jones	.06
514	Jeff Cornell	.06
515	Dave Concepcion	.12
516	Roy Lee Jackson	.06
517	Jerry Martin	.06
518	Chris Chambliss	.08
519	Doug Rader	.06
520	LaMarr Hoyt	.06
521	Rick Dempsey	.08
522	Paul Molitor	.15
523	Candy Maldonado	.10
524	Rob Wilfong	.06
525	Darrell Porter	.08
526	Dave Palmer	.06
527	Checklist 397-528	.06
528	Bill Krueger	.06
529	Rich Gedman	.10
530	Dave Dravecky	.10
531	Joe Lefebvre	.06

620 Dwight Gooden

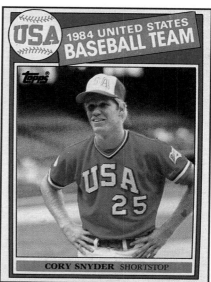

403 1984 US Baseball Team

192 Howard Johnson

575	Pedro Guerrero	.25
576	Jaime Cocanower	.06
577	Chris Speier	.06
578	Terry Francona	.06
579	*Ron Romanick*	.10
580	*Dwight Evans	.12
581	Mark Wagner	.06
582	Ken Phelps (FC)	.20
583	Bobby Brown	.06
584	Kevin Gross	.10
585	Butch Wynegar	.06
586	Bill Scherrer	.06
587	Doug Frobel	.06
588	Bobby Castillo	.06
589	Bob Dernier	.06
590	Ray Knight	.10
591	Larry Herndon	.06
592	*Jeff Robinson*	.30
593	Rick Leach	.06
594	Curt Wilkerson (FC)	.08
595	Larry Gura	.06
596	Jerry Hairston	.06
597	Brad Lesley	.06
598	Jose Oquendo	.08
599	Storm Davis	.12
600	Pete Rose	1.00
601	Tom Lasorda	.12
602	*Jeff Dedmon*	.10
603	Rick Manning	.06
604	Daryl Sconiers	.06
605	Ozzie Smith	.15
606	Rich Gale	.06
607	Bill Almon	.06
608	Craig Lefferts	.08
609	Broderick Perkins	.06
610	Jack Morris	.25
611	Ozzie Virgil	.06
612	Mike Armstrong	.06
613	Terry Puhl	.06
614	Al Williams	.06
615	Marvell Wynne	.06
616	Scott Sanderson	.06
617	Willie Wilson	.10
618	Pete Falcone	.06

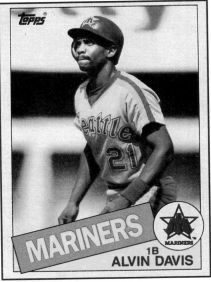

145 Alvin Davis

532	Frank DiPino	.06
533	Tony Bernazard	.06
534	Brian Dayett (FC)	.06
535	Pat Putnam	.06
536	*Kirby Puckett* (FC)	16.00
537	Don Robinson	.10
538	Keith Moreland	.08
539	Aurelio Lopez	.06
540	Claudell Washington	.10
541	Mark Davis	.08
542	Don Slaught	.06
543	Mike Squires	.06
544	Bruce Kison	.06
545	Lloyd Moseby	.10
546	Brent Gaff	.06
547	Pete Rose	.60
548	Larry Parrish	.08
549	Mike Scioscia	.08
550	Scott McGregor	.08
551	Andy Van Slyke	.40
552	Chris Codiroli	.06
553	Bob Clark	.06
554	Doug Flynn	.06
555	Bob Stanley	.06
556	Sixto Lezcano	.06
557	Len Barker	.06
558	Carmelo Martinez	.06
559	Jay Howell	.08
560	Bill Madlock	.12
561	Darryl Motley	.06
562	Houston Jimenez	.06
563	Dick Ruthven	.06
564	Alan Ashby	.06
565	Kirk Gibson	.35
566	Ed Vande Berg	.06
567	Joel Youngblood	.06
568	Cliff Johnson	.06
569	Ken Oberkfell	.06
570	Darryl Strawberry	3.00
571	Charlie Hough	.08
572	Tom Paciorek	.06
573	*Jay Tibbs* (FC)	.15
574	Joe Altobelli	.06

280 1982 #1 Draft Pick

619	Jeff Leonard	.10
620	*Dwight Gooden*	9.00
621	Marvis Foley	.06
622	Luis Leal	.06
623	Greg Walker	.10
624	Benny Ayala	.06
625	*Mark Langston*	3.75
626	German Rivera	.06
627	*Eric Davis* (FC)	16.00
628	Rene Lachemann	.06
629	Dick Schofield	.12
630	Tim Raines	.35
638	*Mike Pagliarulo* (FC)	.75
649	Sid Fernandez (FC)	.90
660	Tony Gwynn	.80
665	Don Mattingly	10.00
670	Tom Seaver	.30
690	Alan Trammell	.35
694	Joe Carter (FC)	3.00
698	Jorge Bell	.40
700	Eddie Murray	.50
701	Eddie Murray AS	.30
703	George Brett AS	.35
704	Cal Ripken AS	.30
705	Dave Winfield AS	.20
706	Rickey Henderson AS	.30
707	Tony Armas AS	.08
708	Lance Parrish AS	.15
709	Mike Boddicker AS	.15
710	Frank Viola AS	.12
711	Dan Quisenberry AS	.10
712	Keith Hernandez AS	.20
713	Ryne Sandberg AS	.20
714	Mike Schmidt AS	.30
715	Ozzie Smith AS	.12
716	Dale Murphy AS	.35
717	Tony Gwynn AS	.35
718	Jeff Leonard AS	.10
719	Gary Carter AS	.20
720	Rick Sutcliffe AS	.12
721	Bob Knepper AS	.08
722	Bruce Sutter AS	.10
723	Dave Stewart	.12

724	Oscar Gamble	.08
725	Floyd Bannister	.10
726	Al Bumbry	.08
727	Frank Pastore	.06
728	Bob Bailor	.06
729	Don Sutton	.30
730	Dave Kingman	.15
731	Neil Allen	.06
732	John McNamara	.06
733	Tony Scott	.06
734	John Henry Johnson	.06
735	Garry Templeton	.08
736	Jerry Mumphrey	.06
737	Bo Diaz	.06
738	Omar Moreno	.06
739	Ernie Camacho	.06
740	Jack Clark	.25
741	John Butcher	.06
742	Ron Hassey	.06
743	Frank White	.10
744	Doug Bair	.06
745	Buddy Bell	.10
746	Jim Clancy	.06

747	Alex Trevino	.06
748	Lee Mazzilli	.08
749	Julio Cruz	.06
750	Rollie Fingers	.20
751	Kelvin Chapman	.06
752	Bob Owchinko	.06
753	Greg Brock	.08
754	Larry Milbourne	.06
755	Ken Singleton	.08
756	Rob Picciolo	.06
757	Willie McGee	.30
758	Ray Burris	.06
759	Jim Fanning	.06
760	Nolan Ryan	1.00
761	Jerry Remy	.06
762	Eddie Whitson	.08
763	Kiko Garcia	.06
764	Jamie Easterly	.06
765	Willie Randolph	.10
766	Paul Mirabella	.06
767	Darrell Brown	.06
768	Ron Cey	.10
769	Joe Cowley	.06

770	Carlton Fisk	.45
771	Geoff Zahn	.06
772	Johnnie LeMaster	.06
773	Hal McRae	.10
774	Dennis Lamp	.06
775	Mookie Wilson	.10
776	Jerry Royster	.06
777	Ned Yost	.06
778	Mike Davis	.08
779	Nick Esasky	.15
780	Mike Flanagan	.10
781	Jim Gantner	.08
782	Tom Niedenfuer	.08
783	Mike Jorgensen	.06
784	Checklist 661-792	.06
785	Tony Armas	.08
786	Enos Cabell	.06
787	Jim Wohlford	.06
788	Steve Comer	.06
789	Luis Salazar	.06
790	Ron Guidry	.25
791	Ivan DeJesus	.06
792	Darrell Evans	.10

1985 TOPPS TRADED

Collectors began evaluating the Traded set based only on the players who would be included in the fall extension series. In 1985, the pickings were slim and the lack of appealing names caused a drastic drop in demand for the set. Meanwhile, the hobby debate about the legitimacy of the Traded set continued. Card purists maintained that the 132-card set wasn't a real collectible because it wasn't marketed through retail chains and candy stores like standard baseball cards. Milwaukee Brewers pitcher Ted Higuera and New York Mets reliever Roger McDowell head the list of first-card originals, while Rickey Henderson and Howard Johnson top the slate of included veterans.

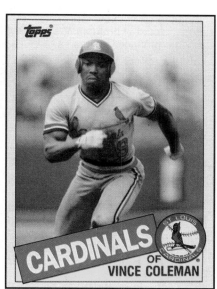

24 Vince Coleman

		MINT
Complete set		**$15.00**
Commons		**.10**

1	Don Aase	$ .10
2	Bill Almon	.10
3	Benny Ayala	.10
4	Dusty Baker	.15
5	George Bamberger	.10
6	Dale Berra	.10
8	Daryl Boston (FC)	.20
9	Hubie Brooks	.25
10	Chris Brown (FC)	.25
11	Tom Browning (FC)	1.25
12	Al Bumbry	.10
13	Ray Burris	.10
14	Jeff Burroughs	.15
15	Bill Campbell	.10
16	Don Carman (FC)	.35
17	Gary Carter	.75
18	Bobby Castillo	.10
19	Bill Caudill	.10

20	Rick Cerone	.10
22	Jack Clark	.35
23	Pat Clements (FC)	.20
24	Vince Coleman (FC)	4.00
25	Dave Collins	.15
26	Danny Darwin	.15
27	Jim Davenport	.10
29	Brian Dayett	.10
30	Ivan DeJesus	.10
31	Ken Dixon	.10
32	Mariano Duncan (FC)	.20
34	Mike Fitzgerald	.10
35	Ray Fontenot	.10
36	Greg Gagne (FC)	.35
37	Oscar Gamble	.15
38	Scott Garrelts	.60
39	Bob Gibson	.10
40	Jim Gott	.10
41	David Green	.10
42	Alfredo Griffin	.15
43	Ozzie Guillen (FC)	1.00
44	Eddie Haas	.10

46	Toby Harrah	.15
47	Greg Harris	.10
48	Ron Hassey	.10
49	Rickey Henderson	2.00
50	Steve Henderson	.10
51	George Hendrick	.15
52	Joe Hesketh (FC)	.20
53	Teddy Higuera (FC)	2.50
54	Donnie Hill	.10

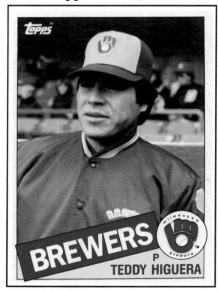

53 Teddy Higuera

55	Al Holland	.10
56	Burt Hooton	.15
57	Jay Howell	.15
58	Ken Howell (FC)	.15
59	LaMarr Hoyt	.10
60	Tim Hulett (FC)	.15
61	Bob James	.10
62	Steve Jeltz (FC)	.10
64	Howard Johnson	2.00
65	Ruppert Jones	.10
66	Steve Kemp	.10
71	Dave LaPoint	.20
73	Vance Law	.15
77	Fred Lynn	.30
78	*Billy Martin	.20
81	Gene Mauch	.15
82	Oddibe McDowell	.60
83	Roger McDowell (FC)	1.00
88	Al Oliver	.30
89	Joe Orsulak (FC)	.20
92	Jim Presley (FC)	.75
93	Rick Reuschel	.25
100	Paul Runge (FC)	.15

101	Mark Salas (FC)	.15
102	Luis Salazar	.10
104	Rick Schu (FC)	.20
106	Larry Sheets (FC)	.50
108	Roy Smalley	.15
109	Lonnie Smith	.15
110	Nate Snell	.20
112	Mike Stenhouse	.15
114	Jim Sundberg	.15
115	*Bruce Sutter	.25
116	Don Sutton	.65
117	Kent Tekulve	.15
119	Walt Terrell	.15
120	Mickey Tettleton (FC)	1.25
122	Rich Thompson	.15
124	John Tudor	.25
125	Jose Uribe (FC)	.25
126	Bobby Valentine	.10
127	Dave Von Ohlen	.10
128	U.L. Washington	.10
129	*Earl Weaver	.15
130	Eddie Whitson	.10
131	Herm Winningham (FC)	.20

1986 DONRUSS

The 660-card Donruss set for 1986 kept the Memphis company popular among collectors. The simply designed set offers a unique blend of single-player cards and unusual subsets. Specialty cards include two honoring record-breaker Pete Rose, a card of brothers Joe and Phil Niekro, and a shot of the base-stealing tandem of Vince Coleman and Willie McGee. The Rated Rookie cards, however, remain the favorite subset in the issue. Jose Canseco, Fred McGriff, Andres Galarraga, Kal Daniels, Cory Snyder, Todd Worrell, and Danny Tartabull star in the 20-card run. Canseco's card alone makes up more than half of the set's total value.

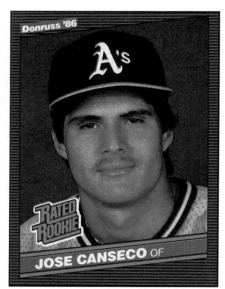

39 Jose Canseco

		MINT
Complete set		**$155.00**
Commons		**.06**

1	Kirk Gibson (DK)	$ .30
4	George Bell (DK)	.30
11	Bret Saberhagen (DK)	.25
18	Orel Hershiser (DK)	1.00
19	Johnny Ray (DK)	.12
20	Gary Ward (DK)	.10
25	Andre Dawson (DK)	.30
26	Dwight Gooden (DK)	1.00
27	*Kal Daniels* (RR) (FC)	4.00
28	*Fred McGriff* (RR) (FC)	16.00
29	*Cory Snyder* (RR) (FC)	3.00
30	*Jose Guzman* (RR) (FC)	.30
31	*Ty Gainey* (RR) (FC)	.10
33	*Andres Galarraga* (RR) (FC)	4.50
35	*Mark McLemore* (RR) (FC)	.20
37	*Paul O'Neill* (RR) (FC)	.85
38	*Danny Tartabull* (RR)	.85
39	*Jose Canseco* (RR) (FC)	85.00

40	*Juan Nieves* (RR) (FC)	.40
41	*Lance McCullers* (RR) (FC)	.35
42	*Rick Surhoff* (RR) (FC)	.08
43	*Todd Worrell* (RR) (FC)	1.00
44	*Bob Kipper* (RR) (FC)	.20
45	*John Habyan* (RR) (FC)	.15
46	*Mike Woodard* (RR) (FC)	.10
47	Mike Boddicker	.15
48	Robin Yount	.90
49	Lou Whitaker	.30
50	"Oil Can" Boyd	.08
51	Rickey Henderson	.65
52	Mike Marshall	.15
53	George Brett	.50
54	Dave Kingman	.15
55	Hubie Brooks	.12
56	*Oddibe McDowell* (FC)	.35
57	Doug DeCinces	.10
58	Britt Burns	.06
59	Ozzie Smith	.15
60	Jose Cruz	.12
61	Mike Schmidt	.50
62	Pete Rose	.80
63	Steve Garvey	.40

64	Tony Pena	.10
65	Chili Davis	.10
66	Dale Murphy	.60
67	Ryne Sandberg	.40
68	Gary Carter	.35
69	Alvin Davis	.35
70	Kent Hrbek	.25
71	George Bell	.30
72	Kirby Puckett	4.50
73	Lloyd Moseby	.10
74	Bob Kearney	.06
75	Dwight Gooden	3.00

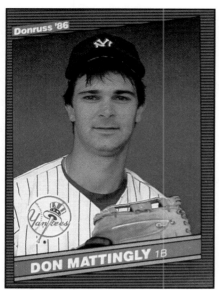

173 Don Mattingly

76	Gary Matthews	.10
77	Rick Mahler	.06
78	Benny Distefano	.06
79	Jeff Leonard	.08
80	Kevin McReynolds	.30
81	Ron Oester	.06
82	John Russell	.06
83	Tommy Herr	.10
84	Jerry Mumphrey	.06
85	Ron Romanick	.06
86	Daryl Boston	.08
87	Andre Dawson	.30
88	Eddie Murray	.40
89	Dion James	.08
90	Chet Lemon	.08
91	Bob Stanley	.06
92	Willie Randolph	.10
93	Mike Scioscia	.08
94	Tom Waddell	.06
95	Danny Jackson	.30
96	Mike Davis	.08
97	Mike Fitzgerald	.06
98	Gary Ward	.08
99	Pete O'Brien	.10
100	Bret Saberhagen	.40
101	Alfredo Griffin	.08
102	Brett Butler	.08
103	Ron Guidry	.20
104	Jerry Reuss	.08
105	Jack Morris	.25
106	Rick Dempsey	.08
107	Ray Burris	.06
108	Brian Downing	.10
109	Willie McGee	.15
110	Bill Doran	.10
111	Kent Tekulve	.08
112	Tony Gwynn	.45
113	Marvell Wynne	.06
114	David Green	.06
115	Jim Gantner	.06
116	George Foster	.15
117	Steve Trout	.06
118	Mark Langston	.30

119	Tony Fernandez	.20
120	John Butcher	.06
121	Ron Robinson	.08
122	Dan Spillner	.06
123	Mike Young	.06
124	Paul Molitor	.15
125	Kirk Gibson	.35
126	Ken Griffey	.12
127	Tony Armas	.08
128	Mariano Duncan (FC)	.15
129	Pat Tabler	.08
130	Frank White	.10
131	Carney Lansford	.10
132	Vance Law	.08
133	Dick Schofield	.06
134	Wayne Tolleson	.06
135	Greg Walker	.10
136	Denny Walling	.06
137	Ozzie Virgil	.06
138	Ricky Horton	.08
139	LaMarr Hoyt	.06
140	Wayne Krenchicki	.06
141	Glenn Hubbard	.06
142	Cecilio Guante	.06
143	Mike Krukow	.08
144	Lee Smith	.10
145	Edwin Nunez	.06
146	Dave Stieb	.12
147	Mike Smithson	.06
148	Ken Dixon	.06
149	Danny Darwin	.06
150	Chris Pittaro	.06
151	Bill Buckner	.12
152	Mike Pagliarulo	.20
153	Bill Russell	.08
154	Brook Jacoby	.15
155	Pat Sheridan	.06
156	Mike Gallego (FC)	.15
157	Jim Wohlford	.06
158	Gary Pettis	.06
159	Toby Harrah	.08
160	Richard Dotson	.10
161	Bob Knepper	.08

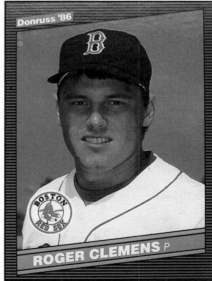

172 Roger Clemens

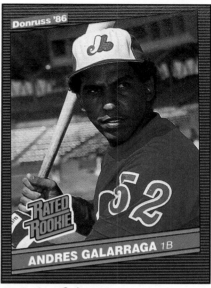

33 Andres Galarraga

162	Dave Dravecky	.08
163	Greg Gross	.06
164	Eric Davis	3.50
165	Gerald Perry	.10
166	Rick Rhoden	.10
167	Keith Moreland	.08
168	Jack Clark	.20
169	Storm Davis	.15
170	Cecil Cooper	.12
171	Alan Trammell	.35
172	Roger Clemens	5.00
173	Don Mattingly	7.00
174	Pedro Guerrero	.20
175	Willie Wilson	.10
176	Dwayne Murphy	.06
177	Tim Raines	.40
179	Mike Witt	.10
180	Harold Baines	.15
181	Vince Coleman (FC)	2.00
182	Jeff Heathcock (FC)	.10
183	Steve Carlton	.40
184	Mario Soto	.08
185	Goose Gossage	.20
186	Johnny Ray	.12
187	Dan Gladden	.08
188	Bob Horner	.15
189	Rick Sutcliffe	.12
190	Keith Hernandez	.35
191	Phil Bradley	.20
192	Tom Brunansky	.15
193	Jesse Barfield	.20
194	Frank Viola	.20
195	Willie Upshaw	.08
196	Jim Beattie	.06
197	Darryl Strawberry	3.00
198	Ron Cey	.10
199	Steve Bedrosian	.12
200	Steve Kemp	.08
201	Manny Trillo	.08
202	Garry Templeton	.08
203	Dave Parker	.25
204	John Denny	.06
205	Terry Pendleton	.15

72 Kirby Puckett

206	Terry Puhl	.06
207	Bobby Grich	.10
208	*Ozzie Guillen* (FC)	.50
209	Jeff Reardon	.12
210	Cal Ripken, Jr	.50
211	Bill Schroeder	.06
212	Dan Petry	.08
213	Jim Rice	.40
214	Dave Righetti	.20
215	Fernando Valenzuela	.35
216	Julio Franco	.12
217	Darryl Motley	.06
218	Dave Collins	.08
219	Tim Wallach	.12
220	George Wright	.06
221	Tommy Dunbar	.06
222	Steve Balboni	.08
223	Jay Howell	.10
224	Joe Carter	.25
225	Ed Whitson	.08
226	Orel Hershiser	1.25
228	Lee Lacy	.06
229	Rollie Fingers	.20
230	*Bob Boone	.08
234	Eric Show	.08
235	Jose DeLeon	.12
236	*Jose Uribe* (FC)	.25
237	Moose Haas	.06
239	Dennis Eckersley	.12
240	Mike Moore	.10
242	Tim Teufel	.06
243	Dave Concepcion	.12
244	Floyd Bannister	.10
245	Fred Lynn	.20
246	Charlie Moore	.06
247	Walt Terrell	.06
248	Dave Winfield	.40
249	*Dwight Evans	.12
250	*Dennis Powell* (FC)	.08
251	Andre Thornton	.10
253	Mike Heath	.06
254	David Palmer ("P" on front)	1.00

255	Donnie Moore	.06
257	Julio Cruz	.06
258	Nolan Ryan	.75
259	Jeff Stone	.06
262	Jay Tibbs	.06
265	Mark Davis	.10
266	Bob Dernier	.06
267	Matt Young	.06
268	Jim Clancy	.08
271	Bob Gibson	.06
273	Rich Gedman	.06
275	Ken Howell	.06
276	Mel Hall	.08
279	*Herman Winningham* (FC)	.12
280	Rod Carew	.40
281	Don Slaught	.06
283	Bill Dawley	.06
286	Nick Esasky	.15
289	Jody Davis	.06
290	Darrell Porter	.10
292	Ted Simmons	.12
295	Dale Berra	.06
296	Greg Brock	.08
297	Charlie Leibrandt	.06
298	Bill Krueger	.06
299	Bryn Smith	.06
300	Burt Hooton	.08
301	*Stu Cliburn* (FC)	.08
302	Luis Salazar	.06
303	Ken Dayley	.06
304	Frank DiPino	.06
305	Von Hayes	.10
306	Gary Redus (1983 2B is 20)	1.00
310	Rick Cerone	.06
311	Shawon Dunston	.25
312	Howard Johnson	.25
313	Jim Presley	.10
314	Gary Gaetti	.20
315	Luis Leal	.06
316	Mark Salas	.06
317	Bill Caudill	.06
318	Dave Henderson	.10

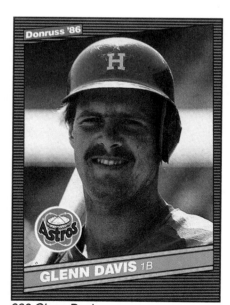

380 Glenn Davis

27 Kal Daniels

319	Rafael Santana	.06
320	Leon Durham	.08
321	Bruce Sutter	.15
323	Bob Brenly	.08
325	Eddie Milner	.06
326	Juan Samuel	.15
327	Tom Nieto	.06
328	Dave Smith	.10
329	*Urbano Lugo* (FC)	.08
330	Joel Skinner	.06
333	Ben Oglivie	.08
334	Lance Parrish	.30
336	Dennis Rasmussen	.10
338	Neal Heaton	.06
339	Jorge Orta	.06
340	Donnie Hill	.06
341	Joe Hesketh	.06
342	Charlie Hough	.10
343	Dave Rozema	.06
344	Greg Pryor	.06
345	*Mickey Tettleton* (FC)	.50
347	Don Baylor	.12
348	Carlos Diaz	.06
350	Larry Sheets	.10
351	*Ted Higuera* (FC)	1.50
353	Bob Forsch	.08
354	Mark Bailey	.06
358	Jim Gott	.06
359	*Earnest Riles* (FC)	.20
360	*John Christensen* (FC)	.10
362	Spike Owen	.06
363	Jim Acker	.06
364	Ron Davis (last line in highlights reads "…relievers (9).")	1.00
364	Ron Davis (last line in highlights reads "…in May.")	.08
365	Tom Hume	.06
366	Carlton Fisk	.35
367	Nate Snell	.06
369	Darrell Evans	.15
370	Ron Hassey	.06

371	Wade Boggs	2.50
373	Chris Bando	.06
374	Bud Black	.06
376	Charlie Lea	.06
377	Reggie Jackson	.40
378	Dave Schmidt	.06
379	Bob James	.06
380	Glenn Davis (FC)	4.00
381	Tim Corcoran	.06
382	Danny Cox	.10
384	Tom Browning	.15
385	Rick Camp	.06
388	Davey Lopes	.08
389	Al Cowens	.06
390	Doyle Alexander	.10
391	Tim Laudner	.06
392	Don Aase	.06
395	Mike Easler	.08
396	Scott Bradley	.06
399	Lonnie Smith	.08
400	Bruce Bochte	.06
402	Jim Slaton	.06
403	Bill Stein	.06
404	Tim Hulett	.06
405	Alan Ashby	.06
408	Ted Power	.06
409	Len Barker	.08
412	Andy Van Slyke	.12
413	Jim Dwyer	.06
417	Dan Pasqua	.15
418	Enos Cabell	.06
419	Mike Jones	.06
420	Steve Kiefer	.06
421	Tim Burke (FC)	.35
422	Mike Mason	.06
427	Don Carman (FC)	.25
428	Tony Perez	.15
429	Jerry Davis	.06
430	Bob Walk	.06
432	Terry Forster	.08
433	Billy Hatcher	.12
434	Clint Hurdle	.06
435	Ivan Calderon (FC)	.50

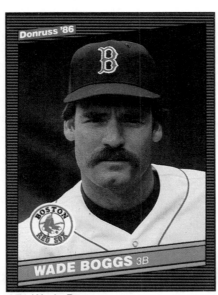

371 Wade Boggs

436	Pete Filson	.06
437	Tom Henke	.08
438	Dave Engle	.06
439	Tom Filer	.06
440	Gorman Thomas	.10
441	Rick Aguilera (FC)	.25
443	Jeff Dedmon	.06
444	Joe Orsulak (FC)	.15
446	Jerry Royster	.06
447	Buddy Bell	.10
448	Dave Rucker	.06
456	Bob Melvin (FC)	.10
459	Bob Welch	.12
462	Tim Birtsas (FC)	.10
464	Chris Welsh	.06
465	Greg Harris	.06
466	Lynn Jones	.06
467	Dusty Baker	.08
468	Roy Smith	.06
474	Kirk McCaskill (FC)	.35
475	Jeff Lahti	.06
476	Mike Scott	.20
477	Darren Daulton (FC)	.10
478	Graig Nettles	.15
479	Bill Almon	.06
480	Greg Minton	.06
481	Randy Ready (FC)	.10
482	*Lenny Dykstra (FC)	.75
483	Thad Bosley	.06
484	Harold Reynolds (FC)	.65
485	Al Oliver	.12
486	Roy Smalley	.06
487	John Franco	.15
489	Al Pardo	.06
490	Bill Wegman (FC)	.20
491	Frank Tanana	.10
492	Brian Fisher (FC)	.30
493	Mark Clear	.06
496	John Wathan	.08
500	Duane Walker	.06
501	Gene Nelson	.06
506	Joe Price	.06
507	Milt Thompson (FC)	.25

509	Vida Blue	.10
510	Steve Engel	.06
511	Karl Best	.06
512	Cecil Fielder (FC)	3.00
514	Tippy Martinez	.06
515	Billy Robidoux (FC)	.10
517	Bruce Hurst	.12
518	Rich Bordi	.06
519	Steve Yeager	.06
521	Hal McRae	.10
522	Jose Rijo	.10
523	Mitch Webster (FC)	.20
524	Jack Howell (FC)	.35
526	Ron Kittle	.10
527	Phil Garner	.08
529	Kevin Gross	.08
530	Bo Diaz	.08
532	Rick Reuschel	.10
538	Al Nipper	.06
539	Billy Sample	.06
540	Steve Sax	.25
541	Dan Quisenberry	.10
543	Floyd Youmans (FC)	.25
544	Steve Buechele (FC)	.25
545	Craig Gerber	.06
546	Joe DeSa	.06
548	Kevin Bass	.10
549	Tom Foley	.06
551	Bruce Bochy	.06
553	Chris Brown (FC)	.15
556	Danny Heep	.06
557	Darnell Coles	.08
558	Greg Gagne	.08
559	Ernie Whitt	.08
561	Jimmy Key	.15
562	Billy Swift (FC)	.15
563	Ron Darling	.15
565	Zane Smith (FC)	.20
566	Sid Bream	.10
567	Joel Youngblood ("IF" on front)	1.00
567	Joel Youngblood ("P" on front)	.08

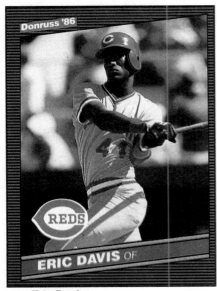

164 Eric Davis

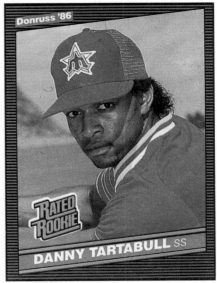

38 Danny Tartabull

570	Rick Schu	.06
573	Al Holland	.06
576	Mike Flanagan	.10
577	Tim Leary (FC)	.35
578	Mike Laga	.06
580	Phil Niekro	.30
583	Mark Gubicza	.12
584	*Stan Javier* (FC)	.15
585	Bill Laskey	.06
586	Jeff Russell	.10
588	Steve Farr	.08
589	*Steve Ontiveros* (FC)	.10
593	Larry Herndon	.08
595	Carlos Ponce	.06
596	*Pat Perry* (FC)	.12
597	Ray Knight	.10
598	*Steve Lombardozzi* (FC)	.20
600	*Pat Clements* (FC)	.12

601	Joe Niekro	.10
603	*Dwayne Henry* (FC)	.10
604	Mookie Wilson	.10
608	Joe Cowley	.06
609	Tom Seaver (green stripes around name)	.40
609	Tom Seaver (yellow stripes around name)	2.00
610	Neil Allen	.06
611	Don Sutton	.30
612	*Fred Toliver* (FC)	.15
613	Jay Baller	.06
615	John Grubb	.06
616	Bruce Kison	.06
617	Bill Madlock	.12
619	Dave Stewart	.12
620	Tim Lollar	.06
621	Gary Lavelle	.06

625	Sid Fernandez	.12
629	*Roger McDowell* (FC)	.50
631	Ed Lynch	.06
632	Rudy Law	.06
634	*Mike Felder* (FC)	.15
636	Bob Ojeda	.08
642	Mike Brown	.06
644	Ty-Breaking Hit (Pete Rose)	.50
645	*Knuckle Brothers (Joe Niekro, Phil Niekro)	.15
648	Cesar Cedeno	.10
649	Bert Blyleven	.15
651	Fleet Feet (Vince Coleman (FC), Willie McGee)	.35
653	King of Kings (Pete Rose)	.75

1986 DONRUSS ROOKIES ▬▬

Donruss followed the leaders in 1986 by creating "The Rookies," a subset issued in the fall to rival Topps and Fleer. Unlike the other companies, however, Donruss did not bother with cards of traded players. This streamlined concept resulted in 55 cards of the leading rookies of 1986, along with a rather useless unnumbered checklist. Border colors switched to green from the blue used on the regular issue of 660 cards. In addition, "The Rookies" logo is found on the lower left of each card front. High-powered rookie stars include Jose Canseco, Will Clark, Bo Jackson, Kevin Mitchell, and Ruben Sierra. The value of the set tripled in its first year.

22 Jose Canseco

	MINT
Complete set	**$55.00**
Commons	**.15**

1	Wally Joyner (FC)	$4.00
2	Tracy Jones (FC)	.50
3	Allan Anderson (FC)	.40
4	Ed Correa (FC)	.25
5	Reggie Williams	.20
6	Charlie Kerfeld	.20
7	Andres Galarraga	.80
8	Bob Tewksbury	.20
9	Al Newman	.15
10	Andres Thomas (FC)	.40
11	Barry Bonds (FC)	1.75
12	Juan Nieves	.20
13	Mark Eichhorn (FC)	.25
14	Dan Plesac (FC)	.40
15	Cory Snyder	1.75
16	Kelly Gruber	.20
17	Kevin Mitchell (FC)	9.00
19	Mitch Williams	.60
20	John Cerutti (FC)	.25
21	Todd Worrell	.50
22	Jose Canseco	15.00
23	Pete Incaviglia (FC)	.90
24	Jose Guzman	.25
25	Scott Bailes (FC)	.25
26	Greg Mathews (FC)	.25
27	Eric King (FC)	.20

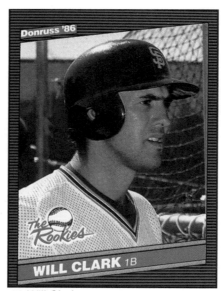
32 Will Clark

28	Paul Assenmacher	.20
29	Jeff Sellers	.25
30	Bobby Bonilla (FC)	.90
31	Doug Drabek (FC)	.30
32	Will Clark (FC)	15.00
33	Leon "Bip" Roberts	.20

34	Jim Deshaies (FC)	.25
35	Mike Lavalliere (LaValliere) (FC)	.30
36	Scott Bankhead (FC)	.20
37	Dale Sveum (FC)	.25
38	Bo Jackson (FC)	12.00
39	Rob Thompson (FC)	.50
40	Eric Plunk	.25
41	Bill Bathe	.20
42	John Kruk (FC)	.40
43	Andy Allanson	.20
44	Mark Portugal	.20
45	Danny Tartabull	1.00
47	Gene Walter	.20
48	Rey Quinones	.30
49	Bobby Witt (FC)	.60
52	Ruben Sierra (FC)	8.00

1986 FLEER

Striking photographs and a simple card design make the 1986 Fleer set a winner. Maximum space on each of the 660 cards is devoted to photos, which are surrounded by a dark blue border. Card backs are bleak and no longer contain the black-and-white photo of past years, but Fleer was the only company to provide complete major and minor league stats for all players. Popular with collectors is a run of 10 Major League Prospect cards, on which two potential rookie sensations, usually teammates, share a card front. Notables in this subset include Jose Canseco, Cory Snyder, and Kal Daniels. Canseco (who would later get a solo card in the 1986 Fleer Update) is the most expensive card in the standard set.

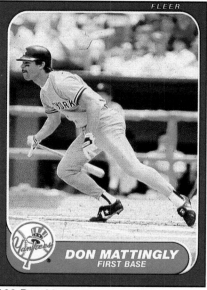
109 Don Mattingly

		MINT
Complete set		$100.00
Commons		.06

4	Bud Black	$ .06
5	George Brett	.50
7	Steve Farr	.08
8	Mark Gubicza	.12
9	Dane Iorg	.06
10	Danny Jackson	.20
11	Lynn Jones	.06
12	Mike Jones	.06
14	Hal McRae	.10
17	Jorge Orta	.06
19	Bret Saberhagen	1.50
23	John Wathan	.08
24	Frank White	.10
25	Willie Wilson	.12
27	Steve Braun	.06
30	Jack Clark	.20
31	*Vince Coleman*	1.75
32	Danny Cox	.10
33	Key Dayley	.06
35	Bob Forsch	.08
37	Tom Herr	.10
40	Jeff Lahti	.06
42	Willie McGee	.15
43	Tom Nieto	.06
44	Terry Pendleton	.15
46	Ozzie Smith	.15
47	John Tudor	.10
48	Andy Van Slyke	.15
49	*Todd Worrell* (FC)	.90
50	Jim Acker	.06
52	Jesse Barfield	.20
53	George Bell	.30
56	Jim Clancy	.06
57	Tony Fernandez	.06
58	Tom Filer	.06
60	Tom Henke	.12
61	Garth Iorg	.06
63	Jimmy Key	.15
64	Dennis Lamp	.06
67	Lloyd Moseby	.10
69	Al Oliver	.10
70	Dave Stieb	.12
72	Willie Upshaw	.08
73	Ernie Whitt	.08
74	*Rick Aguilera* (FC)	.25

76	Gary Carter	.25
77	Ron Darling	.15
78	*Len Dykstra* (FC)	.60
79	Sid Fernandez	.12
80	George Foster	.15
81	Dwight Gooden	2.00
82	Tom Gorman	.06
83	Danny Heep	.06
84	Keith Hernandez	.30
85	Howard Johnson	.15
86	Ray Knight	.08
87	Terry Leach	.08
88	Ed Lynch	.06
89	*Roger McDowell* (FC)	.40
94	Doug Sisk	.06
95	Rusty Staub	.10
96	Darryl Strawberry	1.50
97	Mookie Wilson	.10
98	Neil Allen	.06
99	Don Baylor	.12
100	Dale Berra	.06
101	Rich Bordi	.06
103	Joe Cowley	.06
104	*Brian Fisher*	.25
105	Ken Griffey	.10
106	Ron Guidry	.20
108	Rickey Henderson	.50
109	Don Mattingly	5.00
112	Phil Niekro	.25
113	Mike Pagliarulo	.20

114	Dan Pasqua	.20
115	Willie Randolph	.10
116	Dave Righetti	.20
118	Billy Sample	.06
120	Ed Whitson	.06
121	Dave Winfield	.35
124	Bob Bailor	.06
125	Greg Brock	.08
126	Enos Cabell	.06
128	Carlos Diaz	.06
129	*Mariano Duncan*	.15
130	Pedro Guerrero	.25
131	Orel Hershiser	1.25
133	Ken Howell	.06
135	Bill Madlock	.12
136	Candy Maldonado	.10
137	Mike Marshall	.15
143	Steve Sax	.25
145	Fernando Valenzuela	.30
146	Bob Welch	.12
149	*Bob Boone	.08
150	John Candelaria	.10
151	Rod Carew	.30
152	*Stewart Cliburn* (FC)	.12

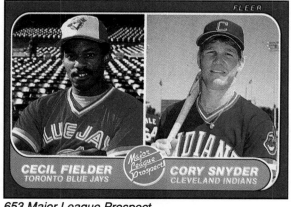
653 Major League Prospect

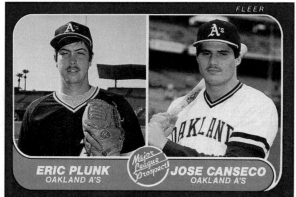

649 Major League Prospect

153	Doug DeCinces	.10
155	Ken Forsch	.06
157	Bobby Grich	.10
159	Al Holland	.06
160	Reggie Jackson	.35
162	*Urbano Lugo*	.08
163	*Kirk McCaskill* (FC)	.35
165	Gary Pettis	.06
169	Jim Slaton	.06
170	Don Sutton	.25
171	Mike Witt	.06
172	Buddy Bell	.10
173	Tom Browning	.30
174	Dave Concepcion	.12
175	Eric Davis	3.00
176	Bo Diaz	.08
177	Nick Esasky	.15
178	John Franco	.12
179	Tom Hume	.06
183	Ron Oester	.06
184	Dave Parker	.20
186	Tony Perez	.15
187	Ted Power	.08
188	Joe Price	.06
189	Gary Redus	.08
191	Pete Rose	.75
192	Mario Soto	.08
193	John Stuper	.06
194	Jay Tibbs	.06
196	Max Venable	.06
197	Juan Agosto	.06
198	Harold Baines	.15
200	Britt Burns	.06
201	Julio Cruz	.06
202	*Joel Davis* (FC)	.08
203	Richard Dotson	.10
204	Carlton Fisk	.30
205	Scott Fletcher	.08
206	*Ozzie Guillen*	.40
207	Jerry Hairston	.06
208	Tim Hulett	.06
209	Bob James	.06
210	Ron Kittle	.10
211	Rudy Law	.06
212	Bryan Little	.06
213	Gene Nelson	.06
214	Reid Nichols	.06
215	Luis Salazar	.06
216	Tom Seaver	.40

217	Dan Spillner	.06
218	Bruce Tanner	.06
219	Greg Walker	.08
220	Dave Wehrmeister	.06
221	Juan Berenguer	.06
222	Dave Bergman	.06
223	Tom Brookens	.06
224	Darrell Evans	.12
225	Barbaro Garbey	.06
226	Kirk Gibson	.30
227	John Grubb	.06
230	Chet Lemon	.06
231	Aurelio Lopez	.06
232	Jack Morris	.20
233	Randy O'Neal	.06
234	Lance Parrish	.20
235	Dan Petry	.08
236	Alex Sanchez	.06
237	Bill Scherrer	.06
239	Frank Tanana	.10
241	Alan Trammell	.25
242	Lou Whitaker	.30
243	Milt Wilcox	.06
244	Hubie Brooks	.10
245	*Tim Burke* (FC)	.30
246	Andre Dawson	.20
249	Bill Gullickson	.06
250	Joe Hesketh	.06
251	Bill Laskey	.06
252	Vance Law	.08

253	Charlie Lea	.06
254	Gary Lucas	.06
255	David Palmer	.06
256	Tim Raines	.30
257	Jeff Reardon	.15
258	Bert Roberge	.06
259	Dan Schatzeder	.06
260	Bryn Smith	.08
262	Scot Thompson	.06
263	Tim Wallach	.12
264	U.L. Washington	.06
265	*Mitch Webster* (FC)	.25
266	*Herm Winningham*	.15
267	*Floyd Youmans* (FC)	.25
268	Don Aase	.06
270	Rich Dauer	.06
271	Storm Davis	.10
273	Ken Dixon	.06
274	Jim Dwyer	.06
276	Wayne Gross	.06
277	Lee Lacy	.06
278	Fred Lynn	.20
282	Eddie Murray	.40
283	Floyd Rayford	.06
284	Cal Ripken Jr.	.40
286	Larry Sheets	.20
287	John Shelby	.06
288	Nate Snell	.06
291	Mike Young	.06
292	Alan Ashby	.06
293	Mark Bailey	.06
294	Kevin Bass	.10
296	Jose Cruz	.15
297	Glenn Davis	.75
298	Bill Dawley	.06
300	Bill Doran	.10
301	Phil Garner	.08
303	*Charlie Kerfeld* (FC)	.15
304	Bob Knepper	.08
305	Ron Mathis	.06
306	Jerry Mumphrey	.06
307	Jim Pankovits	.06
308	Terry Puhl	.06
309	Craig Reynolds	.06
310	Nolan Ryan	.50
311	Mike Scott	.15
312	Dave Smith	.08
313	Dickie Thon	.08
316	Al Bumbry	.06
317	Jerry Davis	.06

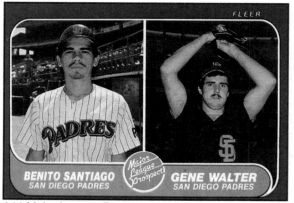

644 Major League Prospect

318	Luis DeLeon	.06
321	Steve Garvey	.30
322	Goose Gossage	.20
323	Tony Gwynn	.80
324	Andy Hawkins	.06
330	*Lance McCullers* (FC)	.25
331	Kevin McReynolds	.30
332	Graig Nettles	.15
334	Eric Show	.08
338	Ed Wojna	.06
339	Tony Armas	.08
340	Marty Barrett	.10
341	Wade Boggs	2.75
343	Bill Buckner	.10
344	Mark Clear	.06
345	Roger Clemens	3.00
346	Steve Crawford	.06
347	Mike Easler	.08
348	*Dwight Evans	.12
349	Rich Gedman	.08
350	Jackie Gutierrez	.06
351	Glenn Hoffman	.06
352	Bruce Hurst	.15
353	Bruce Kison	.06
354	Tim Lollar	.06
355	Steve Lyons	.08
356	Al Nipper	.06
357	Bob Ojeda	.08
358	Jim Rice	.30
359	Bob Stanley	.06
361	Thad Bosley	.06
363	Ron Cey	.10
364	Jody Davis	.06
365	Bob Dernier	.06
366	Shawon Dunston	.15
367	Leon Durham	.08
368	Dennis Eckersley	.12
369	Ray Fontenot	.06
371	Bill Hatcher	.10
372	Dave Lopes	.10
373	Gary Matthews	.10
377	Dick Ruthven	.06
378	Ryne Sandberg	.40
380	Lee Smith	.10

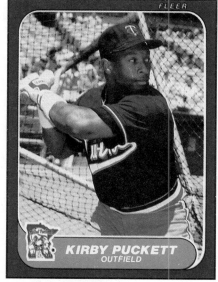

401 Kirby Puckett

646 Major League Prospect

382	Chris Speier	.06
383	Rick Sutcliffe	.12
384	Steve Trout	.06
385	Gary Woods	.06
386	Bert Blyleven	.15
387	Tom Brunansky	.15
388	Randy Bush	.06
390	Ron Davis	.06
391	Dave Engle	.06
393	Pete Filson	.06
394	Gary Gaetti	.20
395	Greg Gagne	.10
396	Mickey Hatcher	.06
397	Kent Hrbek	.25
398	Tim Laudner	.06
399	Rick Lysander	.06
400	Dave Meier	.06
401	Kirby Puckett	4.00
402	Mark Salas	.06
403	Ken Schrom	.06
404	Roy Smalley	.06
405	Mike Smithson	.06
406	Mike Stenhouse	.06
407	Tim Teufel	.06
408	Frank Viola	.15
409	Ron Washington	.06
410	Keith Atherton	.06
411	Dusty Baker	.08
412	*Tim Birtsas*	.10
413	Bruce Bochte	.06
414	Chris Codiroli	.08
415	Dave Collins	.08
416	Mike Davis	.08
417	Alfredo Griffin	.08
418	Mike Heath	.06
419	Steve Henderson	.06
420	Donnie Hill	.06
421	Jay Howell	.10
422	Tommy John	.20
423	Dave Kingman	.15
424	Bill Krueger	.06
425	Rick Langford	.06
426	Carney Lansford	.10
427	Steve McCatty	.06
428	Dwayne Murphy	.06
429	*Steve Ontiveros* (FC)	.10
430	Tony Phillips	.08
431	Jose Rijo	.10
432	*Mickey Tettleton*	.85

433	Luis Aguayo	.06
434	Larry Andersen	.06
435	Steve Carlton	.30
436	*Don Carman*	.25
437	Tim Corcoran	.06
438	*Darren Daulton*	.10
439	John Denny	.08
440	Tom Foley	.06
441	Greg Gross	.06
442	Kevin Gross	.06
443	Von Hayes	.12
444	Charles Hudson	.06
445	Garry Maddox	.08
446	Shane Rawley	.06
447	Dave Rucker	.06
448	John Russell	.06
449	Juan Samuel	.12
450	Mike Schmidt	.50
451	Rick Schu	.06
452	Dave Shipanoff	.06
453	*Dave Stewart	.12
454	Jeff Stone	.06
455	Kent Tekulve	.08
456	Ozzie Virgil	.06
457	Glenn Wilson	.08
458	Jim Beattie	.06
459	Karl Best	.06
460	Barry Bonnell	.06
461	Phil Bradley	.20
462	*Ivan Calderon*	.40
463	Al Cowens	.06
464	Alvin Davis	.30
465	Dave Henderson	.10
466	Bob Kearney	.06
467	Mark Langston	.35
468	Bob Long	.06
469	Mike Moore	.12
470	Edwin Nunez	.06
471	Spike Owen	.06
472	Jack Perconte	.06
473	Jim Presley	.12
474	Donnie Scott	.06
475	Bill Swift (FC)	.10
476	Danny Tartabull	.50
477	Gorman Thomas	.10
478	Roy Thomas	.06
479	Ed Vande Berg	.06
480	Frank Wills	.06
481	Matt Young	.06

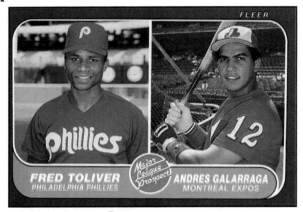

647 Major League Prospect

482	Ray Burris	.06
483	Jaime Cocanower	.06
484	Cecil Cooper	.10
485	Danny Darwin	.06
486	Rollie Fingers	.20
487	Jim Gantner	.06
488	Bob Gibson	.06
489	Moose Haas	.06
490	*Teddy Higuera*	1.25
491	Paul Householder	.06
492	Pete Ladd	.06
493	Rick Manning	.06
494	Bob McClure	.06
495	Paul Molitor	.15
496	Charlie Moore	.06
497	Ben Oglivie	.08
498	Randy Ready	.06
499	*Earnie Riles*	.20
500	Ed Romero	.06
503	Ted Simmons	.15
505	Rick Waits	.06
506	Robin Yount	.30
507	Len Barker	.08
508	Steve Bedrosian	.12
510	Rick Camp	.06
513	Jeff Dedmon	.08
514	Terry Forster	.08
515	Gene Garber	.08
516	Terry Harper	.06
517	Bob Horner	.15
521	Rick Mahler	.08
522	Dale Murphy	.50
524	Pascual Perez	.10
525	Gerald Perry	.08
527	*Steve Shields* (FC)	.10
528	Zane Smith	.08
529	Bruce Sutter	.12
530	*Milt Thompson* (FC)	.30
533	Vida Blue	.10
534	Bob Brenly	.08
535	*Chris Brown*	.15
536	Chili Davis	.10
537	Mark Davis	.15
538	Rob Deer	.10
541	Dan Gladden	.08
542	Jim Gott	.08
543	David Green	.06
548	Jeff Leonard	.10
549	Greg Minton	.06

552	*Jose Uribe*	.20
558	*Steve Buechele* (FC)	.20
559	*Jose Guzman* (FC)	.30
560	Toby Harrah	.08
563	Burt Hooton	.08
564	Charlie Hough	.08
566	*Oddibe McDowell*	.30
568	Pete O'Brien	.10
569	Larry Parrish	.10
572	Don Slaught	.08
574	Duane Walker	.06
575	Gary Ward	.08
578	George Wright	.06
579	Chris Bando	.06
581	Brett Butler	.08
583	Joe Carter	.20
586	Julio Franco	.15
587	Mel Hall	.08
589	Neal Heaton	.06
590	Brook Jacoby	.10
591	*Otis Nixon* (FC)	.10
592	Jerry Reed	.06
593	Vern Ruhle	.06
594	Pat Tabler	.06
600	Curt Wardle	.06
602	Bill Almon	.06
603	Mike Bielecki	.06
604	Sid Bream	.10
605	Mike Brown	.06
606	*Pat Clements*	.10
607	Jose DeLeon	.15
610	Steve Kemp	.08
615	*Joe Orsulak*	.15
616	Tony Pena	.10
617	Johnny Ray	.12
618	Rick Reuschel	.12
620	Rick Rhoden	.10
623	Lee Tunnell	.06
626	Gooden In Action (Dwight Gooden)	.50
627	Mattingly In Action (Don Mattingly)	1.50
628	4,192! (Pete Rose)	.50
629	3,000 Career Hits (Rod Carew)	.20
630	300 Career Wins (Phil Niekro, Tom Seaver)	.20
632	Instant Offense (Tim Raines, Darryl Strawberry)	.30

633	Shortstops Supreme (Cal Ripken, Jr., Alan Trammell)	.30
634	Boggs & "Hero" (Wade Boggs, George Brett)	.60
635	Braves Dynamic Duo (Bob Horner, Dale Murphy)	.30
636	Cardinal Ignitors (Vince Coleman, Willie McGee)	.35
637	Terror on the Basepaths (Vince Coleman)	.35
638	Charlie Hustle & Dr. K (Dwight Gooden, Pete Rose)	.70
639	1984 and 1985 AL Batting Champs (Wade Boggs, Don Mattingly)	1.75
640	NL West Sluggers (Steve Garvey, Dale Murphy, Dave Parker)	.30
641	Staff Aces (Dwight Gooden, Fernando Valenzuela)	.40
644	Major League Prospect (*Benito Santiago, Gene Walter* (FC))	5.00
646	Major League Prospect (*Kal Daniels, Paul O'Neill* (FC))	4.00
647	Major League Prospect (*Andres Galarraga, Fred Toliver* (FC))	4.00
648	Major League Prospect (*Curt Ford, Bob Kipper* (FC))	.25
649	Major League Prospect (*Jose Canseco, Eric Plunk* (FC))	52.00
653	Major League Prospect (*Cecil Fielder, Cory Snyder* (FC))	6.00

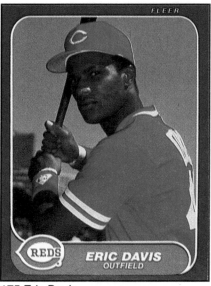

175 Eric Davis

1986 FLEER UPDATE

What a difference a year makes! With the inclusion of popular players such as Jose Canseco, Kevin Mitchell, Ruben Sierra, and Wally Joyner, the 1986 Fleer Update set of 132 cards became an immediate hit. In contrast to Topps, the Fleer "extension" set contains a higher percentage of rookies in its 131 cards (and complete set checklist). Although the company skipped Bo Jackson, it scooped Topps by including the phenomenal Ruben Sierra of the Rangers. The Fleer Update cards differ from the standard 1986 cards only by a "U" prefix on the card numbers (omitted from the following lists). To satisfy collectors of rookie cards, hobby dealers divided sets and sold popular cards in lots of 50 or 100 cards.

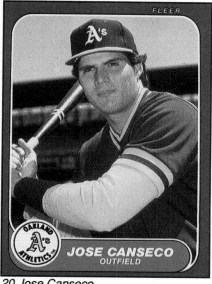

20 Jose Canseco

25 Will Clark

		MINT
Complete set		**$32.00**
Commons		.08

1	Mike Aldrete (FC)	$ .35
2	Andy Allanson (FC)	.20
3	Neil Allen	.10
4	Joaquin Andujar	.10
5	Paul Assenmacher (FC)	.15
6	Scott Bailes (FC)	.25
7	Jay Baller (FC)	.15
8	Scott Bankhead (FC)	.20
9	Bill Bathe	.10
10	Don Baylor	.15
11	Billy Beane	.15
12	Steve Bedrosian	.15
14	Barry Bonds (FC)	1.50
15	Bobby Bonilla (FC)	1.50
16	Rich Bordi	.08
17	Bill Campbell	.08
18	Tom Candiotti	.10
19	John Cangelosi (FC)	.10
20	Jose Canseco	13.00
21	Chuck Cary (FC)	.10
22	Juan Castillo (FC)	.10
23	Rick Cerone	.10
24	John Cerutti (FC)	.25
25	Will Clark (FC)	15.00
26	Mark Clear	.08
27	Darnell Coles (FC)	.20
28	Dave Collins	.10
29	Tim Conroy	.08
30	Ed Correa (FC)	.20
31	Joe Cowley	.10
33	Rob Deer	.15
34	John Denny	.15
35	Jim DeShaies (Deshaies) (FC)	.25
36	Doug Drabek (FC)	.35
37	Mike Easler	.10
38	Mark Eichhorn (FC)	.20
41	Scott Fletcher	.15
42	Terry Forster	.10
44	Andres Galarraga	1.00
45	Lee Guetterman (FC)	.20
48	Moose Haas	.08
49	Billy Hatcher	.15
50	Mike Heath	.08
52	Tom Hume	.08

53	Pete Incaviglia (FC)	.50
54	Dane Iorg	.08
55	Chris James (FC)	.60
56	Stan Javier (FC)	.25
57	Tommy John	.20
58	Tracy Jones (FC)	.40
59	Wally Joyner (FC)	3.00
61	John Kruk (FC)	.35
62	Mike LaCoss	.08
64	Dave LaPoint	.10
65	Mike LaValliere (FC)	.25
66	Rudy Law	.08
67	Dennis Leonard	.10
68	Steve Lombardozzi (FC)	.15
69	Aurelio Lopez	.08
71	Candy Maldonado	.15
72	Roger Mason (FC)	.10
73	Greg Mathews (FC)	.25
75	Joel McKeon (FC)	.12
76	Kevin Mitchell (FC)	7.00
77	Bill Mooneyham (FC)	.10
78	Omar Moreno	.08
80	Al Newman (FC)	.10
81	Phil Niekro	.30

82	Randy Niemann	.08
83	Juan Nieves (FC)	.20
84	Bob Ojeda	.10
88	Jeff Parrett (FC)	.25
89	Pat Perry (FC)	.15
90	Dan Plesac (FC)	.35
91	Darrell Porter	.10
92	Luis Quinones (FC)	.12
93	Rey Quinonez (FC)	.15
94	Gary Redus	.10
95	Jeff Reed (FC)	.10
96	Bip Roberts	.15
97	Billy Joe Robidoux	.15
100	Angel Salazar	.08
101	Joe Sambito	.08
102	Billy Sample	.08
103	Dave Schmidt	.15
104	Ken Schrom	.08
105	Ruben Sierra (FC)	7.00
106	Ted Simmons	.20
108	Kurt Stillwell (FC)	.30
109	Dale Sveum (FC)	.20
110	Tim Teufel	.15
111	Bob Tewksbury	.20
112	Andres Thomas (FC)	.25
113	Jason Thompson	.10
114	Milt Thompson	.15
115	Rob Thompson (FC)	.40
117	Fred Toliver	.10
120	Manny Trillo	.10
122	Ozzie Virgil	.08
123	Tony Walker	.15
124	Gene Walter	.10
125	Duane Ward (FC)	.25
127	Mitch Williams (FC)	.65
128	Reggie Williams (FC)	.15
129	Bobby Witt (FC)	.50

219

1986 TOPPS

At 792 cards, the 1986 Topps set continued to be the biggest on the market. With the team identified in large letters at the top of each card, this design was one of Topps' boldest of the decade. Due to the large size of the edition, there was room for several specialty subsets. Topps remained the only company to give each team manager a card (with a team checklist on the back). Twenty-two All-Star cards are included, along with a seven-card subset of all-time hit king Pete Rose. On the negative side, Topps included few rookies in the set, opting to save them for the fall Traded set.

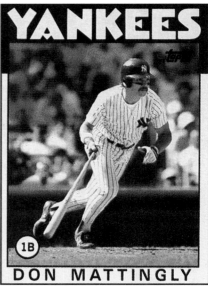

180 Don Mattingly

661 Roger Clemens

		MINT
Complete set		$35.00
Commons		.05

1	Pete Rose	$1.00
2	Rose Special 1963-1966	.35
3	Rose Special 1967-1970	.35
4	Rose Special 1971-1974	.35
5	Rose Special 1975-1978	.35
6	Rose Special 1979-1982	.35
7	Rose Special 1983-1985	.35
8	Dwayne Murphy	.07
9	Roy Smith	.05
10	Tony Gwynn	.50
11	Bob Ojeda	.07
12	Jose Uribe (FC)	.20
13	Bob Kearney	.05
14	Julio Cruz	.05
15	Eddie Whitson	.05
16	Rick Schu (FC)	.07
17	Mike Stenhouse	.05
18	Brent Gaff	.05
19	Rich Hebner	.07
20	Lou Whitaker	.25
21	George Bamberger	.05
22	Duane Walker	.05
23	Manny Lee (FC)	.15
24	Len Barker	.07
25	Willie Wilson	.12
26	Frank DiPino	.05
27	Ray Knight	.07
28	Eric Davis	3.00
29	Tony Phillips	.10
30	Eddie Murray	.40
31	Jamie Easterly	.05
32	Steve Yeager	.05
33	Jeff Lahti	.05
34	Ken Phelps (FC)	.07
35	Jeff Reardon	.12
36	Tigers Ldrs (Lance Parrish)	.12
37	Mark Thurmond	.05
38	Glenn Hoffman	.05
39	Dave Rucker	.05
40	Ken Griffey	.10
41	Brad Wellman	.05
42	Geoff Zahn	.05
43	Dave Engle	.05
44	Lance McCullers (FC)	.25
45	Damaso Garcia	.05
46	Billy Hatcher (FC)	.20

47	Juan Berenguer	.05
48	Bill Almon	.05
49	Rick Manning	.05
50	Dan Quisenberry	.07
51	Not Issued	
52	Chris Welsh	.05
53	Len Dykstra (FC)	.60
54	John Franco	.12
55	Fred Lynn	.15
56	Tom Niedenfuer	.07
57	Bobby Wine	.05
57	Bill Doran	.10
58	Bill Krueger	.05
59	Andre Thornton	.07
60	*Dwight Evans	.12
61	Karl Best	.05
62	*Bob Boone	.07
63	Ron Roenicke	.05
64	Floyd Bannister	.07
65	Dan Driessen	.07
66	Cardinals Ldrs (Bob Forsch)	.07
67	Carmelo Martinez	.07
68	Ed Lynch	.05
69	Luis Aguayo	.05
70	Dave Winfield	.30
71	Ken Schrom	.05

72	Shawon Dunston	.20
73	Randy O'Neal (FC)	.07
74	Rance Mulliniks	.07
75	Jose DeLeon	.15
76	Dion James	.07
77	Charlie Leibrandt	.07
78	Bruce Benedict	.05
79	Dave Schmidt	.07
80	Darryl Strawberry	.75
81	Gene Mauch	.07
82	Tippy Martinez	.05
83	Phil Garner	.07
84	Curt Young	.07
85	Tony Perez	.15
86	Tom Waddell	.05
87	Candy Maldonado	.10
88	Tom Nieto	.05
89	Randy St. Claire (FC)	.07
90	Garry Templeton	.07
91	Steve Crawford	.05
92	Al Cowens	.05
93	Scot Thompson	.05
94	Rick Bordi	.05
95	Ozzie Virgil	.05
96	Blue Jays Ldrs (Jim Clancy)	.07
97	Gary Gaetti	.20
98	Dick Ruthven	.05
99	Buddy Biancalana	.05
100	Nolan Ryan	.75
101	Dave Bergman	.05
102	Joe Orsulak	.15
103	Luis Salazar	.05
104	Sid Fernandez	.12
105	Gary Ward	.07
106	Ray Burris	.05
107	Rafael Ramirez	.05
108	Ted Power	.05
109	Len Matuszek	.05
110	Scott McGregor	.07
111	Roger Craig	.07
112	Bill Campbell	.05
113	U.L. Washington	.05

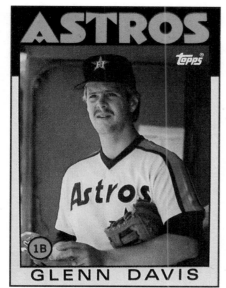

ASTROS

Topps

GLENN DAVIS

1B

389 Glenn Davis

114	Mike Brown	.05
115	Jay Howell	.07
116	Brook Jacoby	.10
117	Bruce Kison	.05
118	Jerry Royster	.05
119	Barry Bonnell	.05
120	Steve Carlton	.30
121	Nelson Simmons	.05
122	Pete Filson	.05
123	Greg Walker	.10
124	Luis Sanchez	.05
125	Dave Lopes	.07
126	Mets Ldrs (Mookie Wilson)	.07
127	*Jack Howell* (FC)	.35
128	John Wathan	.07
129	Jeff Dedmon (FC)	.05
130	Alan Trammell	.30
131	Checklist 1-132	.05
132	Razor Shines	.05
133	Andy McGaffigan	.05
134	Carney Lansford	.10
135	Joe Niekro	.10
136	Mike Hargrove	.05
137	Charlie Moore	.05
138	Mark Davis	.10
139	Daryl Boston	.07
140	John Candelaria	.10
141	Bob Rodgers	.05
141	Chuck Cottier	.05
142	Bob Jones	.05
143	Dave Van Gorder	.05
144	Doug Sisk	.05
145	Pedro Guerrero	.20
146	Jack Perconte	.05
147	Larry Sheets	.15
148	Mike Heath	.05
149	Brett Butler	.07
150	Joaquin Andujar	.07
151	Dave Stapleton	.05
152	Mike Morgan	.05
153	Ricky Adams	.05
154	Bert Roberge	.05

155	Bob Grich	.10
156	White Sox Ldrs (Richard Dotson)	.07
157	Ron Hassey	.05
158	Derrel Thomas	.05
159	Orel Hershiser	1.50
160	Chet Lemon	.07
161	Lee Tunnell	.05
162	Greg Gagne	.07
163	Pete Ladd	.05
164	Steve Balboni	.07
165	Mike Davis	.07
166	Dickie Thon	.07
167	Zane Smith (FC)	.10
168	Jeff Burroughs	.07
169	George Wright	.06
170	Gary Carter	.25
171	Not Issued	
172	Jerry Reed	.05
173	Wayne Gross	.05
174	Brian Snyder	.05
175	Steve Sax	.25
176	Jay Tibbs	.05
177	Joel Youngblood	.05
178	Ivan DeJesus	.05
179	*Stu Cliburn* (FC)	.10
180	Don Mattingly	4.00
181	Al Nipper	.05
182	Bobby Brown	.05
183	Larry Andersen	.05
184	Tim Laudner	.05
185	Rollie Fingers	.25
186	Astros Ldrs (Jose Cruz)	.07
187	Scott Fletcher	.07
188	Bob Dernier	.05
189	Mike Mason	.05
190	George Hendrick	.07
191	Wally Backman	.07
192	Milt Wilcox	.05
193	Daryl Sconiers	.05
194	Craig McMurtry	.05
195	Dave Concepcion	.12
196	Doyle Alexander	.07

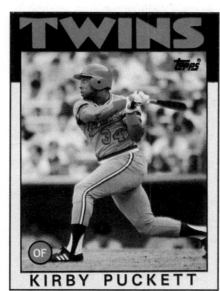

TWINS

Topps

KIRBY PUCKETT

OF

329 Kirby Puckett

REDS

Topps

ERIC DAVIS

OF

28 Eric Davis

197	Enos Cabell	.05
198	Ken Dixon	.05
199	Dick Howser	.05
200	Mike Schmidt	.50
201	Record Breaker (Vince Coleman) (FC)	.30
202	Record Breaker (Dwight Gooden)	.40
203	Record Breaker (Keith Hernandez)	.20
204	Record Breaker (Phil Niekro)	.15
205	Record Breaker (Tony Perez)	.10
206	Record Breaker (Pete Rose)	.50
207	Record Breaker (Fernando Valenzuela)	.20
208	Ramon Romero	.05
209	Randy Ready	.05
210	Calvin Schiraldi (FC)	.10
211	Ed Wojna	.05
212	Chris Speier	.07
213	Bob Shirley	.07
214	Randy Bush	.07
215	Frank White	.10
216	A's Ldrs (Dwayne Murphy)	.07
217	Bill Scherrer	.05
218	Randy Hunt	.05
219	Dennis Lamp	.05
220	Bob Horner	.15
221	Dave Henderson	.10
222	Craig Gerber	.05
223	Atlee Hammaker	.05
224	Cesar Cedeno	.10
225	Ron Darling	.15
226	Lee Lacy	.05
227	Al Jones	.05
228	Tom Lawless	.05
229	Bill Gullickson	.05
230	Terry Kennedy	.07
231	Jim Frey	.05

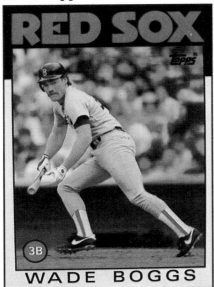

510 Wade Boggs

232	Rick Rhoden	.10
233	Steve Lyons (FC)	.07
234	Doug Corbett	.05
235	Butch Wynegar	.05
236	Frank Eufemia	.05
237	Ted Simmons	.10
238	Larry Parrish	.10
239	Joel Skinner	.05
240	Tommy John	.20
241	Tony Fernandez	.20
242	Rich Thompson	.05
243	Johnny Grubb	.05
244	Craig Lefferts	.05
245	Jim Sundberg	.07
246	Phillies Ldrs (Steve Carlton)	.15
247	Terry Harper	.05
248	Spike Owen	.05
249	Rob Deer (FC)	.40
250	Dwight Gooden	2.00
251	Rich Dauer	.05
252	Bobby Castillo	.05
253	Dann Bilardello	.05
254	Ozzie Guillen	.50
255	Tony Armas	.07
256	Kurt Kepshire	.05
257	Doug DeCinces	.10
258	Tim Burke (FC)	.25
259	Dan Pasqua	.20
260	Tony Pena	.10
261	Bobby Valentine	.05
262	Mario Ramirez	.05
263	Checklist 133-264	.05
264	Darren Daulton (FC)	.10
265	Ron Davis	.05
266	Keith Moreland	.07
267	Paul Molitor	.15
268	Mike Scott	.15
269	Dane Iorg	.05
270	Jack Morris	.20
271	Dave Collins	.07
272	Tim Tolman	.05
273	Jerry Willard	.05

222

274	Ron Gardenhire	.05
275	Charlie Hough	.10
276	Yankees Ldrs (Willie Randolph)	.07
277	Jaime Cocanower	.05
278	Sixto Lezcano	.05
279	Al Pardo	.05
280	Tim Raines	.30
281	Steve Mura	.05
282	Jerry Mumphrey	.05
283	Mike Fischlin	.05
284	Brian Dayett	.05
285	Buddy Bell	.10
286	Luis DeLeon	.05
287	John Christensen (FC)	.10
288	Don Aase	.05
289	Johnnie LeMaster	.05
290	Carlton Fisk	.30
291	Tom Lasorda	.07
292	Chuck Porter	.05
293	Chris Chambliss	.07
294	Danny Cox	.10
295	Kirk Gibson	.30
296	Geno Petralli (FC)	.07
297	Tim Lollar	.05
298	Craig Reynolds	.05
299	Bryn Smith	.05
300	George Brett	.50
301	Dennis Rasmussen	.12
302	Greg Gross	.05
303	Curt Wardle	.05
304	Mike Gallego (FC)	.12
305	Phil Bradley	.15
306	Padres Ldrs (Terry Kennedy)	.07
307	Dave Sax	.05
308	Ray Fontenot	.05
309	John Shelby	.05
310	Greg Minton	.05
311	Dick Schofield	.05
312	Tom Filer	.05
313	Joe DeSa	.05
314	Frank Pastore	.05

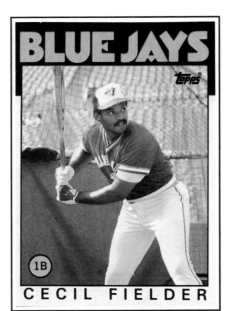

386 Cecil Fielder

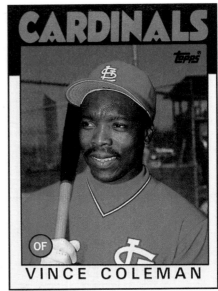

370 Vince Coleman

315	Mookie Wilson	.10
316	Sammy Khalifa	.05
317	Ed Romero	.05
318	Terry Whitfield	.05
319	Rick Camp	.05
320	Jim Rice	.30
321	Earl Weaver	.07
322	Bob Forsch	.07
323	Jerry Davis	.05
324	Dan Schatzeder	.05
325	Juan Beniquez	.05
326	Kent Tekulve	.07
327	Mike Pagliarulo	.20
328	Pete O'Brien	.12
329	Kirby Puckett	3.00
330	Rick Sutcliffe	.12
331	Alan Ashby	.05
332	Darryl Motley	.05
333	Tom Henke (FC)	.12
334	Ken Oberkfell	.05
335	Don Sutton	.25
336	Indians Ldrs (Andre Thornton)	.07
337	Darnell Coles	.07
338	Jorge Bell	.25
339	Bruce Berenyi	.05
340	Cal Ripken	.40
341	Frank Williams	.05
342	Gary Redus	.05
343	Carlos Diaz	.05
344	Jim Wohlford	.05
345	Donnie Moore	.05
346	Bryan Little	.05
347	Teddy Higuera	1.25
348	Cliff Johnson	.05
349	Mark Clear	.05
350	Jack Clark	.20
351	Chuck Tanner	.05
352	Harry Spilman	.05
353	Keith Atherton	.05
354	Tony Bernazard	.05
355	Lee Smith	.10
356	Mickey Hatcher	.05

357	Ed Vande Berg	.05
358	Rick Dempsey	.05
359	Mike LaCoss	.07
360	Lloyd Moseby	.10
361	Shane Rawley	.05
362	Tom Paciorek	.05
363	Terry Forster	.07
364	Reid Nichols	.05
365	Mike Flanagan	.10
366	Reds Ldrs (Dave Concepcion)	.07
367	Aurelio Lopez	.05
368	Greg Brock	.07
369	Al Holland	.05
370	*Vince Coleman*	1.75
371	Bill Stein	.05
372	Ben Oglivie	.07
373	*Urbano Lugo* (FC)	.07
374	Terry Francona	.05
375	Rich Gedman	.07
376	Bill Dawley	.05
377	Joe Carter	.20
378	Bruce Bochte	.05
379	Bobby Meacham	.05
380	LaMarr Hoyt	.05
381	Ray Miller	.05
382	*Ivan Calderon* (FC)	.40
383	*Chris Brown*	.30
384	Steve Trout	.05
385	Cecil Cooper	.10
386	*Cecil Fielder* (FC)	2.00
387	Steve Kemp	.07
388	Dickie Noles	.05
389	Glenn Davis (FC)	3.50
390	Tom Seaver	.40
391	Julio Franco	.15
392	John Russell (FC)	.07
393	Chris Pittaro	.05
394	Checklist 265-396	.05
395	Scott Garrelts	.07
396	Red Sox Ldrs (Dwight Evans)	.07
397	*Steve Buechele* (FC)	.20

53 Len Dykstra

398	*Earnie Riles* (FC)	.15
399	Bill Swift	.10
400	Rod Carew	.35
401	Turn Back the Clock (Fernando Valenzuela)	.15
402	Turn Back the Clock (Tom Seaver)	.15
403	Turn Back the Clock (Willie Mays)	.20
404	Turn Back the Clock (Frank Robinson)	.15
405	Turn Back the Clock (Roger Maris)	.20
409	*Paul Runge*	.07
410	Dave Kingman	.15
415	Hal McRae	.10
420	Von Hayes	.10
426	Brewers Ldrs (Charlie Moore)	.07
430	Kent Hrbek	.20
440	Alvin Davis	.30
441	Whitey Herzog	.10
442	Ron Robinson (FC)	.12
443	Bill Buckner	.10
445	Bert Blyleven	.12
448	*Herm Winningham*	.15
450	Graig Nettles	.15
455	Willie Randolph	.10
456	Braves Ldrs (Dale Murphy)	.25
457	*Mickey Tettleton*	.50
458	Kevin Bass	.10
469	Storm Davis	.10
470	Bill Madlock	.12
474	John Tudor	.10
475	Juan Samuel	.12
479	*Bob Melvin* (FC)	.12
480	*Oddibe McDowell*	.30
481	Scott Bradley (FC)	.10
485	Gary Matthews	.10
486	Angels Ldrs (Bob Grich)	.07
487	Bret Saberhagen	.40
495	Mark Langston	.25
500	Rickey Henderson	.40

505	Jerry Koosman	.10
507	*Steve Ontiveros* (FC)	.12
510	Wade Boggs	2.50
515	Darrell Evans	.12
516	Giants Ldrs (Greg Minton)	.07
517	*Milt Thompson* (FC)	.25
520	Keith Hernandez	.30
524	Darrell Miller (FC)	.07
527	Checklist 397-528	.05
528	Terry Pendleton	.15
530	Rich Gossage	.20
532	*Don Carman*	.25
536	Jose Rijo	.07
538	Dennis Eckersley	.12
545	Jimmy Key	.15
546	Mariners Ldrs (Dave Henderson)	.07
547	*Roger McDowell*	.40
549	Bob Welch	.12
550	Tom Herr	.10
555	Hubie Brooks	.10
557	Gerald Perry	.05
560	Dave Righetti	.20
565	Tom Brunansky	.15
570	Rusty Staub	.10
574	Ron Kittle	.07
575	Mike Boddicker	.07
576	Expos Ldrs (Andre Dawson)	.12
577	Jerry Reuss	.07
580	Willie McGee	.12
581	Bruce Hurst	.15
584	*Brian Fisher* (FC)	.30
589	Sid Bream	.07
592	Frank Tanana	.10
593	Jesse Barfield	.20
595	Dave Parker	.20
598	Jim Presley	.25
599	*Rick Aguilera* (FC)	.25
600	Dale Murphy	.50
602	*Mariano Duncan*	.15
606	Royals Ldrs (Hal McRae)	.07
610	Ron Guidry	.15

159 Orel Hershiser

480 Oddibe McDowell

612	Richard Dotson	.10
615	Johnny Ray	.10
620	Bruce Sutter	.15
628	*Kirk McKaskill* (FC)	.35
629	*Mitch Webster* (FC)	.25
630	Fernando Valenzuela	.30
636	Cubs Ldrs (Lee Smith)	.07
640	Jose Cruz	.10
644	Mark Gubicza	.12
647	Mel Hall	.07
648	Steve Bedrosian	.12
650	Dave Stieb	.12
651	Billy Martin	.12
652	Tom Browning	.25
660	Steve Garvey	.30
661	Roger Clemens	4.00
666	Rangers Ldrs (Charlie Hough)	.07
668	Cecilio Guante	.05
669	Ron Cey	.10
680	George Foster	.15
683	Andy Van Slyke	.12
685	Tim Wallach	.10
689	Dave Stewart	.12
690	Ryne Sandberg	.35
696	Dodgers Ldrs (Bill Russell)	.07
700	Reggie Jackson	.35
701	Keith Hernandez AS	.15
702	Tom Herr AS	.07
703	Tim Wallach AS	.07
704	Ozzie Smith AS	.10
705	Dale Murphy AS	.30
706	Pedro Guerrero AS	.12
707	Willie McGee AS	.12
708	Gary Carter AS	.20
709	Dwight Gooden AS	.40
710	John Tudor AS	.07
711	Jeff Reardon AS	.07

712	Don Mattingly AS	1.00
713	Damaso Garcia AS	.05
714	George Brett AS	.30
715	Cal Ripken AS	.25
716	Rickey Henderson AS	.25
717	Dave Winfield AS	.20
718	Jorge Bell AS	.20
719	Carlton Fisk AS	.12
720	Bret Saberhagen AS	.15
721	Ron Guidry AS	.10
722	Dan Quisenberry AS	.07
726	Orioles Ldrs (Rick Dempsey)	.07
728	Mike Marshall	.12
730	Ozzie Smith	.15
732	*Floyd Youmans* (FC)	.20
734	Marty Barrett	.10
735	Dave Dravecky	.07
736	Glenn Wilson	.07
737	Pete Vuckovich	.07
738	Andre Robertson	.05
739	Dave Rozema	.05
740	Lance Parrish	.20
741	Pete Rose	.40
742	Frank Viola	.15
743	Pat Sheridan	.05
744	Lary Sorensen	.05
745	Willie Upshaw	.05
746	Denny Gonzalez	.05
747	Rick Cerone	.05
748	Steve Henderson	.05
749	Ed Jurak	.05
750	Gorman Thomas	.05
751	Howard Johnson	.15
752	Mike Krukow	.07
753	Dan Ford	.05
754	*Pat Clements*	.10
755	Harold Baines	.15

756	Pirates Ldrs (Rick Rhoden)	.07
757	Darrell Porter	.07
758	Dave Anderson	.05
759	Moose Haas	.05
760	Andre Dawson	.20
761	Don Slaught	.05
762	Eric Show	.07
763	Terry Puhl	.05
764	Kevin Gross	.05
765	Don Baylor	.12
766	Rick Langford	.05
767	Jody Davis	.07
768	Vern Ruhle	.05
769	*Harold Reynolds* (FC)	.75
770	Vida Blue	.10
771	John McNamara	.05
772	Brian Downing	.07
773	Greg Pryor	.05
774	Terry Leach	.05
775	Al Oliver	.10
776	Gene Garber	.05
777	Wayne Krenchicki	.05
778	Jerry Hairston	.05
779	Rick Reuschel	.10
780	Robin Yount	.50
781	Joe Nolan	.05
782	Ken Landreaux	.05
783	Ricky Horton	.07
784	Alan Bannister	.05
785	Bob Stanley	.05
786	Twins Ldrs (Mickey Hatcher)	.07
787	Vance Law	.07
788	Marty Castillo	.05
789	Kurt Bevacqua	.05
790	Phil Niekro	.25
792	Charles Hudson	.05

1986 TOPPS TRADED

After an off year for the regular set in 1986, the Topps Traded set for 1986 delivered the types of big names that rookie-card fans love. Like Fleer and Donruss, Topps provided cards of top rookie stars. Included in the set are Jose Canseco, Will Clark, Bo Jackson, Kevin Mitchell, Wally Joyner, Andres Galarraga, and Pete Incaviglia. The main omission was Ruben Sierra of the Texas Rangers. Today's collectors buying the set should find it still in the specially designed box Topps created. And as usual, the complete sets of 132 cards were distributed only through hobby dealers. For easy handling, the set is numbered in alphabetical order.

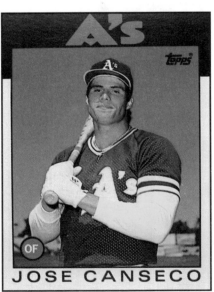

20 Jose Canseco

		MINT
Complete set		**$35.00**
Commons		**.08**

1	Andy Allanson (FC)	$ .20
3	Joaquin Andujar	.10
4	Paul Assenmacher (FC)	.20
5	Scott Bailes (FC)	.20
6	Don Baylor	.15
7	Steve Bedrosian	.15

10	Mike Bielecki (FC)	.35
11	Barry Bonds (FC)	1.00
12	Bobby Bonilla (FC)	.80
16	Rick Burleson	.10
19	John Cangelosi (FC)	.20
20	Jose Canseco (FC)	15.00
23	John Cerutti (FC)	.25
24	Will Clark (FC)	12.00
26	Darnell Coles	.15
27	Dave Collins	.10
30	Joel Davis (FC)	.10

31	Rob Deer	.15
33	Mike Easler	.10
34	Mark Eichhorn (FC)	.20
36	Scott Fletcher	.15
37	Terry Forster	.10
40	Andres Galarraga (FC)	1.75
41	Ken Griffey	.10
43	Jose Guzman (FC)	.35
45	Billy Hatcher	.20
48	Pete Incaviglia (FC)	.50
50	Bo Jackson (FC)	10.00
51	Wally Joyner (FC)	3.00
52	Charlie Kerfeld (FC)	.15
53	Eric King (FC)	.20
54	Bob Kipper (FC)	.10
55	Wayne Krenchicki	.08
56	John Kruk (FC)	.40
57	Mike LaCoss	.08
59	Mike Laga	.08
60	Hal Lanier	.08
61	Dave LaPoint	.12
62	Rudy Law	.08
63	Rick Leach	.08
64	Tim Leary	.08
67	Steve Lyons	.10
68	Mickey Mahler	.08
69	Candy Maldonado	.15
70	Roger Mason (FC)	.10
71	Bob McClure	.08
72	Andy McGaffigan	.08
73	Gene Michael	.08
74	Kevin Mitchell (FC)	7.00
76	Jerry Mumphrey	.08

77	Phil Niekro	.40
78	Randy Niemann	.08
79	Juan Nieves (FC)	.25
80	Otis Nixon (FC)	.10
81	Bob Ojeda	.12
82	Jose Oquendo	.12
83	Tom Paciorek	.10
85	Frank Pastore	.08
86	Lou Piniella	.15
87	Dan Plesac (FC)	.40
88	Darrell Porter	.10
89	Rey Quinones (FC)	.15
90	Gary Redus	.08
91	Bip Roberts	.10
92	Billy Jo Robidoux (FC)	.15
93	Jeff Robinson	.10
94	Gary Roenicke	.08
95	Ed Romero	.08
98	Billy Sample	.08
99	Dave Schmidt	.08
100	Ken Schrom	.08
101	Tom Seaver	.65
102	Ted Simmons	.20
104	Kurt Stillwell (FC)	.30
105	Franklin Stubbs	.12
106	Dale Sveum (FC)	.25
107	Chuck Tanner	.08
108	Danny Tartabull (FC)	1.00
110	Bob Tewksbury (FC)	.15
111	Andres Thomas (FC)	.30
112	Milt Thompson	.12
113	Robby Thompson (FC)	.40
117	Manny Trillo	.10

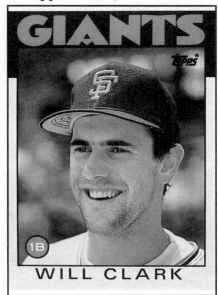

24 Will Clark

120	Bob Walk	.15
121	Gene Walter (FC)	.10
122	Claudell Washington	.15
123	Bill Wegman (FC)	.20
125	Mitch Williams (FC)	.65
126	Bobby Witt (FC)	.40
127	Todd Worrell (FC)	.60

1987 DONRUSS

While Topps and Fleer issued relatively conservative cards in 1987, Donruss broke loose with a wacky design. Look closely at the borders of the 1987 cards and you'll discover that each photo covers a wide gold band of tiny baseballs. But the black border surrounding the photos is problematic: As with the 1971 Topps set, scuffing occurs easily and fewer mint cards remain. Top cards in the 1987 set include specially marked Rated Rookie cards for Bo Jackson, Mark McGwire, Benito Santiago, Greg Swindell, and Devon White. Donruss showed a willingness to include other rookies throughout the set, providing lots of buried treasure for rookie-card fanatics.

35 Bo Jackson

		MINT
Complete set		**$85.00**
Commons		**.05**
1	Wally Joyner (DK)	$1.25
2	Roger Clemens (DK)	.70
3	Dale Murphy (DK)	.40
4	Darryl Strawberry (DK)	.40
5	Ozzie Smith (DK)	.12
6	Jose Canseco (DK)	2.00
7	Charlie Hough (DK)	.07
8	Brook Jacoby (DK)	.10
9	Fred Lynn (DK)	.12
10	Rick Rhoden (DK)	.10
11	Chris Brown (DK)	.10

12	Von Hayes (DK)	.10
13	Jack Morris (DK)	.20
14	Kevin McReynolds (DK) ("Donruss Diamond Kings" in white band on back)	1.25
15	George Brett (DK)	.40
16	Ted Higuera (DK)	.20
17	Hubie Brooks (DK)	.10
18	Mike Scott (DK)	.12
19	Kirby Puckett (DK)	.25
20	Dave Winfield (DK)	.25
21	Lloyd Moseby (DK)	.10
22	Eric Davis (DK) ("Donruss Diamond Kings" in white band on back)	3.00

22	Eric Davis (DK) ("Donruss Diamond Kings" in yellow band on back)	1.00

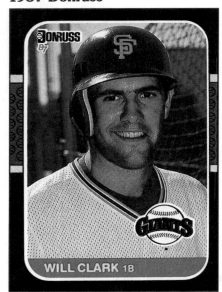

66 Will Clark

61	Glenn Davis	.30
62	Glenn Wilson	.07
63	Tom Browning	.10
64	Tony Gwynn	.35
65	R.J. Reynolds	.07
66	*Will Clark*	12.00
67	Ozzie Virgil	.05
68	Rick Sutcliffe	.12
69	Gary Carter	.30
70	Mike Moore	.10
71	Bert Blyleven	.12
72	Tony Fernandez	.12
73	Kent Hrbek	.15
74	Lloyd Moseby	.10
75	Alvin Davis	.12
76	Keith Hernandez	.25
77	Ryne Sandberg	.35
78	Dale Murphy	.40
79	Sid Bream	.07
80	Chris Brown	.07
81	Steve Garvey	.25
82	Mario Soto	.07
83	Shane Rawley	.05
84	Willie McGee	.12
85	Jose Cruz	.10
86	Brian Downing	.07
87	Ozzie Guillen	.10
88	Hubie Brooks	.10
89	Cal Ripken	.35
90	Juan Nieves	.07
91	Lance Parrish	.20
92	Jim Rice	.30
93	Ron Guidry	.15
94	Fernando Valenzuela	.25
95	*Andy Allanson*	.15
96	Willie Wilson	.10
97	Jose Canseco	10.00
98	Jeff Reardon	.10
99	*Bobby Witt*	.35
100	Checklist 28-133	.05
101	Jose Guzman	.07
102	Steve Balboni	.07
103	Tony Phillips	.05
104	Brook Jacoby	.10

23	Jim Presley (DK)	.12
24	Keith Moreland (DK)	.07
25	Greg Walker (DK) ("Donruss Diamond Kings" in white band on back)	1.25
26	Steve Sax (DK)	.12
28	*B.J. Surhoff* (RR) (FC)	.50
29	*Randy Myers* (RR) (FC)	.85
30	*Ken Gerhart* (RR) (FC)	.15
31	Benito Santiago (RR) (FC)	2.00
32	*Greg Swindell* (RR) (FC)	1.25
33	*Mike Birkbeck* (RR) (FC)	.20
34	*Terry Steinbach* (RR) (FC)	1.00
35	*Bo Jackson* (RR)	12.00
36	*Greg Maddux* (RR) (FC)	1.25
37	*Jim Lindeman* (RR) (FC)	.12
38	*Devon White* (RR) (FC)	1.00
39	*Eric Bell* (RR) (FC)	.12
40	*Will Fraser* (RR) (FC)	.20
41	Jerry Browne (RR) (FC)	.35
42	Chris James (RR) (FC)	.75
43	*Rafael Palmeiro* (RR) (FC)	1.50
44	*Pat Dodson* (RR) (FC)	.12
45	*Duane Ward* (RR) (FC)	.20
46	*Mark McGwire* (RR) (FC)	9.00
47	*Bruce Fields* (RR) (FC) (photo is Darnell Coles)	.10
48	Eddie Murray	.35
49	Ted Higuera	.20
50	Kirk Gibson	.25
51	Oil Can Boyd	.07
52	Don Mattingly	2.50
53	Pedro Guerrero	.25
54	George Brett	.40
55	Jose Rijo	.10
56	Tim Raines	.30
57	*Ed Correa*	.15
58	Mike Witt	.10
59	Greg Walker	.10
60	Ozzie Smith	.15

97 Jose Canseco

585 Mike Greenwell

105	Dave Winfield	.30
106	Orel Hershiser	.40
107	Lou Whitaker	.25
108	Fred Lynn	.15
109	Bill Wegman	.07
110	Donnie Moore	.05
111	Jack Clark	.15
112	Bob Knepper	.05
113	Von Hayes	.10
114	Leon "Bip" Roberts	.05
115	Tony Pena	.08
117	Paul Molitor	.15
118	Darryl Strawberry	.75
119	Shawon Dunston	.10
120	Jim Presley	.07
121	Jesse Barfield	.20
122	Gary Gaetti	.15
123	*Kurt Stillwell*	.65
125	Mike Boddicker	.07
126	Robin Yount	.35
127	Alan Trammell	.25
128	Dave Righetti	.15
129	*Dwight Evans	.12
130	Mike Scioscia	.07
131	Julio Franco	.10
132	Bret Saberhagen	.15
133	Mike Davis	.07
135	*Wally Joyner*	2.00
138	Nolan Ryan	.75
139	Mike Schmidt	.50
140	Tommy Herr	.10
141	Garry Templeton	.07
142	Kal Daniels	1.00
144	Johnny Ray	.10
145	*Rob Thompson*	.30
147	Danny Tartabull	.25
148	Ernie Whitt	.07
149	Kirby Puckett	1.25
152	Frank Tanana	.07
153	Rich Gedman	.07
154	Willie Randolph	.10
155	Bill Madlock (name in brown band)	.12

155	Bill Madlock (name in red band)	.07
156	Joe Carter (name in brown band)	.15
156	Joe Carter (name in red band)	.07
157	Danny Jackson	.15
158	Carney Lansford	.10
161	Oddibe McDowell	.10
162	*John Cangelosi*	.12
163	Mike Scott	.15
164	Eric Show	.07
165	Juan Samuel	.12
166	Nick Esasky	.15
167	Zane Smith	.07
169	Keith Moreland	.07
170	John Tudor	.10
172	Jim Gantner	.07
173	Jack Morris	.20
174	Bruce Hurst	.10
175	Dennis Rasmussen	.10
176	Mike Marshall	.12
177	Dan Quisenberry	.07
178	Eric Plunk (FC)	.10
179	Tim Wallach	.12
180	Steve Buechele	.07
181	Don Sutton	.20
182	Dave Schmidt	.05
183	Terry Pendelton	.10
184	*Jim Deshaies*	.35
185	Steve Bedrosian	.12
186	Pete Rose	.75
187	Dave Dravecky	.07
188	Rick Reuschel	.10
192	Ron Darling	.15
194	Tom Brunansky	.12
195	Dave Stieb	.12
196	Frank Viola	.15
197	Tom Henke	.07
199	Dwight Gooden	1.00
205	Terry Kennedy	.07
208	*Greg Mathews*	.20
209	Charlie Kerfeld	.10
210	Reggie Jackson	.35

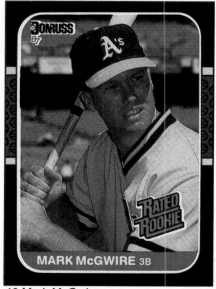

46 Mark McGwire

211	Floyd Bannister	.10
212	Vance Law	.07
213	Rich Bordi	.05
214	*Dan Plesac*	.35
215	Dave Collins	.07
216	Bob Stanley	.05
217	Joe Niekro	.10
218	Tom Niedenfuer	.07
219	Brett Butler	.07
220	Charlie Leibrandt	.07
224	*Pete Incaviglia*	.60
225	Lonnie Smith	.07
227	*Scott Bailes*	.20
228	Rickey Henderson	.35
230	Darnell Coles	.07
232	Tim Leary	.07
233	*Bob Boone	.07
234	Ricky Horton	.07
236	Kevin Gross	.07
237	Lance McCullers	.07
241	Roger McDowell	.12
242	Leon Durham	.07
244	Jimmy Key	.12
246	Bo Diaz	.07
247	Carlton Fisk	.20
248	Larry Sheets	.08
249	*Juan Castillo* (FC)	.10
250	*Eric King*	.20
251	*Doug Drabek*	.30
252	Wade Boggs	1.50
253	Mariano Duncan	.05
254	Pat Tabler	.07
255	Frank White	.10
256	Alfredo Griffin	.07
257	Floyd Youmans	.07
259	Pete O'Brien	.10
261	Dickie Thon	.07
263	Vince Coleman	.25
265	Eric Davis	1.25
266	*Andres Thomas*	.25
267	*Mike Diaz* (FC)	.15
268	Chili Davis	.07
269	Jody Davis	.05

346 Ruben Sierra

270	Phil Bradley	.12
271	George Bell	.25
272	Keith Atherton	.05
273	Storm Davis	.10
274	Rob Deer (FC)	.20
275	Walt Terrell	.07
276	Roger Clemens	2.00
277	Mike Easler	.07
278	Steve Sax	.15
279	Andre Thornton	.07
280	Jim Sundberg	.07
286	Bill Doran	.10
289	John Franco	.10
290	*Paul Assenmacher*	.15
292	Lee Smith	.10
294	Rick Dempsey	.07
298	Mike Pagliarulo	.10
299	Franklin Stubbs	.07
302	*Bill Mooneyham*	.10
303	Andres Galarraga	.25
304	Scott Fletcher	.07
305	Jack Howell	.07
306	*Russ Morman* (FC)	.10
307	Todd Worrell	.20
308	Dave Smith	.07
315	*Jamie Moyer* (FC)	.20
316	Wally Backman	.07
317	Ken Phelps	.07
321	*Mark Eichhorn*	.15
322	*Lee Guetterman*	.15
323	Sid Fernandez	.12
327	Candy Maldonado	.07
328	*John Kruk*	.25
330	Milt Thompson	.07
331	*Mike LaValliere*	.25
334	*Ron Karkovice* (FC)	.10
335	Mitch Webster	.07
337	*Glenn Braggs* (FC)	.30
339	Don Baylor	.12
340	Brian Fisher	.07
341	*Reggie Williams*	.10
344	Curt Young	.07
346	*Ruben Sierra*	7.00
347	*Mitch Williams*	.65

599 Kevin Mitchell

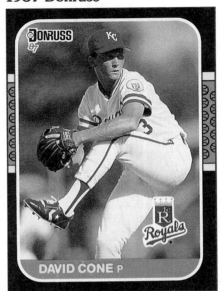

502 David Cone

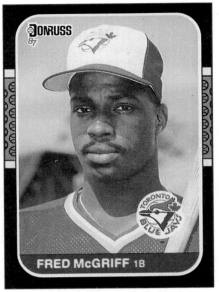

621 Fred McGriff

451	Kevin McReynolds	.15
452	*Rob Murphy* (FC)	.20
453	Kent Tekulve	.07
454	Curt Ford (FC)	.07
455	Davey Lopes	.07
456	Bobby Grich	.10
457	Jose DeLeon	.10
458	Andre Dawson	.20
459	Mike Flanagan	.07
460	*Joey Meyer* (FC)	.20
461	*Chuck Cary* (FC)	.10
462	Bill Buckner	.10
464	*Jeff Hamilton* (FC)	.30
465	Phil Niekro	.20
466	Mark Gubicza	.12
468	*Bob Sebra* (FC)	.10
469	Larry Parrish	.10
470	Charlie Hough	.07
471	Hal McRae	.10
472	*Dave Leiper* (FC)	.10
473	Mel Hall	.07
474	Dan Pasqua	.10
475	Bob Welch	.10
477	Jim Traber	.07
478	*Chris Bosio* (FC)	.30
479	Mark McLemore	.07
481	Billy Hatcher	.07
483	Rich Gossage	.15
487	Mookie Wilson	.10
488	*Dave Martinez* (FC)	.25
489	Harold Reynolds	.10
492	*Barry Larkin* (FC)	3.25
495	*Jim Adduci* (FC)	.07
498	Tony Armas	.07
502	*David Cone* (FC)	3.50
503	Jay Howell	.07
505	*Ray Chadwick* (FC)	.10
506	*Mike Loynd* (FC)	.15
511	Gene Walter	.07
512	*Terry McGriff* (FC)	.12
513	Ken Griffey	.10
515	*Terry Mulholland* (FC)	.12
518	Manny Lee (FC)	.07

351	Ron Kittle	.10
353	Chet Lemon	.07
356	Doug DeCinces	.07
361	*Barry Bonds*	2.00
362	Vida Blue	.10
363	Cecil Cooper	.10
364	Bob Ojeda	.07
365	Dennis Eckersley	.15
367	Willie Upshaw	.07
368	*Allan Anderson* (FC)	.25
369	Bill Gullickson	.07
370	*Bobby Thigpen* (FC)	.45
373	Dan Petry	.07
375	Tom Seaver	.40
379	Dwayne Murphy	.05
381	Kirk McCaskill	.07
383	Rich Dotson	.07
388	Dave Parker	.20
389	Bob Horner	.12
391	Jeff Leonard	.07
397	*Bryan Clutterbuck* (FC)	.10
398	Darrell Evans	.12
401	*Phil Lombardi* (FC)	.10
407	*Chuck Finley* (FC)	.15
408	Toby Harrah	.07
410	Kevin Bass	.10
413	*Tracy Jones*	.25
417	Andy Van Slyke	.12
419	Ben Oglivie	.07
422	*Bob Tewksbury*	.10
424	*Mike Kingery* (FC)	.15
425	Dave Kingman	.15
426	*Al Newman*	.07
427	Gary Ward	.07
429	Harold Baines	.15
432	Don Carman	.07
435	Rick Rhoden	.10
436	Jose Uribe	.07
439	Jesse Orosco	.10
442	*John Cerutti*	.20
444	Kelly Gruber	.07
446	*Ed Hearn*	.10
450	*Mike Aldrete*	.25

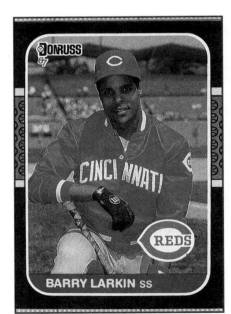

492 Barry Larkin

520	Scott McGregor	.07
522	Willie Hernandez	.07
523	Marty Barrett	.10
525	*Jose Gonzalez* (FC)	.15
526	Cory Snyder	.70
529	*Wilfredo Tejeda* (FC)	.10
531	*Dale Mohorcic* (FC)	.20
535	*Mike Maddux* (FC)	.20
537	Ted Simmons	.12
538	*Rafael Belliard* (FC)	.12
540	Bob Forsch	.07
541	John Stefero	.05
542	*Dale Sveum*	.20
543	Mark Thurmond	.05
544	*Jeff Sellers*	.20
545	Joel Skinner	.05
546	Alex Trevino	.05
547	*Randy Kutcher* (FC)	.10
548	Joaquin Andujar	.07
549	*Casey Candaele* (FC)	.15
550	Jeff Russell	.10
551	John Candelaria	.10
552	Joe Cowley	.05
553	Danny Cox	.07
554	Denny Walling	.05
555	*Bruce Ruffin* (FC)	.20
556	Buddy Bell	.10
557	*Jimmy Jones* (FC)	.20
558	*Bobby Bonilla*	1.75
559	Jeff Robinson	.07
560	Ed Olwine	.05
561	*Glenallen Hill* (FC)	1.75
562	Lee Mazzilli	.07
563	Mike Brown	.05
564	George Frazier	.05
565	*Mike Sharperson* (FC)	.10
566	*Mark Portugal*	.10
567	Rick Leach	.10
568	Mark Langston	.12
569	Rafael Santana	.05
570	Manny Trillo	.07
571	Cliff Speck	.05
572	Bob Kipper	.05

573	*Kelly Downs* (FC)	.30
574	*Randy Asadoor* (FC)	.10
575	*Dave Magadan* (FC)	.35
576	*Marvin Freeman* (FC)	.12
577	Jeff Lahti	.05
578	Jeff Calhoun	.05
579	*Gus Polidor* (FC)	.07
580	Gene Nelson	.05
581	Tim Teufel	.05
582	Odell Jones	.05
583	Mark Ryal	.05
584	Randy O'Neal	.05
585	*Mike Greenwell* (FC)	11.00
586	Ray Knight	.07
587	*Ralph Bryant* (FC)	.12
588	Carmen Castillo	.05
589	Ed Wojna	.05
590	Stan Javier	.05
591	*Jeff Musselman* (FC)	.20
592	*Mike Stanley* (FC)	.20
593	Darrell Porter	.07
594	*Drew Hall* (FC)	.20
595	*Rob Nelson* (FC)	.10
596	Bryan Oelkers	.05
597	*Scott Nielsen* (FC)	.10
598	*Brian Holton* (FC)	.20
599	*Kevin Mitchell*	6.00
600	Checklist 558-660	.05
601	Jackie Gutierrez	.05
602	*Barry Jones* (FC)	.10
603	Jerry Narron	.05
604	Steve Lake	.05
605	Jim Pankovits	.05
606	Ed Romero	.05
607	Dave LaPoint	.05
608	Don Robinson	.07
609	Mike Krukow	.07
610	*Dave Valle* (FC)	.12
611	*Len Dykstra	.25
612	Roberto Clemente puzzle card	.05
613	*Mike Trujillo* (FC)	.05
614	Damaso Garcia	.05
615	Neal Heaton	.05
616	Juan Berenguer	.05
617	Steve Carlton	.25
618	Gary Lucas	.05
619	Geno Petralli	.05
620	Rick Aguilera	.05
621	Fred McGriff	3.00
622	Dave Henderson	.10
623	*Dave Clark* (FC)	.20
624	Angel Salazar	.05
625	Randy Hunt	.05
626	John Gibbons	.05
627	*Kevin Brown* (FC)	.07
628	Bill Dawley	.05
629	Aurelio Lopez	.05
630	Charlie Hudson	.05
632	*Ray Hayward* (FC)	.12
633	Spike Owen	.05
634	Glenn Hubbard	.05
635	*Kevin Elster* (FC)	.40
636	Mike LaCoss	.05
638	*Rey Quinones* (Quinonez)	.15
639	Jim Clancy	.05
640	Larry Andersen	.05
641	Calvin Schiraldi	.07
642	*Stan Jefferson* (FC)	.20
643	Marc Sullivan	.05
644	Mark Grant	.05
645	Cliff Johnson	.05
646	Howard Johnson	.10
647	Dave Sax	.05
648	Dave Stewart	.12
649	Danny Heep	.05
650	Joe Johnson	.05
651	*Bob Brower* (FC)	.20
652	Rob Woodward	.07
653	John Mizerock	.05
654	*Tim Pyznarski* (FC)	.10
655	*Luis Aquino* (FC)	.10
656	*Mickey Brantley* (FC)	.10
657	Doyle Alexander	.07
658	Sammy Stewart	.05
659	Jim Acker	.05
660	Pete Ladd	.05

1987 DONRUSS ROOKIES

For the second year in a row, Donruss issued "The Rookies," a 56-card set highlighting players overlooked in the earlier 660-card issue. Donruss hedged its bets by including Bo Jackson and Mark McGwire in this edition, issued in the fall, even though McGwire had been in the larger 1987 set, and Jackson was a member of The Rookies in 1986. Other appealing names in the set include Mike Greenwell, Ellis Burks, Todd Benzinger, and Kevin Seitzer. The 55 player cards and one checklist card came in a specially designed box. Although the card numbers hold no special prefixes, Donruss altered these cards slightly in comparison to the regular set by changing the border color from black to green and by attaching "The Rookies" logo to each card front.

14 Bo Jackson

		MINT
Complete set		**$20.00**
Commons		**.10**

1	Mark McGwire	$3.25
4	Mike Greenwell	3.75
5	Ellis Burks (FC)	2.50
6	DeWayne Buice (FC)	.20
8	Devon White	.50
10	Lester Lancaster (FC)	.15
11	Ken Williams (FC)	.20
12	Matt Nokes (FC)	.70
13	Jeff Robinson (FC)	.40
14	Bo Jackson	4.00
15	Kevin Seitzer (FC)	1.50
16	Billy Ripken (FC)	.25
17	B.J. Surhoff	.20
21	Les Straker (FC)	.20
22	Mark Davidson (FC)	.15
23	Gene Larkin (FC)	.25
25	Luis Polonia (FC)	.35
26	Terry Steinbach	.25
28	Mike Stanley	.20
30	Todd Benzinger (FC)	.50
31	Fred McGriff	2.25
32	*Mike Henneman (FC)	.30
34	Dave Magadan	.25
35	David Cone	1.25
36	Mike Jackson (FC)	.20
37	John Mitchell (FC)	.20
38	Mike Dunne (FC)	.25
39	John Smiley (FC)	.40
40	Joe Magrane (FC)	1.75
42	Shane Mack (FC)	.25
44	Benito Santiago	.60
45	Matt Williams (FC)	3.00
46	Dave Meads (FC)	.20
47	Rafael Palmeiro	.85
48	Bill Long (FC)	.20
49	Bob Brower	.15
51	Paul Noce (FC)	.15
52	Greg Maddux	.65
55	Chuck Jackson (FC)	.20

1987 FLEER

Fleer produced an attractive and innovative set of baseball cards in 1987. Each of the 660 cards in the annual set features a light blue border fading to white down the sides as it approaches a solid blue bottom. Photos extend into the top border, creating a novel three-dimensional look. The only obstruction on the card fronts are team logos in the lower corners (which seem senseless, considering that the same logos often appear on the player's cap or uniform). Fleer produced its last Pete Rose card, number 213, labeling him a "player-manager." The card of Will Clark, number 269, has turned out to be the most valuable rookie card in the bunch.

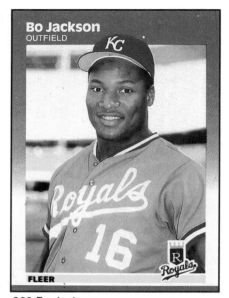

369 Bo Jackson

269 Will Clark

		MINT
Complete set		**$105.00**
Commons		**.06**

1	Rick Aguilera	$ .30
3	Wally Backman	.08
4	Gary Carter	.25
5	Ron Darling	.15
6	Len Dykstra	.20
7	*Kevin Elster* (FC)	.50
8	Sid Fernandez	.12
9	Dwight Gooden	.90
10	*Ed Hearn* (FC)	.10
11	Danny Heep	.06
12	Keith Hernandez	.25
13	Howard Johnson	.65
14	Ray Knight	.08
15	Lee Mazzilli	.08
16	Roger McDowell	.12
17	*Kevin Mitchell*	9.00
19	Bob Ojeda	.08
20	Jesse Orosco	.08
21	Rafael Santana	.06
22	Doug Sisk	.06
23	Darryl Strawberry	1.00
24	Tim Teufel	.06
25	Mookie Wilson	.10
26	Tony Armas	.08
27	Marty Barrett	.10
28	Don Baylor	.12
29	Wade Boggs	2.00
30	Oil Can Boyd	.08
31	Bill Buckner	.10
32	Roger Clemens	1.50
33	Steve Crawford	.06
34	*Dwight Evans	.12
35	Rich Gedman	.08
36	Dave Henderson	.10
37	Bruce Hurst	.10
38	Tim Lollar	.06
39	Al Nipper	.06
40	Spike Owen	.06
41	Jim Rice	.30
42	Ed Romero	.06
43	Joe Sambito	.06
44	Calvin Schiraldi	.08
45	Tom Seaver	.40
46	*Jeff Sellers* (FC)	.20
47	Bob Stanley	.06
48	Sammy Stewart	.06

49	Larry Andersen	.06
50	Alan Ashby	.06
51	Kevin Bass	.10
52	Jeff Calhoun	.06
53	Jose Cruz	.12
54	Danny Darwin	.06
55	Glenn Davis	.30
56	*Jim Deshaies*	.25
57	Bill Doran	.10
58	Phil Garner	.06
59	Billy Hatcher	.08
60	Charlie Kerfeld	.06
62	Dave Lopes	.08
65	Terry Puhl	.06
67	Nolan Ryan	1.00
68	Mike Scott	.15
69	Dave Smith	.08
70	Dickie Thon	.08
71	Tony Walker	.06
73	*Bob Boone	.08
75	John Candelaria	.10
76	Doug Corbett	.06
78	Brian Downing	.08
79	*Chuck Finley* (FC)	.15
80	Terry Forster	.08

81	Bobby Grich	.10
83	Jack Howell (FC)	.10
84	Reggie Jackson	.35
86	Wally Joyner	2.00
87	Gary Lucas	.06
88	Kirk McCaskill	.08
89	Donnie Moore	.06
90	Gary Pettis	.06
91	Vern Ruhle	.06
93	Don Sutton	.20
94	Rob Wilfong	.06
95	Mike Witt	.10
96	*Doug Drabek*	.35
97	Mike Easler	.08
99	Brian Fisher	.08
100	Ron Guidry	.15
101	Rickey Henderson	.50
102	Tommy John	.20
103	Ron Kittle	.10
104	Don Mattingly	3.00
106	Joe Niekro	.10
108	Dan Pasqua	.10
109	Willie Randolph	.10
111	Dave Righetti	.15
112	Gary Roenicke	.06
113	Rod Scurry	.06
114	Bob Shirley	.06
115	Joel Skinner	.06
116	Tim Stoddard	.06
117	*Bob Tewksbury*	.12
118	Wayne Tolleson	.06
120	Dave Winfield	.30
121	Steve Buechele	.08
122	*Ed Correa*	.15
123	Scott Fletcher	.08
124	Jose Guzman	.08
125	Toby Harrah	.08
126	Greg Harris	.06
127	Charlie Hough	.08
128	*Pete Incaviglia*	.60
129	Mike Mason	.06
130	Oddibe McDowell	.10
131	*Dale Mohorcic* (FC)	.20

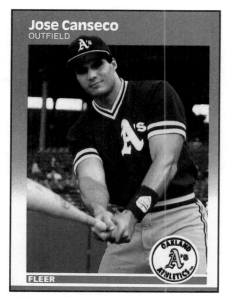

Jose Canseco
OUTFIELD

389 Jose Canseco

132	Pete O'Brien	.10
133	Tom Paciorek	.06
134	Larry Parrish	.08
135	Geno Petralli	.06
136	Darrell Porter	.08
137	Jeff Russell	.10
138	*Ruben Sierra*	12.00
139	Don Slaught	.06
140	Gary Ward	.08
142	*Mitch Williams*	.65
143	*Bobby Witt*	.35
144	Dave Bergman	.06
145	Tom Brookens	.06
146	Bill Campbell	.06
147	*Chuck Cary*	.10
148	Darnell Coles	.08
149	Dave Collins	.08
150	Darrell Evans	.12
151	Kirk Gibson	.25
152	John Grubb	.06
155	*Eric King*	.25
156	Chet Lemon	.08
157	Dwight Lowry	.06
158	Jack Morris	.20
159	Randy O'Neal	.06
160	Lance Parrish	.20
161	Dan Petry	.08
162	Pat Sheridan	.06
163	Jim Slaton	.06
164	Frank Tanana	.08
165	Walt Terrell	.08
167	Alan Trammell	.25
168	Lou Whitaker	.25
169	Luis Aguayo	.06
170	Steve Bedrosian	.12
171	Don Carman	.10
173	Greg Gross	.06
174	Kevin Gross	.08
175	Von Hayes	.15
177	Tom Hume	.06
178	Steve Jeltz	.06
179	*Mike Maddux* (FC)	.20
181	Gary Redus	.06

183	*Bruce Ruffin* (FC)	.20
184	John Russell	.06
185	Juan Samuel	.12
187	Mike Schmidt	.60
188	Rick Schu	.06
189	Jeff Stone	.06
190	Kent Tekulve	.08
191	Milt Thompson	.08
192	Glenn Wilson	.08
193	Buddy Bell	.10
194	Tom Browning	.10
195	Sal Butera	.06
196	Dave Concepcion	.12
197	Kal Daniels	.80
198	Eric Davis	1.50
199	John Denny	.06
200	Bo Diaz	.08
201	Nick Esasky	.15
202	John Franco	.12
204	*Barry Larkin* (FC)	4.00
205	Eddie Milner	.06
206	*Rob Murphy* (FC)	.20
207	Ron Oester	.06
208	Dave Parker	.20
209	Tony Perez	.15
210	Ted Power	.06
211	Joe Price	.06
213	Pete Rose	.60
214	Mario Soto	.08
215	*Kurt Stillwell*	.50
217	Chris Welsh	.06
218	*Carl Willis* (FC)	.10
219	Jesse Barfield	.15
220	George Bell	.25
221	Bill Caudill	.06
222	*John Cerutti*	.20
223	Jim Clancy	.08
224	*Mark Eichhorn*	.15
225	Tony Fernandez	.12
227	Kelly Gruber	.08
228	Tom Henke	.08
229	Garth Iorg	.06
230	Cliff Johnson	.06

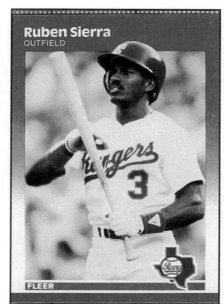

Ruben Sierra
OUTFIELD

138 Ruben Sierra

Kevin Mitchell
INFIELD—OF

17 Kevin Mitchell

231	Joe Johnson	.06
232	Jimmy Key	.12
233	Dennis Lamp	.06
234	Rick Leach	.06
235	Buck Martinez	.06
236	Lloyd Moseby	.10
238	Dave Stieb	.12
240	Ernie Whitt	.08
241	*Andy Allanson*	.15
242	*Scott Bailes*	.20
243	Chris Bando	.06
245	John Butcher	.06
246	Brett Butler	.08
249	Joe Carter	.20
251	Julio Franco	.10
252	Mel Hall	.08
253	Brook Jacoby	.10
254	Phil Niekro	.20
255	Otis Nixon	.06
258	Ken Schrom	.06
259	Don Schulze	.06
260	Cory Snyder	.70
261	Pat Tabler	.08
263	*Rich Yett* (FC)	.12
264	*Mike Aldrete*	.25
266	Vida Blue	.10
267	Bob Brenly	.06
268	Chris Brown	.08
269	*Will Clark*	36.00
270	Chili Davis	.08
271	Mark Davis	.12
272	*Kelly Downs* (FC)	.30
273	Scott Garrelts	.06
274	Dan Gladden	.06
275	Mike Krukow	.08
277	Mike LaCoss	.06
278	Jeff Leonard	.08
280	Roger Mason	.06
281	Bob Melvin (FC)	.08
282	Greg Minton	.06
283	Jeff Robinson	.08
284	Harry Spilman	.06
285	*Rob Thompson*	.35

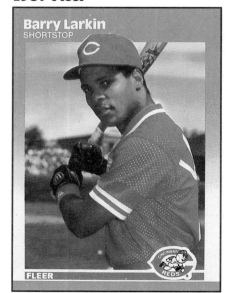

204 Barry Larkin

286	Jose Uribe	.08
287	Frank Williams	.06
289	Jack Clark	.15
290	Vince Coleman	.25
291	Tim Conroy	.06
292	Danny Cox	.08
293	Ken Dayley	.06
294	Curt Ford	.06
295	Bob Forsch	.08
296	Tom Herr	.10
297	Ricky Horton	.08
298	Clint Hurdle	.06
299	Jeff Lahti	.06
300	Steve Lake	.06
301	Tito Landrum	.06
302	*Mike LaValliere*	.25
303	*Greg Mathews* (FC)	.20
304	Willie McGee	.12
305	Jose Oquendo	.10
306	Terry Pendleton	.10
307	Pat Perry	.06
308	Ozzie Smith	.15
309	Ray Soff	.06
310	John Tudor	.10
311	Andy Van Slyke	.12
312	Todd Worrell	.20
314	Hubie Brooks	.10
315	Tim Burke	.12
316	Andre Dawson	.25
318	Tom Foley	.06
319	Andres Galarraga	.40
320	Joe Hesketh	.06
323	Vance Law	.08
325	Bob McClure	.06
327	*Al Newman*	.08
328	Tim Raines	.35
329	Jeff Reardon	.10
330	*Luis Rivera* (FC)	.10
331	*Bob Sebra* (FC)	.10
332	Bryn Smith	.08
333	Jay Tibbs	.06
334	Tim Wallach	.12
335	Mitch Webster	.08

336	Jim Wohlford	.06
337	Floyd Youmans	.06
338	*Chris Bosio* (FC)	.25
339	*Glenn Braggs* (FC)	.30
340	Rick Cerone	.06
341	Mark Clear	.06
342	*Bryan Clutterbuck* (FC)	.10
343	Cecil Cooper	.12
344	Rob Deer	.10
345	Jim Gantner	.08
346	Ted Higuera	.20
348	Tim Leary (FC)	.30
350	Paul Molitor	.15
351	Charlie Moore	.06
352	Juan Nieves	.10
353	Ben Oglivie	.08
354	*Dan Plesac*	.35
355	Ernest Riles	.06
357	Bill Schroeder	.06
358	*Dale Sveum*	.20
360	Bill Wegman (FC)	.10
361	Robin Yount	.25
362	Steve Balboni	.08
363	*Scott Bankhead*	.30
365	Bud Black	.08
366	George Brett	.40
367	Steve Farr	.08
368	Mark Gubicza	.12
369	*Bo Jackson*	20.00
370	Danny Jackson	.15
371	*Mike Kingery*	.15
372	Rudy Law	.06
375	Hal McRae	.10
376	Jorge Orta	.06
377	Jamie Quirk	.06
379	Bret Saberhagen	.20
380	Angel Salazar	.06
381	Lonnie Smith	.10
382	Jim Sundberg	.08
383	Frank White	.10
384	Willie Wilson	.12
386	Doug Bair	.06
387	Dusty Baker	.08

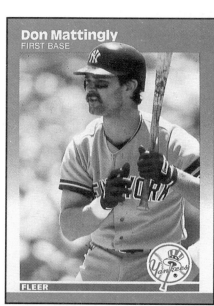

104 Don Mattingly

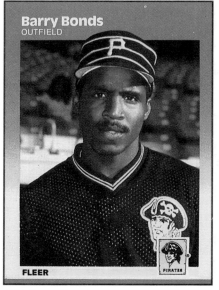

604 Barry Bonds

388	Bruce Bochte	.06
389	Jose Canseco	13.00
391	Mike Davis	.08
392	Alfredo Griffin	.08
393	Moose Haas	.06
394	Donnie Hill	.06
395	Jay Howell	.10
396	Dave Kingman	.15
397	Carney Lansford	.12
398	*David Leiper* (FC)	.12
399	*Bill Mooneyham*	.10
400	Dwayne Murphy	.08
402	Tony Phillips	.10
403	Eric Plunk	.08
404	Jose Rijo	.10
405	*Terry Steinbach* (FC)	.90
406	Dave Stewart	.12
407	Mickey Tettleton	.10
409	Jerry Willard	.06
410	Curt Young	.08
411	Bruce Bochy	.06
413	Tim Flannery	.06
414	Steve Garvey	.25
415	Goose Gossage	.15
416	Tony Gwynn	.35
418	LaMarr Hoyt	.06
420	*John Kruk*	.25
421	Dave LaPoint	.08
422	Craig Lefferts	.06
425	Kevin McReynolds	.15
426	Graig Nettles	.12
427	Bip Roberts	.06
429	Benito Santiago	.85
430	Eric Show	.08
433	Gene Walter	.06
434	Ed Whitson	.08
437	Greg Brock	.08
438	Enos Cabell	.06
440	Pedro Guerrero	.15
441	Orel Hershiser	.40
443	Ken Howell	.08
445	Bill Madlock	.12
446	Mike Marshall	.10

451	Jerry Reuss	.08
452	Bill Russell	.08
453	Steve Sax	.15
457	Fernando Valenzuela	.25
459	Bob Welch	.15
460	*Reggie Williams*	.08
461	Don Aase	.06
465	Rich Bordi	.06
466	Storm Davis	.15
468	Ken Dixon	.06
469	Jim Dwyer	.06
473	Lee Lacy	.06
474	Fred Lynn	.15
476	Eddie Murray	.35
478	Cal Ripken Jr.	.35
481	Nate Snell	.06
482	Jim Traber (FC)	.10
483	Mike Young	.06
484	Neil Allen	.06
485	Harold Baines	.15
487	Daryl Boston	.06
488	Ivan Calderon	.08
489	*John Cangelosi*	.12
490	Steve Carlton	.25
492	Julio Cruz	.06
493	Bill Dawley	.06
494	Jose DeLeon	.15
496	Carlton Fisk	.15
497	Ozzie Guillen	.10
500	Tim Hulett	.06
501	Bob James	.06
507	*Bobby Thigpen* (FC)	.40
508	Greg Walker	.10
509	Jim Acker	.06
511	*Paul Assenmacher*	.15
515	Gene Garber	.06
516	Ken Griffey	.10
518	Bob Horner	.12
520	Rick Mahler	.06
522	Dale Murphy	.40
524	Ed Olwine	.06
527	Billy Sample	.06
528	Ted Simmons	.12

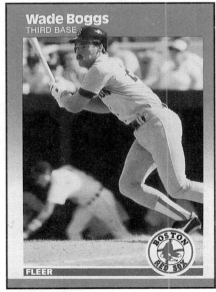

644 Major League Prospects

529	Zane Smith	.08
530	Bruce Sutter	.12
531	*Andres Thomas*	.25
532	Ozzie Virgil	.06
533	**Allan Anderson* (FC)	.25
535	Billy Beane	.06
536	Bert Blyleven	.12
537	Tom Brunansky	.10
538	Randy Bush	.06
540	Gary Gaetti	.15
541	Greg Gagne	.06
543	Neal Heaton	.06
544	Kent Hrbek	.15
546	Tim Laudner	.06
549	Kirby Puckett	1.75
550	Jeff Reed	.06
551	Mark Salas	.06
554	Frank Viola	.15
556	Ron Cey	.10
557	Jody Davis	.08
558	Ron Davis	.06
561	Shawon Dunston	.10
563	Dennis Eckersley	.12
566	Guy Hoffman	.08
567	Ed Lynch	.06
570	*Jamie Moyer* (FC)	.20
572	Ryne Sandberg	.25
574	Lee Smith	.10
575	Chris Speier	.06
576	Rick Sutcliffe	.12
578	Steve Trout	.06
579	Karl Best	.06
580	Phil Bradley	.12
583	Mike Brown	.06
584	Alvin Davis	.12
585	*Lee Guetterman* (FC)	.15
587	Bob Kearney	.06
588	Pete Ladd	.06
589	Mark Langston	.15
590	Mike Moore	.12
592	John Moses	.06
593	Ken Phelps	.06
595	*Rey Quinonez* (Quinones)	.15
596	Harold Reynolds	.15
598	Danny Tartabull	.25
602	*Rafael Belliard* (FC)	.12
604	*Barry Bonds*	2.50
605	*Bobby Bonilla*	2.50

609	*Mike Diaz* (FC)	.15
611	*Barry Jones* (FC)	.12
618	Johnny Ray	.10
619	Rick Reuschel	.10
621	Rick Rhoden	.10
625	Youthful Power (Jose Canseco, Pete Incaviglia)	1.00
628	Rookie All-Stars (Jose Canseco, Wally Joyner)	2.00
629	Magic Mets (Gary Carter, Sid Fernandez, Dwight Gooden, Keith Hernandez, Darryl Strawberry)	.60
633	AL Pitcher's Nightmare (Jose Canseco, Kirby Puckett, Jim Rice)	1.50
634	All-Star Battery (Gary Carter, Roger Clemens)	.25
636	Big Bats at First Sack (Glenn Davis, Eddie Murray)	.20
637	On Base (Wade Boggs, Keith Hernandez)	.35
638	Sluggers from Left Side (Don Mattingly, Darryl Strawberry)	.90
640	Dr. K and Super K (Roger Clemens, Dwight Gooden)	.50
644	Major League Prospects (*Dave Clark, Greg Swindell* (FC))	2.50
646	Major League Prospects (*Willie Fraser, Devon White* (FC))	2.00
647	Major League Prospects (*Jerry Browne, Mike Stanley* (FC))	.65
648	Major League Prospects (*Phil Lombardi, Dave Magadan* (FC))	.85
649	Major League Prospects (*Ralph Bryant, Jose Gonzalez* (FC))	.20
651	Major League Prospects (*Marvin Freeman* (FC), *Tracy Jones*)	.25
652	Major League Prospects (*Kevin Seitzer, John Stefero* (FC))	5.00

29 Wade Boggs

1987 FLEER UPDATE

Following a tradition that began in 1984, Fleer issued another Update edition in 1987. A checklist and 131 player cards are included, numbered U-1 through U-132, and arranged alphabetically (the letter "U" has been omitted from the following list). The cards retain the format of the regular 1987 issue and were available solely through hobby dealers in a specially designed collector's box. Fleer made up for past sins by finally including Mark McGwire in a set. Additional newcomers who make the set appealing are Mike Greenwell, Matt Williams, Kevin Mitchell, Kevin Seitzer, and Matt Nokes. A total of 44 cards are included in this set that are not in the Topps Traded set.

76 Mark McGwire

		MINT
Complete set		**$18.00**
Commons		**.06**

1	Scott Bankhead	$ .15
2	Eric Bell (FC)	.15
5	Mike Birkbeck (FC)	.20
6	Randy Bockus (FC)	.10
7	Rod Booker (FC)	.10
8	Thad Bosley	.10
9	Greg Brock	.10
10	Bob Brower (FC)	.15
11	Chris Brown	.10
12	Jerry Browne	.10
13	Ralph Bryant	.10
14	DeWayne Buice (FC)	.20
15	Ellis Burks (FC)	2.25
16	Casey Candaele (FC)	.15
17	Steve Carlton	.30
19	Chuck Crim (FC)	.15
20	Mark Davidson (FC)	.20
21	Mark Davis	.10
22	Storm Davis	.10
24	Andre Dawson	.40
26	Rick Dempsey	.10
27	Ken Dowell (FC)	.10
28	Dave Dravecky	.10
29	Mike Dunne (FC)	.35
30	Dennis Eckersley	.20
31	Cecil Fielder	1.00
32	Brian Fisher	.10
33	Willie Fraser	.10
34	Ken Gerhart (FC)	.15
35	Jim Gott	.06
36	Dan Gladden	.10
37	Mike Greenwell (FC)	4.00
39	Albert Hall	.06
41	Mickey Hatcher	.15
42	Mike Heath	.08
44	Mike Henneman (FC)	.30
45	Guy Hoffman	.15
47	Chuck Jackson (FC)	.20
48	Mike Jackson (FC)	.20
49	Reggie Jackson	.50
50	Chris James	.35
51	Dion James	.15
52	Stan Javier	.15
53	Stan Jefferson (FC)	.20
54	Jimmy Jones	.10
55	Tracy Jones	.20

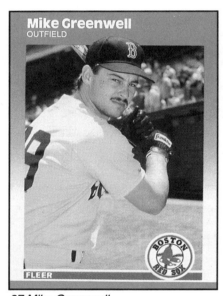

37 Mike Greenwell

56	Terry Kennedy	.15
57	Mike Kingery	.15
58	Ray Knight	.10
59	Gene Larkin (FC)	.30
60	Mike LaValliere	.10
61	Jack Lazorko	.15
62	Terry Leach	.08
63	Rick Leach	.10
65	Jim Lindeman (FC)	.10
66	Bill Long (FC)	.15
67	Mike Loynd (FC)	.15
68	Greg Maddux (FC)	.75
69	Bill Madlock	.20
70	Dave Magadan	.25
71	Joe Magrane (FC)	1.00
72	Fred Manrique (FC)	.15
73	Mike Mason	.06
74	Lloyd McClendon (FC)	.15
75	Fred McGriff (FC)	2.75
76	Mark McGwire (FC)	3.75
78	Kevin McReynolds	.30
79	Dave Meads (FC)	.15
80	Greg Minton	.06
81	John Mitchell (FC)	.10
82	Kevin Mitchell	2.00
83	John Morris	.06

84	Jeff Musselman (FC)	.25
85	Randy Myers (FC)	.65
86	Gene Nelson	.06
87	Joe Niekro	.10
88	Tom Nieto	.06
90	Matt Nokes (FC)	.75
93	Jose Nunez (FC)	.25
94	Paul O'Neill	.10
95	Jim Paciorek	.15
96	Lance Parrish	.20
97	Bill Pecota (FC)	.15
98	Tony Pena	.15
99	Luis Polonia (FC)	.25
100	Randy Ready	.15
101	Jeff Reardon	.15
102	Gary Redus	.08
103	Rick Rhoden	.10
104	Wally Ritchie (FC)	.15
105	Jeff Robinson (FC)	.35
106	Mark Salas	.06
108	Kevin Seitzer	1.50
110	John Smiley (FC)	.35
112	Chris Speier	.10
115	B.J. Surhoff (FC)	.35
116	Greg Swindell	.50
117	Danny Tartabull	.35
118	Dorn Taylor (FC)	.10
119	Lee Tunnell	.06
121	Andy Van Slyke	.15
122	Gary Ward	.06
123	Devon White	.35
125	Bill Wilkinson (FC)	.15
126	Jim Winn	.06
127	Frank Williams	.06
128	Ken Williams (FC)	.20
129	Matt Williams (FC)	3.00
130	Herm Winningham	.06
131	Matt Young	.06

1987 TOPPS

Topps provided collectors with a blast from the past in its 1987 set. Cards use a simulated wood-grain finish for a border, much like the 1962 Topps or 1955 Bowman sets. Aside from the use of the team logo, a generous photo space is largely unobstructed. For the first time since 1972, even player positions were omitted from the card fronts. Although it first appeared in the U.S. Olympic baseball team subset in 1985, Mark McGwire's 1987 Topps card became the hottest "rookie" in this set. Mike Greenwell, Ruben Sierra, Wally Joyner, and Barry Bonds rounded out the popular first-timers spotlighted in 1987.

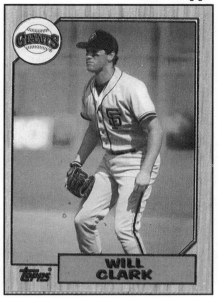

420 Will Clark

		MINT
Complete set		**$45.00**
Commons		**.05**

1	Record Breaker (Roger Clemens)	$ .35
2	Record Breaker (Jim Deshaies)	.07
3	Record Breaker (Dwight Evans)	.07
4	Record Breaker (Dave Lopes)	.07
5	Record Breaker (Dave Righetti)	.07
6	Record Breaker (Ruben Sierra)	.25
7	Record Breaker (Todd Worrell)	.07
8	Terry Pendleton	.07
9	Jay Tibbs	.05
10	Cecil Cooper	.10
11	Indian Ldrs (Jack Aker, Chris Bando, Phil Niekro)	.07
12	*Jeff Sellers* (FC)	.15
13	Nick Esasky	.10
14	Dave Stewart	.20
15	Claudell Washington	.07
16	Pat Clements	.05
17	Pete O'Brien	.10
18	Dick Howser	.05
20	Gary Carter	.20
21	Mark Davis	.10
22	Doug DeCinces	.07
23	Lee Smith	.10
24	Tony Walker	.05
25	Bert Blyleven	.12
26	Greg Brock	.07
27	Joe Cowley	.05
28	Rick Dempsey	.07
29	Jimmy Key	.10
30	Tim Raines	.25
31	Braves Ldrs (Glenn Hubbard, Rafael Ramirez)	.07
32	Tim Leary	.07
33	Andy Van Slyke	.12
34	Jose Rijo	.07
35	Sid Bream	.07
36	*Eric King*	.25
37	Marvell Wynne	.05
38	Dennis Leonard	.07
39	Marty Barrett	.07

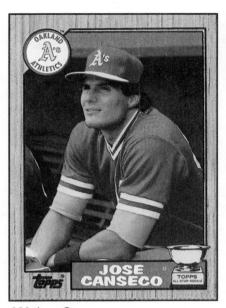

620 Jose Canseco

40	Dave Righetti	.12
41	Bo Diaz	.07
42	Gary Redus	.05
43	Gene Michael	.05
44	Greg Harris	.05
45	Jim Presley	.07
46	Danny Gladden	.05
47	Dennis Powell	.05
48	Wally Backman	.07
49	Terry Harper	.05
50	Dave Smith	.07
51	Mel Hall	.07
52	Keith Atherton	.05
53	Ruppert Jones	.05
54	Bill Dawley	.05
55	Tim Wallach	.10
56	Brewers Ldrs (Jamie Cocanower, Paul Molitor, Charlie Moore, Herm Starrette)	.07
57	*Scott Nielsen* (FC)	.10
58	Thad Bosley	.05
59	Ken Dayley	.05
60	Tony Pena	.07
61	*Bobby Thigpen* (FC)	.45
62	Bobby Meacham	.05

63	Fred Toliver (FC)	.07
64	Harry Spilman	.05
65	Tom Browning	.10
66	Marc Sullivan	.05
67	Bill Swift	.05
68	Tony LaRussa	.07
69	Lonnie Smith	.07
70	Charlie Hough	.07
71	*Mike Aldrete* (FC)	.20
72	Walt Terrell	.07
73	Dave Anderson	.05
74	Dan Pasqua	.10
75	Ron Darling	.12
76	Rafael Ramirez	.05
77	Bryan Oelkers	.05
78	Tom Foley	.05
79	Juan Nieves	.10
80	*Wally Joyner*	2.00
81	Padres Ldrs (Andy Hawkins, Terry Kennedy)	.07
82	*Rob Murphy* (FC)	.15
83	Mike Davis	.07
84	Steve Lake	.05
85	Kevin Bass	.10
86	Nate Snell	.05
87	Mark Salas	.05
88	Ed Wojna	.05
89	Ozzie Guillen	.10
90	Dave Stieb	.12
91	Harold Reynolds	.10
92	Urbano Lugo	.10
93	Jim Leyland	.07
94	Calvin Schiraldi	.07
95	Oddibe McDowell	.07
96	Frank Williams	.05
97	Glenn Wilson	.07
98	Bill Scherrer	.05
99	Darryl Motley	.05
100	Steve Garvey	.20
101	*Carl Willis* (FC)	.10
102	Paul Zuvella	.05
103	Rick Aguilera	.05
104	Billy Sample	.05

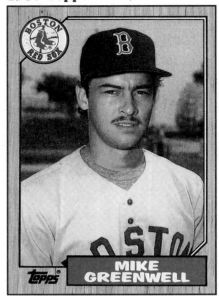

259 Mike Greenwell

148	Dave Collins	.07
149	Ray Searage	.05
150	Wade Boggs	1.25
151	Mike LaCoss	.05
152	Toby Harrah	.05
153	*Duane Ward* (FC)	.12
154	Tom O'Malley	.05
155	Eddie Whitson	.07
156	Mariners Ldrs (Bob Kearney, Phil Regan, Matt Young)	.07
158	Tim Teufel	.05
159	Ed Olwine	.05
160	Julio Franco	.10
161	Steve Ontiveros	.05
162	*Mike LaValliere*	.25
163	Kevin Gross	.05
164	Sammy Khalifa	.05
165	Jeff Reardon	.10
166	*Bob Boone	.07
167	*Jim Deshaies*	.25
168	Lou Piniella	.07
169	Ron Washington	.05
170	Future Stars (Bo Jackson)	4.00
171	*Chuck Cary* (FC)	.10
172	Ron Oester	.05
173	Alex Trevino	.05
174	Henry Cotto	.07
175	Bob Stanley	.05
176	Steve Buechele	.05
177	Keith Moreland	.07
178	Cecil Fielder	.90
180	Chris Brown	.05
181	Cardinals Ldrs (Mike LaValliere, Ozzie Smith, Ray Soff)	.07
182	Lee Lacy	.05
183	Andy Hawkins	.07
184	*Bobby Bonilla*	1.50
185	Roger McDowell	.10
186	Bruce Benedict	.05
187	Mark Huismann	.05
188	Tony Phillips	.07

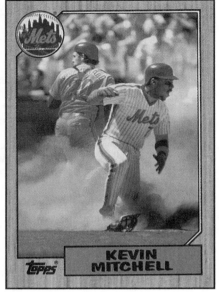

653 Kevin Mitchell

105	Floyd Youmans	.05
106	Blue Jays Ldrs (George Bell, Willie Upshaw)	.07
107	John Butcher	.05
108	Jim Gantner (photo reversed)	.07
109	R.J. Reynolds	.05
110	John Tudor	.10
111	Alfredo Griffin	.07
112	Alan Ashby	.05
113	Neil Allen	.05
115	Donnie Moore	.05
116	Bill Russell	.05
117	Jim Beattie	.05
118	Bobby Valentine	.05
119	Ron Robinson	.05
120	Eddie Murray	.30
121	*Kevin Romine* (FC)	.12
122	Jim Clancy	.07
123	*John Kruk*	.30
124	Ray Fontenot	.05
125	Bob Brenly	.05
126	*Mike Loynd* (FC)	.15
127	Vance Law	.07
129	Rick Cerone	.05
130	Dwight Gooden	.80
131	Pirates Ldrs (Sid Bream, Tony Pena)	.07
132	*Paul Assenmacher*	.15
133	Jose Oquendo	.07
134	*Rich Yett* (FC)	.10
135	Mike Easler	.07
136	Ron Romanick	.05
137	Jerry Willard	.05
138	Roy Lee Jackson	.05
139	*Devon White* (FC)	1.25
140	Bret Saberhagen	.15
141	Herm Winningham	.05
142	Rick Sutcliffe	.10
143	Steve Boros	.05
144	Mike Scioscia	.05
146	*Tracy Jones* (FC)	.25
147	Randy Niemann	.05

170 Bo Jackson

189	Joe Hesketh	.05
190	Jim Sundberg	.07
191	Charles Hudson	.05
192	Cory Snyder (FC)	.70
193	Roger Craig	.07
194	Kirk McCaskill	.07
195	Mike Pagliarulo	.10
196	Randy O'Neal	.05
197	Mark Bailey	.05
198	Lee Mazzilli	.05
199	Mariano Duncan	.05
200	Pete Rose	.60
201	*John Cangelosi*	.12
203	*Mike Kingery* (FC)	.15
204	Sammy Stewart	.05
205	Graig Nettles	.10
206	Twins Ldrs (Tim Laudner, Frank Viola)	.07
207	George Frazier	.05
208	John Shelby	.07
209	Rick Schu	.05
210	Lloyd Moseby	.10
211	John Morris (FC)	.05
212	Mike Fitzgerald	.05
213	*Randy Myers* (FC)	.50
214	Omar Moreno	.05
215	Mark Langston	.15
216	Future Stars (*B.J. Surhoff* (FC))	.50
218	Sparky Anderson	.07
219	Cecilio Guante	.05
220	Joe Carter	.12
221	Vern Ruhle	.05
222	Denny Walling	.05
223	Charlie Leibrandt	.05
224	Wayne Tolleson	.05
225	Mike Smithson	.05
226	Max Venable	.05
227	*Jamie Moyer* (FC)	.20
229	*Mike Birkbeck* (FC)	.15
230	Don Baylor	.10
231	Giants Ldrs (Bob Brenly, Mike Krukow)	.07

No.	Card	Price
232	*Reggie Williams*	.10
233	*Russ Morman* (FC)	.10
234	Pat Sheridan	.05
235	Alvin Davis	.12
236	Tommy John	.15
238	Bill Krueger	.05
239	Juan Espino	.05
240	Steve Balboni	.07
241	Danny Heep	.05
242	Rick Mahler	.05
243	Whitey Herzog	.07
244	Dickie Noles	.05
245	Willie Upshaw	.05
246	Jim Dwyer	.05
247	Jeff Reed (FC)	.07
248	Gene Walter	.05
249	Jim Pankovits	.05
250	Teddy Higuera	.15
251	Rob Wilfong	.05
252	Denny Martinez	.07
253	Eddie Milner	.05
254	*Bob Tewksbury*	.10
255	Juan Samuel	.10
256	Royals Ldrs (George Brett, Frank White)	.10
257	Bob Forsch	.07
258	Steve Yeager	.05
259	*Mike Greenwell* (FC)	5.00
260	Vida Blue	.07
261	*Ruben Sierra* (FC)	3.50
262	Jim Winn	.05
263	Stan Javier (FC)	.05
265	Darrell Evans	.10
266	*Jeff Hamilton* (FC)	.25
267	Howard Johnson	.10
268	Pat Corrales	.05
270	Jody Davis	.05
271	Mike Brown	.05
272	Andres Galarraga	1.00
273	Gene Nelson	.05
274	*Jeff Hearron* (FC)	.05
275	LaMarr Hoyt	.05
276	Jackie Gutierrez	.05
277	Juan Agosto	.05
278	Gary Pettis	.05
279	*Dan Plesac*	.30
280	Jeffrey Leonard	.10
281	Reds Ldrs (Bo Diaz, Bill Gullickson, Pete Rose)	.10
282	Jeff Calhoun	.05
283	*Doug Drabek* (FC)	.25
284	John Moses	.05
285	Dennis Boyd	.05
286	Mike Woodard (FC)	.05
287	Dave Von Ohlen	.05
288	Tito Landrum	.05
289	Bob Kipper	.05
290	Leon Durham	.05
291	*Mitch Williams* (FC)	.65
292	Franklin Stubbs	.07
293	Bob Rodgers	.07
294	Steve Jeltz	.05
295	*Len Dykstra	.20
296	*Andres Thomas*	.25
297	Don Schulze	.05
298	Larry Herndon	.05
299	Joel Davis	.05
300	Reggie Jackson	.40
301	*Luis Aquino* (FC)	.10
302	Bill Schroeder	.07
303	Juan Berenguer	.05
304	Phil Garner	.07
305	John Franco	.10
306	Red Sox Ldrs (Rich Gedman, John McNamara, Tom Seaver)	.07
307	*Lee Guetterman* (FC)	.15
308	Don Slaught	.05
309	Mike Young	.05
310	Frank Viola	.15
311	Turn Back the Clock (Rickey Henderson)	.10
312	Turn Back the Clock (Reggie Jackson)	.10
313	Turn Back the Clock (Roberto Clemente)	.15
314	Turn Back the Clock (Carl Yastrzemski)	.10
315	Turn Back the Clock (Maury Wills)	.07
316	Brian Fisher	.05
317	Clint Hurdle	.05
318	Jim Fregosi	.07
319	*Greg Swindell* (FC)	1.00
320	*Barry Bonds*	1.75
321	Mike Laga	.05
322	Chris Bando	.05
323	*Al Newman*	.07
324	Dave Palmer	.05
325	Garry Templeton	.07
326	Mark Gubicza	.10
327	*Dale Sveum*	.20
328	Bob Welch	.10
329	Ron Roenicke	.05
330	Mike Scott	.12
331	Mets Ldrs (Gary Carter, Keith Hernandez, Dave Johnson, Darryl Strawberry)	.10
332	Joe Price	.05
333	Ken Phelps	.05
334	*Ed Correa*	.15
335	Candy Maldonado	.07
336	*_Allan Anderson_ (FC)	.25
337	Darrell Miller	.05
338	Tim Conroy	.05
339	Donnie Hill	.05
340	Roger Clemens	1.00
342	Bob James	.07
343	Hal Lanier	.07
344	Joe Niekro	.10
345	Andre Dawson	.20
346	Shawon Dunston	.07
347	Mickey Brantley (FC)	.07
348	Carmelo Martinez	.05
349	Storm Davis	.15
350	Keith Hernandez	.20
351	Gene Garber	.07
352	Mike Felder (FC)	.05

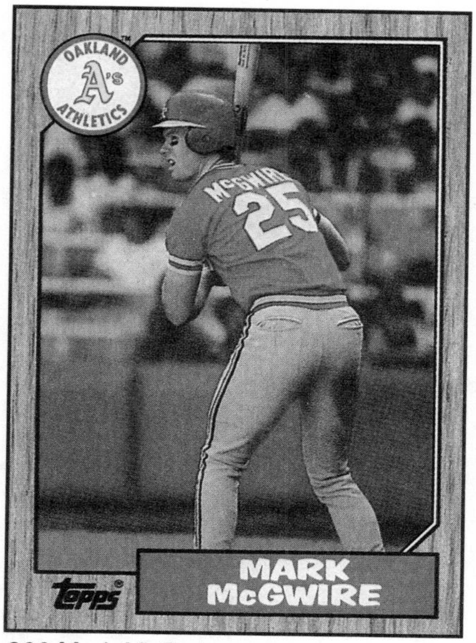

366 Mark McGwire

261 Ruben Sierra

500 Don Mattingly

648 Barry Larkin

429	Tim Pyznarski (FC)	.10
430	Mike Schmidt	.40
431	Dodgers Ldrs (Tom Niedenfuer, Ron Perranoski, Alex Trevino)	.07
432	Jim Slaton	.05
433	Ed Hearn (FC)	.10
434	Mike Fischlin	.05
435	Bruce Sutter	.15
436	Andy Allanson	.15
437	Ted Power	.05
438	Kelly Downs (FC)	.30
439	Karl Best	.05
440	Willie McGee	.10
441	Dave Leiper (FC)	.10
442	Mitch Webster	.05
443	John Felske	.05
444	Jeff Russell	.07
445	Dave Lopes	.07
446	Chuck Finley (FC)	.25
447	Bill Almon	.05
448	Chris Bosio (FC)	.25
449	Pat Dodson (FC)	.10
450	Kirby Puckett	.30
451	Joe Sambito	.05
452	Dave Henderson	.10
453	Scott Terry (FC)	.12
454	Luis Salazar	.05
455	Mike Boddicker	.07
456	A's Ldrs (Carney Lansford, Tony LaRussa, Mickey Tettleton, Dave Von Ohlen)	.07
457	Len Matuszek	.05
458	*Kelly Gruber (FC)	.15
459	Dennis Eckersley	.10
460	Darryl Strawberry	.35
461	Craig McMurtry	.05
462	Scott Fletcher	.05
463	Tom Candiotti	.07
464	Butch Wynegar	.05
465	Todd Worrell	.30
466	Kal Daniels (FC)	1.25

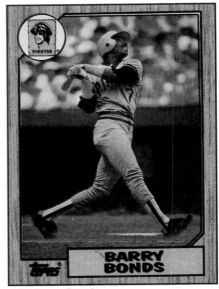

320 Barry Bonds

467	Randy St. Claire	.05
468	George Bamberger	.05
469	Mike Diaz (FC)	.15
470	Dave Dravecky	.07
472	Bill Doran	.07
476	Danny Tartabull	.90
479	Bob Sebra (FC)	.10
480	Jim Rice	.25
481	Phillies Ldrs (Von Hayes, Juan Samuel, Glenn Wilson)	.07
484	Jim Traber (FC)	.15
485	Tony Fernandez	.10
490	Dale Murphy	.40
491	Ron Karkovice (FC)	.10
494	Barry Jones (FC)	.12
495	Gorman Thomas	.10
497	Dale Mohorcic (FC)	.15
499	Bruce Ruffin (FC)	.20
500	Don Mattingly	2.50
506	Orioles Ldrs (Rich Bordi, Rick Dempsey, Earl Weaver)	.07
508	Scott Bankhead	.15
512	Dave Magadan (FC)	.50
516	Ted Simmons	.10
520	Jack Clark	.15
521	Rick Reuschel	.10
525	Phil Bradley	.10
530	Tony Gwynn	.35
531	Astros Ldrs (Yogi Berra, Hal Lanier, Denis Menke, Gene Tenace)	.07
536	Terry Mulholland (FC)	.10
541	Rafael Belliard (FC)	.10
547	Rob Deer	.10
548	Bill Mooneyham (FC)	.10
550	Pete Incaviglia	.40
553	Mike Maddux (FC)	.15
555	Dennis Rasmussen	.10
556	Angels Ldrs (Bob Boone, Marcel Lachemann, Mike Witt)	.07

353	Ernie Camacho	.05
354	Jamie Quirk	.05
355	Don Carman	.07
356	White Sox Ldrs (Ed Brinkman, Julio Cruz)	.07
357	Steve Fireovid (FC)	.07
358	Sal Butera	.05
359	Doug Corbett	.05
360	Pedro Guerrero	.15
366	Mark McGwire	3.00
370	Fred Lynn	.15
371	Mark Eichhorn	.15
375	Ron Guidry	.12
380	Rich Gossage	.15
385	Orel Hershiser	.30
393	Pete Rose	.40
400	George Brett	.35
404	Doug Sisk	.05
405	Brook Jacoby	.10
406	Yankees Ldrs (Rickey Henderson, Don Mattingly)	.15
407	Jim Acker	.05
408	John Mizerock	.05
409	Milt Thompson	.10
410	Fernando Valenzuela	.25
411	Darnell Coles	.05
412	Eric Davis	.90
413	Moose Haas	.05
414	Joe Orsulak	.05
415	Bobby Witt	.30
416	Tom Nieto	.05
417	Pat Perry (FC)	.07
418	Dick Williams	.05
419	Mark Portugal (FC)	.10
420	Will Clark	5.25
421	Jose DeLeon	.07
422	Jack Howell	.07
423	Jaime Cocanower	.05
424	Chris Speier	.05
425	Tom Seaver	.35
427	Ed Nunez	.05
428	Bruce Bochy	.05

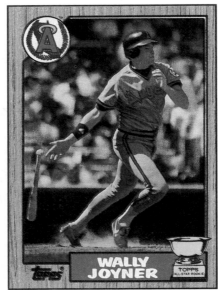

80 Wally Joyner

557	John Cerutti	.15
559	Lance McCullers	.07
560	Glenn Davis	.25
561	Rey Quinones (Quinonez)	.15
562	Bryan Clutterbuck (FC)	.10
567	Greg Mathews (FC)	.20
568	Earl Weaver	.07
569	Wade Rowdon (FC)	.07
570	Sid Fernandez	.10
581	Cubs Ldrs (Ron Cey, Steve Trout)	.07
585	Scott Bailes	.15
587	Eric Plunk (FC)	.10
590	Vince Coleman	.25
595	Keith Hernandez AS	.12
596	Steve Sax AS	.07
597	Mike Schmidt AS	.20
598	Ozzie Smith AS	.07
599	Tony Gwynn AS	.20
600	Dave Parker AS	.10
601	Darryl Strawberry AS	.20
602	Gary Carter AS	.15
603	Dwight Gooden AS	.40
604	Fernando Valenzuela AS	.12
605	Todd Worrell AS	.10
606	Don Mattingly AS	1.00
608	Wade Boggs AS	.40
609	Cal Ripken AS	.15
610	Jim Rice AS	.15

611	Kirby Puckett AS	.15
612	George Bell AS	.12
613	Lance Parrish AS	.10
614	Roger Clemens AS	.30
615	Teddy Higuera AS	.10
616	Dave Righetti AS	.10
620	Jose Canseco	6.25
622	Glenn Braggs (FC)	.30
623	Kurt Stillwell (FC)	.25
631	Tigers Ldrs (Sparky Anderson, Mike Heath, Willie Hernandez)	.07
634	Future Stars (Rafael Palmeiro (FC))	1.50
639	Gerald Perry	.10
645	*Dwight Evans	.12
648	Barry Larkin	2.50
652	Terry Forster	.07
653	Kevin Mitchell	4.00
655	Jesse Barfield	.15
656	Rangers Ldrs (Bobby Valentine, Rickey Wright)	.07
658	Robby Thompson	.30
660	Bob Horner	.12
661	Lou Whitaker	.15
664	Mike Marshall	.10
673	Don Sutton	.15
679	Kent Hrbek	.20
680	Ryne Sandberg	.25

1987 Topps/1987 Topps Traded

681	George Bell	.25
687	Alan Trammell	.25
691	Dave Parker	.15
694	Phil Niekro	.20
705	Bruce Hurst	.10
709	Dave Kingman	.10
710	Gary Gaetti	.15
718	Steve Carlton	.25
731	Dave Concepcion	.10
734	Bill Madlock	.10
735	Rickey Henderson	.30
736	Steve Bedrosian	.10
741	Paul Molitor	.12
749	Ozzie Smith	.15
756	Carlton Fisk	.20
757	Nolan Ryan	.60
765	Kirk Gibson	.20
769	Steve Sax	.15
770	Dave Winfield	.25
771	Shane Rawley	.07
772	Harold Baines	.12
773	Robin Yount	.25
775	Joaquin Andujar	.07
776	Tom Brunansky	.10
777	Chris Chambliss	.07
778	Jack Morris	.20
783	Willie Wilson	.10
784	Cal Ripken	.30
791	Lance Parrish	.15

1987 TOPPS TRADED

One of the least expensive Topps Traded sets of the past decade, this 132-card issue features more than a few notable first-card appearances. Fred McGriff, Matt Williams, David Cone, Joe Magrane, Benny Santiago, Kevin Seitzer, and Terry Steinbach lead the parade of newcomers. One surprising new face in the Traded set is veteran outfielder Kevin McReynolds. The Mets outfielder refused to sign baseball card contracts for several years before finally relenting in 1987. Managers Larry Bowa, Tom Trebelhorn, and Cal Ripken, Sr., are also included. These extras had been overlooked by other card companies.

14 Ellis Burks

		MINT
Complete set		**$16.00**
Commons		**.06**

1	Bill Almon	$ .06
2	Scott Bankhead	.08
3	Eric Bell (FC)	.15
5	Juan Berenguer	.06
7	Thad Bosley	.06
8	Larry Bowa	.10
9	Greg Brock	.10
10	Bob Brower (FC)	.15
11	Jerry Browne (FC)	.30
12	Ralph Bryant (FC)	.10
13	DeWayne Buice (FC)	.15
14	Ellis Burks (FC)	2.00
15	Ivan Calderon	.12
17	Casey Candaele (FC)	.10
18	John Cangelosi	.06
19	Steve Carlton	.30

20	Juan Castillo (FC)	.06
21	Rick Cerone	.06
22	Ron Cey	.10
24	Dave Cone (FC)	1.75
25	Chuck Crim (FC)	.15
26	Storm Davis	.06
27	Andre Dawson	.40
28	Rick Dempsey	.10
29	Doug Drabek	.10
30	Mike Dunne	.40
31	Dennis Eckersley	.25
32	Lee Elia	.06
33	Brian Fisher	.10
34	Terry Francona	.06
35	Willie Fraser (FC)	.15
37	Ken Gerhart (FC)	.15
39	Jim Gott	.06
46	Mike Henneman (FC)	.30
49	Brian Holton (FC)	.15
51	Danny Jackson (FC)	.50
52	Reggie Jackson	.50

53	Chris James (FC)	.40
54	Dion James	.40
55	Stan Jefferson (FC)	.20
56	Joe Johnson (FC)	.08
57	Terry Kennedy	.08
58	Mike Kingery	.08

24 Dave Cone

59	Ray Knight	.10
60	Gene Larkin (FC)	.25
61	Mike LaValliere	.10
65	Jim Lindeman (FC)	.10
67	Bill Long (FC)	.20
68	Barry Lyons (FC)	.15
69	Shane Mack	.20
70	Greg Maddux (FC)	.65
71	Bill Madlock	.15
72	Joe Magrane (FC)	1.25
73	Dave Martinez (FC)	.25
74	Fred McGriff (FC)	3.00
75	Mark McLemore (FC)	.10
76	Kevin McReynolds (FC)	.65
77	Dave Meads (FC)	.15
80	John Mitchell (FC)	.15
81	Kevin Mitchell	1.75
83	Jeff Musselman (FC)	.25
85	Graig Nettles	.10
88	Tom Niedenfuer	.08
89	Joe Niekro	.10
91	Matt Nokes (FC)	.70
93	Pat Pacillo	.15
94	Lance Parrish	.20

95	Tony Pena	.10
96	Luis Polonia (FC)	.30
98	Jeff Reardon	.12
99	Gary Redus	.08
101	Rick Rhoden	.10
103	Wally Ritchie (FC)	.10
104	Jeff Robinson (FC)	.40
109	Benny Santiago (FC)	1.25
110	Dave Schmidt	.08
111	Kevin Seitzer (FC)	1.00
113	Steve Shields (FC)	.08
114	John Smiley (FC)	.40
116	Mike Stanley (FC)	.20
117	Terry Steinbach (FC)	.75
118	Les Straker (FC)	.20
119	Jim Sundberg	.08
120	Danny Tartabull	.35
121	Tom Trebelhorn	.08
122	Dave Valle (FC)	.15
124	Andy Van Slyke	.20
127	Bill Wilkinson (FC)	.15
128	Frank Williams	.08
129	Matt Williams (FC)	3.00
131	Matt Young	.10

1988 DONRUSS

Known for gutsy speculation on unknowns while playing down prospective retirees, the 1988 Donruss set includes beginners such as Mark Grace and Gregg Jefferies. The 660-card set of standard-sized cards features the usual bizarre Donruss design with off-beat borders of red, black, and blue; Diamond Kings artwork; and a series of Rated Rookies. New was a 26-card separately numbered Bonus Card series with stars such as Cal Ripken, Jr., and Darryl Strawberry. These cards came only in random wax packs. High-numbered cards—600 and up—were scarce early in 1988, causing a permanent price hike. Superstars commanding top dollar here include Don Mattingly, Mark McGwire, and Wade Boggs.

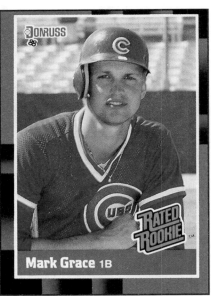

40 Mark Grace

		MINT
Complete set		**$30.00**
Commons		**.05**

1	Mark McGwire (DK)	$1.00
2	Tim Raines (DK)	.25
3	Benito Santiago (DK)	.30
4	Alan Trammell (DK)	.25
5	Danny Tartabull (DK)	.20
6	Ron Darling (DK)	.12
7	Paul Molitor (DK)	.12
8	Devon White (DK)	.20
9	Andre Dawson (DK)	.20
10	Julio Franco (DK)	.10
11	Scott Fletcher (DK)	.07
12	Tony Fernandez (DK)	.12
13	Shane Rawley (DK)	.07
14	Kal Daniels (DK)	.20
15	Jack Clark (DK)	.15
16	*Dwight Evans (DK)	.12
17	*Tommy John (DK)	.15
18	Andy Van Slyke (DK)	.15
19	Gary Gaetti (DK)	.12

20	Mark Langston (DK)	.10
21	Will Clark (DK)	.85
22	Glenn Hubbard (DK)	.07
23	Billy Hatcher (DK)	.07
24	Bob Welch (DK)	.10
25	Ivan Calderon (DK)	.10
26	Cal Ripken, Jr. (DK)	.35
27	Checklist 1-27	.10
28	*Mackey Sasser* (RR) (FC)	.20
29	*Jeff Treadway* (RR) (FC)	.40
30	*Mike Campbell* (RR) (FC)	.25
31	*Lance Johnson* (RR) (FC)	.40
32	*Nelson Liriano* (RR) (FC)	.25
33	*Shawn Abner* (RR) (FC)	.20
34	*Roberto Alomar* (RR) (FC)	1.75
35	*Shawn Hillegas* (RR) (FC)	.25
36	Joey Meyer (RR)	.15
37	Kevin Elster (RR)	.30
38	*Jose Lind* (RR) (FC)	.30
39	*Kirt Manwaring* (RR) (FC)	.35
40	*Mark Grace* (RR) (FC)	8.00
41	*Jody Reed* (RR) (FC)	.50

42	*John Farrell* (RR) (FC)	.25
43	*Al Leiter* (RR) (FC)	.70
44	*Gary Thurman* (RR) (FC)	.35
45	*Vicente Palacios* (RR) (FC)	.20
46	*Eddie Williams* (RR) (FC)	.25
47	*Jack McDowell* (RR) (FC)	.30
48	Ken Dixon	.05
49	Mike Birkbeck	.05
50	Eric King	.07
51	Roger Clemens	.75
52	Pat Clements	.05

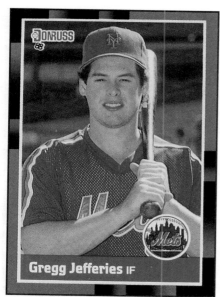

657 Gregg Jefferies

34 Roberto Alomar

96	Bret Saberhagen	.15
97	Curt Young	.07
98	Tim Burke	.07
99	Charlie Hough	.07
100	Checklist 28-133	.10
101	Bobby Witt	.10
102	George Brett	.40
103	Mickey Tettleton	.25
104	Scott Bailes	.07
105	Mike Pagliarulo	.10
106	Mike Scioscia	.07
107	Tom Brookens	.05
108	Ray Knight	.07
109	Dan Plesac	.10
110	Wally Joyner	.40
111	Bob Forsch	.07
112	Mike Scott	.15
113	Kevin Gross	.05
114	Benito Santiago	.35
115	Bob Kipper	.05
116	Mike Krukow	.07
117	Chris Bosio	.07
118	Sid Fernandez	.10
119	Jody Davis	.05
120	Mike Morgan	.05
121	Mark Eichhorn	.07
122	Jeff Reardon	.10
123	John Franco	.10
124	Richard Dotson	.07
125	Eric Bell	.05
126	Juan Nieves	.07
127	Jack Morris	.20
128	Rick Rhoden	.07
129	Rich Gedman	.07
130	Ken Howell	.05
131	Brook Jacoby	.10
132	Danny Jackson	.10
133	Gene Nelson	.05
134	Neal Heaton	.05
135	Willie Fraser	.05
136	Jose Guzman	.07
137	Ozzie Guillen	.15
138	Bob Knepper	.05

53	Fernando Valenzuela	.25
54	Mark Gubicza	.12
55	Jay Howell	.07
56	Floyd Youmans	.05
57	Ed Correa	.05
58	*DeWayne Buice*	.15
59	Jose DeLeon	.10
60	Danny Cox	.07
61	Nolan Ryan	.50
62	Steve Bedrosian	.12
63	Tom Browning	.10
64	Mark Davis	.10
65	R.J. Reynolds	.05
66	*Kevin Mitchell*	.65
67	Ken Oberkfell	.05
68	Rick Sutcliffe	.10
69	Dwight Gooden	.60
70	Scott Bankhead	.07
71	Bert Blyleven	.12
72	Jimmy Key	.10
73	*Les Straker*	.15
74	Jim Clancy	.05
75	Mike Moore	.07
76	Ron Darling	.12
77	Ed Lynch	.05
78	Dale Murphy	.40
79	Doug Drabek	.05
80	Scott Garrelts	.07
81	Ed Whitson	.07
82	Rob Murphy	.07
83	Shane Rawley	.05
84	Greg Mathews	.07
85	Jim Deshaies	.07
86	Mike Witt	.05
87	Donnie Hill	.05
88	Jeff Reed	.05
89	Mike Boddicker	.12
90	Ted Higuera	.10
91	Walt Terrell	.07
92	Bob Stanley	.05
93	Dave Righetti	.15
94	Orel Hershiser	.25
95	Chris Bando	.05

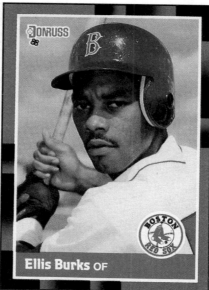

174 Ellis Burks

139	*Mike Jackson*	.20
140	*Joe Magrane*	.50
141	Jimmy Jones	.07
142	Ted Power	.05
143	Ozzie Virgil	.05
144	*Felix Fermin* (FC)	.15
145	Kelly Downs	.10
146	Shawon Dunston	.10
147	Scott Bradley	.07
148	Dave Stieb	.10
149	Frank Viola	.15
150	Terry Kennedy	.07
151	Bill Wegman	.05
152	*Matt Nokes*	.60
153	Wade Boggs	1.00
154	Wayne Tolleson	.05
155	Mariano Duncan	.05
156	Julio Franco	.10
157	Charlie Leibrandt	.07
158	Terry Steinbach	.10
159	Mike Fitzgerald	.05
160	Jack Lazorko	.07
161	Mitch Williams	.07
162	Greg Walker	.07
163	Alan Ashby	.05
164	Tony Gwynn	.35
165	Bruce Ruffin	.07
167	Zane Smith	.05
169	Jamie Moyer	.05
170	Tony Pena	.07
171	Cal Ripken	.35
172	B.J. Surhoff	.10
173	Lou Whitaker	.25
174	*Ellis Burks*	2.00
175	Ron Guidry	.15
176	Steve Sax	.15
177	Danny Tartabull	.20
178	Carney Lansford	.10
180	Scott Fletcher	.07
182	Ivan Calderon	.07
183	Jack Clark	.15
184	Glenn Davis	.15
186	Bo Diaz	.07

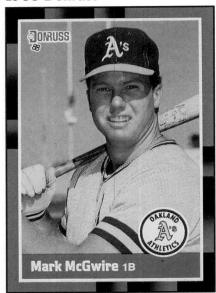

256 Mark McGwire

188	Sid Bream	.07
190	Dion James	.07
191	Leon Durham	.05
192	Jesse Orosco	.07
193	Alvin Davis	.12
194	Gary Gaetti	.15
195	Fred McGriff	.50
198	Rey Quinones	.07
199	Gary Carter	.25
200	Checklist 134-239	.10
201	Keith Moreland	.07
202	Ken Griffey	.07
203	*Tommy Gregg* (FC)	.30
204	Will Clark	1.25
205	John Kruk	.15
206	Buddy Bell	.07
207	Von Hayes	.07
208	Tommy Herr	.07
211	Harold Baines	.12
212	Vance Law	.07
213	Ken Gerhart	.07
215	Chet Lemon	.07
216	Dwight Evans	.12
217	Don Mattingly	1.50
218	Franklin Stubbs	.07
219	Pat Tabler	.07
220	Bo Jackson	1.25
222	Tim Wallach	.10
223	Ruben Sierra	.50
225	Frank White	.07
226	Alfredo Griffin	.07
227	Greg Swindell	.20
228	Willie Randolph	.07
229	Mike Marshall	.12
230	Alan Trammell	.25
231	Eddie Murray	.35
232	Dale Sveum	.07
235	Bill Doran	.07
238	Bobby Bonilla	.15
240	Glenn Braggs	.10
241	Wally Backman	.07
242	Ryne Sandberg	.40
243	Phil Bradley	.10

245	Tom Brunansky	.10
247	Bobby Thigpen	.15
248	Fred Lynn	.15
249	Paul Molitor	.12
250	Darrell Evans	.10
251	Gary Ward	.07
252	Bruce Hurst	.10
253	Bob Welch	.10
254	Joe Carter	.12
255	Willie Wilson	.10
256	Mark McGwire	1.50
257	Mitch Webster	.07
258	Brian Downing	.07
259	Mike Stanley	.10
260	Carlton Fisk	.20
261	Billy Hatcher	.07
262	Glenn Wilson	.07
263	Ozzie Smith	.15
265	Kurt Stillwell	.10
267	Mike Diaz	.07
268	Rob Thompson	.07
269	Andre Dawson	.20
271	Willie Upshaw	.07
273	Larry Sheets	.07
274	Rob Deer	.07
275	Kirk Gibson	.20
276	Marty Barrett	.07
277	Rickey Henderson	.50
278	Pedro Guerrero	.15
279	Brett Butler	.07
280	Kevin Seitzer	.80
281	Mike Davis	.07
282	Andres Galarraga	.15
283	Devon White	.30
284	Pete O'Brien	.07
286	Kevin Bass	.07
287	Carmelo Martinez	.07
288	Juan Samuel	.12
289	Kal Daniels	.20
291	Andy Van Slyke	.12
292	Lee Smith	.10
293	Vince Coleman	.20
294	Tom Niedenfuer	.07

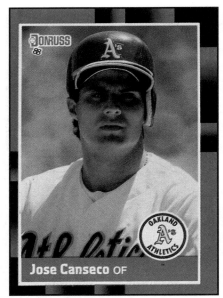

302 Jose Canseco

339 Mike Greenwell

295	Robin Yount	.30
296	*Jeff Robinson*	.40
297	*Todd Benzinger*	.40
298	Dave Winfield	.30
300	Checklist 240-345	.10
302	Jose Canseco	1.50
304	Pete Incaviglia	.15
305	*Bob Boone	.07
306	*Bill Long*	.20
307	Willie McGee	.12
308	*Ken Caminiti* (FC)	.25
310	Tracy Jones	.10
311	Greg Booker	.07
312	Mike LaValliere	.07
313	Chili Davis	.07
315	*Paul Noce*	.10
316	Keith Hernandez	.20
317	Mark Langston	.12
319	Tony Fernandez	.12
320	Kent Hrbek	.15
321	John Cerutti	.07
323	Dave Magadan	.12
324	Rafael Palmeiro	.40
326	Barry Bonds	.12
327	Jeffrey Leonard	.07
329	Dave Concepcion	.07
330	Mike Schmidt	.60
333	Jack Howell	.07
334	*Ken Williams*	.20
336	*Billy Ripken*	.25
337	Greg Brock	.07
339	Mike Greenwell	1.50
340	Claudell Washington	.07
342	Mel Hall	.07
343	Jim Eisenreich	.05
345	Tim Raines	.25
346	Bob Brower	.07
347	Larry Parrish	.10
349	Dennis Eckersley	.15
350	Cory Snyder	.20
355	*Chuck Crim*	.12
359	Lance Parrish	.15
360	*James Steels*	.12

361	*Al Pedrique* (FC)	.15
362	Mike Aldrete	.07
364	Len Dykstra	.10
366	Jim Presley	.10
367	Lloyd Moseby	.10
368	Kirby Puckett	.50
369	Eric Davis	.80
381	Kirk McCaskill	.07
382	Oddibe McDowell	.07
383	Floyd Bannister	.10
385	Don Carman	.05
386	Todd Worrell	.12
387	Eric Show	.07
388	Dave Parker	.20
390	*Mike Dunne*	.20
391	Candy Maldonado	.07
394	Ernie Whitt	.07
398	Willie Hernandez	.07
399	Jim Rice	.30
400	Checklist 346-451	.10
401	Tommy John	.15
402	Brian Holton	.07
405	Dwayne Murphy	.07
406	*Jeff Parrett* (FC)	.25
407	Don Sutton	.20
408	Jerry Browne	.07
409	Jim Winn	.07
411	*Shane Mack*	.15
412	Greg Gross	.05
414	Damaso Garcia	.05
418	*Mark Williamson*	.10
420	*Mike Henneman*	.25
421	*John Marzano* (FC)	.20
422	Ron Kittle	.07
424	Steve Balboni	.07
425	*Luis Polonia*	.25
428	Johnny Ray	.07
430	Ricky Horton	.07
431	*Gerald Young* (FC)	.35
433	Paul O'Neill	.07
434	Rich Gossage	.15
437	Gerald Perry	.07
438	Dave Martinez	.07

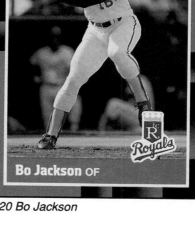

220 Bo Jackson

439	Darryl Strawberry	.35
442	Jesse Barfield	.10
449	*John Smiley*	.35
451	Lance McCullers	.07
452	Guy Hoffman (FC)	.07
453	Chris James	.10
454	Terry Pendleton	.10
455	*Dave Meads*	.15
456	Bill Buckner	.10
457	*John Pawlowski* (FC)	.10
460	*Jay Aldrich* (FC)	.10
461	Frank Tanana	.07
462	Oil Can Boyd	.07
463	Dan Pasqua	.10
464	*Tim Crews* (FC)	.15
465	Andy Allanson	.07
466	*Bill Pecota* (FC)	.15
468	Hubie Brooks	.10
469	*Paul Kilgus* (FC)	.20
471	Dan Quisenberry	.07
472	Dave Stewart	.12
473	Dave Clark	.07
476	Dan Petry	.07
477	*Carl Nichols* (FC)	.12
479	George Hendrick	.07
481	*Manny Hernandez* (FC)	.10
483	Chris Brown	.07
485	Dave Dravecky	.07
488	Jim Sundberg	.07
489	Ken Phelps	.05
490	Tom Henke	.10
492	Barry Larkin	.40
493	*Fred Manrique* (FC)	.15
495	*Mark Knudson* (FC)	.10
496	Bill Madlock	.12
498	*Sam Horn* (FC)	.30
499	*Tracy Woodson* (FC)	.25
500	Checklist 452-557	.10
508	*Robbie Wine* (FC)	.10
513	*Jeff Blauser* (FC)	.25
516	Manny Trillo	.07
519	*Mark Davidson*	.10
520	*Jeff Ballard* (FC)	.35

521	*Dave Stapleton* (FC)	.10
525	Jeff Hamilton	.07
526	*Tommy Hinzo* (FC)	.15
527	Lonnie Smith	.07
528	*Greg Cadaret* (FC)	.20
534	*Eric Nolte* (FC)	.15
535	Kent Tekulve	.07
536	*Pat Pacillo* (FC)	.15
538	*Tom Prince* (FC)	.15
539	Greg Maddux	.15
540	Jim Lindeman	.05
541	*Pete Stanicek* (FC)	.25
545	*Jay Buhner* (FC)	.30
546	*Mike Devereaux* (FC)	.30
548	Jose Rijo	.10
552	Dave LaPoint	.07
553	John Tudor	.10
554	*Rocky Childress* (FC)	.10
555	*Wally Ritchie* (FC)	.15
558	Jeff Robinson	.07
560	Ted Simmons	.10
561	*Lester Lancaster*	.15
562	*Keith Miller* (FC)	.25
563	Harold Reynolds	.10
564	*Gene Larkin*	.20
567	Duane Ward	.07
568	*Bill Wilkinson* (FC)	.15
569	Howard Johnson	.15
571	*Pete Smith* (FC)	.20
572	Darnell Coles	.07
573	Don Robinson	.07
575	Dennis Rasmussen	.10
577	*Tom Pagnozzi* (FC)	.15
582	*Rene Gonzales* (FC)	.15
584	Doyle Alexander	.07
585	Jeff Sellers	.05
587	Tim Belcher (FC)	.35
588	*Doug Jones* (FC)	.50
589	*Melido Perez* (FC)	.30
591	Pascual Perez	.07
593	Steve Howe	.05
594	*John Davis* (FC)	.20
595	Storm Davis	.12

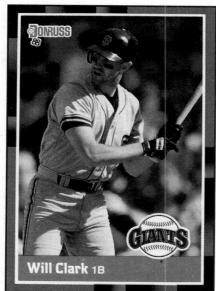

Will Clark 1B

204 Will Clark

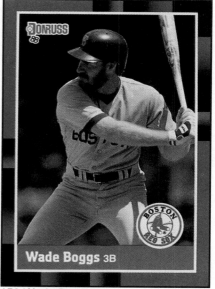

Wade Boggs 3B

153 Wade Boggs

243

598	Alejandro Pena	.07
600	Checklist 558-660	.10
601	*Jose Mesa* (FC)	.20
602	*Don August* (FC)	.25
603	Terry Leach	.07
604	*Tom Newell* (FC)	.20
605	*Randall Byers* (FC)	.20
608	John Candelaria	.10
609	*Mike Brumley* (FC)	.20
610	Mickey Brantley	.07
611	*Jose Nunez* (FC)	.25
613	Rick Reuschel	.10
614	Lee Mazzilli	.10
615	*Scott Lusader* (FC)	.20
617	Kevin McReynolds	.15
619	*Barry Lyons* (FC)	.15
620	Randy Myers	.10

624	*Greg Myers* (FC)	.20
625	Ripken Baseball Family (Billy Ripken, Cal Ripken, Jr., Cal Ripken, Sr.)	.20
627	Andres Thomas	.08
628	*Matt Williams*	1.00
629	*Dave Hengel* (FC)	.20
630	Jeff Musselman	.07
632	Bob Ojeda	.07
633	Rafael Santana	.05
634	*Wes Gardner* (FC)	.25
635	*Roberto Kelly* (FC)	1.00
636	Mike Flanagan	.12
637	*Jay Bell* (FC)	.20
639	*Damon Berryhill* (FC)	.40
640	*David Wells* (FC)	.25
643	*Keith Hughes* (FC)	.20

644	*Tom Glavine* (FC)	.40
645	Al Newman	.05
646	Scott Sanderson	.05
647	Scott Terry	.07
648	Tim Teufel	.10
649	Garry Templeton	.10
650	Manny Lee	.07
651	Roger McDowell	.10
652	Mookie Wilson	.15
653	David Cone	.70
654	*Ron Gant* (FC)	.40
655	Joe Price	.07
656	George Bell	.25
657	*Gregg Jefferies* (FC)	6.00
658	*Todd Stottlemyre* (FC)	.40
659	*Geronimo Berroa* (FC)	.40
660	Jerry Royster	.10

1988 DONRUSS ROOKIES

Donruss marked its third year of producing "The Rookies" in 1988. Once again, a specially designed box held the set of 55 player cards and an unnumbered checklist. A 15-piece puzzle of Hall-of-Famer Stan Musial was even included. The cards differ from the design of the regular set only in border color and "The Rookies" logo in the lower-right portion of each card. Due to a lackluster crop of rookies, the 1988 Donruss set has just three who are in high demand: Mark Grace, Chris Sabo, and Walt Weiss. Collectors have overlooked this edition in favor of the larger and more affordable fall issues from Score, Topps, and Fleer.

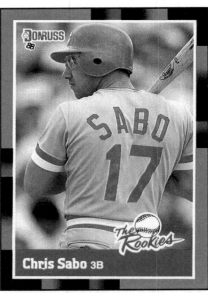

30 Chris Sabo

		MINT
Complete set		**$14.00**
Commons		.10

1	Mark Grace	$6.00
3	Todd Frowirth (FC)	.20
5	Shawn Abner	.20
6	Jose Cecena (FC)	.25
7	Dave Gallagher (FC)	.25
8	Mark Parent (FC)	.25
9	Cecil Espy (FC)	.15
11	Jay Buhner	.20
12	Pat Borders (FC)	.30
13	Doug Jennings (FC)	.25
14	Brady Anderson (FC)	.40
15	Pete Stanicek	.20
16	Roberto Kelly	.25
17	Jeff Treadway	.20
18	Walt Weiss (FC)	1.35
19	Paul Gibson (FC)	.20
21	Melido Perez	.20
22	Steve Peters (FC)	.20
23	Craig Worthington (FC)	.30
27	Al Leiter	.30
28	Tim Belcher	.25
29	Johnny Paredes (FC)	.20
30	Chris Sabo (FC)	2.00
31	Damon Berryhill	.25
32	Randy Milligan (FC)	.20

1 Mark Grace

33	Gary Thurman	.20
34	Kevin Elster	.20
35	Roberto Alomar	.35
36	Edgar Martinez	.25

37	Todd Stottlemyre	.20
38	Joey Meyer	.25
41	Jose Bautista (FC)	.20
42	Sil Campusano (FC)	.25
43	John Dopson (FC)	.20
44	Jody Reed	.25
45	Darrin Jackson (FC)	.20
46	Mike Capel (FC)	.20
47	Ron Gant	.20
50	Cris Carpenter (FC)	.35
51	Mackey Sasser	.25
52	Luis Alicea (FC)	.25
53	Bryan Harvey (FC)	.30
54	Steve Ellsworth (FC)	.15
55	Mike Macfarlane	.25

1988 FLEER

This 660-card, standard-dimension set features backs that carry a wealth of information. Full career statistics and graphs showing performance in various ballparks are complemented by "At Their Best" individualized highlights. Card fronts are white, with a border of busy blue and red diagonals, while player photos feature blended backgrounds. Star combo cards combine players by team or position, with Major League Prospects pairing off rookies, Mark Grace among them. Photos featuring surfboards or players with two gloves pleased some purchasers but offended others. As always, however, the greatest complaints concerned spotty distribution.

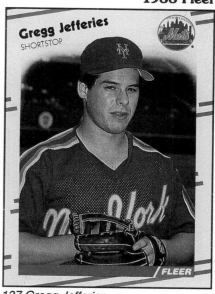

137 Gregg Jefferies

		MINT
Complete set		**$30.00**
Commons		**.06**

2	Don Baylor	$ .10
4	Bert Blyleven	.12
5	Tom Brunansky	.15
6	Randy Bush	.08
7	Steve Carlton	.20
8	*Mark Davidson* (FC)	.12
10	Gary Gaetti	.10
11	Greg Gagne	.08
13	Kent Hrbek	.15
14	*Gene Larkin*	.20
18	Joe Niekro	.08
19	Kirby Puckett	.50
20	Jeff Reardon	.12
21	Dan Schatzader (incorrect spelling)	.40
21	Dan Schatzeder (correct spelling)	.10
24	*Les Straker* (FC)	.15
25	Frank Viola	.15
26	Jack Clark	.15
27	Vince Coleman	.20
28	Danny Cox	.08
33	Bob Forsch	.08
35	Tom Herr	.08
37	*Lance Johnson* (FC)	.40
40	*Joe Magrane*	.50
42	Willie McGee	.12
45	Tony Pena	.08
47	Ozzie Smith	.15
48	John Tudor	.10
50	Todd Worrell	.10
54	Darrell Evans	.10
55	Kirk Gibson	.20
57	*Mike Henneman*	.25
58	Willie Hernandez	.08
60	Eric King	.08
61	Chet Lemon	.08
62	*Scott Lusader* (FC)	.20
63	Bill Madlock	.10
64	Jack Morris	.20
66	*Matt Nokes*	.50
67	Dan Petry	.08
68	*Jeff Robinson* (born 12/13/60 on back)	1.25
68	*Jeff Robinson* (born 12/14/61 on back)	.40

72	Walt Terrell	.08
74	Alan Trammell	.25
75	Lou Whitaker	.25
78	Will Clark	3.25
79	Chili Davis	.08
80	Kelly Downs	.10
82	Scott Garrelts	.06
84	Dave Henderson	.10
88	Jeff Leonard	.10
92	Kevin Mitchell	.20
93	*Jon Perlman* (FC)	.12
94	Rick Reuschel	.10
96	Chris Speier	.06
99	Jose Uribe	.08
100	*Mark Wasinger* (FC)	.15
101	*Matt Williams*	2.00
102	Jesse Barfield	.15
103	George Bell	.25
105	John Cerutti	.06
107	*Rob Ducey* (FC)	.15
109	Tony Fernandez	.12
110	Cecil Fielder	.75
111	Kelly Gruber	.20
112	Tom Henke	.08
114	Jimmy Key	.10
117	*Nelson Liriano* (FC)	.25
118	*Fred McGriff*	1.50
122	*Jose Nunez*	.25
123	Dave Stieb	.10
125	*Duane Ward* (FC)	.08
126	Ernie Whitt	.08
129	*Mark Carreon* (FC)	.12

130	Gary Carter	.25
131	David Cone (FC)	1.25
132	Ron Darling	.12
133	*Len Dykstra	.15
134	Sid Fernandez	.10
135	Dwight Gooden	.60
136	Keith Hernandez	.20
137	*Gregg Jefferies* (FC)	6.00
138	Howard Johnson	.10
140	*Barry Lyons* (FC)	.15
141	Dave Magadan	.12
142	Roger McDowell	.10
143	Kevin McReynolds	.15
144	*Keith Miller* (FC)	.25
145	*John Mitchell* (FC)	.20
146	Randy Myers	.15
147	Bob Ojeda	.08
151	Darryl Strawberry	.35
152	Tim Teufel	.08
155	*Jay Aldrich* (FC)	.12
156	Chris Bosio	.08
157	Glenn Braggs	.08
158	Greg Brock	.06
161	Cecil Cooper	.10
162	*Chuck Crim*	.12

641 Major League Prospects

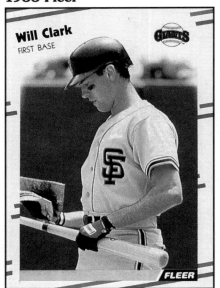

78 Will Clark

163	Rob Deer	.08
166	Ted Higuera	.10
169	Paul Molitor	.12
170	Juan Nieves	.08
171	Dan Plesac	.10
174	*Steve Stanicek* (FC)	.15
175	B.J. Surhoff	.20
176	Dale Sveum	.08
178	Robin Yount	.30
179	Hubie Brooks	.10
180	Tim Burke	.08
183	Tom Foley	.06
184	Andres Galarraga	.15
187	Vance Law	.08
193	Tim Raines	.25
195	Bob Sebra	.08
196	Bryn Smith	.08
198	Tim Wallach	.10
199	Mitch Webster	.08
202	*Brad Arnsberg* (FC)	.15
203	Rick Cerone	.06
205	Henry Cotto	.08
206	Mike Easler	.08
207	Ron Guidry	.15
209	Rickey Henderson	.35
211	Tommy John	.15
212	*Roberto Kelly* (FC)	1.25
213	Ron Kittle	.08
214	Don Mattingly	1.50
216	Mike Pagliarulo	.10
217	Dan Pasqua	.10
219	Rick Rhoden	.08
220	Dave Righetti	.15
221	Jerry Royster	.06
226	Dave Winfield	.30
227	Buddy Bell	.08
228	Tom Browning	.10
230	Kal Daniels	.20
231	Eric Davis	.80
233	Nick Esasky	.12
234	John Franco	.10
237	Tracy Jones	.12
238	*Bill Landrum* (FC)	.10

239	Barry Larkin	.40
241	Rob Murphy	.08
243	Dave Parker	.20
248	Kurt Stillwell	.10
249	*Jeff Treadway* (FC)	.25
252	Bud Black	.08
253	Thad Bosley	.06
254	George Brett	.40
255	John Davis (FC)	.20
256	Steve Farr	.08
257	Gene Garber	.08
259	Mark Gubicza	.12
260	Bo Jackson	3.25
261	Danny Jackson	.12
262	*Ross Jones* (FC)	.12
264	*Bill Pecota*	.15
265	*Melido Perez* (FC)	.30
266	Jamie Quirk	.06
268	Bret Saberhagen	.25
270	Kevin Seitzer	.70
271	Danny Tartabull	.20
272	*Gary Thurman* (FC)	.20
273	Frank White	.08
274	Willie Wilson	.10
276	Jose Canseco	2.50
277	Mike Davis	.08
278	Storm Davis	.12
279	Dennis Eckersley	.12
280	Alfredo Griffin	.08
282	Jay Howell	.08
283	Reggie Jackson	.50
284	Dennis Lamp	.08
285	Carney Lansford	.10
286	Mark McGwire	2.00
288	Gene Nelson	.06
290	Tony Phillips	.08
291	Eric Plunk	.08
292	*Luis Polonia*	.25
294	Terry Steinbach	.12
295	Dave Stewart	.10
296	Curt Young	.08
298	Steve Bedrosian	.12
300	Don Carman	.08

260 Bo Jackson

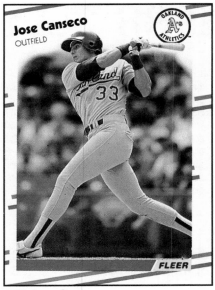

276 Jose Canseco

301	*Todd Frohwirth* (FC)	.20
304	Von Hayes	.12
305	*Keith Hughes* (FC)	.20
306	*Mike Jackson*	.20
307	Chris James	.20
308	Steve Jeltz	.06
309	Mike Maddux	.06
310	Lance Parrish	.17
312	*Wally Ritchie*	.15
313	Bruce Ruffin	.08
314	Juan Samuel	.12
315	Mike Schmidt	.65
318	Kent Tekulve	.08
319	Milt Thompson	.08
320	Glenn Wilson	.08
322	Barry Bonds	.12
323	Bobby Bonilla	.15
324	Sid Bream	.08
326	Mike Diaz	.06
327	Doug Drabek	.06
328	*Mike Dunne*	.25
329	Brian Fisher	.08
334	*Jose Lind* (FC)	.30
335	Junior Ortiz	.06
336	*Vicente Palacios* (FC)	.20
337	*Bob Patterson* (FC)	.12
338	*Al Pedrique* (FC)	.20
339	R.J. Reynolds	.06
340	*John Smiley*	.35
341	Andy Van Slyke	.12
344	*Todd Benzinger* (FC)	.40
345	Wade Boggs	1.00
346	*Tom Bolton* (FC)	.15
348	Ellis Burks	1.75
349	Roger Clemens	.60
351	*Dwight Evans	.12
352	*Wes Gardner* (FC)	.25
354	Mike Greenwell	2.00
355	*Sam Horn* (FC)	.30
356	Bruce Hurst	.10
357	*John Marzano* (FC)	.20
358	Al Nipper	.06
359	Spike Owen	.06

360	*Jody Reed* (FC)	.50
361	Jim Rice	.30
362	Ed Romero	.06
366	Jeff Sellers	.08
367	Bob Stanley	.06
369	Phil Bradley	.10
370	Scott Bradley	.06
372	*Mike Campbell* (FC)	.25
373	Alvin Davis	.12
375	*Dave Hengel* (FC)	.20
377	Mark Langston	.12
378	*Edgar Martinez* (FC)	1.00
379	Mike Moore	.10
380	Mike Morgan	.06
381	John Moses	.06
382	*Donnell Nixon* (FC)	.20
384	Ken Phelps	.06
385	Jim Presley	.08
387	Jerry Reed	.06
388	Harold Reynolds	.10
390	*Bill Wilkinson* (FC)	.15
391	Harold Baines	.12
393	Daryl Boston	.06
394	Ivan Calderon	.10
395	Jose DeLeon	.10
397	Carlton Fisk	.20
398	Ozzie Guillen	.08
399	Ron Hassey	.06
402	Dave LaPoint	.06
403	*Bill Lindsey* (FC)	.12
404	*Bill Long* (FC)	.20
405	Steve Lyons	.06
406	*Fred Manrique*	.15
407	*Jack McDowell* (FC)	.25
408	Gary Redus	.06
409	Ray Searage	.06
410	Bobby Thigpen	.10
411	Greg Walker	.08
412	*Kenny Williams*	.20
413	Jim Winn	.06
414	Jody Davis	.06
415	Andre Dawson	.20
419	Shawon Dunston	.08

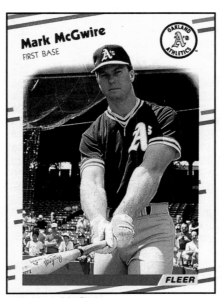

286 Mark McGwire

420	Leon Durham	.06
421	*Les Lancaster* (FC)	.15
422	Ed Lynch	.06
423	Greg Maddux	.25
425	Keith Moreland (bunting, photo is Jody Davis)	3.50
425	Keith Moreland (standing, correct photo)	.10
426	Jamie Moyer	.06
428	*Paul Noce* (FC)	.10
429	Rafael Palmeiro (FC)	.70
430	*Wade Rowdon* (FC)	.06
431	Ryne Sandberg	.25
433	Lee Smith	.10
435	Rick Sutcliffe	.10
436	Manny Trillo	.06
439	Alan Ashby	.06
440	Kevin Bass	.08
441	*Ken Caminiti* (FC)	.35
442	*Rocky Childress* (FC)	.12
443	Jose Cruz	.10
445	Glenn Davis	.15
447	Bill Doran	.08
449	Billy Hatcher	.08
451	Bob Knepper	.06
452	*Rob Mallicoat* (FC)	.10
453	*Dave Meads*	.15
455	Nolan Ryan	.75
456	Mike Scott	.15
457	Dave Smith	.08
459	*Robbie Wine* (FC)	.10
460	*Gerald Young* (FC)	.35
461	Bob Brower	.08
462	Jerry Browne (photo is Bob Brower)	3.50
462	Jerry Browne (correct photo)	.10
464	Edwin Correa	.06
465	*Cecil Espy* (FC)	.30
468	Greg Harris	.06
470	Pete Incaviglia	.15
471	*Paul Kilgus* (FC)	.20
472	Mike Loynd	.06

475	Pete O'Brien	.10
478	Jeff Russell	.10
479	Ruben Sierra	.75
482	Mitch Williams	.10
483	Bobby Witt	.10
484	Tony Armas	.06
485	*Bob Boone	.08
486	Bill Buckner	.10
487	*DeWayne Buice*	.15
489	Chuck Finley	.08
490	Willie Fraser	.06
491	Jack Howell	.08
493	Wally Joyner	.40
495	Gary Lucas	.06
501	Gus Polidor	.06
502	Johnny Ray	.10
503	Mark Ryal (FC)	.06
505	Don Sutton	.20
506	Devon White	.20
507	Mike Witt	.08
509	Tim Belcher (FC)	.40
510	Ralph Bryant	.06
511	*Tim Crews* (FC)	.15
512	*Mike Devereaux* (FC)	.30
514	Pedro Guerrero	.15
515	Jeff Hamilton (FC)	.12
518	Orel Hershiser	.25
519	*Shawn Hillegas* (FC)	.20
520	Ken Howell	.06
521	Tim Leary	.08
522	Mike Marshall	.12
523	Steve Sax	.15
526	John Shelby	.06
528	Fernando Valenzuela	.20
529	Bob Welch	.10
530	Matt Young	.06
531	Jim Acker	.06
533	*Jeff Blauser* (FC)	.25
534	*Joe Boever* (FC)	.15
536	*Kevin Coffman* (FC)	.10
537	Jeff Dedmon	.06
538	*Ron Gant* (FC)	.40
539	*Tom Glavine* (FC)	.40

101 Matt Williams

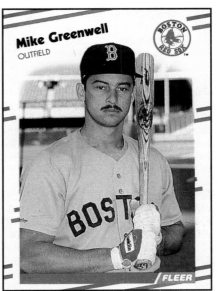

354 Mike Greenwell

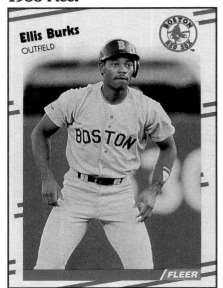

348 Ellis Burks

540	Ken Griffey	.08
541	Al Hall	.06
543	Dion James	.08
544	Dale Murphy	.40
547	Gerald Perry	.08
549	Ted Simmons	.10
550	Zane Smith	.06
552	Ozzie Virgil	.06
553	Don Aase	.06
554	*Jeff Ballard* (FC)	.35
555	Eric Bell	.06
557	Ken Dixon	.06
558	Jim Dwyer	.06
560	*Rene Gonzales* (FC)	.15
564	Ray Knight	.08
565	Lee Lacy	.06
566	Fred Lynn	.15
567	Eddie Murray	.35
569	*Bill Ripken* (FC)	.25
570	Cal Ripken Jr.	35
573	*Pete Stanicek* (FC)	.25
574	*Mark Williamson* (FC)	.10
575	Mike Young	.06
576	Shawn Abner (FC)	.20
577	Greg Booker	.06
578	Chris Brown	.06
579	*Keith Comstock* (FC)	.10
580	*Joey Cora* (FC)	.12
581	Mark Davis	.10
583	Goose Gossage	.15
584	Mark Grant	.06
585	Tony Gwynn	.35
587	Stan Jefferson	.06
589	John Kruk	.10
590	*Shane Mack* (FC)	.20
593	*Eric Nolte* (FC)	.15
594	Randy Ready	.06
595	Luis Salazar	.06
596	Benito Santiago	.35
597	Eric Show	.08
599	Ed Whitson	.08
600	Scott Bailes	.06
601	Chris Bando	.06

602	*Jay Bell* (FC)	.20
603	Brett Butler	.08
604	Tom Candiotti	.06
605	Joe Carter	.12
607	*Brian Dorsett* (FC)	.15
608	*John Farrell* (FC)	.35
609	Julio Franco	.10
610	Mel Hall	.06
611	*Tommy Hinzo* (FC)	.15
612	Brook Jacoby	.08
613	*Doug Jones* (FC)	.45
615	Cory Snyder	.20
617	Greg Swindell	.20
618	Pat Tabler	.06
619	Ed Vande Berg	.06
620	*Eddie Williams* (FC)	.20
621	Rich Yett	.06
622	Slugging Sophomores (Wally Joyner, Cory Snyder)	.40
623	Dominican Dynamite (George Bell, Pedro Guerrero)	.15
624	Oakland's Power Team (Mark McGwire, Jose Canseco)	1.25
625	Classic Relief (Dan Plesac, Dave Righetti)	.08
626	All Star Righties (Jack Morris, Bret Saberhagen, Mike Witt)	.10
627	Game Closers (Steve Bedrosian, John Franco)	.10
628	Masters of the Double Play (Ryne Sandberg, Ozzie Smith)	.12
629	Rookie Record Setter (Mark McGwire)	1.00
630	Changing in the Guard in Boston (Todd Benzinger, Ellis Burks, Mike Greenwell)	1.00
631	NL Batting Champs (Tony Gwynn, Tim Raines)	.15
633	Big Bats At First (Mark McGwire, Pat Tabler)	.50

635	AL Slugging Shortstops (Tony Fernandez, Cal Ripken Jr., Alan Trammell)	.15
636	Tried and True Sluggers (Gary Carter, Mike Schmidt)	.20
637	Crunch Time (Eric Davis, Darryl Strawberry)	.75
639	NL All-Stars (Keith Hernandez, Dale Murphy)	.20
641	Major League Prospects (*Mark Grace, Darrin Jackson*) (FC)	13.00
642	Major League Prospects (*Damon Berryhill, Jeff Montgomery*) (FC)	.50
643	Major League Prospects (*Felix Fermin, Jessie Reid*) (FC)	.20
644	Major League Prospects (*Greg Myers, Greg Tabor*) (FC)	.20
645	Major League Prospects (*Jim Eppard*, Joey Meyer) (FC)	.25
646	Major League Prospects (*Adam Peterson, Randy Velarde*) (FC)	.30
647	Major League Prospects (*Chris Gwynn, Peter Smith*) (FC)	.40
648	Major league Prospects (*Greg Jelks, Tom Newell*) (FC)	.25
649	Major League Prospects (*Mario Diaz, Clay Parker*) (FC)	.25
650	Major League Prospects (*Jack Savage, Todd Simmons*) (FC)	.25
651	Major League Prospects (*John Burkett, Kirt Manwaring*) (FC)	.30
652	Major League Prospects (*Dave Otto, Walt Weiss*) (FC)	1.25
653	Major League Prospects (*Randell Byers (Randall), Jeff King*) (FC)	.25

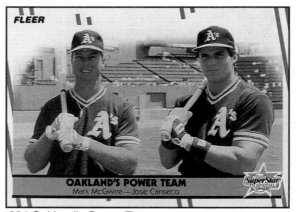

624 Oakland's Power Team

1988 FLEER UPDATE

This traditional 132-card fall "extension" set, the fifth annual from Fleer, failed to successfully compete with the Olympian-filled Topps Traded set. However, the Update set has 131 more cards which repeat the attractive design unveiled in Fleer's 660-card set earlier that summer. The Update set contains one unusual pairing: Card 113-U, supposedly of Tommy Gregg, actually depicts Pirates teammate Randy Milligan, who also gets his own card, number 115-U, which is correct (the "U" has been omitted from the following lists). Unlike the alphabetical system used by Topps, Fleer Updates are arranged by team.

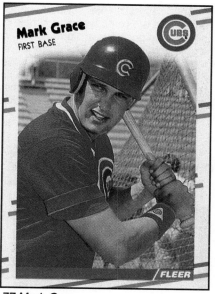

77 Mark Grace

110 Ricky Jordan

		MINT
Complete set		**$16.00**
Commons		**.06**

1	Jose Bautista (FC)	$ .20
4	Craig Worthington (FC)	.75
5	Mike Boddicker	.10
6	Rick Cerone	.06
7	Larry Parrish	.08
8	Lee Smith	.10
10	John Trautwein (FC)	.15
11	Sherman Corbett (FC)	.15
12	Chili Davis	.10
14	Bryan Harvey (FC)	.35
15	John Davis	.08
16	Dave Gallagher (FC)	.25
17	Ricky Horton	.06
18	Dan Pasqua	.08
19	Melido Perez	.10
20	Jose Segura (FC)	.15
21	Andy Allanson	.10
23	Domingo Ramos	.12
25	Willie Upshaw	.08
26	Paul Gibson (FC)	.15
27	Don Heinkel (FC)	.15
28	Ray Knight	.08
29	Gary Pettis	.08
30	Luis Salazar	.10
31	Mike McFarlane (Macfarlane) (FC)	.25
32	Jeff Montgomery	.12
34	Israel Sanchez (FC)	.15
35	Kurt Stillwell	.10
36	Pat Tabler	.08
37	Don August (FC)	.20
38	Darryl Hamilton (FC)	.15
39	Jeff Leonard	.12
40	Joey Meyer	.15
41	Andy Allanson	.10
42	Brian Harper	.08
43	Tom Herr	.10
46	John Candelaria	.10
47	Jack Clark	.15
48	Richard Dotson	.12
49	Al Leiter (FC)	.25
52	Todd Burns (FC)	.25
53	Dave Henderson	.10
54	Doug Jennings (FC)	.15
55	Dave Parker	.12
56	Walt Weiss	.75
57	Bob Welch	.10

59	Mario Diaz	.12
60	Mike Jackson	.12
61	Bill Swift	.12
62	Jose Cecena (FC)	.15
63	Ray Hayward (FC)	.08
64	Jim Steels	.15
65	Pat Borders (FC)	.20
66	Sil Campusano (FC)	.25
67	Mike Flanagan	.08
68	Todd Stottlemyre (FC)	.25
69	David Wells	.20
70	Jose Alvarez (FC)	.15
72	Cesar Jiminez (German) (FC)	.15
73	Pete Smith	.08
74	John Smoltz (FC)	1.50
75	Damon Berryhill	.10
76	Goose Gossage	.15
77	Mark Grace	6.00
78	Darrin Jackson	.10
79	Vance Law	.08
80	Jeff Pico (FC)	.20
81	Gary Varsho (FC)	.15
82	Tim Birtsas	.10
83	Rob Dibble (FC)	.40
84	Danny Jackson	.10

85	Paul O'Neill	.10
86	Jose Rijo	.15
87	Chris Sabo (FC)	1.50
88	John Fishel (FC)	.15
89	Craig Biggio (FC)	1.50
92	Louie Meadows (FC)	.15
93	Kirk Gibson	.15
94	Alfredo Griffin	.12
95	Jay Howell	.08
96	Jesse Orosco	.08
98	Tracy Woodson	.30
99	John Dopson (FC)	.25
100	Brian Holman (FC)	.25
102	Jeff Parrett (FC)	.10
103	Nelson Santovenia (FC)	.25
104	Kevin Elster	.12
105	Jeff Innis (FC)	.20
106	Mackey Sasser (FC)	.10
107	Phil Bradley	.15
108	Danny Clay (FC)	.15
110	Ricky Jordan (FC)	2.75
112	Jim Gott	.08
113	Tommy Gregg (photo is Randy Milligan) (FC)	.10
115	Randy Milligan (FC)	.10
116	Luis Alicea (FC)	.15
117	Tom Brunansky	.15
118	John Costello (FC)	.15
119	Jose DeLeon	.10
120	Bob Horner	.08
121	Scott Terry (FC)	.08
122	Roberto Alomar (FC)	.50
125	Mark Parent (FC)	.25
126	Dennis Rasmussen	.08
128	Brett Butler	.12
129	Donnell Nixon	.12
131	Roger Samuels	.15

1988 SCORE ===

Score's 660-card 1988 set was applauded for information-filled backs and color photo insets. Fronts feature a simple bold border in one of six colors. Player names and positions are prominently centered at the bottom with the Score logo at the lower right. The cards were sold in poly-bags that could not be tampered with and resealed (unlike the wax packs from Donruss, Topps, and Fleer). Initially, many cards from the poly-bags were damaged, but they were replaced by the company. Subsets include Rookie Prospects, 1987 Highlights, and a five-card salute to Reggie Jackson.

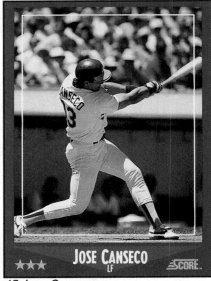

45 Jose Canseco

645 Rookie Prospect

		MINT
Complete set		**$25.00**
Commons		**.04**

1	Don Mattingly	$1.50
2	Wade Boggs	1.00
3	Tim Raines	.20
4	Andre Dawson	.15
5	Mark McGwire	1.00
6	Kevin Seitzer	.60
7	Wally Joyner	.35
8	Jesse Barfield	.10
9	Pedro Guerrero	.12
10	Eric Davis	.60
11	George Brett	.30
12	Ozzie Smith	.12
13	Rickey Henderson	.25
14	Jim Rice	.20
15	*Matt Nokes*	.50
16	Mike Schmidt	.50
17	Dave Parker	.12
18	Eddie Murray	.25
19	Andres Galarraga	.15
20	Tony Fernandez	.15
21	Kevin McReynolds	.15
22	B.J. Surhoff	.10
23	Pat Tabler	.06
24	Kirby Puckett	.25
25	Benny Santiago	.35
26	Ryne Sandberg	.25
27	Kelly Downs	.08
28	Jose Cruz	.06
29	Pete O'Brien	.06
30	Mark Langston	.15
31	Lee Smith	.08
32	Juan Samuel	.10
33	Kevin Bass	.06
34	R.J. Reynolds	.04
35	Steve Sax	.12
36	John Kruk	.12
37	Alan Trammell	.15
38	Chris Bosio	.06
39	Brook Jacoby	.08
40	Willie McGee	.10
41	Dave Magadan	.10
42	Fred Lynn	.10
43	Kent Hrbek	.12
44	Brian Downing	.06
45	Jose Canseco	1.75
46	Jim Presley	.06
47	Mike Stanley	.06

48	Tony Pena	.06
49	David Cone	.75
50	Rick Sutcliffe	.08
51	Doug Drabek	.06
52	Bill Doran	.06
53	Mike Scioscia	.06
54	Candy Maldonado	.06
55	Dave Winfield	.25
56	Lou Whitaker	.20
57	Tom Henke	.06
58	Ken Gerhart	.06
59	Glenn Braggs	.08
60	Julio Franco	.08
61	Charlie Leibrandt	.06
62	Gary Gaetti	.10
63	*Bob Boone	.08
64	*Luis Polonia*	.15
65	*Dwight Evans	.10
66	Phil Bradley	.08
67	Mike Boddicker	.15
68	Vince Coleman	.15
69	Howard Johnson	.08
70	Tim Wallach	.08
71	Keith Moreland	.06
72	Barry Larkin	.20
73	Alan Ashby	.04

74	Rick Rhoden	.06
75	Darrell Evans	.08
76	Dave Stieb	.08
77	Dan Plesac	.08
78	Will Clark	1.25
79	Frank White	.08
80	Joe Carter	.10
81	Mike Witt	.06
82	Terry Steinbach	.10
83	Alvin Davis	.10
84	Tom Herr	.06
85	Vance Law	.06
86	Kal Daniels	.15
87	Rick Honeycutt	.04
88	Alfredo Griffin	.06
89	Bret Saberhagen	.35
90	Bert Blyleven	.10
91	Jeff Reardon	.08
92	Cory Snyder	.15
93	Greg Walker	.06
94	*Joe Magrane*	.50
95	Rob Deer	.06
96	Ray Knight	.06
97	Casey Candaele	.04
98	John Cerutti	.06
99	Buddy Bell	.08
100	Jack Clark	.12
101	Eric Bell	.06
102	Willie Wilson	.08
103	Dave Schmidt	.04
104	Dennis Eckersley	.10
105	Don Sutton	.12
106	Danny Tartabull	.15
107	Fred McGriff	.80
108	*Les Straker*	.15
109	Lloyd Moseby	.06
110	Roger Clemens	.50
111	Glenn Hubbard	.04
112	*Ken Williams*	.20
113	Ruben Sierra	.50
114	Stan Jefferson	.06
115	Milt Thompson	.08
116	Bobby Bonilla	.20

472 Ellis Burks

117	Wayne Tolleson	.04
118	*Matt Williams*	.75
119	Chet Lemon	.06
120	Dale Sveum	.06
121	Dennis Boyd	.06
122	Brett Butler	.06
123	Terry Kennedy	.06
124	Jack Howell	.06
125	Curt Young	.06
126	Dale Valle (first name incorrect)	.25
126	Dave Valle (first name correct)	.12
127	Curt Wilkerson	.04
128	Tim Teufel	.04
129	Ozzie Virgil	.04
130	Brian Fisher	.06
131	Lance Parrish	.12
132	Tom Browning	.08
133	Larry Anderson (incorrect spelling)	.25
133	Larry Andersen (correct spelling)	.10
134	Bob Brenley (incorrect spelling)	.25
134	Bob Brenly (correct spelling)	.10
135	Mike Marshall	.10
136	Gerald Perry	.06
137	Bobby Meacham	.04
138	Larry Herndon	.04
139	*Fred Manrique*	.12
140	Charlie Hough	.06
141	Ron Darling	.10
142	Herm Winningham	.04
143	Mike Diaz	.06
144	*Mike Jackson*	.15
145	Denny Walling	.04
146	Rob Thompson	.06
147	Frankling Stubbs	.06
148	Albert Hall	.04
149	Bobby Witt	.08
150	Lance McCullers	.06

151	Scott Bradley	.04
152	Mark McLemore	.04
153	Tim Laudner	.04
154	Greg Swindell	.15
155	Marty Barrett	.06
156	Mike Heath	.04
157	Gary Ward	.06
158	Lee Mazilli (incorrect spelling)	.25
158	Lee Mazzilli (correct spelling)	.10
159	Tom Foley	.04
160	Robin Yount	.20
161	Steve Bedrosian	.10
162	Bob Walk	.04
163	Nick Esasky	.15
164	*Ken Caminiti*	.35
165	Jose Uribe	.04
166	Dave Anderson	.04
167	Ed Whitson	.06
168	Ernie Whitt	.06
169	Cecil Cooper	.08
170	Mike Pagliarulo	.08
171	Pat Sheridan	.04
172	Chris Bando	.04
173	Lee Lacy	.04
174	Steve Lombardozzi	.04
175	Mike Greenwell	1.50
176	Greg Minton	.04
177	Moose Haas	.04
178	Mike Kingery	.04
179	Greg Harris	.04
180	Bo Jackson	.50
181	Carmelo Martinez	.06
182	Alex Trevino	.04
183	Ron Oester	.04
184	Danny Darwin	.04
185	Mike Krukow	.06
186	Rafael Palmeiro	.35
187	Tim Burke	.06
188	Roger McDowell	.08
189	Garry Templeton	.06
190	Terry Pendleton	.06

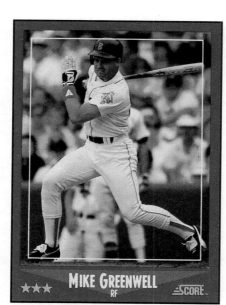

175 Mike Greenwell

1 Don Mattingly

191	Larry Parrish	.06
192	Rey Quinones	.04
193	Joaquin Andujar	.04
194	Tom Brunansky	.10
195	Donnie Moore	.04
196	Dan Pasqua	.08
197	Jim Gantner	.04
198	Mark Eichhorn	.06
199	John Grubb	.04
200	*Bill Ripken*	.20
201	*Sam Horn*	.30
202	Todd Worrell	.08
203	Terry Leach	.04
204	Garth Iorg	.04
205	Brian Dayett	.04
206	Bo Diaz	.04
207	Craig Reynolds	.04
208	Brian Holton	.08
209	Marvelle Wynne (Marvell)	.04
210	Dave Concepcion	.06
211	Mike Davis	.06
212	Devon White	.15
213	Mickey Brantley	.04
214	Greg Gagne	.04
215	Oddibe McDowell	.06
216	Jimmy Key	.06
217	Dave Bergman	.04
218	Calvin Schiraldi	.04
219	Larry Sheets	.06
220	Mike Easler	.06
221	Kurt Stillwell	.08
222	*Chuck Jackson*	.15
223	Dave Martinez	.06
224	Tim Leary	.06
225	Steve Garvey	.20
226	Greg Mathews	.06
227	Doug Sisk	.04
228	Dave Henderson	.08
229	Jimmy Dwyer	.04
230	Larry Owen	.04
231	Andre Thornton	.06
232	Mark Salas	.04
233	Tom Brookens	.04

78 Will Clark

234	Greg Brock	.06
235	Rance Mulliniks	.04
236	Bob Brower	.06
237	Joe Niekro	.06
238	Scott Bankhead	.06
239	Doug DeCinces	.06
240	Tommy John	.12
241	Rich Gedman	.04
242	Ted Power	.04
243	*Dave Meads*	.10
244	Jim Sundberg	.06
245	Ken Oberkfell	.04
246	Jimmy Jones	.04
247	Ken Landreaux	.04
248	Jose Oquendo	.08
249	*John Mitchell*	.15
250	Don Baylor	.08
251	Scott Fletcher	.06
252	Al Newman	.04
253	Carney Lansford	.08
254	Johnny Ray	.06
255	Gary Pettis	.04
256	Ken Phelps	.06
257	Tim Stoddard	.04
260	Sid Bream	.06
261	Tom Neidenfuer (incorrect spelling)	.25
261	Tom Niedenfuer (correct spelling)	.08
262	Rick Dempsey	.06
263	Lonnie Smith	.06
264	Bob Forsch	.06
265	Barry Bonds	.10
266	Willie Randolph	.06
270	Jerry Reuss	.06
273	Steve Balboni	.06
275	John Tudor	.08
276	*Gene Larkin*	.25
277	Harold Reynolds	.08
278	Jerry Browne	.06
279	Willie Upshaw	.06
280	Ted Higuera	.08
283	*Mark Wasinger*	.10

285	Ted Simmons	.08
287	*John Smiley*	.30
290	Dan Quisenberry	.06
293	John Candelaria	.06
297	Terry Franconia (incorrect spelling)	.25
297	Terry Francona (correct spelling)	.08
299	Andres Thomas	.06
301	*Alfredo Pedrique*	.12
302	Jim Lindeman	.06
303	Wally Backman	.06
304	Paul O'Neill	.06
305	Hubie Brooks	.08
307	Bobby Thigpen	.15
308	George Hendrick	.06
310	Ron Guidry	.12
312	*Jose Nunez*	.12
315	Scott McGregor	.06
322	Jose Guzman	.06
325	Gary Carter	.15
326	Tracy Jones	.10
329	*Paul Noce*	.10
331	Goose Gossage	.12
335	Mike Scott	.10
336	Randy Myers	.10
338	Eric Show	.06
339	Mitch Williams	.10
340	Paul Molitor	.10
344	Bob Knepper	.04
345	Mitch Webster	.06
350	Dwight Gooden	.40
351	Dave Righetti	.12
360	Darryl Strawberry	.30
376	*DeWayne Buice*	.15
377	*Bill Pecota*	.15
385	Tony Gwynn	.25
400	Keith Hernandez	.15
414	*Shane Mack*	.15
419	John Christansen (incorrect spelling)	.25
419	John Christensen (correct spelling)	.08

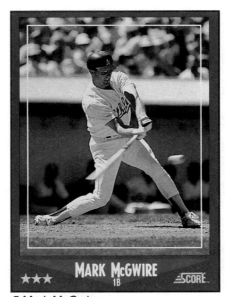

5 Mark McGwire

107 Fred McGriff

432	*Mike Dunne*	.20
436	*Donnell Nixon*	.15
442	*Gerald Young*	.30
450	Dale Murphy	.30
460	Glenn Davis	.12
470	Orel Hershiser	.20
472	*Ellis Burks*	1.50
481	Kevin Mitchell	.75
485	Pete Incaviglia	.12
495	Jesse Orosco	.06
496	*Robby Wine Jr.*	.10
497	*Jeff Montgomery*	.15
500	Reggie Jackson (1968-75, Oakland Athletics)	.20
501	Reggie Jackson (1976, Baltimore Orioles)	.20
502	Reggie Jackson (1977-81, New York Yankees)	.20
503	Reggie Jackson (1982-86, California Angels)	.20
504	Reggie Jackson (1987, Oakland Athletics)	.20
505	Billy Hatcher	.06
507	Willie Hernandez	.06
508	Jose DeLeon	.08
510	Bob Welch	.08
513	Juan Nieves	.06
515	Von Hayes	.12
516	Mark Gubicza	.10
519	Rick Reuschel	.08
520	*Mike Henneman*	.20
522	Jay Howell	.06
524	Manny Trillo	.06
525	Kirk Gibson	.15
526	*Wally Ritchie*	.12
527	Al Nipper	.04
529	Shawon Dunston	.08
530	Jim Clancy	.06
535	John Franco	.08
536	*Paul Kilgus*	.20
537	Darrell Porter	.06
538	Walt Terrell	.06
539	*Bill Long*	.15

540	George Bell	.20
541	Jeff Sellers	.06
542	*Joe Boever*	.12
543	Steve Howe	.06
545	Jack Morris	.15
546	*Todd Benzinger*	.30
549	*Jeff Robinson*	.35
550	Cal Ripken Jr.	.25
551	Jody Davis	.06
552	Kirk McCaskill	.06
554	Darnell Coles	.06
555	Phil Niekro	.25
556	Mike Aldrete	.06
559	Rob Murphy	.06
560	Dennis Rasmussen	.08
562	*Jeff Blauser*	.20
563	Bob Ojeda	.06
564	Dave Dravecky	.06
567	*Tommy Hinzo*	.12
568	*Eric Nolte*	.12
570	*Mark Davidson*	.12
571	*Jim Walewander*	.12
573	Jamie Moyer	.06
575	Nolan Ryan	.50
578	*Jay Aldrich*	.10
579	Claudell Washington	.06
580	Jeff Leonard	.06
583	*Jeff DeWilis*	.15
584	*John Marzano*	.20
585	Bill Gullickson	.06
586	Andy Allanson	.08
589	Dave LaPoint	.06
590	Harold Baines	.10
591	Bill Buckner	.08
592	Carlton Fisk	.25
594	*Doug Jones*	.50
597	*Jose Lind*	.25
598	*Ross Jones*	.12
599	Gary Matthews	.06
600	Fernando Valenzuela	.15
601	Dennis Martinez	.06
602	*Les Lancaster*	.15
603	Ozzie Guillen	.06

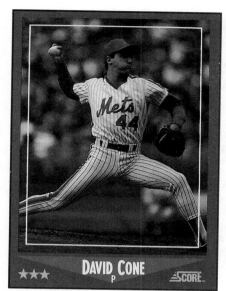
49 David Cone

605	Chili Davis	.06
607	Ivan Calderon	.08
610	Doyle Alexander	.06
611	Mike Bielecki	.06
612	*Shawn Hillegas*	.15
614	Eric Plunk	.06
615	Sid Fernandez	.08
616	Dennis Lamp	.06
619	Don Robinson	.06
620	*John Farreli*	.30
621	*Nelson Liriano*	.15
622	Floyd Bannister	.06
623	Rookie Prospect (*Randy Milligan*)	.25
624	Rookie Prospect (Kevin Elster)	.30
625	Rookie Prospect (*Jody Reed*)	.35
626	Rookie Prospect (Shawn Abner)	.20
627	Rookie Prospect (*Kirt Manwaring*)	.30
628	Rookie Prospect (*Pete Stanicek*)	.20
629	Rookie Prospect (*Rob Ducey*)	.12
631	Rookie Prospect (*Gary Thurman*)	.25
632	Rookie Prospect (*Darrel Akerfelds*)	.12
633	Rookie Prospect (Dave Clark)	.10
634	Rookie Prospect (*Roberto Kelly*)	.80
635	Rookie Prospect (*Keith Hughes*)	.15
636	Rookie Prospect (*John Davis*)	.15
637	Rookie Prospect (*Mike Devereaux*)	.30
638	Rookie Prospect (*Tom Glavine*)	.45
639	Rookie Prospect (*Keith Miller*)	.20

640	Rookie Prospect (*Chris Gwynn*)	.20
641	Rookie Prospect (*Tim Crews*)	.15
642	Rookie Prospect (*Mackey Sasser*)	.20
643	Rookie Prospect (*Vicente Palacios*)	.15
644	Rookie Prospect (Kevin Romine)	.06
645	Rookie Prospect (*Gregg Jefferies*)	3.25
646	Rookie Prospect (*Jeff Treadway*)	.30
647	Rookie Prospect (*Ronnie Gant*)	.30
648	Rookie Sluggers (Mark McGwire, Matt Nokes)	.30
649	Speed and Power (Eric Davis, Tim Raines)	.25
650	Game Breakers (Jack Clark, Don Mattingly)	.60
651	Super Shortstops (Tony Fernandez, Cal Ripken Jr., Alan Trammell)	.15
652	1987 Highlights (Vince Coleman)	.08
653	1987 Highlights (Kirby Puckett)	.12
654	1987 Highlights (Benito Santiago)	.10
655	1987 Highlights (Juan Nieves)	.06
656	1987 Highlights (Steve Bedrosian)	.06
657	1987 Highlights (Mike Schmidt)	.15
658	1987 Highlights (Don Mattingly)	.60
660	1987 Highlights (Paul Molitor)	.08

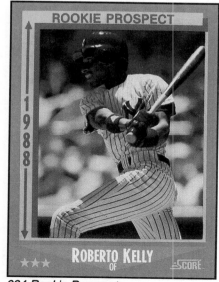
634 Rookie Prospect

118 Matt Williams

253

1988 SCORE ROOKIE & TRADED

This modest, 110-card offering from Score became the sleeper hit of the year in the hobby world. Although Score's debut set of 660 cards earlier in the year was an immediate success, the cards were taken for granted due to their abundant supply. Hobbyists slow to pick up the sets have found that a lesser supply of the fall extension set exists. As with other companies, Score maintained the same card design and marketing formula for the Rookie & Traded set. However, Score grouped all the first-time players in the last half of the set, making things easier for rookie-card specialists. Score rookies include Mark Grace, Ricky Jordan, Chris Sabo, and Walt Weiss. This set is three times as valuable as the 660-card Score set for 1988.

74 Greg Briley

		MINT
Complete set		**$75.00**
Commons		**.08**
1	Jack Clark	$ .20
2	Danny Jackson	.20
4	Kurt Stillwell	.25
5	Tom Brunansky	.20
6	Dennis Lamp	.10
7	Jose DeLeon	.10
8	Tom Herr	.10
10	Kirk Gibson	.20
14	Goose Gossage	.15
15	Bob Welch	.10
18	Dan Quisenberry	.10
20	Lee Smith	.10
25	Graig Nettles	.10
26	Dan Petry	.10
27	Jose Rijo	.15
28	Chili Davis	.15
29	Dickie Thon	.10
30	Mackey Sasser (FC)	.10
34	Phil Bradley	.10
36	Bill Buckner	.10
38	Gary Pettis	.08
44	Ron Kittle	.15
46	Steve Balboni	.08
48	Henry Cotto	.06
49	Dave Henderson	.10
50	Dave Parker	.15
51	Mike Young	.06
52	Mark Salas	.06
53	Mike Davis	.08
55	Don Baylor	.15
56	Dan Pasqua	.10
57	Ernest Riles	.06
61	Jerry Reuss	.10
62	Mike Jackson	.08
63	Floyd Bannister	.10
65	Larry Parrish	.08
66	Jeff Bittiger (FC)	.15
67	Ray Hayward (FC)	.08
68	Ricky Jordan (FC)	5.75
69	Tommy Gregg (FC)	.10
70	Brady Anderson (FC)	.50
71	Jeff Montgomery (FC)	.10

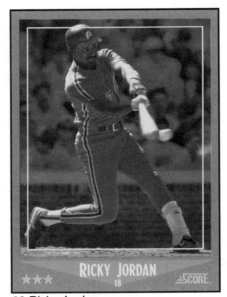
68 Ricky Jordan

72	Darryl Hamilton (FC)	.25
73	Cecil Espy (FC)	.15
74	Greg Briley (FC)	3.25
75	Joey Meyer (FC)	.20
76	Mike Macfarlane (FC)	.25
77	Oswald Peraza (FC)	.20
78	Jack Armstrong (FC)	1.50
79	Don Heinkel (FC)	.20
80	Mark Grace (FC)	27.00
81	Steve Curry (FC)	.20
82	Damon Berryhill (FC)	.25
83	Steve Ellsworth (FC)	.20
84	Pete Smith (FC)	.20
85	Jack McDowell (FC)	.20
86	Rob Dibble (FC)	1.25
87	Brian Harvey (FC)	.25
88	John Dopson (FC)	.25
89	Dave Gallagher (FC)	.25
90	Todd Stottlemyre (FC)	.35
91	Mike Schooler (FC)	1.00
92	Don Gordon (FC)	.10

93	Sil Campusano (FC)	.25
94	Jeff Pico (FC)	.25
95	Jay Buhner (FC)	.45
96	Nelson Santovenia (FC)	.25
97	Al Leiter (FC)	.30
98	Luis Alicea (FC)	.20
99	Pat Borders (FC)	.25
100	Chris Sabo (FC)	3.25
101	Tim Belcher (FC)	1.00
102	Walt Weiss (FC)	2.75
103	Craig Biggio (FC)	3.25
104	Don August (FC)	.25
105	Roberto Alomar (FC)	.60
106	Todd Burns (FC)	.30
107	John Costello (FC)	.20
108	Melido Perez (FC)	.30
109	Darrin Jackson (FC)	.10
110	Orestes Destrade (FC)	.10

103 Craig Biggio

1988 TOPPS

Size and number were Topps' standards this year, although the design was simple—often compared to a magazine cover. Sharply focused action photos have soft backgrounds, while white borders with bold team names across the top are partially obscured by players' heads. Diagonal strips in the lower right-hand corner contain the player name, and backs are gray with complete major league stats. Subsets in this 792-card issue include 26 team leaders with vintage photos, 22 All-Stars, 26 managers, seven Record Breakers (McGwire and Mattingly, among others), five Future Stars (including Kevin Elster), and 10 All-Star rookies honored with special trophy designations (such as second-year player Matt Nokes).

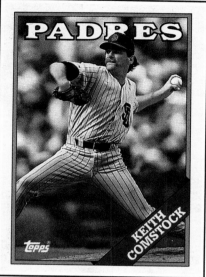

778 Keith Comstock

		MINT
Complete set		$27.00
Commons		.04

1	'87 Record Breakers (Vince Coleman)	$ .08
2	'87 Record Breakers (Don Mattingly)	.60
3	'87 Record Breakers (Mark McGwire)	.60
4	'87 Record Breakers (Eddie Murray) (record headline on front)	2.00
4	'87 Record Breakers (Eddie Murray) (no headline)	.40
5	'87 Record Breakers (Joe Niekro, Phil Niekro)	.10
6	'87 Record Breakers (Nolan Ryan)	.10
7	'87 Record Breakers (Benito Santiago)	.15
8	Kevin Elster (FC)	.25
10	Ryne Sandberg	.15
18	*Al Leiter* (FC) (photo is Steve George; no "NY" on jersey)	1.00
18	*Al Leiter* (FC) (correct photo; "NY" on jersey)	.80
19	*Mark Davidson* (FC)	.12
21	Red Sox Ldrs (Wade Boggs, Spike Owen)	.15
22	Greg Swindell	.15
25	Andres Galarraga	.12
28	*Jose Nunez* (FC)	.20
30	Sid Fernandez	.08
35	Harold Baines	.10
39	Gerald Perry	.08
40	Orel Hershiser	.20
42	*Bill Landrum* (FC)	.20
45	Kent Hrbek	.12
49	Dave Clark (FC)	.10
50	Hubie Brooks	.10
51	Orioles Ldrs (Eddie Murray, Cal Ripken)	.12
55	Phil Bradley	.10
57	*Tim Crews* (FC)	.15
58	Dave Magadan	.10
60	Rickey Henderson	.25

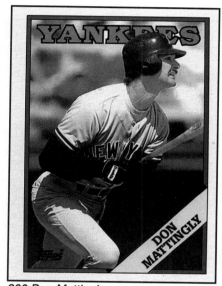

300 Don Mattingly

61	*Mark Knudson* (FC)	.10
62	Jeff Hamilton	.08
63	Jimmy Jones (FC)	.10
64	*Ken Caminiti* (FC)	.35
69	*Mike Hart* (FC)	.10
70	Roger Clemens	.50
72	Dennis Eckersley	.10
75	Joe Carter	.10
80	Mark Langston	.10
81	Reds Ldrs (John Franco, Ron Robinson)	.06
82	*Darrel Akerfelds* (FC)	.12
85	Howard Johnson	.08
89	*Gary Thurman* (FC)	.20
90	Dale Murphy	.30
91	*Joey Cora* (FC)	.12
94	*Chuck Jackson* (FC)	.15
95	Lance Parrish	.12
96	*Todd Benzinger* (FC)	.30
98	*Rene Gonzales* (FC)	.15
100	Jack Clark	.12
102	Barry Larkin	.35
106	*Jim Walewander* (FC)	.12
110	Teddy Higuera	.08

111	Expos Ldrs (Hubie Brooks, Vance Law)	.06
112	*Les Lancaster* (FC)	.15
117	*James Steels* (FC)	.10
118	Bob Welch	.08
119	*Robbie Wine* (FC)	.12
120	Kirby Puckett	.45
125	Bruce Hurst	.10
130	Buddy Bell	.08
135	Dennis Rasmussen	.08
140	Jesse Barfield	.10
141	Royals Ldrs (Bret Saberhagen)	.12
142	Andy Van Slyke	.10
144	*Don Gordon* (FC)	.08
145	Bill Madlock	.08
146	*Donell Nixon* (FC)	.15
147	Bill Buckner	.08
148	Carmelo Martinez	.06
150	Eric Davis	.60
152	*Jody Reed* (FC)	.40
155	Bruce Sutter	.10
159	*Brad Arnsberg* (FC)	.12
160	Willie McGee	.10
165	Robin Yount	.35
166	*Rick Rodriguez* (FC)	.10
169	*Ross Jones* (FC)	.12
170	Rich Gossage	.12
171	Cubs Ldrs (Shawon Dunston, Manny Trillo)	.06
172	*Lloyd McClendon* (FC)	.10
175	Kevin Bass	.06
181	Dave Cone	.80
184	Ivan Calderon	.08
186	Rafael Palmeiro	.35
189	*Wes Gardner* (FC)	.20
192	Devon White	.20

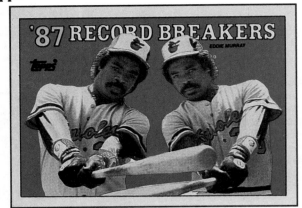

4 '87 Record Breakers

199	*Dave Meads*	.12
200	Wade Boggs	.80
201	Rangers Ldrs (Steve Buechele, Pete Incaviglia, Pete O'Brien, Bobby Valentine)	.06
204	Paul O'Neill (FC)	.08
205	*Nelson Liriano* (FC)	.20
207	*John Mitchell* (FC)	.15
223	Stan Jefferson	.06
229	Jeff Musselman	.06
231	Pirates Ldrs (Barry Bonds, Bobby Bonilla)	.10
238	*Luis Polonia*	.20
240	Lee Smith	.08
246	*Mike Campbell* (FC)	.20
248	Storm Davis	.12
249	Mike Marshall	.10
250	Nolan Ryan	.65
259	Ron Kittle	.06
260	Vince Coleman	.15
261	Giants Ldrs (Will Clark, Candy Maldonado, Kevin Mitchell, Robby Thompson, Jose Uribe)	.10
262	Drew Hall (FC)	.12
263	Glenn Braggs	.08
264	*Les Straker*	.15
265	Bo Diaz	.06
267	*Billy Bean* (FC)	.10
268	Bruce Ruffin	.06
269	*Ellis Burks*	1.25
270	Mike Witt	.08
271	Ken Gerhart	.06
275	Kevin Seitzer	.60
277	Alejando Pena	.06
278	Jose Cruz	.08
280	Pete Incaviglia	.12
283	Phil Lombardi (FC)	.10
284	Larry Bowa	.06
285	Jim Presley	.08
286	*Chuck Crim*	.12
287	Manny Trillo	.06
288	Pat Pacillo	.10
290	Tony Fernandez	.10
291	Astros Ldrs (Kevin Bass, Billy Hatcher)	.06
292	Carney Lansford	.08
293	*Doug Jones* (FC)	.45

294	*Al Pedrique* (FC)	.12
295	Bert Blyleven	.10
297	Zane Smith	.06
300	Don Mattingly	1.75
303	Eric Show	.06
305	Steve Sax	.15
306	Billy Hatcher	.06
308	Lee Mazzilli	.06
309	*Bill Long*	.15
310	Tom Herr	.06
312	Joey Meyer (FC)	.25
315	Dave Parker	.12
316	Jose Rijo	.08
318	Mel Hall	.06
320	Alan Trammell	.15
321	White Sox Ldrs (Harold Baines, Carlton Fisk)	.08
322	*Vicente Palacios* (FC)	.15
324	Danny Jackson	.20
327	Larry Sheets	.06
328	*Greg Cadaret* (FC)	.15
330	Eddie Whitson	.06
331	Brian Downing	.06
333	Wally Backman	.06
335	Claudell Washington	.06
337	Jim Gantner	.06
338	Brian Holton	.08
339	Kurt Stillwell	.08
340	Jack Morris	.15
343	Greg Gagne	.06
344	Tony LaRussa	.06
345	Scott Fletcher	.06
346	Vance Law	.06
348	Jim Eisenreich	.06
350	Will Clark	1.00
351	Cardinals Ldrs (Tony Pena, Red Schoendienst)	.07
352	*Billy Ripken* (FC)	.20
353	Ed Olwine	.06
355	Roger McDowell	.10
360	Tony Gwynn	.25
361	Greg Maddux	.35
363	Willie Fraser	.06
364	Nick Esasky	.15
366	Chet Lemon	.06
367	Tim Leary	.06
368	*Gerald Young* (FC)	.30
370	Jose Canseco	1.50
372	*Matt Williams*	.75

375	Tom Brunansky	.10
376	*Bill Wilkinson*	.12
377	*Sam Horn* (FC)	.30
378	*Todd Frohwirth* (FC)	.15
380	*Joe Magrane*	.50
381	Angels Ldrs (Jack Howell, Wally Joyner)	.12
382	*Keith Miller* (FC)	.20
383	Eric Bell	.06
385	Carlton Fisk	.20
386	Don Mattingly AS	.60
387	Willie Randolph AS	.06
388	Wade Boggs AS	.35
389	Alan Trammell AS	.08
390	George Bell AS	.10
391	Kirby Pucket AS	.12
392	Dave Winfield AS	.12
393	Matt Nokes AS	.15
394	Roger Clemens AS	.15
395	Jimmy Key AS	.06
396	Tom Henke AS	.06
397	Jack Clark AS	.06
398	Juan Samuel AS	.06
399	Tim Wallach AS	.06
400	Ozzie Smith AS	.08
401	Andre Dawson AS	.10
402	Tony Gwynn AS	.15
403	Tim Raines AS	.12
404	Benny Santiago AS	.10
405	Dwight Gooden AS	.15
406	Shane Rawley AS	.06
407	Steve Bedrosian AS	.08
408	Dion James	.06
409	Joel McKeon (FC)	.06
410	Tony Pena	.10
412	Randy Myers	.10
415	Don Carman	.06
416	Keith Moreland	.06
417	*Mark Ciardi* (FC)	.10
419	Scott McGregor	.08
420	Wally Joyner	.35
422	Dave Concepcion	.10
423	*John Smiley*	.30

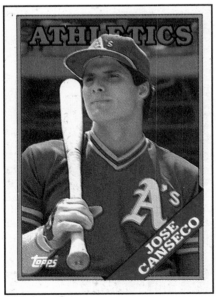

370 Jose Canseco

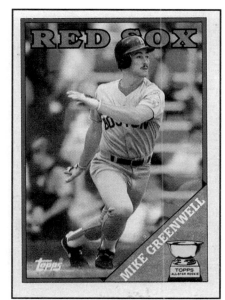

493 Mike Greenwell

750 Bo Jackson

485	Harold Reynolds	.10
486	*Pat Keedy* (FC)	.10
489	Dodgers Ldrs (Pedro Guerrero, Fernando Valenzuela)	.08
490	Larry Parrish	.06
491	B.J. Surhoff	.10
492	Doyle Alexander	.06
493	Mike Greenwell	1.50
494	*Wally Ritchie*	.12
495	Eddie Murray	.25
497	Kevin Mitchell	.30
498	*Bob Boone	.06
500	Andre Dawson	.15
501	Tim Birtsas (FC)	.06
502	Danny Gladden	.06
503	*Junior Noboa* (FC)	.10
505	Willie Upshaw	.06
507	Mark Gubicza	.10
508	Tim Teufel	.06
510	Dave Winfield	.20
511	Joel Davis	.06
512	Alex Trevino	.06
515	Juan Nieves	.08
516	Jim Sundberg	.06
517	Ron Robinson	.06
519	Mariners Ldrs (Phil Bradley, Harold Reynolds)	.08
520	Dave Smith	.08
522	*Bob Patterson* (FC)	.12
525	Marty Barrett	.06
526	Juan Berenguer	.06
528	Checklist 397-528 (number 455 is Steve Carlton)	.40
528	Checklist 397-528 (number 455 is Shawn Hillegas)	.08
529	Tim Burke	.06
530	Gary Carter	.15
533	*John Farrell* (FC)	.30
534	John Wathan	.06
535	Ron Guidry	.15
539	Mike LaValliere	.06
540	Bret Saberhagen	.20

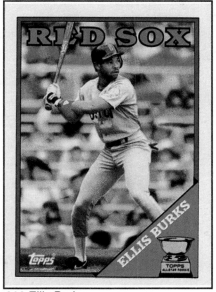

269 Ellis Burks

425	Jeff Reardon	.08
427	*Paul Kilgus* (FC)	.20
428	John Shelby	.06
429	Tigers Ldrs (Kirk Gibson, Alan Trammell)	.08
430	*Glenn Davis*	1.00
432	Mike Moore	.08
433	*Bill Pecota* (FC)	.15
434	Rick Aguilera	.06
435	Mike Pagliarulo	.06
436	Mike Bielecki	.06
437	*Fred Manrique* (FC)	.12
438	*Rob Ducey* (FC)	.12
439	Dave Martinez	.08
440	Steve Bedrosian	.10
442	*Tom Bolton* (FC)	.15
443	Ken Griffey	.08
444	Cal Ripken, Sr.	.06
445	Mike Krukow	.06
446	Doug DeCinces	.08
447	*Jeff Montgomery* (FC)	.30
448	Mike Davis	.06
449	*Jeff Robinson*	.35
450	Barry Bonds	.10
452	Willie Wilson	.10
455	*Shawn Hillegas* (FC)	.15
457	Terry Leach	.06
459	Yankees Ldrs (Willie Randolph, Dave Winfield)	.08
460	Ozzie Smith	.12
463	*Fred McGriff*	1.00
465	Paul Molitor	.10
466	Jerry Mumphrey	.06
470	*Dwight Evans	.10
472	Robby Thompson	.06
473	Joe Niekro	.06
475	*Pete Rose	.20
476	Dave Stewart	.08
478	Sid Bream	.06
479	Brett Butler	.06
480	Dwight Gooden	.40
482	Mark Davis	.10
483	*Rod Booker* (FC)	.12

542	*Paul Noce* (FC)	.10
543	Kent Tekulve	.08
544	Jim Traber	.06
545	Don Baylor	.08
546	John Candelaria	.08
547	*Felix Fermin* (FC)	.12
548	*Shane Mack*	.15
549	Braves Ldrs (Ken Griffey, Dion James, Dale Murphy, Gerald Perry)	.08
550	Pedro Guerrero	.15
551	Terry Steinbach	.15
553	Tracy Jones	.10
555	Brook Jacoby	.08
556	*Stan Clarke* (FC)	.12
558	Bob Ojeda	.08
559	*Ken Williams* (FC)	.15
560	Tim Wallach	.08
561	Rick Cerone	.04
562	Jim Lindeman	.08
563	Jose Guzman	.06
564	Frank Lucchesi	.04
565	Lloyd Moseby	.08
566	*Charlie O'Brien* (FC)	.12
567	Mike Diaz	.04
568	Chris Brown	.04
569	Charlie Leibrandt	.06
570	Jeffrey Leonard	.08
571	Mark Williamson (FC)	.12
572	Chris James	.15
574	Graig Nettles	.08
575	Don Sutton	.12
576	*Tommy Hinzo* (FC)	.12
577	Tom Browning	.08
578	Gary Gaetti	.10
579	Mets Ldrs (Gary Carter, Kevin McReynolds)	.08
580	Mark McGwire	1.00
581	Tito Landrum	.04
582	*Mike Henneman*	.20
583	Dave Valle (FC)	.06
584	Steve Trout	.04
585	Ozzie Guillen	.06

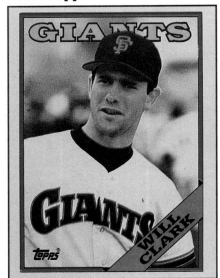

350 Will Clark

586	Bob Forsch	.06
588	*Jeff Parrett* (FC)	.20
590	George Bell	.20
591	Doug Drabek	.06
592	Dale Sveum	.06
593	Bob Tewksbury	.04
594	Bobby Valentine	.04
595	Frank White	.06
596	John Kruk	.12
597	Gene Garber	.06
598	Lee Lacy	.04
599	Calvin Schiraldi	.08
600	Mike Schmidt	.50
602	Mike Aldrete	.06
603	Rob Murphy	.06
604	Chris Bando	.04
605	Kirk Gibson	.15
606	Moose Haas	.04
607	Mickey Hatcher	.04
608	Charlie Kerfeld	.04
609	Twins Ldrs (Gary Gaetti, Kent Hrbek)	.08
610	Keith Hernandez	.15
611	Tommy John	.12
612	Curt Ford	.04
613	Bobby Thigpen	.15
614	Herm Winningham	.04
615	Jody Davis	.06
616	*Jay Aldrich* (FC)	.10
617	Oddibe McDowell	.06
618	Cecil Fielder	.75
619	*Mike Dunne*	.15
620	Cory Snyder	.15
621	Gene Nelson	.04
622	Kal Daniels	.12
623	Mike Flanagan	.06
624	Jim Leyland	.04
625	Frank Viola	.12
626	Glenn Wilson	.06
627	*Joe Boever* (FC)	.12
628	Dave Henderson	.10
629	Kelly Downs	.08
630	Darrell Evans	.08

631	Jack Howell	.06
632	*Steve Shields*	.06
633	*Barry Lyons*	.12
634	Jose DeLeon	.12
635	Terry Pendleton	.08
636	Charles Hudson	.04
637	*Jay Bell* (FC)	.15
638	Steve Balboni	.06
639	Brewers Ldrs (Glenn Braggs, Tony Muser)	.06
640	Garry Templeton	.06
641	Rick Honeycutt	.04
642	Bob Dernier	.04
643	*Rocky Childress* (FC)	.12
644	Terry McGriff (FC)	.06
645	*Matt Nokes*	.50
647	Pascual Perez	.08
648	Al Newman	.04
649	*DeWayne Buice*	.15
650	Cal Ripken	.25
651	*Mike Jackson* (FC)	.15
652	Bruce Benedict	.04
653	Jeff Sellers	.04
654	Roger Craig	.06
655	*Len Dykstra	.12
656	Lee Guetterman	.06
657	Gary Redus	.04
658	Tim Conroy	.04
659	Bobby Meacham	.04
660	Rick Reuschel	.10
661	Turn Back The Clock (Nolan Ryan)	.25
662	Turn Back The Clock (Jim Rice)	.08
663	Turn Back The Clock (Ron Blomberg)	.04
664	Turn Back The Clock (Bob Gibson)	.08
665	Turn Back The Clock (Stan Musial)	.12
666	Mario Soto	.06
667	Luis Quinones	.04
668	Walt Terrell	.06

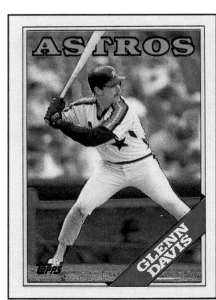

430 Glenn Davis

463 Fred McGriff

669	Phillies Ldrs (Lance Parrish, Mike Ryan)	.06
670	Dan Plesac	.08
671	Tim Laudner	.04
672	*John Davis* (FC)	.15
673	Tony Phillips	.08
674	Mike Fitzgerald	.04
675	Jim Rice	.20
676	Ken Dixon	.04
677	Eddie Milner	.04
678	Jim Acker	.04
679	Darrell Miller	.04
680	Charlie Hough	.08
681	Bobby Bonilla	.12
682	Jimmy Key	.08
683	Julio Franco	.08
684	Hal Lanier	.04
685	Ron Darling	.10
686	Terry Francona	.04
687	Mickey Brantley	.04
688	Jim Winn	.04
689	*Tom Pagnozzi*	.12
690	Jay Howell	.08
691	Dan Pasqua	.08
692	Mike Birkbeck	.06
693	Benny Santiago	.60
694	*Eric Nolte* (FC)	.12
695	Shawon Dunston	.08
696	Duane Ward	.06
697	Steve Lombardozzi	.08
698	Brad Havens	.04
699	Padres Ldrs (Tony Gwynn, Benny Santiago)	.12
700	George Brett	.30
701	Sammy Stewart	.04
702	Mike Gallego	.04
703	Bob Brenly	.04
704	Dennis Boyd	.06
705	Juan Samuel	.10
706	Rick Mahler	.06
707	Fred Lynn	.10
708	Gus Polidor (FC)	.06
709	George Frazier	.04

710	Darryl Strawberry	.30	740	Rick Sutcliffe .08
711	Bill Gullickson	.06	741	Mike Easler .04
712	John Moses	.04	742	Mark Clear .04
713	Willie Hernandez	.06	743	Larry Herndon .04
717	Jay Baller (FC)	.06	744	Whitey Herzog .06
718	Mike Felder	.04	745	Bill Doran .08
719	Denny Walling	.04	746	*Gene Larkin* .25
720	Tim Raines	.20	747	Bobby Witt .08
721	Pete O'Brien	.10	748	Reid Nichols .06
722	Manny Lee	.04	749	Mark Eichhorn .06
723	Bob Kipper	.04	750	Bo Jackson 1.25
724	Danny Tartabull	.15	751	Jim Morrison .04
725	Mike Boddicker	.06	752	Mark Grant .06
726	Alfredo Griffin	.06	753	Danny Heep .04
727	Greg Booker	.04	754	Mike LaCoss .04
728	Andy Allanson	.04	755	Ozzie Virgil .04
729	Blue Jays Ldrs (George Bell, Fred McGriff)	.10	756	Mike Maddux .04
			757	*John Marzano* .20
730	John Franco	.10	758	Eddie Williams (FC) .20
731	Rick Schu	.04	759	A's Ldrs (Jose Canseco, Mark McGwire) .45
732	Dave Palmer	.04		
733	Spike Owen	.04	760	Mike Scott .10
734	Craig Lefferts	.06	761	Tony Armas .06
735	Kevin McReynolds	.20	762	Scott Bradley .04
736	Matt Young	.04	763	Doug Sisk .04
737	Butch Wynegar	.04	764	Greg Walker .04
738	Scott Bankhead	.06	765	Neal Heaton .04
739	Daryl Boston	.04	766	Henry Cotto .06

1988 Topps/1988 Topps Traded

767	*Jose Lind* (FC)	.20
768	Dickie Noles	.04
769	Cecil Cooper	.08
770	Lou Whitaker	.20
771	Ruben Sierra	.35
772	Sal Butera	.04
774	Gene Mauch	.06
775	Dave Stieb	.08
777	Lonnie Smith	.06
778	*Keith Comstock* (FC) (team name in white)	7.00
778	*Keith Comstock* (FC) (team name in blue)	.12
779	*Tom Glavine* (FC)	.25
780	Fernando Valenzuela	.15
781	*Keith Hughes* (FC)	.12
782	*Jeff Ballard* (FC)	.30
783	Ron Roenicke	.04
784	Joe Sambito	.04
785	Alvin Davis	.10
786	Joe Price	.04
787	Bill Almon	.04
788	Ray Searage	.04
789	Indians Ldrs (Joe Carter, Cory Snyder)	.08
790	Dave Righetti	.12
791	Ted Simmons	.08
792	John Tudor	.08

1988 TOPPS TRADED

Topps revitalized its standard 132-card Traded set by infusing the series with a subset portraying players from the 1988 U.S. Olympic Team wearing their colorful Team USA uniforms. The Olympians won the gold medal, and the cards feature big-name rookies who enjoy above-average acclaim. Jim Abbott, Andy Benes, and Robin Ventura highlight this 20-card subset. The 1988 edition promises to be a quality investment as more Olympians achieve fame in the big leagues. Other notables in the remainder of the set include Mark Grace and Chris Sabo. The Traded set maintains the Topps' tradition of being sold only through hobby dealers in complete, boxed sets.

1 Jim Abbott

		MINT
Complete set		**$39.00**
Commons		**.06**

1	Jim Abbott (FC) (USA)	$13.00
3	Luis Alicea (FC)	.15
4	Roberto Alomar (FC)	1.75
5	Brady Anderson (FC)	.40
6	Jack Armstrong (FC)	.75
7	Don August	.15
9	Brett Barberie (FC) (USA)	.40
10	Jose Bautista (FC)	.10
11	Don Baylor	.10
12	Tim Belcher	.20
13	Buddy Bell	.10
14	Andy Benes (FC) (USA)	3.75
15	Damon Berryhill (FC)	.35

17	Pat Borders (FC)	.20
18	Phil Bradley	.10
19	Jeff Branson (FC) (USA)	.40
20	Tom Brunansky	.15
21	Jay Buhner (FC)	.35
23	Jim Campanis (FC) (USA)	.40
24	Sil Campusano (FC)	.25
26	Jose Cecena (FC)	.15
28	Jack Clark	.15
29	Kevin Coffman (FC)	.10
30	Pat Combs (FC) (USA)	2.00
34	*Jose DeLeon	.10
35	Richard Dotson	.10
36	Cecil Espy (FC)	.08
38	Mike Fiore (FC) (USA)	.60
39	Ron Gant (FC)	.30
40	Kirk Gibson	.15

41	Rich Gossage	.15
42	Mark Grace (FC)	3.00
44	Ty Griffin (FC) (USA)	1.25
45	Bryan Harvey (FC)	.35

259

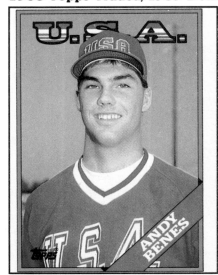

14 Andy Benes

47	Ray Hayward (FC)	.08
48	Dave Henderson	.15
49	Tom Herr	.10

50	Bob Horner	.10
51	Ricky Horton	.08
52	Jay Howell	.10
54	Jeff Innis (FC)	.15
55	Danny Jackson	.15
56	Darrin Jackson (FC)	.10
57	Roberto Kelly (FC)	.75
58	Ron Kittle	.15
59	Ray Knight	.08
60	Vance Law	.08
62	Mike Macfarlane (FC)	.20
63	Scotti Madison (FC)	.15
64	Kirt Manwaring (FC)	.20
66	Tino Martinez (FC) (USA)	1.50
67	Billy Masse (FC) (USA)	.40
68	Jack McDowell (FC)	.20
71	Mickey Morandini (FC) (USA)	.50
72	Keith Moreland	.08
74	Charles Nagy (FC) (USA)	.65
80	Mark Parent (FC)	.20
81	Dave Parker	.15
82	Dan Pasqua	.10
83	Melido Perez (FC)	.30
84	Steve Peters (FC)	.15
85	Dan Petry	.08
87	Jeff Pico (FC)	.15
88	Jim Poole (FC) (USA)	.40

91	Dennis Rasmussen	.10
92	Jose Rijo	.08
94	Luis Rivera (FC)	.08
95	Doug Robbins (FC) (USA)	.40
96	*Frank Robinson	.10
98	Chris Sabo (FC)	1.50
102	Nelson Santovenia (FC)	.20
103	Mackey Sasser (FC)	.10
105	Mike Schooler (FC)	.35
106	Scott Servais (FC) (USA)	.40
107	Dave Silvestri (FC) (USA)	.40
109	Joe Slusarski (FC) (USA)	.40
110	Lee Smith	.10
111	*Pete Smith (FC)	.10
113	Ed Sprague (FC) (USA)	.60
114	Steve Stanicek (FC)	.15
115	Kurt Stillwell	.10
116	Todd Stottlemyre (FC)	.30
119	Scott Terry (FC)	.10
122	Jeff Treadway (FC)	.20
123	Willie Upshaw	.08
124	Robin Ventura (FC) (USA)	3.00
126	Walt Weiss (FC)	1.00
127	Bob Welch	.10
128	David Wells (FC)	.08
129	Glenn Wilson	.10
130	Ted Wood (FC) (USA)	.60

1989 DONRUSS

Once again a Diamond King from each team appears at the beginning of this 660-card, standard-dimension set. The painted portraits display striking colors, while the borders contrast white and black stripes on the sides and use fading neon colors for the tops and bottoms. Player names appear in a simple print style, with the upper right-hand corner reserved for more elaborate team names or subset designations, including Rated Rookies. The white backs, while criticized for having few statistics, are packed with full names, team records, specifics of a player's acquisition, and detailed career highlights.

33 Ken Griffey Jr.

		MINT
Complete set		**$25.00**
Commons		**.04**

1	Mike Greenwell (DK)	$ .60
2	Bobby Bonilla (DK)	.12
3	Pete Incaviglia (DK)	.12
4	Chris Sabo (DK)	.80
5	Robin Yount (DK)	.25
6	Tony Gwynn (DK)	.35
7	Carlton Fisk (DK)	.12
8	Cory Snyder (DK)	.15
9	David Cone (DK)	.35
10	Kevin Seitzer (DK)	.25
11	Rick Reuschel (DK)	.10
12	Johnny Ray (DK)	.10
14	Andres Galarraga (DK)	.15
15	Kirk Gibson (DK)	.20
16	Fred McGriff (DK)	.25
17	Mark Grace (DK)	1.25
18	Jeff Robinson (DK)	.12

19	Vince Coleman (DK)	.20
20	Dave Henderson (DK)	.10
22	Gerald Perry (DK)	.10
23	Frank Viola (DK)	.15
24	Steve Bedrosian (DK)	.10
25	Glenn Davis (DK)	.15
26	Don Mattingly (DK)	1.25
28	*Sandy Alomar Jr.* (FC) (RR)	2.00
29	*Steve Searcy* (FC)(RR)	.30
30	*Cameron Drew* (FC)(RR)	.30
31	*Gary Sheffield* (FC) (RR)	2.00
32	*Erik Hanson* (FC) (RR)	.35
33	*Ken Griffey Jr.* (FC) (RR)	7.50
34	*Greg Harris* (FC) (RR)	.30
35	Gregg Jefferies (RR)	2.50
36	*Luis Medina* (FC) (RR)	.40
37	*Carlos Quintana* (RR)	.45
38	*Felix Jose* (FC) (RR)	.25
39	*Cris Carpenter* (FC) (RR)	.35
40	*Ron Jones* (FC) (RR)	.35

41	*Dave West* (FC) (RR)	.60
42	*Randy Johnson* (FC) (RR)	.45
43	*Mike Harkey* (FC) (RR)	.40
44	*Pete Harnisch* (FC) (RR)	.30
45	*Tom Gordon* (FC) (RR)	2.00
46	*Gregg Olson* (FC) (RR)	1.50
47	*Alex Sanchez* (FC) (RR)	.25

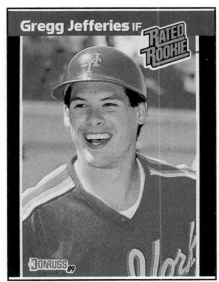

35 Gregg Jefferies

48	Ruben Sierra	.50
49	Rafael Palmeiro	.25
50	Ron Gant	.15
51	Cal Ripken, Jr.	.30
52	Wally Joyner	.20
53	Gary Carter	.20
54	Andy Van Slyke	.12
55	Robin Yount	.25
56	Pete Incaviglia	.10
57	Greg Brock	.06
58	Melido Perez	.06
60	Gary Pettis	.06
61	Danny Tartabull	.15
63	Ozzie Smith	.12
64	Gary Gaetti	.12
65	Mark Davis	.08
66	Lee Smith	.08
67	Dennis Eckersley	.10
68	Wade Boggs	.90
69	Mike Scott	.10
70	Fred McGriff	.50
73	Mel Hall	.06
74	Don Mattingly	1.50
76	Juan Samuel	.10
78	Dave Righetti	.12
80	Eric Davis	.40
82	Todd Worrell	.08
83	Joe Carter	.12
84	Steve Sax	.12
85	Frank White	.06
86	John Kruk	.10
88	Alan Ashby	.04
90	Frank Tanana	.06
91	Jose Canseco	1.50
92	Barry Bonds	.12
95	Mark McGwire	.60
96	Eddie Murray	.25
97	Tim Raines	.25
99	Kevin McReynolds	.12
101	Carlton Fisk	.20
104	Dale Murphy	.30
105	Ryne Sandberg	.25
110	Mike Marshall	.10

112	Tom Brunansky	.10
115	Keith Brown (FC)	.20
116	Matt Nokes	.15
117	Keith Hernandez	.20
118	Bob Forsch	.06
119	Bert Blyleven	.10
122	Jim Rice	.25
124	Danny Jackson	.12
126	Brian Fisher	.06
128	Tony Gwynn	.30
130	Andres Galarraga	.15
131	Jose Uribe	.04
132	Kirk Gibson	.20
135	Greg Walker	.06
136	Kirk McKaskill	.06
139	Rob Murphy	.04
140	Mike Aldrete	.06
142	Scott Fletcher	.06
143	Steve Balboni	.06
144	Bret Saberhagen	.15
145	Ozzie Virgil	.04
146	Dale Sveum	.04
147	Darryl Strawberry	.35
148	Harold Baines	.12
149	George Bell	.25
150	Dave Parker	.12
151	Bobby Bonilla	.12
152	Mookie Wilson	.06
153	Ted Power	.04
154	Nolan Ryan	.50
155	Jeff Reardon	.08
156	Tim Wallach	.08
157	Jamie Moyer	.04
158	Rich Gossage	.10
159	Dave Winfield	.25
160	Von Hayes	.10
161	Willie McGee	.10
163	Tony Pena	.06
164	Mike Morgan	.04
166	Mike Stanley	.04
167	Andre Dawson	.20
168	Joe Boever (FC)	.08
169	Pete Stanicek	.06

28 Sandy Alomar Jr.

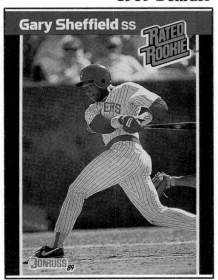

31 Gary Sheffield

170	*Bob Boone	.08
171	Ron Darling	.10
172	Bob Walk	.06
173	Rob Deer	.08
175	Ted Higuera	.08
176	Ozzie Guillen	.12
178	Doyle Alexander	.06
179	Mark Gubicza	.10
180	Alan Trammell	.15
181	Vince Coleman	.15
182	Kirby Puckett	.45
183	Chris Brown	.06
185	Stan Javier	.04
186	Mike Greenwell	.60
187	Billy Hatcher	.06
188	Jimmy Key	.08
189	Nick Esasky	.12
190	Don Slaught	.04
191	Cory Snyder	.15
193	Mike Schmidt	.50
194	Kevin Gross	.04
195	John Tudor	.10
196	Neil Allen	.04
197	Orel Hershiser	.25
198	Kal Daniels	.15
199	Kent Hrbek	.15
201	*Joe Magrane	.08
202	Scott Bailes	.04
203	Tim Belcher	.10
204	George Brett	.30
205	Benito Santiago	.15
206	Tony Fernandez	.10
207	Gerald Young	.10
208	Bo Jackson	.85
209	Chet Lemon	.06
210	Storm Davis	.10
211	Doug Drabek	.06
213	Devon White	.10
214	Dave Stewart	.10
216	Bryn Smith	.06
217	Brett Butler	.06
218	Bob Ojeda	.06
219	Steve Rosenberg (FC)	.20

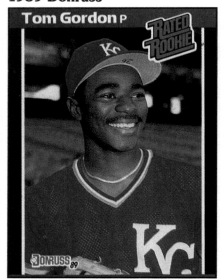

45 Tom Gordon

280	Roger Clemens	.50
281	Greg Mathews	.06
283	Paul Kilgus	.20
284	Jose Guzman	.08
286	Charlie Puleo	.06
287	Joe Orsulak	.06
288	Jack Howell	.06
289	Kevin Elster	.08
290	Jose Lind	.10
291	Paul Molitor	.12
292	Cecil Espy	.08
293	Bill Wegman	.04
294	Dan Pasqua	.08
298	Lou Whitaker	.20
299	Ken Dayley	.04
301	Tommy Herr	.06
303	Ellis Burks	.60
304	Curt Young	.06
305	Jody Reed	.10
306	Bill Doran	.08
307	David Wells	.06
310	Julio Franco	.10
311	Jack Clark	.15
312	Chris James	.08
314	John Shelby	.04
315	Al Leiter	.15
316	Mike Davis	.06
317	*Chris Sabo*	.70
318	Greg Gagne	.06
320	John Farrell	.10
322	Kurt Stillwell	.06
323	Shawn Abner	.10
325	Kevin Bass	.06
326	Pat Tabler	.06
329	John Smiley	.10
331	Johnny Ray	.08
332	Bob Welch	.08
333	Larry Sheets	.06
334	Jeff Parrett	.06
336	Randy Myers	.10
337	Ken Williams	.06
339	Joey Meyer	.06
340	Dion James	.04

255 Mark Grace

220	Hubie Brooks	.08
221	B.J. Surhoff	.08
222	Rick Mahler	.06
223	Rick Sutcliffe	.08
224	Neal Heaton	.04
225	Mitch Williams	.10
227	Mark Langston	.12
232	Greg Swindell	.10
233	John Franco	.10
234	Jack Morris	.15
235	Howard Johnson	.15
236	Glenn Davis	.15
237	Frank Viola	.15
238	Kevin Seitzer	.25
240	*Dwight Evans	.10
242	Bo Diaz	.06
245	Rickey Henderson	.35
246	Roberto Alomar	.25
247	Jimmy Jones	.04
249	Will Clark	.80
250	Fernando Valenzuela	.15
252	Sid Bream	.06
253	Steve Lyons	.06
255	Mark Grace	2.00
257	Barry Larkin	.20
258	Mike Krukow	.06
259	Billy Ripken	.06
260	Cecilio Guante	.04
261	Scott Bradley	.04
263	Pete Smith	.08
265	Roger McDowell	.10
266	Bobby Thigpen	.08
268	Terry Steinbach	.08
269	Mike Dunne	.06
270	Dwight Gooden	.20
271	Mike Heath	.04
272	Dave Smith	.08
274	Tim Burke	.06
275	Damon Berryhill	.12
276	Vance Law	.06
277	Rich Dotson	.06
278	Lance Parrish	.12
279	Denny Walling	.04

624 Ricky Jordan

342	Tom Foley	.04
343	Geno Petralli	.04
344	Dan Petry	.06
345	Alvin Davis	.12
348	Danny Cox	.06
349	Dave Stieb	.08
350	Jay Bell	.04
351	Jeff Treadway	.10
352	Luis Salazar	.04
355	Gene Larkin	.10
356	Steve Farr	.06
358	Todd Benzinger	.12
360	Paul O'Neill	.04
361	Ron Hassey	.04
362	Jim Gott	.04
363	Ken Phelps	.06
365	Randy Ready	.04
366	*Nelson Santovenia* (FC)	.20
367	Kelly Downs	.08
369	Phil Bradley	.10
372	Mike Witt	.08
373	Greg Maddux	.10
375	Jose Rijo	.08
376	Joe Price	.04
379	Jim Presley	.06
380	Brad Wellman	.04
381	Tom Glavine	.10
382	Dan Plesac	.08
384	*Dave Gallagher*	.25
385	Tom Henke	.06
386	Luis Polonia	.08
387	Junior Ortiz	.04
388	David Cone	.35
389	Dave Bergman	.04
390	Danny Darwin	.04
391	Dan Gladden	.04
392	*John Dopson*	.25
393	Frank DiPino	.04
394	Al Nipper	.04
395	Willie Randolph	.06
396	Don Carman	.04
397	Scott Terry	.06
398	Rick Cerone	.04

399	Tom Pagnozzi	.04
401	Mickey Tettleton	.08
402	Curtis Wilkerson	.04
403	Jeff Russell	.08
404	Pat Perry	.04
405	*Jose Alvarez* (FC)	.15
406	Rick Schu	.06
407	*Sherman Corbett* (FC)	.15
408	Dave Magadan	.10
409	Bob Kipper	.04
410	Don August	.06
412	Chris Bosio	.06
413	Jerry Reuss	.08
416	*Mike Macfarlane*	.20
417	Pat Sheridan	.04
418	Pedro Guerrero	.15
419	*Alan Anderson	.06
420	*Mark Parent*	.20
423	Bruce Hurst	.08
424	Dave Meads	.06
425	Jesse Barfield	.06
426	*Rob Dibble* (FC)	.45
427	Joel Skinner	.04
428	Ron Kittle	.10
429	Rick Rhoden	.06
433	Roberto Kelly	.10
436	Al Newman	.04
437	Jose DeLeon	.12
438	Doug Jones	.10
443	*John Fishel* (FC)	.20
445	*Paul Gibson*	.15
446	Walt Weiss	.50
447	Glenn Wilson	.06
448	Mike Moore	.10
449	Chili Davis	.08
451	*Jose Bautista*	.20
452	Rex Hudler	.04
453	Bob Brenly	.04
458	Bruce Sutter	.08
460	Joe Hesketh	.04
461	Bobby Witt	.08
464	*Ramon Martinez* (FC)	.50
466	Luis Alicea	.20

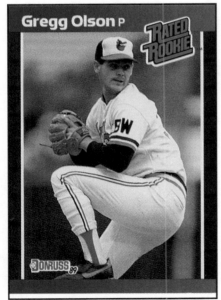

46 Gregg Olson

Don Mattingly 1B

74 Don Mattingly

469	Jeff Reed	.04
470	Jeff Robinson	.12
471	Sid Fernandez	.08
472	Terry Puhl	.04
473	Charlie Lea	.04
474	*Israel Sanchez* (FC)	.15
479	Greg Cadaret	.10
480	*Randy Kramer* (FC)	.15
481	*Dave Eiland* (FC)	.20
482	Eric Show	.06
483	Garry Templeton	.06
485	Kevin Mitchell	.60
486	Tim Crews	.04
487	Mike Maddux	.04
488	Dave LaPoint	.06
491	*Doug Dascenzo* (FC)	.25
492	Willie Upshaw	.06
493	*Jack Armstrong* (FC)	.65
494	Kirt Manwaring	.10
495	Jeff Ballard	.06
496	Jeff Kunkel	.04
497	Mike Campbell	.08
498	Gary Thurman	.10
499	Zane Smith	.06
501	Mike Birkbeck	.06
502	Terry Leach	.04
504	Manny Lee	.04
505	*Doug Jennings*	.20
507	Tim Teufel	.04
510	Fred Toliver	.04
511	*Brian Holman* (FC)	.30
513	*Jeff Pico* (FC)	.25
514	Charles Hudson	.04
515	Bruce Ruffin	.04
517	Jeff Sellers	.06
518	*John Costello* (FC)	.20
519	*Brady Anderson*	.35
522	Drew Hall	.08
523	*Mark Lemke* (FC)	.20
524	*Oswald Peraza* (FC)	.20
525	*Bryan Harvey*	.25
527	Tom Prince	.06
528	Mark Clear	.04

529	Jerry Browne	.06
532	Chris Speier	.04
533	Darrell Evans	.08
535	Eric King	.04
536	*Ken Hill* (FC)	.25
537	Randy Bush	.04
538	Shane Mack	.06
540	Gene Nelson	.04
541	Wes Gardner	.06
542	Ken Caminiti	.10
543	Duane Ward	.06
544	*Norm Charlton* (FC)	.25
545	*Hal Morris* (FC)	.20
547	*Hensley Meulens* (FC)	.60
548	Greg Harris	.04
552	Tim Leary	.06
555	*Tim Jones* (FC)	.15
556	Bud Black	.04
558	*Jose DeJesus* (FC)	.20
559	Dennis Rasmussen	.08
560	*Pat Borders*	.20
561	*Craig Biggio* (FC)	.90
562	*Luis de los Santos* (FC)	.15
563	Fred Lynn	.10
564	*Todd Burns* (FC)	.30
567	Willie Fraser	.04
569	*Craig Worthington*	.30
570	*Johnny Paredes*	.20
572	Barry Lyons	.04
573	Bill Long	.06
574	Tracy Jones	.10
575	Juan Nieves	.06
576	Andres Thomas	.06
577	*Rolando Roomes* (FC)	.35
579	*Chad Kreuter* (FC)	.20
580	Tony Armas	.06
581	Jay Buhner	.10
582	Ricky Horton	.06
583	Andy Hawkins	.06
584	*Sil Campusano*	.20
585	Dave Clark	.06
586	*Van Snider* (FC)	.20
589	*William Brennan* (FC)	.20

91 Jose Canseco

17 Mark Grace (DK)

590	German Gonzalez (FC)	.20
591	Ernie Whitt	.08
592	Jeff Blauser	.08

593	Spike Owen	.04
594	Matt Williams	.35
596	Steve Ontiveros	.04
597	Scott Medvin (FC)	.20
598	Hipolito Pena (FC)	.15
599	Jerald Clark (FC)	.25
601	Carmelo Martinez	.04
602	Mike LaCoss	.04
603	Mike Devereaux	.15
604	Alex Madrid (FC)	.15
605	Gary Redus	.04
606	Lance Johnson	.15
607	Terry Clark (FC)	.15
609	Scott Jordan (FC)	.15
610	Jay Howell	.06
611	Francisco Melendez (FC)	.25
613	Kevin Brown	.20
614	Dave Valle	.06
615	Tim Laudner	.04
616	Andy Nezelek (FC)	.20
617	Chuck Crim	.06
618	Jack Savage (FC)	.10
619	Adam Peterson (FC)	.10
620	Todd Stottlemyre	.10
621	Lance Blankenship (FC)	.25
622	Miguel Garcia (FC)	.15
624	Ricky Jordan (FC)	1.75
626	John Moses	.04

628	Mike Smithson	.04
629	Scott Sanderson	.05
631	Marvin Freeman	.05
632	Mike Young	.04
633	Dennis Lamp	.04
634	Dante Bichette (FC)	.35
635	Curt Schilling (FC)	.15
636	Scott May (FC)	.15
637	Mike Schooler (FC)	.40
638	Rick Leach	.04
639	Tom Lampkin (FC)	.15
640	Brian Meyer (FC)	.15
642	John Smoltz (FC)	.60
643	40/40 Club (Jose Canseco)	.85
645	Edgar Martinez (FC)	.45
646	Dennis Cook (FC)	.50
648	59 and Counting (Orel Hershiser)	.15
649	Rod Nichols (FC)	.15
650	Jody Davis	.06
651	Bob Milacki (FC)	.25
652	Mike Jackson	.06
653	Derek Lilliquist (FC)	.35
655	Mike Diaz	.06
657	Jerry Reed	.04
658	Kevin Blankenship (FC)	.20
660	Eric Hetzel (FC)	.20

1989 DONRUSS ROOKIES

Rookie fever raged on in 1989, as evidenced by the popularity of the 1989 Donruss set called "The Rookies." The concept was originated by Donruss in 1986, and the company continued in 1989 to feature 55 players and a checklist card in a boxed, complete set. Ironically, more than a third of the 55 depicted "rookies" actually had made prior appearances in Donruss sets, some more than a year before. This hobby-wise company, however, gave leading newcomers encore appearances in their season-ending set. The cards closely resemble the standard 660-card set from earlier in the year except for "The Rookies" logo found on the upper right of each card.

26 Jerome Walton

		MINT
Complete set		**$32.00**
Commons		**.10**

1	Gary Sheffield	$1.00
2	Gregg Jefferies	1.00
3	Ken Griffey, Jr.	5.50
4	Tom Gordon	2.50
5	Billy Spiers (FC)	.40
6	Deion Sanders (FC)	1.25
8	Steve Carter (FC)	.20
9	Francisco Oliveras (FC)	.15
11	Bob Geren (FC)	.50
12	Tony Castillo	.20
13	Kenny Rogers (FC)	.20
14	Carlos Martinez (FC)	.20

16	Jim Abbott	3.50
18	Mark Carreon	.20
20	Luis Medina	.20
21	Sandy Alomar, Jr.	.60
23	Joe Girardi	.35
25	Craig Worthington	.30
26	Jerome Walton	5.50
27	Gary Wayne (FC)	.20
30	Alexis Infante (FC)	.15
32	Dwight Smith	1.65
34	Eric Yelding (FC)	.20
35	Gregg Olson	1.00
38	Rick Wrona (FC)	.35
41	Jeff Brantley (FC)	.20

42	Ron Jones	.20
45	Ramon Martinez	.40
46	Greg Harris	.20
47	Steve Finley	.35

1989 FLEER

Some of Fleer's best photos were not well cropped in the standard-sized 1989 set. The gray pin-striped borders are broad and diagonally cut by poorly edited player photos. Bats are often missing, or, even worse, arms are cut off, marring the dynamic concept. And print within the pin-striped background is too busy. Gray card backs include "Did You Know" trivia quizzes and charts marking player progress before and after the All-Star break. Informal group cards, star tribute cards, and duo rookie cards are rounded out by a dozen All-Stars with bios on backs.

38 Gregg Jefferies

		MINT
Complete set		**$35.00**
Commons		**.05**

1	Don Baylor	$ .10
2	*Lance Blankenship* (FC)	.25
3	*Todd Burns*	.30
5	Jose Canseco	1.50
6	Storm Davis	.10
7	Dennis Eckersley	.12
10	Dave Henderson	.10
11	Rick Honeycutt	.05
12	Glenn Hubbard	.05
13	Stan Javier	.05
14	*Doug Jennings*	.20
15	*Felix Jose* (FC)	.25
17	Mark McGwire	.75
19	Dave Parker	.12
20	Eric Plunk	.07
22	Terry Steinbach	.10
23	Dave Stewart	.10
24	Walt Weiss	.30
25	Bob Welch	.10
26	Curt Young	.07
30	Gary Carter	.20
31	David Cone	.40
32	Ron Darling	.12
33	Len Dykstra	.15
34	Kevin Elster	.10
35	Sid Fernandez	.10
36	Dwight Gooden	.50
37	Keith Hernandez	.25
38	Gregg Jefferies	2.00
39	Howard Johnson	.10
40	Terry Leach	.05
41	Dave Magadan	.10
43	Roger McDowell	.10
44	Kevin McReynolds	.15
45	Keith Miller	.20
46	Randy Myers	.10
47	Bob Ojeda	.07
49	Darryl Strawberry	.40
50	Tim Teufel	.05
51	*Dave West* (FC)	.60
54	Tim Belcher	.10
55	Mike Davis	.07
56	Mike Devereaux	.15
57	Kirk Gibson	.20
59	Chris Gwynn	.12
61	Danny Heep (home: San Antonio, TX)	1.00

548 Ken Griffey Jr.

62	Orel Hershiser	.25
64	Jay Howell	.10
65	Tim Leary	.07
66	Mike Marshall	.10
67	*Ramon Martinez* (FC)	.65
70	Steve Sax	.15
75	John Tudor	.10
76	Fernando Valenzuela	.20
77	Tracy Woodson	.10
79	Todd Benzinger	.12
81	Wade Boggs	1.50
83	Ellis Burks	.60
85	Roger Clemens	.50
86	*Steve Curry* (FC)	.20
87	*Dwight Evans	.10
90	Mike Greenwell	1.00
91	Bruce Hurst	.10
93	Spike Owen	.05
95	*Carlos Quintana* (FC)	.40
96	Jody Reed	.12
97	Jim Rice	.25
98	Kevin Romine (photo is Randy Kutcher, batting follow through)	.50
98	Kevin Romine (correct photo, arms crossed on chest)	.60

99	Lee Smith	.10
101	Bob Stanley	.05
105	Bert Blyleven	.12
106	*Eric Bullock* (FC)	.25
107	Randy Bush	.05
109	Mark Davidson	.07
110	Gary Gaetti	.15
111	Greg Gagne	.07
112	Dan Gladden	.05
113	*German Gonzalez* (FC)	.20
114	Brian Harper	.05
115	Tom Herr	.07
116	Kent Hrbek	.20
117	Gene Larkin	.10
121	John Moses (Home: Phoenix, AZ)	1.00
122	Al Newman	.05
124	Kirby Puckett	.35
125	Jeff Reardon	.10
127	Frank Viola	.15
129	Dave Bergman	.05
130	Tom Brookens (Mike Heath stats on back)	2.25
130	Tom Brookens (correct stats)	.30
131	*Paul Gibson*	.15
132	Mike Heath (Tom Brookens stats on back)	2.25
132	Mike Heath (correct stats)	.30
133	*Don Heinkel*	.15
134	Mike Henneman	.10
136	Eric King	.05
137	Chet Lemon	.07
138	Fred Lynn	.10
139	Jack Morris	.15
140	Matt Nokes	.20
143	Jeff M. Robinson	.12
145	*Steve Searcy* (FC)	.30
148	Alan Trammell	.20
151	Lou Whitaker	.20
152	Tim Birtsas	.05
153	Tom Browning	.10

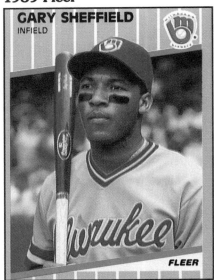

196 Gary Sheffield

154	*Keith Brown* (FC)	.20
155	*Norm Charlton* (FC)	.25
157	Kal Daniels	.15
158	Eric Davis	.50
159	Bo Diaz	.07
160	*Rob Dibble*	.35
161	Nick Esasky	.10
162	John Franco	.10
163	Danny Jackson	.15
164	Barry Larkin	.25
165	Rob Murphy	.05
166	Paul O'Neill	.07
167	Jeff Reed	.05
168	Jose Rijo	.10
170	*Chris Sabo*	.60
171	*Candy Sierra* (FC)	.15
172	*Van Snider* (FC)	.20
173	Jeff Treadway	.15
174	Frank Williams	.05
177	Don August	.10
179	Chris Bosio	.07
180	Glenn Braggs	.07
181	Greg Brock	.05
182	Mark Clear	.05
183	Chuck Crim	.07
184	Rob Deer	.07
185	Tom Filer	.05
187	*Darryl Hamilton*	.15
188	Ted Higuera	.12
189	Odell Jones	.05
191	Joey Meyer	.07
193	Paul Molitor	.15
195	Dan Plesac	.10
196	*Gary Sheffield* (FC)	2.00
197	B.J. Surhoff	.10
198	Dale Sveum	.07
200	Robin Yount	.25
202	Barry Bonds	.20
203	Bobby Bonilla	.20
204	Sid Bream	.07
206	Doug Drabek	.07
207	Mike Dunne	.07
208	Felix Fermin	.05

209	Brian Fisher	.05
210	Jim Gott	.05
214	Jose Lind	.10
217	Tom Prince (FC)	.10
218	Gary Redus	.05
220	Jeff Robinson	.07
221	John Smiley	.12
222	Andy Van Slyke	.15
223	Bob Walk	.05
224	Glenn Wilson	.05
225	Jesse Barfield	.10
226	George Bell	.25
227	*Pat Borders*	.25
228	John Cerutti	.07
229	Jim Clancy	.07
230	Mark Eichhorn	.07
231	Tony Fernandez	.12
233	Mike Flanagan	.10
234	Kelly Gruber	.15
235	Tom Henke	.10
236	Jimmy Key	.10
237	Rick Leach	.05
240	Fred McGriff	.50
241	Lloyd Moseby	.10
244	Dave Stieb	.10
245	Todd Stottlemyre	.10
246	Duane Ward	.07
247	David Wells	.10
248	Ernie Whitt	.07
250	Neil Allen (Home: Sarasota, FL)	1.50
252	Jack Clark	.15
254	Rickey Henderson	.35
255	Tommy John	.12
256	Roberto Kelly	.20
257	Al Leiter	.15
258	Don Mattingly	1.50
259	Dale Mohorcic	.05
260	*Hal Morris* (FC)	.20
261	Scott Nielsen (FC)	.10
262	Mike Pagliarulo	.10
263	*Hipoleto Pena* (FC)	.20
264	Ken Phelps	.05

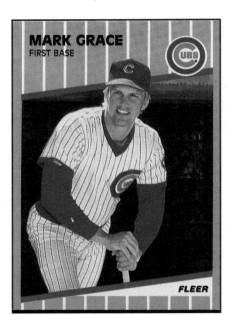

426 Mark Grace

284 Tom Gordon

265	Willie Randolph	.07
266	Rick Rhoden	.07
267	Dave Righetti	.12
271	Don Slaught	.05
272	Claudell Washington	.07
273	Gary Ward	.07
274	Dave Winfield	.30
276	Floyd Bannister	.07
277	George Brett	.35
278	Bill Buckner	.10
279	*Nick Capra* (FC)	.20
280	*Jose DeJesus* (FC)	.15
281	Steve Farr	.05
283	Mark Gubicza	.10
284	*Tom Gordon* (FC)	1.75
285	Bo Jackson	.70
286	Charlie Leibrandt	.07
287	*Mike Macfarlane*	.20
288	Jeff Montgomery	.07
289	Bill Pecota	.07
291	Bret Saberhagen	.15
292	Kevin Seitzer	.30
293	Kurt Stillwell	.07
294	Pat Tabler	.07
295	Danny Tartabull	.20
296	Gary Thurman	.12
297	Frank White	.07
298	Willie Wilson	.10
299	Roberto Alomar	.50
300	*Sandy Alomar Jr.* (FC)	1.75
301	Chris Brown	.05
302	Mike Brumley (FC)	.07
303	Mark Davis	.07
304	Mark Grant	.05
305	Tony Gwynn	.35
306	*Greg Harris* (FC)	.30
308	Jimmy Jones	.05
309	John Kruk	.12
310	Dave Leiper	.05
312	Lance McCullers	.07
313	Keith Moreland	.07
314	Dennis Rasmussen	.10
315	Randy Ready	.05

316	Benito Santiago	.15
317	Eric Show	.07
318	Todd Simmons	.20
319	Garry Templeton	.07
321	Ed Whitson	.07
323	Mike Aldrete	.07
324	Brett Butler	.07
325	Will Clark	1.00
326	Kelly Downs	.10
327	Dave Dravecky	.07
330	Charlie Hayes (FC)	.15
331	Mike Krukow	.07
333	Candy Maldonado	.07
334	Kirt Manwaring	.10
335	Bob Melvin	.05
336	Kevin Mitchell	.65
338	Tony Perezchica (FC)	.15
339	Joe Price	.05
340	Rick Reuschel	.10
343	Chris Speier	.05
344	Robby Thompson	.07
345	Jose Uribe	.05
346	Matt Williams	.12
347	Trevor Wilson (FC)	.25
348	Juan Agosto	.05
350	Alan Ashby	.05
351	Kevin Bass	.07
352	Buddy Bell	.07
353	Craig Biggio	.60
355	Glenn Davis	.25
357	Bill Doran	.07
358	John Fishel	.20
359	Billy Hatcher	.10
361	Louie Meadows	.15
362	Dave Meads	.05
364	Terry Puhl	.05
367	Mike Scott	.12
368	Nolan Ryan	.50
369	Dave Smith	.07
370	Gerald Young	.12
371	Hubie Brooks	.10
372	Tim Burke	.07
373	John Dopson	.25

81 Wade Boggs

375	Tom Foley	.05
376	Andres Galarraga	.15
378	Joe Hesketh	.05
379	Brian Holman	.35
380	Rex Hudler	.05
381	Randy Johnson (FC)	.35
382	Wallace Johnson	.05
383	Tracy Jones	.10
384	Dave Martinez	.07
385	Dennis Martinez	.07
387	Otis Nixon	.05
388	Johnny Paredes (FC)	.20
389	Jeff Parrett	.10
390	Pascual Perez	.07
391	Tim Raines	.25
392	Luis Rivera	.05
393	Nelson Santovenia	.25
394	Bryn Smith	.07
395	Tim Wallach	.10
397	Rod Allen	.15
398	Scott Bailes	.05
400	Joe Carter	.12
402	Dave Clark	.05
403	John Farrell	.10
404	Julio Franco	.10
405	Don Gordon	.05
406	Mel Hall	.05
408	Brook Jacoby	.10
409	Doug Jones	.20
410	Jeff Kaiser (FC)	.15
411	Luis Medina (FC)	.25
412	Cory Snyder	.15
413	Greg Swindell	.15
414	Ron Tingley (FC)	.15
415	Willie Upshaw	.05
417	Rich Yett	.05
418	Damon Berryhill	.10
420	Doug Dascenzo (FC)	.30
421	Jody Davis	.05
422	Andre Dawson	.20
424	Shawon Dunston	.10
425	"Goose" Gossage	.12
426	Mark Grace	2.00

5 Jose Canseco

427	Mike Harkey (FC)	.35
428	Darrin Jackson	.07
429	Les Lancaster	.07
430	Vance Law	.07
431	Greg Maddux	.12
433	Al Nipper	.05
434	Rafael Palmeiro	.15
435	Pat Perry	.05
436	Jeff Pico	.25
437	Ryne Sandberg	.35
439	Rick Sutcliffe	.10
441	Gary Varsho	.20
442	Mitch Webster	.07
443	Luis Alicea	.20
444	Tom Brunansky	.12
445	Vince Coleman	.15
446	John Costello	.20
447	Danny Cox	.07
449	Jose DeLeon	.10
450	Curt Ford	.05
451	Pedro Guerrero	.15
452	Bob Horner	.10
453	Tim Jones (FC)	.15
454	Steve Lake	.05
455	*Joe Magrane	.10
456	Greg Mathews	.05
457	Willie McGee	.12
460	Tony Pena	.07
461	Terry Pendleton	.10
462	Steve Peters (FC)	.15
463	Ozzie Smith	.15
464	Scott Terry	.08
466	Todd Worrell	.10
467	Tony Armas	.07
468	Dante Bichette (FC)	.25
469	*Bob Boone	.07
470	Terry Clark (FC)	.15
472	Mike Cook (FC)	.15
473	Sherman Corbett	.15
474	Chili Davis	.07
475	Brian Downing	.07
476	Jim Eppard	.05
479	Bryan Harvey	.25

258 Don Mattingly

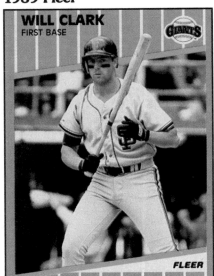

WILL CLARK
FIRST BASE

325 Will Clark

480	Jack Howell	.07
481	Wally Joyner	.25
483	Kirk McCaskill	.07
486	Dan Petry	.07
487	Johnny Ray	.07
489	Devon White	.10
490	Mike Witt	.07
491	Harold Baines	.12
492	Ivan Calderon	.07
495	Carlton Fisk	.20
496	*Dave Gallagher*	.25
497	Ozzie Guillen	.15
498	Shawn Hillegas	.07
499	Lance Johnson	.07
501	Bill Long	.07
503	Fred Manrique	.07
504	Jack McDowell	.10
505	*Donn Pall*	.20
506	Kelly Paris	.05
507	Dan Pasqua	.10
508	*Ken Patterson*	.20
509	Melido Perez	.10
510	Jerry Reuss	.07
511	Mark Salas	.05
512	Bobby Thigpen	.15
514	Bob Brower	.05
516	*Jose Cecena*	.15
517	Cecil Espy	.07
518	Scott Fletcher	.07
520	Jose Guzman	.07
522	Charlie Hough	.07
523	Pete Incaviglia	.12
525	Paul Kilgus	.15
526	*Chad Kreuter* (FC)	.20
528	Oddibe McDowell	.07
529	Pete O'Brien	.07
532	Ruben Sierra	.50
536	Mitch Williams	.15
537	Bobby Witt	.10
538	Steve Balboni	.07
542	Jay Buhner (FC)	.15
543	Mike Campbell	.10
544	Darnell Coles	.07

268

546	Alvin Davis	.15
547	Mario Diaz	.20
548	*Ken Griffey Jr.* (FC)	7.00
549	*Erik Hanson* (FC)	.30
550	Mike Jackson	.07
551	Mark Langston	.15
552	Edgar Martinez	.25
553	*Bill McGuire* (FC)	.15
554	Mike Moore	.07
555	Jim Presley	.07
558	Harold Reynolds	.12
559	*Mike Schooler* (FC)	.35
561	Dave Valle	.07
562	Steve Bedrosian	.12
563	Phil Bradley	.10
564	Don Carman	.05
568	Greg Gross	.05
569	Kevin Gross	.05
571	Von Hayes	.10
572	Chris James	.10
574	*Ron Jones* (FC)	.35
575	*Ricky Jordan*	1.50
578	Lance Parrish	.15
581	Juan Samuel	.12
582	Mike Schmidt	.45
585	*Jose Alvarez*	.15
588	Jeff Blauser	.10
589	*Terry Blocker* (FC)	.15
590	Ron Gant	.15
591	Tom Glavine	.10
592	Tommy Gregg	.10
596	Dale Murphy	.40
597	Gerald Perry	.07
599	Ted Simmons	.10
600	Pete Smith	.10
601	Zane Smith	.07
602	*John Smoltz*	.60
603	Bruce Sutter	.10
604	Andres Thomas	.07
606	*Brady Anderson* (FC)	.35
607	Jeff Ballard	.07
608	*Jose Bautista*	.20
609	Ken Gerhart	.05

RICKY JORDAN
FIRST BASE

575 Ricky Jordan

BO JACKSON
OUTFIELD

285 Bo Jackson

611	Eddie Murray	.30
612	Carl Nichols (FC)	.20
615	*Oswaldo Peraza (Oswald)* (FC)	.20
616	Bill Ripken (obscenity on bat)	25.00
616	Bill Ripken (obscenity on bat blacked out)	1.00
616	Bill Ripken (obscenity on bat scribbled out in black)	20.00
616	Bill Ripken (obscenity on bat painted out)	35.00
617	Cal Ripken Jr.	.35
619	Rick Schu	.05
622	Pete Stanicek	.10
623	Mickey Tettleton	.12
625	Jim Traber	.07
627	*Craig Worthington*	.40
628	Speed and Power (Jose Canseco)	.60
630	Like Father Like Sons (Roberto Alomar, Sandy Alomar Jr.)	.50
631	NL All-Stars (Will Clark, Rafael Palmeiro)	.40
632	Home Runs Coast to Coast (Will Clark, Darryl Strawberry)	.35
633	Hot Corners' Hot Hitters (Wade Boggs, Carney Lansford)	.40
634	Triple A's (Jose Canseco, Mark McGwire, Terry Steinbach)	.75
635	Dual Heat (Mark Davis, Dwight Gooden)	.25
636	NL Pitching Power (David Cone, Danny Jackson)	.15

637	Cannon Arms (Bobby Bonilla, Chris Sabo)	.20
639	Power Center (Eric Davis, Kirby Puckett)	.30
640	Major League Prospects (*Cameron Drew, Steve Wilson*) (FC)	.25
641	Major League Prospects (*Kevin Brown, Kevin Reimer*) (FC)	.30
642	Major League Prospects (*Jerald Clark, Brad Pounders*) (FC)	.30
643	Major League Prospects (*Mike Capel, Drew Hall*) (FC)	.25
644	Major League Prospects (*Joe Girardi, Rolando Roomes*) (FC)	.50
645	Major League Prospects (*Marty Brown, Lenny Harris*) (FC)	.30
646	Major League Prospects (*Luis de los Santos, Jim Campbell*) (FC)	.25
647	Major League Prospects (*Miguel Garcia, Randy Kramer*) (FC)	.25
648	Major League Prospects (*Torey Lovullo, Robert Palacios*) (FC)	.25
649	Major League Prospects (*Jim Corsi, Bob Milacki*) (FC)	.25
650	Major League Prospects (*Grady Hall, Mike Rochford*) (FC)	.25
651	Major League Prospects (*Vance Lovelace, Terry Taylor*) (FC)	.25
652	Major League Prospects (*Dennis Cook, Ken Hill*) (FC)	.40

1989 FLEER UPDATE

Tradition dictated the production and distribution of another Update set for 1989. And thanks to the fact that some hot rookie names were included, the 132-card subset zoomed in value immediately after its fall release. Rookie card fanatics embraced popular cards of Todd Zeile, Jerome Walton, Greg Vaughn, Jim Abbott, Dwight Smith, Robin Ventura, and Joey Belle. Fleer also included a special card commemorating Mike Schmidt's retirement. Unfortunately, the Updates retain the gaudy design of their 1989 Fleer counterparts. Cards are arranged by team, and then alphabetically by player within each team. A "U" prefix is added to distinguish the Update cards from the 660-card set issued earlier (the letter "U" has been omitted from the following list).

41 Greg Vaughn

122 Todd Zeile

		MINT
Complete set		**$22.00**
Commons		**.07**
1	Phil Bradley	$ .15
2	Mike Devereaux	.15
3	Steve Finley	.40
6	Bob Milacki	.25
7	Randy Milligan	.20
8	John Dopson	.20
9	Nick Esasky	.25
11	Jim Abbott (FC)	2.75
12	Bert Blyleven	.25
13	Jeff Manto (FC)	.35
15	Lance Parrish	.20
16	Lee Stevens (FC)	.50
17	Claudell Washington	.15
18	Mark Davis	.20
19	Eric King	.12
21	Matt Merullo (FC)	.20
22	Steve Rosenberg	.15
23	Robin Ventura	1.50
25	Joey Belle (FC)	1.00
29	Pete O'Brien	.15
31	Tracy Jones	.15
32	Mike Schwabe (FC)	.20
35	Kevin Appier	.25
36	*Bob Boone	.15
37	Luis de los Santos	.20
38	Jim Eisenreich	.12
39	Jamie Navarro (FC)	.50
40	Bill Spiers (FC)	.35
41	Greg Vaughn (FC)	3.00

42	Randy Veres (FC)	.20
46	Jesse Barfield	.15
47	Alvaro Espinoza	.15
48	Bob Geren (FC)	.40
50	Andy Hawkins	.15
51	Hensley Meulens	.60
52	Steve Sax	.20

53	Deion Sanders (FC)	1.50
54	Rickey Henderson	.40
55	Mike Moore	.20
57	Greg Briley	1.00
58	Gene Harris (FC)	.30
59	Randy Johnson	.15
60	Jeffrey Leonard	.20
62	Omar Vizquel (FC)	.30
63	Kevin Brown	.15
64	Julio Franco	.20
66	Rafael Palmeiro	.20
67	Nolan Ryan	1.85
68	Francisco Cabrera (FC)	.30
69	Junior Felix (FC)	1.00
70	Al Leiter	.12
71	Alex Sanchez	.25
73	Derek Lilliquist	.25
74	Lonnie Smith	.15
75	Jeff Treadway	.12

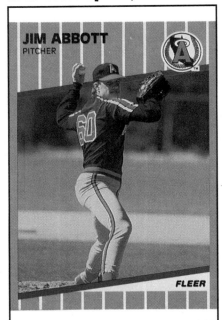

11 Jim Abbott

79	Dwight Smith	1.75
80	Jerome Walton	3.25
81	Mitch Williams	.25

82	Steve Wilson	.15
83	Todd Benzinger	.15
84	Ken Griffey	.20
86	Rolando Roomes	.20
87	Scott Scudder (FC)	.25
91	Mike Morgan	.15
92	Eddie Murray	.20
93	Willie Randolph	.15
97	Mark Langston	.25
101	Barry Lyons	.15
102	Juan Samuel	.25
103	Wally Whitehurst	.25
104	Dennis Cook	.12
105	Lenny Dykstra	.15
106	Charlie Hayes	.15
109	John Kruk	.15
110	Roger McDowell	.15
111	Terry Mulholland	.15
112	Jeff Parrett	.15
114	Jeff King	.15
115	Randy Kramer	.12
116	Bill Landrum	.20
117	Cris Carpenter	.15
119	Ken Hill	.10
120	Dan Quisenberry	.15
121	Milt Thompson	.20
122	Todd Zeile (FC)	4.00
123	Jack Clark	.15
124	Bruce Hurst	.20
125	Mark Parent	.15
126	Bip Roberts	.15

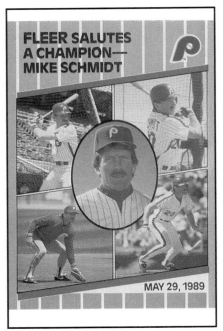

131 Mike Schmidt

127	Jeff Brantley (FC)	.20
130	Greg Litton (FC)	.30
131	Mike Schmidt	2.00

1989 SCORE

Card backs had been neglected for years, but Score's second set of 660 cards maintained its reputation for having baseball's most glorious card backs. The company continued to adorn backs with color photos, stats, and interesting bios. Unfortunately, the company insisted on including action photos on the front of every card. Several shots are dark or blurred, some show player faces shrouded by helmets, and others catch players with their backs turned to the camera. Score also began to get repetitive in photo selection. Most non-pitchers are shown in their batting stances; pitchers are displayed in their windups. Numbers 620-651 are specially designated in a 1989 Rookie subset.

		MINT
Complete set		**$22.00**
Commons		**.03**

1	Jose Canseco	$1.35
2	Andre Dawson	.15
3	Mark McGwire	.60
4	Benny Santiago	.12
5	Rick Reuschel	.08
6	Fred McGriff	.35
7	Kal Daniels	.10
8	Gary Gaetti	.15
9	Ellis Burks	.50
10	Darryl Strawberry	.35
11	Julio Franco	.08
12	Lloyd Moseby	.06
13	*Jeff Pico*	.20
14	Johnny Ray	.06
15	Cal Ripken Jr.	.30

17	Mel Hall	.06
18	Bill Ripken	.06
19	Brook Jacoby	.08
20	Kirby Puckett	.35
21	Bill Doran	.06
22	Pete O'Brien	.06
23	Matt Nokes	.15
24	Brian Fisher	.06
25	Jack Clark	.15
28	Willie Wilson	.08
29	Curt Young	.06
30	Dale Murphy	.30
31	Barry Larkin	.10
32	Dave Stewart	.08
33	Mike LaValliere	.06
35	Ryne Sandberg	.25
36	Tony Pena	.06
37	Greg Walker	.06
38	Von Hayes	.08

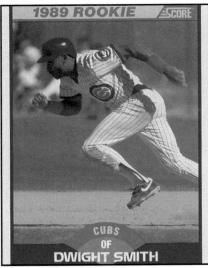

642 1989 Rookie

39	Kevin Mitchell	.50
40	Tim Raines	.25
41	Keith Hernandez	.20
42	Keith Moreland	.06
43	Ruben Sierra	.35
44	Chet Lemon	.06

600 Gregg Jefferies

94	Eddie Murray	.25
95	Lance Parrish	.15
96	Ron Kittle	.06
97	Gerald Young	.10
98	Ernie Whitt	.06
99	Jeff Reed	.03
100	Don Mattingly	1.50
101	Gerald Perry	.08
102	Vance Law	.06
104	*Chris Sabo*	.50
105	Danny Tartabull	.15
106	Glenn Wilson	.06
107	Mark Davidson	.06
108	Dave Parker	.10
109	Eric Davis	.35
110	Alan Trammell	.15
112	Frank Tanana	.06
114	Dennis Martinez	.06
115	Jose DeLeon	.08
116	Bob Ojeda	.06
117	Doug Drabek	.06
119	Greg Maddux (FC)	.10
120	Cecil Fielder (photo on back reversed)	.75
121	Mike Scioscia	.06
122	Dan Petry	.06
124	Kelly Downs	.08
125	Greg Gross (first name incorrect on back)	.20
126	Fred Lynn	.10
127	Barry Bonds	.20
128	Harold Baines	.10
130	Kevin Elster	.08
132	Teddy Higuera	.08
135	Ray Knight (photo reversed)	.25
136	Howard Johnson	.08
137	Terry Pendleton	.08
142	*Rich Renteria* (FC)	.10
143	Jose Guzman	.08
144	Andres Galarraga	.15
145	Rick Horton	.06
147	Glenn Braggs	.06

630 1989 Rookie

45	Willie Randolph	.06
47	Candy Maldonado	.06
48	Sid Bream	.06
49	Denny Walling	.03
50	Dave Winfield	.25
51	Alvin Davis	.10
52	Cory Snyder	.15
53	Hubie Brooks	.08
54	Chili Davis	.06
55	Kevin Seitzer	.25
57	Tony Fernandez	.10
58	Tim Teufel	.03
59	Oddibe McDowell	.06
60	Les Lancaster	.06
61	Billy Hatcher	.06
63	Marty Barrett	.06
64	Nick Esasky	.08
65	Wally Joyner	.20
66	Mike Greenwell	.60
67	Ken Williams	.06
68	Bob Horner	.08
69	Steve Sax	.15
70	Rickey Henderson	.40
71	Mitch Webster	.06
72	Rob Deer	.06
73	Jim Presley	.06
75	George Brett	.40
76	Brian Downing	.06
77	Dave Martinez	.06
78	Scott Fletcher	.06
79	Phil Bradley	.08
80	Ozzie Smith	.15
81	Larry Sheets	.06
82	Mike Aldrete	.06
83	Darnell Coles	.06
84	Len Dykstra	.08
85	Jim Rice	.20
86	Jeff Treadway	.10
87	Jose Lind	.08
88	Willie McGee	.10
90	Tony Gwynn	.35
92	Milt Thompson	.06
93	Kevin McReynolds	.15

362 Mark Grace

148	John Kruk	.10
149	Mike Schmidt	.50
150	Lee Smith	.08
151	Robin Yount	.25
152	Mark Eichhorn	.06
154	B.J. Surhoff	.08
155	Vince Coleman	.15
158	Lance McCullers	.06
160	Jesse Barfield	.08
161	Mark Langston	.10
162	Kurt Stillwell	.06
164	Glenn Davis	.15
165	Walt Weiss	.15
166	Dave Concepcion	.08
167	Alfredo Griffin	.06
168	*Don Heinkel*	.15
170	Shane Rawley	.06
171	Darrell Evans	.08
173	Jody Davis	.06
174	Andy Van Slyke	.15
175	Wade Boggs	.90
179	Carney Lansford	.06
180	Ron Darling	.10
181	Kirk McCaskill	.06
182	Tony Armas	.06
184	Tom Brunansky	.10
185	*Bryan Harvey*	.20
186	Mike Marshall	.10
187	Bo Diaz	.06
189	Mike Pagliarulo	.08
190	Mike Krukow	.06
191	Tommy Herr	.06
193	*Dwight Evans	.10
195	Bobby Bonilla	.20
197	Dave Stieb	.08
198	*Pat Borders*	.20
199	Rafael Palmeiro	.15
200	Doc Gooden	.40
201	Pete Incaviglia	.08
202	Chris James	.08
205	Don Baylor	.08
207	Pete Smith	.08
210	Kirk Gibson	.15

100 Don Mattingly

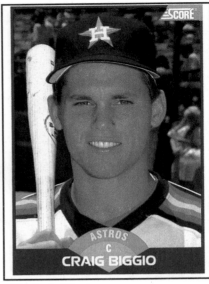

237 Craig Biggio

278	Rich Dotson	.06
280	Gene Larkin	.08
281	Roger McDowell	.08
282	Greg Swindell	.10
284	Jeff Robinson	.06
285	Mike Dunne	.08
286	Greg Mathews	.06
287	Kent Tekulve	.06
289	Jack McDowell	.08
290	Frank Viola	.15
291	Mark Gubicza	.10
293	Mike Henneman	.08
295	Charlie Hough	.06
298	Mike Witt	.06
299	Pascual Perez	.06
300	Nolan Ryan	.65
301	Mitch Williams	.08
302	Mookie Wilson	.06
303	Mackey Sasser	.06
304	John Cerutti	.06
305	Jeff Reardon	.08
306	Randy Myers	.08
307	Greg Brock	.06
308	Bob Welch	.08
309	Jeff Robinson	.15
310	Harold Reynolds	.06
312	Dave Magadan	.08
314	Walt Terrell	.06
315	Wally Backman	.06
317	Rick Rhoden	.06
318	Tom Henke	.06
319	*Mike Macfarlane*	.20
320	Dan Plesac	.08
323	Devon White	.10
325	Bruce Hurst	.08
330	Bo Jackson	.35
331	Ivan Calderon	.06
336	Damon Berryhill	.15
338	Dan Pasqua	.08
339	Bill Pecota	.06
340	Greg Cadaret	.06
342	Ron Guidry	.15
345	Rich Gedman	.06

211	Claudell Washington	.06
213	Joe Carter	.10
214	Bill Buckner	.08
215	Bert Blyleven	.15
216	Brett Butler	.06
217	Lee Mazzilli	.06
220	Tim Wallach	.08
221	David Cone	.30
222	Don Carman	.06
223	Rich Gossage	.10
225	Dave Righetti	.10
226	Kevin Bass	.06
227	Kevin Gross	.06
230	Lou Whitaker	.15
231	*Luis Alicea*	.15
232	Roberto Alomar	.45
233	*Bob Boone	.06
235	Shawon Dunston	.08
236	Pete Stanicek	.08
237	*Craig Biggio*	.65
238	Dennis Boyd	.06
240	Gary Carter	.15
242	Ken Phelps	.06
244	Les Straker	.06
245	Dave Smith	.06
247	Joe Orsulak	.06
248	Storm Davis	.10
250	Jack Morris	.15
251	Bret Saberhagen	.15
254	Eric Show	.06
255	Juan Samuel	.10
256	Dale Sveum	.06
260	Steve Bedrosian	.08
261	Jack Howell	.06
265	Todd Worrell	.10
266	John Farrell	.08
267	Dave Collins	.06
268	Sid Fernandez	.08
270	Shane Mack	.06
271	Paul Kilgus	.20
273	Bob Knepper	.04
276	Dennis Eckersley	.10
277	Graig Nettles	.10

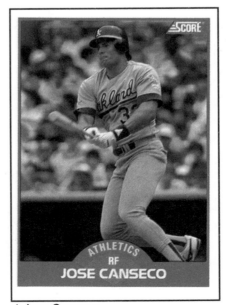

1 Jose Canseco

346	*Nelson Santovenia*	.20
347	George Bell	.20
350	Roger Clemens	.50
351	Bill Long	.06
352	Jay Bell (FC)	.06
353	Steve Balboni	.06
356	Jesse Orosco	.06
360	Darrin Jackson (FC)	.08
362	Mark Grace	2.00
365	Terry Steinbach	.08
367	Jeff Montgomery	.06
369	Chris Brown	.06
370	Orel Hershiser	.20
371	Todd Benzinger	.10
372	Ron Gant	.15
374	Joey Meyer	.08
376	Mike Davis	.06
377	Jeff Parrett (FC)	.08
378	Jay Howell	.06
380	Luis Polonia	.06
382	Kent Hrbek	.15
384	Dave LaPoint	.06
386	Melido Perez	.08
387	Doug Jones	.10
389	Alejandro Pena	.06
390	Frank White	.06
391	Pat Tabler	.06
394	Allan Anderson (FC)	.06
397	Scott Terry (FC)	.08
398	Mike Jackson	.06
399	Bobby Thigpen	.08
400	Don Sutton	.15
401	Cecil Espy	.06
406	Andres Thomas	.06
407	Rick Sutcliffe	.08
409	John Smiley	.10
410	Juan Nieves	.06
411	Shawn Abner	.08
412	Wes Gardner (FC)	.06
418	Tim Belcher	.08
419	Don August	.08
425	Bruce Sutter	.08
429	Tim Leary	.06

433	Ozzie Guillen	.06
435	Gary Ward	.06
437	Fernando Valenzuela	.15
442	*Tom Glavine	.08
449	Carlton Fisk	.15
450	Will Clark	.50
453	Todd Stottlemyre	.15
455	*Dave Gallagher*	.20
457	Fred Manrique	.06
459	*Doug Jennings* (FC)	.20
460	*Joe Magrane	.08
462	*Jack Armstrong*	.35
463	Bobby Witt	.08
464	Keith Miller	.06
465	*Todd Burns*	.30
466	John Dopson	.20
473	*Sil Campusano*	.20
475	Mike Flanagan	.06
476	Greg Harris	.03
477	Tommy John	.10
478	Dave Anderson	.03
479	Fred Toliver	.03
480	Jimmy Key	.08
483	Tom Pagnozzi	.06
486	Jody Reed	.10
487	Roberto Kelly	.25
488	Shawn Hillegas	.06
489	Jerry Reuss	.06
490	Mark Davis	.10
491	Jeff Sellers	.03
492	Zane Smith	.06
493	Al Newman (FC)	.03
494	Mike Young	.03
495	Larry Parrish	.06
498	Joe Hesketh	.03
499	Darrell Miller	.03
500	Mike LaCoss	.03
503	Charlie Lea	.03
505	Tim Crews	.06
506	Ken Gerhart	.06
507	Brian Holton	.15
508	Dennis Lamp	.06
509	Bobby Meacham	.20

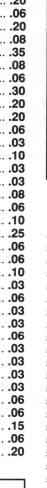

300 Nolan Ryan

510	Tracy Jones	.08
511	Mike Fitzgerald	.03
512	*Jeff Bittiger*	.12
513	Tim Flannery	.03
514	Ray Hayward (FC)	.03
515	Dave Leiper	.03
516	Rod Scurry	.03
517	Carmelo Martinez	.03
518	Curtis Wilkerson	.03
520	Dan Quisenberry	.06
521	Lloyd McClendon (FC)	.03
522	Steve Trout	.03
523	Larry Andersen	.03
524	Don Aase	.03
525	Bob Forsch	.06
526	Geno Petralli	.03
527	Angel Salazar	.03
528	*Mike Schooler*	.20
529	Jose Oquendo	.06
530	Jay Buhner	.15
531	Tom Bolton (FC)	.06
532	Al Nipper	.03
533	Dave Henderson	.08
534	*John Costello* (FC)	.20
535	Donnie Moore	.03
536	Mike Laga	.03
537	Mike Gallego	.03
538	Jim Clancy	.06
539	Joel Youngblood	.03
540	Rick Leach	.03
541	Kevin Romine	.03
542	Mark Salas	.03
543	Greg Minton	.03
544	Dave Palmer	.03
545	Dwayne Murphy	.03
546	Jim Deshaies	.03
547	Don Gordon (FC)	.03
548	*Ricky Jordan*	1.50
549	Mike Boddicker	.10
550	Mike Scott	.10
551	Jeff Ballard (FC)	.08
552	Jose Rijo	.20
553	Danny Darwin	.03

554	Tom Browning	.08
555	Danny Jackson	.15
556	Rick Dempsey	.06
557	Jeffrey Leonard	.06
558	Jeff Musselman	.06
559	Ron Robinson	.03
560	John Tudor	.08
561	Don Slaught	.06
562	Dennis Rasmussen	.08
563	*Brady Anderson*	.30
564	Pedro Guerrero	.15
565	Paul Molitor	.15
566	*Terry Clark* (FC)	.15
567	Terry Puhl	.03
568	Mike Campbell (FC)	.08
569	Paul Mirabella	.03
570	Jeff Hamilton (FC)	.06
571	*Oswald Peraza*	.20
572	Bob McClure	.03
573	*Jose Bautista* (FC)	.15
574	Alex Trevino	.03
575	John Franco	.08
576	*Mark Parent* (FC)	.15
577	Nelson Liriano	.06
578	Steve Shields	.03
579	Odell Jones	.03
580	Al Leiter	.20
581	Dave Stapleton (FC)	.06
582	1988 World Series (Jose Canseco, Kirk Gibson, Orel Hershiser, Dave Stewart)	.20
583	Donnie Hill	.03
584	Chuck Jackson	.06
585	Rene Gonzales (FC)	.06
586	Tracy Woodson (FC)	.08
587	Jim Adduci (FC)	.03
588	Mario Soto	.06
589	Jeff Blauser	.08
590	Jim Traber	.06
591	Jon Perlman (FC)	.03
592	Mark Williamson (FC)	.06
593	Dave Meads	.03

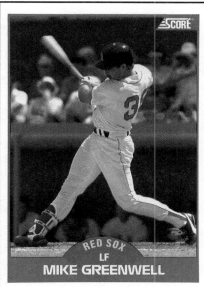

66 Mike Greenwell

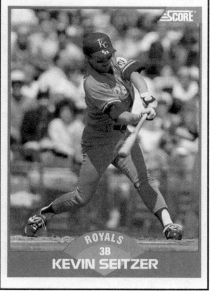

55 Kevin Seitzer

594	Jim Eisenreich	.03	625	1989 Rookie (Gary Sheffield) (FC)	1.75	643	1989 Rookie (Cameron Drew) (FC)	.20
595	Paul Gibson (FC)	.15	626	1989 Rookie (Tom Prince) (FC)	.08	644	1989 Rookie (Jerald Clark) (FC)	.20
596	Mike Birkbeck	.06	627	1989 Rookie (Steve Searcy) (FC)	.25	645	1989 Rookie (Randy Johnson) (FC)	.25
597	Terry Francona	.03	628	1989 Rookie (Charlie Hayes) (FC)	.15	646	1989 Rookie (Norm Charlton) (FC)	.20
598	Paul Zuvella (FC)	.03	629	1989 Rookie (Felix Jose) (FC)	.20	647	1989 Rookie (Todd Frohwirth) (FC)	.08
599	Franklin Stubbs	.03	630	1989 Rookie (Sandy Alomar) (FC)	1.50	648	1989 Rookie (Luis de los Santos) (FC)	.20
600	Gregg Jefferies	2.00	631	1989 Rookie (Derek Lilliquist) (FC)	.40	649	1989 Rookie (Tim Jones) (FC)	.15
601	John Cangelosi	.03	632	1989 Rookie (Geronimo Berroa) (FC)	.06	650	1989 Rookie (Dave West) (FC)	.50
602	Mike Sharperson (FC)	.03	633	1989 Rookie (Luis Medina) (FC)	.35	651	1989 Rookie (Bob Milacki) (FC)	.25
603	Mike Diaz	.06	634	1989 Rookie (Tom Gordon) (FC)	1.00	652	1988 Highlights (Wrigley Field)	.08
604	Gary Varsho (FC)	.20	635	*1989 Rookie (Ramon Martinez) (FC)	.45	653	1988 Highlights (Orel Hershiser)	.10
605	Terry Blocker (FC)	.10	636	1989 Rookie (Craig Worthington) (FC)	.50	654	1988 Highlights (Wade Boggs)	.40
606	Charlie O'Brien (FC)	.03	637	1989 Rookie (Edgar Martinez) (FC)	.25	655	1988 Highlights (Jose Canseco)	.60
607	Jim Eppard (FC)	.08	638	1989 Rookie (Chad Krueter) (FC)	.20	657	1988 Highlights (Rickey Henderson)	.12
608	John Davis	.03	639	1989 Rookie (Ron Jones) (FC)	.30	658	1988 Highlights (Tom Browning)	.06
609	Ken Griffey Sr.	.08	640	1989 Rookie (Van Snider) (FC)	.20	659	1988 Highlights (Mike Greenwell)	.30
610	Buddy Bell	.06	641	1989 Rookie (Lance Blankenship) (FC)	.25	660	1988 Highlights (Boston Red Sox 24 home-game winning streak)	.06
611	Ted Simmons	.08	642	1989 Rookie (Dwight Smith) (FC)	3.00			
612	*Matt Williams	.10						
613	Danny Cox	.06						
614	Al Pedrique	.03						
615	Ron Oester	.03						
616	John Smoltz (FC)	.50						
617	Bob Melvin	.03						
618	Rob Dibble	.25						
619	Kirt Manwaring	.10						
620	1989 Rookie (Felix Fermin) (FC)	.06						
621	1989 Rookie (Doug Dascenzo) (FC)	.25						
622	1989 Rookie (Bill Brennan) (FC)	.20						
623	1989 Rookie (Carlos Quintana) (FC)	.35						
624	1989 Rookie (Mike Harkey) (FC)	.40						

1989 SCORE ROOKIE & TRADED

After hobbyists overwhelmed Score with their ceaseless demands for its initial Rookie & Traded set in 1988, the company was prepared for collectors in 1989. Greater availability and fewer hot rookie names kept the second-year set of 110 cards from booming in price immediately. However, it seemed just as popular as the regular Score set. The company even scooped its competition by becoming the only card manufacturer with a photo of Los Angeles Dodgers rookie hurler John Wetteland. Following the lead of the other companies, Score sold their extension set only through hobby dealers in boxed, complete sets.

		MINT
Complete set		**$17.00**
Commons		**.06**
1	Rafael Palmeiro	$ .12
2	Nolan Ryan	1.50
3	Jack Clark	.12
5	Mike Moore	.20
6	Pete O'Brien	.15
7	Jeffrey Leonard	.20
9	Tom Herr	.10
10	Claudell Washington	.15
11	Mike Pagliarulo	.12
14	Andy Hawkins	.15
15	Todd Benzinger	.15
16	Mookie Wilson	.15
17	Bert Blyleven	.25
18	Jeff Treadway	.12
19	Bruce Hurst	.20
20	Steve Sax	.15
21	Juan Samuel	.20
22	Jesse Barfield	.15
23	Carmelo Castillo	.12
24	Terry Leach	.08
25	Mark Langston	.20
26	Eric King	.12
27	Steve Balboni	.15
28	Lenny Dykstra	.15
29	Keith Moreland	.10
31	Eddie Murray	.15
32	Mitch Williams	.15
33	Jeff Parrett	.12
34	Wally Backman	.12
35	Julio Franco	.12
36	Lance Parrish	.20
37	Nick Esasky	.15
38	Luis Polonia	.12
39	Kevin Gross	.08
41	Willie Randolph	.15
43	Tracy Jones	.12
44	Phil Bradley	.15

45	Milt Thompson	.20
46	Chris James	.12
47	Scott Fletcher	.12
48	Kal Daniels	.12
49	Steve Bedrosian	.15
50	Rickey Henderson	.50
51	Dion James	.15
52	Tim Leary	.12
53	Roger McDowell	.15
54	Mel Hall	.12
56	Zane Smith	.10
57	Danny Heep	.10
58	Bob McClure	.10
59	Brian Holton	.12
62	Harold Baines	.20
64	Jody Davis	.12
65	Darrell Evans	.15
67	Frank Viola	.15
69	Greg Cadaret	.12
70	John Kruk	.15
72	Oddibe McDowell	.12
73	Tom Brookens	.10
74	*Bob Boone	.15
75	Walt Terrell	.15
77	Randy Johnson	.15
79	Rick Mahler	.10
80	Rich Dotson	.15

81	Cris Carpenter	.25
82	Billy Spiers (FC)	.30
83	Junior Felix (FC)	**1.00**
84	Joe Girardi (FC)	.35
85	Jerome Walton	**3.00**
86	Greg Litton (FC)	.35
87	Greg Harris	.20
88	Jim Abbott	**2.00**
89	Kevin Brown	.20
90	John Wetteland (FC)	.40
91	Gary Wayne (FC)	.25
92	Rich Monteleone (FC)	.25
93	Bob Geren (FC)	.35
94	Clay Parker	.15
95	Steve Finley	.30
96	Gregg Olson	**1.35**
97	Ken Patterson	.15
98	Ken Hill	.25
99	Scott Scudder (FC)	.30
100	Ken Griffey, Jr.	**5.50**
101	Jeff Brantley (FC)	.20
102	Donn Pall	.15
103	Carlos Martinez (FC)	.20
104	Joe Oliver (FC)	.35
105	Omar Vizquel (FC)	.30
106	Joey Belle (FC)	**1.00**
107	Kenny Rogers (FC)	.20

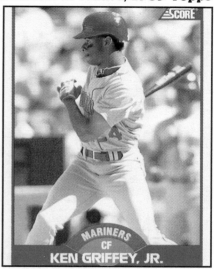

100 Ken Griffey, Jr.

108	Mark Carreon	.15
109	Rolando Roomes	.25
110	Pete Harnisch	.20

1989 TOPPS

Although Topps maintained the size of its annual 792-card set at 2 1/2 by 3 1/2 inches, the Brooklyn company offered several alterations in its design for 1989. While retaining simple white front borders and crisp, well-cropped photos, bold border lettering sometimes turned overwhelmingly neon (shades of 1972 Topps!). Player positions are omitted from card fronts, while player names are dwarfed by team designations. Topps saved the day by including several appealing subsets. A group of 10 cards, called #1 Draft Picks, consists of promising rookies (mostly former Olympians) in their college uniforms. Jim Abbott, Robin Ventura, and Andy Benes are big names in this category. Top rookies like Gregg Jefferies, Sandy Alomar, Jr., and Gary Sheffield are spotlighted with specially marked Future Star cards.

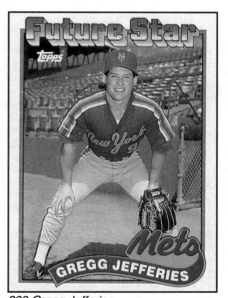

233 Gregg Jefferies

		MINT
Complete set		**$27.00**
Commons		**.03**
2	Record Breaker (Wade Boggs)	$ .35
3	Record Breaker (Gary Carter)	.10
5	Record Breaker (Orel Hershiser)	.10
6	Record Breaker (Doug Jones)	.06
8	*Dave Eiland* (FC)	.20
9	Tim Teufel	.03
10	Andre Dawson	.15
11	Bruce Sutter	.10
12	Dale Sveum	.06
13	Doug Sisk	.03

14	Tom Kelly	.03
15	Robby Thompson	.06
16	Ron Robinson	.03
17	Brian Downing	.06
18	Rick Rhoden	.06
19	Greg Gagne	.03
20	Steve Bedrosian	.08
22	Tim Crews	.06
25	Frank White	.06
27	*Orestes Destrade* (FC)	.12
28	Mike Moore	.03
29	Kelly Gruber	.03
30	Doc Gooden	.40
33	B.J. Surhoff	.08
34	Ken Williams	.06
35	John Tudor	.08
36	Mitch Webster	.06
40	Steve Sax	.15

45	Kal Daniels	.10
48	Tim Burke	.06
49	*Craig Biggio* (FC)	.75
50	George Bell	.25
53	Ruben Sierra	.35
54	Steve Trout	.03
55	Julio Franco	.06

465 Mark Grace

56	Pat Tabler	.03
59	Mark Davis	.10
60	Tom Brunansky	.10
63	Mark Clear	.03
65	Rick Reuschel	.08
69	Jeff Ballard	.06
70	Mark McGwire	.65
73	Pascual Perez	.06
75	Tom Henke	.06
76	*Terry Blocker* (FC)	.12
77	Doyle Alexander	.06
78	Jim Sundberg	.06
80	Cory Snyder	.15
83	*Jeff Blauser* (FC)	.15
84	#1 Draft Pick	
	(*Bill Bene*) (FC)	.50
85	Kevin McReynolds	.15
88	*Darryl Hamilton* (FC)	.12
89	Dave LaPoint	.03
90	Vince Coleman	.12
95	Gerald Young	.10
97	Greg Mathews	.06
98	Larry Sheets	.06
99	*Sherman Corbett* (FC)	.12
100	Mike Schmidt	.35
101	Les Straker	.03
103	Tim Birtsas	.03
105	Ron Darling	.10
106	Willie Upshaw	.06
107	Jose DeLeon	.10
109	*Hipolito Pena* (FC)	.10
110	Paul Molitor	.15
112	Jim Presley	.06
115	Jody Davis	.06
119	Terry Puhl	.03
120	Frank Viola	.15
122	Lance Johnson (FC)	.12
124	Jim Traber	.06
126	Sid Bream	.06
127	Walt Terrell	.06
129	*Terry Clark* (FC)	.20
130	Gerald Perry	.06
132	Curt Ford	.03

133	Bill Long	.06
135	Jose Rijo	.08
136	Joey Meyer	.06
141	Indians Ldrs	
	(Brook Jacoby)	.06
142	Mike Diaz	.06
143	Mike Campbell	.06
144	Jay Bell	.06
145	Dave Stewart	.08
148	Bill Pecota	.06
149	*Doug Dascenzo* (FC)	.25
150	Fernando Valenzuela	.15
154	Don Carman	.03
155	Marty Barrett	.06
156	*Dave Gallagher* (FC)	.20
157	Tom Glavine	.12
160	Jeffrey Leonard	.06
161	#1 Draft Pick	
	(*Gregg Olson*) (FC)	**1.00**
162	John Davis	.03
163	Bob Forsch	.06
164	Hal Lanier	.03
165	Mike Dunne	.06
166	*Doug Jennings* (FC)	.20
167	FS (*Steve Searcy*) (FC)	.25
168	Willie Wilson	.08
169	Mike Jackson	.06
170	Tony Fernandez	.10
173	Mel Hall	.06
174	*Todd Burns* (FC)	.25
176	Jeff Parrett	.06
177	#1 Draft Pick	
	(*Monty Fariss*) (FC)	.50
178	Mark Grant	.03
180	Mike Scott	.15
181	*Craig Worthington* (FC)	.35
183	Oddibe McDowell	.06
184	*John Costello*	.20
186	Pat Perry	.03
189	Kevin Mitchell	.50
190	Mike Witt	.08
191	*Sil Campusano*	.20
194	*Greg W. Harris* (FC)	.25

358 Ricky Jordan

648 Sandy Alomar

195	Ozzie Guillen	.10
199	*Mike Schooler*	.35
200	George Brett	.45
202	*Brad Moore* (FC)	.12
203	Rob Ducey	.03
205	*Dwight Evans	.10
206	Roberto Alomar	.40
208	Tom Pagnozzi	.03
209	*Jeff Bittiger* (FC)	.12
210	Dale Murphy	.30
215	Kevin Gross	.03
216	Jack Howell	.06
217	Joe Price	.03
219	Jim Clancy	.06
220	Gary Gaetti	.12
221	Cecil Espy	.06
222	#1 Draft Pick	
	(*Mark Lewis*) (FC)	.50
223	Jay Buhner	.15
224	Tony LaRussa	.06
225	*Ramon Martinez* (FC)	.45
226	Bill Doran	.06
227	John Farrell	.08
228	*Nelson Santovenia*	.20
229	Jimmy Key	.08
230	Ozzie Smith	.15
232	Ricky Horton	.06
233	FS (Gregg Jefferies) (FC)	3.50
234	Tom Browning	.08
235	John Kruk	.10
238	Eric King	.03
240	Greg Maddux	.10
241	Brett Butler	.06
243	*Bob Boone	.06
244	Jim Acker	.03
245	Jim Rice	.20
247	Shawn Hillegas	.06
249	Tim Leary	.06
250	Cal Ripken	.30
251	*John Dopson* (FC)	.25
252	Billy Hatcher	.06
253	*Jose Alvarez* (FC)	.12
254	Tom Lasorda	.06

255	Ron Guidry	.12
256	Benny Santiago	.15
260	Dave Winfield	.25
262	*Jeff Pico*	.20
264	**Rob Dibble* (FC)	.35
265	Kent Hrbek	.15
268	Keith Miller	.06
269	Tom Bolton	.06
270	Wally Joyner	.25
271	Jay Tibbs	.03
273	Jose Lind	.06
275	Danny Tartabull	.15
276	Paul Kilgus	.10
277	Mike Davis	.06
280	Bob Knepper	.03
281	Gary Redus	.03
282	*Cris Carpenter* (FC)	.30
286	Darrin Jackson	.08
287	Juan Nieves	.06
289	Ernie Whitt	.06
290	John Franco	.08
291	Mets Ldrs (Darryl Strawberry)	.12
292	*Jim Corsi* (FC)	.15
293	Glenn Wilson	.06
295	Scott Fletcher	.06
296	Ron Gant	.15
297	*Oswald Peraza* (FC)	.15
298	Chris James	.08
299	*Steve Ellsworth* (FC)	.12
300	Darryl Strawberry	.35
302	Gary Ward	.06
303	Felix Fermin	.06
305	Dave Smith	.06
309	Mario Diaz (FC)	.20
310	Rafael Palmeiro	.25
311	Chris Bosio	.03
315	Greg Swindell	.10
316	Walt Weiss	.50
317	*Jack Armstrong*	.35
318	Gene Larkin	.08
320	Lou Whitaker	.15
321	Red Sox Ldrs (Jody Reed)	.06

700 Don Mattingly

322	John Smiley	.10
323	Gary Thurman	.10
324	*Bob Milacki* (FC)	.25
326	Dennis Boyd	.06
327	*Mark Lemke* (FC)	.20
329	Bob Melvin	.03
330	Eric Davis	.35
332	Tony Armas	.06
333	Bob Ojeda	.06
334	Steve Lyons	.06
335	Dave Righetti	.10
336	Steve Balboni	.06
337	Calvin Schiraldi	.03
338	Jim Adduci (FC)	.03
339	Scott Bailes	.03
340	Kirk Gibson	.15
343	FS (*Gary Sheffield*) (FC)	1.50
349	*Ron Jones* (FC)	.30
350	Andy Van Slyke	.15
351	Giants Ldrs (Bob Melvin)	.06
352	Rick Schu	.03
354	Larry Parrish	.06
355	Mark Langston	.12
356	Kevin Elster	.08
357	Jerry Reuss	.06
358	*Ricky Jordan* (FC)	1.50
359	Tommy John	.10
360	Ryne Sandberg	.20
361	Kelly Downs	.08
363	Rich Yett	.03
364	Rob Deer	.06
365	Mike Henneman	.06
367	*Johnny Paredes* (FC)	.20
368	Brian Holton	.06
369	Ken Caminiti	.06
370	Dennis Eckersley	.10
371	Manny Lee	.03
373	Tracy Jones	.08
374	John Wathan	.06
375	Terry Pendleton	.08
377	Mike Smithson	.03
379	Tim Flannery	.03
380	Rickey Henderson	.30

382	*John Smoltz* (FC)	.50
383	Howard Johnson	.08
384	Mark Salas	.03
385	Von Hayes	.08
386	Andres Galarraga AS	.08
387	Ryne Sandberg AS	.10
388	Bobby Bonilla AS	.08
389	Ozzie Smith AS	.10
390	Darryl Strawberry AS	.15
391	Andre Dawson AS	.12
392	Andy Van Slyke AS	.12
393	Gary Carter AS	.10
394	Orel Hershiser AS	.12
395	Danny Jackson AS	.08
396	Kirk Gibson AS	.08
397	Don Mattingly AS	.60
398	Julio Franco AS	.08
399	Wade Boggs AS	.35
400	Alan Trammell AS	.08
401	Jose Canseco AS	.50
402	Mike Greenwell AS	.20
403	Kirby Puckett AS	.15
404	Bob Boone AS	.06
405	Roger Clemens AS	.15
406	Frank Viola AS	.08
407	Dave Winfield AS	.15
408	Greg Walker	.06
409	Ken Dayley	.03
410	Jack Clark	.15
411	Mitch Williams	.08
412	Barry Lyons	.03
414	Jim Fregosi	.03
415	Rich Gossage	.10
416	Fred Lynn	.10
419	Tom Filer	.03
420	Joe Carter	.10
421	Kirk McCaskill	.06
422	Bo Diaz	.06
423	Brian Fisher	.06
424	Luis Polonia	.06
425	Jay Howell	.06
427	Eric Show	.06
429	Twins Ldrs (Greg Gagne)	.06

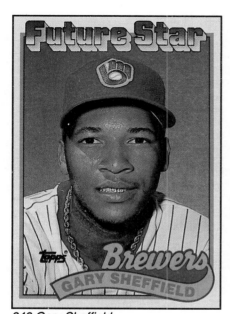

343 Gary Sheffield

764 #1 Draft Pick

573 #1 Draft Pick

430	Mark Gubicza	.08
431	Luis Rivera	.06
432	*Chad Kreuter* (FC)	.20
433	Albert Hall	.03
434	*Ken Patterson* (FC)	.15
435	*Len Dykstra	.15
437	#1 Draft Pick (*Andy Benes*)	1.00
438	Greg Gross	.03
440	Bobby Bonilla	.15
441	Jerry Reed	.03
442	Jose Oquendo	.08
443	*Rod Nichols* (FC)	.15
444	Moose Stubing	.03
445	Matt Nokes	.15
446	Rob Murphy	.03
448	Eric Plunk	.03
450	Roger Clemens	.40
451	Mark Davidson	.06
452	*Israel Sanchez*	.12
453	Tom Prince (FC)	.08
455	Johnny Ray	.06
456	Tim Belcher	.06
457	Mackey Sasser	.06
458	*Donn Pall* (FC)	.20
460	Dave Stieb	.08
461	Buddy Bell	.06
462	Jose Guzman	.06
463	Steve Lake	.03
464	Bryn Smith	.06
465	Mark Grace	1.50
466	Chuck Crim	.06
468	Henry Cotto	.06
469	*Jose Bautista*	.20
470	Lance Parrish	.12
471	*Steve Curry* (FC)	.20
472	Brian Harper	.06
474	Bob Rodgers	.03
475	Dave Parker	.10
476	Jon Perlman (FC)	.06
478	Doug Drabek	.06
479	*Mike Macfarlane*	.20
480	Keith Hernandez	.20

481	Chris Brown	.03
482	*Steve Peters*	.12
484	Steve Shields	.03
485	Hubie Brooks	.08
486	Jack McDowell	.06
487	Scott Lusader (FC)	.08
488	Kevin Coffman	.06
489	Phillies Ldrs (Mike Schmidt)	.12
490	*Chris Sabo*	.60
492	Alan Ashby	.03
493	Todd Benzinger	.10
494	Shane Rawley	.06
497	Pete Stanicek	.12
498	Dave Valle	.03
499	*Don Heinkel* (FC)	.15
500	Jose Canseco	1.00
501	Vance Law	.06
502	Duane Ward	.03
504	Bob Walk	.03
505	*Pete Rose	.25
506	Kirt Manwaring	.10
507	Steve Farr	.03
508	Wally Backman	.06
509	Bud Black	.03
510	Bob Horner	.08
512	Donnie Hill	.03
513	Jesse Orosco	.06
514	Chet Lemon	.06
515	Barry Larkin	.20
516	Eddie Whitson	.06
517	Greg Brock	.06
518	Bruce Ruffin	.03
520	Rick Sutcliffe	.08
521	Mickey Tettleton	.08
522	*Randy Kramer* (FC)	.12
523	Andres Thomas	.06
524	Checklist 397-528	.03
525	Chili Davis	.06
526	Wes Gardner	.06
527	Dave Henderson	.10
528	*Luis Medina* (FC)	.25
529	Tom Foley	.03

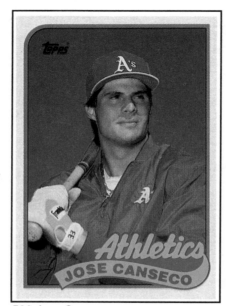

500 Jose Canseco

713 #1 Draft Pick

530	Nolan Ryan	.50
531	Dave Hengel (FC)	.08
532	Jerry Browne	.03
533	Andy Hawkins	.06
534	Doc Edwards	.03
535	Todd Worrell	.08
536	Joel Skinner	.03
537	Pete Smith	.08
538	Juan Castillo	.03
539	Barry Jones	.06
540	Bo Jackson	.50
541	Cecil Fielder	.25
543	Damon Berryhill	.15
544	Jeff Sellers	.06
545	Mookie Wilson	.10
548	Bobby Witt	.08
550	Orel Hershiser	.25
551	Randy Ready	.03
552	Greg Cadaret	.06
554	Nick Esasky	.12
555	Bert Blyleven	.12
556	Bruce Fields (FC)	.06
557	*Keith Miller* (FC)	.15
558	Dan Pasqua	.08
560	Rock Raines	.25
562	Danny Cox	.06
564	Russ Nixon	.03
565	Jeff Russell	.06
567	David Wells	.08
569	*German Jimenez* (FC)	.03
570	Tony Gwynn	.30
571	Billy Ripken	.06
573	#1 Draft Pick (*Jim Abbott*) (FC)	1.25
574	Dave Clark	.06
575	Juan Samuel	.10
576	Greg Minton	.03
577	Randy Bush	.06
578	John Morris	.03
579	Astros Ldrs (Glenn Davis)	.08
580	Harold Reynolds	.08
581	Gene Nelson	.03
582	Mike Marshall	.10

583	*Paul Gibson* (FC)	.20
584	Randy Velarde (FC)	.10
585	Harold Baines	.10
588	*Luis Alicea*	.15
589	Dave Meads	.03
590	Andres Galarraga	.12
593	Drew Hall	.10
594	Jimy Williams	.03
595	Ted Higuera	.08
596	Kurt Stillwell	.06
597	*Terry Taylor* (FC)	.20
598	Ken Gerhart	.06
600	Wade Boggs	.90
601	Dave Dravecky	.06
602	Devon White	.10
603	Frank Tanana	.06
604	Paul O'Neill	.06
605	Bob Welch	.08
606	Rick Dempsey	.06
607	#1 Draft Pick (*Willie Ansley*) (FC)	.75
608	Phil Bradley	.08
609	Tigers Ldrs (Frank Tanana)	.06
610	Randy Myers	.08
611	Don Slaught	.03
612	Dan Quisenberry	.08
613	*Gary Varsho* (FC)	.15
614	Joe Hesketh	.03
615	Robin Yount	.35
616	*Steve Rosenberg* (FC)	.15
617	*Mark Parent*	.15
619	Checklist 529-660	.03
620	Barry Bonds	.10
621	Rick Mahler	.06
622	Stan Javier	.06
623	Fred Toliver	.03
625	Eddie Murray	.25
626	Jeff Reed	.03
628	*Matt Williams	.15
629	Pete O'Brien	.08
630	Mike Greenwell	.60
632	*Bryan Harvey*	.20
633	Daryl Boston	.03

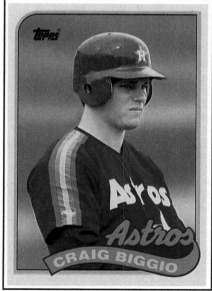

600 Wade Boggs

634	Marvin Freeman (FC)	.08
635	Willie Randolph	.06
636	Bill Wilkinson	.06
639	Athletics Ldrs (Walt Weiss)	.15
640	Willie McGee	.10
641	Curt Young	.06
643	*Louie Meadows* (FC)	.12
645	Jack Morris	.12
646	Kevin Bass	.06
647	*Randy Johnson* (FC)	.35
648	FS (*Sandy Alomar*) (FC)	1.50
650	Kirby Puckett	.25
651	Tom Niedenfuer	.03
652	Rich Gedman	.03
653	*Tommy Barrett* (FC)	.12
654	Whitey Herzog	.06
655	Dave Magadan	.08
656	Ivan Calderon	.06
657	*Joe Magrane	.08
659	Al Leiter	.15
660	Will Clark	.50
661	Turn Back the Clock (Dwight Gooden)	.20
662	Turn Back the Clock (Lou Brock)	.08
663	Turn Back the Clock (Hank Aaron)	.15
664	Turn Back the Clock (Gil Hodges)	.06
665	Turn Back the Clock (Tony Oliva)	.06
669	Dodgers Ldrs (Orel Hershiser)	.12
670	Kevin Seitzer	.25
672	Allan Anderson	.06
673	Don Baylor	.08
674	Otis Nixon	.03
675	Bruce Hurst	.08
676	Ernie Riles	.06
678	Dion James	.06
679	Willie Fraser	.03
680	Gary Carter	.15
681	Jeff Robinson	.10

682	Rick Leach	.03
683	*Jose Cecena*	.15
684	Dave Johnson	.03
685	Jeff Treadway	.10
686	Scott Terry	.08
687	Alvin Davis	.10
688	Zane Smith	.06
690	Doug Jones	.10
691	Roberto Kelly	.25
693	*Pat Borders*	.20
694	Les Lancaster	.06
695	Carlton Fisk	.20
696	Don August	.06
699	Pirates Ldrs (Al Pedrique)	.06
700	Don Mattingly	1.50
701	Storm Davis	.08
702	Jamie Quirk	.03
704	*Carlos Quintana* (FC)	.35
705	Terry Kennedy	.06
706	Pete Incaviglia	.10
707	Steve Jeltz	.03
709	Tom Herr	.06
710	Dave Cone	.30
711	*Candy Sierra* (FC)	.12
712	Bill Swift	.06
713	#1 Draft Pick (*Ty Griffin*)	1.00
714	Joe Morgan	.03
715	Tony Pena	.06
717	Jamie Moyer	.03
718	Glenn Braggs	.06
719	Danny Darwin	.03
720	Tim Wallach	.08
721	*Ron Tingley* (FC)	.12
722	Todd Stottlemyre	.15
723	Rafael Belliard	.03
725	Terry Steinbach	.08
726	Dickie Thon	.03
727	Joe Orsulak	.03
728	Charlie Puleo	.03
729	Rangers Ldrs (Steve Buechele)	.06
730	Danny Jackson	.12
731	Mike Young	.03

161 #1 Draft Pick

49 Craig Biggio

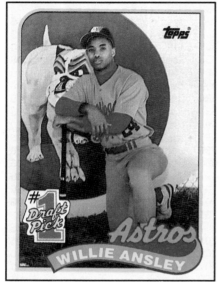

607 #1 Draft Pick

733	*Randy Bockus* (FC)	.06
734	Jody Reed	.10
735	Roger McDowell	.08
736	Jeff Hamilton	.06
737	*Norm Charlton* (FC)	.35
738	Darnell Coles	.06
739	Brook Jacoby	.08
740	Dan Plesac	.08
741	Ken Phelps	.06
742	FS (*Mike Harkey*) (FC)	.35
743	Mike Heath	.03
744	Roger Craig	.06
745	Fred McGriff	.40
746	*German Gonzalez* (FC)	.20
747	Will Tejada (FC)	.06
748	Jimmy Jones	.03
750	Bret Saberhagen	.15
752	Jim Gott	.03
753	Jose Uribe	.03
754	Bob Brower	.03
756	*Scott Medvin* (FC)	.20
757	*Brady Anderson*	.30
758	Gene Walter	.03

759	Brewers Ldrs (Rob Deer)	.06
760	Lee Smith	.08
761	*Dante Bichette* (FC)	.20
762	Bobby Thigpen	.08
763	Dave Martinez	.06
764	#1 Draft Pick (*Robin Ventura*)	1.25
765	Glenn Davis	.20
767	*Mike Capel* (FC)	.15
768	Bill Wegman	.03
770	Alan Trammell	.15
771	Ron Kittle	.06
773	Keith Moreland	.06
774	Frank Robinson	.08
775	Jeff Reardon	.08
776	Nelson Liriano	.06
780	Pedro Guerrero	.15
781	*Greg Briley* (FC)	.50
783	*Trevor Wilson* (FC)	.15
784	#1 Draft Pick (*Steve Avery*) (FC)	.75
785	Ellis Burks	.50
786	Melido Perez	.08

1989 TOPPS TRADED

Topps stuck with tradition by releasing a ninth annual 132-card Traded set in 1989. The company maintained the same format for the set (which copied the 792-card Topps set from the same year), and packaged the 131 individual cards plus a checklist card in a specially designed box. However, for the first time, the company experimented with selling complete sets in selected retail outlets such as toy stores. This added a new phase to the continuing debate over whether collectors would have to consider Traded cards as official "rookie" cards. Hot cards in the set include Jerome Walton, Tom Gordon, and Ken Griffey, Jr., all of whom are pictured on Topps cards for the first time.

41 Ken Griffey, Jr.

		MINT
Complete set		**$16.00**
Commons		**.05**

2	Jim Abbott	$1.25
3	Kent Anderson (FC)	.20
6	Steve Balboni	.10
7	Jesse Barfield	.12
8	Steve Bedrosian	.20
9	Todd Benzinger	.15
11	Bert Blyleven	.20
12	*Bob Boone	.15
13	Phil Bradley	.20
14	Jeff Brantley (FC)	.30
15	Kevin Brown	.20
16	Jerry Browne	.15
17	Chuck Cary	.25
20	Jack Clark	.20
23	Mike Devereaux	.20
26	John Dopson	.10
28	Jim Eisenreich	.15

29	Nick Esasky	.25
30	Alvaro Espinoza	.10
31	Darrell Evans	.10
32	Junior Felix (FC)	.90
34	Julio Franco	.20
37	Bob Geren (FC)	.65
38	Tom Gordon	1.25
39	Tommy Gregg	.15
40	Ken Griffey	.15
41	Ken Griffey, Jr.	5.50
43	Lee Guetterman	.10
44	Mel Hall	.10
45	Erik Hanson	.20
46	Gene Harris (FC)	.35
47	Andy Hawkins	.10
48	Rickey Henderson	.35
49	Tom Herr	.10
50	Ken Hill	.20
51	Brian Holman	.30
52	Brian Holton	.12
54	Ken Howell	.10

55	Bruce Hurst	.15
56	Chris James	.10
57	Randy Johnson	.30
61	Eric King	.12
62	Ron Kittle	.10
63	John Kruk	.12
66	Mark Langston	.35
70	Jim Lefebvre	.10

71 Al Leiter .15
72 Jeffrey Leonard .15
73 Derek Lilliquist .20
75 Tom McCarthy (FC) .15
76 Lloyd McClendon .10
79 Roger McDowell .15
81 Randy Milligan .20
82 Mike Moore .20
83 Keith Moreland .10
84 Mike Morgan .10
86 Rob Murphy .10
87 Eddie Murray .25
88 Pete O'Brien .15
89 Gregg Olson .85
90 Steve Ontiveros .10
91 Jesse Orosco .10
92 Spike Owen .10
93 Rafael Palmeiro .20
94 Clay Parker .25
95 Jeff Parrett .10
96 Lance Parrish .20
99 Doug Rader .08
100 Willie Randolph .15
103 Bip Roberts .15
104 Kenny Rogers (FC) .20
106 Nolan Ryan 1.35
108 Juan Samuel .15
109 Alex Sanchez .25
110 Deion Sanders (FC) .90
111 Steve Sax .20
112 Rick Schu .08
113 Dwight Smith 1.25
114 Lonnie Smith .15
115 Billy Spiers (FC) .45
116 Kent Tekulve .10
117 Walt Terrell .10
118 Milt Thompson .20
120 Jeff Torborg .10
121 Jeff Treadway .15
122 Omar Vizquel (FC) .25
123 Jerome Walton 3.00
124 Gary Ward .10
125 Claudell Washington .12
127 Eddie Williams .15
130 Mitch Williams .20
131 Steve Wilson .20

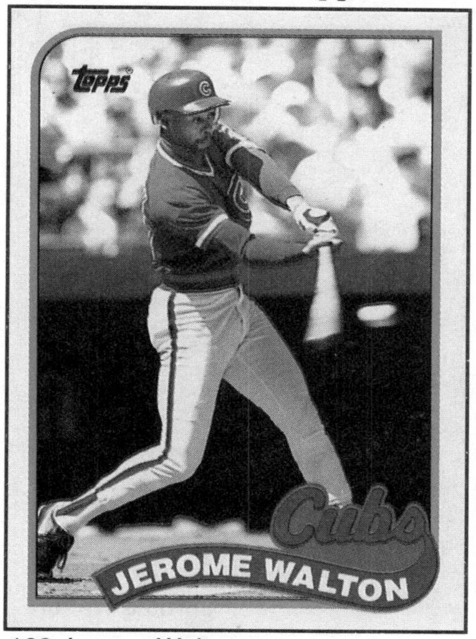

123 Jerome Walton

1989 UPPER DECK

The biggest hobby event of 1989 was the arrival of a new card company. Upper Deck, a card manufacturer from Anaheim, California, managed to penetrate the market shared by Topps, Fleer, Donruss, and Score. The Upper Deck cards feature large color photos both on the front and back, and are printed on glossy stock of a heavy weight. The company sold the cards in foil packs containing 15 cards for 89 cents per pack. Within weeks, the price shot up to $1.50 a pack. Upper Deck announced that no more than 60,000 to 70,000 foil pack cases were produced in 1989. The set, originally thought to number 700, grew to 800 when the company issued a second series in July, though factory-collated sets contain all 800 cards. Each card includes a small hologram on the back that is said to be counterfeit-proof.

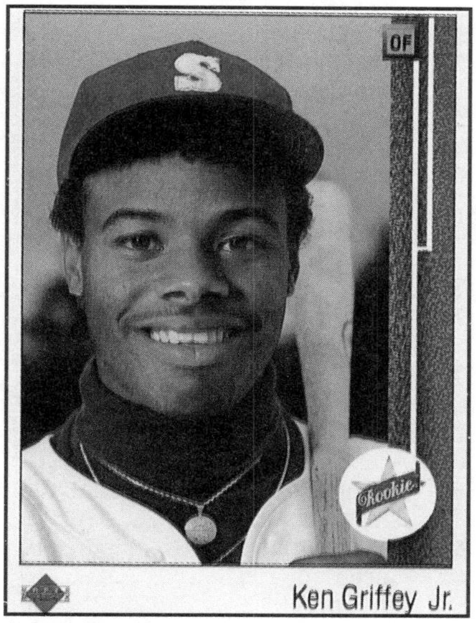

1 Star Rookie

	MINT
Complete set (1-700)	**$58.00**
Commons (1-700)	**.08**
Complete set (1-800)	**90.00**
Commons (701-800)	**.10**

1 Star Rookie (*Ken Griffey Jr.*) $25.00
2 Star Rookie (*Luis Medina*) .30
3 Star Rookie (*Tony Chance*) .20
4 Star Rookie (*Dave Otto*) .10
5 Star Rookie (*Sandy Alomar Jr.*) 2.00
6 Star Rookie (*Rolando Roomes*) .40
7 Star Rookie (*David West*) .40
8 Star Rookie (*Cris Carpenter*) .30
9 Star Rookie (*Gregg Jefferies*) 2.50
10 Star Rookie (*Doug Dascenzo*) .35
11 Star Rookie (*Ron Jones*) .35
12 Star Rookie (*Luis de los Santos*) .25
13 Star Rookie (*Gary Sheffield*) (SS designation on front is inverted) 4.00
13 Star Rookie (*Gary Sheffield*) (SS position correct) 2.50
14 Star Rookie (*Mike Harkey*) .45
15 Star Rookie (*Lance Blankenship*) .25
16 Star Rookie (*William Brennan*) .20
17 Star Rookie (*John Smoltz*) 1.00
18 Star Rookie (*Ramon Martinez*) .75
19 Star Rookie (*Mark Lemke*) .25
20 Star Rookie (*Juan Bell*) .50
21 Star Rookie (*Rey Palacios*) .25
22 Star Rookie (*Felix Jose*) .25
23 Star Rookie (*Van Snider*) .25
24 Star Rookie (*Dante Bichette*) .25
25 Star Rookie (*Randy Johnson*) .45
26 Star Rookie (*Carlos Quintana*) .35
28 *Mike Schooler* .25
30 *Jerald Clark* .20
31 Kevin Gross .08
32 *Dan Firova* .20
35 *Ricky Jordan* 2.00
37 Bret Saberhagen .15

Jerome Walton

765 Jerome Walton

39	Dave Dravecky	.08
41	Jeff Musselman	.10
45	*Sil Campusano*	.20
46	Mike Krukow	.08
47	*Paul Gibson*	.15
53	Steve Sax	.20
54	Pete O'Brien	.12
56	Rick Rhoden	.10
57	*John Dopson*	.25
58	Casey Candaele	.08
59	Dave Righetti	.15
66	John Tudor	.08
68	Mike Devereaux	.15
69	Brian Fisher	.08
70	Mike Marshall	.12
71	Zane Smith	.08
72	Brian Holton (photo is Shawn Hillegas)	2.00
73	Jose Guzman	.10
83	Les Straker	.08
84	Les Lancaster	.10
85	Allan Anderson	.12
86	Junior Ortiz	.08
87	Jesse Orosco	.10
88	Felix Fermin	.10
92	Cecil Espy	.10
94	Tim Leary	.08
95	Mitch Williams	.12
96	Tracy Jones	.10
97	Danny Darwin	.08
98	Gary Ward	.08
101	Bill Doran	.10
102	Tim Wallach	.12
103	*Joe Magrane	.12
105	Alvin Davis	.12
107	Shawon Dunston	.12
108	Tracy Woodson	.10
109	Nelson Liriano	.10
110	Devon White	.15
111	Steve Balboni	.08
112	Buddy Bell	.10
114	Ken Dayley	.08
115	Andres Galarraga	.15

116	Mike Scioscia	.10
118	Ernie Whitt	.10
119	*Bob Boone	.10
120	Ryne Sandberg	.25
122	Hubie Brooks	.10
123	Mike Moore	.10
125	Bob Horner	.10
126	Chili Davis	.10
128	Chet Lemon	.10
130	Orel Hershiser	.25
131	Terry Pendleton	.10
132	Jeff Blauser	.10
135	Gerald Young	.10
137	Alejandro Pena	.08
138	Jack Howell	.10
139	Tony Fernandez	.12
140	Mark Grace	2.00
141	Ken Caminiti	.15
142	Mike Jackson	.08
144	Andres Thomas	.08
145	Nolan Ryan	1.25
146	Mike Davis	.08
149	Jesse Barfield	.10
150	Matt Nokes	.25
151	Jerry Reuss	.10
152	Rick Cerone	.08
153	Storm Davis	.12
155	Will Clark	1.00
158	Randy Bush	.08
159	Ron Darling	.15
160	Kal Daniels	.12
161	Spike Owen	.08
162	Luis Polonia	.10
163	Kevin Mitchell	.65
164	*Dave Gallagher*	.25
165	Benito Santiago	.15
166	Greg Gagne	.08
167	Ken Phelps	.08
168	Sid Fernandez	.10
169	Bo Diaz	.08
170	Cory Snyder	.15
171	Eric Show	.10
172	Rob Thompson	.10

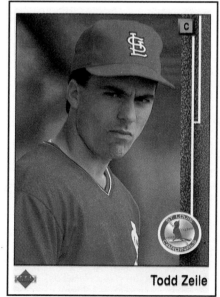

Todd Zeile

754 Todd Zeile

Nolan Ryan

774 Nolan Ryan

173	Marty Barrett	.10
174	Dave Henderson	.12
175	Ozzie Guillen	.10
176	Barry Lyons	.08
177	*Kelvin Torve* (FC)	.35
178	Don Slaught	.08
180	*Chris Sabo*	.75
181	Jose Uribe	.08
182	Shane Mack	.10
184	Todd Benzinger	.10
185	Dave Stewart	.15
186	Julio Franco	.10
188	Wally Backman	.08
189	Randy Velarde	.10
190	Joe Carter	.20
191	Bob Welch	.12
192	Kelly Paris	.08
193	Chris Brown	.08
194	Rick Reuschel	.12
195	Roger Clemens	.50
196	Dave Concepcion	.10
197	Al Newman	.08
198	Brook Jacoby	.12
199	Mookie Wilson	.10
200	Don Mattingly	2.00
202	Mark Gubicza	.12
203	Gary Gaetti	.15
204	Dan Pasqua	.10
205	Andre Dawson	.20
207	Kent Tekulve	.10
208	Rod Scurry	.08
210	Rickey Henderson	.35
211	Harold Baines	.15
212	Tony Armas	.08
213	Kent Hrbek	.25
214	Darrin Jackson	.10
215	George Brett	.35
218	Brett Butler	.10
219	Steve Jeltz	.08
220	Jay Buhner	.15
221	Bo Jackson	.75
222	Angel Salazar	.08
223	Kirk McCaskill	.10

224	Steve Lyons	.08
225	Bert Blyleven	.15
226	Scott Bradley	.08
227	Bob Melvin	.08
228	Ron Kittle	.10
229	Phil Bradley	.12
230	Tommy John	.12
231	Greg Walker	.08
233	Pat Tabler	.08
234	*Terry Clark*	.20
235	Rafael Palmeiro	.25
236	Paul Zuvella	.08
237	Willie Randolph	.10
238	Bruce Fields	.08
239	Mike Aldrete	.10
240	Lance Parrish	.15
241	Greg Maddux	.15
242	John Moses	.08
243	Melido Perez	.12
244	Willie Wilson	.12
245	Mark McLemore	.08
246	Von Hayes	.15
247	*Matt Williams	.15
248	John Candelaria	.10
249	Harold Reynolds	.12
250	Greg Swindell	.15
251	Juan Agosto	.08
252	Mike Felder	.08
253	Vince Coleman	.15
254	Larry Sheets	.10
255	George Bell	.25
256	Terry Steinbach	.12
257	*Jack Armstrong*	.35
258	Dickie Thon	.08
259	Ray Knight	.10
260	Darryl Strawberry	.45
261	Doug Sisk	.08
262	Alex Trevino	.08
263	Jeff Leonard	.12
264	Tom Henke	.10
265	Ozzie Smith	.15
266	Dave Berman	.08
267	Tony Phillips	.08

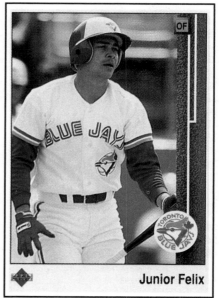

723 Gregg Olson

Gregg Olson

268	Mark Davis	.12
269	Kevin Elster	.12
270	Barry Larkin	.25
271	Manny Lee	.08
272	Tom Brunansky	.15
273	*Craig Biggio*	.75
274	Jim Gantner	.08
275	Eddie Murray	.25
276	Jeff Reed	.08
277	Tim Teufel	.08
280	John Kruk	.15
281	*Luis Alicea*	.20
282	Jim Clancy	.10
283	Billy Ripken	.10
285	Robin Yount	.35
286	Jimmy Jones	.08
287	Ron Oester	.08
288	Terry Leach	.08
289	Dennis Eckersley	.15
290	Alan Trammell	.25
291	Jimmy Key	.12
292	Chris Bosio	.08
293	Jose DeLeon	.12
294	Jim Traber	.10
295	Mike Scott	.15
296	Roger McDowell	.12
297	Garry Templeton	.10
298	Doyle Alexander	.10
299	Nick Esasky	.15
300	Mark McGwire	.75
301	*Darryl Hamilton*	.15
302	Dave Smith	.10
303	Rick Sutcliffe	.12
305	Alan Ashby	.08
306	Pedro Guerrero	.15
307	Ron Guidry	.15
308	Steve Farr	.08
309	Curt Ford	.08
311	Tom Prince	.10
312	*Chad Kreuter*	.15
313	Ken Oberkfell	.08
314	Jerry Browne	.08
315	R.J. Reynolds	.08

316	Scott Bankhead	.08
317	Milt Thompson	.08
318	Mario Diaz	.20
319	Bruce Ruffin	.08
320	Dave Valle	.08
321	*Gary Varsho* (photo is Mike Bielecki on card back, batting right-handed)	2.00
321	*Gary Varsho* (correct photo, batting left-handed)	.25
324	Drew Hall	.12
325	Don August	.12
326	*Israel Sanchez*	.20
327	Denny Walling	.08
328	Joel Skinner	.08
329	Danny Tartabull	.20
330	Tony Pena	.10
331	Jim Sundberg	.10
332	Jeff Robinson	.15
333	Oddibe McDowell	.10
334	Jose Lind	.12
335	Paul Kilgus	.20
336	Juan Samuel	.15
337	Mike Campbell	.12
338	Mike Maddux	.08
339	Darnell Coles	.10
340	Bob Dernier	.08
341	Rafael Ramirez	.08
342	Scott Sanderson	.08
343	B.J. Surhoff	.12
344	Billy Hatcher	.10
345	Pat Perry	.08
346	Jack Clark	.15
347	Gary Thurman	.15
348	*Timmy Jones*	.20
349	Dave Winfield	.35
350	Frank White	.10
351	Dave Collins	.10
352	Jack Morris	.15
353	Eric Plunk	.10
354	Leon Durham	.08
355	Ivan DeJesus	.08

Sandy Alomar Jr.

5 Star Rookie

Junior Felix

743 Junior Felix

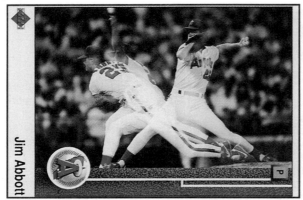

755 Jim Abbott

356	*Brian Holman*	.35
357	Dale Murphy (front photo reversed, jersey logo backwards)	150.00
357	Dale Murphy (correct photo)	.35
358	Mark Portugal	.08
360	Tom Glavine	.15
361	Keith Moreland	.10
362	Todd Stottlemyre	.20
363	Dave Leiper	.08
364	Cecil Fielder	.85
366	*Dwight Evans	.12
367	Kevin McReynolds	.15
368	Rich Gedman	.08
369	Len Dykstra	.12
370	Jody Reed	.15
371	Jose Canseco	1.50
372	Rob Murphy	.08
373	Mike Henneman	.15
374	Walt Weiss	.45
375	*Rob Dibble*	.25
376	Kirby Puckett	.35
377	Denny Martinez	.10
378	Ron Gant	.15
379	Brian Harper	.08
380	*Nelson Santovenia*	.20
381	Lloyd Moseby	.10
383	Dave Stieb	.12
384	Tony Gwynn	.35
385	Mike Flanagan	.10
386	Bob Ojeda	.10
387	Bruce Hurst	.15
388	Dave Magadan	.15
389	Wade Boggs	1.00
390	Gary Carter	.25
391	Frank Tanana	.10
392	Curt Young	.10
393	Jeff Treadway	.12
394	Darrell Evans	.12
395	Glenn Hubbard	.08
396	Chuck Cary	.08
397	Frank Viola	.15
398	Jeff Parrett	.12
399	*Terry Blocker*	.15
400	Dan Gladden	.08
401	*Louie Meadows*	.20
402	Tim Raines	.25
403	Joey Meyer	.08
406	Mike Schmidt	1.00

407	John Franco	.12
408	*Brady Anderson*	.30
409	Don Carman	.08
410	Eric Davis	.40
412	Pete Smith	.10
413	Jim Rice	.25
414	Bruce Sutter	.10
415	Oil Can Boyd	.08
416	Ruben Sierra	.60
417	Mike LaValliere	.08
420	Scott Fletcher	.08
421	Dale Sveum	.08
422	Bob Knepper	.08
424	Ted Higuera	.12
425	Kevin Bass	.10
426	Ken Gerhart	.08
427	Shane Rawley	.08
431	Gerald Perry	.10
432	Mike Greenwell	.60
434	Ellis Burks	.60
437	Charlie Hough	.10
440	Barry Bonds	.20
442	Rob Deer	.10
443	Glenn Davis	.15
444	Dave Martinez	.08
450	Don Aase	.08
451	Lou Whitaker	.15
452	Goose Gossage	.12
453	Ed Whitson	.10
455	Damon Berryhill	.12
456	Tim Burke	.10
460	Mark Salas	.08
461	Jeff Russell	.10
464	*Sherman Corbett*	.20
466	Bud Black	.08
467	Cal Ripken, Jr.	.35
468	John Farrell	.10
469	Terry Kennedy	.08
471	Roberto Alomar	.40
472	Jeff Robinson	.12
473	Vance Law	.08
475	Walt Terrell	.08
476	Kelly Downs	.10
477	*Johnny Paredes*	.20
478	Shawn Hillegas	.08
481	Johnny Ray	.10
484	Pete Incaviglia	.12
485	Brian Downing	.10
486	Jeff Stone	.08
488	Tom Niedenfuer	.08

489	Jay Bell	.08
490	Rick Schu	.08
491	*Jeff Pico*	.20
492	*Mark Parent*	.20
498	Pascual Perez	.10
499	Bill Long	.08
500	Kirt Manwaring	.12
501	Chuck Crim	.08
504	Glenn Braggs	.10
505	Joe Price	.08
506	Ken Williams	.08
507	Bill Pecota	.08
509	*Jeff Bittiger*	.15
510	Kevin Seitzer	.30
511	Steve Bedrosian	.12
512	Todd Worrell	.12
513	Chris James	.10
514	Jose Oquendo	.08
516	John Smiley	.12
517	Dave Clark	.08
518	Mike Dunne	.08
521	Lee Smith	.10
525	Paul Molitor	.15
526	Mark Langston	.15
530	Jack McDowell	.10
531	Greg Mathews	.08
533	Dan Quisenberry	.08
535	Danny Cox	.08
537	Andy Van Slyke	.15
538	Mel Hall	.08
539	Jim Gott	.08
540	Doug Jones	.15
541	Craig Lefferts	.08
542	Mike Boddicker	.12
543	Greg Brock	.10
545	Tom Bolton	.08
546	*Mike Macfarlane*	.20
547	*Rich Renteria*	.15
552	Dan Petry	.08
553	Mickey Tettleton	.12
555	Mike Witt	.10
556	Sid Bream	.08
557	Bobby Witt	.10

780 Dwight Smith

756 Ozzie Canseco

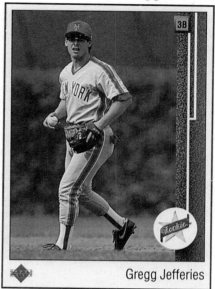

Gregg Jefferies

9 Star Rookie

622	Mark Grant	.08
625	*John Costello*	.20
627	Bill Schroeder (photo is Ronn Reynolds, holding shin guards)	2.00
628	Fred Manrique (photo is Ozzie Guillen, throwing)	2.00
629	Ricky Horton	.08
630	Dan Plesac	.12
631	Alfredo Griffin	.10
633	Kirk Gibson	.20
634	Randy Myers	.15
639	Bill Buckner	.10
640	Danny Jackson	.15
642	Jim Presley	.08
645	Dennis Rasmussen	.10
646	Juan Nieves	.08
647	Bobby Thigpen	.12
648	Tim Belcher	.10
651	*Oswaldo Peraza*	.20
652	Pat Sheridan (no position listed on front)	35.00
652	Pat Sheridan (outfielder listed)	.10
656	Fernando Valenzuela	.20
658	Frank Viola (AL Cy Young)	.15
659	Jose Canseco (AL MVP)	.25
660	Walt Weiss (AL Rookie of Year)	.08
661	Orel Hershiser (NL Cy Young)	.10
662	Kirk Gibson (NL MVP)	.10
663	Chris Sabo (NL Rookie of Year)	.08
664	Dennis Eckersley (ALCS MVP)	.10
665	Orel Hershiser (NLCS MVP)	.10
667	Orel Hershiser (WS MVP)	.10
669	Astros Checklist (Nolan Ryan)	.12

558	Tommy Herr	.08
559	Randy Milligan	.10
560	*Jose Cecena*	.20
561	Mackey Sasser	.10
562	Carney Lansford	.12
565	Dwight Gooden	.50
569	Mike Pagliarulo	.10
570	Ted Simmons	.10
572	Fred McGriff	.45
573	Wally Joyner	.35
574	*Jose Bautista*	.20
575	Kelly Gruber	.15
578	Bobby Bonilla	.15
580	Gene Larkin	.12
582	Howard Johnson	.12
583	Mike Gallego (photo on card back reversed)	2.00
584	David Cone	.35
585	*Doug Jennings*	.20
588	Al Leiter	.15
590	Roberto Kelly	.25
592	Pete Stanicek	.10
593	*Pat Borders*	.25
594	*Bryan Harvey*	.25
595	Jeff Ballard	.10
596	Jeff Reardon	.12
597	Doug Drabek	.08
601	Don Baylor	.12
602	Tom Pagnozzi	.08
605	Dave Parker	.20
607	Chris Gwynn	.10
609	Carlton Fisk	.15
610	Jay Howell	.12
611	Tim Crews	.10
612	Keith Hernandez	.20
614	Jim Eppard	.08
615	Jeff Hamilton	.08
616	Kurt Stillwell	.08
617	Tom Browning	.15
618	Jeff Montgomery	.10
619	Jose Rijo	.10
621	Willie McGee	.12

736 Tom Gordon

Tom Gordon

670	Athletics Checklist (Jose Canseco)	.15
678	Giants Checklist (Will Clark)	.15
693	Yankees Checklist (Don Mattingly)	.25
701	Checklist 701-800	.20
702	Jesse Barfield	.12
703	Walt Terrell	.10
704	Dickie Thon	.10
705	Al Leiter	.12
706	Dave LaPoint	.10
707	Charlie Hayes (FC)	.15
708	Andy Hawkins	.12
709	Mickey Hatcher	.10
710	Lance McCullers	.10
711	Ron Kittle	.10
712	Bert Blyleven	.20
713	Rick Dempsey	.10
714	Ken Williams	.10
715	Steve Rosenberg (FC)	.15
716	Joe Skalski (FC)	.20
717	Spike Owen	.10
718	Todd Burns (FC)	.25
719	Kevin Gross	.10
720	Tommy Herr	.10
721	Rob Ducey (FC)	.15
722	Gary Green (FC)	.15
723	Gregg Olson (FC)	3.50
724	Greg W. Harris (FC)	.15
725	Craig Worthington (FC)	.75
726	Tom Howard (FC)	.35
727	Dale Mohoric	.10
728	Rich Yett	.10
729	Mel Hall	.10
730	Floyd Youmans	.10
731	Lonnie Smith	.15
732	Wally Backman	.10
733	Trevor Wilson (FC)	.20
734	Jose Alvarez (FC)	.15
735	Bob Milacki (FC)	.15
736	Tom Gordon (FC)	2.75
737	Wally Whitehurst (FC)	.25

738	Mike Aldrete	.10	759	Rob Murphy	.10	780	Dwight Smith (FC)	3.00
739	Keith Miller (FC)	.12	760	Rick Mahler	.10	781	Lenny Harris (FC)	.20
740	Randy Milligan	.15	761	Fred Lynn	.15	782	Torey Lovullo (FC)	.12
741	Jeff Parrett	.12	762	Kevin Blankenship (FC)	.15	783	Norm Charlton (FC)	.15
742	Steve Finley (FC)	.35	763	Eddie Murray	.15	784	Chris Brown	.10
743	Junior Felix (FC)	3.00	764	Steve Searcy (FC)	.20	785	Todd Benzinger	.15
744	Pete Harnisch (FC)	.15	765	Jerome Walton (FC)	9.00	786	Shane Rawley	.10
745	Bill Spiers (FC)	.75	766	Erik Hanson (FC)	.25	787	Omar Vizquel (FC)	.25
746	Hensley Meulens (FC)	.75	767	*Bob Boone	.15	788	LaVel Freeman (FC)	.40
747	Juan Bell	.20	768	Edgar Martinez (FC)	.15	789	Jeffrey Leonard	.20
748	Steve Sax	.25	769	Jose DeJesus (FC)	.15	790	Eddie Williams	.15
749	Phil Bradley	.15	770	Greg Briley (FC)	.40	791	Jamie Moyer	.10
750	Rey Quinones	.10	771	Steve Peters (FC)	.15	792	Bruce Hurst	.15
751	Tommy Gregg (FC)	.15	772	Rafael Palmeiro	.20	793	Julio Franco	.15
752	Kevin Brown (FC)	.20	773	Jack Clark	.20	794	Claudell Washington	.15
753	Derek Lilliquist (FC)	.15	774	Nolan Ryan	6.00	795	Jody Davis	.10
754	Todd Zeile (FC)	7.00	775	Lance Parrish	.20	796	Oddibe McDowell	.12
755	Jim Abbott (FC)	8.00	776	Joe Girardi (FC)	.35	797	Paul Kilgus	.15
756	Ozzie Canseco (FC)	2.50	777	Willie Randolph	.20	798	Tracy Jones	.12
757	Nick Esasky	.20	778	Mitch Williams	.30	799	Steve Wilson (FC)	.25
758	Mike Moore	.25	779	Dennis Cook (FC)	.20	800	Pete O'Brien	.12

1990 DONRUSS

The nicest part about the 1990 Donruss set is its clean design. While other manufacturers cluttered cards with team logos, company trademarks, and other ornamentation, Donruss chose to use large rectangular photos, unblemished by frills. The top of each card contains only the player name in cursive print, followed by the position, team name, and "Donruss 90." Orange card backs are easy to read, thanks to the placement of player statistics in a white box. Following tradition, the 1990 set begins with 26 Diamond Kings (with paintings by Dick Perez), followed by a like number of Rated Rookies. This year's subset should be an investment winner in future years thanks to the popularity of Ben McDonald, Eric Anthony, Todd Zeile, Robin Ventura, Sandy Alomar, Jr., and Steve Avery. Donruss concludes the set with a commemorative card of late commissioner, A. Bartlett Giamatti. Flipped negatives, inverted pairs of card backs, and statistical glitches have created numerous error/variation challenges for advanced collectors.

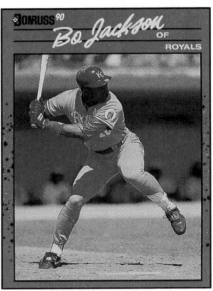

61 Bo Jackson

		MINT
Complete set		**$29.00**
Commons		**.05**

1	Bo Jackson (DK)	$ .65
2	Steve Sax (DK)	.20
3	Ruben Sierra (DK) (no line on top border)	1.00
3	Ruben Sierra (DK) (correct border)	.35
4	Ken Griffey Jr. (DK)	1.00
5	Mickey Tettleton (DK)	.10
6	Dave Stewart (DK)	.15
7	Jim Deshaies (DK)	.07
8	John Smoltz (DK)	.25
9	Mike Bielecki (DK)	.07
10	Brian Downing (DK) (negative reversed)	1.50
10	Brian Downing (DK) (correct photo)	.25
11	Kevin Mitchell (DK)	.35
12	Kelly Gruber (DK)	.15
13	Joe Magrane (DK)	.07
14	John Franco (DK)	.10
15	Ozzie Guillen (DK)	.20
16	Lou Whitaker (DK)	.08
17	John Smiley (DK)	.07
18	Howard Johnson (DK)	.30
19	Willie Randolph (DK)	.08
20	Chris Bosio (DK)	.07
21	Tommy Herr (DK)	.07
22	Dan Gladden (DK)	.07
23	Ellis Burks (DK)	.25
24	Pete O'Brien (DK)	.07
25	Bryn Smith (DK)	.07
26	Ed Whitson (DK)	.07
27	Checklist (DK)	.07
28	Robin Ventura (FC) (RR)	.65
29	Todd Zeile (FC) (RR)	1.65
30	Sandy Alomar, Jr. (RR)	.50
31	Kent Mercker (FC) (RR)	.30
32	Ben McDonald (FC) (RR)	2.25
33	Juan Gonzalez (FC) (RR) (negative reversed)	5.00
33	Juan Gonzalez (FC) (RR) (correct photo)	.60
34	Eric Anthony (FC) (RR)	2.00
35	Mike Fetters (FC) (RR)	.20
36	Marquis Grissom (FC) (RR)	1.00
37	Greg Vaughn (FC) (RR)	1.50
38	Brian Dubois (FC) (RR)	.25
39	Steve Avery (FC) (RR)	.65
40	Mark Gardner (FC) (RR)	.25
41	Andy Benes (FC) (RR)	.65

711 John Olerud

42	Delino DeShields (FC) (RR)	.85
43	Scott Coolbaugh (FC) (RR)	.30
44	Pat Combs (FC) (RR)	.50
45	Alex Sanchez (RR)	.15
46	Kelly Mann (FC) (RR)	.25
47	Julio Machado (FC) (RR)	.30
48	Pete Incaviglia	.07
49	Shawon Dunston	.07
50	Jeff Treadway	.05
51	Jeff Ballard	.04
53	Juan Samuel	.05
54	John Smiley	.05
55	Rob Deer	.05
57	Chris Bosio	.06
58	Carlton Fisk	.12
59	Kirt Manwaring	.07
60	Chet Lemon	.04
61	Bo Jackson	.65
63	Pedro Guerrero	.12
64	Allan Anderson	.07
65	Greg Harris	.07
66	Mike Greenwell	.25
67	Walt Weiss	.08
68	Wade Boggs	.35
69	Jim Clancy	.04
70	Junior Felix	.40
71	Barry Larkin	.15
74	Jesse Barfield	.06
76	Ricky Jordan	.25
77	Eddie Murray	.10
78	Steve Sax	.12
79	Tim Belcher	.08
81	Kent Hrbek	.12
83	Brook Jacoby	.08
84	Mike Marshall	.08
85	Kevin Seitzer	.08
86	Tony Gwynn	.15
87	Dave Stieb	.15
88	Dave Smith	.06
89	Bret Saberhagen	.15
90	Alan Trammell	.10

92	Doug Drabek	.08
93	Jeffrey Leonard	.06
94	Wally Joyner	.08
95	Carney Lansford	.08
96	Cal Ripken	.15
97	Andres Galarraga	.15
98	Kevin Mitchell	.35
99	Howard Johnson	.12
101	Melido Perez	.07
102	Spike Owen	.05
103	Paul Molitor	.10
105	Ryne Sandberg	.20
106	Bryn Smith	.06
108	Jim Abbott	.60
109	Alvin Davis	.10
110	Lee Smith	.06
111	Roberto Alomar	.10
112	Rick Reuschel	.08
113	Kelly Gruber	.10
114	Joe Carter	.10
115	Jose Rijo	.06
117	Bob Ojeda	.04
118	Glenn Davis	.08
119	Jeff Reardon	.06
120	Kurt Stillwell	.05
121	John Smoltz	.10
122	Dwight Evans	.08
123	Eric Yelding	.08
124	John Franco	.06
125	Jose Canseco	.50
126	Barry Bonds	.15
128	Jack Clark	.08
129	Dave Valle	.04
130	Hubie Brooks	.05
134	Jeff Robinson	.05
135	Ozzie Guillen	.09
136	Chili Davis	.05
138	Jerry Browne	.05
139	Bo Diaz	.04
140	Robby Thompson	.07
141	Craig Worthington	.10
142	Julio Franco	.10
143	Brian Holman	.07
144	George Brett	.10

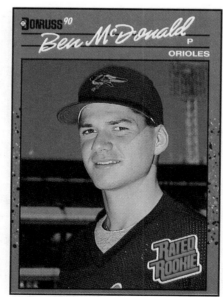

32 Ben McDonald

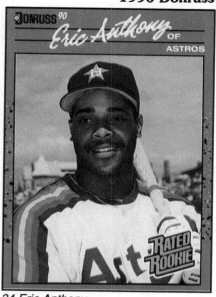

34 Eric Anthony

145	Tom Glavine	.10
146	Robin Young	.20
147	Gary Carter	.06
148	Ron Kittle	.07
149	Tony Fernandez	.07
150	Dave Stewart	.08
151	Gary Gaetti	.07
152	Kevin Elster	.05
154	Jesse Orosco	.04
157	Rick Sutcliffe	.06
158	Greg Maddux	.10
159	Andy Hawkins	.05
160	John Kruk	.06
162	John Dopson	.06
163	Joe Magrane	.06
164	Billy Ripken	.04
166	Nolan Ryan	.35
168	Dale Murphy	.10
169	Mickey Tettleton	.08
171	Dwight Gooden	.15
172	Jose Lind	.04
173	B.J. Surhoff	.04
174	Ruben Sierra	.12
175	Dan Plesac	.08
176	Dan Pasqua	.05
177	Kelly Downs	.05
178	Matt Nokes	.05
180	Frank Tanana	.05
181	Tony Pena	.07
182	Dan Gladden	.05
183	Bruce Hurst	.05
184	Roger Clemens	.25
185	Mark McGwire	.35
186	Rob Murphy	.04
188	Fred McGriff	.20
190	Don Mattingly	.90
192	Roberto Kelly	.08
193	Dennis Cook	.05
195	Alfredo Griffin	.05
196	Eric Plunk	.05
197	Orel Hershiser	.12
199	Randy Bush	.04
201	Ozzie Smith	.10

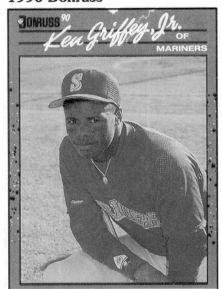

365 Ken Griffey, Jr.

258	Don Robinson	.05
259	Phil Bradley	.08
260	Cecil Espy	.05
262	Frank White	.07
265	David Cone	.10
266	Bobby Thigpen	.10
268	Terry Steinbach	.07
269	Kirby Puckett	.35
270	Gregg Jefferies	.35
271	Jeff Blauser	.05
272	Cory Snyder	.07
273	Roy Smith	.05
274	Tom Foley	.05
275	Mitch Williams	.08
276	Paul Kilgus	.05
278	Von Hayes	.10
279	Vince Coleman	.10
280	Mike Boddicker	.07
281	Ken Dayley	.05
283	*Kenny Rogers*	.10
284	Jeff Russell	.06
285	*Jerome Walton*	1.00
287	Joe Orsulak	.05
289	Ron Darling	.08
290	Bobby Bonilla	.15
292	Bobby Witt	.05
293	Greg Brock	.05
294	Ivan Calderon	.07
295	Steve Bedrosian	.06
296	Mike Henneman	.07
297	Tom Gordon	.20
298	Lou Whitaker	.08
299	Terry Pendleton	.06
300	Checklist	.05
302	Mark Davis	.07
303	Nick Esasky	.06
304	Rickey Henderson	.25
305	Rick Cerone	.05
306	Craig Biggio	.15
307	Duane Ward	.05
308	Tom Browning	.08
310	Greg Swindell	.08
311	Dave Righetti	.07

29 Todd Zeile

202	Pete O'Brien	.06
203	Jay Howell	.06
204	Mark Gubicza	.08
205	Ed Whitson	.05
206	George Bell	.10
207	Mike Scott	.08
209	Mike Heath	.05
210	Dennis Eckersley	.10
213	Lance Parrish	.07
214	Mike Moore	.06
215	*Steve Finley*	.20
216	Tim Raines	.10
217	Scott Garrelts	.07
218	Kevin McReynolds	.09
219	Dave Gallagher	.06
220	Tim Wallach	.08
221	Chuck Crim	.05
222	Lonnie Smith	.06
223	Andre Dawson	.12
224	Nelson Santovenia	.06
225	Rafael Palmeiro	.08
226	Devon White	.07
227	Harold Reynolds	.07
228	Ellis Burks	.20
230	Will Clark	.70
231	Jimmy Key	.07
233	Eric Davis	.35
234	Johnny Ray	.06
235	Darryl Strawberry	.35
236	Bill Doran	.05
237	Greg Gagne	.05
240	Marty Barrett	.05
242	Chris Sabo	.10
243	Dave Henderson	.08
244	Andy Van Slyke	.08
245	Alvaro Espinosa	.08
247	Gene Harris	.05
249	Brett Butler	.07
250	Willie Randolph	.07
251	Roger McDowell	.07
254	Jack Howell	.05
256	Tom Candiotti	.06
257	Todd Benzinger	.06

285 Jerome Walton

312	Mike Maddux	.05
313	*Lenny Dykstra	.08
316	Mike Scioscia	.07
317	Ron Oester	.05
318	*Gary Wayne*	.10
319	Todd Worrell	.06
320	Doug Jones	.07
322	Danny Tartabull	.08
323	Chris James	.05
325	Gerald Young	.05
326	Bob Boone	.10
328	Dave Parker	.10
329	Sid Bream	.05
330	Mike Schooler	.06
331	Bert Blyleven	.08
332	Bob Welch	.08
334	Tim Burke	.06
336	Randy Myers	.08
337	Eric King	.04
338	Mark Langston	.10
339	Ted Higuera	.07
342	Pascual Perez	.05
343	Kevin Brown	.06
344	Chuck Finley	.05
345	Erik Hanson	.07
346	Rich Gedman	.04
347	Bip Roberts	.05
348	Matt Williams	.20
349	Tom Henke	.07
351	Jeff Reed	.04
353	Frank Viola	.15
354	Terry Puhl	.04
355	Brian Harper	.04
356	Steve Farr	.04
357	Joe Boever	.05
358	Danny Heep	.04
362	Bob Kipper	.04
363	Clay Parker	.06
365	Ken Griffey, Jr.	1.75
366	Rex Hudler	.04
368	Kirk Gibson	.08
369	Jeff Parrett	.04
370	Bob Walk	.04

373	Mike Bielecki	.06
374	Tom McGrann (FC)	.20
375	Rick Mahler	.04
377	Gregg Olson	.15
378	Jamie Moyer	.04
379	Randy Johnson	.10
380	Jeff Montgomery	.06
381	Marty Clary	.04
382	Bill Spiers	.15
383	Dave Magadan	.07
384	Greg Hibbard (FC)	.20
387	Dave West	.07
388	Keith Hernandez	.06
390	Joey Belle (FC)	.65
391	Rick Aguilera	.08
393	Dwight Smith	.75
394	Steve Wilson	.12
395	Bob Geren	.20
397	Ken Hill	.05
398	Jody Reed	.05
399	Tom Brunansky	.07
402	Harold Baines	.07
404	Joe Girardi	.08
405	Sergio Valdez (FC)	.15
407	Glenn Hoffmann	.04
408	Jeff Innis (FC)	.15
410	Charlie O'Brien (FC)	.04
411	Charlie Hough	.06
412	Gus Polidor	.04
414	Trevor Wilson (FC)	.10
415	Kevin Ritz (FC)	.20
422	Jim Corsi (FC)	.04
424	Ken Caminiti	.05
425	David Wells	.04
426	Norm Charlton	.06
427	*Deion Sanders	.75
428	Dion James	.04
429	Chuck Cary	.04
430	Ken Howell	.04
431	Steve Lake	.04
432	Kal Daniels	.06
434	Lenny Harris (FC)	.08
435	Scott Scudder (FC)	.20

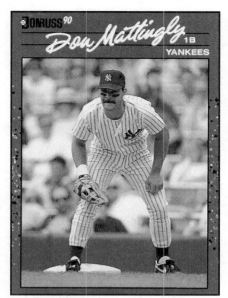

125 Jose Canseco

436	Gene Larkin	.04
438	Steve Olin (FC)	.20
440	Willie Wilson	.05
441	Mark Grant	.04
442	Mookie Wilson	.05
443	Alex Trevino	.04
444	Pat Tabler	.04
446	Todd Burns	.04
448	Jay Buhner	.08
449	Lee Stevens (FC)	.20
450	Ron Hassey	.04
451	Bob Melvin	.04
453	Greg Litton (FC)	.25
454	Mark Carreon	.06
457	Tony Fossas (FC)	.12
458	John Russell	.04
460	Zane Smith	.04
461	Jack Daugherty	.12
462	Rich Monteleone (FC)	.15
463	Greg Briley (FC)	.25
465	Benito Santiago	.15
466	Jeff Brantley	.15
467	Jose Nunez	.04
469	Ken Griffey	.05
473	Kevin Tapani (FC)	.20
474	Bill Buckner	.05
475	Ron Gant	.06
476	Kevin Romine (FC)	.05
477	Juan Agosto	.04
479	Storm Davis	.06
480	Jeff King (FC)	.15
481	Kevin Mmahat (FC)	.20
483	Omar Vizquel	.10
484	Jim Dwyer	.04
487	Ron Jones	.06
488	Jay Bell	.04
489	Sammy Sosa (FC)	.65
490	Kent Anderson (FC)	.15
492	Dave Clark	.04
493	Tim Birtsas	.04
495	Larry Sheets	.04
496	Jeff Kunkel	.04
497	Jim Presley	.04

499	Pete Smith	.06
500	Checklist	.04
501	Gary Sheffield	.35
502	Terry Bross (FC)	.15
503	Jerry Kutzler (FC)	.15
504	Lloyd Moseby	.06
505	Curt Young	.04
506	Al Newman	.04
507	Keith Miller	.04
508	Mike Stanton (FC)	.20
509	Rich Yett	.04
510	Tim Drummond (FC)	.20
512	Rick Wrona	.12
514	Hal Morris	.08
516	John Morris	.04
517	Carlos Quintana	.08
518	Frank DiPino	.04
519	Randy Milligan	.06
520	Chad Kreuter	.05
522	Mike Harkey	.10
525	Tony Armas	.04
527	Rick Reed (FC)	.20
528	Jerry Reuss	.05
529	Dean Palmer (FC)	.65
530	Jeff Petarek (FC)	.20
531	Carlos Martinez	.20
533	Mike Brumley	.04
534	Terry Leach	.04
535	Doug Strange (FC)	.15
536	Jose DeLeon	.07
538	Joey Cora (FC)	.10
539	Eric Hetzel	.06
543	Al Leiter	.05
544	*Jack Armstrong	.10
546	Rod Nichols	.04
548	Charlie Hayes (FC)	.15
549	Dickie Thon	.04
550	Tim Crews	.04
551	Dave Winfield	.15
552	Mike Davis	.04
556	Bud Black	.06
558	Jim Acker	.04
559	Eric Show	.04

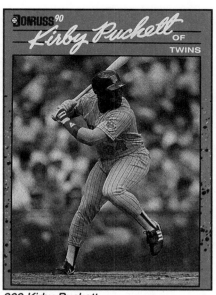

190 Don Mattingly

269 Kirby Puckett

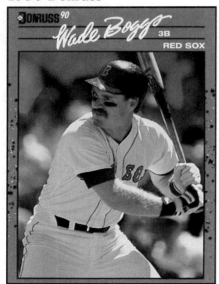

68 Wade Boggs

562	*Rick Luecken* (FC)	.20
563	Edwin Nunez	.04
564	Felix Jose	.05
566	Billy Swift	.04
567	Bill Schroeder	.04
568	Stan Javier	.04
569	Jim Traber	.04
572	Sid Fernandez	.06
573	Lance Johnson	.08
576	*Tommy Greene* (FC)	.25
577	Mark Grace	.25
578	*Larry Walker* (FC)	.25
580	Mike Witt	.04
582	Greg Harris	.07
583	Kevin Hickey	.04
585	Jeff Pico	.04
586	*Joe Oliver* (FC)	.35
587	Willie Fraser	.04
589	Kevin Bass	.05
590	John Moses	.04
592	*Tony Castillo*	.10
593	Jerald Clark	.05
597	Gary Redus	.04
598	Mel Hall	.04
599	Rick Schu	.04
600	Checklist	.04
604	Don Carman	.04
605	Jim Gott	.04
606	Donn Pall	.05
609	Mike Felder	.04
611	Candy Maldonado	.06
613	Rick Leach	.04
614	Jerry Reed	.04
616	Billy Hatcher	.05
617	Don August	.05
618	Tim Teufel	.04
620	Manny Lee	.04
621	Gary Ward	.05
622	*Mark Guthrie* (FC)	.20
624	Mark Lemke	.04
625	Fernando Valenzuela	.09
626	*Paul Sorrento* (FC)	.15
627	Glenallen Hill	.20

628	Les Lancaster	.05
629	Vance Law	.04
630	Randy Velarde (FC)	.10
632	Willie McGee	.07
633	Oil Can Boyd	.06
634	Cris Carpenter	.05
636	Tracy Jones	.04
637	Terry Steinbach AS	.10
638	Brady Anderson	.07
639	Jack Morris	.06
640	*Jaimie Navarro* (FC)	.20
641	Darrin Jackson	.04
642	*Mike Dyer* (FC)	.15
643	Mike Schmidt	.45
644	Henry Cotto	.04
646	*Francisco Cabrera* (FC)	.35
650	Bo Jackson AS (back reads "Recent Major League Performance")	3.00
650	Bo Jackson AS (correct card-back reads "All-Star Game Performance")	.50
651	Steve Lyons	.04
653	Ted Power	.04
654	Howard Johnson AS	.10
655	*Mauro Gozzo* (FC)	.15
656	*Mike Blowers* (FC)	.25
657	Paul Gibson	.04
658	Neal Heaton	.06
659	5000 K (Nolan Ryan) (card number 665 on back)	12.00
659	5000 K (Nolan Ryan) (correct card)	1.25
660	Harold Baines AS (back reads "Recent Major League Performance")	5.00
660	Harold Baines AS (line through star on front, incorrect back)	15.00
661	Gary Pettis	.05
662	*Clint Zavaras* (FC)	.20
663	Rick Reuschel	.06

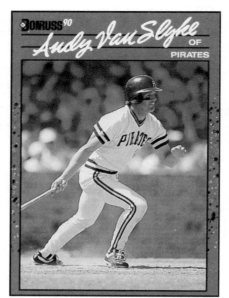

244 Andy Van Slyke

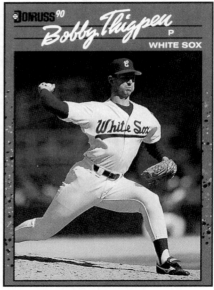

266 Bobby Thigpen

665	King of Kings (Nolan Ryan) (number 659 on back)	12.00
665	King of Kings (Nolan Ryan) (correct card)	1.25
668	Bill Landrum (FC)	.05
669	Todd Stottlemyre	.05
670	Tim Leary	.05
671	*John Wetteland* (FC)	.25
673	Ruben Sierra AS	.10
674	Pedro Guerrero AS	.10
676	Cal Ripken AS	.10
678	Goose Gossage	.04
679	*Gary Mielke* (FC)	.20
680	Bill Bathe	.04
682	*Xavier Hernandez* (FC)	.20
683	Kirby Puckett AS	.10
685	*Ramon Martinez	.15
686	Tim Jones	.04
687	Tom Filer	.04
689	*Bernie Williams* (FC)	.15
690	*Chip Hale* (FC)	.25
691	*Beau Allred* (FC)	.20
692	Ryne Sandberg AS	.10
693	*Jeff Huson* (FC)	.25
695	Eric Davis AS	.10
697	Mark McGwire AS	.10
698	*Steve Cummings* (FC)	.20
699	*George Canale* (FC)	.20
701	Julio Franco AS	.10
702	*Dave Johnson* (FC)	.10
703	Dave Stewart AS	.10
704	*Dave Justice* (FC)	.20
705	Tony Gwynn AS	.12
706	Greg Myers	.06
707	Will Clark AS	.15
708	Benito Santiago AS	.10
710	Ozzie Smith AS	.10
711	*John Olerud* (FC)	3.00
712	Wade Boggs AS	.10
713	*Gary Eave* (FC)	.10
715	Kevin Mitchell AS	.10
716	Bart Giamatti	1.00

1990 DONRUSS ROOKIES

Although Donruss was one of the leading card makers of 1990 with its attractive standard set, the company lost steam with "The Rookies," its 56-card extension set. Due to a limited concept, fewer cards, and high cost relative to its competition, collectors were able to restrain their enthusiasm for the set. In fact, "The Rookies" paled in comparison with the larger fall sets from Fleer, Score, Topps, and Upper Deck. Each of these companies produced more cards in their season-ending subsets than Donruss, and each included traded players within its run. In a way, Donruss became a victim of the success of its earlier edition, since so many noted newcomers were featured in the Rated Rookies subset that was part of the standard Donruss edition. The only hot cards in this Rookies set are those of Dave Justice, Ben McDonald, and John Olerud. Special logos on the card fronts and bright green borders identify the Donruss Rookies, in contrast to the red borders used on the earlier set.

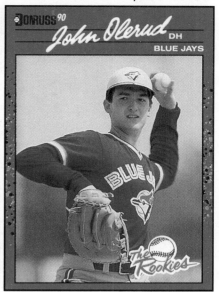

2 John Olerud

		MINT
Complete set		**$12.00**
Commons		**.07**
1	Sandy Alomar	$ .30
2	John Olerud	1.50
3	Pat Combs	.15
4	Brian Dubois	.07
5	Felix Jose	.15
6	Delino DeShields	.50
7	Mike Stanton	.10
8	Mike Munoz	.10
9	Craig Grebeck	.15
11	Joe Kraemer	.10
12	Bill Sampen	.25
13	Brian Bohanon	.10
14	Dave Justice	1.75
15	Robin Ventura	.15
16	Greg Vaughn	.45
17	Wayne Edwards	.15
18	Shawn Boskie	.25
19	Carlos Baerga	.35
20	Mark Gardner	.20
21	Kevin Appier	.35
22	Mike Harkey	.25
23	Tim Layana	.15
26	Mike Blowers	.15
27	Scott Ruskin	.15
28	Dana Kiecker	.20
29	Willie Blair	.10
30	Ben McDonald	.85
31	Todd Zeile	.35
32	Scott Coolbaugh	.15
34	Mike Hartley	.20
36	Kevin Wickander	.10
37	Carlos Hernandez	.10
38	Brian Traxler	.12
39	Marty Brown	.12
40	Scott Radinsky	.15
41	Julio Machado	.15
42	Steve Avery	.30
45	Marquis Grissom	.35
46	Greg Olson	.20
47	Dave Hollins	.15
48	Jerald Clark	.15
49	Eric Anthony	.35
50	Tim Drummond	.10
51	John Burkett	.25
52	Brent Knackert	.07
53	Jeff Shaw	.10
54	John Orton	.15
55	Terry Shumpert	.20
56	Checklist	.07

1990 FLEER

A modest card design and a set smaller in number than some of its competition prevented the 1990 Fleer set from becoming a popular collectible. Card fronts with small photos and large white borders seem unimaginative, while backs, using red-and-blue ink (along with annoying pink-and-white stripes), are hard to read. For cards of younger players with fewer statistics, Fleer chose in many cases to leave the remaining space unoccupied. However, the Philadelphia-based company's newest innovation was its most successful: A "Players of the Decade" subset highlights memorable stars from the 1980s on a year-by-year basis. While Fleer's 1990 set includes numerous rookies, many important names wind up sharing cards. In an outdated practice from previous years, Fleer created a subset for rookie stars using photos of two players. Surprisingly, several of these two-photo cards pair rookies of different teams and unrelated positions. Set collectors appreciate the numbering system Fleer uses: Cards are numbered consecutively by team, starting with last year's champion Oakland A's.

		MINT
Complete set		**$23.00**
Commons		**.05**
2	Todd Burns	$ .06
3	Jose Canseco	.75
5	Storm Davis	.07
6	Dennis Eckersley	.15
9	Dave Henderson	.10
10	Rickey Henderson	.35
12	Stan Javier	.06
13	Felix Jose	.10
14	Carney Lansford	.09
15	Mark McGwire	.75

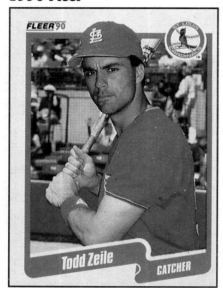

265 Todd Zeile

76	George Bell	.10
77	Pat Borders	.07
78	John Cerutti	.05
79	*Junior Felix*	.75
80	Tony Fernandez	.09
82	*Mauro Gozzo* (FC)	.15
83	Kelly Gruber	.12
84	Tom Henke	.07
85	Jimmy Key	.06
86	Manny Lee	.05
89	Fred McGriff	.25
90	Lloyd Moseby	.07
92	Alex Sanchez	.06
93	Dave Stieb	.09
94	Todd Stottlemyre	.09
95	Duane Ward	.05
96	David Wells	.05
97	Ernie Whitt	.05
99	Mookie Wilson	.07
100	*Kevin Appier* (FC)	.20
102	Bob Boone	.08
103	George Brett	.15
104	Jose DeJesus	.06
107	Steve Farr	.05
108	Tom Gordon	.50
109	Mark Gubicza	.09
110	Bo Jackson	.35
111	Terry Leach	.05
113	*Rick Luecken* (FC)	.20
115	Jeff Montgomery	.06
116	Bret Saberhagen	.10
117	Kevin Seitzer	.09
118	Kurt Stillwell	.08
119	Pat Tabler	.05
122	Frank White	.07
123	Willie Wilson	.06
124	*Matt Winters* (FC)	.15
125	Jim Abbott	.90
126	Tony Armas	.05
127	Dante Bichette	.09
128	Bert Blyleven	.09
129	Chili Davis	.06
130	Brian Downing	.06

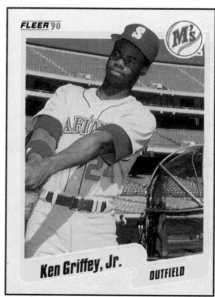

513 Ken Griffey, Jr.

44 Jerome Walton

16	Mike Moore	.10
17	Gene Nelson	.05
18	Dave Parker	.12
19	Tony Phillips	.05
20	Terry Steinbach	.10
21	Dave Stewart	.15
22	Walt Weiss	.10
23	Bob Welch	.10
27	Mike Bielecki	.08
29	Andre Dawson	.15
30	Shawon Dunston	.07
31	Joe Girardi	.20
32	Mark Grace	.25
33	Mike Harkey	.12
35	Les Lancaster	.06
36	Vance Law	.05
37	Greg Maddux	.10
39	Jeff Pico	.05
40	Ryne Sandberg	.25
42	Dwight Smith	.65
43	Rick Sutcliffe	.08
44	*Jerome Walton*	1.00
47	*Dean Wilkins* (FC)	.15
48	Mitch Williams	.15
49	Steve Wilson	.05
50	Steve Bedrosian	.07
51	*Mike Benjamin* (FC)	.35
52	*Jeff Brantley*	.15
53	Brett Butler	.07
54	Will Clark	.60
55	Kelly Downs	.05
56	Scott Garrelts	.07
58	Terry Kennedy	.05
61	*Greg Litton*	.20
62	Candy Maldonado	.08
63	Kirt Manwaring	.06
64	*Randy McCament* (FC)	.20
65	Kevin Mitchell	.30
68	Rick Reuschel	.09
72	Chris Speier	.05
73	Robby Thompson	.07
74	Jose Uribe	.05
75	Matt Williams	.20

131	*Mike Fetters* (FC)	.35
132	Chuck Finley	.06
133	Willie Fraser	.05
135	Jack Howell	.05
136	Wally Joyner	.10
137	*Jeff Manto*	.20
138	Kirk McKaskill	.06
140	Greg Minton	.06
141	Lance Parrish	.08
142	Dan Petry	.05
143	Johnny Ray	.05
144	Dick Schofield	.06
145	*Lee Stevens*	.25
147	Devon White	.08
148	Mike Witt	.05
149	Roberto Alomar	.10
150	*Sandy Alomar Jr.	.45
151	Andy Benes (FC)	1.00
152	Jack Clark	.06
154	Joey Cora	.05
155	Mark Davis	.08
156	Mark Grant	.05
157	Tony Gwynn	.25
158	Greg Harris	.08
159	Bruce Hurst	.06
161	Chris James	.05
164	Mark Parent	.05
166	Bip Roberts	.08
167	Benito Santiago	.15
169	Eric Show	.05
171	Ed Whitson	.05
172	Brady Anderson	.06
173	Jeff Ballard	.05
174	Phil Bradley	.08
176	*Steve Finley*	.20
177	Pete Harnisch (FC)	.10
178	Kevin Hickey	.05
180	*Ben McDonald* (FC)	2.00
181	Bob Melvin	.05
182	Bob Milacki	.05
183	Randy Milligan	.07
184	Gregg Olson (FC)	.65
185	Joe Orsulak	.05

186	Bill Ripken	.05
187	Cal Ripken Jr.	.15
189	Larry Sheets	.05
190	Mickey Tettleton	.08
192	Jay Tibbs	.05
193	Jim Traber	.05
195	Craig Worthington	.15
196	Don Aase	.05
197	*Blaine Beatty* (FC)	.35
198	Mark Carreon	.10
199	Gary Carter	.08
200	David Cone	.10
201	Ron Darling	.06
202	Kevin Elster	.05
203	Sid Fernandez	.08
204	Dwight Gooden	.20
205	Keith Hernandez	.06
206	*Jeff Innis*	.15
207	Gregg Jefferies	.50
208	Howard Johnson	.15
209	Barry Lyons	.05
210	Dave Magadan	.07
211	Kevin McReynolds	.07
213	Randy Myers	.08
214	Bob Ojeda	.05
215	Juan Samuel	.06
217	Darryl Strawberry	.35
218	Tim Teufel	.05
219	Frank Viola	.15
220	Juan Agosto	.05
222	*Eric Anthony* (FC)	2.25
223	Kevin Bass	.06
224	Craig Biggio	.10
225	Ken Caminiti	.06
226	Jim Clancy	.05
228	Glenn Davis	.15
229	Jim Deshaies	.06
230	Bill Doran	.05
237	Mike Scott	.08
238	Dave Smith	.06
239	Alex Trevino	.05
241	Gerald Young	.05
242	Tom Brunansky	.06

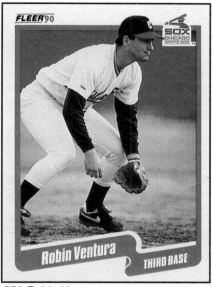

550 Robin Ventura

243	Cris Carpenter	.07
244	*Alex Cole* (FC)	.15
245	Vince Coleman	.10
247	Ken Dayley	.05
248	Jose DeLeon	.10
249	Frank DiPino	.05
250	Pedro Guerrero	.12
251	Ken Hill	.06
252	Joe Magrane	.07
253	Willie McGee	.07
254	John Morris	.05
255	Jose Oquendo	.05
256	Tony Pena	.06
257	Terry Pendleton	.06
258	Ted Power	.05
260	Ozzie Smith	.12
261	Scott Terry	.05
262	Milt Thompson	.05
263	Denny Walling	.05
264	Todd Worrell	.06
265	*Todd Zeile*	2.00
267	Mike Boddicker	.09
268	Wade Boggs	.40
269	Ellis Burks	.35
270	Rick Cerone	.05
271	Roger Clemens	.30
272	John Dopson	.06
273	Nick Esasky	.07
274	*Dwight Evans	.09
275	Wes Gardner	.05
276	Rich Gedman	.05
277	Mike Greenwell	.40
279	Eric Hetzel	.08
282	Joe Price	.05
283	Carlos Quintana	.20
284	Jody Reed	.06
287	Lee Smith	.07
290	Harold Baines	.09
291	Kevin Brown	.06
293	*Scott Coolbaugh* (FC)	.25
294	*Jack Daugherty* (FC)	.25
295	Cecil Espy	.06
296	Julio Franco	.07

297	*Juan Gonzalez* (FC)	.85
299	Drew Hall	.05
300	Charlie Hough	.05
303	Chad Krueter	.06
304	Jeff Kunkel	.05
307	Jamie Moyer	.05
308	Rafael Palmeiro	.07
309	Geno Petralli	.05
310	Kevin Reimer	.05
311	*Kenny Rogers* (FC)	.20
312	Jeff Russell	.06
313	*Nolan Ryan	.60
314	Ruben Sierra	.15
315	Bobby Witt	.05
316	Chris Bosio	.06
317	Glenn Braggs	.07
318	Greg Brock	.05
319	Chuck Crim	.05
320	Rob Deer	.06
321	Mike Felder	.05
322	Tom Filer	.05
323	*Tony Fossas* (FC)	.10
324	Jim Gantner	.05
326	Ted Higuera	.08
328	Bill Krueger	.05
329	*Tim McIntosh* (FC)	.25
330	Paul Molitor	.08
331	*Jaime Navarro*	.20
332	Charlie O'Brien	.05
333	*Jeff Peterek* (FC)	.25
334	Dan Plesac	.07
336	Gary Sheffield	.35
337	*Bill Spiers*	.35
338	B.J. Surhoff	.05
339	*Greg Vaughn*	2.00
340	Robin Yount	.25
342	Tim Burke	.06
344	Tom Foley	.05
345	Andres Galarraga	.15
347	*Marquis Grissom* (FC)	.85
349	Joe Hesketh	.05
350	*Jeff Huson* (FC)	.25
352	Mark Langston	.07

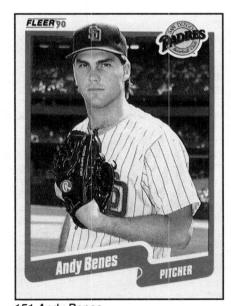

151 Andy Benes

447 Don Mattingly

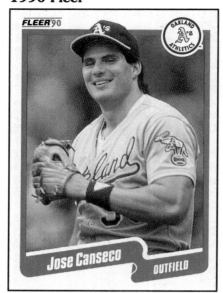

3 Jose Canseco

354	Dennis Martinez	.06
356	Otis Nixon	.05
357	Spike Owen	.05
358	Pascual Perez	.06
359	Tim Raines	.10
360	Nelson Santovenia	.08
361	Bryn Smith	.06
362	Zane Smith	.05
363	*Larry Walker* (FC)	.25
364	Tim Wallach	.07
365	Rick Aguilera	.10
366	Allan Anderson	.06
370	Randy Bush	.05
372	*Mike Dyer* (FC)	.15
373	Gary Gaetti	.07
374	Greg Gagne	.05
377	Brian Harper	.05
378	Kent Hrbek	.10
379	Gene Larkin	.05
382	Al Newman	.05
383	Kirby Puckett	.40
385	Jeff Reardon	.07
386	Roy Smith	.05
387	*Gary Wayne* (FC)	.15
388	Dave West	.25
389	Tim Belcher	.10
390	Tim Crews	.05
391	Mike Davis	.05
393	Kirk Gibson	.08
395	Alfredo Griffin	.05
396	Jeff Hamilton	.05
397	Lenny Harris	.05
399	Orel Hershiser	.12
400	Jay Howell	.06
401	Mike Marshall	.06
402	*Ramos Martinez	.25
403	Mike Morgan	.05
404	Eddie Murray	.10
407	Mike Scioscia	.07
409	Fernando Valenzuela	.10
410	*Jose Viscaino* (FC)	.40
411	*John Wetteland* (FC)	.40
412	*Jack Armstrong	.12

413	Todd Benzinger	.07
415	Tom Browning	.07
416	Norm Charlton	.06
417	Eric Davis	.25
418	Rob Dibble	.15
419	John Franco	.07
421	*Chris Hammond* (FC)	.25
422	Danny Jackson	.06
423	Barry Larkin	.15
424	Tim Leary	.06
425	Rick Mahler	.05
426	*Joe Oliver* (FC)	.30
427	Paul O'Neill	.07
429	Jeff Reed	.05
430	Jose Rijo	.07
433	Chris Sabo	.20
434	*Scott Scudder*	.30
437	Jesse Barfield	.07
438	*Mike Blowers* (FC)	.25
439	Tom Brookens	.05
441	*Alvaro Espinosa*	.25
442	*Bob Geren*	.25
444	Mel Hall	.06
445	Andy Hawkins	.06
446	Roberto Kelly	.15
447	Don Mattingly	.85
449	Hensley Muelens	.35
451	Clay Parker	.10
452	Eric Plunk	.05
453	Dave Righetti	.07
454	*Deion Sanders*	.50
455	Steve Sax	.12
456	Don Slaught	.05
457	Walt Terrell	.05
458	Dave Winfield	.15
459	Jay Bell	.05
461	Barry Bonds	.12
462	Bobby Bonilla	.12
463	Sid Bream	.06
465	Doug Drabek	.06
466	Jim Gott	.05
467	Billy Hatcher	.07
468	Neal Heaton	.07

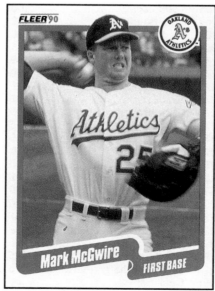

15 Mark McGwire

79 Junior Felix

469	Jeff King	.20
472	Bill Landrum	.06
474	Jose Lind	.06
476	Gary Redus	.06
477	*Rick Reed* (FC)	.20
480	John Smiley	.07
481	Andy Van Slyke	.09
482	Bob Walk	.05
485	*Joey Belle*	.65
486	Bud Black	.06
487	Jerry Browne	.06
488	Tom Candiotti	.07
489	Joe Carter	.08
493	Brook Jacoby	.07
494	Dion James	.05
495	Doug Jones	.07
498	Pete O'Brien	.07
499	*Steve Olin* (FC)	.35
500	Jesse Orosco	.05
502	Cory Snyder	.06
503	Greg Swindell	.10
504	Rich Yett	.05
505	Scott Bankhead	.06
506	Scott Bradley	.05
507	Greg Briley	.15
508	Jay Buhner	.10
509	Darnell Coles	.05
511	Henry Cotto	.05
512	Alvin Davis	.12
513	*Ken Griffey, Jr.	1.75
514	Erik Hanson	.20
515	Gene Harris	.10
516	Brian Holman	.07
517	Mike Jackson	.05
518	Randy Johnson	.15
519	Jeffrey Leonard	.06
520	Edgar Martinez	.10
521	Dennis Powell	.05
522	Jim Presley	.05
523	Jerry Reed	.05
524	Harold Reynolds	.07
525	Mike Schooler	.07
526	Bill Swift	.05

527	David Valle .05
528	*Omar Vizquel* .10
529	Ivan Calderon .06
530	Carlton Fisk .12
532	Dave Gallagher .06
533	Ozzie Guillen .10
534	*Greg Hibbard* (FC) .15
536	Lance Johnson .07
537	Eric King .05
538	Ron Kittle .07
539	Steve Lyons .05
540	Carlos Martinez .15
541	*Tom McCarthy* (FC) .15
542	*Matt Merullo* .25
543	Donn Pall .05
544	Dan Pasqua .06
546	Melido Perez .07
548	*Sammy Sosa* (FC) .35
549	Bobby Thigpen .07
550	Robin Ventura **1.00**
551	Greg Walker .05
552	Don Carman .05
553	*Pat Combs* (FC) .50
554	Dennis Cook .20
556	*Lenny Dykstra .10
557	Curt Ford .05
559	Von Hayes .09
560	Tom Herr .06
561	Ken Howell .05
562	Steve Jeltz .05
563	Ron Jones .20
564	Ricky Jordan .35
565	John Kruk .07
566	Steve Lake .05
567	Roger McDowell .05
570	Jeff Partrett .06
571	Randy Ready .05
572	Bruce Ruffin .05
573	Dickie Thon .05
574	Jose Alvarez .05
576	Jeff Blauser .05
577	Joe Boever .07
578	Marty Clary .05

195 Craig Worthington

579	Jody Davis .05
580	Mark Eichorn .05
582	Ron Gant .10
583	Tom Glavin .09
584	*Tommy Greene* (FC) .40
585	Tommy Gregg .15
586	*David Justice* (FC) .35
587	Mark Lemke (FC) .10
588	Derek Lilliquist .06
589	Oddibe McDowell .06
590	*Kent Mercker* (FC) .40
591	Dale Murphy .15
592	Gerald Perry .06
594	Pete Smith .07
595	John Smoltz .15
596	*Mike Stanton* (FC) .35
597	Andres Thomas .05
598	Jeff Treadway .07
601	*Brian Dubois* (FC) .35
602	Paul Gibson .05
603	Mike Heath .05
604	Mike Henneman .07
606	*Shawn Holman* (FC) .20
607	Tracy Jones .05
608	Chet Lemon .05
609	Fred Lynn .06
610	Jack Morris .07
611	Matt Nokes .06
612	Gary Pettis .05
613	*Kevin Ritz* (FC) .15
614	Jeff Robinson .07
616	Frank Tanana .06
617	Alan Trammell .10
618	Gary Ward .05
619	Lou Whitaker .09
621	Players of the Decade, 1980 (George Brett) .50
622	Players of the Decade, 1981 (Fernando Valenzuela) .20
623	Players of the Decade, 1982 (Dale Murphy) .20
624	Players of the Decade, 1983 (Cal Ripken Jr.) .20

54 Will Clark

625	Players of the Decade, 1984 (Ryne Sandberg) .25
626	Players of the Decade, 1985 (Don Mattingly) .50
627	Players of the Decade, 1986 (Roger Clemens) .25
628	Players of the Decade, 1987 (George Bell) .20
629	Players of the Decade, 1988 (Jose Canseco) .75
630	Players of the Decade, 1989 (Will Clark) .65
635	Human Dynamos .10
636	300 Strikeout Club .10
637	The Dynamic Duo .10
640	*Rudy Seanez* (FC), *Colin Charland* (FC) .20
641	*George Canale* (FC), *Kevin Maas* (FC) .20
642	*Kelly Mann* (FC), *Dave Hansen* (FC) .25
643	*Greg Smith* (FC), *Stu Tate* (FC) .20
644	*Tom Drees* (FC), *Dan Howitt* (FC) .20
645	*Mike Roesler* (FC), *Derrick May* (FC) .25
646	*Scott Hemond* (FC), *Mark Gardner* (FC) .30
647	*John Orton* (FC), *Scott Leuis* (FC) .20
648	*Rich Monteleone* (FC), *Dana Williams* (FC) .15
649	*Mike Huff* (FC), *Steve Frey* (FC) .20
650	*Chuck McElroy* (FC), *Moises Alou* (FC) .40
651	*Bobby Rose* (FC), *Mike Hartley* (FC) .25
652	*Matt Kinzer* (FC), *Wayne Edwards* (FC) .25
653	*Delino DeShields* (FC), *Jason Grimsley* (FC) .75

110 Bo Jackson

1990 FLEER UPDATE

Although this set is Fleer's tenth anniversary edition, there is nothing remarkable about it. Following tradition, the Update cards use exactly the same design used by the larger Fleer set issued earlier in the year. Unfortunately, Fleer (and most other companies) continued the practice of distributing its extension sets only through hobby dealers. By limiting the means available to collectors to obtain them, all extension sets become more expensive. One customer benefit Fleer provided in 1990 was to shrink-wrap individual sets in an effort to deter tampering. This positive move could make it harder for dealers to break open sets and offer individual cards for sale. Notable single cards include a three-image card honoring Nolan Ryan's 300 career victories and 6 no-hitters, along with cards of newcomers Frank Thomas, Kevin Maas, John Olerud, and Delino DeShields. Fleer continues as the only major manufacturer that groups and numbers players by team.

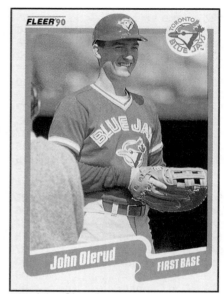

128 John Olerud

		MINT
Complete set		**$14.00**
Commons		**.07**

1	Steve Avery	$ .35
2	Francisco Cabrera	.10
3	Nick Esasky	.07
4	Jimmy Kremers	.12
5	Greg Olson	.25
7	Shawn Boskie	.25
8	Joe Kraemer	.07
9	Luis Salazar	.07
10	Hector Villanueva	.20
11	Glenn Braggs	.07
12	Mariano Duncan	.07
13	Billy Hatcher	.15
14	Tim Layana	.20
15	Hal Morris	.35
16	Javier Ortiz	.15
17	Dave Rohde	.10
18	Eric Yelding	.20
19	Hubie Brooks	.07
20	Kal Daniels	.10
21	Dave Hansen	.15
22	Mike Hartley	.20
23	Stan Javier	.07
24	Jose Offerman	.50
25	Juan Samuel	.07
26	Dennis Boyd	.07
27	Delino DeShields	1.00
28	Steve Frey	.20
29	Mark Gardner	.25
30	Chris Nabholz	.30
31	Bill Sampen	.30
32	Dave Schmidt	.07
33	Daryl Boston	.07
34	Chuck Carr	.15
35	John Franco	.10
36	Todd Hundley	.20
37	Julio Machado	.20
38	Alejandro Pena	.07
39	Darren Reed	.15
40	Kelvin Torve	.12

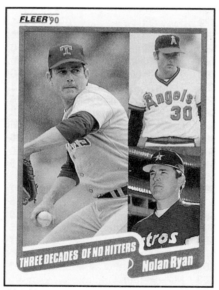

131 Nolan Ryan

41	Darrel Akerfelds	.10
42	Jose DeJesus	.25
43	Dave Hollins	.15
44	Carmelo Martinez	.07
45	Brad Moore	.15
46	Dale Murphy	.12
47	Wally Backman	.07
48	Stan Belinda	.20
49	Bob Patterson	.07
50	Ted Power	.07
51	Don Slaught	.07
52	Geronimo Pena	.20
53	Lee Smith	.15
54	John Tudor	.07
55	Joe Carter	.15
56	Tom Howard	.15
57	Craig Lefferts	.07
58	Rafael Valdez	.30
59	Dave Anderson	.07

60	Kevin Bass	.07
61	John Burkett	.25
62	Gary Carter	.12
63	Rick Parker	.15
64	Trevor Wilson	.15
65	Chris Hoiles	.30
66	Tim Hulett	.07
67	Dave Johnson	.07
68	Curt Schilling	.07
69	David Segui	.35
70	Tom Brunansky	.07
71	Greg Harris	.07
72	Dana Kiecker	.20
73	Tim Naehring	.25
74	Tony Pena	.07
75	Jeff Reardon	.10
76	Jerry Reed	.07
77	Mark Eichhorn	.07
78	Mark Langston	.12
79	John Orton	.15
80	Luis Polonia	.07
81	Dave Winfield	.15
82	Cliff Young	.15
83	Wayne Edwards	.25
84	Alex Fernandez	.45
85	Craig Grebeck	.15
86	Scott Radinsky	.20
87	Frank Thomas	3.50
88	Beau Allred	.25
89	Sandy Alomar, Jr.	.40
90	Carlos Baerga	.25
91	Kevin Bearse	.20
92	Chris James	.07
93	Candy Maldonado	.07
94	Jeff Manto	.10
95	Cecil Fielder	.35
96	Travis Fryman	.35
97	Lloyd Moseby	.07
98	Edwin Nunez	.07
99	Tony Phillips	.07
100	Larry Sheets	.07
101	Mark Davis	.07
102	Storm Davis	.07

103	Gerald Perry	.07
104	Terry Shumpert	.25
105	Edgar Diaz	.10
106	Dave Parker	.15
107	Tim Drummond	.12
108	Junior Ortiz	.07
110	Kevin Tapani	.35
111	Oscar Azocar	.20
112	Jim Leyritz	.25

113	Kevin Maas	3.50
114	Alan Mills	.20
115	Matt Nokes	.07
116	Pascual Perez	.07
117	Ozzie Canseco	.50
118	Scott Sanderson	.08
119	Tino Martinez	.75
120	Jeff Schaefer	.07
121	Matt Young	.07

1990 Fleer Update/1990 Score

122	Brian Bohanon	.15
123	Jeff Huson	.20
126	Willie Blair	.20
127	Glenallen Hill	.25
128	John Olerud	2.00
129	Luis Sojo	.20
130	Mark Whiten	.25
131	Nolan Ryan	2.00
132	Checklist	.06

1990 SCORE

Score was the surprise hit of the hobby world in 1990. After a mediocre 1989 showing, the 704 cards in its 1990 set surpassed the $40 mark before the All-Star break. Decreased availability, due to a rumored short printing, drove 1990 Score prices up throughout the summer. One of the hottest cards in the set remains number 697, a black-and-white reproduction of Bo Jackson's football/baseball Nike poster, which shows him posing in football shoulder pads and toting a bat across his shoulders. Special subsets include cards of top draft picks from each team and a 13-card Dream Team. The latter uses tinted photographs of top stars in a tobacco-card format. Card backs include one-paragraph tributes from famous sportswriters. Score's biggest error/correction involves Ryne Sandberg's card. The initial cards carry an on-front designation of Sandberg as a third baseman, while the more common variety carry no infield position.

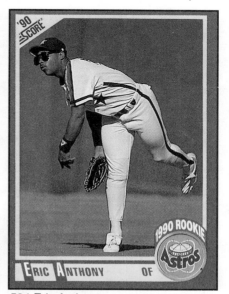

584 Eric Anthony

		MINT
Complete set		**$50.00**
Commons		**.05**

1	Don Mattingly	$1.50
2	Cal Ripken Jr.	.25
3	Dwight Evans	.08
4	Barry Bonds	.20
5	Kevin McReynolds	.12
6	Ozzie Guillen	.10
9	Alan Trammell	.09
10	Cory Snyder	.09
11	Jody Reed	.05
12	Roberto Alomar	.20
13	Pedro Guerrero	.12
16	Ricky Jordan	.35
17	Joe Magrane	.06
18	Sid Fernandez	.07
20	Jack Clark	.09
21	Bob Walk	.05
23	Lenny Harris (FC)	.20
24	Phil Bradley	.09
25	Andres Galarraga	.15
26	Brian Downing	.06
28	Eric King	.05
31	Mike Boddicker	.09
32	Tom Foley	.05
33	Brady Anderson	.07
35	Lance Parrish	.06
36	Von Hayes	.10
37	Lee Smith	.08
40	Mike Scott	.08
43	Gerald Young	.05
45	Dave Smith	.06
46	Dave Magadan	.07

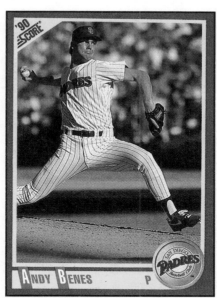

578 Andy Benes

50	Orel Hershiser	.12
51	Bip Roberts (FC)	.10
52	Jerry Browne	.08
54	Fernando Valenzuela	.10
55	Matt Nokes	.07
56	Brook Jacoby	.09
57	Frank Tanana	.06
60	Bob Boone	.08
63	Gregg Olson	.65
64	Todd Burns	.05

65	Todd Benzinger	.07
66	Dale Murphy	.15
69	Cecil Espy	.07
70	Chris Sabo	.20
72	Tom Brunansky	.08
74	B.J. Surhoff	.06
75	Lou Whitaker	.09
76	Ken Caminiti	.08
78	Tommy Gregg	.08
80	Eddie Murray	.12
81	Joe Boever	.08
83	Jose Lind	.06
86	Dan Plesac	.06
89	Tony Fernandez	.09
90	Ryne Sandberg	.45
91	Nick Esasky	.06
93	Pete Incaviglia	.07
94	Ivan Calderon	.07
95	Jeff Treadway	.06
97	Gary Sheffield	.50
98	Jeffrey Leonard	.07
100	Roberto Kelly	.15
101	Alvaro Espinoza (FC)	.15
102	Greg Gagne	.05
108	Chuck Crim	.05
109	Dave Valle	.05

697 Bo Jackson (NIKE poster photo)

110	Walt Weiss	.15
115	Dave Gallagher	.07
119	Mark Parent	.05
120	Wally Joyner	.15
121	Mark Gubicza	.08
122	Tony Pena	.07
124	Howard Johnson	.20
125	Steve Sax	.20
126	Tim Belcher	.10
127	Tim Burke	.08
128	Al Newman	.05
130	Doug Jones	.08
131	Fred Lynn	.07
132	Jeff Hamilton	.05
134	John Morris	.05
135	Dave Parker	.10
136	Gary Pettis	.06
137	Dennis Boyd	.07
138	Candy Maldonado	.08
139	Rick Cerone	.05
140	George Brett	.15
141	Dave Clark	.05
142	Dickie Thon	.05
143	Junior Ortiz	.05
144	Don August	.05
145	Gary Gaetti	.12
146	Kirt Manwaring	.08
147	Jeff Reed	.05
149	Mike Schooler	.09
150	Mark Grace	.65
152	Barry Jones	.05
154	Jim Deshaies	.08
155	Barry Larkin	.20
157	Tom Henke	.08
159	Bob Welch	.10
160	Julio Franco	.10
162	Terry Steinbach	.10
164	Tim Crews	.05
165	Tom Browning	.10
167	Harold Reynolds	.10
168	Ron Hassey	.05
169	Shawon Dunston	.10
170	Bobby Bonilla	.20
171	Tom Herr	.06
172	Mike Heath	.05
174	Bill Ripken	.05
175	Pete O'Brien	.08
176	Lloyd McClendon (back lists uniform number 1)	2.00

176	Lloyd McClendon (correct card—uniform number 10)	.25
180	Bert Blyleven	.10
182	Bill Doran	.07
183	Curt Ford	.05
184	Mike Henneman	.07
185	Eric Davis	.35
187	*Steve Davis* (FC)	.25
188	Bill Wegman	.05
190	Mike Moore	.10
192	Tim Wallach	.10
193	Keith Hernandez	.07
194	Dave Righetti	.08
195	Bret Saberhagen	.15
197	Bud Black	.07
198	Juan Samuel	.07
199	Kevin Seitzer	.15
200	Darryl Strawberry	.45
201	Dave Stieb	.10
203	Jack Morris	.07
205	Alvin Davis	.15
206	Jack Howell	.05
208	Terry Pendleton	.09
210	Kevin Brown (FC)	.10
211	Dan Petry	.05
214	Kevin Hickey (FC)	.06
215	Mike Krukow	.06
217	Kirk McKaskill	.07
219	Bob Forsch	.05
222	Jesse Barfield	.09
225	Pete Smith	.09
226	Mike Witt	.06
227	Jay Howell	.06
229	*Jerome Walton*	1.00
230	Greg Swindell	.15
233	Ken Hill	.05
234	Craig Worthington	.15
235	Scott Terry	.08
236	Brett Butler	.09
240	Dwight Smith	.50
244	Danny Tartabull	.12
245	Wade Boggs	.35
250	Nolan Ryan	.65
251	Kevin Gross	.05
252	Randy Milligan	.07
253	Mike LaCoss	.05
254	Dave Bergman	.05
255	Tony Gwynn	.35
256	Felix Fermin	.04

257	Greg Harris	.07
258	*Junior Felix*	.50
259	Mark Davis	.08
260	Vince Coleman	.15
261	Paul Gibson	.05
262	Mitch Williams	.10
263	Jeff Russell	.06
264	*Omar Vizquel*	.15
265	Andre Dawson	.20
266	Storm Davis	.06
268	Mike Felder	.05
269	Tom Candiotti	.08
270	Bruce Hurst	.09
271	Fred McGriff	.30
272	Glenn Davis	.15
273	John Franco	.10
274	Rich Yett	.05
275	Craig Biggio	.15
276	Gene Larkin	.05
277	*Rob Dibble	.20
278	Randy Bush	.05
279	Kevin Bass	.07
280	Bo Jackson	.60
281	Wally Backman	.06
283	Chris Bosio	.07
284	Juan Agosto	.05
285	Ozzie Smith	.10
286	George Bell	.10
287	Rex Hudler	.05
288	Pat Borders	.10
289	Danny Jackson	.06
290	Carlton Fisk	.12
291	Tracy Jones	.05
292	Allan Anderson	.07
293	Johnny Ray	.07
295	Paul O'Neill	.07
296	Carney Lansford	.10
297	Tom Brookens	.05
298	Claudell Washington	.07
299	Hubie Brooks	.07
300	Will Clark	.85
301	*Kenny Rogers*	.20
302	Darrell Evans	.07
303	Greg Briley	.25

589 John Olerud

304	Donn Pall	.07
305	Teddy Higuera	.08
306	Dan Pasqua	.07
307	Dave Winfield	.20
308	Dennis Powell	.05
309	Jose DeLeon	.10
310	Roger Clemens	.25
311	Melido Perez	.10
312	Devon White	.10
313	Doc Gooden	.25
314	*Carlos Martinez*	.20
315	Dennis Eckersley	.10
316	Clay Parker	.08
317	Rick Honeycutt	.06
318	Tim Laudner	.05
319	Joe Carter	.12
320	Robin Yount	.20
321	Felix Jose	.10
322	Mickey Tettleton	.08
323	Mike Gallego	.05
324	Edgar Martinez	.08
325	Dave Henderson	.09
326	Chili Davis	.08
330	Jim Abbott	.65
331	John Dopson	.10
333	Jeff Robinson	.08
334	John Smiley	.06
335	Bobby Thigpen	.09
338	Ken Griffey, Sr. (lists uniform number 25)	**2.25**
338	Ken Griffey, Sr. (correct card—uniform number 30)	.15
340	Ellis Burks	.30
343	Kevin Mitchell	.40
345	Mike Greenwell	.60
349	Jeff Ballard	.06
351	Randy Myers	.10
352	Shawn Abner	.07
353	Jesse Orosco	.05
355	Pete Harnisch	.08
356	Steve Farr	.05
358	Willie Fraser	.05
360	Rickey Henderson	.50

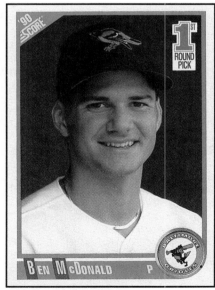

680 Ben McDonald

363	Mark Carreon	.10
364	Ron Jones	.10
365	Jeff Montgomery	.08
369	*Greg Hibbard* (FC)	.20
370	John Smoltz	.20
371	*Jeff Brantley*	.15
372	Frank White	.08
373	Ed Whitson	.06
374	Willie McGee	.09
375	Jose Canseco	.75
379	Steve Bedrosian	.07
380	Chuck Finley	.07
381	Kent Hrbek	.12
383	Mel Hall	.06
384	Mike Marshall	.07
385	Mark McGwire	.75
388	*John Wetteland*	.35
390	Rob Deer	.07
392	Todd Worrell	.07
394	Stan Javier	.05
395	Willie Randolph	.07
396	Bill Buckner	.06
397	Robby Thompson	.07
398	Mike Scioscia	.08
399	Lonnie Smith	.08
400	Kirby Puckett	.45
401	Mark Langston	.12
403	Greg Maddux	.15
404	Lloyd Moseby	.07
405	Rafael Palmeiro	.08
406	Chad Kreuter	.10
407	Jimmy Key	.09
409	Tim Raines	.15
410	Dave Stewart	.12
411	*Eric Yelding* (FC)	.20
412	*Kent Anderson* (FC)	.20
415	Randy Johnson	.10
416	Gary Carter	.07
419	Bryn Smith	.07
420	Ruben Sierra	.20
423	Sid Bream	.05
424	Jim Clancy	.05
425	Kelly Gruber	.15

583 Milt Cuyler

426	Rick Leach	.05
427	*Lenny Dykstra	.12
428	Jeff Pico	.05
430	David Cone	.10
431	Jeff Kunkel	.05
433	Ernie Whitt	.05
434	Bo Diaz	.05
435	Steve Lake	.05
436	Pat Perry	.05
437	Mike Davis	.05
439	Duane Ward	.05
440	Andy Van Slyke	.12
441	Gene Nelson	.05
443	Kevin Elster	.06
445	Roger McDowell	.06
446	Ron Darling	.08
449	*Bill Spiers* (birthdate reads "19")	**20.00**
449	*Bill Spiers* (birthdate reads "1966")	.25
450	Rick Sutcliffe	.07
451	Nelson Santovenia	.08
454	Benny Santiago	.15
455	Jose Uribe	.05
456	Bill Landrum (FC)	.08
460	Paul Molitor	.10
461	*Ramon Martinez (FC)	.35
463	Walt Terrell	.05
464	*Bob Geren*	.30
465	Rick Reuschel	.09
466	Mark Grant	.05
467	John Kruk	.07
468	Gregg Jefferies	.75
470	Harold Baines	.08
472	Tom Gordon	.50
473	Terry Puhl	.05
477	Zane Smith	.05
480	Jay Tibbs	.05
481	Tom Glavine	.09
482	Manny Lee	.05
483	Joe Hesketh	.05
484	Mike Bielecki	.06
485	Greg Brock	.06
486	Pascual Perez	.06

176 Lloyd McClendon

585 Greg Vaughn

595 Robin Ventura

487	Kirk Gibson	.09
490	Kal Daniels	.10
491	David Wells (negative reversed on back)	**7.00**
491	David Wells (correct card)	.05
493	Eric Show	.05
495	Ron Robinson	.05
497	*Greg Litton*	.25
498	Chris James	.05
500	Frank Viola	.15
501	Tim Teufel	.05
502	Terry Leach	.05
503	Matt Williams	.20
504	Tim Leary	.06
505	Doug Drabek	.08
507	Charlie Hayes	.10
508	*Joey Belle*	**1.00**
511	Jose Rijo	.07
513	Gary Ward	.06
515	Jim Gott	.05
517	Doug Bair	.05
518	*Scott Scudder*	.20
519	Rick Aguilera	.09
521	Jay Buhner	.08
522	Jeff Reardon	.07
523	Steve Rosenberg (FC)	.09
524	Randy Velarde (FC)	.09
526	Bill Long	.05
527	*Gary Wayne*	.12
528	*Dave Johnson* (FC)	.15
529	Ron Kittle	.08
530	Erik Hanson (FC)	.25
531	Steve Wilson (FC)	.20
533	Curt Young	.05
534	Kelly Downs	.06
535	Joe Girardi	.10
536	Lance Blankenship	.10
539	Mark Knudson (FC)	.08
540	*Jeff Wetherby* (FC)	.30
543	Eric Hetzel (FC)	.15
544	*Rick Reed* (FC)	.30
545	Dennis Cook (FC)	.15
548	*Gene Harris* (FC)	.20
549	Jeff King (FC)	.20

550	*Dave Dravecky (tribute)	.10
551	Randy Kutcher (FC)	.07
553	*Jim Corsi* (FC)	.10
554	Todd Stottlemyre	.15
555	Scott Bankhead	.08
556	Ken Dayley	.05
557	*Rick Wrona* (FC)	.25
558	*Sammy Sosa* (FC)	.45
560	Ken Griffey, Jr.	1.75
561	Ryne Sandberg (No Errors) ("3B" on front)	25.00
561	Ryne Sandberg (No Errors) (no position on front)	.35
562	Billy Hatcher	.06
563	Jay Bell (FC)	.07
564	*Jack Daugherty* (FC)	.30
565	*Rich Monteleone*	.20
566	Bo Jackson (All-Star MVP)	.75
567	*Tony Fossas* (FC)	.10
568	*Roy Smith* (FC)	.15
569	*Jaime Navarro* (FC)	.35
570	Lance Johnson (FC)	.20
571	*Mike Dyer* (FC)	.25
572	*Kevin Ritz* (FC)	.20
573	Dave West	.10
574	*Gary Mielke* (FC)	.25
575	Scott Lusader (FC)	.07
576	*Joe Oliver*	.30
577	Sandy Alomar Jr.	.75
578	Andy Benes (FC)	.75
579	Tim Jones	.05
580	*Randy McCament* (FC)	.25
581	Curt Schilling (FC)	.15
582	*John Orton* (FC)	.25
583	*Milt Cuyler* (FC) (back reads "pitched in 989 games")	2.25
583	*Milt Cuyler* (FC) (back reads "pitched in 98 games")	.45
584	*Eric Anthony* (FC)	2.50
585	*Greg Vaughn* (FC)	2.00
586	*Deion Sanders* (FC)	.45
587	Jose DeJesus (FC)	.15

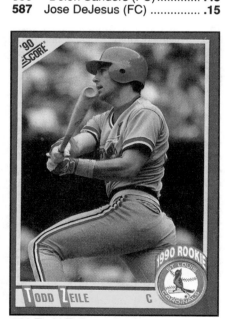

600 Todd Zeile

588	Chip Hale (FC)	.25
589	*John Olerud* (FC)	2.75
590	*Steve Olin* (FC)	.35
591	Marquis Grissom (FC)	1.35
592	*Moises Alou* (FC)	.50
593	Mark Lemke (FC)	.08
594	*Dean Palmer* (FC)	.25
595	Robin Ventura (FC)	.75
596	*Tino Martinez* (FC)	.75
597	*Mike Huff* (FC)	.25
598	*Scott Hemond* (FC)	.25
599	*Wally Whitehurst* (FC)	.20
600	Todd Zeile (FC)	2.00
601	Glenallen Hill (FC)	.35
602	Hal Morris (FC)	.20
603	Juan Bell (FC)	.15
604	*Bobby Rose* (FC)	.25
605	*Matt Merullo* (FC)	.20
606	*Kevin Maas* (FC)	.20
607	*Randy Mosek* (FC)	.25
608	*Billy Bates* (FC)	.20
609	*Mike Stanton* (FC)	.25
610	*Goose Gozzo* (FC)	.25
611	*Charles Nagy* (FC)	.25
612	Scott Coolbaugh (FC)	.35
613	*Jose Vizcaino* (FC)	.40
614	*Greg Smith* (FC)	.20
615	Jeff Huson (FC)	.25
616	*Mickey Weston* (FC)	.20
617	John Pawlowski (FC)	.20
618	*Joe Skalski* (FC)	.20
619	*Bernie Williams* (FC)	.90
620	*Shawn Holman* (FC)	.25
621	*Gary Eave* (FC)	.15
622	*Darrin Fletcher* (FC)	.25
623	*Pat Combs* (FC)	.90
624	*Mike Blowers* (FC)	.25
625	*Kevin Appier* (FC)	.30
626	*Pat Austin* (FC)	.25
627	*Kelly Mann* (FC)	.40
628	*Matt Kinzer* (FC)	.25
629	*Scott Hammond* (FC)	.25
630	*Dean Wilkins* (FC)	.25
631	*Larry Walker* (FC)	.30

632	Blaine Beatty (FC)	.40
633	Tom Barrett (FC)	.10
634	Stan Belinda (FC)	.25
635	Tex Smith (FC)	.25
636	Hensley Meulens (FC)	.40
637	Juan Gonzalez (FC)	.60
638	Lenny Webster (FC)	.25
639	Mark Gardner (FC)	.35
640	Tommy Greene (FC)	.25
641	Mike Hartley (FC)	.25
642	Phil Stephenson (FC)	.15
643	Kevin Mmahat (FC)	.15
644	Ed Whited (FC)	.15
645	Delino DeShields (FC)	.90
646	Kevin Blankenship (FC)	.15
647	Paul Sorrento (FC)	.40
648	Mike Roesler (FC)	.25
649	Jason Grimsley (FC)	.25
650	Dave Justice (FC)	.50
651	Scott Cooper (FC)	.25
652	Dave Eiland (FC)	.10
653	Mike Munoz (FC)	.25
654	Jeff Fischer (FC)	.25
655	Terry Jorgenson (FC)	.20
656	George Canale (FC)	.40
657	Brian DuBois (FC)	.40
658	Carlos Quintana	.12
660	Jerald Clark	.08
661	Donald Harris (FC) (#1 Draft Pick)	.30
662	Paul Coleman (FC) (#1 Draft Pick)	.45
663	Frank Thomas (FC) (#1 Draft Pick)	.65
664	Brent Mayne (FC) (#1 Draft Pick)	.20
665	Eddie Zosky (FC) (#1 Draft Pick)	.20
666	Steve Hosey (FC) (#1 Draft Pick)	.25
667	Scott Bryant (FC) (#1 Draft Pick)	.20
668	Tom Goodwin (FC) (#1 Draft Pick)	.40

300 Will Clark

591 Marquis Grissom

669	Cal Eldred (FC) (#1 Draft Pick)	.20
670	Earl Cunningham (FC) (#1 Draft Pick)	.50
671	Alan Zinter (FC) (#1 Draft Pick)	.25
672	Chuck Knoblauch (FC) (#1 Draft Pick)	.25
673	Kyle Abbott (FC) (#1 Draft Pick)	.25
674	Roger Salkeld (FC) (#1 Draft Pick)	.50
675	Maurice Vaughn (FC) (#1 Draft Pick)	.30
676	Keith "Kiki" Jones (FC) (#1 Draft Pick)	.25
677	Tyler Houston (FC) (#1 Draft Pick)	.45
678	Jeff Jackson (FC) (#1 Draft Pick)	.35

679	Greg Gohr (FC) (#1 Draft Pick)	.25
680	Ben McDonald (FC) (#1 Draft Pick)	2.50
681	Greg Blosser (FC) (#1 Draft Pick)	.25
682	Willie Green (FC) (#1 Draft Pick)	.25
683	Wade Boggs (Dream Team)	.30
684	Will Clark (Dream Team)	.35
685	Tony Gwynn (Dream Team)	.30
686	Rickey Henderson (Dream Team)	.30
687	Bo Jackson (Dream Team)	.50
688	Mark Langston (Dream Team)	.20
689	Barry Larkin (Dream Team)	.25
690	Kirby Puckett (Dream Team)	.25
691	Ryne Sandberg (Dream Team)	.25
692	Mike Scott (Dream Team)	.20
693	Terry Steinbach (Dream Team)	.20
694	Bobby Thigpen (Dream Team)	.20
695	Mitch Williams (Dream Team)	.20
696	Nolan Ryan (5000 K)	.50
697	Bo Jackson (NIKE poster photo)	17.00
698	Rickey Henderson (ALCS MVP)	.25
699	Will Clark (NLCS MVP)	.35
700	World Series Games 1 and 2	.35
701	Lights Out: Candlestick	.50
702	World Series Game 3	.35
703	World Series Game 4	.35
704	Wade Boggs (200 hits)	.25

560 Ken Griffey, Jr.

1 Don Mattingly

1990 SCORE ROOKIE & TRADED

Score's popularity continued with its Rookie & Traded set of 110 cards. Unlike other companies, for the convenience of collectors Score divided its updated set into two parts. Cards numbered 1 through 66 portray traded players in their new uniforms. Cards from 67 to 110 depict rookies and newcomers. This second group of cards, though no more difficult to find than the first 66, are generally more valuable. Top names in the rookies group include Frank Thomas, Ray Lankford, Bernard Gilkey, Scott Chiamparino, and Steve Avery. Surprisingly, the most talked about cards feature two of the least-known players. Card number 97 features D.J. Dozier, a football star attempting to start a second career with the Mets, a move similar to Bo Jackson's. Card number 100 shows Blue Jays prospect Eric Lindros, another two-sport man, who will also pop up in current hockey sets. This 1990 set, Score's third annual entry, is available mainly from hobby dealers. The demand for Score's regular 1990 set should help boost the value for this smaller extension set as well.

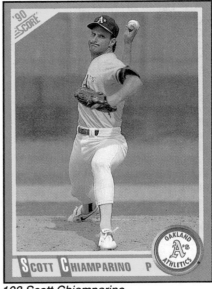

108 Scott Chiamparino

		MINT
Complete set		**$17.00**
Commons		**.07**

1	Dave Winfield	.15
2	Kevin Bass	.07
3	Nick Esasky	.07
4	Mitch Webster	.07
5	Pascual Perez	.07
6	Gary Pettis	.07
7	Tony Pena	.07
8	Candy Maldonado	.07
9	Cecil Fielder	.45
10	Carmelo Martinez	.07
11	Mark Langston	.12
12	Dave Parker	.12
13	Don Slaught	.07
14	Tony Phillips	.07
15	John Franco	.12
16	Randy Myers	.12
17	Jeff Reardon	.10
18	Sandy Alomar Jr	.25
19	Joe Carter	.12
20	Fred Lynn	.07
21	Storm Davis	.07
22	Craig Lefferts	.07
23	Pete O'Brien	.07
24	Dennis Boyd	.09
25	Lloyd Moseby	.07
26	Mark Davis	.07
27	Tim Leary	.07
28	Gerald Perry	.07
29	Don Aase	.07
30	Ernie Whitt	.07
31	Dale Murphy	.10
32	Alejandro Pena	.07
33	Juan Samuel	.07
34	Hubie Brooks	.07

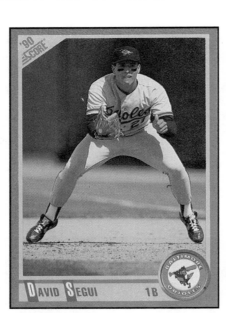

95 David Segui

35	Gary Carter	.10
36	Jim Presley	.07
37	Wally Backman	.07
38	Matt Nokes	.07
39	Dan Petry	.07
40	Franklin Stubbs	.07
41	Jeff Huson	.10
42	Billy Hatcher	.15
43	Terry Leach	.07
44	Phil Bradley	.07
45	Claudell Washington	.07
46	Luis Polonia	.07
47	Daryl Boston	.07
48	Lee Smith	.12

49	Tom Brunansky	.10
50	Mike Witt	.07
51	Willie Randolph	.07
52	Stan Javier	.07
53	Brad Komminsk	.07
54	John Candelaria	.07
55	Bryn Smith	.07
56	Glenn Braggs	.07
57	Keith Hernandez	.10
60	Chris James	.07
67	Francisco Cabrera	.20
68	Gary DiSarcina	.20
69	Greg Olson	.25
70	Beau Allred	.20
71	Oscar Azocar	.20
72	Kent Mercker	.12
73	John Burkett	.25
74	Carlos Baerga	.35
75	Dave Hollins	.20

100 Eric Lindros

76	Todd Hundley	.25
77	Rick Parker	.12
78	Steve Cummings	.15
79	Bill Sampen	.30
80	Jerry Kutzler	.12
81	Derek Bell	.20
82	Kevin Tapani	.35
83	Jim Leyritz	.25
84	Ray Lankford	.90
85	Wayne Edwards	.25
86	Frank Thomas	1.50
87	Tim Naehring	.25

88	Willie Blair	.12
89	Alan Mills	.20
90	Scott Radinsky	.20
91	Howard Farmer	.20
92	Julio Machado	.15
93	Rafael Valdez	.25
94	Shawn Boskie	.25
95	David Segui	.30
96	Chris Hoiles	.30
97	D.J. Dozier	.75
98	Hector Villanueva	.30
99	Eric Gunderson	.15

100	Eric Lindros	2.75
101	Dave Otto	.12
102	Dana Kiecker	.20
103	Tim Drummond	.15
104	Mickey Pina	.15
105	Craig Grebeck	.15
106	Bernard Gilkey	.40
107	Tim Layana	.20
108	Scott Chiamparino	.30
109	Steve Avery	.45
110	Terry Shumpert	.20

1990 TOPPS

Topps unveiled an eye-popping card design for one of its wildest-looking sets in nearly two decades. Not since 1972 had the usually conservative company dabbled with such a gaudy array of multi-colored borders. Surprisingly, the two-tone, partially speckled borders are contrasted with traditional, plain backs of yellow-and-black ink on gray card stock. One of the most popular features of the 1990 set is the return of #1 Draft Pick cards, which show pre-rookies in collegiate uniforms. Another repeat is the traditional subset of All-Star cards. In a new twist, future Hall-of-Famer Nolan Ryan is honored on the first five cards of the set, four of which depict him with the Mets, Angels, Astros, and Rangers. Due to what seemed like a higher-than-normal public distribution of cards and the abundance of prepackaged factory sets in retail stores, Topps prices have remained lower than most other 1990 sets.

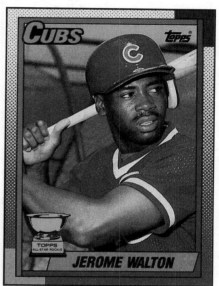

464 Jerome Walton

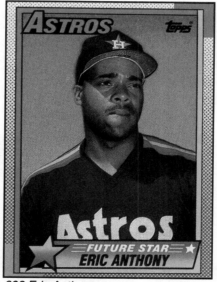

608 Eric Anthony

		MINT
Complete set		**$26.00**
Commons		**.05**

1	Nolan Ryan	$ .50
2	Nolan Ryan (The Mets Years)	.20
3	Nolan Ryan (The Angels Years)	.20
4	Nolan Ryan (The Astros Years)	.20
5	Nolan Ryan (The Rangers)	.25
6	1989 Record Breaker (Vince Coleman)	.10
7	1989 Record Breaker (Rickey Henderson)	.20
8	1989 Record Breaker (Cal Ripken)	.15
10	Barry Larkin	.15
11	Paul Gibson	.04
12	Joe Girardi (FC)	.15
14	*Mike Fetters* (FC)	.20
15	Teddy Higuera	.08
16	*Kent Anderson*	.10
17	Kelly Downs	.05
18	Carlos Quintana	.09
20	Mark Gubicza	.10
23	Randy Velarde	.07
25	Willie Randolph	.08
28	Duane Ward	.04
30	David Cone	.10
32	John Farrell	.05
33	Greg Walker	.05

34	*Tony Fossas* (FC)	.07
35	Benito Santiago	.12
40	Jay Howell	.06
41	Matt Williams	.15
42	Jeff Robinson	.07
43	Dante Bichette	.07
44	*Roger Salkeld* (#1 Draft Pick) (FC)	.50
45	Dave Parker	.08

46	*Rob Dibble	.12
48	Zane Smith	.03
50	Glenn Davis	.10
57	*Greg Vaughn* (FC)	1.35
60	George Brett	.15
61	*Deion Sanders*	.50
62	*Ramon Martinez	.15
65	Devon White	.07
66	*Greg Litton* (FC)	.25
67	Scott Sanderson	.04
68	Dave Henderson	.06
70	Mike Greenwell	.30
71	Allan Anderson	.05
72	*Jeff Huson* (FC)	.25
73	Bob Milacki	.05
74	*Jeff Jackson* (#1 Draft Pick) (FC)	.25
75	Doug Jones	.07
76	Dave Valle	.03
79	Ron Kittle	.07
80	Jeff Russell	.05
83	Hensley Meulens	.30
85	Juan Samuel	.08

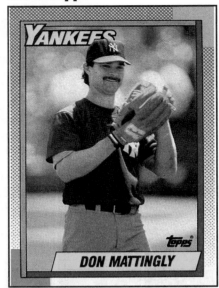

200 Don Mattingly

144	Bud Black	.04
145	Terry Steinbach	.09
146	*Rob Richie* (FC)	.20
147	Chuck Finley	.05
148	Edgar Martinez (FC)	.15
149	Steve Farr	.04
150	Kirk Gibson	.09
152	Lonnie Smith	.05
153	Randy Milligan	.06
155	Ellis Burks	.25
157	Craig Biggio	.15
160	Dave Righetti	.06
161	Harold Reynolds	.06
162	*Todd Zeile* (FC)	1.25
163	Phil Bradley	.06
164	*Jeff Juden* (#1 Draft Pick) (FC)	.35
165	Walt Weiss	.08
166	Bobby Witt	.03
167	*Kevin Appier* (FC)	.20
168	Jose Lind	.04
170	George Bell	.12
172	Tom Lampkin (FC)	.07
173	Tim Belcher	.12
175	Mike Moore	.07
177	Mike Henneman	.07
178	Chris James	.05
180	Rock Raines	.10
183	Steve Lake	.03
185	Ruben Sierra	.20
186	Dave LaPoint	.03
187	*Rick Wrona* (FC)	.15
190	Rick Reuschel	.07
191	Pat Borders	.07
193	Andy Benes	.35
194	Glenallen Hill (FC)	.25
195	Tim Burke	.07
197	Doug Drabek	.07
198	Mike Marshall	.06
199	*Sergio Valdez* (FC)	.20
200	Don Mattingly	.90
201	Cito Gaston	.03
203	*Mike Roesler* (FC)	.15

86	Paul Kilgus	.03
87	*Rick Luecken* (FC)	.15
88	Glenn Braggs	.04
89	*Clint Zavaras* (FC)	.15
90	Jack Clark	.07
91	*Steve Frey* (FC)	.20
95	Todd Worrell	.06
97	Curt Schilling (FC)	.10
98	Jose Gonzalez (FC)	07
99	*Rich Monteleone* (FC)	.15
100	Will Clark	.75
101	Shane Rawley	.04
102	Stan Javier	.04
103	Marvin Freeman	.07
104	Bob Knepper	.03
105	Randy Myers	.07
107	Fred Lynn	.06
109	Roberto Kelly	.08
111	Ed Whited	.20
113	Manny Lee	.04
114	Mike Bielecki	.05
115	Tony Pena	.06
117	Mike Sharperson (FC)	.08
118	Erik Hanson	.15
119	Billy Hatcher	.05
120	John Franco	.07
121	Robin Ventura	.40
125	Kent Hrbek	.15
127	Mike Devereaux	.06
129	Ron Jones	.10
130	Bert Blyleven	.06
131	Matt Nokes	.06
132	Lance Blankenship (FC)	.10
134	*Earl Cunningham* (#1 Draft Pick) (FC)	.65
135	Dave Magadan	.07
136	Kevin Brown	.05
137	*Marty Pevey* (FC)	.12
138	Al Leiter	.04
139	Greg Brock	.04
140	Andre Dawson	.15
141	*John Hart* (FC)	.15
142	*Jeff Wetherby* (FC)	.20

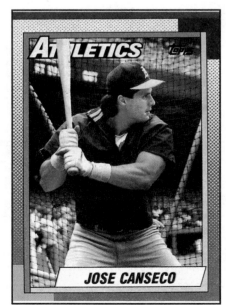

250 Jose Canseco

300 Bo Jackson

205	Mark Davis	.07
206	Nick Esasky	.05
207	Bob Ojeda	.04
208	Brook Jacoby	.06
210	Ryne Sandberg	.25
213	Scott Bankhead	.05
216	Ricky Jordan	.30
219	Donn Pall	.03
220	Barry Bonds	.20
221	*Gary Mielke* (FC)	.20
222	Kurt Stillwell	.05
223	Tommy Gregg	.06
224	*Delino DeShields* (FC)	.75
227	*Kevin Tapani* (FC)	.30
230	Keith Hernandez	.05
233	Ken Hill	.03
236	Hal Morris (FC)	.10
237	*Kevin Ritz* (FC)	.20
238	Felix Jose (FC)	.15
239	Eric Show	.04
240	Mark Grace	.45
243	Barry Jones	.03
245	Roger Clemens	.24
247	Jerry Reed	.03
249	*Mike Smith* (FC)	.20
250	Jose Canseco	.75
252	Otis Nixon	.03
255	Bobby Thigpen	.06
257	Jose DeLeon	.07
260	Eric Davis	.35
261	Whitey Herzog	.05
263	*Mel Stottlemyre Jr.* (FC)	.15
265	Pete O'Brien	.06
268	Rob Murphy	.03
269	Dickie Thon	.03
270	Dave Stewart	.09
271	Chet Lemon	.04
273	Bobby Bonilla	.15
274	*Goose Gozzo* (FC)	.20
275	Mickey Tettleton	.06
277	Lenny Harris (FC)	.10
278	Pascual Perez	.06
280	Lou Whitaker	.07

281	Kevin Bass	.06
282	Derek Lilliquist	.05
283	*Joey Belle* (FC)	.85
284	*Mark Gardner* (FC)	.35
285	Willie McGee	.06
287	Vance Law	.05
288	Greg Briley	.15
289	Norm Charlton	.10
290	Robin Yount	.20
292	Jim Gott	.04
295	Fred McGriff	.25
296	Jeff Ballard	.04
297	Tom Herr	.05
299	Adam Peterson (FC)	.09
300	Bo Jackson	.50
301	Don Aase	.03
302	*Marcus Lawton* (FC)	.07
304	Marty Clary (FC)	.08
305	Eddie Murray	.15
307	Bip Roberts	.08
309	*Eric Yelding* (FC)	.20
311	Dwight Smith	.90
314	*Donald Harris* (#1 Draft Pick) (FC)	.30
315	Bruce Hurst	.07
316	Carney Lansford	.09
317	*Mark Guthrie* (FC)	.20
319	Dion James	.03
320	Dave Stieb	.10
321	Joe Morgan	.03
322	Junior Ortiz	.03
324	Pete Harnisch (FC)	.10
325	Robby Thompson	.06
326	*Tom McCarthy*	.10
327	Ken Williams	.03
328	Curt Young	.03
330	Ron Darling	.07
331	*Juan Gonzalez* (FC)	.45
332	Paul O'Neill	.08
334	Johnny Ray	.05
335	Andy Hawkins	.05
336	Ken Griffey Jr.	1.50
339	Dave Clark	.03

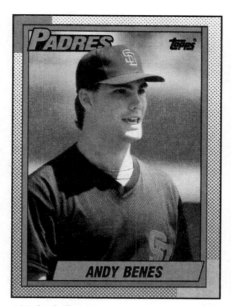

193 Andy Benes

340	Fernando Valenzuela	.08
341	Tom Foley	.03
343	Frank Tanana	.05
344	*George Canale* (FC)	.25
345	Harold Baines	.07
347	*Junior Felix*	.45
348	*Gary Wayne* (FC)	.15
349	*Steve Finley* (FC)	.30
350	Bret Saberhagen	.10
351	Roger Craig	.03
352	Bryn Smith	.05
353	*Sandy Alomar	.35
354	*Stan Belinda* (FC)	.20
357	Dave West	.12
360	Paul Molitor	.08
361	*Randy McCament* (FC)	.25
363	Dan Petry	.04
364	*Rolando Roomes* (FC)	.12
365	Ozzie Guillen	.10
366	Mike Heath	.03
368	Bill Doran	.04
370	Tim Wallach	.07
371	Jimmy Key	.08
373	Alvin Davis	.12
374	*Steve Cummings* (FC)	.20
375	Dwight Evans	.09
377	*Mickey Weston* (FC)	.20
380	Dave Winfield	.15
381	Frank Robinson	.03
384	*Pat Combs*	.50
385	Fred McGriff AS	.15
386	Julio Franco AS	.12
387	Wade Boggs AS	.20
388	Cal Ripken AS	.15
389	Robin Yount AS	.20
390	Ruben Sierra AS	.20
391	Kirby Puckett AS	.20
392	Carlton Fisk AS	.12
393	Bret Saberhagen AS	.10
394	Jeff Ballard AS	.08
395	Jeff Russell AS	.08
396	A. Bartlett Giamatti	.15
397	Will Clark AS	.20

398	Ryne Sandberg AS	.20
399	Howard Johnson AS	.15
400	Ozzie Smith AS	.10
401	Kevin Mitchell AS	.20
402	Eric Davis AS	.20
403	Tony Gwynn AS	.20
404	Craig Biggio AS	.08
405	Mike Scott AS	.08
406	Joe Magrane AS	.08
407	Mark Davis AS	.08
408	Trevor Wilson	.07
409	Tom Brunansky	.07
410	Joe Boever	.06
411	Ken Phelps	.03
412	Jamie Moyer	.04
413	*Brian Dubois* (FC)	.20
414	*Frank Thomas* (#1 Draft Pick) (FC)	.65
416	*Dave Johnson* (FC)	.15
417	Jim Gantner	.06
418	Tom Browning	.08
419	*Beau Allred* (FC)	.20
420	Carlton Fisk	.10
421	Greg Minton	.03
422	Pat Sheridan	.03
424	Jerry Reuss	.04
425	Bill Landrum	.06
426	Jeff Hamilton	.03
428	*Steve Davis* (FC)	.12
429	Tom Kelly	.03
430	Pete Incaviglia	.06
431	Randy Johnson	.12
433	*Steve Olin* (FC)	.15
434	Mark Carreon (FC)	.10
435	Kevin Seitzer	.10
436	Mel Hall	.05
438	Greg Myers (FC)	.10
439	Jeff Parrett	.06
440	Alan Trammell	.09
442	Jerry Browne	.07
443	Cris Carpenter	.05
444	*Kyle Abbott* (#1 Draft Pick) (FC)	.30

690 Mark McGwire

57 Greg Vaughn

692 Sammy Sosa

446	Dan Pasqua	.06
448	Greg Gagne	.03
450	Rickey Henderson	.35
451	Mark Lemke (FC)	.10
453	Jody Davis	.03
454	Jeff King (FC)	.15
455	Jeffrey Leonard	.06
456	Chris Gwynn (FC)	.09
457	Gregg Jefferies	.50
459	Jim Lefebvre	.03
460	Mike Scott	.09
461	*Carlos Martinez* (FC)	.25
463	Drew Hall	.03
464	*Jerome Walton*	1.00
465	Kevin Gross	.05
468	Billy Ripken	.03
469	John Kruk	.05
470	Frank Viola	.15
472	Jose Uribe	.05
473	Joe Price	.03
475	Bob Welch	.08
477	Willie Fraser	.03
479	Frank White	.06
480	Sid Fernandez	.08
482	*Steve Carter* (FC)	.20
486	Jeff Treadway	.05
489	Nick Leyva	.03
490	Dan Plesac	.07
491	*Dave Cochrane* (FC)	.20
493	*Jason Grimsley* (FC)	.25
494	Terry Puhl	.03
495	Lee Smith	.06
496	Cecil Espy	.04
498	Rick Schu	.03
499	Bill Long	.03
500	Kevin Mitchell	.35
505	Kelly Gruber	.10
506	Tom Glavine	.10
508	Terry Leach	.03
510	Doc Gooden	.25
511	Clay Parker	.06
515	*Len Dykstra	.12
516	Tim Leary	.05

517	Roberto Alomar	.20
519	Bucky Dent	.03
520	Mitch Williams	.09
521	Craig Worthington	.15
523	Jay Bell	.03
525	Wally Joyner	.15
526	Checklist 397-528	.03
528	*Kevin Wickander* (FC)	.20
529	Greg Harris	.05
530	Mark Langston	.10
531	Ken Caminiti	.06
533	Tim Jones (FC)	.05
535	John Smoltz	.15
536	*Bob Geren*	.15
537	Mark Grant	.03
538	*Billy Spiers*	.20
539	Neal Heaton	.06
540	Danny Tartabull	.08
541	Pat Perry	.03
544	Dennis Boyd	.05
545	Kevin McReynolds	.09
546	Kevin Hickey	.04
547	Jack Howell	.05
549	Don Zimmer	.03
550	Julio Franco	.10
551	Tim Crews	.03
552	*Mike Smith* (FC)	.15
553	*Scott Scudder* (FC)	.25
554	Jay Buhner	.08
555	Jack Morris	.07
557	*Jeff Innis*	.15
560	Steve Sax	.12
561	Ken Dayley	.03
562	Chad Kreuter	.09
563	Alex Sanchez	.09
564	*Tyler Houston* (#1 Draft Pick) (FC)	.60
567	Ron Gant	.07
568	John Smiley	.06
569	Ivan Calderon	.06
570	Cal Ripken	.15
571	Brett Butler	.06
572	Greg Harris	.09

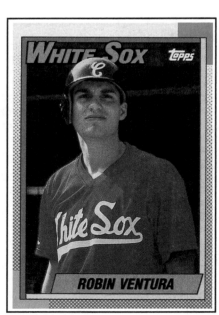

121 Robin Ventura

457 Gregg Jeffries

574	Bill Swift	.04
575	Lance Parrish	.07
576	*Mike Dyer* (FC)	.20
577	Charlie Hayes (FC)	.10
578	Joe Magrane	.07
579	Art Howe	.03
580	Joe Carter	.15
581	Ken Griffey	.05
584	*Phil Stephenson* (FC)	.09
585	Kal Daniels	.10
586	Ed Nunez	.03
587	Lance Johnson	.10
588	Rick Rhoden	.04
589	Mike Aldrete	.05
590	Ozzie Smith	.12
591	Todd Stottlemyre	.08
593	Scott Bradley	.04
594	*Luis Sojo* (FC)	.20
595	Greg Swindell	.10
596	Jose DeJesus (FC)	.10
597	Chris Bosio	.07
598	Brady Anderson	.05
599	Frank Williams	.04
600	Darryl Strawberry	.45
601	Luis Rivera	.05
602	Scott Garrelts	.07
603	Tony Armas	.03
604	Rob Robinson	.03
605	Mike Scioscia	.06
606	Storm Davis	.07
607	Steve Jeltz	.03
608	*Eric Anthony* (FC)	2.00
609	Sparky Anderson	.03
610	Pedro Guerrero	.10
611	Walt Terrell	.03
612	Dave Gallagher	.05
613	Jeff Pico	.04
614	Nelson Santovenia	.08
615	Rob Deer	.07
616	Brian Holman	.10
617	Geronimo Berroa	.05
618	Eddie Whitson	.05
619	Rob Ducey	.08

620	*Tony Castillo* (FC)	.20
621	Melido Perez	.08
622	Sid Bream	.05
623	Jim Corsi	.04
624	Darrin Jackson	.04
625	Roger McDowell	.07
626	Bob Melvin	.04
627	Jose Rijo	.07
628	Candy Maldonado	.08
629	Eric Hetzel (FC)	.10
630	Gary Gaetti	.12
631	*John Wetteland* (FC)	.25
632	Scott Lusader	.05
633	Dennis Cook (FC)	.15
634	Luis Polonia	.06
635	Brian Downing	.05
636	Jesse Orosco	.03
637	Craig Reynolds	.03
638	Jeff Montgomery	.07
639	Tony LaRussa	.03
640	Rick Sutcliffe	.06
641	*Doug Strange* (FC)	.20
642	*Jack Armstrong	.12
643	Alfredo Griffin	.05
644	Paul Assenmacher	.04
645	Jose Oquendo	.06
647	Rex Hudler	.03
648	Jim Clancy	.03
649	*Dan Murphy* (FC)	.15
650	Mike Witt	.06
651	Rafael Santana	.06
652	Mike Boddicker	.09
653	John Moses	.03
654	*Paul Coleman* (#1 Draft Pick) (FC)	.35
656	Mackey Sasser	.05
657	Terry Mulholland	.07
658	Donnell Nixon	.03
659	Greg Cadaret	.03
660	Vince Coleman	.10
666	Brian Fisher	.05
667	Curt Wilkerson	.03
668	*Joe Oliver* (FC)	.30

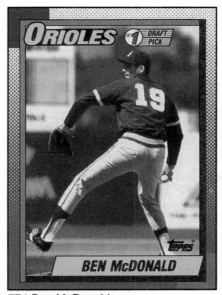
774 Ben McDonald

669	Tom Lasorda	.03
670	Dennis Eckersley	.10
671	Bob Boone	.09
672	Roy Smith	.03
673	Joey Meyer	.03
674	Spike Owen	.05
675	Jim Abbott	.75
676	Randy Kutcher (FC)	.07
677	Jay Tibbs	.04
678	Kirt Manwaring	.09
679	Gary Ward	.04
680	Howard Johnson	.15
681	Mike Schooler	.08
682	Dann Bilardello	.03
683	*Kenny Rogers*	.10
684	*Julio Machado* (FC)	.20
685	Tony Fernandez	.09
686	Carmelo Martinez	.08
687	Tim Birtsas	.04
688	Milt Thompson	.05
689	Rich Yett	.04
690	Mark McGwire	.50
691	Chuck Cary	.03
692	Sammy Sosa	.50
693	Calvin Schiraldi	.03
694	*Mike Stanton* (FC)	.15
695	Tom Henke	.07
696	B.J. Surhoff	.04
697	Mike Davis	.03
698	*Omar Vizquel*	.10
699	Jim Leyland	.03
700	Kirby Puckett	.25
701	*Bernie Williams* (FC)	.25
702	Tony Phillips	.05
703	*Jeff Brantley*	.12
704	*Chip Hale* (FC)	.20
705	Claudell Washington	.07
706	Geno Petralli	.03
707	Luis Aquino	.03
708	Larry Sheets	.03
709	Juan Berenguer	.03
710	Von Hayes	.09
711	Rick Aguilera	.08

712	Todd Benzinger	.07
713	*Tim Drummond* (FC)	.15
714	*Marquis Grissom* (FC)	.85
715	Greg Maddux	.10
716	Steve Balboni	.03
717	Ron Karkovice	.03
718	Gary Sheffield	.40
719	*Wally Whitehurst* (FC)	.15
720	Andres Galarraga	.15
721	Lee Mazzilli	.03
722	Felix Fermin	.03
723	Jeff Robinson	.05
724	Juan Bell (FC)	.10
725	Terry Pendleton	.07
726	Gene Nelson	.03
727	Pat Tabler	.04
728	Jim Acker	.03
729	Bobby Valentine	.03
730	Tony Gwynn	.20
731	Don Carman	.03
732	Ernie Riles	.03
733	John Dopson	.08
734	Kevin Elster	.06
735	Charlie Hough	.06
736	Rick Dempsey	.03
737	Chris Sabo	.15
738	*Gene Harris*	.10
739	Dale Sveum	.04
740	Jesse Barfield	.08
741	Steve Wilson	.10
742	Ernie Whitt	.04
743	Tom Candiotti	.07
744	*Kelly Mann* (FC)	.25
745	Hubie Brooks	.05
746	Dave Smith	.06
747	Randy Bush	.03
748	Doyle Alexander	.04
749	Mark Parent	.04
750	Dale Murphy	.10
751	Steve Lyons	.03
752	Tom Gordon	.50
753	Chris Speier	.03
754	Bob Walk	.03

216 Ricky Jordan

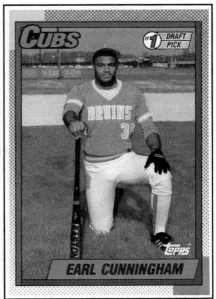
134 Earl Cunningham

755	Rafael Palmeiro	.08
756	Ken Howell	.03
757	*Larry Walker* (FC)	.35
758	Mark Thurmond	.03
759	Tom Trebelhorn	.03
760	Wade Boggs	.45
761	Mike Jackson	.05
762	Doug Dascenzo	.07
764	Tim Teufel	.05

765	Chili Davis	.07
766	Brian Meyer (FC)	.07
767	Tracy Jones	.04
768	Chuck Crim	.04
769	*Greg Hibbard* (FC)	.15
770	Cory Snyder	.09
771	Pete Smith	.07
772	Jeff Reed	.03
773	Dave Leiper	.03

774	*Ben McDonald* (FC)	**2.25**
775	Andy Van Slyke	.09
776	Charlie Leibrandt	.04
779	Lloyd Moseby	.07
780	Orel Hershiser	.12
785	Jim Rice	.07
786	Eric King	.04
790	Gary Carter	.07
792	Gerald Perry	.06

1990 TOPPS TRADED

Topps wasn't the first company to issue an updated set, but its yearly fall issue continues as one of the most popular. Card fronts duplicate the gaudy, multi-colored borders found in the 792-card set issued earlier in the year. The company scooped the competition with its annual practice of creating manager cards. World Championship manager Lou Piniella made his first appearance in a Reds uniform, and yet another card was issued for Hall-of-Famer Red Schoendienst (because of his brief interim service as a Cardinals manager). Again, rookie newcomers remain the most popular traded-set entries with collectors. In terms of value, cards of Kevin Maas, Dave Justice, John Olerud, and Ben McDonald are tops with hobbyists. The Traded sets were issued in a specially designed box, available mainly through hobby dealers.

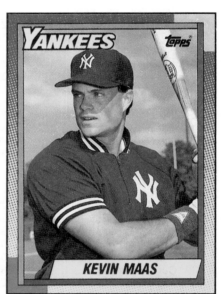

63 Kevin Maas

		MINT
Complete set		**$15.00**
Commons		**.06**

1	Darrel Akerfelds	$ .06
2	Sandy Alomar	.50
3	Brad Arnsberg	.10
4	Steve Avery	.50
5	Wally Backman	.06
6	Carlos Baerga	.35
7	Kevin Bass	.06
8	Willie Blair	.15
9	Mike Blowers	.25
10	Shawn Boskie	.25
16	John Burkett	.25
17	Casey Candaele	.08
19	Gary Carter	.10
20	Joe Carter	.15
22	Scott Coolbaugh	.20
26	Edgar Diaz	.08
27	Wayne Edwards	.15
29	Scott Erickson	.15
31	Cecil Fielder	.35
32	John Franco	.10
33	Travis Fryman	.50
35	Darryl Hamilton	.08
36	Mike Harkey	.25
38	Billy Hatcher	.10
41	Dave Hollins	.08
43	Steve Howard	.10

83 John Olerud

44	Todd Hundley	.15
45	Jeff Huson	.12
48	Dave Justice	2.25
49	Jeff Kaiser	.15
50	Dana Kiecker	.20
51	Joe Klink	.15
52	Brent Knackert	.10
54	Mark Langston	.10

55	Tim Layana	.15
61	Jim Leyritz	.25
63	Kevin Maas	2.50
65	Candy Maldonado	.10
69	John Marzano	.08
70	Ben McDonald	1.25
71	Jack McDowell	.12
74	Stump Merrill	.06
75	Alan Mills	.20
76	Hal Morris	.35
77	Lloyd Moseby	.08
78	Randy Myers	.10
79	Tim Naehring	.25
80	Junior Noboa	.06
81	Matt Nokes	.06
82	Pete O'Brien	.06
83	John Olerud	2.25
84	Greg Olson	.25
85	Junior Ortiz	.06
86	Dave Parker	.12

87	Rick Parker	.12
88	Bob Patterson	.06
89	Alejandro Pena	.08
90	Tony Pena	.10
91	Pascual Perez	.08
92	Gerald Perry	.06
93	Dan Petry	.06
94	Gary Pettis	.06
95	Tony Phillips	.08
96	Lou Piniella	.10
97	Luis Polonia	.06
98	Jim Presley	.12
99	Scott Radinsky	.20
100	Willie Randolph	.08
101	Jeff Reardon	.12
102	Greg Riddoch	.06
103	Jeff Robinson	.06
104	Ron Robinson	.08
105	Kevin Romine	.06
106	Scott Ruskin	.20
107	John Russell	.06
108	Bill Sampen	.25
109	Juan Samuel	.12

110	Scott Sanderson	.08
111	Jack Savage	.06
112	Dave Schmidt	.06
113	Red Schoendienst	.20
114	Terry Shumpert	.20
115	Matt Sinatro	.06
116	Don Slaught	.06
117	Bryn Smith	.06
118	Lee Smith	.15
119	Paul Sorrento	.12
120	Franklin Stubbs	.10
121	Russ Swan	.08
122	Bob Tewksbury	.08
123	Wayne Tolleson	.06
124	John Tudor	.06
125	Randy Veres	.12
126	Hector Villanueva	.25
127	Mitch Webster	.06
128	Ernie Whitt	.06
129	Frank Wills	.06
130	Dave Winfield	.12
131	Matt Young	.06
132	Checklist	.06

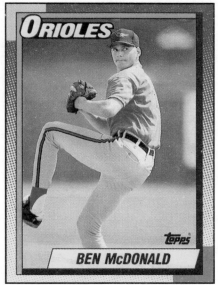

70 Ben McDonald

1990 UPPER DECK

After its incredible 1989 debut, only a few changes were made to the popular Upper Deck set for 1990. The color photos are larger due to the elimination of the ornamentation on the right side of the card fronts, and the Upper Deck logo was moved from the lower left corner to the upper right. But apart from the presence of the team logo, this design is closest to the simple beauty of the stunning 1953 Bowman Color edition. Although the initial printing contained a few notable errors, they were quickly corrected. For example, Ben McDonald's card first appeared with an Orioles rather than a Rookies logo; Mickey Weston was incorrectly identified as "Jamie," both on his card and on the Orioles checklist; and incorrect photos were used for both Scott Garrelts and Jim Gott. As in 1989, team checklist cards display star portraits by artist Vernon Wells, who also created cards honoring Mike Schmidt's retirement and Nolan Ryan's 5,000th strikeout. The final 100 cards of the 1990 set were issued in a popular mid-season, high-number series, 701-800. This final series came both in foil packs and in a factory-collated, complete "set."

56 John Olerud

	MINT
Complete set (1-700)	**$60.00**
Commons (1-700)	**.07**
Complete set (1-800)	**95.00**
Commons (701-800)	**.10**

2	*Randy Mosek* (FC)	$ .15
3	*Tom Drees* (FC)	.15
4	Curt Young	.07
6	Luis Salazar	.06
8	Jose Bautista	.07
9	*Marquis Grissom* (FC)	1.35
11	Rick Aguilera	.14
13	*Deion Sanders* (FC)	.65
14	Marvell Wynne	.07
15	David West	.15

17	*Sammy Sosa* (FC)	.90
19	Jack Howell	.08
20	Mike Schmidt (special card)	1.50
21	Robin Ventura (FC)	.75
22	Brian Meyer (FC)	.20
23	*Blaine Beatty* (FC)	.25
25	Greg Vaughn (FC)	2.15
26	Xavier Hernandez (FC)	.15
27	*Jason Grimsley* (FC)	.25
28	*Eric Anthony* (FC)	3.00
30	David Wells	.08
31	Hal Morris (FC)	.15
33	*Kelly Mann* (FC)	.15
34	Nolan Ryan (special card)	1.75
35	*Scott Service* (FC)	.20

37	*Tino Martinez* (FC)	.65
38	Chili Davis	.10
39	Scott Sanderson	.07
42	*Scott Coolbaugh* (FC)	.40
43	*Jose Cano* (FC)	.15
44	*Jose Vizcaino* (FC)	.50
45	*Bob Hamelin* (FC)	1.25
46	*Jose Offerman* (FC)	1.35
47	Kevin Blankenship	.10
49	*Tommy Greene* (FC)	.90

309

Ben McDonald

54 Ben McDonald

50	Will Clark (special card)	.50
51	Rob Nelson (FC)	.09
52	*Chris Hammond* (FC)	.15
54	*Ben McDonald* (Orioles logo) (FC)	65.00
54	*Ben McDonald* (Rookies logo) (FC)	4.00
55	Andy Benes (FC)	1.00
56	*John Olerud* (FC)	4.25
58	Tony Armas	.07
59	*George Canale* (FC)	.50
60	Orioles Checklist (reads "Jamie Weston")	10.00
60	Orioles Checklist (correct card—reads "Mickey Weston")	.15
61	*Mike Stanton* (FC)	.15
63	*Kent Mercker* (FC)	.90

64	*Francisco Cabrera* (FC)	.30
65	Steve Avery (FC)	.75
66	Jose Canseco	1.00
67	*Matt Merullo* (FC)	.15
69	Ron Karkovice	.07
70	*Kevin Maas* (FC)	.50
71	Dennis Cook	.10
72	*Juan Gonzalez* (FC)	1.00
74	*Dean Palmer* (FC)	.40
75	Bo Jackson (special card)	.50
76	*Rob Richie* (FC)	.20
77	*Bobby Rose* (FC)	.40
78	*Brian DuBois* (FC)	.15
80	Gene Nelson	.07
83	Greg Minton	.07
85	Willie Fraser	.07
86	Neal Heaton	.08
87	*Kevin Tapani* (FC)	.25
89	Jim Gott (photo is Rick Reed)	12.00

Terry Shumpert

733 Terry Shumpert

Todd Zeile

545 Todd Zeile

116	Eric Davis	.25
117	Kevin Mitchell	.40
118	Ron Oester	.07
119	Brett Butler	.09
122	Ken Caminiti	.10
123	Kevin Brown	.10
124	George Brett	.15
125	Mike Scott	.10
126	Cory Snyder	.10
127	George Bell	.15
128	Mark Grace	.50
129	Devon White	.10
130	Tony Fernandez	.10
131	Don Aase	.07
135	Mark Carreon (FC)	.15
139	John Franco	.09
141	Jeff Treadway	.08
142	Pat Tabler	.07

Eric Anthony

28 Eric Anthony

89	Jim Gott (correct photo)	.25
90	Lance Johnson (FC)	.10
92	Jeff Parrett	.08
93	*Julio Machado* (FC)	.25
94	Ron Jones	.10
98	*Kevin Ritz* (FC)	.25
102	*Kevin Appier* (FC)	.30
103	Julio Franco	.10
104	Craig Biggio	.30
105	Bo Jackson	.90
106	*Junior Felix*	.75
107	Mike Harkey (FC)	.35
108	Fredd McGriff	.25
109	Rick Sutcliffe	.09
110	Pete O'Brien	.08
111	Kelly Gruber	.12
112	Pat Borders	.08
113	Dwight Evans	.10
114	Dwight Gooden	.20
115	*Kevin Batiste* (FC)	.15

Todd Hundley

726 Todd Hundley

156	Ken Griffey Jr.	2.50
157	Gary Sheffield	.50
161	Paul O'Neill	.09
162	*Jeff McKnight* (FC)	.20
163	*Alvaro Espinosa* (FC)	.15
164	*Scott Scudder* (FC)	.20
166	Gregg Jefferies	.60
167	Barry Larkin	.15
168	Gary Carter	.09
169	Robby Thompson	.09
170	Rolando Roomes	.15
171	Mark McGwire	.60
172	Steve Sax	.15
174	Mitch Williams	.15
176	Rob Deer	.08
177	Tim Raines	.15
178	Mike Felder	.07
179	Harold Reynolds	.10
181	Chris Sabo	.15
182	Darryl Strawberry	.25

Robin Ventura

21 Robin Ventura

233	*Omar Vizquel*	.10
235	Erik Hanson	.15
236	Kirby Puckett	.50
237	*Bill Spiers*	.25
241	Ron Darling	.08
242	Joe Magrane	.08
243	Dave Magadan	.09
244	Pedro Guerrero	.12
245	Glenn Davis	.15
246	Terry Steinbach	.12
247	Fred Lynn	.09
248	Gary Redus	.07
250	Sid Bream	.08
251	Bob Welch	.12
252	Bill Buckner	.07
253	Carney Lansford	.09
254	Paul Molitor	.12
255	Jose DeJesus	.15
256	Orel Hershiser	.25
257	Tom Brunansky	.10

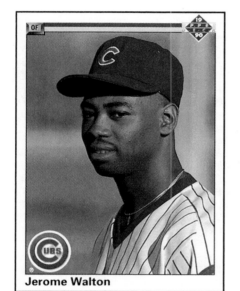

Jerome Walton

345 Jerome Walton

213	Greg Maddux	.20
214	Mike Schooler	.09
215	Lonnie Smith	.08
216	Jose Rijo	.09
217	Greg Gagne	.07
218	Jim Gantner	.08
219	Allan Anderson	.09
220	Rick Mahler	.08
221	Jim Deshaies	.09
222	Keith Hernandez	.10
223	Vince Coleman	.12
224	David Cone	.20
225	Ozzie Smith	.20
226	Matt Nokes	.09
227	Barry Bonds	.20
228	Felix Jose	.10
231	Shawon Dunston	.10
232	Ron Gant	.10

Kevin Bearse

715 Kevin Bearse

183	Willie Randolph	.09
186	Todd Benzinger	.09
187	Kevin Elster	.07
188	Jose Uribe	.07
189	Tom Browning	.10
190	Keith Miller	.09
191	Don Mattingly	.85
192	Dave Parker	.12
193	Roberto Kelly	.12
194	Phil Bradley	.09
195	Ron Hassey	.07
197	Hubie Brooks	.08
198	Bill Doran	.08
199	Al Newman	.07
201	Terry Puhl	.07
204	Bob Ojeda	.07
206	Dave Henderson	.10
207	Henry Cotto	.07
209	Stan Javier	.07
210	Jerry Reed	.07
212	Andre Thomas	.07

Marquis Grissom

9 Marquis Grissom

258	Mike Davis	.08
259	Jeff Ballard	.09
260	Scott Terry	.09
261	Sid Fernandez	.10
262	Mike Marshall	.08
263	Howard Johnson	.20
264	Kirk Gibson	.09
265	Kevin McReynolds	.15
266	Cal Ripken Jr.	.15
267	Ozzie Guillen	.10
268	Jim Traber	.07
269	Bobby Thigpen	.10
271	Bob Boone	.09
272	Dave Stewart	.10
273	Tim Wallach	.09
275	Mike Moore	.10
276	Tony Pena	.09
277	Eddie Murray	.15
278	Milt Thompson	.08
280	Ken Dayley	.07
282	Tom Henke	.09

34 Nolan Ryan

Jose Offerman

46 Jose Offerman

285	Manny Lee	.07
286	Dan Pasqua	.08
287	Larry Sheets	.07
291	Spike Owen	.08
292	Storm Davis	.09
293	Chris Bosio	.09
295	Don August	.09
297	Mickey Tettleton	.09
298	Mike Scioscia	.10
301	Shawn Abner	.07
302	Kevin Bass	.08
303	Bip Roberts (FC)	.10
304	Joe Girardi	.10
305	Danny Darwin	.07
306	Mike Heath	.07
307	Mike Macfarlane	.07
308	Ed Whitson	.09
309	Tracy Jones	.07
310	Scott Fletcher	.08
311	Darnell Coles	.07
312	Mike Brumley	.07
313	Bill Swift	.08
314	Charlie Hough	.08
315	Jim Presley	.07
316	Luis Polonia	.08

317	Mike Morgan	.07
319	Jose Oquendo	.07
321	Jody Reed	.07
323	Roger Clemens	.45
324	Ryne Sandberg	.20
325	Benito Santiago	.15
326	Bret Saberhagen	.15
327	Lou Whitaker	.10
328	Dave Gallagher	.10
331	Jeffrey Leonard	.09
332	Torey Lovullo	.20
333	Pete Incaviglia	.09
334	Rickey Henderson	.15
335	Rafael Palmeiro	.10
336	Ken Hill	.08
337	Dave Winfield	.15
338	Alfredo Griffin	.08
339	Andy Hawkins	.08
340	Ted Power	.07
341	Steve Wilson	.10
342	Jack Clark	.10
343	Ellis Burks	.25
344	Tony Gwynn	.20
345	*Jerome Walton*	2.00
346	Roberto Alomar	.12
347	*Carlos Martinez* (FC)	.15
348	Chet Lemon	.07
349	Willie Wilson	.07
350	Greg Walker	.07
351	Tom Bolton	.07
353	Harold Baines	.09
354	Mike Greenwell	.50
355	Ruben Sierra	.20
357	Andre Dawson	.25
358	*Jeff Brantley* (FC)	.12
359	Mike Bielecki	.09
361	Kurt Stillwell	.09
362	Brian Holman	.10
363	Kevin Seitzer	.10
364	Alvin Davis	.12
365	Tom Gordon	.65
366	Bobby Bonilla	.15
367	Carlton Fisk	.10
368	*Steve Carter* (FC)	.15
369	Joel Skinner	.07
371	Cecil Espy	.08
372	*Gary Wayne* (FC)	.25
373	Jim Rice	.08
374	*Mike Dyer* (FC)	.15
375	Joe Carter	.15

376	Dwight Smith	.75
377	*John Wetteland* (FC)	.25
378	Ernie Riles	.07
379	Otis Nixon	.07
380	Vance Law	.07
382	Frank White	.09
383	Scott Bradley	.07
385	Gary Pettis	.08
386	Donn Pall (FC)	.09
387	John Smiley	.09
388	Tom Candiotti	.10
389	Junior Ortiz	.07
390	Steve Lyons	.07
391	Brian Harper	.07
392	Fred Manrique	.07
393	Lee Smith	.09
394	Jeff Kunkel	.07
396	John Tudor	.09
397	Terry Kennedy	.07

Delino DeShields

746 Delino DeShields

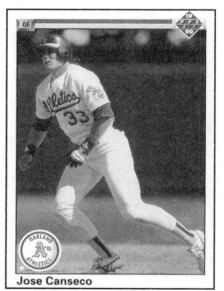

Jose Canseco

66 Jose Canseco

Will Clark

50 Will Clark

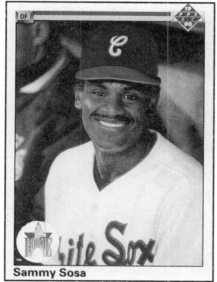

Sammy Sosa

17 Sammy Sosa

20 Mike Schmidt

399	Craig Lefferts	.07
400	Checklist 301-400	.07
401	Keith Moreland	.07
402	Rich Gedman	.07
403	Jeff Robinson	.08
404	Randy Ready	.07
405	Rick Cerone	.07
406	Jeff Blauser	.07
407	Larry Anderson	.07
408	Joe Boever	.08
409	Felix Fermin	.07
410	Glenn Wilson	.07
411	Rex Hudler	.07
412	Mark Grant	.07
413	Dennis Martinez	.08
414	Darrin Jackson	.07
415	Mike Aldrete	.07
416	Roger McDowell	.09
417	Jeff Reardon	.10

418	Darren Daulton	.07
419	Tim Laudner	.07
420	Don Carman	.07
421	Lloyd Moseby	.09
422	Doug Drabek	.09
423	Lenny Harris	.09
424	Jose Lind	.07
425	*Dave Johnson* (FC)	.30
426	Jerry Browne	.09
427	*Eric Yelding* (FC)	.12
429	Jody Davis	.06
430	Mariano Duncan (FC)	.09
431	Mark Davis	.12
432	Nelson Santovenia	.10
433	Bruce Hurst	.10
434	*Jeff Huson* (FC)	.25
435	Chris James	.08
436	*Mark Guthrie* (FC)	.15
437	*Charlie Hayes* (FC)	.10
438	Shane Rawley	.08
439	Dickie Thon	.07
440	Juan Berenguer	.07
441	Kevine Romine	.07
442	Bill Landrum	.09
443	Todd Frohwirth	.07
444	Craig Worthington	.10
445	Fernando Valenzuela	.10
446	*Joey Belle* (FC)	1.00
447	*Ed Whited* (FC)	.15
448	Dave Smith	.08
449	Dave Clark	.07
450	Juan Agosto	.07
451	Dave Valle	.07
452	Kent Hrbek	.15
453	Von Hayes	.10
454	Gary Gaetti	.15
455	Greg Briley	.40
456	Glenn Braggs	.07
457	Kirt Manwaring	.09
458	Mel Hall	.07
459	Brook Jacoby	.08
460	Pat Sheridan	.07
461	Rob Murphy	.07
462	Jimmy Key	.10
463	Nick Esasky	.09
464	Rob Ducey	.09
465	Carlos Quintana	.09
466	*Larry Walker* (FC)	.50
467	Todd Worrell	.10
468	Kevin Gross	.07

469	Terry Pendleton	.09
470	Dave Martinez	.07
471	Gene Larkin	.07
472	*Len Dykstra	.12
473	Barry Lyons	.07
474	Terry Mulholland (FC)	.10
475	*Chip Hale* (FC)	.15
476	Jesse Barfield	.08
477	Dan Plesac	.08
478	Scott Garrelts (photo is Bill Bathe)	5.00
478	Scott Garrelts (correct photo)	.25
479	Dave Righetti	.10
480	Gus Polidor (FC)	.07
481	Mookie Wilson	.08
482	Luis Rivera	.07
483	Mike Flanagan	.08
484	Dennis "Oil Can" Boyd	.07
485	John Cerutti	.07
486	John Costello	.07
487	Pascual Perez	.08
488	Tommy Herr	.07
489	Tom Foley	.07
490	Curt Ford	.07

Nolan Ryan

734 Nolan Ryan's Sixth No-Hitter

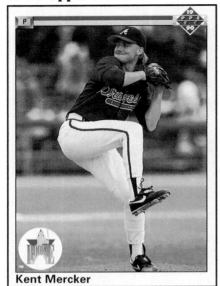

Kent Mercker

63 Kent Mercker

510	Dave Anderson	.07
511	Chuck Crim	.07
512	Joe Hesketh	.07
513	Dennis Eckersley	.12
514	Greg Brock	.07
515	Tim Burke	.09
516	Frank Tanana	.08
517	Jay Bell	.07
518	Guillermo Hernandez	.07
519	Randy Kramer (FC)	.07
520	Charles Hudson	.07
521	Jim Corsi (FC)	.08
522	Steve Rosenberg	.08
523	Cris Carpenter	.10
524	*Matt Winters* (FC)	.12
525	Melido Perez	.08
526	Chris Gwynn	.07
527	Bert Blyleven	.09
528	Chuck Cary	.07
529	Daryl Boston	.08

Tim Layana

717 Tim Layana

491	Steve Lake	.07
492	Tim Teufel	.07
493	Randy Bush	.07
494	Mike Jackson	.08
495	Steve Jeltz	.07
496	Paul Gibson	.07
497	Steve Balboni	.07
498	Bud Black	.08
499	Dale Sveum	.07
500	Checklist 401-500	.07
501	Timmy Jones	.07
502	Mark Portugal	.07
503	Ivan Calderon	.07
504	Rick Rhoden	.07
505	Willie McGee	.09
506	Kirk McKaskill	.08
507	Dave LaPoint	.07
508	Jay Howell	.08
509	Johnny Ray	.08

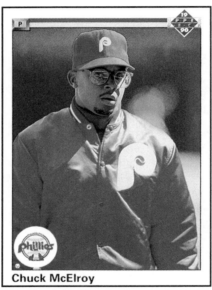

Chuck McElroy

706 Chuck McElroy

551	*Tony Castillo* (FC)	.12
552	Jeff Robinson	.08
553	*Steve Olin* (FC)	.15
554	Alan Trammell	.10
555	Wade Boggs	.75
556	Will Clark	1.00
557	Jeff King (FC)	.12
558	Mike Fitzgerald	.07
559	Ken Howell	.07
560	Bob Kipper	.07
561	Scott Bankhead	.09
562	*Jeff Innis* (FC)	.12
563	Randy Johnson	.15
564	*Wally Whitehurst*	.10
565	*Gene Harris* (FC)	.10
566	Norm Charlton	.09
567	Robin Yount	.25
568	*Joe Oliver* (FC)	.25
569	Mark Parent	.07

Mark Davis

710 Mark Davis

530	Dale Mohoric	.07
531	Geronimo Berroa (FC)	.08
532	Edgar Martinez	.10
533	Dale Murphy	.15
534	Jay Buhner	.09
535	John Smoltz	.15
536	Andy Van Slyke	.15
537	Mike Henneman	.09
538	Miguel Garcia (FC)	.07
539	Frank Williams	.07
540	R.J. Reynolds	.07
541	Shawn Hillegas	.07
542	Walt Weiss	.10
543	*Greg Hibbard* (FC)	.15
544	Nolan Ryan	1.25
545	*Todd Zeile* (FC)	2.25
546	Hensley Meulens	.20
547	Tim Belcher	.09
548	Mike Witt	.07
549	Greg Cadaret	.07
550	Franklin Stubbs	.07

Mark Gardner

743 Mark Gardner

570	John Farrell	.07
571	Tom Glavine	.10
572	Rod Nichols (FC)	.10
573	Jack Morris	.09
574	Greg Swindell	.12
575	Steve Searcy (FC)	.09
576	Ricky Jordan	.50
577	Matt Williams	.35
578	Mike LaValliere	.07
579	Bryn Smith	.08
580	Bruce Ruffin	.07
581	Randy Myers	.10
582	*Rick Wrona* (FC)	.15
583	Juan Samuel	.09
584	Les Lancaster	.07
585	Jeff Musselman	.07
586	*Rob Dibble	.12
587	Eric Show	.07
588	Jesse Orosco	.07
589	Herm Winningham	.07

751 Alex Cole

611	*Jeff Wetherby* (FC)	.15
612	*Gary Mielke* (FC)	.15
613	Pete Smith	.09
614	*Jack Daugherty* (FC)	.15
616	Don Robinson	.07
617	Jose Guzman	.07
618	Steve Bedrosian	.08
619	Jamie Moyer	.07
621	*Rick Luecken* (FC)	.15
622	Greg W. Harris	.09
623	Pete Harnisch	.10
624	Jerald Clark	.10
625	Jack McDowell	.07
626	Frank Viola	.20
627	Ted Higuera	.10
628	*Marty Pevey* (FC)	.15
630	Eric Plunk	.07
631	Drew Hall	.07
635	Bob Milacki (FC)	.08

"Rookie Threats"

702 Rookie Threats

590	Andy Allanson	.07
591	Dion James	.07
592	Carmelo Martinez	.08
593	Luis Quinones (FC)	.09
594	Dennis Rasmussen	.08
595	Rich Yett	.07
596	Bob Walk	.07
597	Andy McGaffigan	.07
598	Billy Hatcher	.08
599	Bob Knepper	.07
600	Checklist 501-600	.07
601	Joey Cora (FC)	.10
602	*Steve Finley*	.15
603	Kal Daniels	.10
604	Gregg Olson	.50
605	Dave Stieb	.10
606	*Kenny Rogers* (FC)	.15
607	Zane Smith	.07
608	*Bob Geren* (FC)	.25
609	Chad Kreuter	.10
610	Mike Smithson	.07

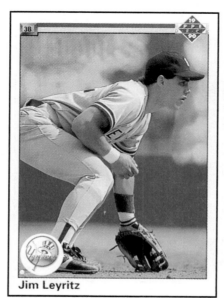
Jim Leyritz

723 Jim Leyritz

636	Bobby Witt	.07
637	Trevor Wilson	.08
638	Jeff Russell	.08
640	Rick Leach	.07
642	Terry Leach	.07
645	Jim Abbott	1.25
646	*Jaime Navarro* (FC)	.25
647	Mark Langston	.10
648	Juan Nieves	.08
651	Eric King	.07
652	Mike Boddicker	.09
653	Duane Ward	.07
655	Sandy Alomar Jr.	.65
656	Danny Tartabull	.10
662	Tim Leary	.07
663	Randy Milligan	.08
664	Bo Diaz	.07
665	Mark Lemke	.08
667	Chuck Finley	.08
668	John Kruk	.08

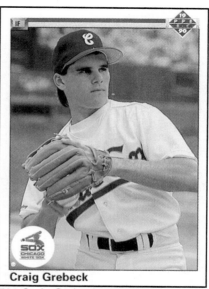
Craig Grebeck

721 Craig Grebeck

670	Tim Crews	.07
671	John Dopson	.09
672	*John Orton* (FC)	.15
673	Eric Hetzel (FC)	.10
674	Lance Parrish	.10
675	*Ramon Martinez	.20
676	Mark Gubicza	.09
677	Greg Litton	.20
680	Steve Farr	.07
681	Mike Devereaux	.08
682	Ken Griffey Sr.	.08
683	*Jamie Weston* (first name incorrect) (FC)	10.00
683	*Mickey Weston* (correct name) (FC)	.30
684	*Jack Armstrong	.12
686	Bryan Harvey	.07
688	Dante Bichette	.09
689	Todd Burns	.09
690	Dan Petry	.07
691	*Kent Anderson* (FC)	.15

315

John Burkett

735 John Burkett

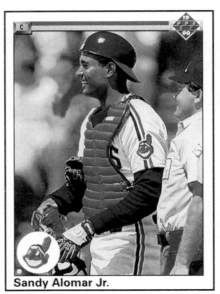

Sandy Alomar Jr.

756 Sandy Alomar Jr.

Storm Davis

712 Storm Davis

692	Todd Stottlemyre	.09
693	Wally Joyner	.15
694	Mike Rochford (FC)	.10
696	Rick Reuschel	.09
697	Jose DeLeon	.09
700	Checklist 601-700 (lists "Jamie Weston")	10.00
700	Checklist 601-700 (correct card—lists "Mickey Weston")	.25
701	Jim Gott	.10
702	Rookie Threats (Delino DeShields, Marquis Grissom, Larry Walker)	.50
703	Alejandro Pena	.10
704	Willie Randolph	.10
705	Tim Leary	.10
706	*Chuck McElroy* (FC)	.15

707	Gerald Perry	.10
708	Tom Brunansky	.10
709	John Franco	.15
710	Mark Davis	.10
711	Dave Justice	.20
712	Storm Davis	.10
713	Scott Ruskin (FC)	.15
714	Glenn Braggs	.10
715	*Kevin Bearse* (FC)	.20
716	Jose Nunez	.10
717	*Tim Layana* (FC)	.20
718	Greg Myers (FC)	.12
719	Pete O'Brien	.10
720	John Candelaria	.10
721	*Craig Grebeck* (FC)	.20
722	*Shawn Boskie* (FC)	.25
723	*Jim Leyritz* (FC)	.25
724	*Bill Sampen* (FC)	.25
725	Scott Radinsky	.10

726	*Todd Hundley* (FC)	.30
727	*Scott Hemond* (FC)	.15
728	*Lenny Webster* (FC)	.15
729	Jeff Reardon	.12
730	Mitch Webster	.10
731	*Brian Bohanon* (FC)	.15
732	*Rick Parker* (FC)	.20
733	*Terry Shumpert* (FC)	.30
734	Nolan Ryan's Sixth No-Hitter (with "300th WIN!" stripe on front)	1.00
734	Nolan Ryan's Sixth No-Hitter (w/o "300th WIN!" stripe on front)	4.00
735	*John Burkett* (FC)	.25
736	*Derrick May* (FC)	.25
737	Carlos Baerga	.10
738	*Greg Smith*	.15
739	Scott Sanderson	.10

Dave Winfield

745 Dave Winfield

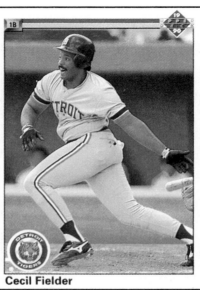

Cecil Fielder

786 Cecil Fielder

Shawn Boskie

722 Shawn Boskie

John Franco

709 John Franco

Bill Sampen

724 Bill Sampen

Derrick May

736 Derrick May

740 Joe Kraemer .... .10	759 Stan Belinda .... .15	778 Billy Hatcher .... .10
741 *Hector Villanueva* (FC) .... .20	760 Jim Presley .... .10	780 Candy Maldonado .... .10
742 Mike Fetters .... .15	761 *Gary DiSarcina* (FC) .... .15	781 Mike Marshall .... .10
743 Mark Gardner .... .25	762 *Wayne Edwards* (FC) .... .15	783 Mark Langston .... .12
744 Matt Nokes .... .10	763 Pat Combs .... .10	784 Paul Sorrento .... .20
745 Dave Winfield .... .15	764 *Mickey Pina* (FC) .... .15	785 *Dave Hollins* (FC) .... .25
746 *Delino DeShields* (FC) 1.25	765 *Wilson Alvarez* (FC) .... .25	786 Cecil Fielder .... .45
747 *Dann Howitt* (FC) .... .20	766 Dave Parker .... .15	787 Matt Young .... .10
748 Tony Pena .... .15	767 *Mike Blowers* (FC) .... .25	788 Jeff Huson .... .10
749 Oil Can Boyd .... .10	768 Tony Phillips .... .10	789 Lloyd Moseby .... .10
750 *Mike Benjamin* (FC) .... .20	769 Pascual Perez .... .10	791 Hubie Brooks .... .10
751 *Alex Cole* (FC) .... .65	770 Gary Pettis .... .10	792 Craig Lefferts .... .10
752 Eric Gunderson .... .10	771 Fred Lynn .... .10	793 Kevin Bass .... .10
753 Howard Farmer .... .10	772 *Mel Rojas* (FC) .... .25	794 Bryn Smith .... .12
754 Joe Carter .... .20	773 *David Segui* (FC) .... .35	795 Juan Samuel .... .12
755 *Ray Lankford* (FC) .... .65	774 Gary Carter .... .15	796 Sam Horn .... .10
756 Sandy Alomar Jr. .... .35	775 Rafael Valdez .... .10	797 Randy Myers .... .15
757 Alex Sanchez .... .10	776 Glenallen Hill .... .10	799 Bill Gullickson .... .10
758 Nick Esasky .... .10	777 Keith Hernandez .... .12	800 Checklist 701-800 .... .10

David Segui

773 David Segui

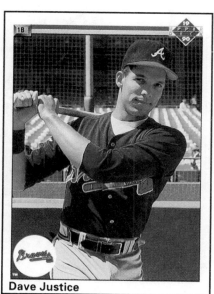

Dave Justice

711 Dave Justice

Mark Langston

783 Mark Langston

1991'S HOTTEST CARDS

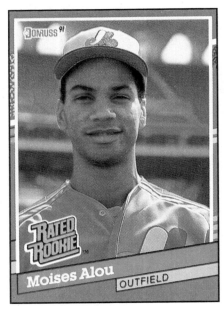

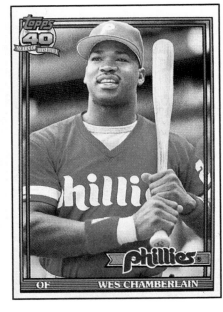

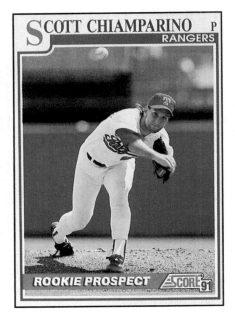

MOISES ALOU

1991 Set	Card Number	Value
Donruss	**38**	**.50- .75**
Fleer	No Card	—
Score	No Card	—
Topps	526	.50- .75
Upper Deck	665	.75-1.00

WES CHAMBERLAIN

1991 Set	Card Number	Value
Donruss	No Card	—
Fleer	291	.75- .90
Score	No Card	—
Topps	**603**	**.75- .90**
Upper Deck	626	1.00-1.25

SCOTT CHIAMPARINO

1991 Set	Card Number	Value
Donruss	42	1.25-1.50
Fleer	No Card	—
Score	**352**	**1.50-1.75**
Topps	676	1.00-1.25
Upper Deck	8	1.75-2.00

STEVE DECKER

1991 Set	Card Number	Value
Donruss	No Card	—
Fleer	260	1.00-1.25
Score	No Card	—
Topps	No Card	—
Upper Deck	**25**	**1.50-1.75**

LANCE DICKSON

1991 Set	Card Number	Value
Donruss	No Card	—
Fleer	No Card	—
Score	385	1.00-1.25
Topps	**114**	**.75-1.00**
Upper Deck	9	1.50-1.75

DAVE EILAND

1991 Set	Card Number	Value
Donruss	**354**	**1.25-1.50**
Fleer	661	1.00-1.25
Score	No Card	—
Topps	611	1.25-1.50
Upper Deck	No Card	—

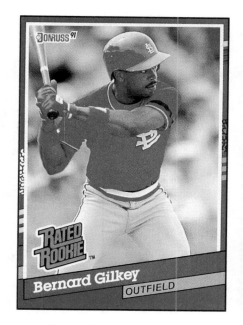

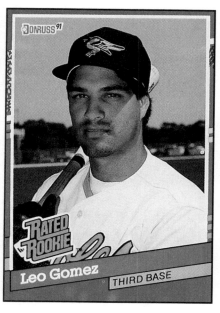

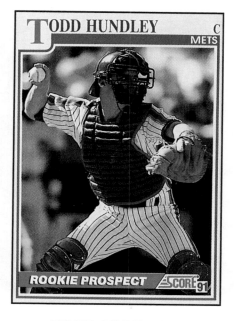

BERNARD GILKEY

1991 Set	Card Number	Value
Donruss	30	**1.00-1.25**
Fleer	633	1.00-1.25
Score	No Card	—
Topps	126	1.25-1.50
Upper Deck	16	1.75-2.00

LEO GOMEZ

1991 Set	Card Number	Value
Donruss	35	**.75-1.00**
Fleer	472	.50- .75
Score	No Card	—
Topps	No Card	—
Upper Deck	6	1.00-1.25

TODD HUNDLEY

1991 Set	Card Number	Value
Donruss	No Card	—
Fleer	150	1.25-1.50
Score	340	**1.50-1.75**
Topps	457	1.25-1.50
Upper Deck	440	2.00-2.25

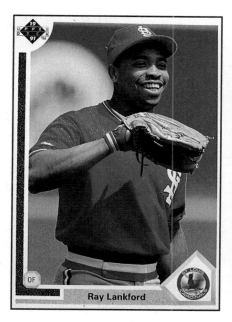

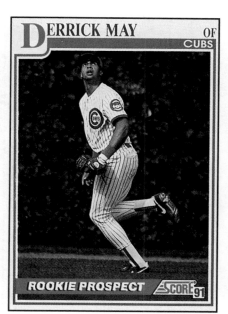

RAY LANKFORD

1991 Set	Card Number	Value
Donruss	43	1.75-2.00
Fleer	637	1.50-1.75
Score	No Card	—
Topps	682	1.50-1.75
Upper Deck	346	**2.00-2.25**

DERRICK MAY

1991 Set	Card Number	Value
Donruss	36	1.25-1.50
Fleer	427	1.00-1.25
Score	379	**1.50-1.75**
Topps	288	1.25-1.50
Upper Deck	334	1.75-2.00

TIM McINTOSH

1991 Set	Card Number	Value
Donruss	No Card	—
Fleer	589	.40- .45
Score	347	.50- .75
Topps	561	**.40- .45**
Upper Deck	547	.75- 1.00

1991'S HOTTEST CARDS

BRIAN McRAE

1991 Set	Card Number	Value
Donruss	No Card	—
Fleer	563	.75- .90
Score	331	1.00-1.25
Topps	**222**	**.90-1.00**
Upper Deck	543	1.25-1.50

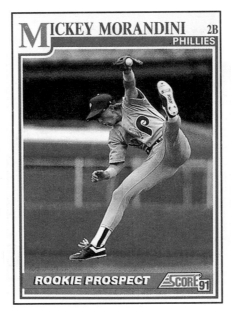

MICKEY MORANDINI

1991 Set	Card Number	Value
Donruss	44	.75- .90
Fleer	407	.55- .75
Score	**376**	**1.00-1.25**
Topps	342	.55- .75
Upper Deck	18	1.25-1.50

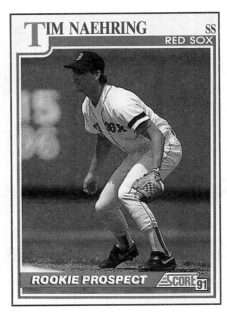

TIM NAEHRING

1991 Set	Card Number	Value
Donruss	367	1.00-1.25
Fleer	105	.75-1.00
Score	**356**	**1.25-1.50**
Topps	702	1.00-1.25
Upper Deck	527	1.50-1.75

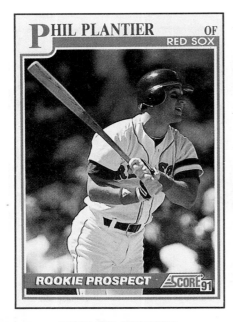

PHIL PLANTIER

1991 Set	Card Number	Value
Donruss	41	1.50-1.75
Fleer	107	1.25-1.50
Score	**348**	**1.75-2.00**
Topps	474	1.25-1.50
Upper Deck	2	2.00-2.25

DAVID SEGUI

1991 Set	Card Number	Value
Donruss	No Card	—
Fleer	492	1.00-1.25
Score	362	1.25-1.50
Topps	**724**	**1.00-1.25**
Upper Deck	No Card	—

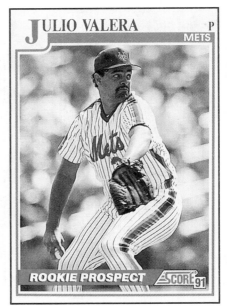

JULIO VALERA

1991 Set	Card Number	Value
Donruss	39	1.00-1.25
Fleer	164	.75-1.00
Score	**353**	**1.25-1.50**
Topps	504	1.00-1.25
Upper Deck	534	1.50-1.75